SUPERSTAR PHARAOHS

CALOUSTE GULBENKIAN
MUSEUM

INTRODUCTION

ESSAYS

1

THE IMMORTALS

2

THE IMMORTALS

3

THE IMMORTALS

MEETING THE PHARAOHS

Guilherme d'Oliveira Martins
TRUSTEE OF THE CALOUSTE GULBENKIAN FOUNDATION

'Such beauty, such civilisation!' This would be a fitting caption for the famous photograph of Calouste Sarkis Gulbenkian, taken in 1934 at the temple of Horus, in Edfu, Egypt, which documents the fulfilment of a dream. The statue next to the Foundation's headquarters faithfully recreates that moment. This expression of astonishment and admiration demonstrates just how perennial this long-held affection was. The Collector had long wished to go and discover the world of the pharaohs and once there he completely immersed himself in the environment he had so craved. His passion for Egyptian antiquities stretched back to at least 1907, when he had acquired the breccia bowl. And, especially after 1920, he regularly acquired works to satisfy his penchant for the magical Nile civilisation. Thus he approached the famous British Egyptologist Howard Carter, who, in 1922, would discover the untouched tomb of the young pharaoh Tutankhamun in the Valley of the Kings, a hundred years after Champollion had deciphered the Rosetta Stone hieroglyphs. Indeed, Carter acted as Calouste Gulbenkian's advisor as he sought out and acquired some of the emblematic works in his collection.

The exhibition *Superstar Pharaohs*, conceived from an idea by Egyptologist Frédéric Mougenot, and first held at the Mucem – Musée des civilisations de l'Europe et de la Méditerranée, in Marseille, and then at the Calouste Gulbenkian Foundation, embraces an enduring cultural phenomenon. Its aim is to provide an opportunity to reflect on historical knowledge as a key phenomenon in the societies inhabiting Europe and the eastern shores of the Mediterranean. The contribution of great Egyptologists has allowed us to understand subjects as diverse as the Egyptians' knowledge of their past and their history, the presence of the pharaohs in Greco-Roman literature, and the impact of images and their destruction in the construction of an official history of Egypt. Of course, we cannot forget the issue of 'Egyptomania' and the reference to emblematic figures from Egyptian culture. Calouste S. Gulbenkian was an exemplary figure in this field, and it was João Carvalho Dias who, based on a study of the Collector's archives, revealed the important connections, meetings and missed opportunities with Howard Carter, discoverer of the most famous media figure of all, Tutankhamun.

Until now, no other exhibition has sought to present the history of the pharaohs in imagery and culture, from the ancient Egyptians to the present day. In 2017 and 2018, a short investigation in Cairo and Luxor allowed us to understand the specific situation in the territory, as we gathered important documents and pieces for this exhibition in order to elucidate the precise conditions and implications of an exceptional historical phenomenon. It has been wrongly claimed

50

Statue of a falcon-god protecting a pharaoh, probably Nectanebo II, Egypt, probably reign of Nectanebo II (360–342 BCE).

To establish their legitimacy, the early Ptolemys perpetuated the cult of statues of the last Egyptian pharaoh, with the appellation 'Nectanebo the Falcon'.

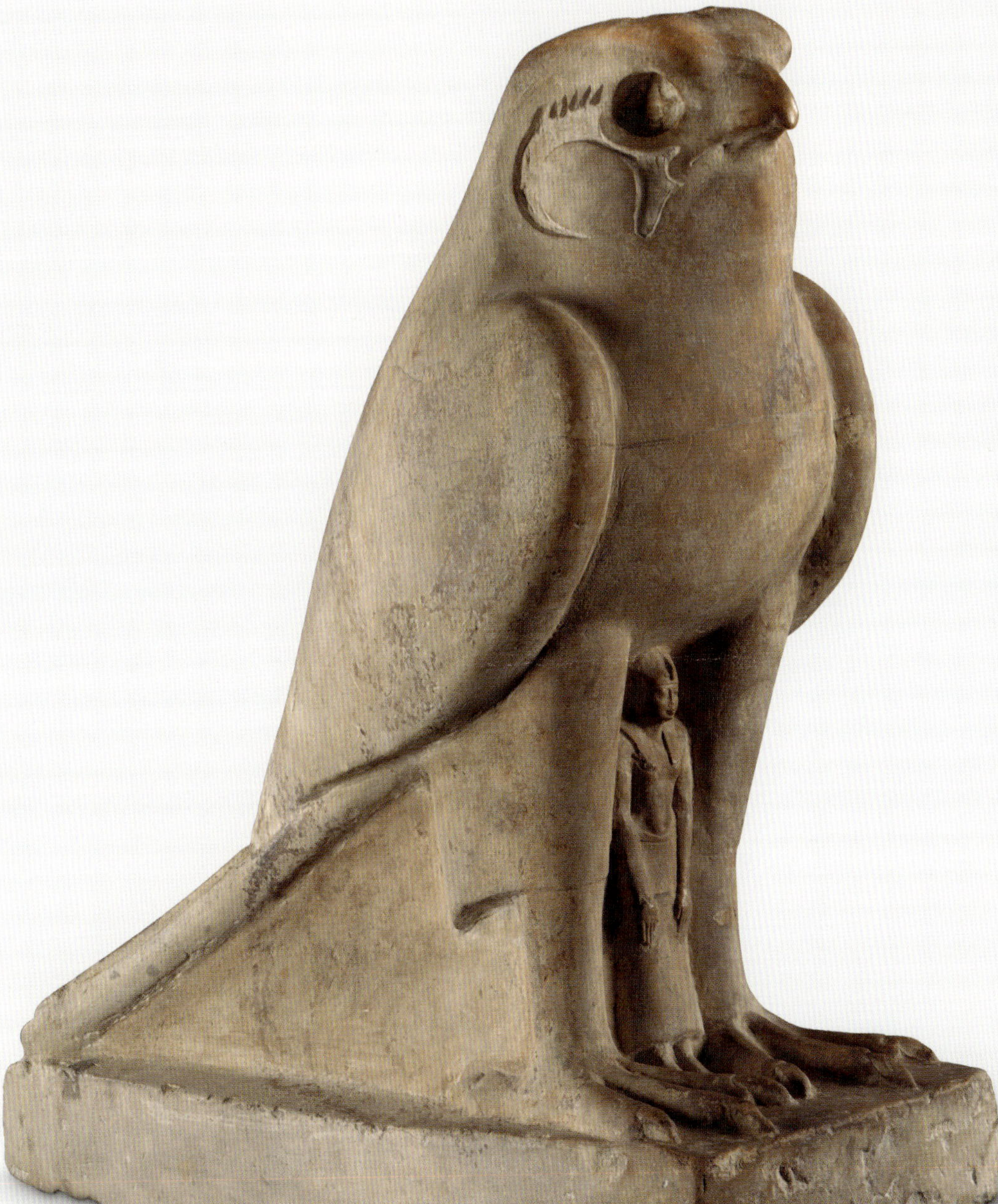

that the Egyptian people were not interested in the past, particularly the pre-Islamic past. Recent work has revealed that modern opinion has created such an illusion. However, the work of Egyptologist Fayza Haikal has drawn attention to the cultural and affective links between the peoples of the Mediterranean Levant and the civilisation of the pharaohs.

Today, knowledge is advancing faster than ever before thanks to the demanding and largely unseen work of the anthropologists, archaeologists, palaeobotanists, pottery experts and philologists who study the daily life of the peoples of the Nile valley. Even the most experienced and knowledgeable Egyptologists cannot hide their excitement when it comes to the celebrity pharaohs, in much the same way as Egyptian mythology enthusiasts and ordinary visitors to the Egyptian museums or the Louvre, keenly following recent investigations into the hypothetical presence of Nefertiti's tomb behind that of Tutankhamun. They are all equally thrilled by the exhibition of the latter's treasure at the Grande Halle de la Villette (Paris), which has revived the enthusiasm of laymen and scholars alike for the magic of Egyptian antiquity.

Calouste S. Gulbenkian's acquisition of the head of King Senwosret III, father of Amenemhat III, of the Twelfth Dynasty, is a good illustration of his intricate knowledge and passion in this regard. Indeed, the aforementioned magic of Egyptian culture is clearly apparent, proving that the pharaohs are still veritable superstars today!

This exhibition would not have been possible without the commitment shown from the outset by Jean-François Chougnet, President of the Mucem, the teams from the two museums whose work formed the basis of the project, and all the national and international lenders who supported this initiative. We thank you all.

ON THE NAME OF THINGS

António Filipe Pimentel
DIRECTOR OF THE CALOUSTE GULBENKIAN MUSEUM

The Calouste Gulbenkian Museum has just opened its doors to the *Superstar Pharaohs* exhibition, a fascinating and particularly complex project resulting from a remarkable partnership with the Mucem – Musée des civilisations de l'Europe et de la Méditerranée (Marseille), following an idea by Frédéric Mougenot, with João Carvalho Dias, deputy director of the Lisbon museum, as co-curator. The chosen title (deliberately bewildering) appears to evoke the timely paraphrase of an anthology by Miguel Esteves Cardoso, precisely named *A Causa das Coisas* (The Cause of Things): for in a project of this type, it is the things themselves that always lie behind the respective name.

Certainly, this programme could not have a more canonical leitmotif: the simultaneous occasion of the centenary of famous archaeologist Howard Carter's discovery of Tutankhamun's tomb (1922) and the bicentenary of Jean-François Champollion deciphering hieroglyphic writing (1822). Indeed, Carter himself played an important role in establishing the Gulbenkian Collection's Egyptian section, which explains the Gulbenkian Museum's inevitable association with this project. What is equally certain is that the exhibition is being offered to the public (in Marseille and Lisbon) under an impressive seal of approval from the remarkably large number of generous lenders: more than forty, from Portugal and abroad. The latter in particular (including the most important public and private Egyptology collections in the world) make up more than three quarters of the total.

In fact, it is thanks to their invaluable support that the exhibition boasts such a plethora of objects (more than two hundred and fifty), ranging from the minuscule (such as the small gold jewels) to the colossal (such as the fist of Ramesses II) and evoking more than five thousand years of history: from the Old Kingdom to the present day. It is, therefore, thanks to this extensive and generous international network that the original idea is able to come to full fruition. Meanwhile, two prestigious but very different international institutions have come together to create this exhibition: one that opened its doors in 2013, the other going back more than six decades. The former is known for its irreverent programmes, while the latter is careful to preserve its good name, long-established among its peers, making it quite averse to epistemological adventures.

251

Joana Vasconcelos,
Cleópatra (PA), Lisbon, 2021.

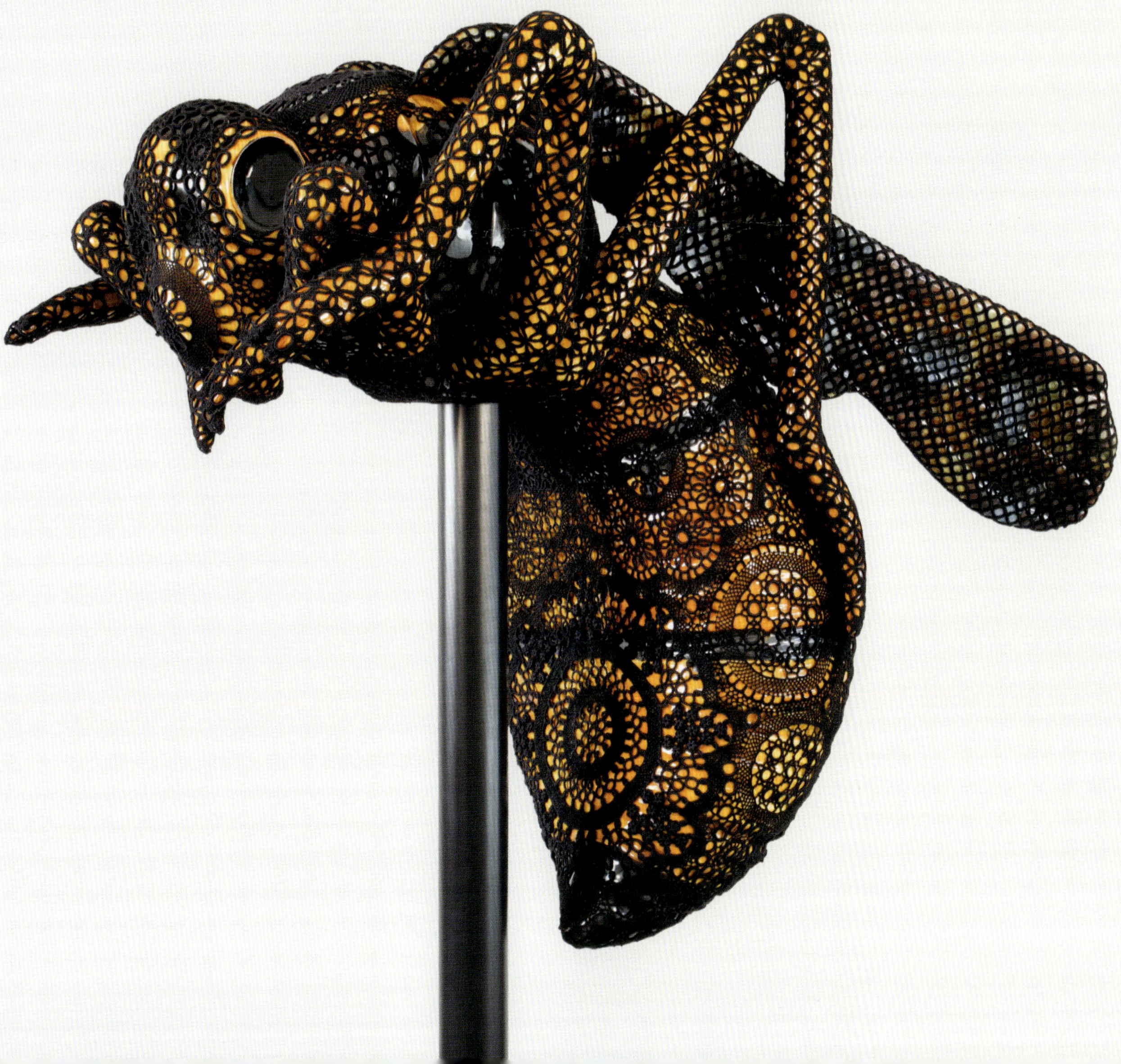

However, history here is more than evoked, it is summoned — and therein lies the true importance of this name, *Superstar Pharaohs*, with an exhibition designed to deliberately navigate between Egyptology and *Egyptomania*: between what the past actually was and the successive images that issued from it. Hence the apparent contradiction in terms that this name implies; hence its deliberate and simultaneous evocation of the values of continuity and rupture — the reference to 'pharaohs' evoking more than three thousand years of tradition and stability, with the consequent projection (itself two thousand years old) onto Western culture; the term 'superstars' refers rather to contemporary references, which from the outset are associated with the notion of fleeting transitoriness, which we link to the (vertiginous) rise and fall of products generated by consumer society.

All the more reason, therefore, to be mindful of its semantic charge, which is explained in detail in the splendid text by Frédéric Mougenot that opens this volume. Thus we can focus on *the cause of things*, within the context of a process in which Carter himself would, ultimately, establish the Egyptology *star system*. And the same would occur, in fact, with the very figure of Tutankhamun, the *superstar pharaoh* by antonomasia. Irrelevant as it would be, from the point of view of Egyptian memory (as opposed to others, who would see their names swallowed up by history, despite the critical fortune they would enjoy as exemplary metaphors of good government), it allows us to elucidate the true process addressed by the exhibition: that of memory and its fundamental power, between remembering and forgetting. These are tools that ancient Egypt learned to master and manipulate, as so many others would, thus justifying its status as the cradle of our culture and civilisation.

Above all, however, it amply explains the underlying reason why the Egyptian model was used as a basis for this kind of *memory game*, something in which the exhibition itself delights. So this is also about names (of the pharaohs, of course, whose hieroglyphic symbols Champollion's work would help us to decipher) and about the respective processes of re-appropriation and/or elimination, which are, after all, as old as humanity itself. For that very reason, this is a journey into the fleeting time in which we live. On the importance (the causes) of things — and the names we give them and/or choose to forget. And that is why this adventure does not only take place between two museums in Marseille and Lisbon, which give it the scientific seal of approval: the rare combination of efforts that underpins it also bears witness to its huge wider significance.

INTRODUCTION

REMEMBERING THE PHARAOHS

FRÉDÉRIC MOUGENOT

It all began with a condom. It entered the collections of Mucem (Musée des civilisations de l'Europe et da la Méditerrannée) in 2003, in the context of a wide-ranging study into the history of HIV prevention, and the wrapping was labelled, in capital letters, with a simple name: Ramses (cat. 229; fig. 1). A brand name, the name of an American subsidiary of Durex; but also the name of a king, the pharaoh who ruled over Egypt from 1279 to 1213 BCE, and who boasted of having fathered about a hundred children. When you come across this object in the museum's inventory, the irony jumps out at you: it seems like an enlightening and amusing subject for a museum of civilizations. How and why was a contraceptive device named after a Near Eastern sovereign who died more than three thousand years ago? What did Ramesses — the second so-named and by far the most famous — do to deserve this doubtful honour? What conclusions can we draw, if not about the monarch's achievements, at least about the society that wrenched him from his mummified rest for commercial purposes and about the image that society has of the pharaohs? A few exciting finds in Mucem's archives and in other collections have confirmed our early intuitions. The most remarkable and conclusive is undoubtedly a print evoking the Napoleonic cult, inherited from the old Musée national des Arts et Traditions populaires in Paris, which shows the French general and emperor being welcomed into the pantheon of war leaders by an operatic Sesostris in tights, who no longer has much connection with the various conquerors, builders and reformers bearing his name in books of Egyptology (cat. 105).

27

Head of Amenhotep III,
Egypt, New Kingdom, Eighteenth
Dynasty (c. 1402–1364 BCE).

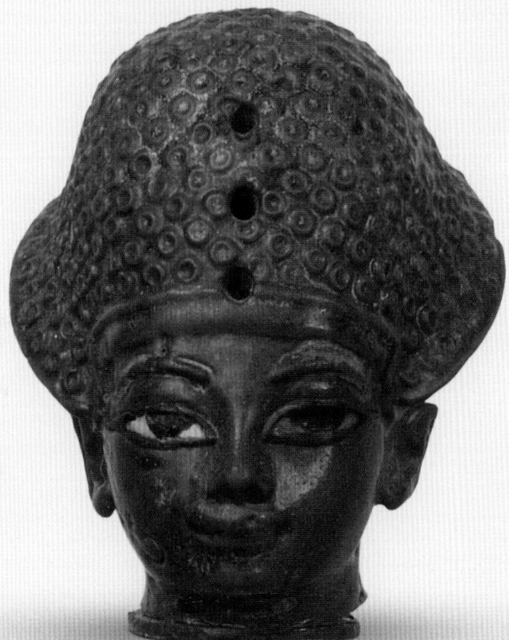

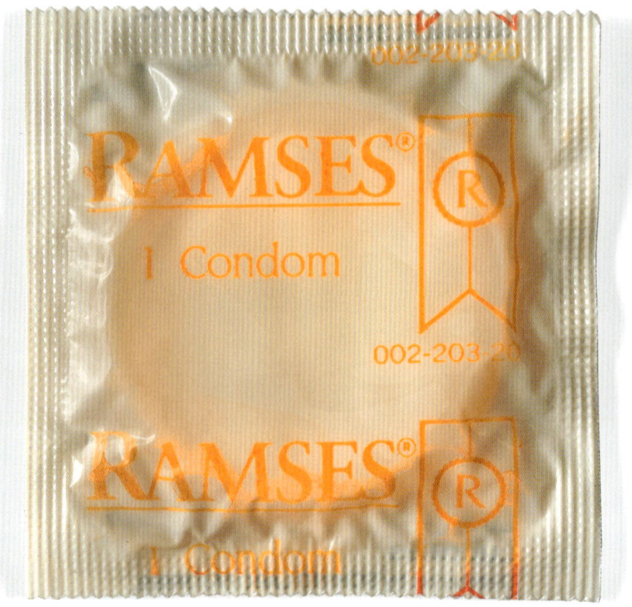

→ FIG. 1
Condom, Ramses brand, Canada, early 2000s, plastic, latex, 5.1 x 5.1 cm. Mucem, inv. 2003.125.429.

The consequence of these interesting finds, whose piquancy resides in the chronological and cultural gulf between the historical sovereign and what we have done with him thousands of years later, is the exhibition *Superstar Pharaohs*. The title, deliberately anachronistic and dissonant, sums up the sometimes disrespectful irony and incongruity that distinguishes modern interest in ancient Egypt. Underlying its 'popular' aspect, there is also a nod to the posthumous destiny desired by all the pharaohs: to join the 'Immortals', the circumpolar stars that shine all night and all through the year. The exhibition's name, deliberately in the plural, highlights individuals rather than the royal institution: celebrities juxtaposed as in a popular magazine. It also attempts to signal the perilous leap that this exhibition is making: describing, in one go, five thousand years of pharaonic fame. This means bringing together in one place authentic Egyptian antiquities, loaned by the greatest collections in the field, illustrious examples of Western and Eastern fine art, photographs, films, archival records, creations by contemporary artists, and — the supreme challenge — everyday objects that are wholly trivial but extremely significant: one of the historical specialities of Mucem's ethnographical collections.

Mission: pharaoh

The exhibition's theme is therefore the posthumous memory — or the image we have reconstructed — of sovereigns known as 'pharaohs' and some of their spouses. 'Pharaoh' was a title held by the king of Egypt in antiquity, from the Eighteenth Dynasty onwards, in a similar vein to the Persian monarch being known as 'King of Kings' or the Roman emperor as 'Augustus'. It is the transcription, by way of Greek, of the ancient Egyptian expression *per-aa*, 'the great house' which initially designated the royal palace and later, as a function of metonymy, its most important resident — just as the Élysée Palace represents the French president or the Vatican represents the pope. The name's bearers may have been mortal, but the monarchy was assumed to be immutable and unshakeable. Established in mythical times, when the god Horus entrusted the running of the kingdom to his human representative, the institution appears in tangible sources towards the end of the fourth millennium BCE. Until the Roman conquest in 31 BCE, which signalled a definitive break in the history of the Egyptian state, when the ruler was permanently abroad and the country was administered as a subjugated province, Egypt was governed by more than three hundred and forty pharaohs. Whatever their exact number — the subject of many studies, but so far impossible to ascertain — it is inevitable that the royal institution saw as many changes in three thousand years as did religion, art, material culture, ecology and the economy. But these hundreds of sovereigns all subscribed to the same conservative and astonishingly coherent tradition, over and above almost incidental developments, so it is possible to give a fairly consistent definition of the pharaoh and his aspirations.

The pharaoh was the temporal incarnation of the divine power that organized the universe. From the moment he completed the crowning ritual, he assumed a function and powers that were divine in their nature. His main role was to maintain *maat*, the order of things established by the deity at the time the world was created: a cosmic, political and social order. To achieve this, he had to appease the gods by building them temples — their earthly homes — and serving them with offerings and the care of statues and sacred animals, their earthly manifestations. In return, when the gods were satisfied, the universe functioned properly: astral cycles were regular, there were no climatic catastrophes and, every year, the Nile's fertilizing inundation reached a reasonable height, neither too meagre nor too destructive. It is impossible to establish an infallible equation between the flood's abundance, which must have been systematically reported in annals that have not always survived, and posthumous glory. We can only observe some coincidences: for example, one of the most significant spates of history occurred during the reign of Sneferu (twenty-seventh century BCE), one of the most popular pharaohs, who was remembered as 'a benevolent king throughout the country' ('Prophecy of Neferti', twentieth century BCE). Flood guaranteed the economic prosperity of the country and the full stomachs of its inhabitants, who were in turn grateful to their ruler for making the cosmic machine operate for everyone's benefit. To achieve this, the sovereign had to eliminate all troublemakers or drive them away from Egypt. War was therefore considered to be one of the pharaoh's essential missions, as the earthly lieutenant of the gods. War was always presented by official sources as an act of defence against the agents of chaos, who would be repulsed to the far reaches of the world, into foreign territories. It was less a case of growing the Egyptian Empire than of stabilizing its frontiers — which were however sufficiently far away that it was possible to sleep peacefully in the Lower Nile Valley — and above all of guaranteeing the provision of products that the country consumed in abundance: gold, tin, copper, wood for construction, incense for religious rites and manpower. The riches brought back from military and mining expeditions, like tributes and diplomatic gifts exchanged with neighbouring states, fed into the Egyptian economy, especially the temples. The pharaoh who succeeded in all these missions was remembered posthumously with lavish praise, as summarized in the account known as the 'Eloquent Peasant' (eighteenth century BCE): '*Maat* is eternal. It goes down to the necropolis with the one who accomplishes it. He is put in the tomb and earth covers him, but his name is not erased from the Earth and he is remembered for the good he has done.'

Wives of the pharaohs and female pharaohs

The monarch was supported in his role by the great royal wife. While it is used for the sake of convenience — in this book too — the term 'queen' is not strictly accurate in the sense that classical Egyptian did not have a female equivalent for the word 'king'. On the other hand, while the pharaoh could take several wives, to satisfy his carnal desires or his diplomatic ambitions, theoretically only one of them was the 'great' wife. Aside from the political support that her lineage could offer, which is often rather difficult to establish when she was not a princess by blood, her role was above all religious — and therefore political, in a theocracy where the head of state was also a religious figure. She and her husband formed the divine couple who daily ensured the renewal of creation, the maintenance of *maat* and the country's prosperity. This was a particularly prominent role during the reign of Akhenaten, who was routinely accompanied by Nefertiti. Several queens had an influential role at court or in the country's governance, especially in the event of the sovereign's incapacity to reign, as in the case of Ahmose-Nefertari, of whom we will hear more in this work, or Hatshepsut before she became pharaoh. Seeing herself as the most legitimate member of the royal family, owing to her lineage and her experience, Hatshepsut gradually assumed the role and attributes of king, a virile function given by a male god to a representative of the same sex. Since her rediscovery, the reign of this female pharaoh of the sixteenth century BCE has sparked many fantasies, tinged with male chauvinism or feminism depending on the period and the author, in which she has been viewed either as a harridan or as an emblem of 'girl power'.

The only thing that can be said objectively is that it shows the force of the Egyptian monarchic institution's inertia, bending neither to the gender of its representative, nor their ethnic origin, nor to the passage of time.

In the name of kings

The royal function thus passed from titulary to titulary and should have been impersonal, each new pharaoh being nothing more than the umpteenth materialisation of a divine immortal principle, theoretically detached from historical circumstances. Yet, from the start, the kings were seen as individuals, if only in their names. From the Middle Kingdom, all sovereigns had up to four royal names in addition to the one they had received at birth as mortal individuals. These titles, confirmed by the priests at the coronation, represented a plan, a roadmap that was supposed to mark out their reign, setting it apart from predecessors, but very often also paying homage to them and reclaiming their heritage. The birth name and the coronation name, those that were most used, were written inside a 'cartouche', a knotted, elongated loop (cat. 1), symbolizing the pharaoh's dominion over everything encompassed by the passage of the sun. One or two of these cartouches can easily be recognised on most monuments referring to the kings of Egypt. In fact, it was with the help of these graphic reference points that Jean-François Champollion identified the names of Ptolemy, Cleopatra, Thutmose III and Ramesses II on the first monuments he analysed.

The ups and downs of memory

While the typical figure of the pharaoh, whose personality is subsumed in an atemporal function, is fascinating precisely because of its stability, the ancient monuments of Egypt, the accounts of Greco-Roman historians, as well as the anecdotal but symbolic Ramses condom mentioned above, also show that some sovereigns stood out in the long list of titleholders. The preparatory work for the exhibition has involved extracting all posthumous mentions and appearances of kings and queens from ancient documentation, literature and iconography from the Middle Ages right up to contemporary advertising and performing arts. Proper names, which are revealing in every era, are also included: for example, the popularity of the name Ramses among the Copts, since the beginning of the twentieth century, expresses their claim to be direct descendants of the pharaohs. From this initial corpus, gathered without any chronological or geographical preconceptions, it has become clear that some characters are better represented than others, a useful statistical reflection of their importance in general culture. Thus Cleopatra, who was hardly remembered in her own country before the end of antiquity, wins hands down as the most prominent Egyptian sovereign in Western art to this day.

The list of memorable sovereigns does in fact vary over time. Who today knows about Sneferu, Amenemhat III or Thutmose III? Yet the Egyptians remembered them as exceptional rulers, comparable to gods. Who has heard of Psamtik, Amasis or Nectanebo? Yet for a long time they were the only pharaohs known in the West, symbols of Egypt, its power, its knowledge and its strangeness. But everyone has heard of Tutankhamun and Nefertiti, who are iconic figures today, although the Egyptians had quickly erased them from their memory. Only Cheops (now usually called Khufu), Ramesses II and Cleopatra seem to have enjoyed uninterrupted fame, though there have been ups and downs, from the moment they ascended the throne until the twenty-first century. The stars of today are not always those of yesterday, nor of tomorrow.

We may well ask ourselves what these few chosen ones did to deserve such celebrity. Khufu commissioned the building of the most monumental and enduring tomb in history, constructed according to plans that verge on geometric perfection. Ramesses II took advantage of his very long reign to mobilize all the riches of Egypt, Nubia and the Near East to glorify the royal function and his own person. As for Psamtik and Amasis, they opened their kingdom up to the Greeks, who therefore wrote about them extensively. Much was also written about Cleopatra, this time by the historians of the Roman Empire: she embodied their fear and fascination for the Orient, whose legacy they linked to the whole of the modern West. Conversely, Tutankhamun's fame is based on little more than the fact that his tomb and his grave goods, covered by rubble and fallen rocks, escaped the looters. Nefertiti, for her part, was lucky that her husband's political and religious reform failed and that his capital was abandoned overnight, along with her striking portrait made by the royal sculptor and now on display in Berlin. These two have been particular beneficiaries of extensive media attention since their rediscovery at the beginning of the twentieth century.

Finally, historical reality is not really important in this history of pharaonic popularity. A few military, economic or artistic achievements launch a career, but they are themselves fleeting, relative and subjective. The fame of some sovereigns ends in overtaking them and acquires an existence of its own, which survives long beyond them, even though it may be distorted. That fame can in due course be extinguished, but it can also be rekindled and shine more brightly, as the consequence of events now entirely beyond the individuals' control. It does need, however, some material support, a text or an image, which can be forgotten or put aside and then rediscovered, like those films that the public shuns in the cinema but that a new generation, brought up on cassettes, videos or streaming, defines a classic.

Superstars at the museum

This fickleness of history and fame has shaped the concept of the exhibition, which attempts to embrace a cultural phenomenon over a long period and to explore contemporary society's real or imagined roots in a civilization that is both 'Oriental' and African. The exhibition gives the Western viewer the opportunity to consider the fact, not immediately self-evident, that ancient and exotic royal figures have just as much of a place in our general culture as the European Middle Ages or the Age of Enlightenment — perhaps even more. The transmission of historical knowledge is a fundamental phenomenon for the societies that inhabit Europe and the Mediterranean shores. In terms of Egyptology, it has been studied by eminent scholars who have produced key works of reference, such as Dietrich Wildung, Pascal Vernus, Jan Assmann and Khaled el-Enany. No less qualified than these are the three Egyptologists who have been invited to explore more detailed aspects of the subject here: with contributions from their chosen fields, they shed light on Egyptian antiquity's paths of memory. Bernard Mathieu focuses on the knowledge that the ancient Egyptians had of their own past and history. Michel Chauveau offers a more detailed study of the royal figures in late literature recovered by Greco-Roman historians, while Simon Connor analyses the impact of images and their destruction in the creation of an official history of the monarchy.

Some monographic exhibitions have already addressed the posthumous memory of various royal Egyptian figures, often logically at the end of the exhibition.[1] None until now has considered the phenomenon for its own sake, as it applies to all the sovereigns, nor taken it up to the present day. In this context, Jean-Marcel Humbert, who has an almost inexhaustible stock of information about Egyptomania, gives us a hit parade revealing the figures who have most strongly represented the Western fascination for Egyptian royalty. In terms of this enthusiasm for Egypt, Calouste Gulbenkian stands out at a moment in the twentieth century that was decisive for the perception of pharaonic art as a noble art. João Carvalho Dias, who has long been studying the collector's archives, reveals the significant ties that history has weaved between the founder of the Gulbenkian Museum and Howard Carter, the unwitting inventor of the media superstar and national icon that is Tutankhamun.

No previous exhibition has ever tried to present the memory of famous pharaohs in the material culture and imaginary of Egyptians today. In 2017 and 2018, a short survey in Cairo and Luxor made it possible to observe the situation on the ground, to collect documents and objects that would be significant for the exhibition, and to understand the key points and challenges of the issue.[2] Westerners have long considered, more or less implicitly, that the Egyptians were not interested in the pre-Islamic past. Yet recent work, particularly by Donald Reid, has revealed that it is these same Westerners who have largely influenced this situation. Modern Egyptians have also advanced the history

1 For example: *Cléopâtre dans le miroir de l'art occidental* at the Musée Rath, Geneva, in 2004; *Reines d'Égypte, d'Hétephérès à Cléopâtre* at the Grimaldi Forum, Monaco, in 2008; *Im Licht von Amarna. 100 Jahre Fund der Nofretete* at the Neues Museum, Berlin, in 2012; *Sésostris III, pharaon de légende* at the Palais des Beaux-Arts, Lille, and *Le Mythe Cléopâtre* at the Pinacothèque de Paris in 2014; *Khâemouaset, le prince archéologue* at the Musée Départemental Arles Antique, and *Ramses — Göttlicher Herrscher am Nil* at the Badisches Landesmuseum, Karlsruhe, in 2016.

2 The study, undertaken by Mohamed Alaa Sadek and Frédéric Mougenot, also enriched Mucem's collection in this field.

of Pharaonism and Egyptian Egyptology, with certain exponents such as Zahi Hawass leading the way, by promoting this ancient heritage to their fellow citizens. The work of Fayza Haikal, who has long highlighted the cultural and affective ties that bind her compatriots to the pharaohs' civilization, made her the perfect author to address these questions at the beginning of this catalogue.

Today, knowledge is advanced more than ever by the painstaking work undertaken by ceramologists, anthropologists, archeo-zoologists, paleobotanists and philologists, who are studying ordinary daily life among the people who lived in the Nile Valley. Yet these eminent Egyptologists, despite their extensive experience, their scientific rigour and their critical knowledge, must still surely succumb to the charms of pharaonic celebrities, just like any visitor to the Louvre or any admirer of Joseph L. Mankiewicz's *Cleopatra*. The latest discoveries in the eastern deserts that refer to the name of Khufu and the construction of his pyramid, recent publications on the hypothetical presence of Nefertiti's tomb behind that of Tutankhamun, and the blockbuster exhibition of Tutankhamun's treasure in the Grande Halle de La Villette in Paris, must have suddenly sounded the fanfare of fame and reawakened childhood dreams in these scholars as much as in ordinary people.

ESSAYS

THE EGYPTIANS AND THE PHARAOHS TODAY

FAYZA HAIKAL

How can the dichotomy that the pharaoh's image conjures up in the memory of Egyptians be explained? For today, the word evokes not only grandeur and power but despotism and intolerance — in fact in some Arab dialects it has produced a verb, *yatafar'an*, which emphasises the arrogant and tyrannical qualities of those it describes. The negative image of the pharaoh comes to us from the Bible and the Qur'an, where it relates principally to the Pharaoh of Exodus, identified by his title rather than his name. The Qur'an explains that when Moses returned to Egypt to bring his people away, he challenged Pharaoh with the power of his own religion and his own God, proving his superiority in a competition with the magicians of his court. When the magicians were defeated, they turned to Moses and his God, rejecting the despot Pharaoh, who condemned them to death. We witness here political, religious and social conflict — which could perhaps be compared to the conflict that occurred in the time of Akhenaten, when he wanted to impose his god Aten and his 'monotheism'.

200

Edition of the magazine *Mickey*, 17 August 1967, Cairo.

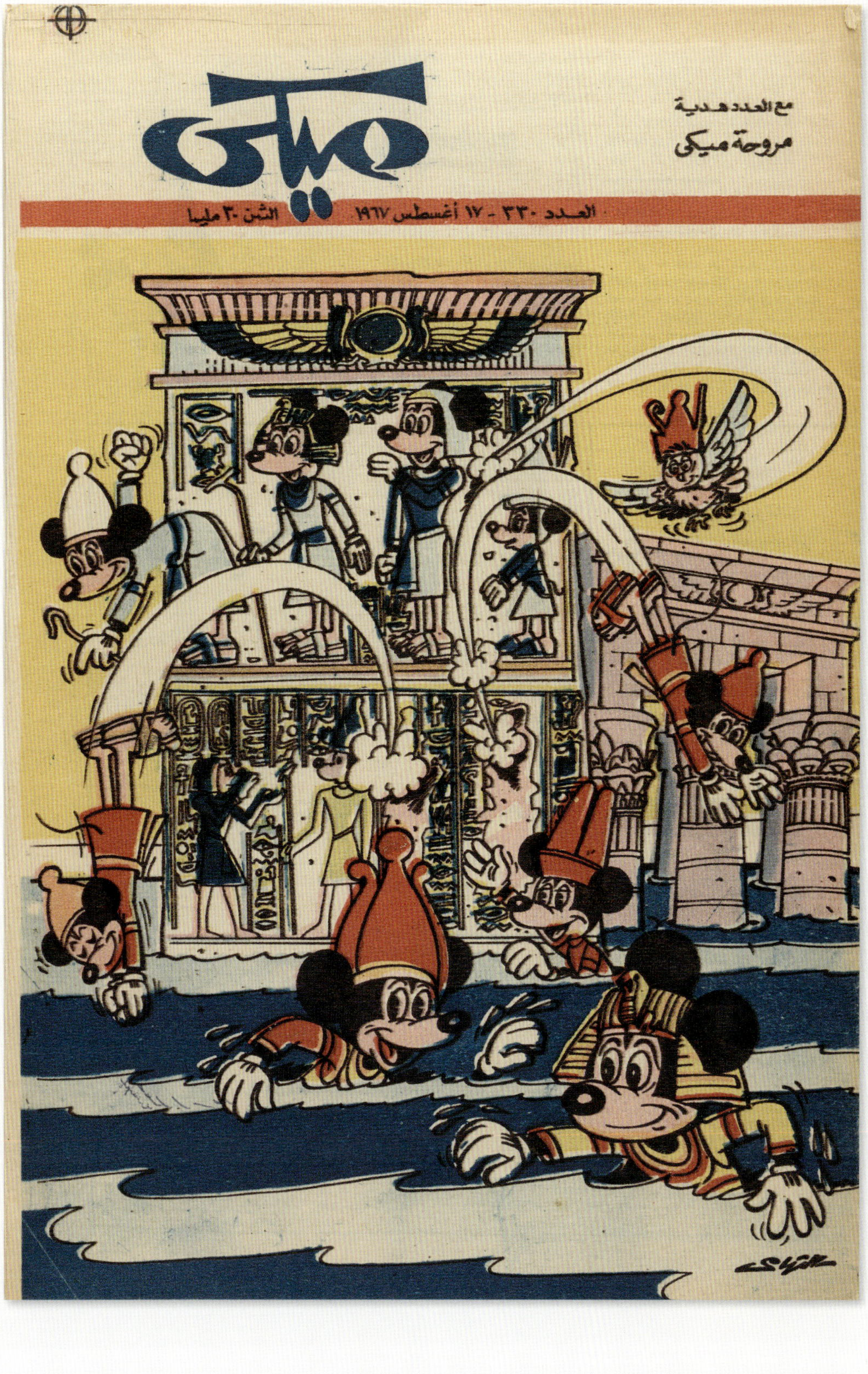

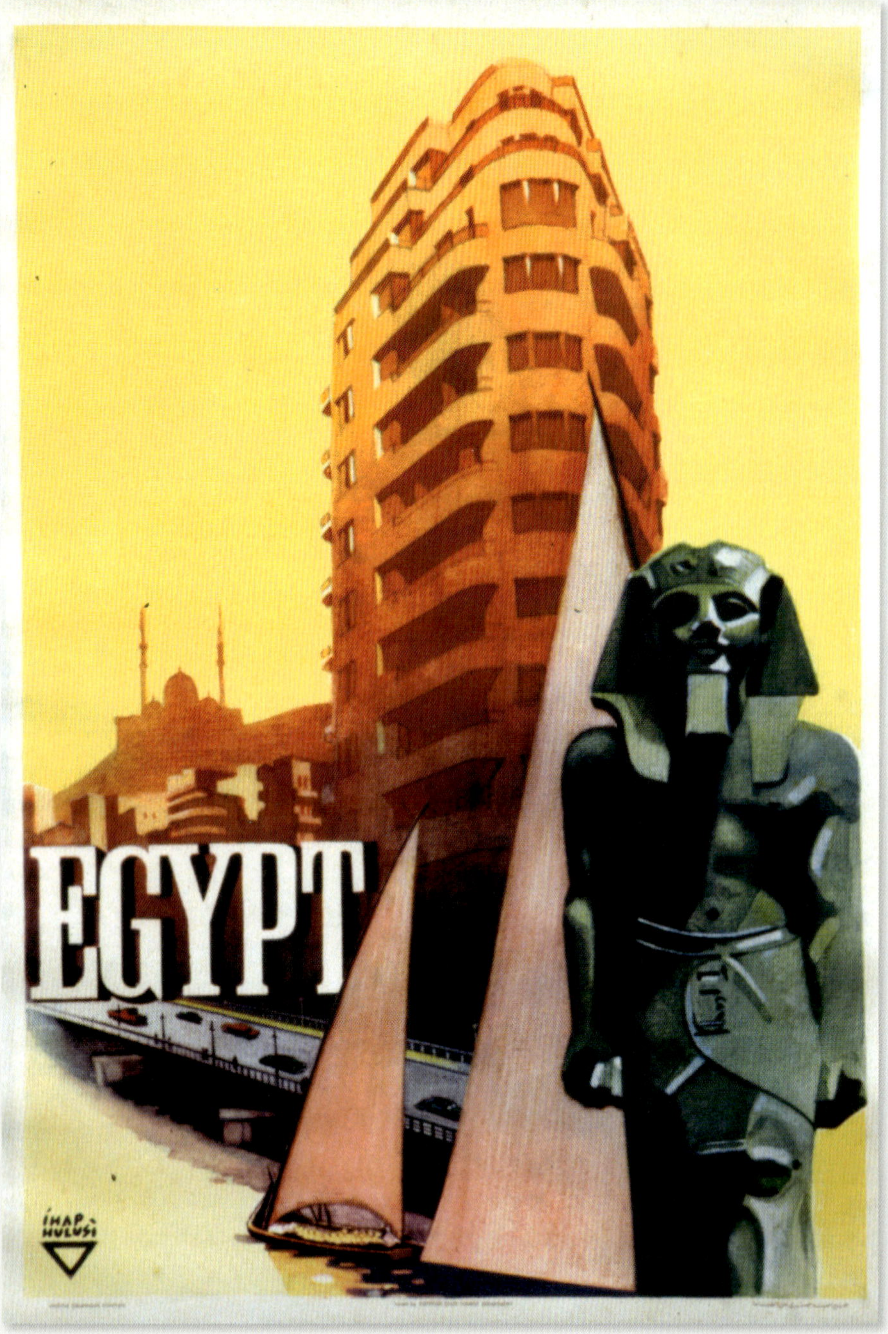

188

İhap Hulusi Görey (1898–1986) and Institut Graphique Égyptien, poster promoting tourism in Egypt, Cairo, 1960.

The pharaohs today: popular pride and nationalist emblem

It is true that the paganism of the pharaonic ideology, which saw the pharaoh as the son of gods, has no appeal for today's Egyptians, who are all monotheists. They are nevertheless proud of descending from great conquerors such as Ahmose, who freed Egypt from the domination of the Hyksos (cat. 198); Thutmose III and Ramesses II, who turned Egypt into a great empire; Hatshepsut the 'pharaoh queen'; Akhenaten and his wife, the beautiful Nefertiti; Tutankhamun with his sumptuous treasure; and Cleopatra with her storybook life. This, in a nutshell, is what most Egyptians remember today when they leave school. Their pride is reinforced by the fact that after the seventh century Arab conquest, Muhammad, the prophet of Islam, married an Egyptian woman and never hid his admiration for this great civilisation, as was also the case for his immediate disciples and later the Arab historians who visited the country. There was even an attempt to match the Egyptian gods with the prophets mentioned in the Qur'an. In everyone's eyes, ancient Egypt was a glorious period thanks to the power of the pharaohs. And through the might of the creative word, mentioned in all religions, the word 'pharaoh' on its own still embodies that power and transmits it to whoever bears the name. That is why the Egyptian national football team is called the 'Pharaohs', and it is also why the State reminds the people that they are descended from the pharaohs every time they want them to sign up to some major project to benefit the country's future — for example the Aswan High Dam. The last kings of Egypt, Fuad I and his son Farouk, had themselves portrayed as pharaohs and commissioned the building of monuments in a very Egyptianising style. In Fuad I's parliament, a huge hall, entirely decorated with scenes derived from ancient Egypt, featured his name inscribed in hieroglyphs in cartouches. As for Farouk, he commissioned a hunting pavilion built in a pharaonic style, at the foot of the pyramids of Giza; its façade was adorned with statues showing him as a pharaoh, again with his name inscribed in cartouches. After the 1952 revolution, which forced King Farouk to abdicate and go into exile, and which led to the kingdom of Egypt becoming a republic two years later, presidents often had themselves shown with the Great Sphinx or the pyramids of Giza in the background: no monument could evoke Egypt more clearly.

But thirty years later, with the military revolt and the emergence of the Muslim Brotherhood on the country's political scene, the image of the despot pharaoh resurfaced. On 6 October 1981, one of Sadat's assassins shouted 'I've killed Pharaoh!'.[1] Sadat was buried in a very simple rectangular sarcophagus, beneath the open-sided pyramid erected as a memorial commemorating the soldiers who fell on the field of honour in the 1973 war, a clear symbol of the Egyptomania of the time[2] (cat. 173).

[1] Lewis, 1984.
[2] Haikal, 2003.

171

Edition of *Al-Musawar*, 14 January 1927: Saad Zaghloul, prime minister of Egypt, visits the building site of *Egypt's Renaissance* by Mahmoud Mokhtar, Dar Al-Hilalc (publisher), Cairo.

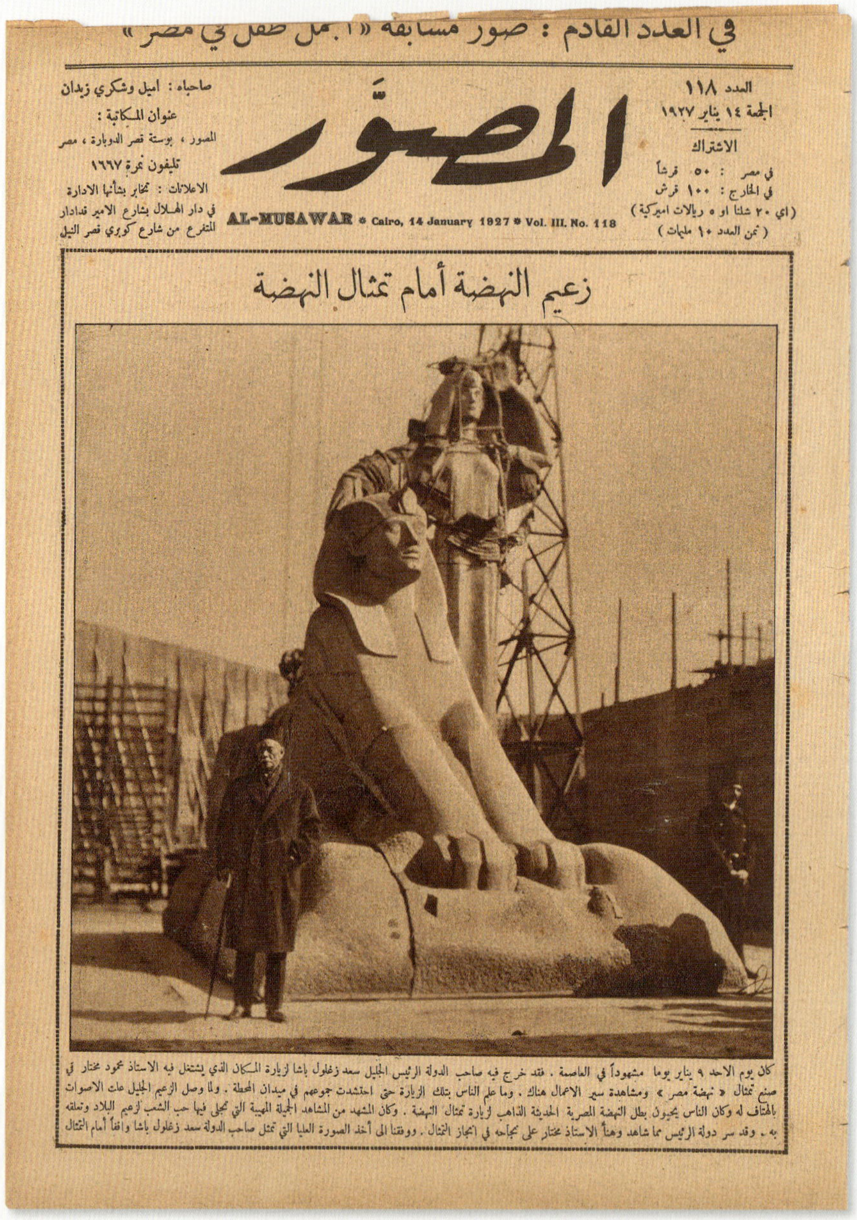

في العدد القادم : صور مسابقة «أجمل طفل في مصر»

المصوَّر

العدد ١١٨
الجمعة ١٤ يناير ١٩٢٧

الاشتراك
في مصر : ٥٠ قرشاً
في الخارج : ١٠٠ قرش
(اي ٢٠ شلنا او ٥ ريالات اميركية)
(ثمن العدد ١٠ مليمات)

صاحباه : اميل وشكري زيدان
عنوان المكاتبة :
المصور ، بوستة قصر الدوبارة ، مصر
تليفون نمرة ١٦٦٧
الاعلانات : تخابر بشأنها الادارة
في دار الهلال بشارع الامير قدادار
المتفرع من شارع كوبري قصر النيل

AL-MUSAWAR * Cairo, 14 January 1927 * Vol. III. No. 118

زعيم النهضة أمام تمثال النهضة

كان يوم الاحد ٩ يناير يوما مشهوداً في العاصمة . فقد خرج فيه صاحب الدولة الرئيس الجليل سعد زغلول باشا لزيارة المكان الذي يشتغل فيه الاستاذ محمود مختار في صنع تمثال « نهضة مصر » ومشاهدة سير الاعمال هناك . وما علم الناس بتلك الزيارة حتى احتشدت جموعهم في ميدان المحطة . ولما وصل الزعيم الجليل علت الاصوات بالهتاف له وكان الناس يحيون بطل النهضة المصرية الحديثة الذاهب لزيارة تمثال النهضة . وكان المشهد من المشاهد الجميلة المهيبة التي تجلى فيها حب الشعب لزعيم البلاد وتعلقه به . وقد سر دولة الرئيس مما شاهد وهنأ الاستاذ مختار على نجاحه في انجاز التمثال . ووفقنا الى أخذ الصورة العليا التي تمثل صاحب الدولة سعد زغلول باشا واقفاً أمام التمثال

But while the Egyptians are proud of their glorious past and celebrate it, do they know enough about it? Who knows now that ancient Egypt survives in Egyptian daily life, in some of its customs, in part of its mindset and in its contemporary culture?

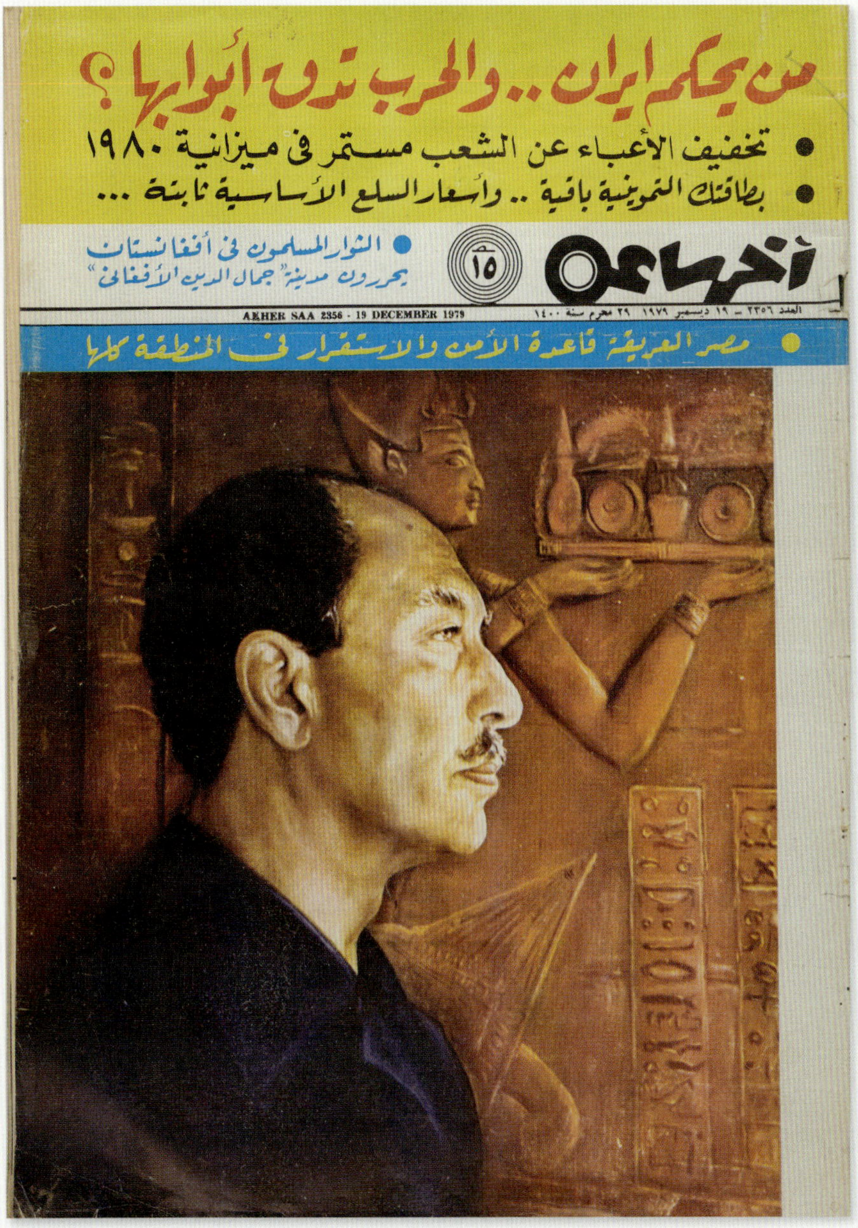

173

Edition of *Akher Sa'aa*, 19 December 1979, Cairo.

The profile of President Anwar Sadat stands out against an image in relief of a pharaoh holding up a tray of offerings.

What remains of ancient Egypt?

IN TOPOGRAPHY, TOPONOMY AND PROPER NAMES

From the time of the unification of Egypt around the end of the fourth millennium BCE, pharaohs reigned over the 'Two Lands' (Upper and Lower Egypt). Many towns have retained their ancient names, like the town of Damanhur/*Demi-en-Hor* south of Alexandria, which means 'the town of Horus' in Egyptian; Ehnasia/*Hut-nen-nesut*, 'the compound of the royal child'; Asyut/*Zawty*, 'the protected' in Middle Egypt; and Aswan /*Swen*, 'the market' or 'the trading place', in Upper Egypt. As in the case of towns, many first names have an ancient Egyptian origin, and most are used as much by Christians as by Muslims: Isis, Nefertiti and Cleopatra are classic examples, but in recent years many little girls have also been named Taia or Maia (Tutankhamun's wet nurse). There are even more male names: Ahmes, Ramses, Horus, Bakhoum/ Beshay, Bekhyt, and so on.[3]

IN WRITING AND LANGUAGE

Although Egyptian writing has left no traces in Arabic, Egyptian language and culture are certainly still in evidence. To appreciate this, it only takes a glance at the day's date marked on *Al-Ahram*, the best-known daily newspaper in Egypt. It is written in the Gregorian calendar (international), the Arabic Muslim calendar and the Coptic calendar, which has names for the months that go back to ancient Egypt. In modern Egyptian folk culture, the Coptic months are the basis for counting rhymes that children can easily remember, describing seasonal weather and crops. The Nilotic and societal environment is the basis for many metaphors in the Egyptian language. They can often be found in literary texts and some have passed into Arabic. For example, two people who get on very well are literally described as 'fat on honey' in both Egyptian and Arab dialect. 'Showing people the red eye', i.e. to threaten them, also goes back to ancient Egypt, alluding to the eye of the goddess Sekhmet when she is angry. 'Having a big eye', in both languages, means to be greedy or gluttonous. Because the Nile is so important in the lives of Egyptians, water sometimes stands in for all alimentary resources: so the expression 'to cut off someone's water' means, in both languages, to cut off their supplies. Everyday words have also found their way into Arabic: the Egyptian verb *ini*, normally translated as 'to bring' can also mean 'to reach' in both languages. Other words such as *ta-ta*, which a mother traditionally uses to encourage her children to walk, or *mebou*, when she gives them water, probably derive respectively from *titi*, 'to tread' and

[3] Nureddin, 1998.

[4] Haikal, 2014.

mou, 'water' in Egyptian. Such cases occur quite frequently in Egyptian Arabic dialect. Some words have even crossed over into other countries. The word 'alchemy' probably derives from *Kemet*, a name for pharaonic Egypt. Adobe, the brick made from earth mixed with straw, comes from the Egyptian word *djebet*, meaning 'brick' which acquired the definite article when it passed into Arabic and became *adobe* when it reached Spain.[4]

IN FOLK CULTURE

The sound of music made by ancient instruments is still often heard in Egypt, along with the echoes of tales and poems, sometimes with later material added. Egyptologists also recognise superstitions nearly five centuries old, adapted to modern circumstances, such as the breaking of one or several pieces of pottery after the departure of unwelcome visitors to stop them returning. The ancient Egyptians broke pots that they had used for the embalming and funeral of their loved ones, to prevent death returning to their family too soon. Another tradition that has been preserved is writing magic words on healing statues or on the sides and rim of a bowl, so that the text's magic dissolves into the water poured into it, and cures the ailing body of the patient who is given the water to drink or is bathed with it.

There is also the habit of not naming illnesses or problems, to stop them being conjured up through the creative power of the word. As was the practice among ancient Egyptians, danger is averted by alluding to ills without naming them, or by redirecting them towards the sick person's 'enemies'. In the Papyrus Vandier, to indicate that the pharaoh was ill, it was written that 'the enemies' of the pharaoh were suffering and a doctor must be called. Today as then, when speaking of someone we do not wish to see, we say 'the one far away' or 'the unnameable one'.

Reminders of religion or ancient tales are also numerous in modern folklore. 'The eye of the sun' is a common expression in the modern language, like the nursery rhymes that allude to nurturing goddesses appearing in the form of trees or cows. It is likely that the children who sing them and the mothers who teach them no longer know what they mean, but the tradition endures: they are modified a little, while the rhyme and rhythm is retained.

IN FUNERARY TRADITIONS AND RITUALS

The most tenacious and remarkable traditions in modern Egypt are those that concern the unknown, death and the afterlife. For example, the coffin in which the deceased is carried to the tomb is known as *neb-ânkh*, 'lord of life', echoed by its Arab equivalent *al naash* ('the one who brings alive again'), probably because the word's power will assist the deceased's resurrection. The food offerings called *hetepu* — 'mercy' or 'peace' in Egyptian — are called *rahma* in Arabic, which has the same meaning. According to Judeo-Christian and Muslim tradition, the deceased has no need of food: today these offerings are no longer made for the dead but they are distributed among the poor in the name of the deceased, so that God will forgive and bless them. The offering bread still goes by the Egyptian name *sherek*, and resembles its ancestor. The visit to the cemetery is called 'going up' to the cemetery, like the word *peret* in ancient Egypt. Finally, in modern Egypt there are many tombs constructed as 'houses of eternity', as they were in ancient Egypt, so that visitors can be more easily received when they come to make food offerings for their dead, decorate their tombs with flowers or plants symbolising rebirth, and often even sharing a meal in their company: this does not reflect either Christian or Muslim tradition. The administrative organisation of large cemeteries can also be compared with the way things were managed in ancient Egypt.[5]

IN EGYPTIAN SPIRITUALITY

The Egyptians have always been a very religious people and their spirituality manifests itself in different ways, depending on their cultural level and the depth of their faith. They have always been very attached to their 'saints', to whom they attribute powers similar to those of deified figures in ancient Egypt, and they often appeal for their help to resolve everyday problems, because they consider them to be the best able to intercede with God. As in ancient Egypt, they still write to them, handing their letters over to officials in the churches or in the mausolea where they lie, sticking them into the frames of icons, or placing them on tombstones or in mosques. The day of their death, or 'rebirth' in heaven, is the subject of major celebrations and pilgrimages are organised by the church or by Muslim brotherhoods for the faithful. Cattle are sacrificed to honour the saint and important guests are invited to the meal. But since antiquity, these religious festivals have also included community support rituals: the poor are fed by the organisers and they are also often presented with offerings made by benefactors devoted to the celebrated saint, who use these occasions to demonstrate their charitable commitment. On an economic and social level, these are opportunities for interesting meetings and exchanges.[6]

[5] El-Shohoumi, 2014.
[6] Haikal, 2007.

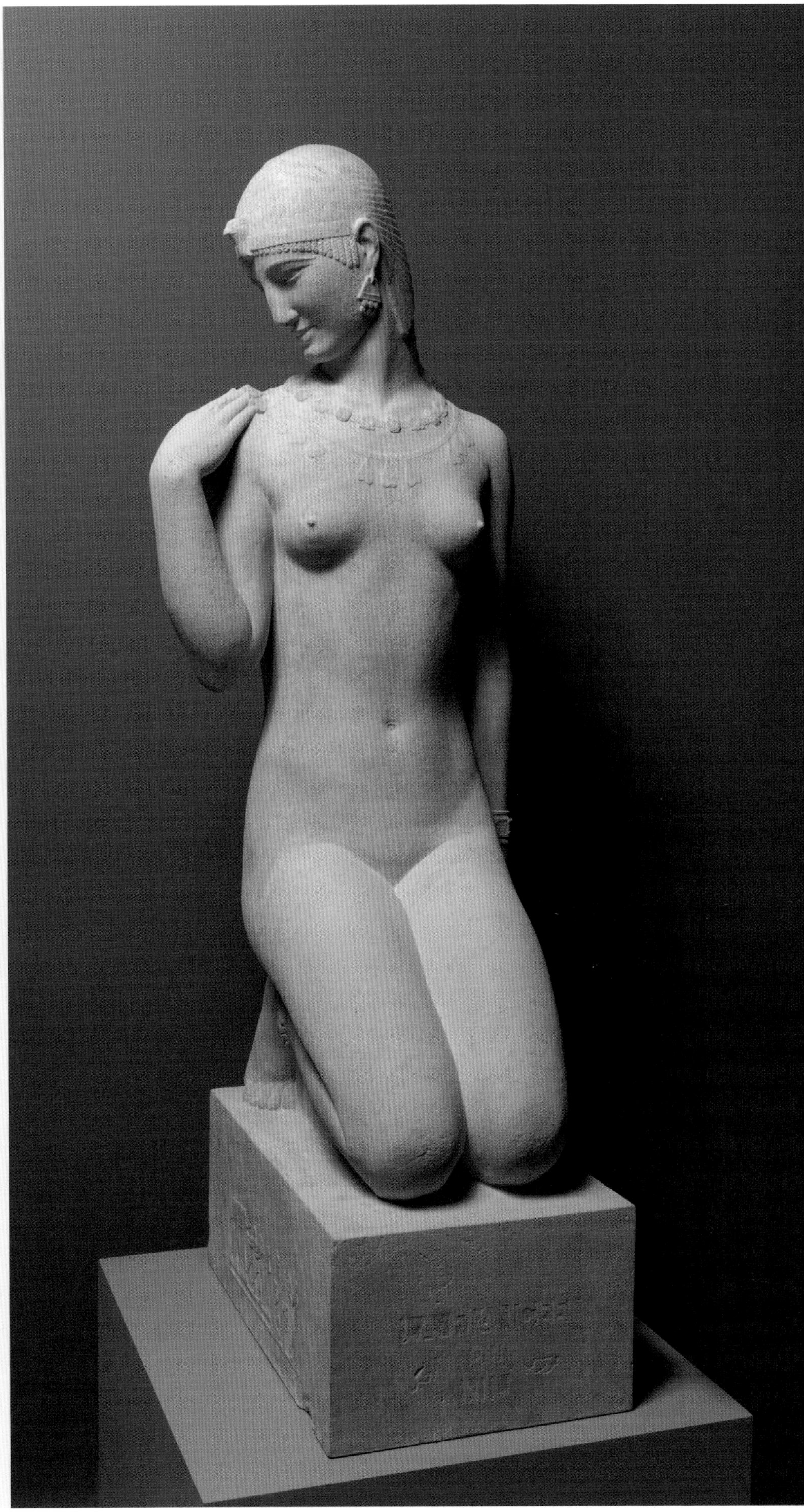

172

Mahmoud Mokhtar, *Arus el-Nil, La Fiancée du Nil* (known in English as *The Bride of the Nile*), Cairo, c. 1929.

The Egyptians' Egyptomania

As a national experience, Egyptomania began in the nineteenth century after the return of Rifa'a al-Tahtawi, a senior official working for Mohamed Ali Pasha, the ruler of Egypt under the Ottoman Empire, who was sent to France by the Egyptian government, as escort to the first group of scholarship students sent abroad. He later became responsible for Egypt's national education and cultural affairs. However, Egyptomania did not truly blossom until after the epic poem by Hafez Ibrahim, which glorified ancient Egypt and recalled the great moments of its history (*Egypt talks about herself*, 1894). After this text came other great literary works: the best-known in the West are probably those of Naguib Mahfouz (1911–2006, cat. 198). In the visual arts, it was the discovery of the tomb of Tutankhamun in 1922 that unleashed a new wave of international Egyptomania: in Egypt, this discovery coincided with a burst of nationalist energy and militant opposition to the British, who were still occupying the country despite the declaration of independence. This was when Mahmoud Mokhtar created his famous statue, *Egypt's Renaissance* (designed in 1919–20, cat. 171): pharaonic in its size and in the perfect polish of its rose granite, this sculpture represents an Egyptian peasant woman standing beside the Great Sphinx, rising, as she pushes aside her veil, to symbolise the nation's reawakening. Many other painters and sculptors followed in this path — adopting a form of 'Egyptian-ness' rather than 'Egyptomania' (cat. 172).

↓ FIG. 1
Léopold Savine (1861–1934), statue of Mustafa Kamil (1910) erected in Mustafa Kamil Square in Cairo in 1940.

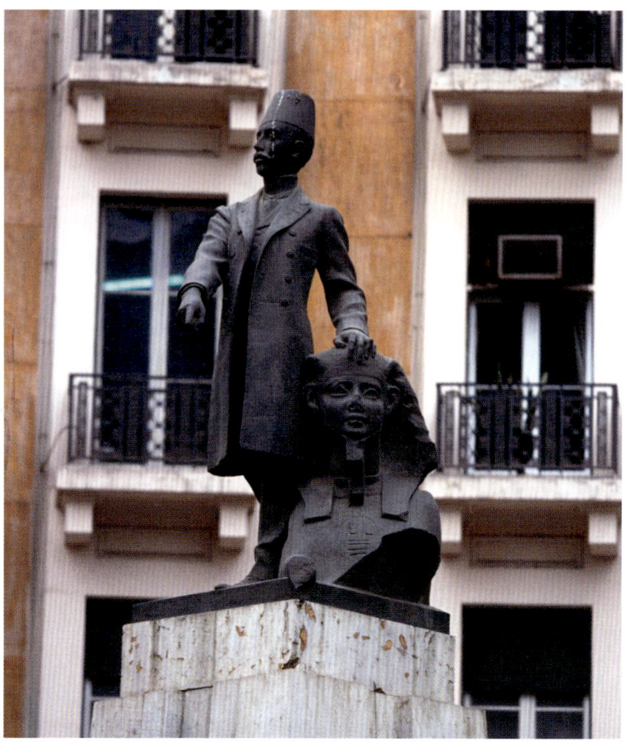

198

Children's edition of *Kifâh Tiba* (Thebes at War) by Naguib Mahfouz, adapted by Mohamed Al-Mou'alim, illustrated by Mostafa Hussein, Dar Al-Shorouk (publisher), Cairo, 2009.

This 1944 novel, which describes King Ahmose's battle to free Egypt from the foreign Hyksos dynasty, was originally a pamphlet opposing British occupation and turned Ahmose into a national hero who is still studied in schools.

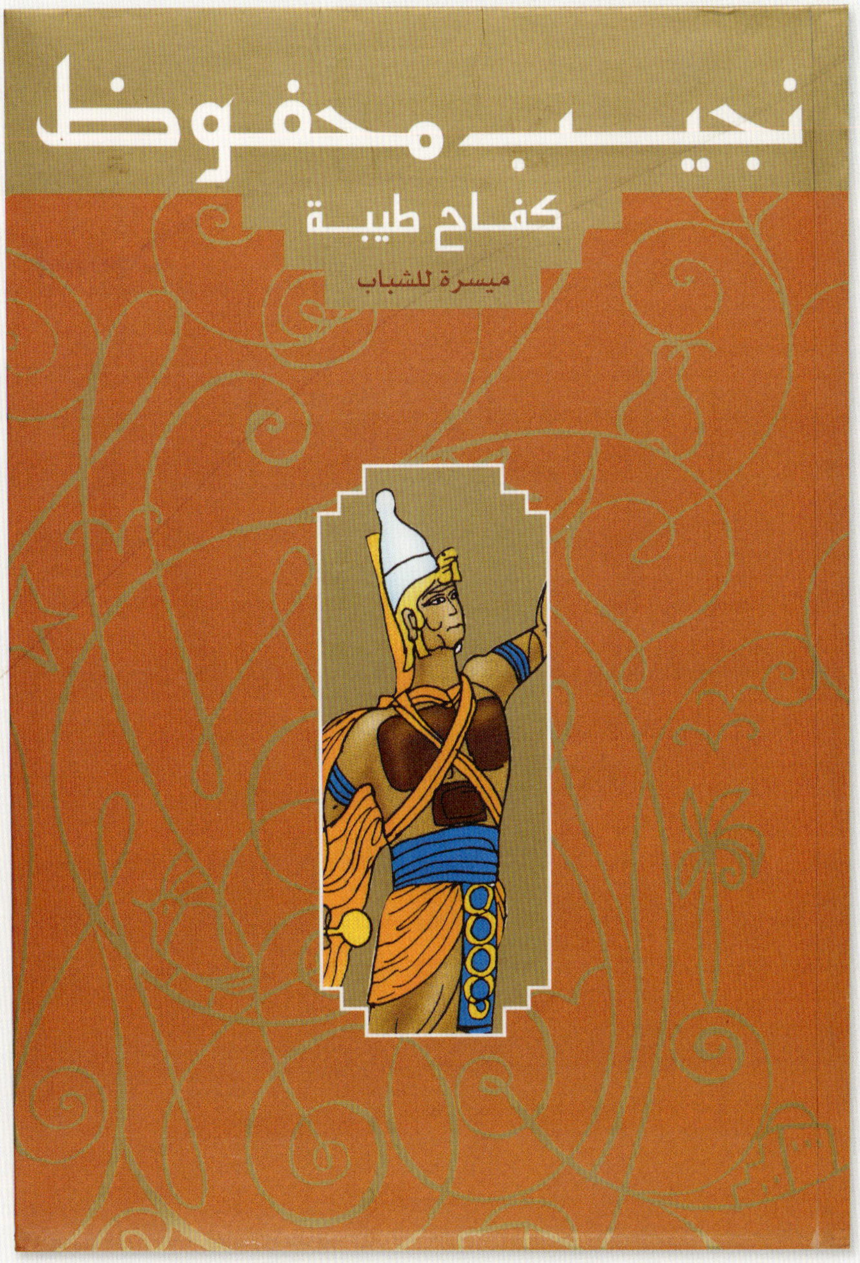

Between World Wars I and II, a great number of official monuments continued to be built in this style. The most remarkable were: the mausoleum in the shape of an ancient temple façade, built to honour Saad Zaghloul Pasha, a great national hero who died in 1927; the railway station at Giza, decorated with columns and other motifs drawn from ancient architecture; the entry to the zoo at Giza with its Egyptianising bas-reliefs; and the statue of Mustafa Kamil, his hand resting on the head of a sphinx in the middle of the roundabout that bears his name (fig. 1). Finally, the great Egyptian institutions — universities, insurance and tourism companies, the airline Egypt Air, the Supreme Constitutional Court and even certain ministries — sourced their emblems from ancient Egypt (cat. 188).[7]

[7] Haikal, 2004.

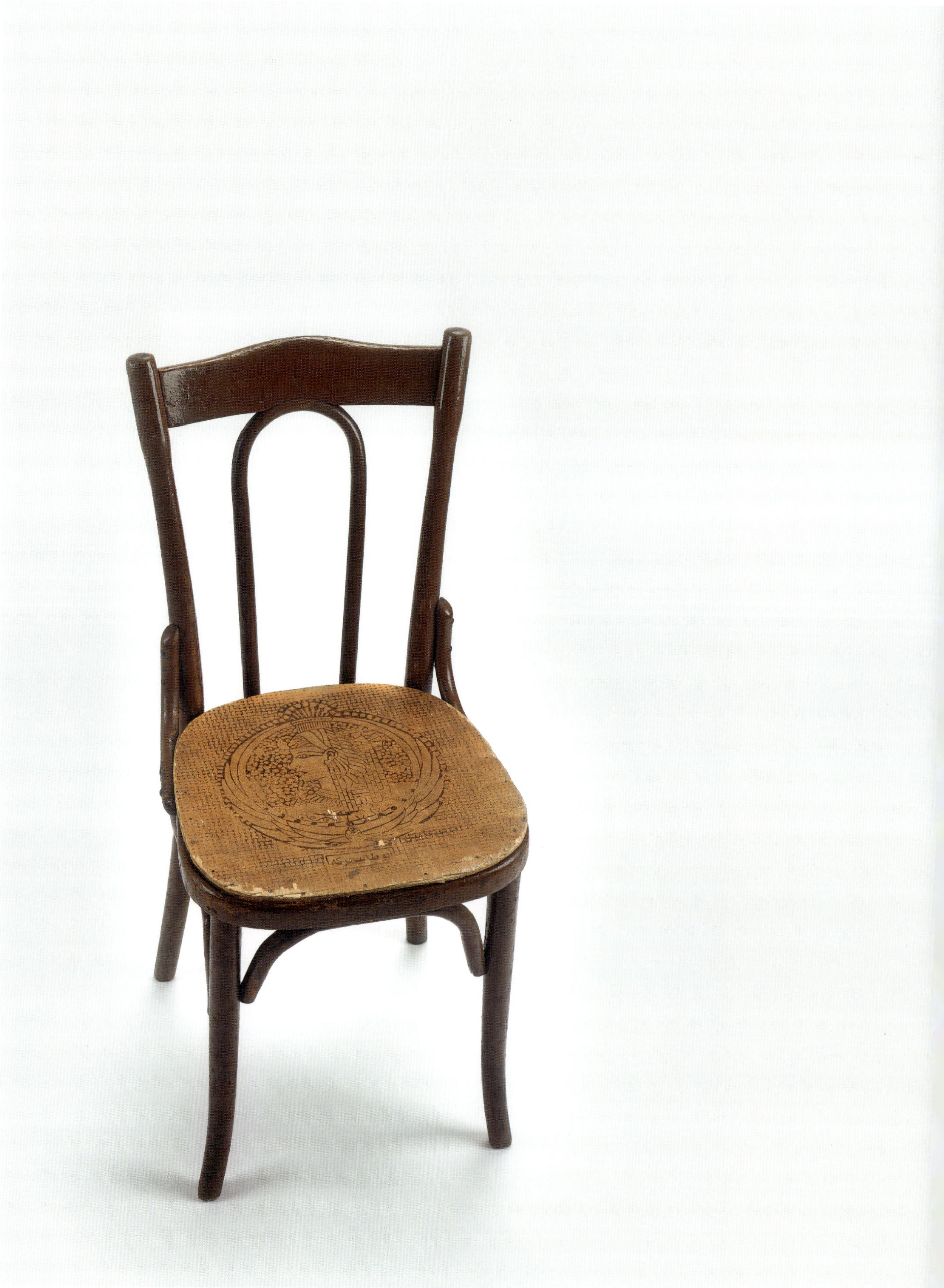

181–182

Café and shopkeepers' chairs: one decorated with an image of the Misr business logo, sometimes known as 'Cleopatra', burnt into the wood using pyrography (left), the other with the mask of Tutankhamun (right), Cairo, twentieth to twenty-first century.

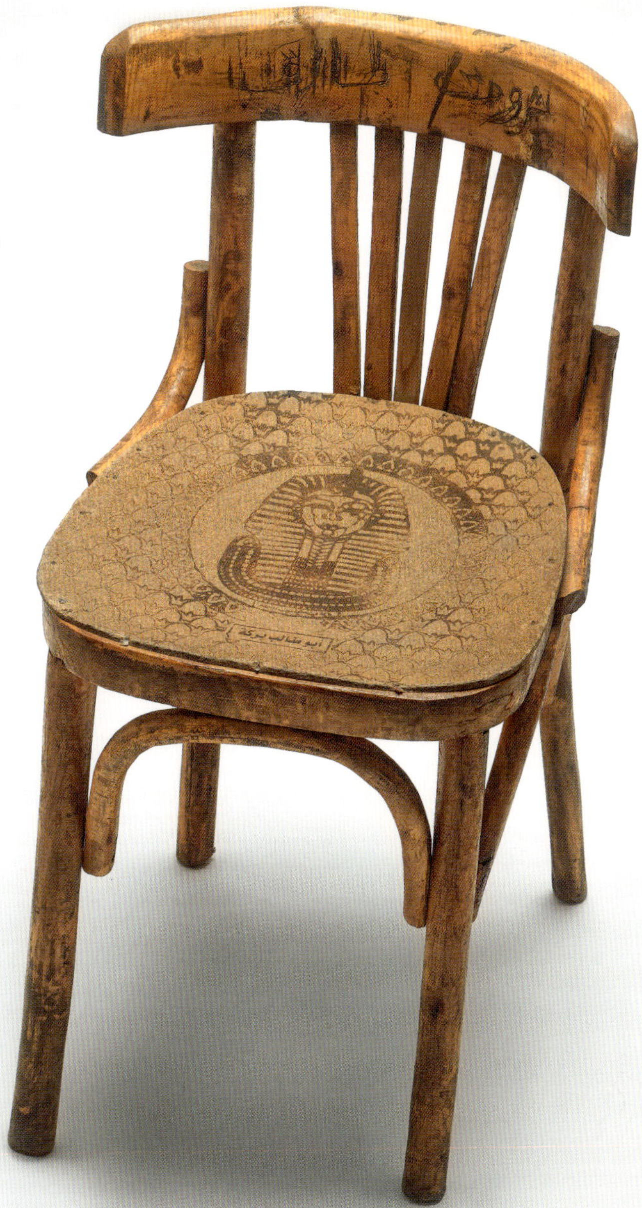

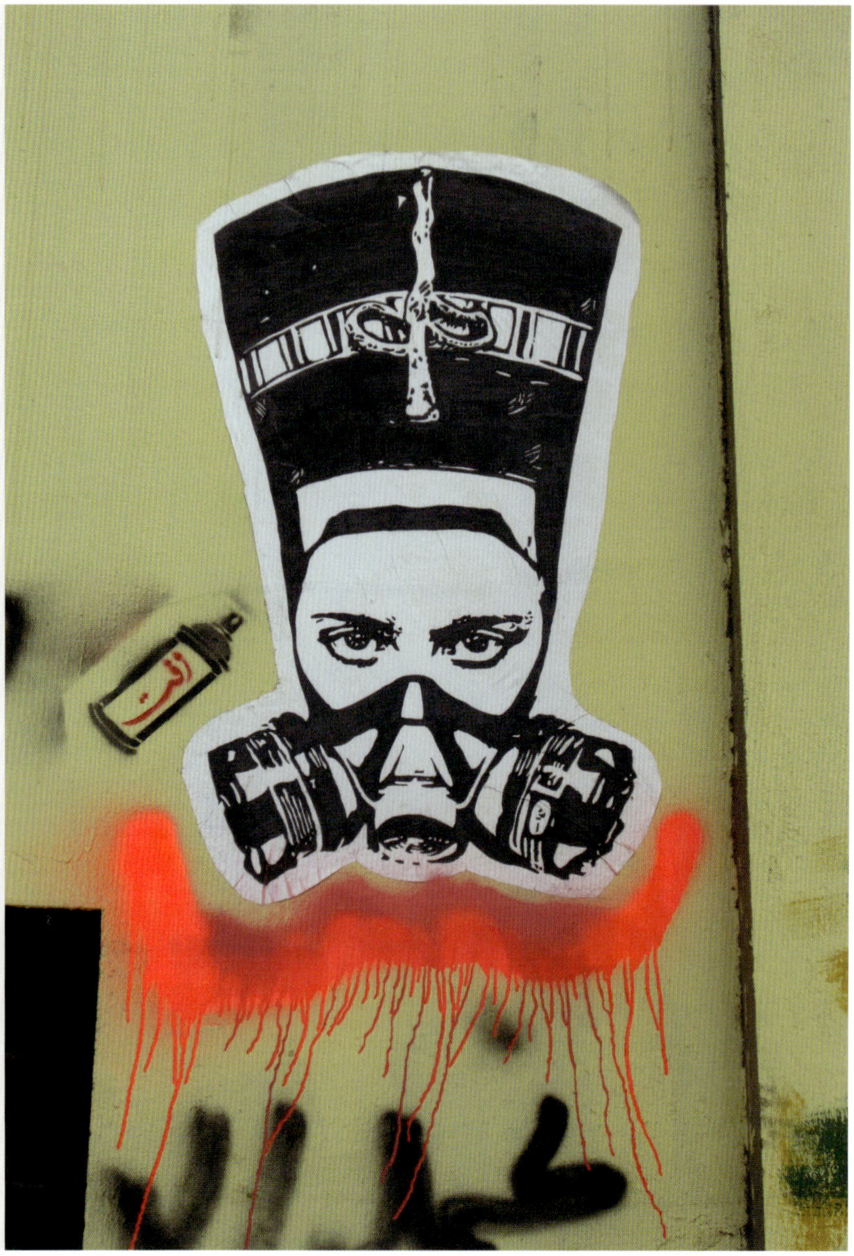

202

El-Zeft, *Nefertiti*, allegory of the Revolution, Cairo, 2013.

After the 1952 revolution, President Nasser, seeking to encourage Egyptian industry, named the first car to be produced in Egypt 'Ramses' (cat. 174), while the first sewing machine that came out of the national factories was given the name 'Nefertiti' (cat. 180). In the cafés, wooden chairs were decorated with images of Cleopatra or Tutankhamun (cats. 181–182).

Finally, it is impossible to mention Egyptomania in contemporary arts without acknowledging its role as graffiti in the 2011 revolution and the ensuing upheaval (cat. 202). Ancient Egypt is everywhere around: with its watching pharaohs, its people lamenting and mourning their martyrs, its hieroglyphic texts alongside. The Egyptian people express their emotion through the art that represents them and that they know best.[8]

[8] Haikal, 2014.

State and NGOs efforts to preserve the heritage

Aware of the unrivalled value of their heritage, the State and Egyptian intellectuals are battling today not only to create new museums that are worthy of it, but also to protect it, despite the modest means at their disposal. NGOs and other committed charitable organisations are sharing the task of spreading knowledge among the poorest classes of society; meanwhile the Ministry of Antiquities has returned to its former policy in relation to primary schools and colleges, encouraging pupils and students to visit the country's museums.

TO WHAT EXTENT WERE THE EGYPTIANS AWARE OF THEIR OWN HISTORY?

BERNARD MATHIEU

A review of their profuse written output leaves no doubt that the Egyptians of antiquity took pains to record their own history scrupulously. This is noted by Diodorus of Sicily, who asserted in the first century BCE that 'the priests possessed records in their sacred books about all of them [the rulers of Egypt], which from antiquity were unfailingly handed down to their successors, describing the stature of each king, his character, and the achievements of his reign'.[1]

[1] Diodorus, *The Library of History*, 1.44,4.

48

Fragment of a statue dedicated by Senwosret I to King Sneferu, Serabit el-Khadim, Egypt, reign of Senwosret I (c. 1944–1900 BCE).

This statue comes from the turquoise mines of Sinai, where the pharaoh Sneferu had sent expeditions about seven hundred years earlier.

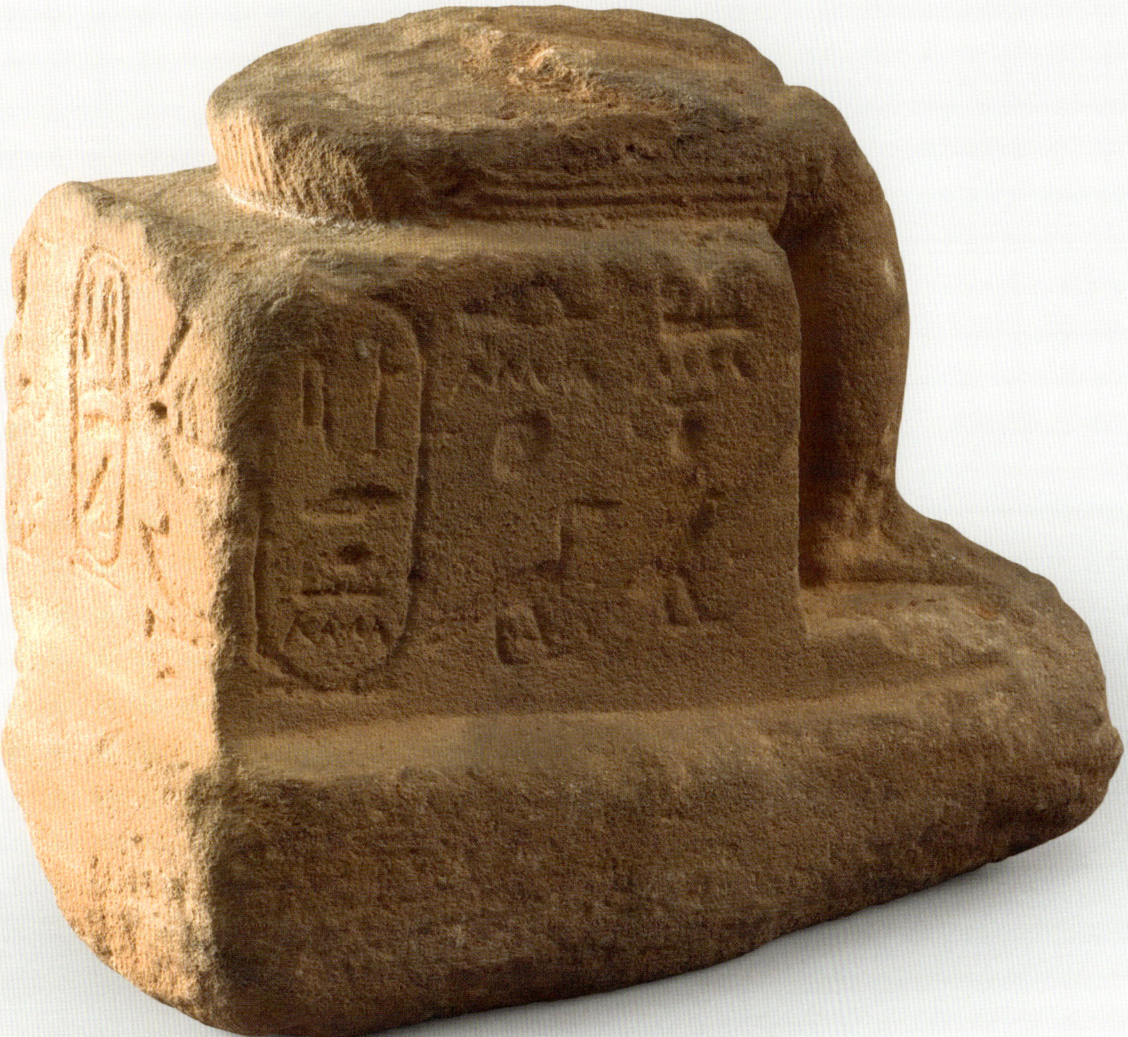

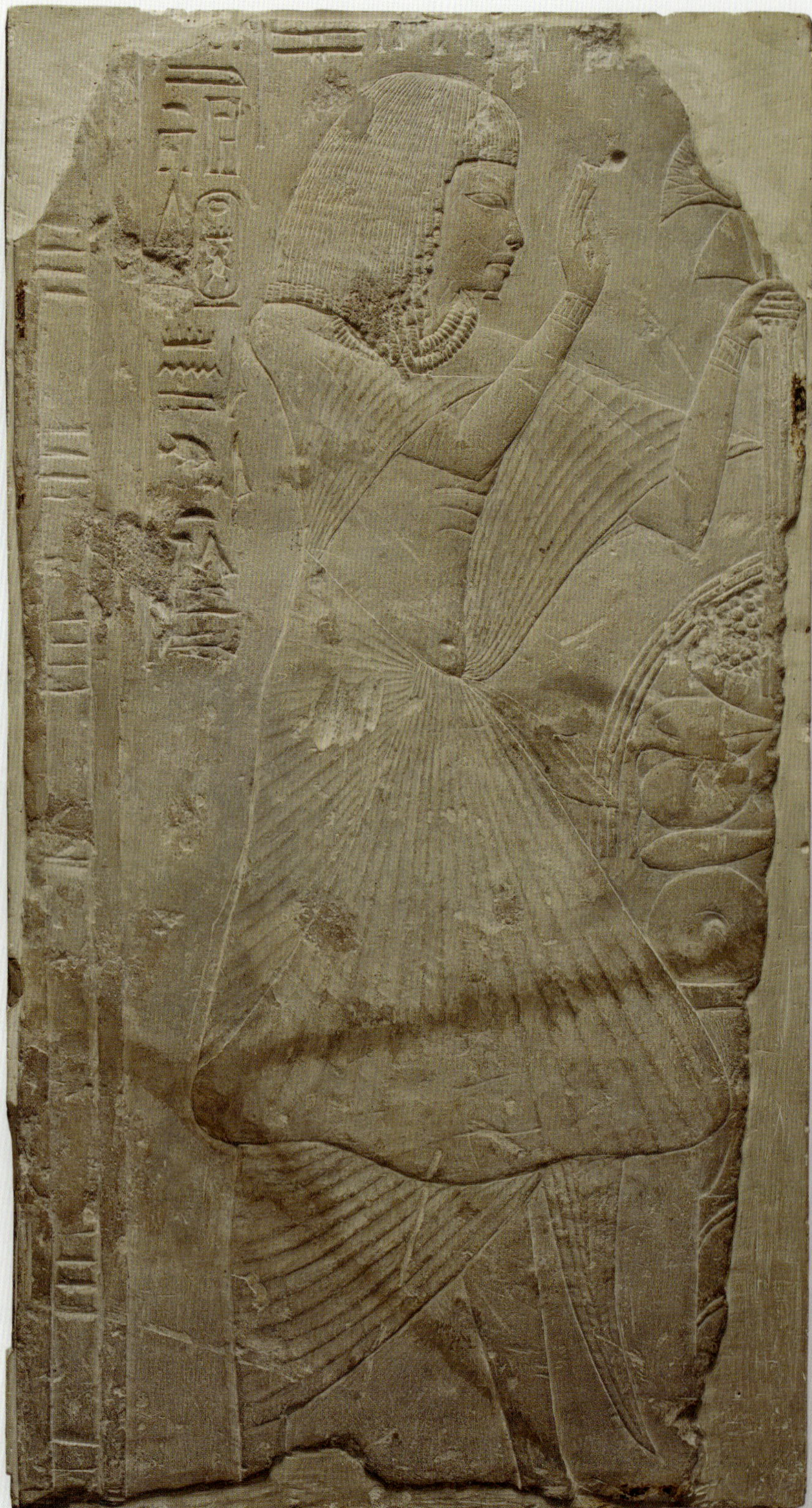

56

Low relief of the priest Ameneminet, Saqqara, Egypt, late Eighteenth Dynasty, c. 1320 BCE.

Ameneminet was a functionary in a temple dedicated to Thutmose III, still active a century after the pharaoh's death.

The history of major events, as seen by the elite

Archaeology, whose journey of discovery is far from complete, has supported Diodorus' assertion, revealing the huge popularity of the annalistic genre in ancient Egypt.[2] We have only to think of the famous Palermo Stone, which supplies the list of kings from 'Dynasty 0' to the Fifth Dynasty, their principal achievements and even the annual height of the Nile in flood.[3] Or the South Saqqara Stone, a basalt sarcophagus lid which was reused as a support for royal annals at the end of the Sixth Dynasty.[4] Or the famous Chamber of the Ancestors of Thutmose III, in the temple of Amun at Karnak, the original of which is now in the Musée du Louvre.[5] Or of the impressive Gallery of the Ancestors in the Temple of Seti I at Abydos, which lists seventy-six pharaohs from Meni onwards. Or the Turin Royal Canon, written under Ramesses II, which lists all the preceding reigns with their respective lengths[6] — now in fragments: the papyrus apparently disintegrated while it was being carried away on a donkey! Or the Saqqara Tablet, discovered in the tomb of a certain Tjuneroy, 'conductor of ritual for all the gods, overseer of works for all the king's buildings, royal scribe and chief lector priest' under Ramesses II, which contains the names of fifty-eight rulers since Adjib, the sixth king of the First Dynasty.[7] And we must not forget the offering table of Qenherkhopshef (cat. 1), a notable figure who held sway in the Deir el-Medina community in the second half of the Nineteenth Dynasty: extremely corrupt, with a reputation for many kinds of embezzlement, this 'scribe of the tomb' nevertheless had the good taste to create a distinctive little monument, dedicated to the memory of sixteen past kings and two queens, beginning with the founder of the Middle Kingdom, Mentuhotep II, all of whom were buried in the Theban necropolis.[8]

This tally of records of this type — Manetho's *Aegyptiaca*, at the beginning of the Ptolemaic Period, was the last major example[9] — is far from exhaustive. The annalistic sources at our disposal tell us mostly about the literate elite — because it was they who created them — the scribes, priests and other *hierogrammateis* whose training and duties gave them a more or less detailed knowledge of their past, depending on the extent of their erudition. The cupbearer Djehuty, a contemporary of Thutmose III, had no qualms about asserting in his autobiography: '[I was someone] who researched history, who announced what had not yet happened, with the wisdom to look into the future, understanding the past and intuiting the future, an expert in what would happen.'[10] The king, for his part, was endowed with omniscience because of his divine nature and was understood to have a complete knowledge of history, as the vizier Rekhmire confirmed with reference to Thutmose III: 'His Majesty knows the past. There is absolutely nothing He doesn't know, because He is Thoth in every way.'[11]

2 Redford, 1986; Baud, 2003.
3 Palermo, Museo Archeologico, inv. no. 1028.
4 Cairo, Egyptian Museum, JE 65908.
5 Paris, Musée du Louvre, E13481bis.
6 Turin, Museo Egizio, cat. 1874.
7 Cairo, Egyptian Museum, CG 34516.
8 Marseille, Musée d'Archéologie Méditerranéenne.
9 Waddell, 1940; Loprieno, 2003; Aufrère, 2008.
10 Davies, 1932, pl. 39, l. 11–12.
11 *Urkunden* IV, 1074, 2–9.

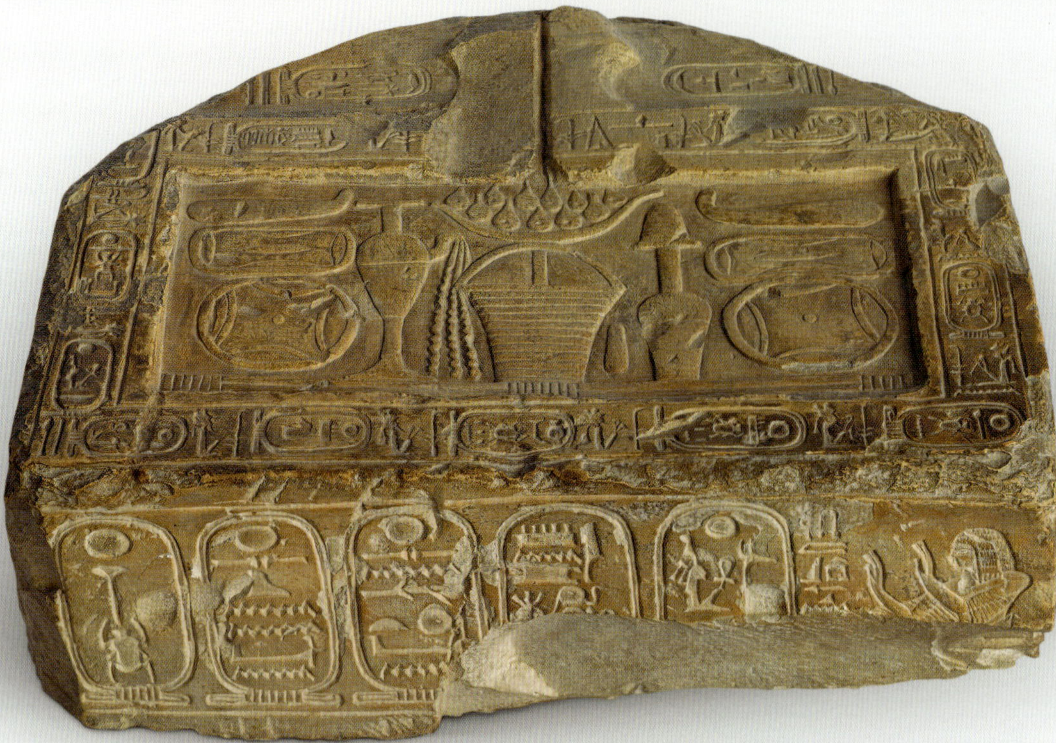

1

Offering table of Qenherkhepechef, author of the inscriptions, dedicated to sixteen past kings and two queens, Deir el-Medina, Egypt, reigns of Ramesses II and Merenptah (c. 1279–1202 BCE).

The history of major events, as seen by the people

But we must guard against simplistic interpretations: this propensity to record events, like the portrait of a king as a 'historian' or 'archivist', was dictated by concerns that were essentially political: reference to ancestral tradition was useful to a power in search of permanent legitimacy (cat. 54). As for the simple craftsman, the farmer, the shepherd, the fisherman-fowler, they were inevitably less attuned to this ideological imperative: it is difficult to evaluate what they knew about successive dynasties and events forming part of the country's history. But it seems reasonable to assume that they must have known, at least through oral transmission, some great figures from the past and some important historical events, which found their way into narratives mixing true facts with fictional extrapolations.

The tales in the Papyrus Westcar, a literary text dating to the late Middle Kingdom at the earliest,[12] usually known as 'King Cheops and the Magicians', could reflect a historiographical tradition that was more widespread, perhaps, than that conveyed by official ideology. According to this, each pharaoh was expected to do more than his predecessors, as part of the 'requirement to outperform' which was demanded of him as it was of all his subjects.[13] The account transports us to the court of Khufu/Cheops, a pharaoh of the Fourth Dynasty, famous for having built the Great Pyramid of Giza. The royal sons stand up in turn to entertain their father with the story of a miracle. The tales, each of which takes place under a different reign, represent an opportunity to paint contrasting pictures of the various rulers. Thus, the portrait of the renowned Djoser is followed by that of the cruel Nebka, who made no bones about sentencing two adulterous lovers to death. Then comes the story of the easygoing Sneferu, happy in his contemplation of young, lightly dressed oarswomen. In contrast to this cheerful figure, his son Khufu is told off by the magician Djedi for having unduly proposed sacrificing a prisoner's life for the sake of an experiment. A similar approach, alternating good and bad kings, is found in the Book of Deuteronomy. It is not impossible that this alternative historiography was fairly widely circulated among the Egyptian population, especially as it could be broadly confirmed by lived experience (!) — rulers, as in every civilisation, succeeding each other without resembling each other. Additionally, classical authors, such as Herodotus and Manetho, continued to refer to Khufu's bad reputation, which seems to suggest a lively tradition, although it has no confirmed historical basis.

[12] Berlin, Ägyptisches Museum, ÄM 3033.

[13] Vernus, 1995.

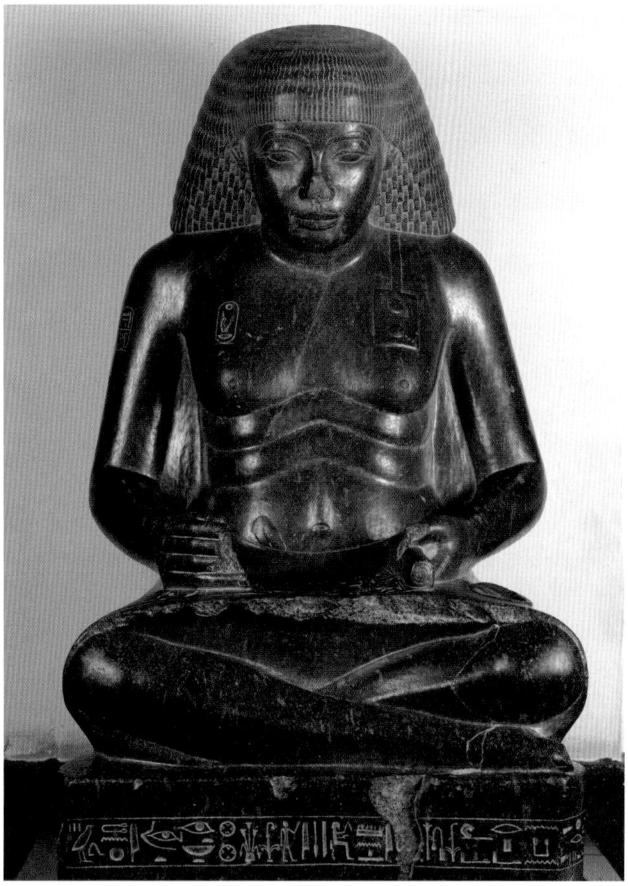

← FIG. 1
Statue of Amenhotep, son of Hapu, found in front of the 10th pylon of the temple of Amun in Karnak, Egypt, reign of Amenhotep III (c. 1388–1349 BCE), granite, 128 × 74.5 × 69.5 cm, Egyptian Museum, Cairo, inv. JE 44861.

Remembering important historical figures

The early pharaoh Djoser, the good king Sneferu, Pepi II — who had the longest reign in pharaonic history and was the subject of a humorous account suggesting he had intimate relations with one of his generals — the Senwosret pharaohs of the Middle Kingdom, Thutmose III the conqueror and Ramesses, the 'victor' of Qadesh — all these left some trace in the collective memories of the inhabitants of the Nile Valley. But there is no doubt that there were also great figures from the past who, though not royal, became exceptionally famous too. This is true of Imhotep, architect of Djoser's funerary complex: it was in the Ramesside period that he was first thought to be the son of the god Ptah, then from the Saite period (Twenty-sixth Dynasty) he was considered a healing god, before becoming the hero of Demotic narratives and being assimilated by the Greeks to Asclepius (their god of medicine). The 'sun pharaoh', Amenhotep III, had a scribe, the illustrious Amenhotep son of Hapu, who was similarly celebrated and soon after his death became the subject of a popular cult, portrayed in many statues (fig. 1). Installed in or around various sanctuaries, notably at the south entrance of the Temple of Karnak, these cult effigies made him a prominent intercessor, as can be seen from the wear of the stone at the level of the papyrus unrolled upon his knees, resulting from the repeated touch of pilgrims' hands.

54

Fragment of a wall from the tomb of Inkef, priest serving the funerary cult of King Sened, who died about two hundred years earlier, Saqqara, Egypt, reign of Khufu (c. 2636–2605 BCE).

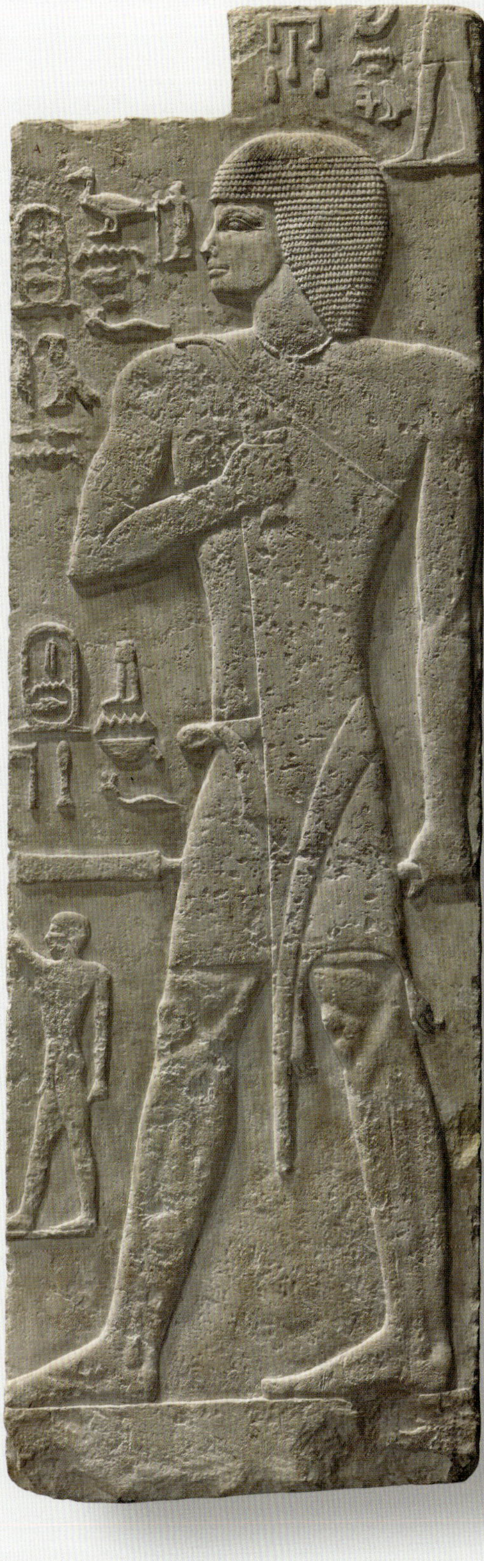

Remembering local luminaries

It was not only kings and individuals who enjoyed 'national' popularity. The Egyptians of antiquity, whether or not they were literate, must chiefly have had an awareness and knowledge of 'local' history relating to the town of their birth or their province. If we could question, today, a *lambda* Egyptian mummy, following a spectacular advance in technology — though the mummy in question would have to be able to understand the Egyptologists' jargon! — it would be a good bet that it would give us more information about the micro-history of local prominent figures than about the ruling pharaoh's policies or the achievements of his royal predecessors. In ancient Egypt there were many local 'saints': these were sometimes deceased kings (cat. 56), but were more often simply individuals who had held important roles, who enjoyed a significant reputation in a limited geographical area, and in some cases were really revered by the people. Several Egyptologists have addressed this important aspect of pharaonic civilisation. However, as J. Quaegebeur underlined, a complete study of the cult of saints in Pharaonic and Graeco-Roman Egypt has yet to be written.[14]

Thus, for example, the vizier and nomarch Isi, who lived during the last two reigns of the Fifth Dynasty and the first three of the Sixth, had a role as an intercessor until the beginning of the New Kingdom in the city of Edfu: that is to say for more than six centuries. The governor Pepinakht, known as Heqaib, who died at the end of the Sixth Dynasty, was honoured with sanctuaries on the island of Elephantine, which became true places of pilgrimage until the Second Intermediate Period; his posthumous cult lasted for four centuries. The discovery of the tomb of the ritualist priest Khuennemti, in the necropolis of Tabbet el-Guesh, has revealed the existence of three individuals, Heti, Ny(ui)nesu and Nyankhmin, who seem to have been prestigious ancestors, venerated at the end of the Old Kingdom in the Saqqara region; this evidence, as yet unpublished, remains to be investigated. Better-known are Nyuserre, a sovereign with an extended reign in the Fifth Dynasty, honoured in the Abusir region until the Middle Kingdom; Menkauhor, his successor (cat. 37); Unas, the last king of the same dynasty; Teti, the founder of the next dynasty, who was for a long time revered in Saqqara; King Mentuhotep II, already mentioned, the 'Theban saint par excellence'; and Amenhotep I and his mother Ahmose-Nefertari, true 'patrons' of the village of Deir el-Medina, on the west bank of Thebes; the celebrations, processions and oracular processes devoted to them lent a rhythm to daily life in the community of artisans during the Ramesside period (cats. 64, 67, 68 and 69).

The 'god's treasurer' Urdjededba, who lived in the time of King Djedkare Isesi, the last but one king of the Fifth Dynasty, could be added to this list. This figure, so it seems, made an impression with far flung expeditions; the two autobiographies of Harkhuf and Weni, later by several generations, mention him explicitly. His tomb in the Memphis necropolis has still not been located. And of course there were also the

[14] Quaegebeur, 1977.

37

Fragment of a tomb wall depicting King Menkauhor, Saqqara, Egypt, late Eighteenth Dynasty (c. 1330–1295 BCE).

The cult of Menkauhor experienced a revival a thousand years after his reign, probably near his pyramid at Saqqara.

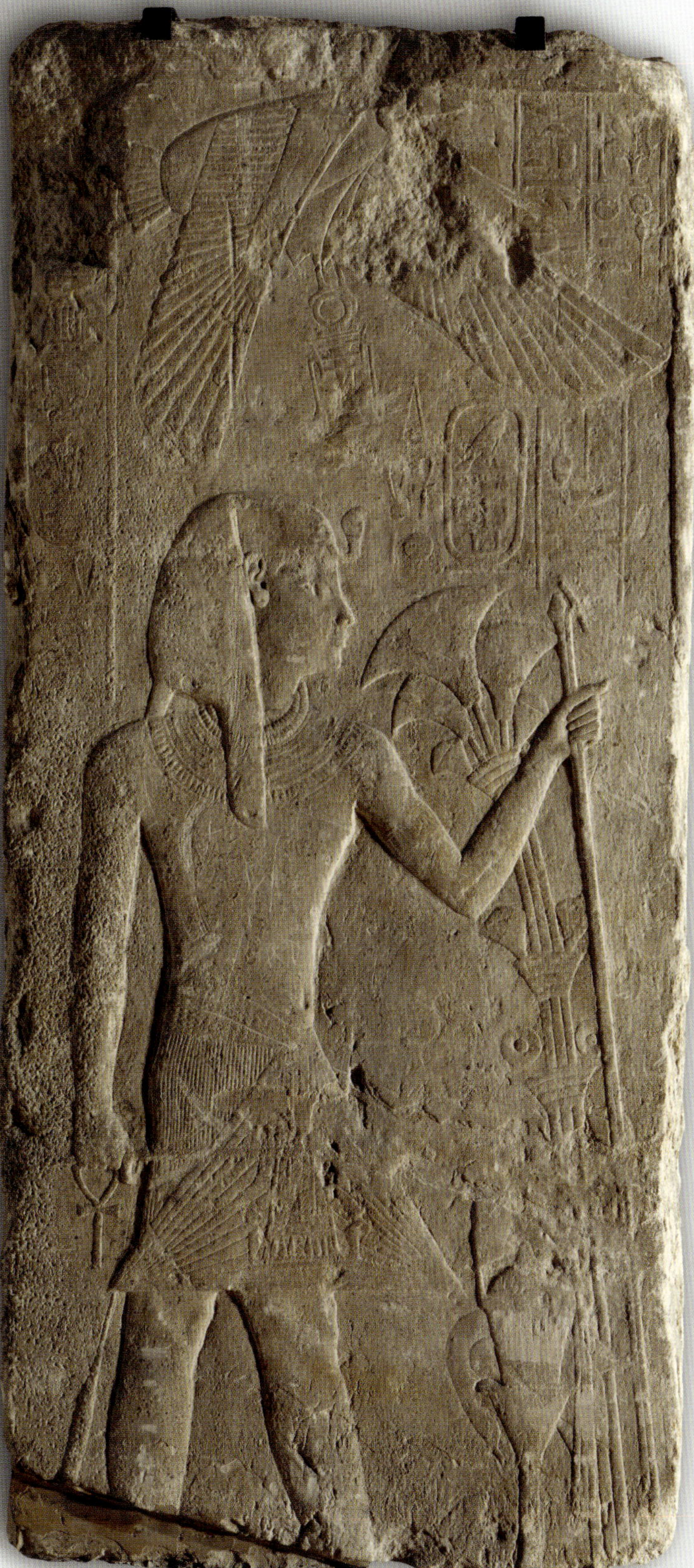

viziers Gemnikai, Ptahhotep and Mehu, in Saqqara; the governors Ibu and Wahka (II), venerated at Qau el-Kebir, in Middle Egypt; the nomarch Tjauti, whose tomb in Qasr es-Sayyad, in the seventh nome of Upper Egypt, is exceptionally large; the obscure Horemheb, a native of Naukratis; and the female 'saint' Udjarenes, part of the local pantheon in Hu, a city also in the seventh nome of Upper Egypt. Examples proliferate in later centuries.

The large number of these luminaries from the past, who were 'deified' and venerated to varying extents, testifies to a widespread phenomenon of collective memory, feeding mainly off local history, linked to the practice of recourse to intercession, sometimes to oracular consultation and finally to the social dimension which the Egyptians ascribed to the deceased. This collective history was quite separate from the official history codified by central authorities, or from theological speculations concerning the great cycles of the world's progress since the time of the 'First Time'.[15] Anchored to a confined area, enshrined in a festive calendar, renewed at every celebration, it must have united the whole population — the ordinary people as well as the elite — around common references and a shared memory.

[15] Uphill, 2003.

FROM SCRIBES TO GREEK HISTORIANS: THE PHARAOHS AS FIGURES IN LITERATURE

MICHEL CHAUVEAU

The fragments of Egyptian narrative works that have come down to us through chance archaeological finds mostly feature kings and princes, and much more rarely queens. This is hardly surprising, given the extent to which the pharaonic figure structured ancient Egyptian culture, to the point where its disappearance as a focus for society and unique intermediary between this society and the divine world led to the collapse of the old religion and its cultural context. There was no ancient Egypt without the pharaohs, even when these were simply Persian, Greeks and Romans in disguise. The real identity of the incumbent was not important, so long as he was wearing the costume, or at least could be represented as doing so. All accounts of real or fictional events thus had to include a pharaoh, historical or invented, even if only as a background detail.

58

Literary *ostracon*: beginning of the *Instruction of Amenemhat I to His Son Senwosret*, Luxor, Egypt, New Kingdom (c. 1539–1069 BCE).

This copy of the text is more than four hundred years later than the reign of Amenemhat I.

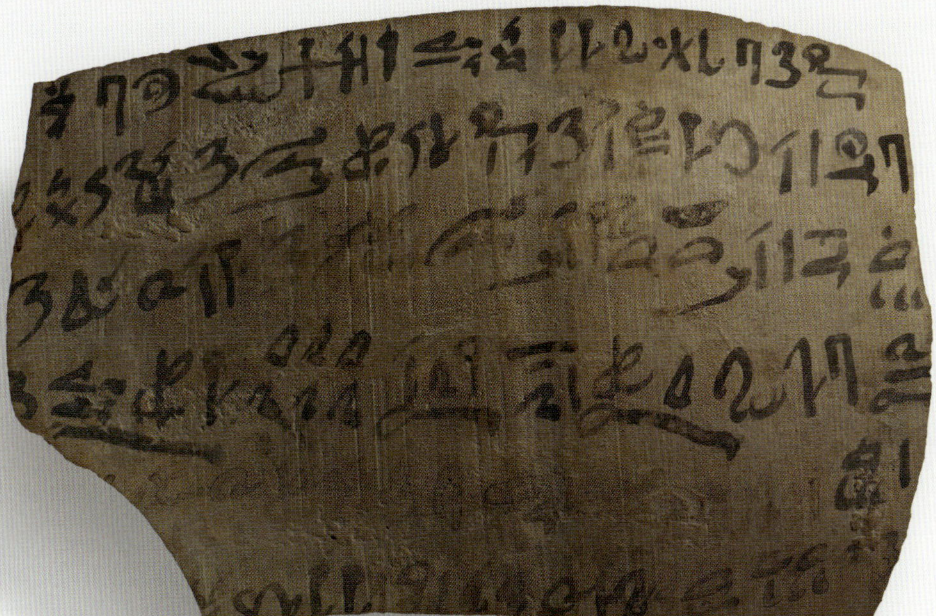

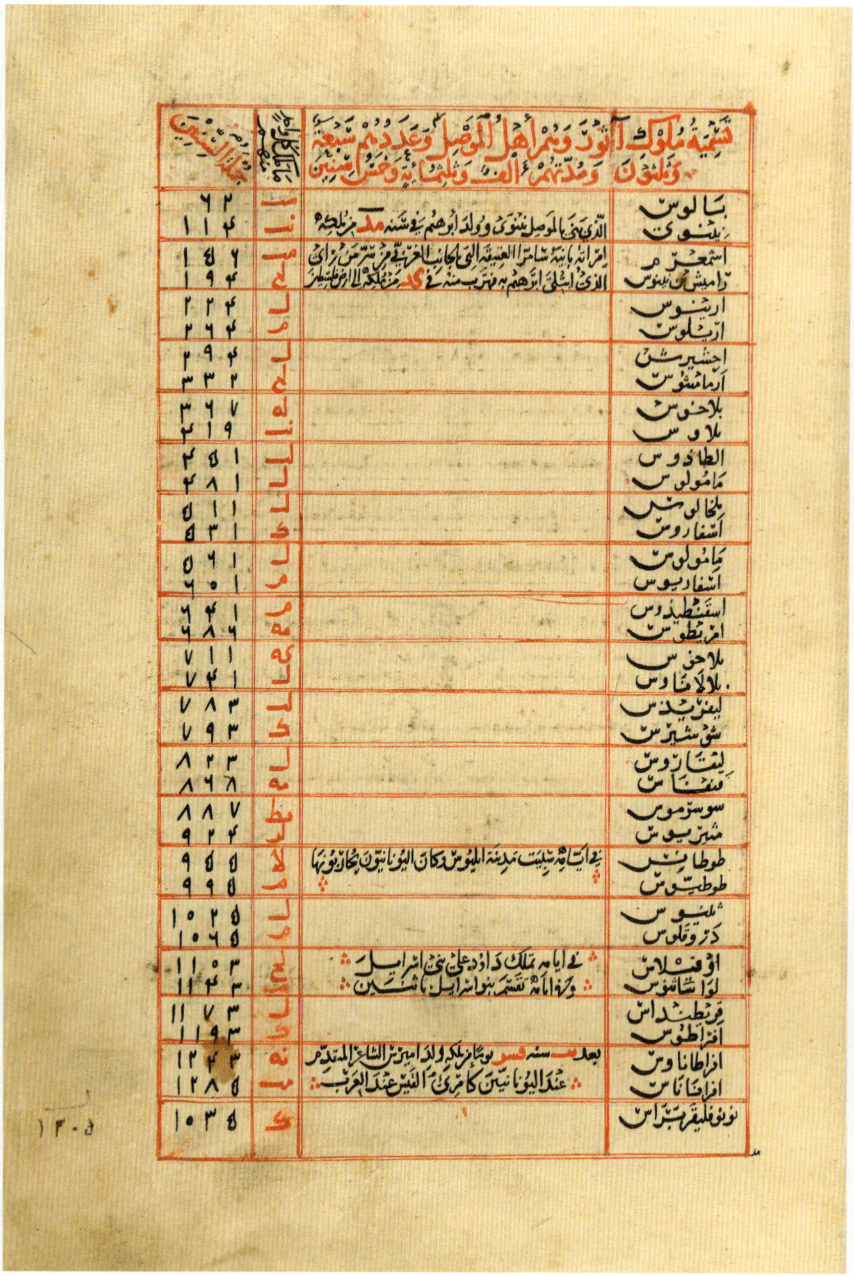

82

Abu Rayhan Al-Biruni, 'Names of the Coptic kings in Egypt', in the *Chronology of Ancient Nations*, Iran, manuscript dated 1307, fol. 44r.

This chronology, taken from Manetho's *Aegyptiaca*, lists the pharaohs of the last ten dynasties and the lengths of their reigns.

Some pharaohs were even thought to be the authors of literary works that had a didactic character, destined to be copied and disseminated, probably for educational purposes in scribe schools. Two wisdom texts with royal paternity survive: the first attributed to the father of King Merikare of the First Intermediate Period, the second to Amenemhat I, addressed to his son and successor, Senwosret I (cat. 58). These two teaching texts, constructed very differently, sketch out a particular concept of pharaonic royalty as well as indirectly providing a portrait of the two presumed authors.[1]

[1] Vernus, 2001, pp. 135–77.

87

Flask in the shape of a Greek soldier's head, with the cartouche of Amasis, Egypt, reign of Amasis (c. 570–527 BCE).

This flask provides evidence of trade between the Greeks of Asia Minor and the Egypt of Amasis.

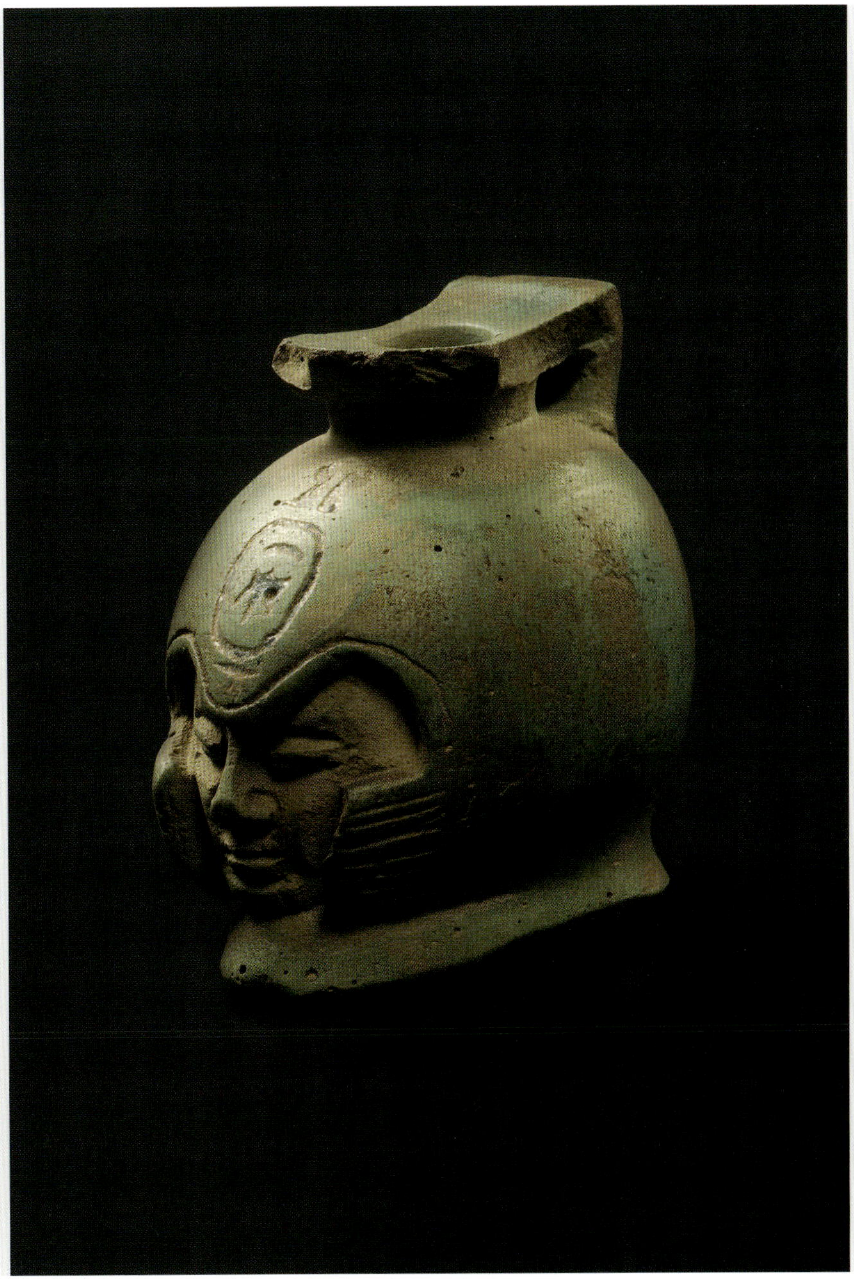

Apart from in these two wisdom texts, the pharaoh hardly ever appears as the sole protagonist in surviving literary works and he is only rarely the only hero, when his role is not confined to serving as a historical marker, enabling the subject to be sited in a clearly defined past. This function is essential when the chronology is emphasised by the prophetic character of the events described. The king therefore always has an interlocutor: mostly, after consulting his courtiers, who prove unable to help him solve a crucial problem, he summons a sage, a magician or a prophet. Most narratives featuring the pharaoh are in fact frame stories which provide an introduction to the discussions or adventures of these characters with exceptional talents, which they put to use for the benefit of the supreme power incarnated by the king.

Which pharaohs?

The pharaohs who appear in literary texts are clearly presented as historical rather than imaginary figures. However, this historicity embraces very variable levels of authenticity, depending on the narrative context; the greater or lesser distance in time between the real sovereign and the date of the work in which he appears; the chance or deliberate corruption of royal names; the possible confusion between several kings bearing more or less the same name; and even the whim of an author who invents a fictional character. While the Egyptians themselves felt no need to record the history of their ancient kings, except in the form of lists and annals containing very scant data (cat. 82), Greek authors, such as Herodotus (fifth century BCE) or Diodorus (first century BCE) compiled biographical summaries — using an approximate chronology — that reflect a certain vision of Egypt and its exceptional culture. Depending on the various periods when these Egyptian or Greek works were produced, a handful of famous or completely unknown kings were preserved, for different reasons, as emblematic and recurring figures in these tales of the imagination (cat. 88).

Thus, several Old Kingdom kings logically appear in tales written during the Middle Kingdom, but also in much later works: Djoser, for example, appears in a tale known through a manuscript dating to the Roman period, but is mentioned as a contemporary and master of the mythical Imhotep, deified in the Late Period.[2]

In later periods, it is notable that the great conquerors of the New Kingdom, Thutmose III and Ramesses II, do not appear in literary tradition as such. It is Sesostris — probably a mix of the first and third Senwosrets in the dynastic lists — who is attributed with glorious and extraordinary military achievements, pre-empting and even outdoing those of Darius and Alexander. On the Greek side, historical and fictional accounts — of which only small shreds survive — testify to a popularity whose real basis is very difficult to establish. On the Egyptian side, fragments of at least three Demotic manuscripts[3] attest to the Egyptian origin of the legend of Sesostris, despite being later than the Greek writers.[4]

The Assyrian followed by the Persian invasions, with periods of restoration in between (the Twenty-sixth and Thirtieth Dynasties), were a more fruitful source of inspiration for Demotic literature of the Greco-Roman period. Inaros of Athribis and Pedubast of Tanis — local princes in the Delta — became the heroes of a whole cycle of military endeavours in a long series of Demotic narratives. Inaros, a symbol of Egyptian resistance to the Asian invasions, derived from a fusion of a prince of Athribis who opposed the Assyrians in the seventh century and a Libyan chief, an enemy of the Persians, two centuries later.[5] Pedubast, on the other hand, who corresponds to the second of three kings known to have been so named, seems to lack any particularly worthy qualities, although paradoxically he appears more frequently in surviving works.

2 Ryholt, 2010, p. 716.
3 'Demotic' is the cursive writing which spread from the seventh century onwards in the vernacular Egyptian language of the time. The term is used to describe texts composed or copied in this writing.
4 Quack, 2013, pp. 63–6.
5 Ryholt, 2009, p. 236, n. 29.

The pharaoh and the sage-magician

This is the most persistent theme in Egyptian literature, at least from the Middle Kingdom until the Roman period. One of the most ancient narratives, preserved in the Papyrus Westcar[6] and dated to the end of the Second Intermediate Period, brings no less than four successive pharaohs face to face with the great magicians of their respective periods. Although the beginning of the frame story is lost, it is evident that King Khufu, feeling bored — like so many monarchs in stories from all around the world! — has gathered together his four sons so that they can entertain him. The first three take it in turns to tell him the story of an episode involving one of his predecessors — Djoser, Nebka and Sneferu — all of whom had witnessed a miracle at the hands of a different magician. The last son, Hordjedef, reveals that if the king consents to him being summoned, he too can test the skills of a venerable magician who is still living. The king wastes no time in doing so. The thaumaturge then performs his favourite trick before Khufu — reattaching severed heads — before making a prophecy about the future of Egypt.

Nearly a thousand years later, another pharaoh appealed to a magician, this time not to entertain him but to heal him. In the Papyrus Vandier,[7] the pharaoh Sisebek — an otherwise unknown king, unless his name is a corruption of the name of King Shabaka of the Twenty-fifth Dynasty — summons the magician Merire to cure an incurable disease. Finally, in the Ptolemaic period, the Tale of Setne-Khamwas and Si-Osire puts Ramesses II himself up against a Nubian sorcerer, who issues a challenge to which only the pharaoh's grandson Si-Osire can respond. In the end, Si-Osire reveals that he is the reincarnation of a magician who fifteen centuries earlier had avenged his king — thought to be Thutmose III, despite the incorrect timeframe — for a brutal humiliation inflicted upon him by the same Nubian sorcerer. The somewhat grotesque misadventures that befall the two most famous pharaohs in Egyptian history, whose great exploits are not mentioned, show that scribes in the later periods were indifferent to their bygone glories.

The pharaoh and the prophet

The end of the Papyrus Westcar takes a distinctive turn. The magician summoned by Khufu tells the king that a miracle is taking place: the wife of one of Ra's priests is about to give birth to three children, whose conception was divine and who would later be called to rule over Egypt. This is one of the earliest examples of a prophetic narrative in which a king receives a revelation concerning the country's future. The genre will endure for a considerable length of time: the

6 Parys, 2017.

7 Posener, 1985, pp. 119–37; a recent translation in Agut-Labordère Chauveau, 2011, pp. 3–11.

Prophecy of Neferti, another magician summoned to entertain King Sneferu, concerns the catastrophes that would apparently befall the country at the end of the Old Kingdom, and the arrival of a saviour named Ameny, who may be identified as the founder of the Twelfth Dynasty, Amenemhat I. The Prophecy of the Lamb, revealed to King Bocchoris of the Twenty-fourth Dynasty, describes the woes that accompany the Persian invasion. The Dream of the Pharaoh Nectanebo II, for which only the frame story survives, must also have warned of the troubles brought by the second Persian conquest. Finally, the Oracle of the Potter, apparently proffered under a King Amenophis who is difficult to identify, alludes to the expected end of Greek and Roman domination and a return of the ancient gods to Memphis.[8]

The 'two bodies' of the pharaoh, beginning in the Old Kingdom...

When he is not only an abstract figure, embodying supreme power in a theocratic society, the pharaoh in these tales is rarely a wholly positive character. While his authority is never truly contested, it is basically linked to his sacred function, symbolised by the abundant regalia (crowns, sceptres, costume) that he makes sure to display. But the man, behind this impressive apparatus, does not escape the depravity of other mortals. It is thus already possible in Egypt to observe the duality of the 'king's two bodies', as revealed by contemporary historiography in the monarchies of the medieval West, distinguishing between the mortal and imperfect body and the eternal body exempt from human transgression. In the Papyrus Westcar, the royal protagonists do not always appear as models of enlightened monarchs: Sneferu is portrayed as an idle potentate, whose only entertainment is watching young girls in erotic outfits rowing in the palace pool. As for Khufu, he has so little regard for his subjects that he is prepared to have one of them decapitated — a prisoner, but the procedure envisaged does not seem to have anything to do with his punishment — solely for the pleasure of seeing whether the magician Djedi can reattach his head. In fact, Djedi disapproves of his master's proposal and substitutes a bull and a duck as subjects for the experiment.

... and in later periods

At the end of the New Kingdom, there were no qualms about narrating the adventures of King Neferkare — probably Pepi II of the Sixth Dynasty, a thousand years earlier — who abased himself in secret trysts with one of his generals.[9] But it is in the Late Period that the discordance observed between the behaviour of the man and the supreme function that he is supposed to incarnate becomes most flagrant. The pharaoh Sisebek in the tale of the Papyrus Vandier does not only send his magician

[8] Chauveau, 1999, pp. 8–9.
[9] Posener, 1957.

Merire to the afterlife in order to persuade the god to prolong his life, but he shamelessly betrays all the promises he made to the magician concerning the protection of his wife and goods while he is absent from the land of the living. In the kingdom of the dead, Merire learns that the wicked king has taken his wife into his harem, has given his house to a courtier and has had his son assassinated. Curiously, it is not the king himself who is held accountable for these crimes but the court magicians who apparently encouraged the pharaoh to commit them, and it is they who finally pay the price by being burned alive. Whatever his actual morals as an individual might be, the sacred nature of his function means that the sovereign cannot shoulder the consequences of any wrongful act: the responsibility must therefore fall to his entourage. It is his entourage that feels the effects of royal ire when it appears that the courtiers have concealed important information from the pharaoh. This theme recurs so frequently, as much in fictional tales as in narratives supposedly describing actual events, that Egyptologists have given episodes constructed in this way the generic appellation *Königsnovelle*. A clear parody of the *Königsnovelle*, in which the king plays a deplorable part, can be found in the Demotic tale of the pharaoh Amasis and the sailor, of which only the beginning survives, in a papyrus of the third century BCE. The king assembles his courtiers to announce his intention of getting drunk on a kind of strongly alcoholic wine; he goes ahead with this plan despite their opposition. Here again, the king's obvious vice does not affect the sacred nature of his function, which has a curious parallel in Herodotus' description of the pharaoh Amasis' drunkenness alongside the importance of his political, legislative and building achievements (cats. 81 and 87).

Herodotus mentions another king who behaves badly, but whose historicity is problematic since his name, Pheron, seems to be simply a corruption of 'pharaoh'. Son of the mythical Sesostris, the gods strike him blind as punishment for sacrilege. After ten years, an oracle promises that he will be healed if he bathes his eyes in the urine of woman who has known no man other than her husband. After fruitlessly trying the experiment with the queen, and then with many other women, he finally discovers the rare pearl who will enable him to recover his sight. He then burns alive all the infidels betrayed by their inability to heal him, including his own wife, and takes as his queen the woman whose urine cured him. A rather mutilated Demotic version of this story has recently been found, with interesting variations showing that the two versions are independent of each other.[10] The Egyptian tale is set in the Saite period, since the king's son bears the dynastic name of Necho. The cause of the blindness seems to the criminal lechery of the king, who had killed the husband of a woman he coveted for his harem. Finally the suggested means of obtaining a potential cure is no longer urine but the tears of a faithful wife.

[10] Quack, 2013, pp. 66–9.

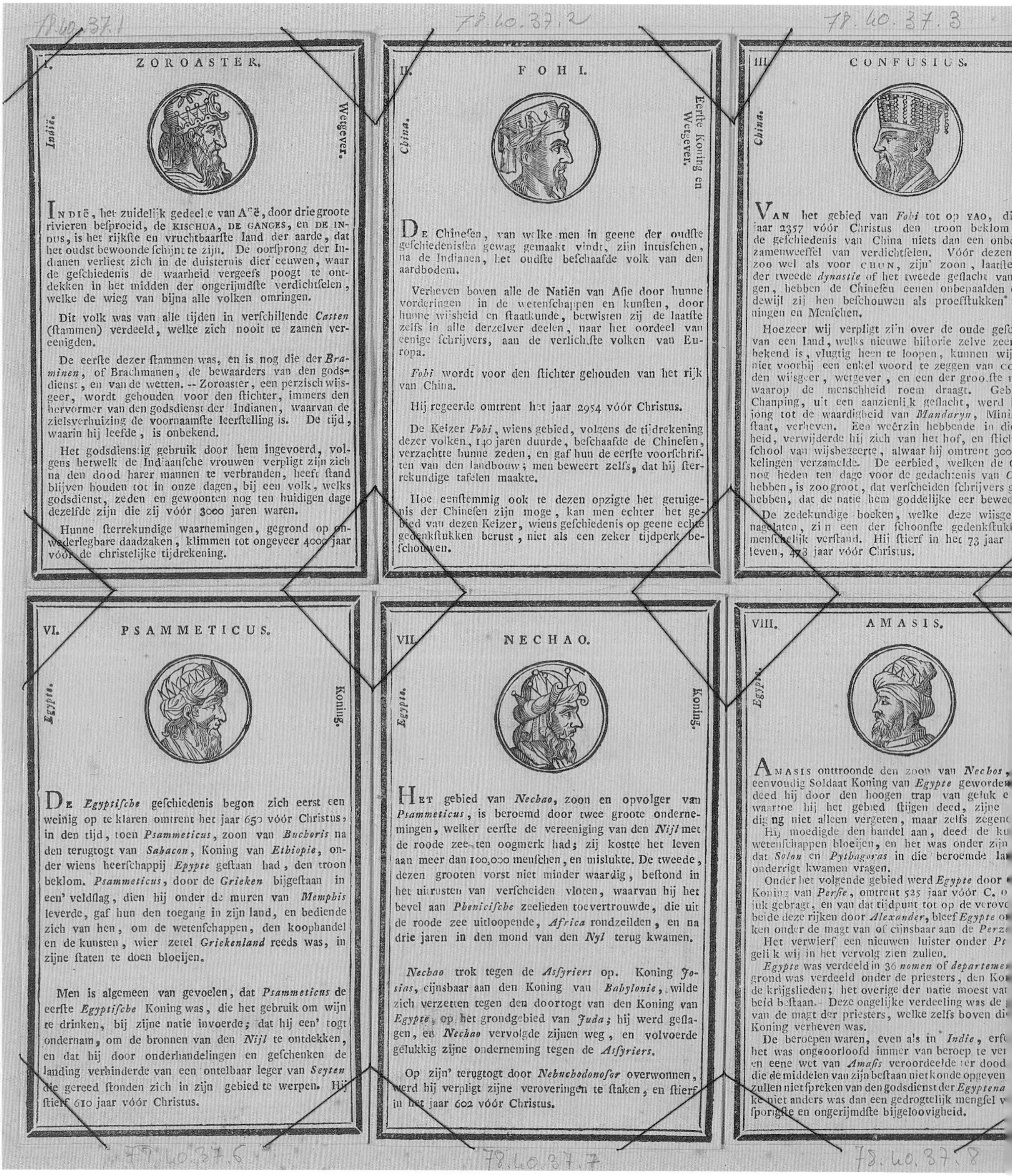

I. ZOROASTER.

Indië. Wetgever.

INDIË, het zuidelijk gedeelte van Asië, door drie groote rivieren besproeid, de KISCHUA, DE GANGES, en DE INDUS, is het rijkste en vruchtbaarste land der aarde, dat het oudst bewoonde schijnt te zijn. De oorsprong der Indianen verliest zich in de duisternis dier eeuwen, waar de geschiedenis de waarheid vergeefs poogt te ontdekken in het midden der ongerijmdste verdichtselen, welke de wieg van bijna alle volken omringen.

Dit volk was van alle tijden in verschillende *Casten* (stammen) verdeeld, welke zich nooit te zamen vereenigden.

De eerste dezer stammen was, en is nog die der *Braminen*, of Brachmanen, de bewaarders van den godsdienst, en van de wetten. -- Zoroaster, een perzisch wijsgeer, wordt gehouden voor den stichter, immers den hervormer van den godsdienst der Indianen, waarvan de zielsverhuizing de voornaamste leerstelling is. De tijd, waarin hij leefde, is onbekend.

Het godsdienstig gebruik door hem ingevoerd, volgens hetwelk de Indiaansche vrouwen verpligt zijn zich na den dood harer mannen te verbranden, heeft stand blijven houden tot in onze dagen, bij een volk, welks godsdienst, zeden en gewoonten nog ten huidigen dage dezelfde zijn die zij vóór 3000 jaren waren.

Hunne sterrekundige waarnemingen, gegrond op onwederlegbare daadzaken, klimmen tot ongeveer 4000 jaar vóór de christelijke tijdrekening.

II. FOHI.

China. Eerste Koning en Wetgever.

DE Chinesen, van welke men in geene der oudste geschiedenissen gewag gemaakt vindt, zijn intusschen, na de Indianen, het oudste beschaafde volk van den aardbodem.

Verheven boven alle de Natiën van Asie door hunne vorderingen in de wetenschappen en kunsten, door hunne wijsheid en staatkunde, betwisten zij de laatste zelfs in alle derzelver deelen, naar het oordeel van eenige schrijvers, aan de verlichtste volken van Europa.

Fohi wordt voor den stichter gehouden van het rijk van China.

Hij regeerde omtrent het jaar 2954 vóór Christus.

De Keizer *Fohi*, wiens gebied, volgens de tijdrekening dezer volken, 140 jaren duurde, beschaafde de Chinesen, verzachtte hunne zeden, en gaf hun de eerste voorschriften van den landbouw; men beweert zelfs, dat hij sterrekundige tafelen maakte.

Hoe eenstemmig ook te dezen opzigte het getuigenis der Chinesen zijn moge, kan men echter het gebied van dezen Keizer, wiens geschiedenis op geene echte gedenkstukken berust, niet als een zeker tijdperk beschouwen.

III. CONFUSIUS.

China.

VAN het gebied van *Fohi* tot op YAO, di[e] jaar 2357 vóór Christus den troon beklom, de geschiedenis van China niets dan een onbe[…] zamenweefsel van verdichtselen. Vóór dezen zoo wel als voor CHUN, zijn' zoon, laatste der tweede *dynastie* of het tweede geslacht van[…] gen, hebben de Chinesen eenen onbepaalden […] dewijl zij hen beschouwen als proefstukken […] ningen en Menschen.

Hoezeer wij verpligt zijn over de oude gesc[…] van een land, welks nieuwe historie zelve zeer […] bekend is, vlugtig heen te loopen, kunnen wij […] niet voorbij een enkel woord te zeggen van Co[…] den wijsgeer, wetgever, en een der grootste m[…] waarop de menschheid roem draagt. Geb[…] Chanping, uit een aanzienlijk geslacht, werd […] jong tot de waardigheid van *Mandaryn*, Minis[…] staat, verheven. Een weêrzin hebbende in die[…] heid, verwijderde hij zich van het hof, en stich[…] school van wijsbegeerte, alwaar hij omtrent 300[…] kelingen verzamelde. De eerbied, welken de C[…] nog heden ten dage voor de gedachtenis van C[…] hebben, is zoo groot, dat verscheiden schrijvers g[…] hebben, dat de natie hem goddelijke eer bewee[…]

De zedekundige boeken, welke deze wijsge[…] nagelaten, zijn een der schoonste gedenkstukk[…] menschelijk verstand. Hij stierf in het 73 jaar […] leven, 473 jaar vóór Christus.

VI. PSAMMETICUS.

Egypte. Koning.

DE *Egyptische* geschiedenis begon zich eerst een weinig op te klaren omtrent het jaar 650 vóór Christus; in den tijd, toen *Psammeticus*, zoon van *Bucboris* na den terugtogt van *Sabacon*, Koning van *Ethiopie*, onder wiens heerschappij *Egypte* gestaan had, den troon beklom. *Psammeticus*, door de *Grieken* bijgestaan in een' veldslag, dien hij onder de muren van *Memphis* leverde, gaf hun den toegang in zijn land, en bediende zich van hen, om de wetenschappen, den koophandel en de kunsten, wier zetel *Griekenland* reeds was, in zijne staten te doen bloeijen.

Men is algemeen van gevoelen, dat *Psammeticus* de eerste *Egyptische* Koning was, die het gebruik om wijn te drinken, bij zijne natie invoerde; dat hij een' togt ondernam, om de bronnen van den *Nijl* te ontdekken, en dat hij door onderhandelingen en geschenken de landing verhinderde van een ontelbaar leger van *Scyten* die gereed stonden zich in zijn gebied te werpen. Hij stierf 610 jaar vóór Christus.

VII. NECHAO.

Egypte. Koning.

HET gebied van *Nechao*, zoon en opvolger van *Psammeticus*, is beroemd door twee groote ondernemingen, welker eerste de vereeniging van den *Nijl* met de roode zee ten oogmerk had; zij kostte het leven aan meer dan 100,000 menschen, en mislukte. De tweede, dezen grooten vorst niet minder waardig, bestond in het uitrusten van verscheiden vloten, waarvan hij het bevel aan *Phenicische* zeelieden toevertrouwde, die uit de roode zee uitloopende, *Africa* rondzeilden, en na drie jaren in den mond van den *Nyl* terug kwamen.

Nechao trok tegen de *Assyriers* op. Koning *Josias*, cijnsbaar aan den Koning van *Babylonie*, wilde zich verzetten tegen den doortogt van den Koning van *Egypte*, op het grondgebied van *Juda*; hij werd geslagen, en *Nechao* vervolgde zijnen weg, en volvoerde gelukkig zijne onderneming tegen de *Assyriers*.

Op zijn' terugtogt door *Nebuchodonosor* overwonnen, werd hij verpligt zijne veroveringen te staken, en stierf in het jaar 602 vóór Christus.

VIII. AMASIS.

Egypte.

AMASIS onttroonde den zoon van *Nechos*, […] eenvoudig Soldaat Koning van *Egypte* geworden […] deed hij door den hoogen trap van geluk e[…] waartoe hij het gebied stijgen deed, zijne […] diging niet alleen vergeten, maar zelfs zegen[…]

Hij moedigde den handel aan, deed de ku[…] wetenschappen bloeijen, en het was onder zijn […] dat *Solon* en *Pythagoras* in die beroemde la[…] onderrigt kwamen vragen.

Onder het volgende gebied werd *Egypte* door […] Koning van *Persie*, omtrent 525 jaar vóór C. o[…] juk gebragt, en van dat tijdpunt tot op de verove[…] beide deze rijken door *Alexander*, bleef *Egypte* o[…] ken onder de magt van of cijnsbaar aan de *Perz*[…]

Het verwierf een nieuwen luister onder *Pt*[…] gelijk wij in het vervolg zien zullen.

Egypte was verdeeld in 36 *nomen* of *departeme*[…] grond was verdeeld onder de priesters, den Ko[…] de krijgslieden; het overige der natie moest va[…] beid bestaan. Deze ongelijke verdeeling was de […] van de magt der priesters, welke zelfs boven di[…] Koning verheven was.

De beroepen waren, even als in *Indie*, erf[…] het was ongeoorloofd immer van beroep te ve[…] en eene wet van *Amasis* veroordeelde ter dood […] die de middelen van zijn bestaan niet konde opgeven […] zullen niet spreken van den godsdienst der *Egyptena*[…] ke niet anders was dan een gedrogtelijk mengsel v[…] sporigste en ongerijmdste bijgeloovigheid.

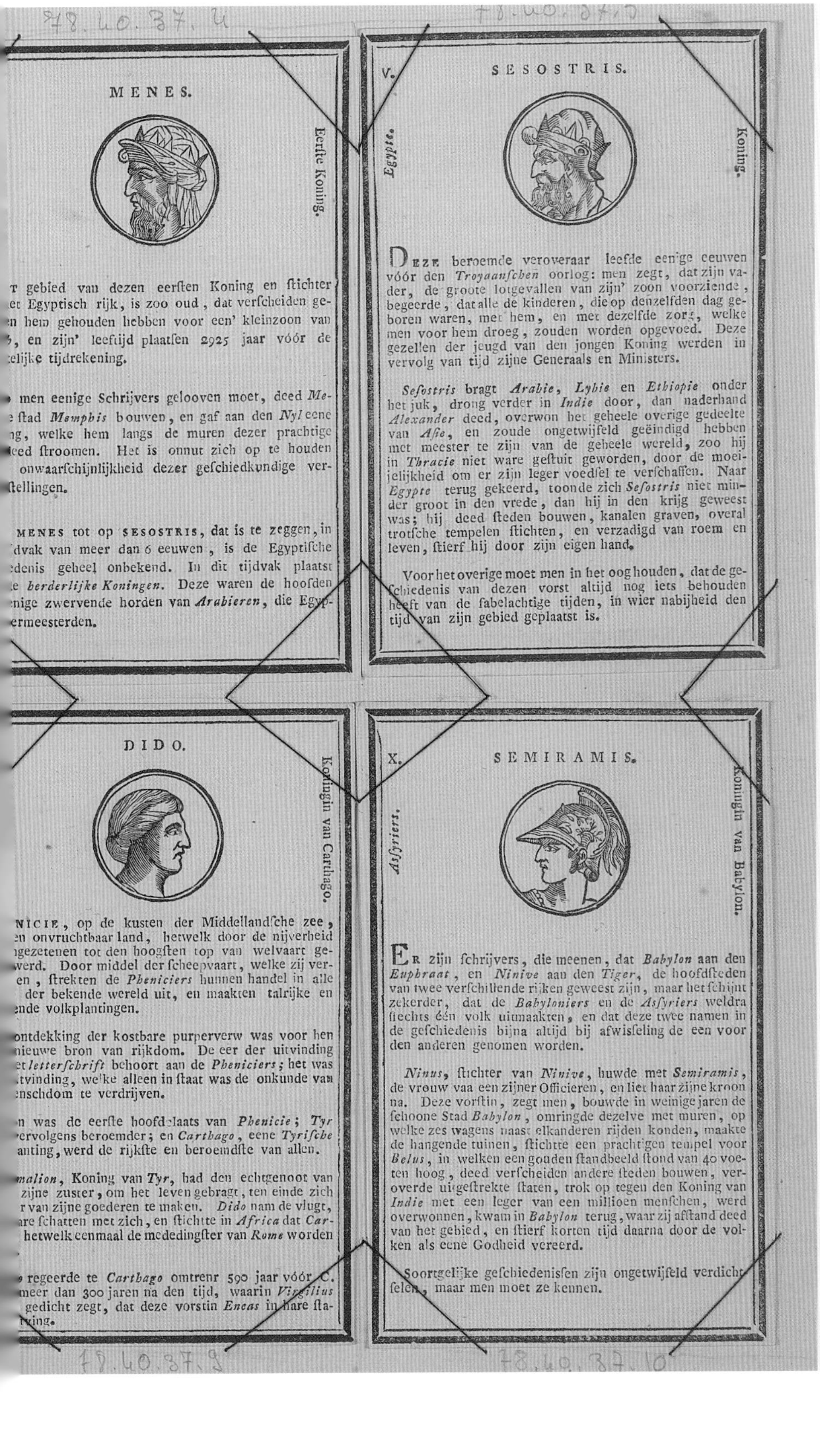

81

Card game used to teach about the great figures of antiquity, Netherlands, first half of the nineteenth century.

This game features a selection of Egyptian kings known from the Renaissance to the nineteenth century: Menes, Sesostris, Psammetichus, Necho and Amasis.

The two bodies of Pedubast

This duality of the pharaoh's persona is still more marked in the Demotic narratives that form part of the cycle of Inaros and Pedubast. The latter, reigning placidly in Tanis, struggles to impose his will on princes who are theoretically his vassals, but who have greater armed forces at their disposal and whose personalities are more aggressive and battle-hardened than his. Appearing completely passive and powerless in the face of events that pass him by, he provokes indifference and even disdain in the other protagonists, who have no qualms in making their feelings known to him.

In the Contest for the Benefice of Amun, the king, who has arrived at Thebes to lead the procession of the god from one bank of the Nile to the other, sees the sacred barge seized by a gang led by a young priest who maintains the benefice is his. Taken by surprise, and after two abortive attacks by the crown prince and the army's senior commander, both of whom are captured by the interlopers, Pedubast is reduced to asking advice from Amun's oracle, who orders him to try nothing on his own, but to appeal to two princes that he had deliberately excluded from the ceremonies. Feeling uneasy about the prospect of asking for their help himself, he begs Prince Pakruru, the father of one of them, to write to them. Very reluctant at first, Pakruru finally agrees, although he forcefully upbraids the sovereign. The furious reaction of the son, Petechonsis, when he reads his father's letter, is remarkable:

> 'This fisherman of small fry from Tanis, this setter of traps with trusses (?) from Buto, this Pedubast son of Khahor whom I did not call Pharaoh! He loads me with flattery when he needs me in his distress, but when he goes to celebrate his gods' festivals without experiencing quarrels or brawls he ignores me...'

Petechonsis seems to be contesting King Pedubast's very legitimacy by using his patronym, as though he were an ordinary individual.

A second episode, still more troubling, presents us with another hero who hurries from Elephantine to chase away the terrorists who have taken possession of the sacred barge. He throws himself straight into battle, proudly ignoring the presence of the pharaoh, and it is only at the end of a first, interminable duel that the pharaoh dares approach to receive homage from the warrior who had arrived in such a timely fashion, who 'took off his helmet and prostrated himself on the ground, [...] filling his mouth with a clod of earth'. But raising him up, the king 'stretched his arms around him and put his mouth to his mouth. He kissed him in this way for a very long time, in the manner of a man honouring the woman he loves!' This gesture by the sovereign, which was certainly not normal protocol, clearly underlines his humiliating dependency on his powerful vassals. It is only his status that places him above them and in the end it is his regalia that is respected by his subjects rather than his own moral authority. A passage in the Contest for the Armour of Inaros highlights this explicitly: Pedubast, having failed to prevent civil war between two princely alliances who are fighting over the dead hero's precious cuirass, tries at least to force the adversaries to observe elementary rules. To this end, he asks Prince Petechonsis to defer the battle. The prince 'looked at the pharaoh Pedubast wearing the crown of Isis, the diadem of the Mistress of the Two Lands, paid homage to him and did not engage in battle that day'. It is the sacred crown that commands the warrior's respect, much more than the individual wearing it.

The evolution of the image of the pharaoh in Egyptian literature, culminating in the anecdotes recounted by Greek authors, certainly indicates a growing disassociation between the sovereign's human and divine natures, with his desacralisation as the ultimate consequence. Without power or prestige, the pharaoh, unlike the Roman emperor who endured for so long, could only join the realm of nostalgic memories in the face of monotheism's triumph.

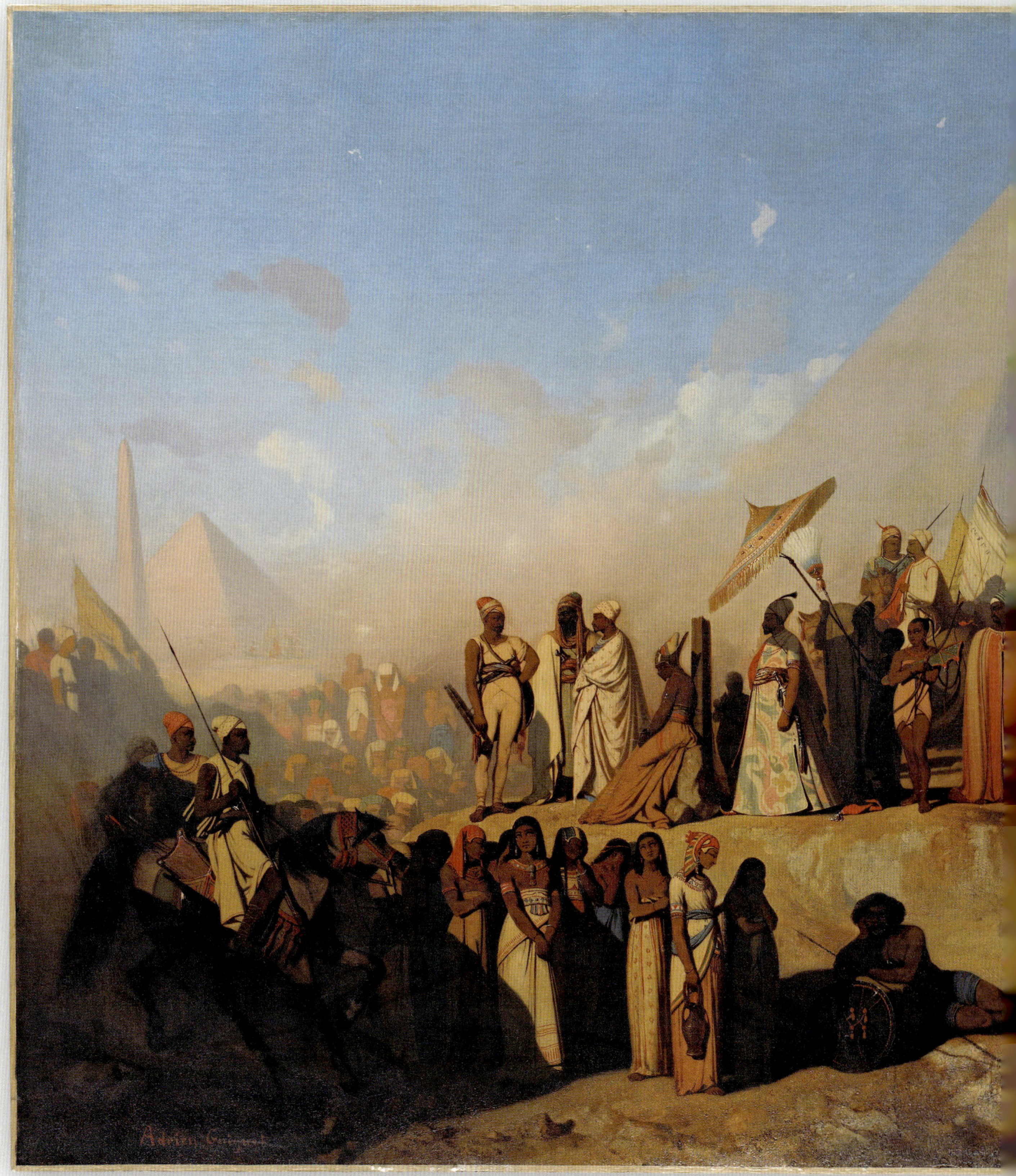

88

Adrien Guignet, *Cambyse et Psamménite* (Cambyses and Psammetichus), France, 1841.

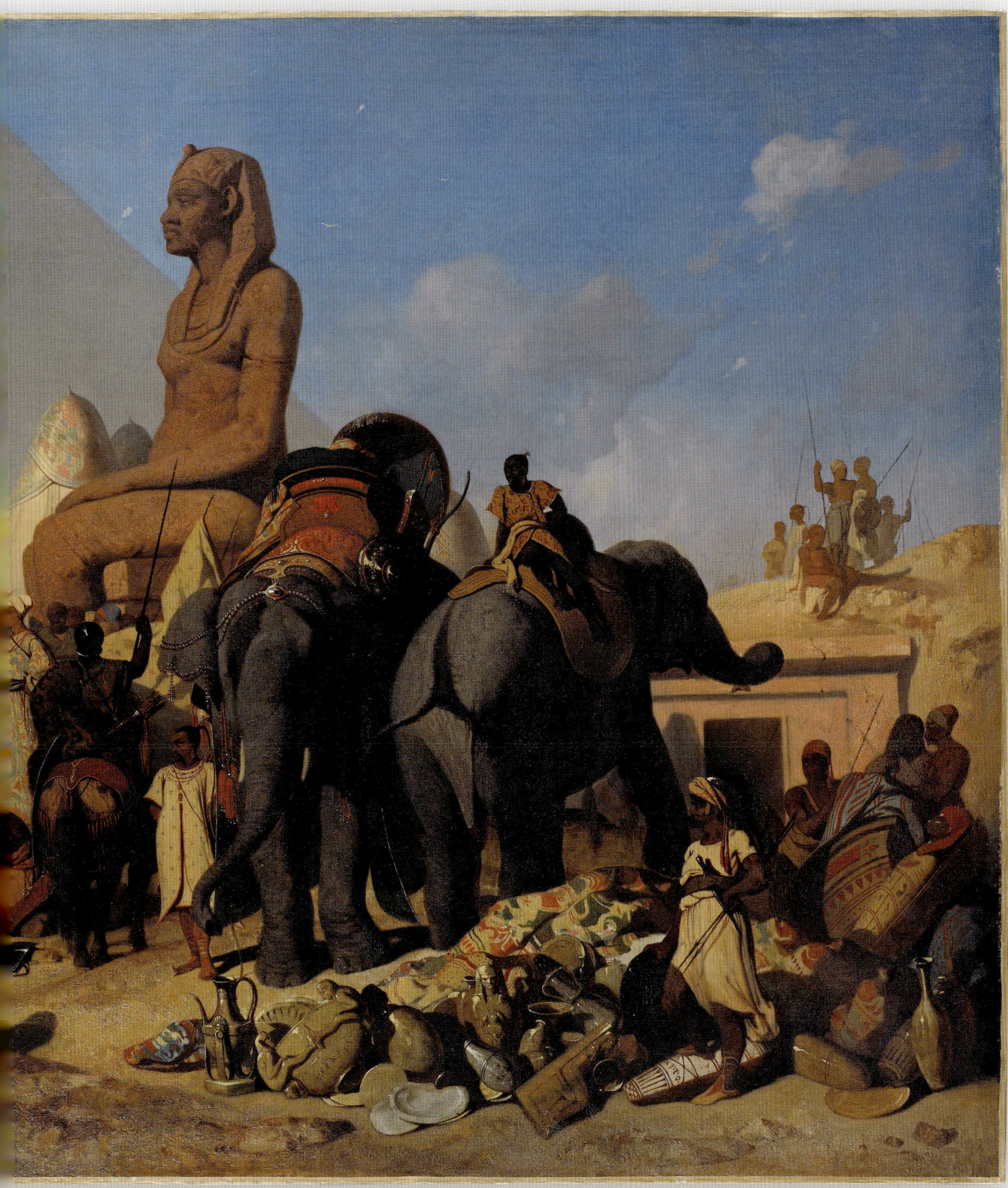

ACTING ON IMAGES – IMAGES THAT ACT

SIMON CONNOR

Some pharaohs were already superstars in antiquity, sometimes even in their own lifetimes. At least, that is how a number of them appear to us: Amenhotep III, Akhenaten, Tutankhamun, Ramesses II and Ramesses III, acclaimed by their courtiers in temple reliefs and on the walls of the tombs of important dignitaries. While it may be difficult to establish the extent to which these images reflect reality, it is known that some images of kings — in particular statues, invested with the power of their presence and endowed with an ability to act — could become the object of a real cult, sometimes persisting for several centuries.

19

Magical figurine depicting a bound Nubian, fortress of Mirgissa, Sudan, first half of the Twelfth Dynasty (c. 1974–1856 BCE).

This statuette is covered in magical formulae for the destruction of Egypt's enemies. It was ritually buried in front of a fortress at the kingdom's southern frontier.

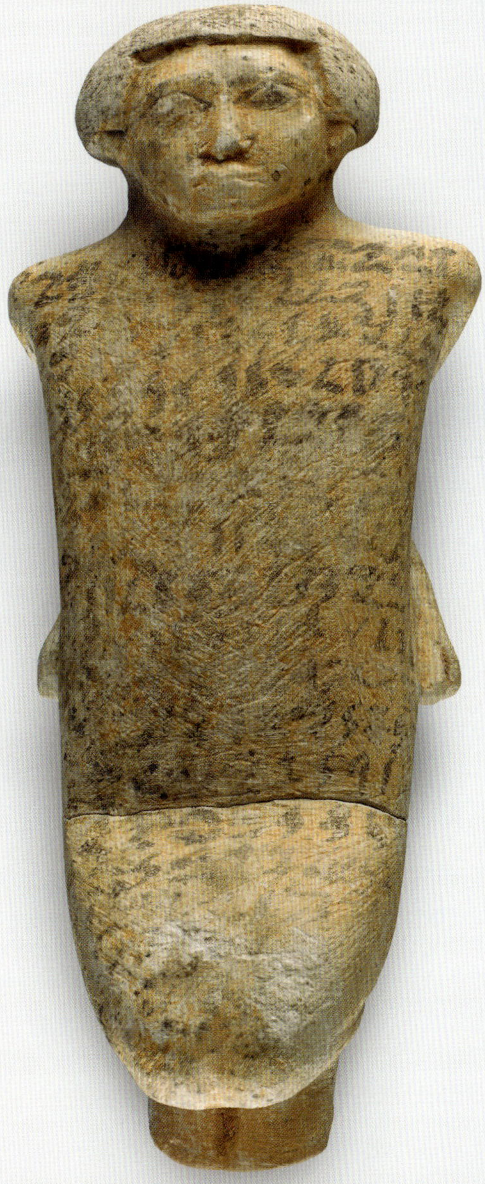

The power of images

Colossal statues were not only markers in the landscape: perhaps they also represented one of the rare ways in which the population could have access to the divine. These majestic three-dimensional images acted as supernatural incarnations of the sovereign, intermediaries between the human world and the mysterious domain that lay behind the sanctuary gates (cat. 43).

These statues, made from hard stone (pink granite, orange quartzite, dark granodiorite, sometimes also indurated white limestone) tangibly represented the king's presence and his role as a privileged intercessor with the world of the gods. Far from being simple decorative elements, and even transcending their function as 'propaganda' — or objects conveying an ideological and political message, if we want to avoid a word that is too modern — in the view of the ancient Egyptians, these images had the ability to hear prayers and take appropriate action. More tangible than the immaterial and often inaccessible deities, they gradually became objects of devotion not only as representatives of the king, but also as monuments invested with real powers to act. This influential means of promoting power gathered real momentum during the New Kingdom. Many stelae of this period bear witness to the cult of royal statues (cat. 44).

It was in this context that the practice developed of giving statues of Ramesses II names that were chosen by the king himself or by his advisors. At Pi-Ramesses, the Nineteenth Dynasty's royal residence, an immense sculpture of the standing king was named 'Sun of Princes'. Only fragments of this colossus now survive: they can be seen at Tanis, where they were reused as masonry blocks for the temples of the first millennium BCE (figs. 1 and 2).

The adoration of royal colossi as a way of communicating with the world of the gods was not restricted to the general population: Ramesses himself chose to be portrayed worshipping his own stone images — either he had a deep conviction of his own divinity or he wanted to set an example and encourage his people to venerate his person (cat. 45). While Ramesses was considered a real superstar, in his lifetime as well as after his death, this communication operation was evidently orchestrated by the royal powers.

Endowed with a real ability to act, statues had an actual 'life'. For them to be born — or activated — a ritual of opening the mouth was required, after which they could become receptacles for prayers and offerings dedicated to the deceased or to the deity. Cult statues concealed in the temples, made from metal or wood, were even washed, clothed, perfumed and fed. Their magical powers could be both beneficial and dangerous: a desire to neutralize this power may be one of the reasons for the fragmentary condition of the sculptures now in museums or on archaeological sites. It is not unusual to hear visitors to such places expressing surprise at the incomplete state of the statues and reliefs around them, especially the almost inevitable absence of the nose, despite the fact that noses are easily broken excrescences. Egyptian antiquities are not excluded from such observations, to the point that doubt may be cast over the authenticity of a sculpture that is 'too well preserved'.

Damnatio memoriae

In the course of Egyptian antiquity, political reasons as well as magical and cult practices may have prompted the mutilation of images, in line with the principle of *damnatio memoriae* or 'condemnation of memory'. Kings, private individuals and even gods were all victims of this practice (cat. 72).

While some kings and queens were worshipped as if they were gods while they were alive and for several generations afterwards, there were others who became 'anti-stars' shortly after their deaths, victims of an official campaign to have them forgotten. Paradoxically, many of these sovereigns who were proscribed by history are today among the most popular: the female pharaoh Hatshepsut (cats. 73, 74 and 75), who usurped the throne of Thutmose III; the Amarna sovereigns Akhenaten and Nefertiti, who instigated a new cult but were also iconoclasts judged unpardonable by their contemporaries, responsible for wrecking Amun's images and name throughout the country; and finally Tutankhamun, the last-born child of that couple, who died prematurely and was buried amidst fabulous treasures, but cast out of the collective memory until 1922.

These rulers were retrospectively considered a destabilizing influence. The message was clear: it was necessary 'to remember to forget them'. This was because these pharaohs had disrupted the established order. They had not fulfilled their mission, which was to ensure that the Two Lands continued to respect *maat*, the principle of cosmic order: as a result, their names had to be erased from inscriptions and it was important to act, often conspicuously, as though they had never existed. Hieroglyphs that had been scratched out were very often not replaced; in mutilated reliefs and statues, the figures attacked with hammers remained visible, displaying their wounds, their faces destroyed and their limbs broken. The case of the Atenist sovereigns (who founded the cult of the universal god Aten) is one of the most explicit. The statues of Akhenaten and Nefertiti discovered in the ruins of Amarna were found reduced to thousands of fragments. Although blocks of stone (*talatats*) from the temples of Aten were often identified in the masonry of temples built in the late Eighteenth and Nineteenth Dynasties (cat. 76), the statues were systematically destroyed. They were toppled, but broken not only by their fall: it is clear that they were relentlessly and meticulously smashed (cats. 77 and 78).

Akhenaten had marked out the territory of the town of Amarna with a series of monumental stelae cut into the cliffs (boundary stelae) (fig. 4), for twenty kilometres alongside the Nile, accompanied by statues of the royal family presenting offerings to the solar disc. After his reign, during the campaign to destroy his memory, these stelae were deliberately pitted; the statues were amputated, disfigured and often decapitated, their bodies left to the mercies of time for the ensuing centuries, displaying their stumps and their headless necks, like a reminder — perhaps even a warning — that such a model was not to be emulated, showing the fate that would await a king who failed in the same way (figs. 3 and 4).

At Amarna, a site destined 'to die', the images were in many cases left clearly visible, like mutilated corpses. By contrast, at Karnak (Thebes), which never stopped 'living', growing and becoming ever finer in the centuries that followed the Amarna episode, the statues of Akhenaten (the famous sandstone colossi showing the king with particularly prominent features) were not savagely attacked but carefully sawn into pieces and separated from their dorsal pillars, sometimes with signs of hammering around the eyes or on other parts of the body, before being buried face down in front of the pedestals that originally supported them — and then disappearing. In the town of Thebes, the desire to rebuild and renew must have taken precedence over parading condemnation of the Atenist pharaoh's memory.

The case of Tutankhamun

Aside from their symbolic condemnation, it would have been difficult for other sovereigns to use the statues of Akhenaten and Nefertiti: their style was too distinctive, too recognizable. Their son Tutankhamun was a different case. Perhaps the young pharaoh, who became a superstar almost by mistake thanks to the discovery of his tomb and its fabulous treasure, was insignificant in the eyes of his successor, Horemheb, and not even worth the bother of a conspicuous *damnatio memoriae*. Although there is evidence that Tutankhamun was the victim of a condemnation of his memory during the reign of Horemheb, it does not seem that this *damnatio* entailed a massive destruction of his images. Instead of destroying them, the former army general who became pharaoh was more inclined to lay claim to the reliefs and statues (cat. 79). Horemheb decided to adopt the same official facial features as the child-king; as a result, it is difficult to distinguish between reappropriated statues of Tutankhamun and those that were actually made for him. By reusing and re-inscribing statues of Tutankhamun, retaining the same facial features — although at the time he ascended the throne, the old general would certainly not have had the same childlike face with plump cheeks — Horemheb probably wanted to replace the young king and usurp his role as 'restorer', while rejecting the memory of the Amarna child. For this reason, we should not be too quick to assign to Horemheb all the damage done to images of the young sovereign.

Two statues in the Musée du Louvre (cat. 80 and fig. 5), both showing the seated god Amun protecting a standing figure of the sovereign with his hands, attest to the *damnatio memoriae* inflicted upon Tutankhamun, since the king's name has been partially erased with a hammer on the dorsal pillars of both statues. Only the hieroglyphs designating the gods Amun and Ra have been spared, while the other signs have been effaced so as to 'break', as it were, the name contained in the cartouches: [Tut-ankh]-Amun [Neb-kheperu]-Ra. It seems likely that this desire to obliterate the identity of the king while respecting the names of the gods was Horemheb's handiwork.

In both these statue groups, the figure of the king standing in front of the god has also been damaged. In the smallest sculpture (cat. 80), it has been almost entirely ripped away, while in the other (fig. 5), a more targeted mutilation focused on the legs (which permit movement), the arms (which express the king's act of worship) and the head (which confers life and identity). It is tempting to see in this a deliberate attack on Tutankhamun, but this is far from certain. In both cases, the figure of Amun was also mutilated and decapitated (the scar from the restoration is still clearly visible).

In the statue on display in this exhibition (cat. 80), Amun has been disfigured by blows to his nose and mouth, while his beard has been carefully pulled off; in the second statue, the god is less badly damaged, but the point of his beard is missing, as are his hands, which once rested on the sovereign's shoulders. We cannot entirely dismiss the possibility that the general-pharaoh's henchmen were responsible for the ravages to the figure of Tutankhamun — but why mutilate it, when it would have been so easy to change the inscription and turn it into an authentic Horemheb? It is also difficult to believe that the damage done to the figures of Amun date to this period, since the restoration of his cult was one of the cornerstones of the policies of post-Amarna sovereigns.

It is true that there are no visible signs of restoration, since the cartouches were not reinscribed, but it is hard to imagine that figures so maimed were installed in temples. Perhaps the effaced cartouches were covered in plaster? It seems that the Louvre group (fig. 5) was the one found in 1857 in the hypostyle hall of the temple of Karnak, built by Seti I and Ramesses II — after the reign of Horemheb. It is therefore likely, that in the Nineteenth Dynasty the sculpture was still presentable enough to be included in the building's sculptural programme.

If Horemheb was not responsible for all the damage to these statues, who should be blamed? The hundreds of sculptures brought to light at Karnak were all found in a fragmentary condition. There are many factors that could account for this: the effect of weather and natural causes (erosion, earthquakes, climatic variations, salinisation, animal excretions and so on) as well as deliberate human actions. In this last case — probably very common, although it is not always easy to prove — a whole series of motives could be put forward. Some reliefs and statues were reused in foundations or walls, but often these pieces seem to have

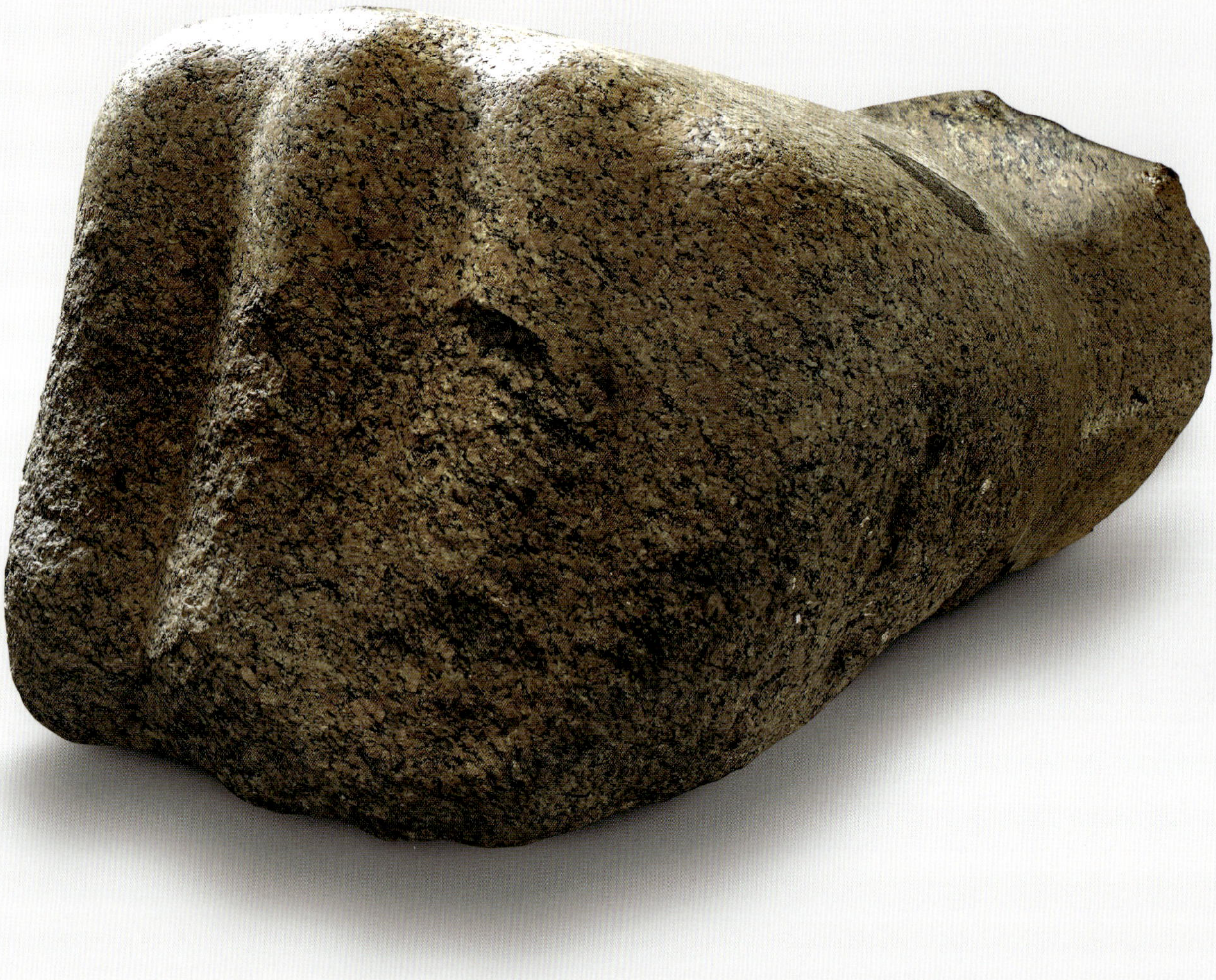

43

Left fist of a colossus of Ramesses II, Mit Rahina, Egypt, reign of Ramesses II (c. 1279–1212 BCE).

Colossal statues placed in front of temple gates were monumental manifestations of the supernatural nature of the king, the intermediary between humans and gods. This enormous hand belonged to the depiction of a standing king whose arms reached down, alongside his body. It comes from one of the gates of the Temple of Ptah at Mit Rahina (the ancient Memphis), where the bases of several monumental statues of Ramesses II can still be found — probably reused statues of a Middle Kingdom pharaoh.

44

Stela depicting a scene of offering to a statue of Ramesses II, Qantir (?), Egypt, reign of Ramesses II (c. 1279–1212 BCE).

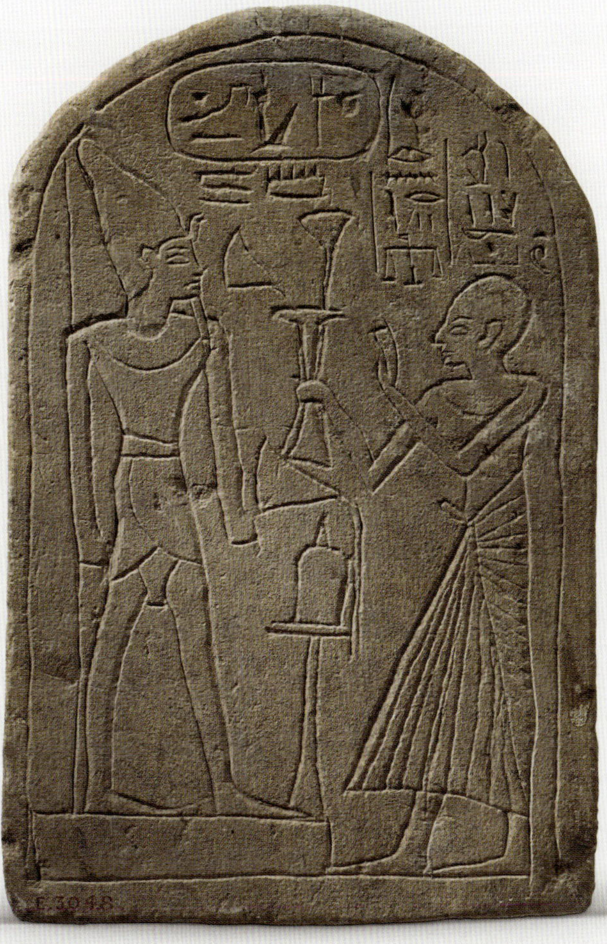

Many traces can be found of the cult of statues portraying the reigning sovereign in the New Kingdom. This small private stela, probably an ex-voto, depicts a certain Setinakht making offerings to a colossus of Ramesses II. We can identify it as the depiction of a statue rather than a figure of the king himself because the sovereign stands very stiffly on a base and against a back pillar.

been mutilated, as if 'deactivated', before being put to this new use. At various times in Egypt's history, we also find references to temples and towns being sacked in times of war or revolt. Finally, at the beginning of the Christian era, many pagan monuments were subjected to fanatical iconoclastic destruction throughout the Mediterranean Basin, which led to many pharaonic remains disappearing or being damaged.
In the case of the statues of Amun protecting Tutankhamun, the mystery persists and the door remains open to interpretations. It is plausible that the damage we see on these objects represents a number of successive campaigns of attack, separated by several centuries.

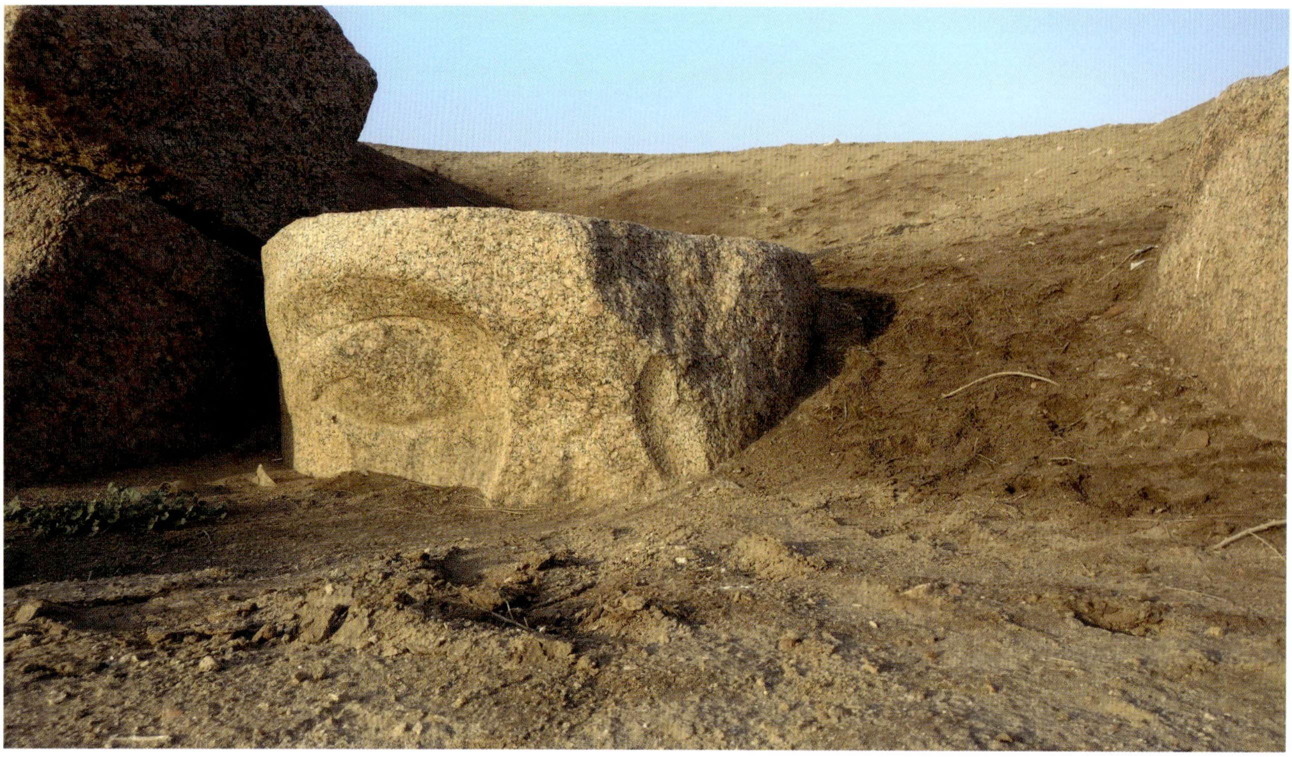

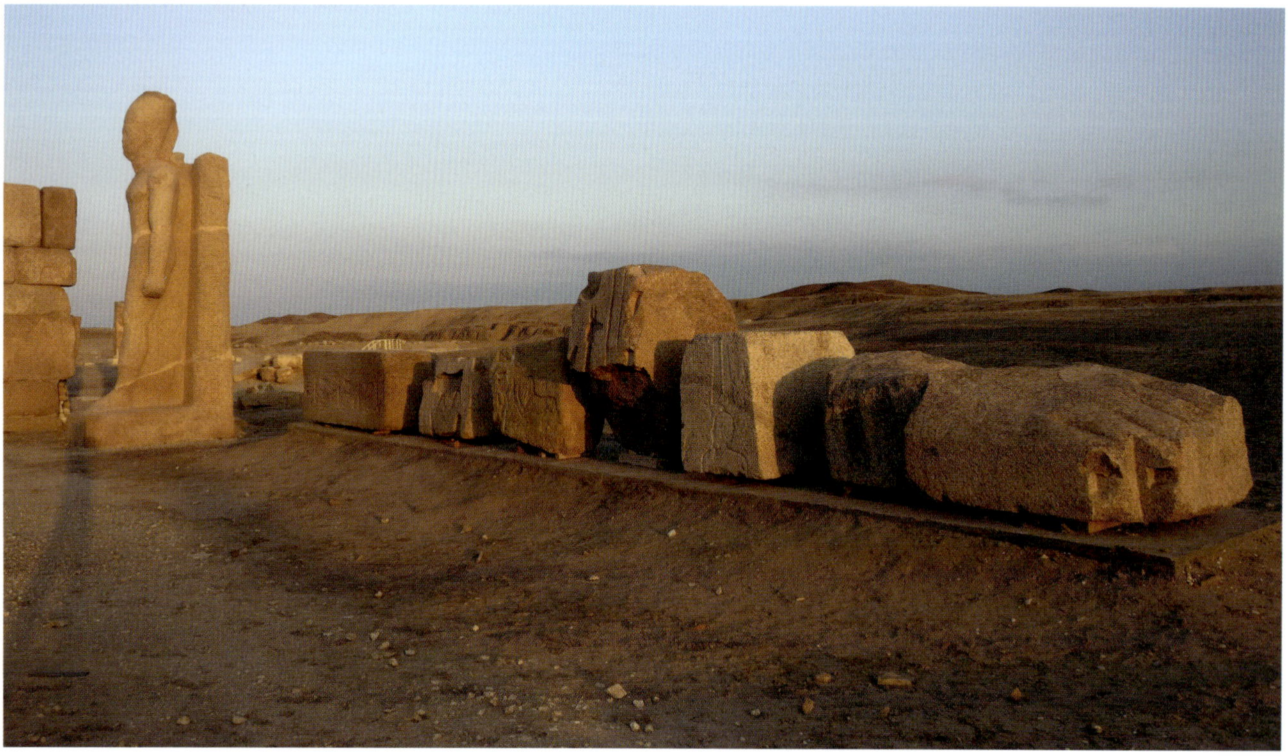

↑ FIGS. 1 AND 2
Fragment of a monumental face and right foot, San el-Hagar (Tanis), Egypt, reign of Ramesses II (1279–1212 BCE), granite.

The elements of the granite statue have been recut into parallelepipedal blocks. This reuse has of course both a practical and an economic role, eliminating the need for new blocks to be transported from the Aswan quarries. However, an image of the famous Ramesses — the quintessential model for the pharaohs who succeeded him — would have been invested with sacred power, so it is conceivable that reusing its body also held a particular appeal for the builders of Tanis.

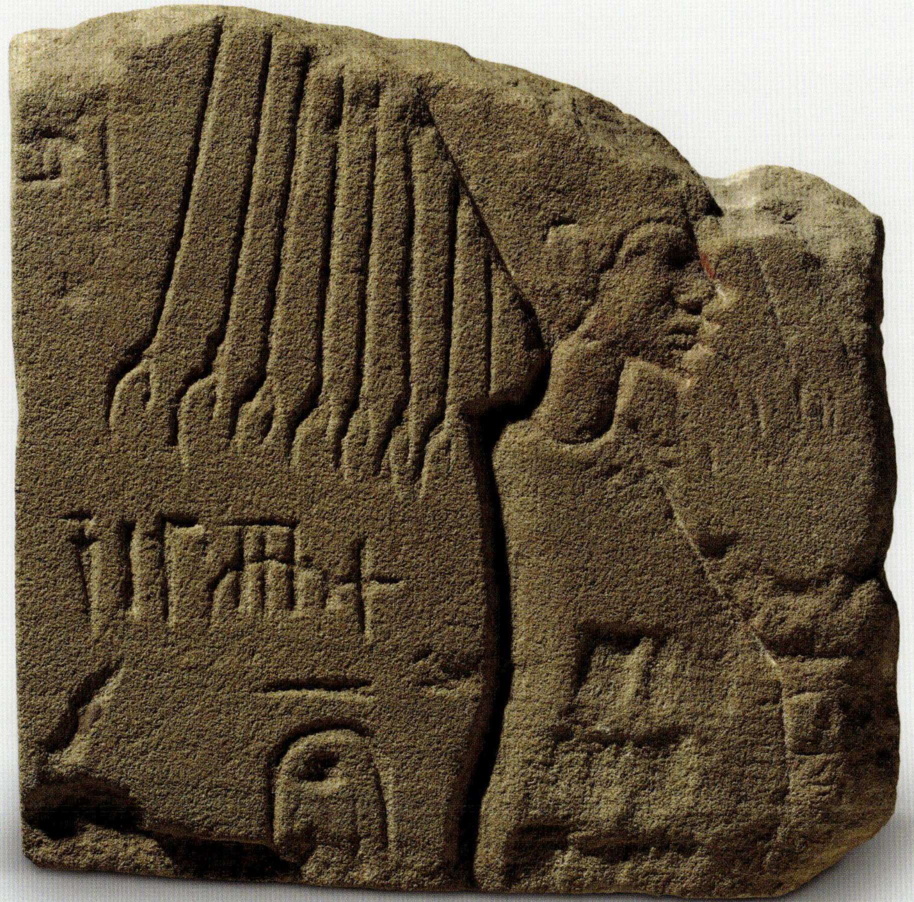

76

Fragment of a building block with chisel marks on the image of Akhenaten, Karnak, Egypt, reign of Akhenaten (c. 1349–1333 BCE), sandstone.

This block is carved in sandstone, which indicates that the relief likely came from Karnak, the domain of Amun, where Amenhotep IV-Akhenaten erected an enormous building, probably a palace, at the beginning of his reign. When this building was dismantled, under Horemheb, the reliefs covering the walls were systematically effaced by hammering and the blocks were reused in the masonry for a new pylon at the nearby temple of Amun. The chisel marks visible on the lower right corner of the block bear witness to the hammering campaign directed at Amarna images.

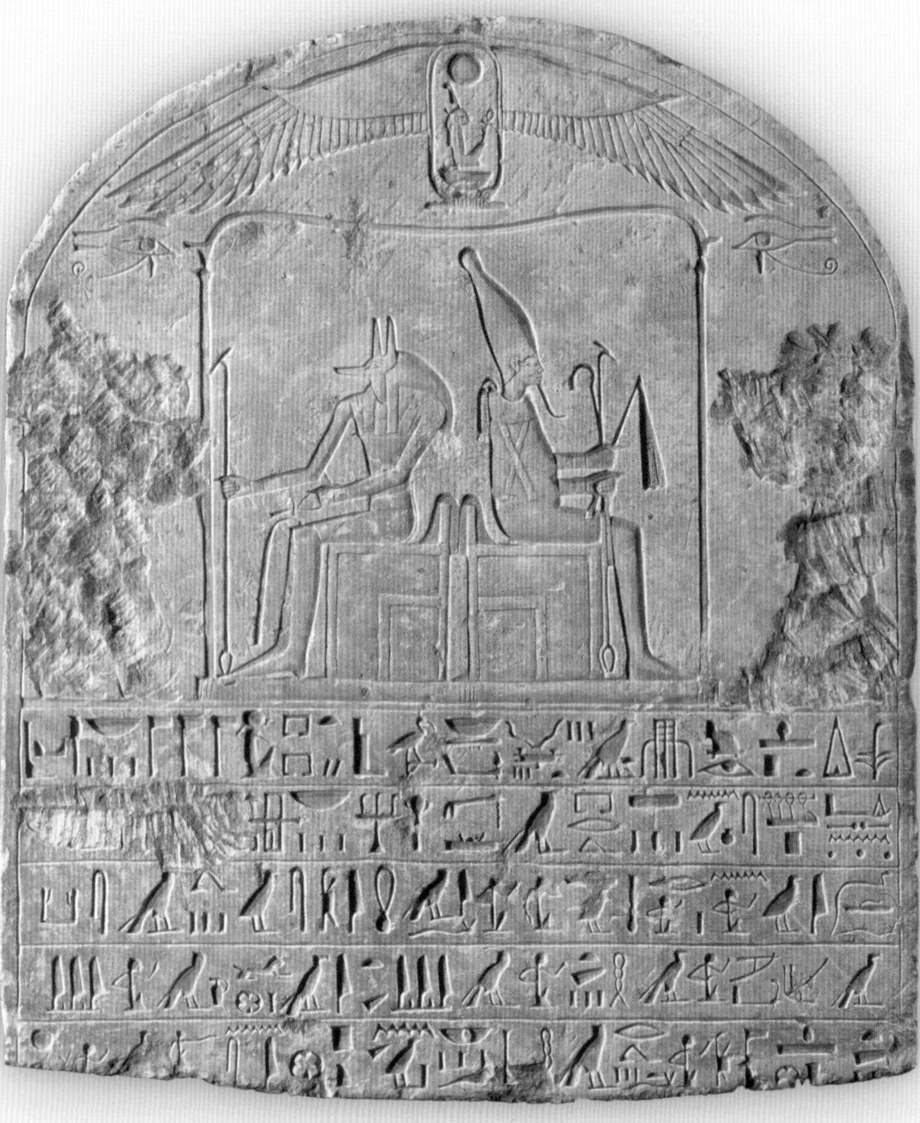

72

Funerary stela dedicated to the gods Osiris and Upuaut, Egypt, reign of Amenhotep III (c. 1388–1349 BCE).

On this stela, a dignitary and contemporary of the king Amenhotep III, according to the cartouche engraved on the arch, is making offerings to the funerary gods Osiris and Upuaut. Perhaps this person had fallen into disgrace: his figure has been literally erased from the surface of his funerary stela: both images of him have been entirely hammered away — so carefully that it is still possible to make out the man's position — and his name has been removed from the second line of the inscription.

75

Head of a statue thought to be Hatshepsut, Egypt, reign of Hatshepsut (c. 1479–1458 BCE).

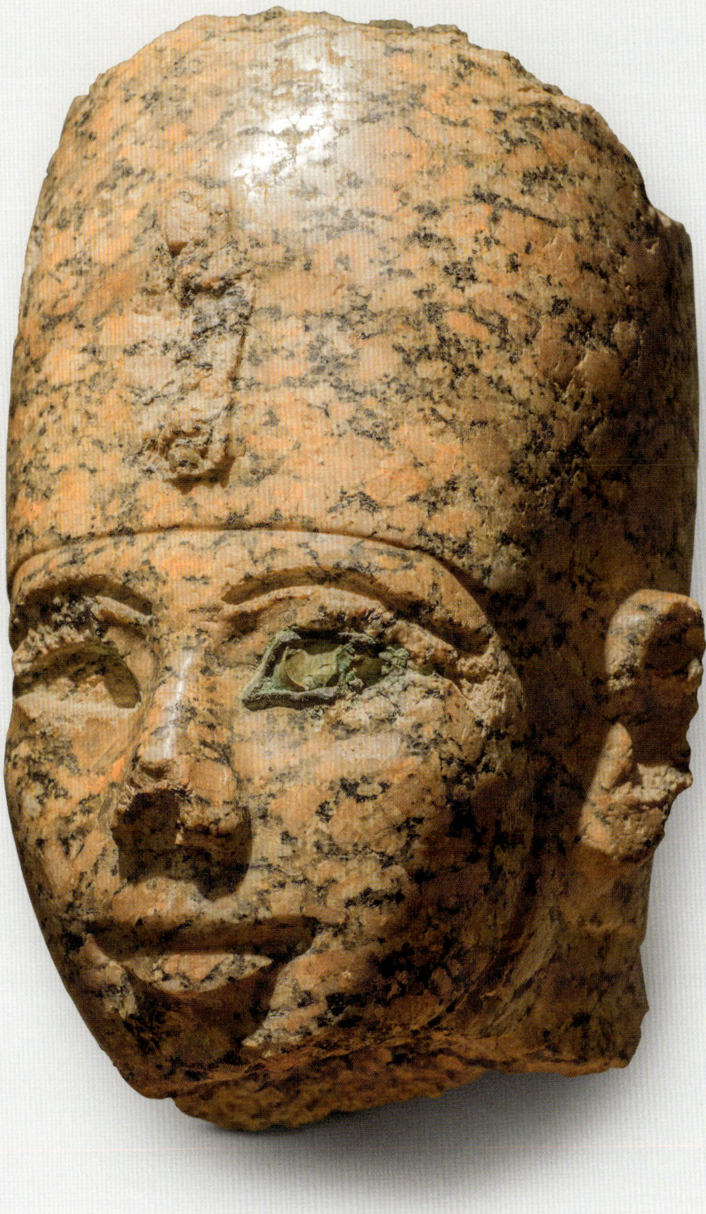

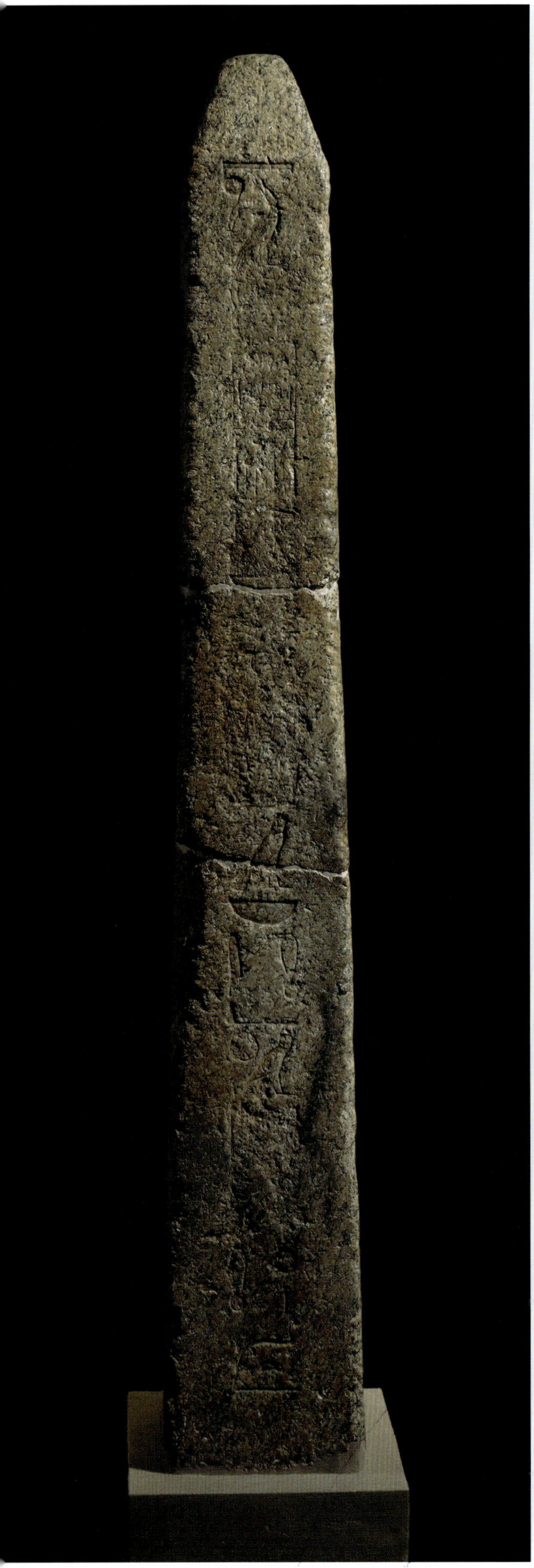

73

Obelisk with Hatshepsut's names effaced by hammering, Qasr Ibrim, Egypt, reign of Hatshepsut and Thutmose III (c. 1479–1458 BCE).

Queen Hatshepsut was subject to a condemnation of her memory from the end of the reign of Thutmose III, not because she was a woman (Egypt had other female pharaohs, although they were rare) but because she seized power when another king, still very much alive, was already on the throne: aunt and step-mother to the child Thutmose III, she took the throne away from him in his youth. Twenty years after the queen's death, the elderly Thutmose decided to ensure that his heir Amenhotep II had a trouble-free succession by conspicuously consigning the usurper Hatshepsut to oblivion. Perhaps to show the fate that would befall those who did not respect the order laid down by the gods, he ordered an organized campaign to obliterate the name and images of the usurper queen. Statues of the female pharaoh were mutilated, disfigured, broken and buried. Some parts of her body were almost systematic targets for the wreckers: the nose, the eyes, and the dangerous cobra *uraeus*, symbol of the supreme protection afforded to royalty. What is more, almost all Hatshepsut's statues were found decapitated.
The granite obelisk in the British Museum provides further evidence of this campaign of *damnatio memoriae*: the inscription it bore, placing the queen under the protection of the god 'Horus, lord of Miam' (the ancient name for the site of Aniba, in Nubia) has been partially mutilated. The queen's names were deliberately damaged, while those of the god were left intact. The monument was not reinscribed with the name of another king, which suggests that it remained visible, in its mutilated form, as though to remind those looking at it that they should remember to forget the queen. Much later, like many Egyptian antiquities, the monument had a second life, reused as the step of a staircase at the fortified site of Qasr Ibrim.

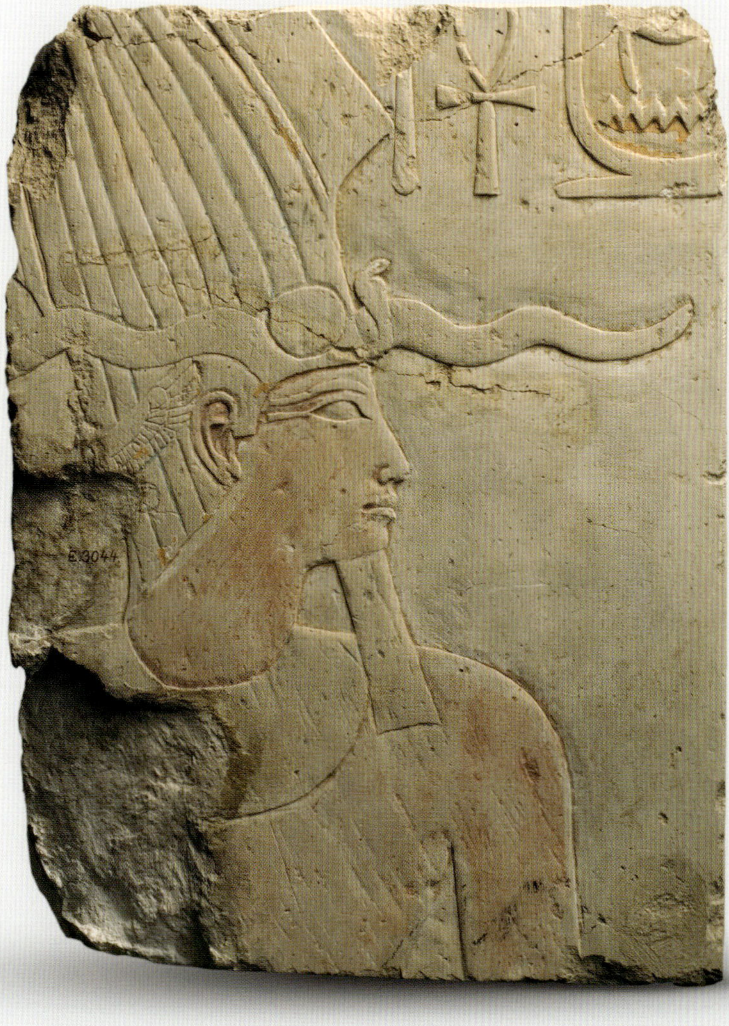

74

Relief representing Hatshepsut,
reassigned to Thutmose II, Deir el-Bahari,
Egypt, reigns of Hatshepsut and Thutmose III
(c. 1479–1425 BCE).

Unlike her statues, reliefs of Hatshepsut were sometimes reassigned, with new inscriptions, to the queen's predecessors. Here, Hatshepsut's cartouche has been modified by scratching out the hieroglyphs composing her name and replacing them with those of Thutmose II, father of Thutmose III. Despite the sculptors' skills, it appears that they were not always literate, because there are some lapses in their modifications. For example, while the partially preserved cartouche gives Thutmose II's throne name, the word that accompanies it, the hieroglyph *ankh*, is followed by the feminine termination *ti* (the vertical sign on the left), which can be translated as 'may she live', thus designating a female sovereign.

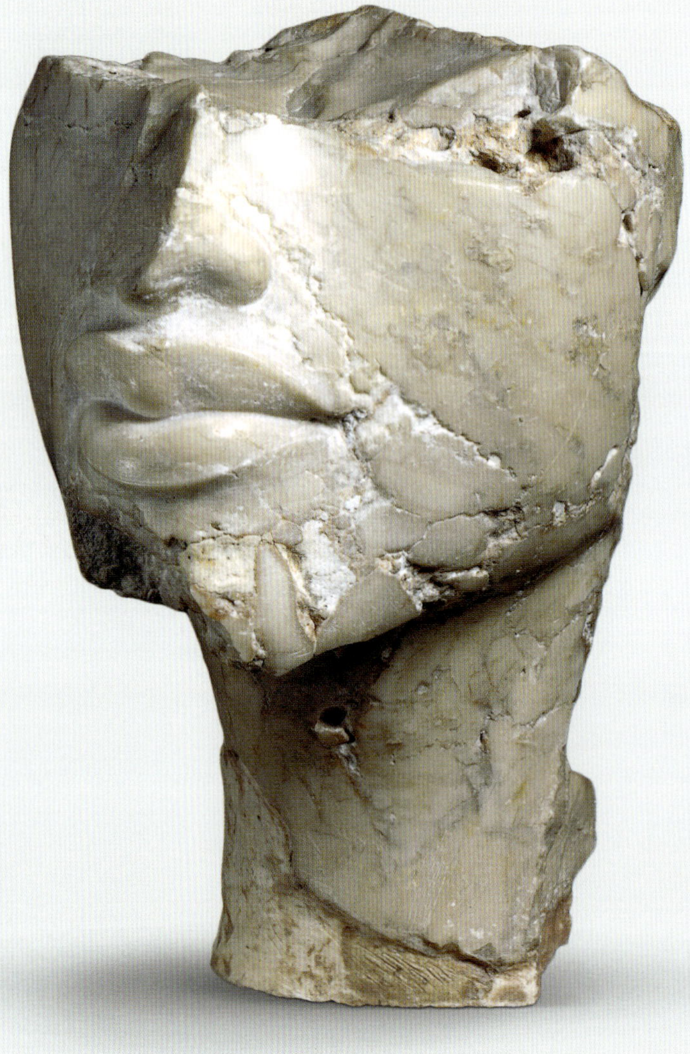

77

Fragment of a face from a statue of Akhenaten, Amarna, Egypt, reign of Akhenaten (c. 1349–1333 BCE).

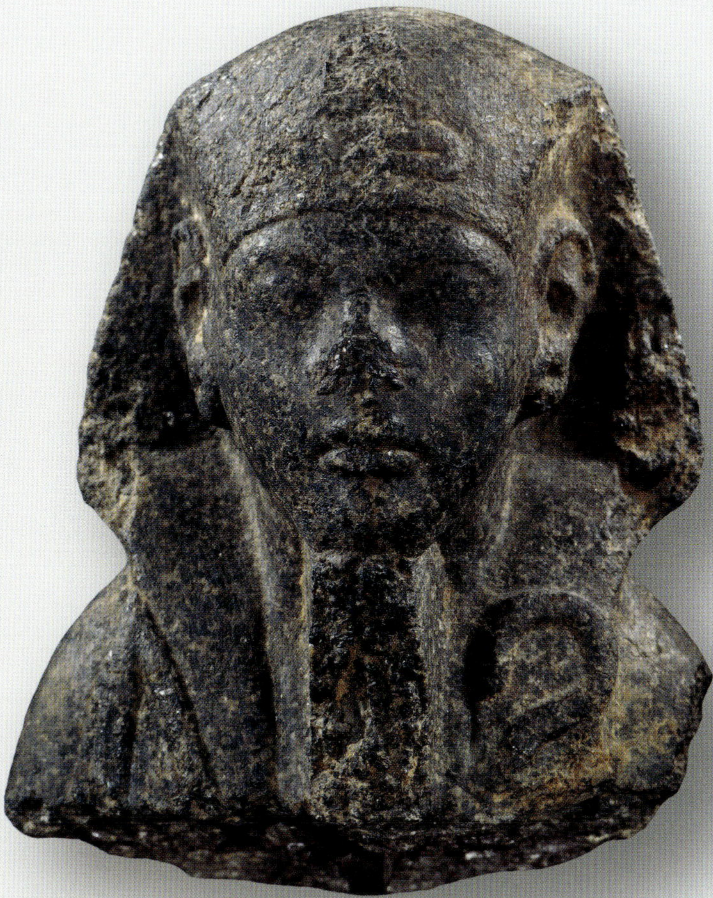

78

Broken funerary statuette of Akhenaten, probably Amarna, Egypt, reign of Akhenaten (c. 1349–1333 BCE).

79

Fragmentary statuette of Tutankhamun usurped by Horemheb, Egypt, reigns of Tutankhamun and Horemheb (1330–1295 BCE), steatite.

In the late Eighteenth Dynasty, during the reign of Horemheb — the army general who became pharaoh — Akhenaten and his entire family were condemned to oblivion. Since Akhenaten had not fulfilled his duty to ensure the country's stability, at least in the eyes of the new king and his supporters, it needed to be made crystal clear that this episode should never have occurred and that the previous sovereigns had failed. The innumerable monuments built in the name of Akhenaten and Nefertiti were dismantled and all the images and inscriptions were erased by hammering. Tutankhamun was included in the campaign of oblivion aimed at his father. However, in his case, Horemheb chose not to destroy his images, but to reuse them for his own benefit. He adopted the same youthful facial features and replaced Tutankhamun's name with his own on temple reliefs and statues of the deceased young king. This steatite statue is an example of this. The king portrayed was originally Tutankhamun — the sovereign's name is still legible on the belt buckle and on the standard he holds in his left hand. The inscription covering the dorsal pillar comprises two cartouches which have been scratched out; only the first of the two displays an aborted attempt at reinscription with Horemheb's name. However, the signs have been engraved back to front. Was the piece abandoned and perhaps destroyed because of this mistake, made by the sculptor charged with adapting the statuette?

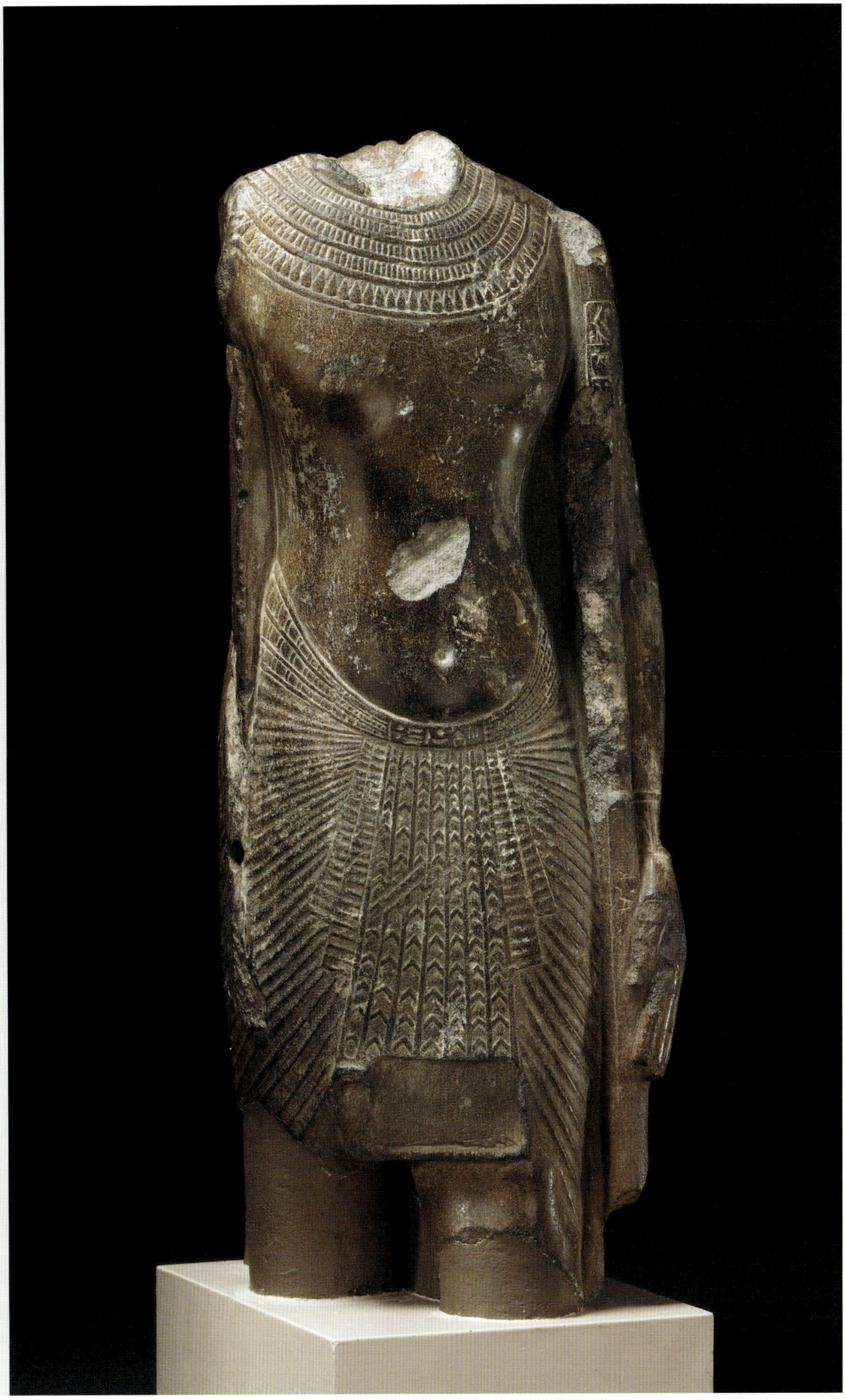

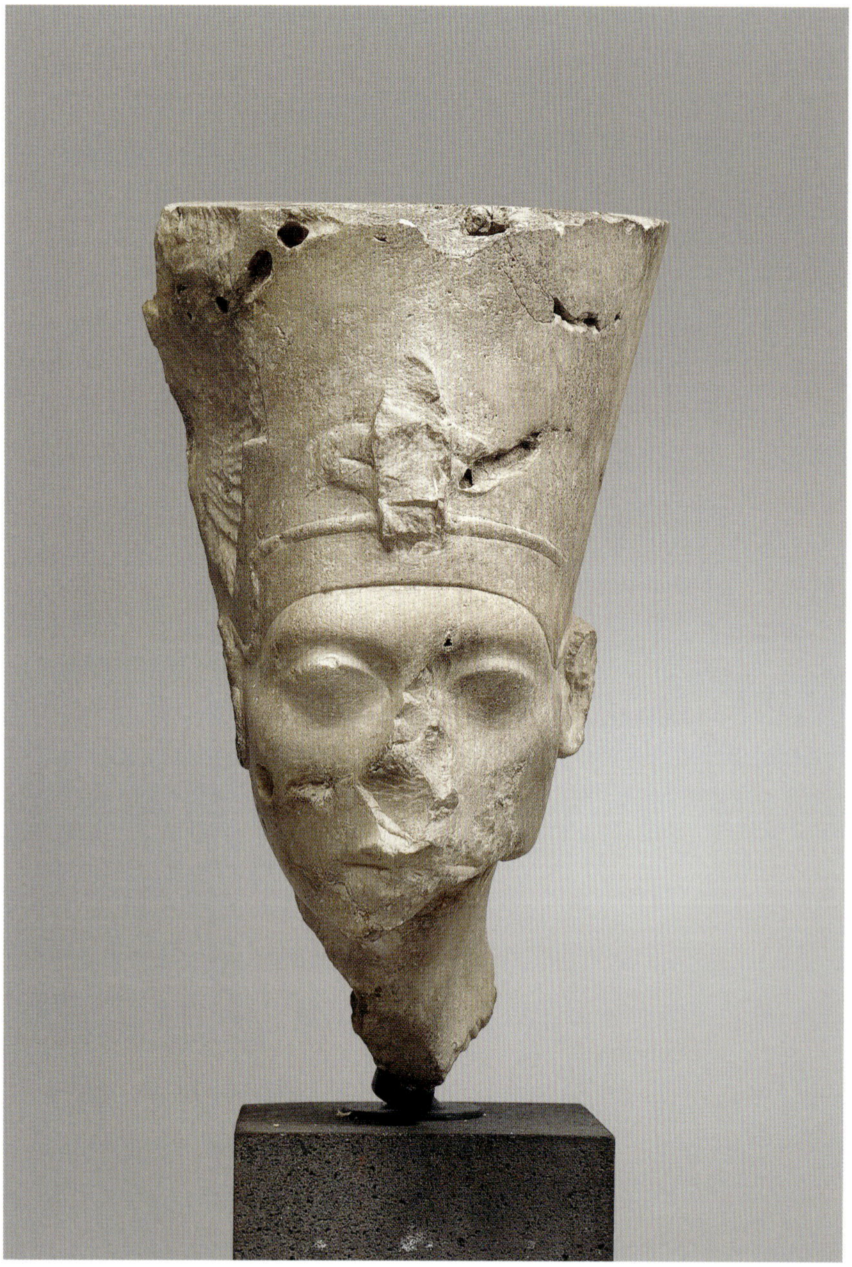

↑ FIG. 3
Head of a mutilated statue of Nefertiti, Amarna, Egypt, reign of Akhenaten (c. 1349–1333 BCE), nummulite limestone, 33.7 × 19.5 × 23.5 cm, Essen, Museum Folkwang.

The provenance of this fragment can be established from the material used to make this sculpture, a limestone studded with tiny fossils: it is one of the boundary stelae cut into the cliff faces surrounding the territory of the town of Amarna. The face has been disfigured, but some parts seem to have been particularly targeted by the iconoclasts: the mouth, which permits speech; the nose, essential for breathing; and the *uraeus*, the rearing snake on the queen's forehead.

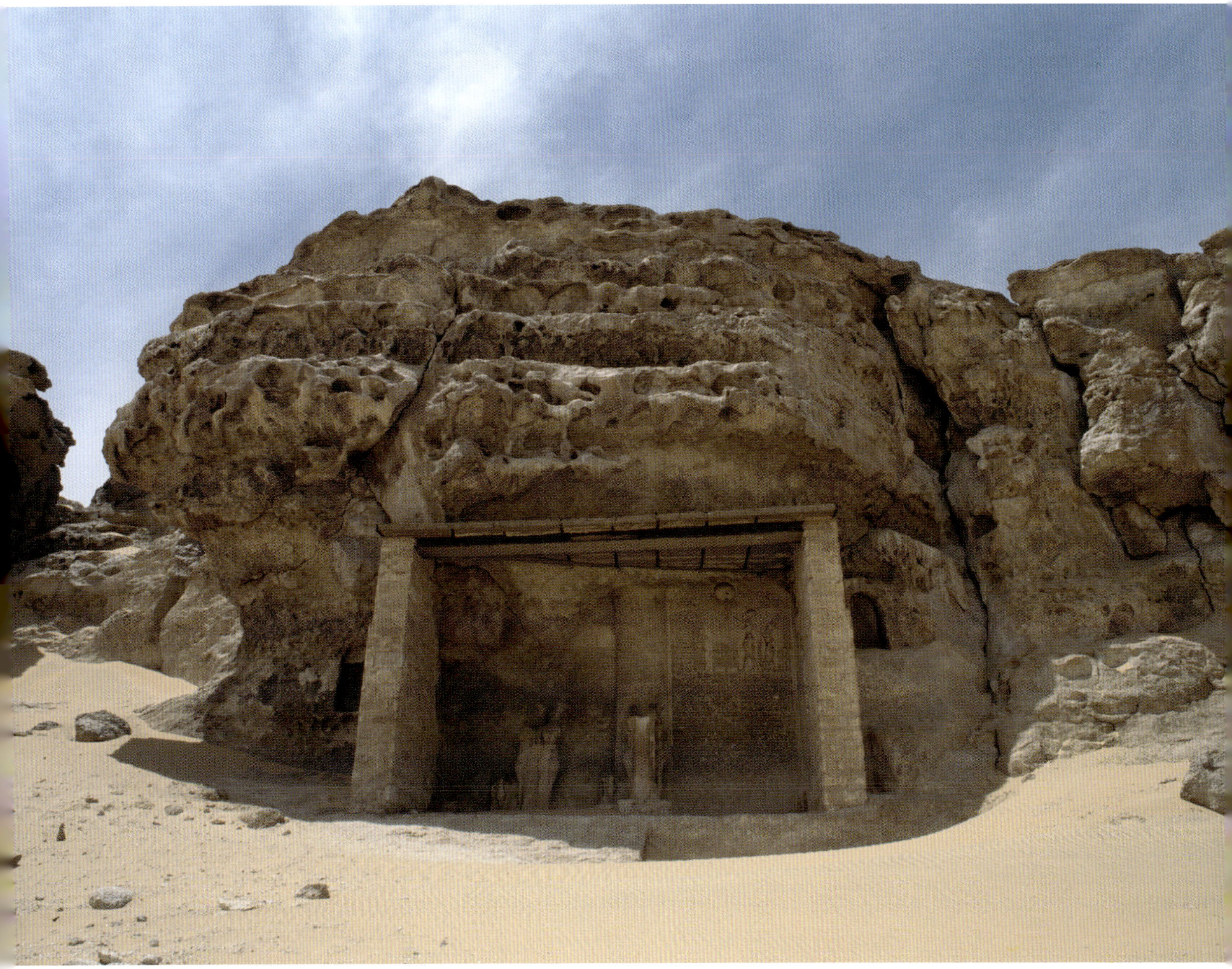

↑ FIG. 4
Boundary stela, Tuna el-Gebel, Egypt, reign of Akhenaten (c. 1349–1333 BCE).

This stela is near the town of Hermopolis, on the west bank of the river, facing Amarna. The royal family is portrayed three times: in bas-relief on the stela itself and in two statue groups in high relief, which stand proud of the rock. The statues and the stela have been scrupulously mutilated: the faces of the figures in relief have been attacked with hammers and the cartouches systematically pitted, while the statues have been decapitated and their arms ripped off.

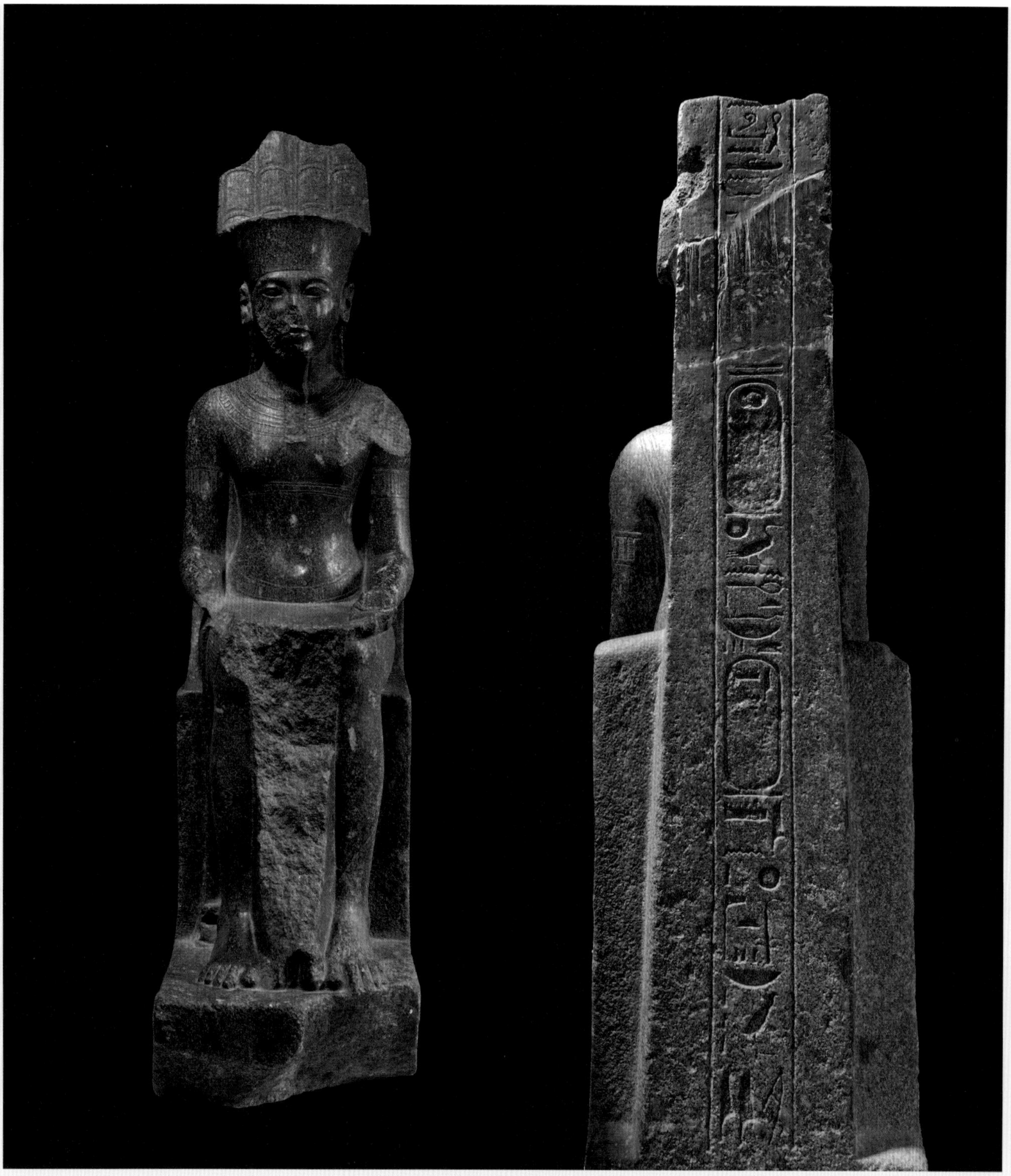

80

Statue of Amun and Tutankhamun, Karnak or Luxor, Egypt, reign of Tutankhamun (c. 1330–1320 BCE).

The god holds out the ankh cross and the symbol of millions of years to the king Tutankhamun, whose figure was facing the god before it was torn off — now all that is left is his feet.

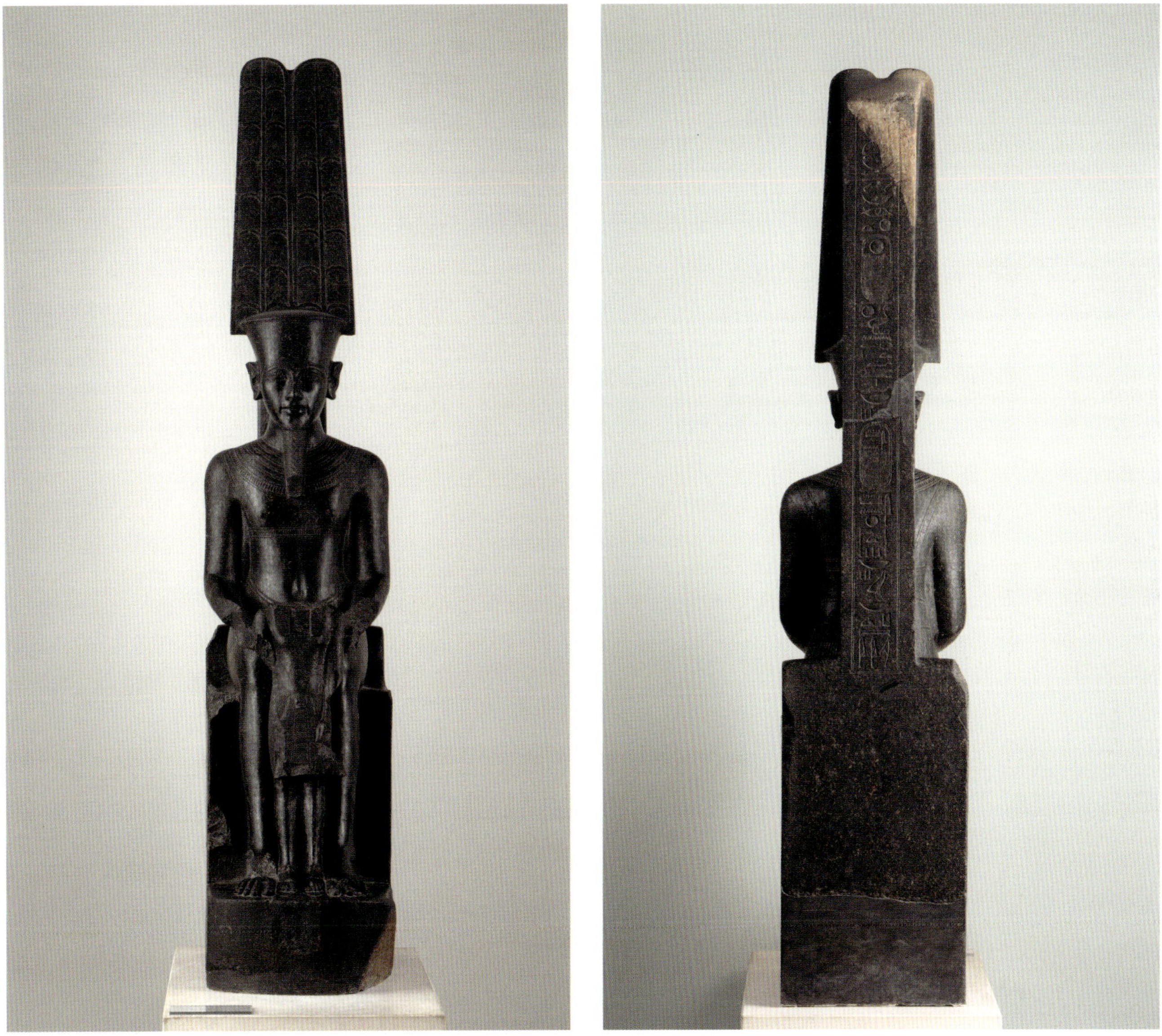

↑ FIG. 5
Statue of Amun and Tutankhamun, Karnak, Egypt, reign of Tutankhamun (c. 1330–1320 BCE), granodiorite, 220 × 44 × 78 cm, Paris, Musée du Louvre, Département des Antiquités égyptiennes, inv. E 11609.

This shows the god Amun, whose hands once protected the figure of Tutankhamun, standing in front of him.

PHARAONIC ICONS AND EGYPTOMANIA

JEAN-MARCEL HUMBERT

For most young people today, Akhenaten and Ramesses are rappers... and as for Egyptian queens, they will cite Nicki Minaj — or Rihanna, who in November 2017, disguised as Nefertiti, made the cover of *Vogue Arabia* (cat. 242). Luckily, in all these cases, humour is never far away. Cleopatra raised some laughs in the film *Carry On Cleo...* (1964) (cat. 219) and Nefertiti has also experienced some fairly entertaining reinterpretations, though some have been controversial. Her famous bust has been transformed into Duckfertiti (Duckomenta, the interDuck collective) and into Marge Simpson. In a series of iterations by the artist Isa Genzken, she was kitted out with sunglasses, while the Hungarian collective Little Warsaw even provided the bust with a body. However, it is only the pastiche principle that makes these mash-ups acceptable — otherwise they would constitute real sacrilege. Why and how has such a strange phenomenon developed over the centuries? These are the questions that the study of Egyptomania seeks to answer.

Tom Chantrell, poster for the film *OK Cleo* by Gerald Thomas, J. Lichtert & Fils, printer, Belgium, 1964.

This comedy came out immediately after Joseph L. Mankiewicz's famous epic starring Elizabeth Taylor, and even parodies its poster.

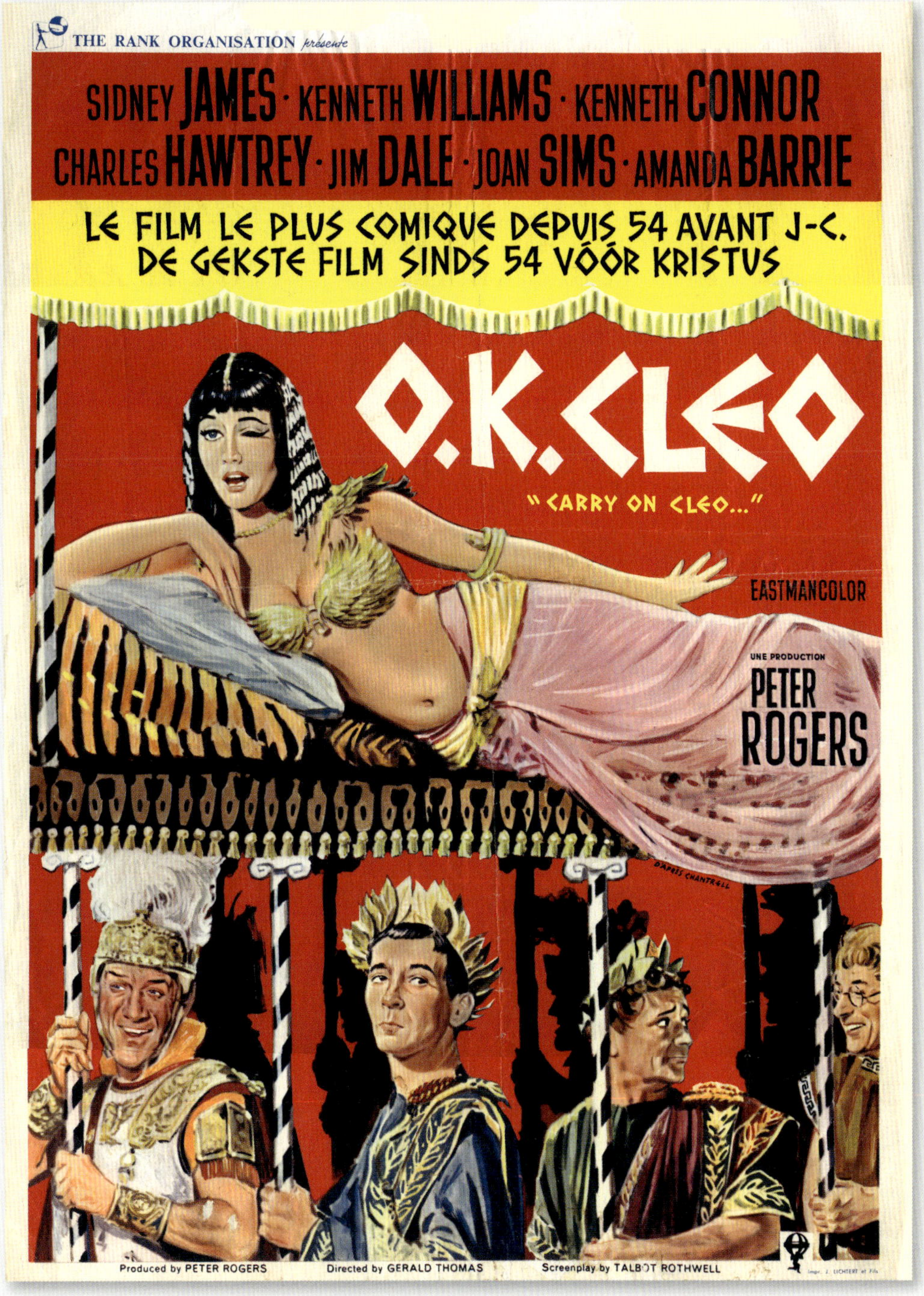

Even more than with the Caesars, Dido, Semiramis or Zenobia, the western world has formed an attachment to ancient Egypt marked by curiosity and admiration, placing its sovereigns on a pedestal that might be envied by Queen Elizabeth I, Napoleon, Queen Victoria or Churchill. This is because, since the mists of time, our connection with the Egyptian kings has been based both on the myths attached to them and on the later clichés which have spread through our society's middle classes during the last two centuries. The pharaohs and queens themselves would be very surprised to know how popular they are with billions of human beings, some of whom only know them from their modern presence: a collective imaginary made up of the knowledge and 'powers' inherited from ancient Egypt.

We may therefore observe on the one hand an ancient Egypt that continues to exert an astonishing fascination and on the other an exploitation of the image of the pharaohs and queens which is close to humbug. This Egyptomania insists on presenting important figures not as they were, as far as we know, but as modern people imagine them to have been, according to the criteria of the period in which we live. This usually means that antiquity — with its costumes, hairstyles and a general allure to which people feel a connection — simply gets transposed into a different key, without any attempt at an accurate historical reconstruction.

What connection can there possibly be between Theda Bara, Claudette Colbert and Elizabeth Taylor? All three have played Cleopatra in films; while each of them created a different character, on each occasion they all perfectly represented the queen that millions of viewers imagined. Thanks to the magic of cinema, Cleopatra became a contemporary of her viewers, as well as a part of them and their ordinary reality. Nefertiti has been portrayed much less often in film (Jeanne Crain in 1961 and Michela Rocco di Torrepadula in 1994). But in both cases, these queens that no man could resist had the potential to inspire women, and the brands that have advertised a wide range of products using their names have continued to play on this identification to reel in female consumers. As for men, they could dream about these temptresses displayed in sumptuous surroundings without running any risks. Nefertiti and Cleopatra were still creating special connections with men and women of all generations...

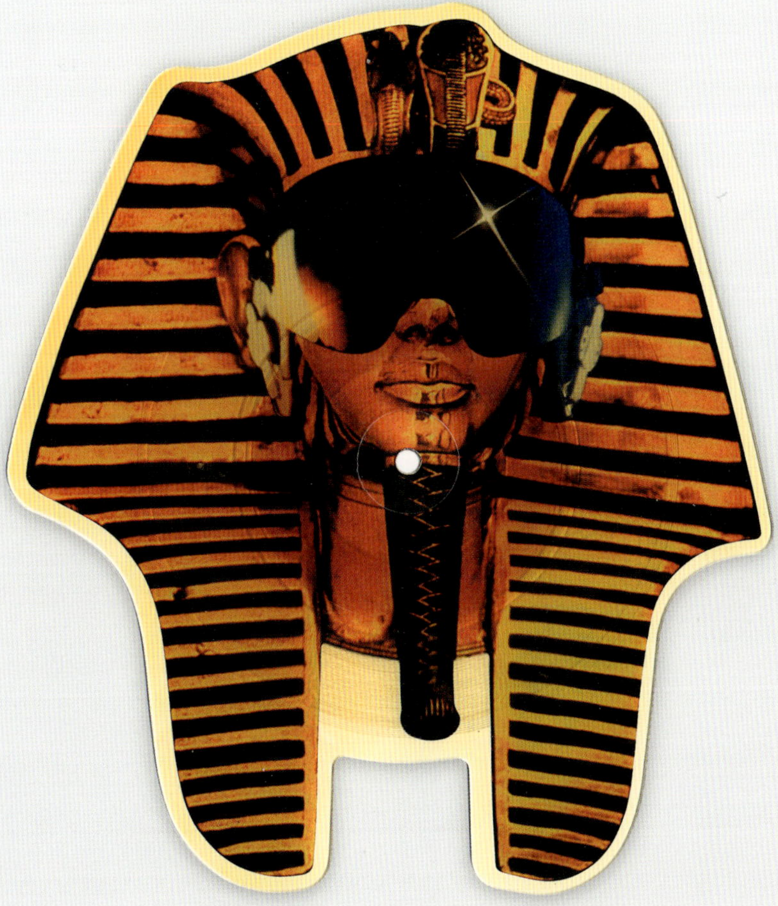

206

Sleeping Bag picture disc,
ZZ Top, UK, 1985.

Literature, opera and the theatre bring these mythical figures to life again

Already fairly well known thanks to the classical humanities, from the seventeenth century onwards the Egyptian sovereigns of antiquity found the means to promote their image and history in literature and then in the iconography peddled by hawkers. Later, illustrated magazines, theatre and cinema used these characters, adapting their appearance to the style and fashion of the time. However, not all of them enjoyed the same popularity: some attempts to bring particular pharaohs back to life failed. This was true of two British five-act tragedies: Edward Young's *Busiris, King of Egypt* (1735) and *Sesostris; or, the Priest and the King* (1853) by C. H. Williams — as well as Voltaire's little allegorical tale, *Sésostris* (1776). Even Ramesses has only managed to inspire a single play: a one-act drama by Joseph de Pesquidoux, performed in 1900 on the stage of the Egyptian Palace at the Exposition Universelle in Paris.

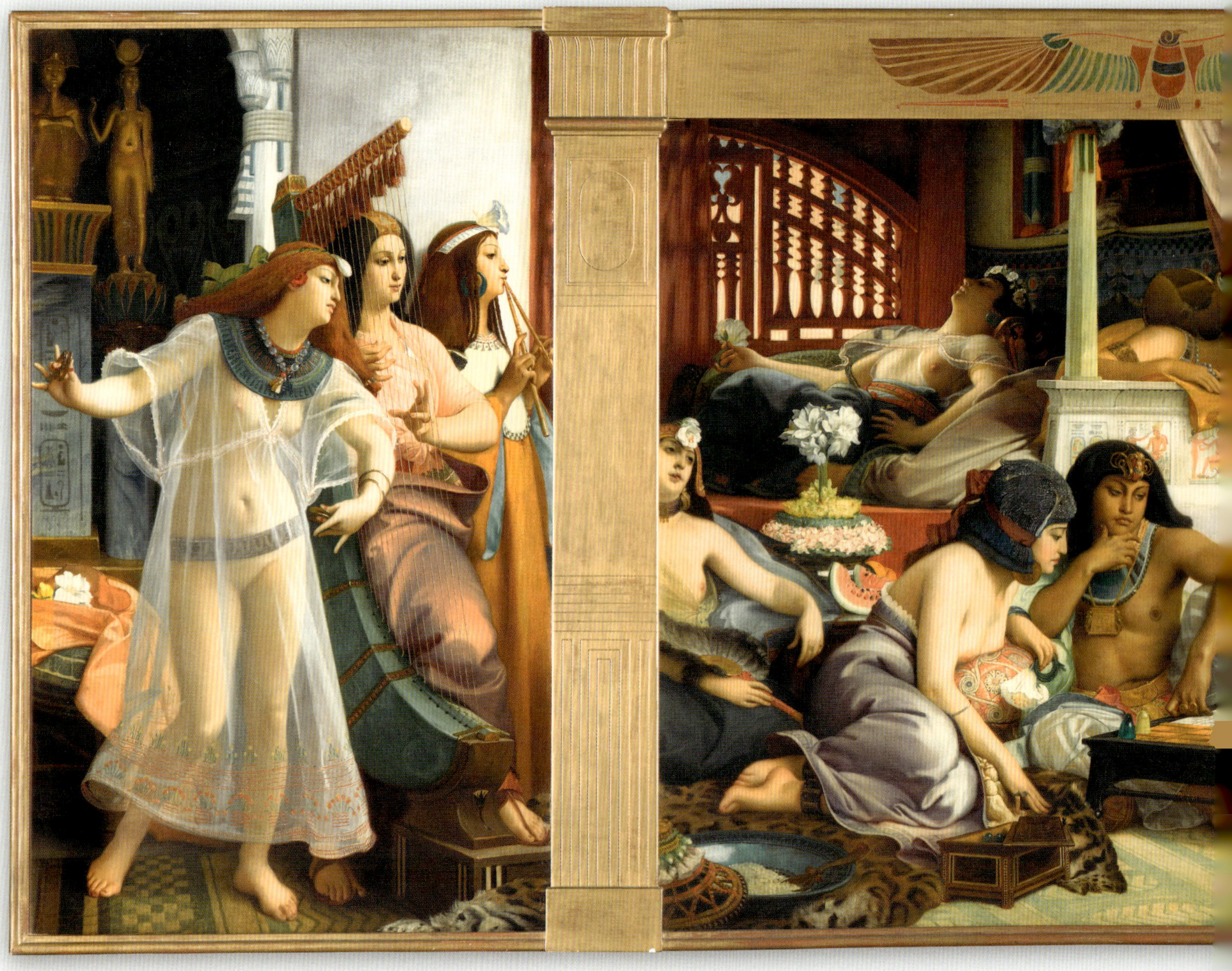

127

Jean Lecomte du Noüy, *Ramsès dans son harem* (Ramesses in his harem), 1885–6.

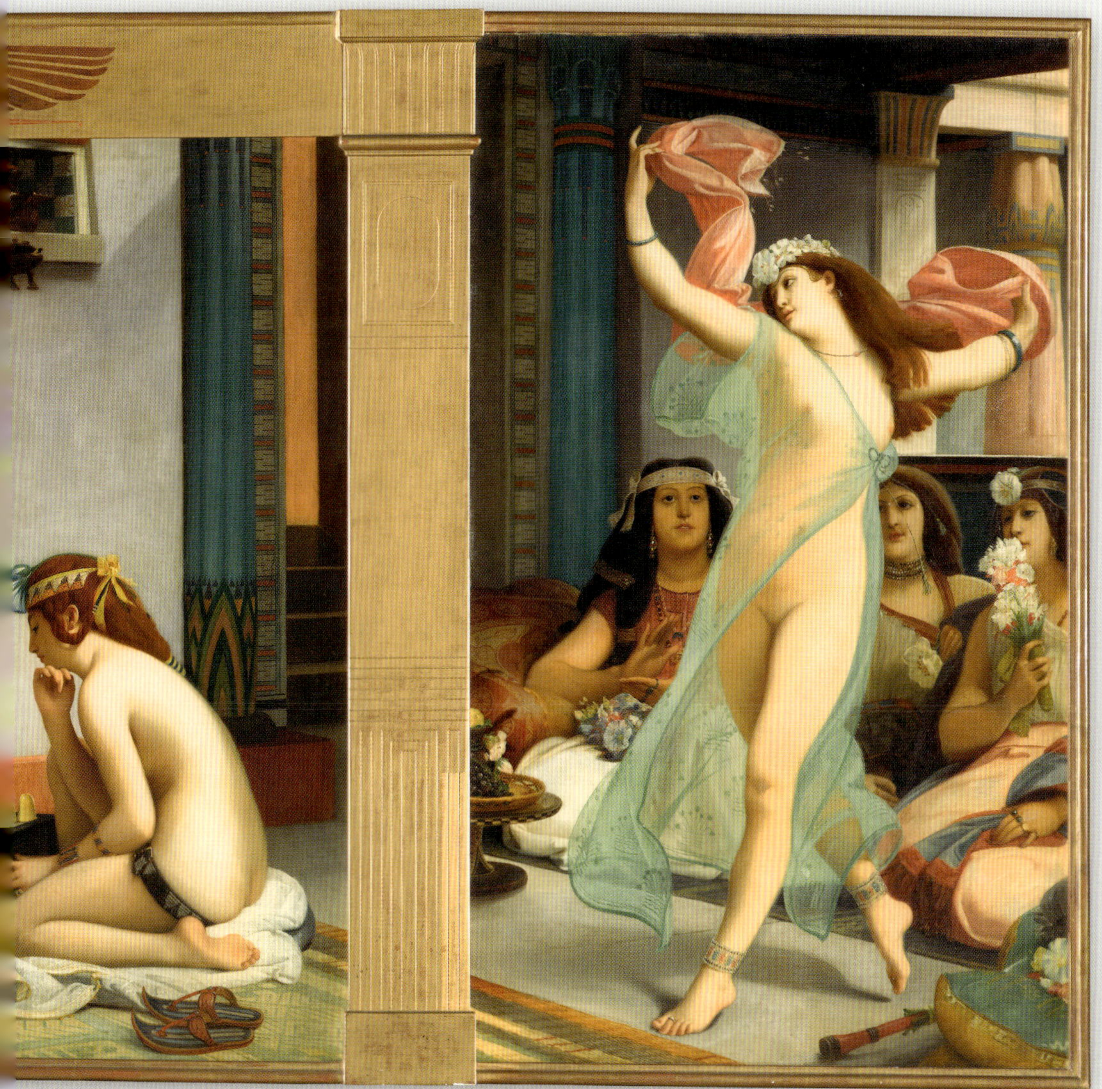

Others, on the other hand, have shown a remarkable capacity for survival. Cleopatra is the best example, and is still today a classic case study. Omnipresent — although somewhat stereotyped — in all forms of Western art, she embodies a wide range of values. Supposedly beautiful and intelligent, she also had a reputation for cunning and double-dealing: skills that enabled her to lead men easily into temptation… For if Cleopatra's reputation has survived over the centuries, it is largely because of the whiff of scandal that accompanied much of her life story. It has been said that she was impious, debauched, a liar and a traitress, extravagant, bewitching, and above all 'Egyptian', which was in itself even more deplorable… 'Money, sex and scandal…': this catchphrase in the publicity for Mankiewicz's film *Cleopatra* (1963) broadly illustrates how this historical figure is received in the modern world.

It is therefore unsurprising that opera — along with literature and the theatre, from Shakespeare to George Bernard Shaw to Victorien Sardou — has taken an interest in this shape-shifting character. More than fifty operas have adapted one or more episodes in the life of the Queen of Egypt, without counting ballets and other kinds of musical theatre, accompaniments and incidental music. Cleopatra is certainly at home on the stage: Handel's *Giulio Cesare in Egitto* (1724) is still the work most often performed, while Graun's *Cleopatra e Cesare* (1742) was revived between 1992 and 1996 at the Deutsche Staatsoper in Berlin. But others have been forgotten, such as *La Morte di Cleopatra* by Sebastiano Nasolini (1791), or *Cleopatra* by Joseph Weigl (1807). And then there are those that never really became popular with the public but are still sometimes performed — such as those by Rossi (1876), Massé (1885) and Massenet (1912). Many others, like *Die Perlen der Cleopatra*, an operetta in two acts by Oscar Straus (1923), were added in the twentieth century to an already long list that included music hall and several musical comedies. Nefertiti, for her part, is much less well represented, with just one operetta by Nico Dostal, *Prinzessin Nofretete* (1936), and a musical comedy by David Spangler, *Nefertiti* (1978). As for Sesostris, he only inspired a single opera, by Domènec Terradellas (1751).

How queens and pharaohs follow fashion, without forsaking their eminent status

As is the case for most sovereigns, pharaohs are associated with the concept of power and queens with the idea of beauty, although it is understood that Cleopatra combines both notions — even though her beauty has often been denied in favour of her charm and intelligence. The many qualities attributed to her have made her the archetype of an exceptional woman: a sovereign with the competence to be a head of state and an unusually effective organiser, commanding admiration. Over the centuries, she has left a transcendent memory. That is why, along with Ramesses, she is specially sought after as a subject for three-dimensional images (in marble, bronze, metal alloy or ceramic), which have proliferated with industrialisation. Over time, we have therefore seen Cleopatras in Victorian, Art Nouveau and Art Deco styles. Literature, both historical and fictional, readily supports her periodical reappearances: in recent times there have been children's books and graphic novels, both Western and Japanese.

But the Egyptian kings embody many other symbols relating to pharaonic Egypt in general: a civilisation that was considered sophisticated, associated with a pleasant kind of lifestyle, construction skills manifested in buildings that defied their age, mystery and science, medicine and magic... Their association with historical figures from a distant antiquity gives all these reinterpretations an undeniable prestige, adding to their intrinsic interest.

How queens and pharaohs became sales reps

The presence of ancient Egypt in advertising imagery has been prevalent from the end of the nineteenth century and throughout the twentieth century. Because of its extraordinary popularity, ancient Egypt helps to sell anything. The name and even the image of queens and pharaohs is used to attach a moral, intellectual or aesthetic endorsement to products that are mostly unconnected to them. So here they are, being invited through no fault of their own to serve the cause of the modern goddess Consumption. Either their name becomes a brand, or they appear in person to promote a wide range of products, whether they be luxury items or essentials (cat. 233). It is in these last circumstances that the identification of the purchaser with the royal figure is at its most effective, the key to the advertising campaign's success...

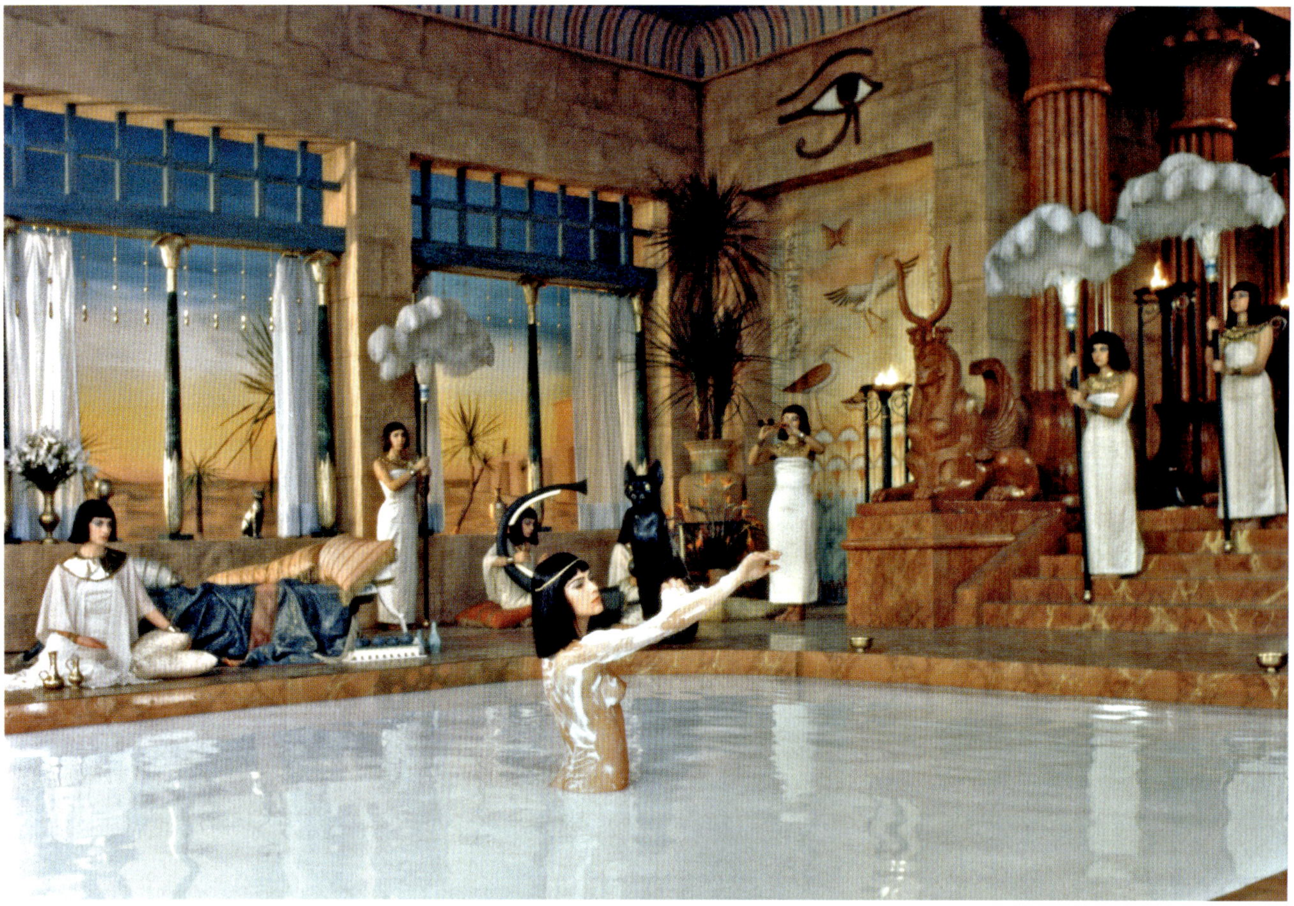

QUEENS OF BEAUTY

Cleopatra, thanks to her fame, has been particularly successful in this field. Since the early twentieth century, she has regularly been called upon, as an allegory of beauty, to sell cosmetics (cat. 234), notably the famous Cleopatra soaps. In 1915, in the USA, Colgate-Palmolive began to use her name to promote their products, made 'to an ancient recipe beloved of the Queen of Egypt'. The theme of this campaign would be regularly revisited, for example in the 1950s and at the end of the 1980s, when we find Cleopatra, in a commercial by Georges Lautner, taking a bath in asses' milk (fig. 1).

Cleopatra's legendary nose was responsible for one of her finest roles in advertising (Polivé tissues, in the mid-1980s), but other choices are much harder to explain: Cleopatra sardines, 'Cléopâtre' glue — 'the queen of glues' — and the fizzy drink 'Cleo Cola' (cat. 222), 'queen of sparkling drinks', from 1935 to about 1945... However, Cleopatra was not able to break away from everyday consumer products. Ramesses, on the other hand, specialised in luxury brands: the company bearing his name, launched in Paris in 1919, would expand internationally.

'Ramsès' face powder — 'a real Egyptian powder' — appears alongside the star product, the perfume 'Secret du Sphinx', whose publicity material boasts some perplexing origins: 'The authentic

↑ FIG. 1
Photo taken on the set of the commercial by Georges Lautner (1926–2013) for Cleopatra soap, 1985, Collection Jean-Marcel Humbert, Paris.

231

Advertisement for Maidenform bras, USA, 1952.

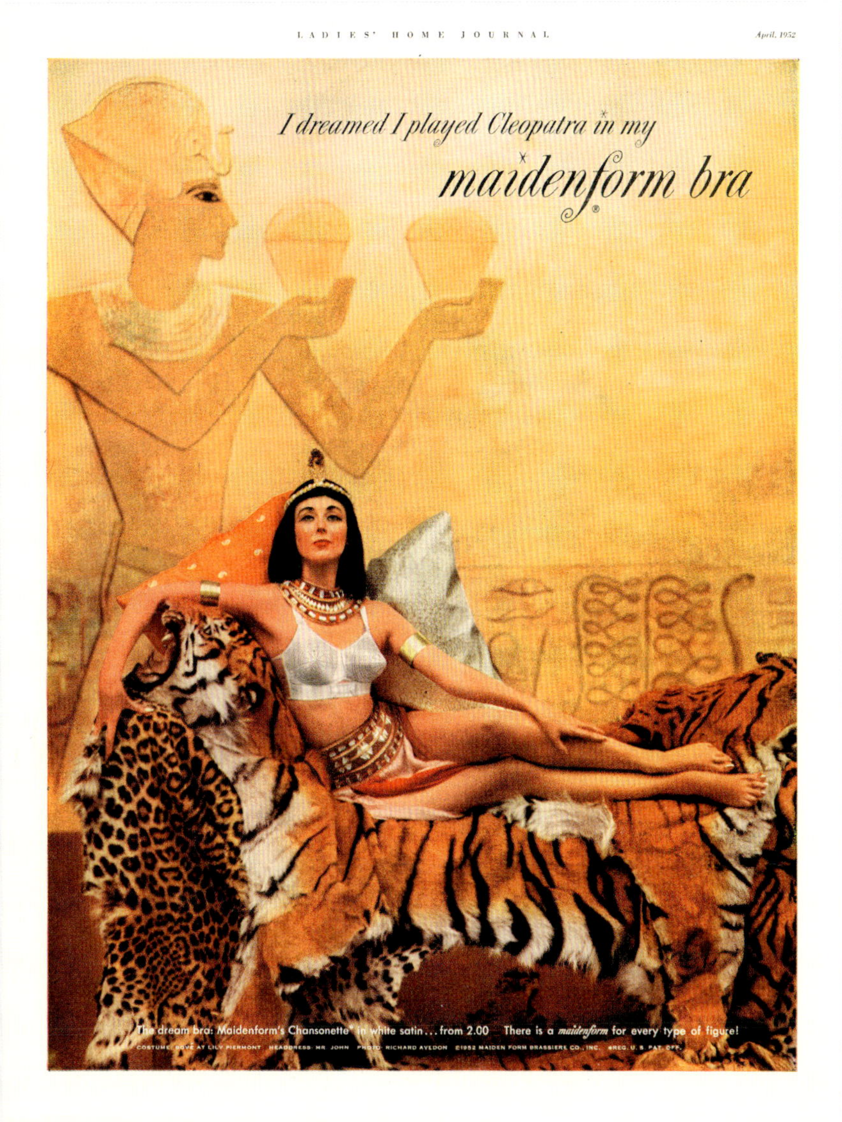

perfume given to Princess Ast, Pharaoh's daughter'. In 1923, the Ramsès company set up business at the corner of Rue Royale and the Faubourg-Saint-Honoré in Paris, in an upmarket shop decorated with five monumental heads of the eponymous pharaoh.

Sticking with beauty, but in a more popular vein, the Mila company decorated their pharmacy shop fronts with a bust of Nefertiti until the 1960s. Tutankhamun also embarked on advertising career in 1923, the year after his tomb was discovered. In his name, a cosmetic cream was launched in America called 'Tutenkamen' (cat. 226) as well as... 'Lady Tut' talcum powder (cat. 228). In France, he also helped to promote several products, including 'Dentol' toothpaste.

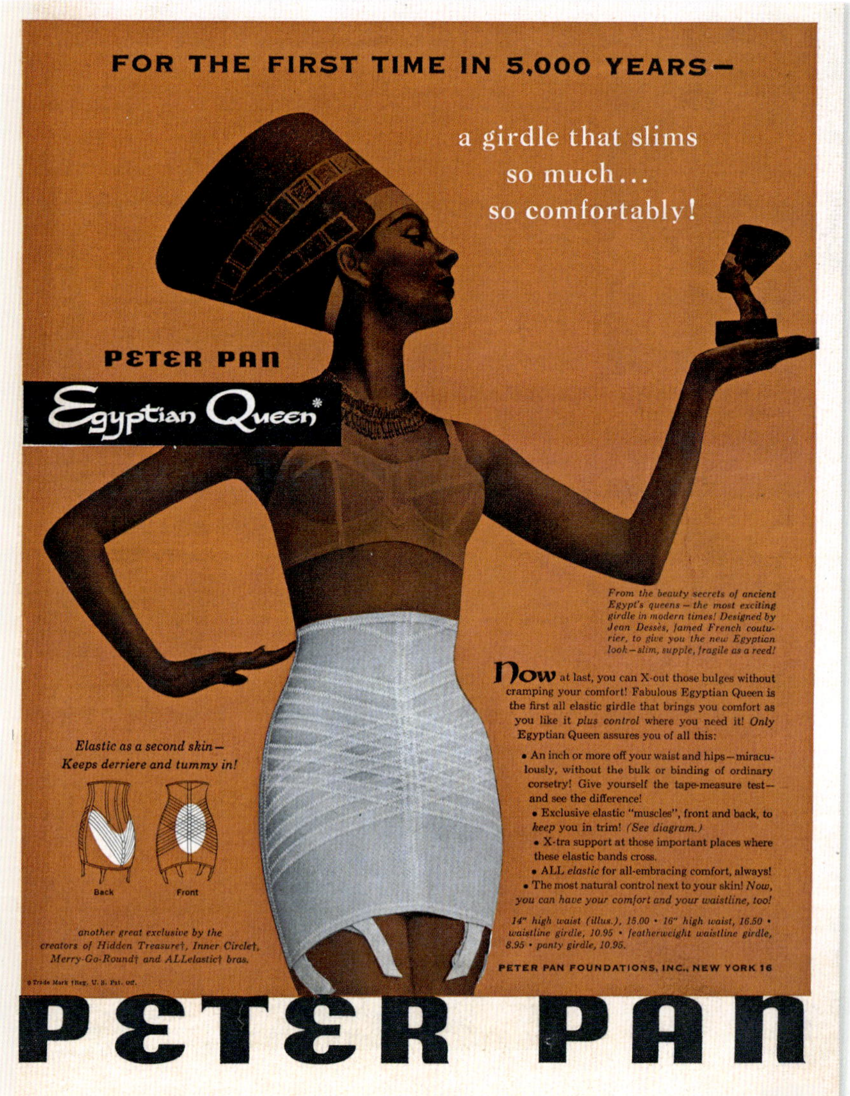

232

Advertisement for the Egyptian Queen girdle, Peter Pan brand, New York, 1954.

When it came to underwear, the sovereigns very astutely split the job according to type. Cleopatra and Nefertiti promoted brassieres (Maidenform bra, 1952 and 1963, cat. 231), Peter Pan Lingerie, with their model 'Egyptian Queen' by Jean Dessès, 1954, cat. 232), while Ramesses focused on underpants in Egyptian cotton (Ramesses brand, 1910s). This fashion was also extended to cotton fabrics: in Paris in the 1930s, the textile company F. Ducharne produced a crushed velvet by the name of 'Sesostris'.

Nefertiti, the ultimate beauty icon, helped to promote Air France in 1985, wearing a headdress incorporating an airplane ticket; and United Arab Airlines took up the same idea.

233

Poster advertising La Seigneurie paints, inspired by the bust of Nefertiti, agency Saatchi & Saatchi Équipement, France, 1989.

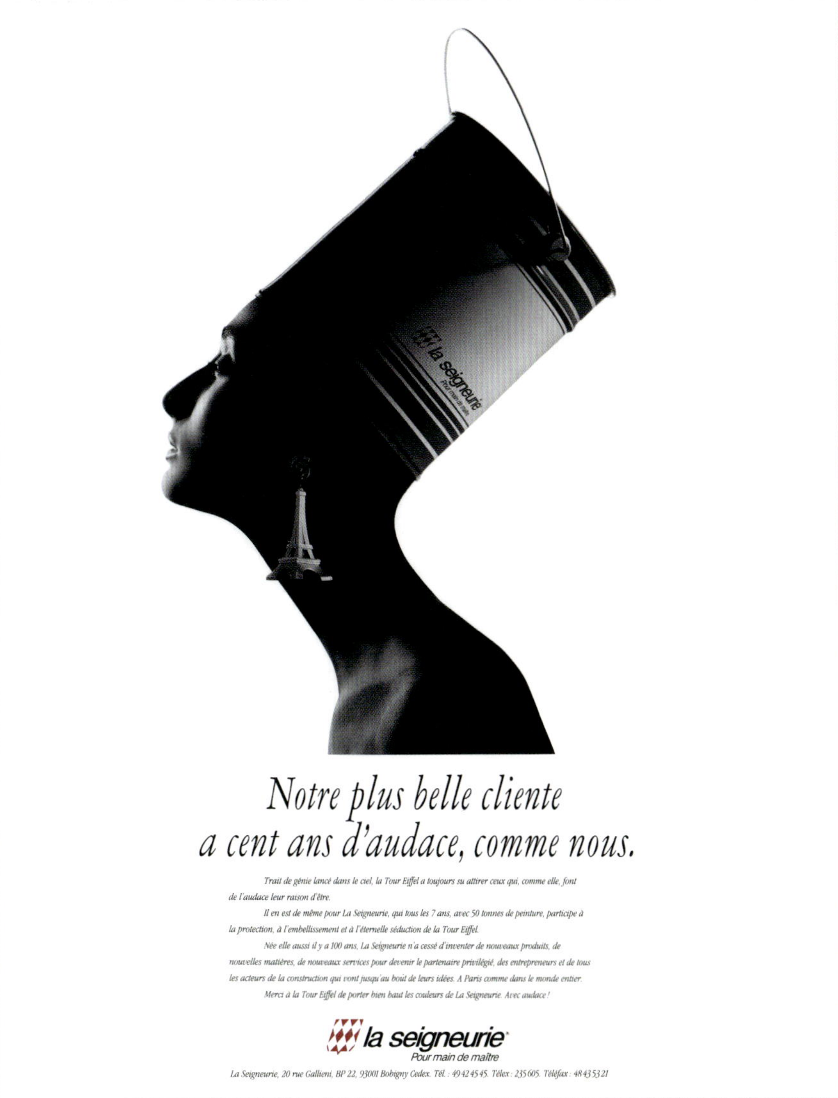

234

Prototype labels for Cleopatra hairspray and self-bronzer, by Comprovex, Estúdio Mário Novais, Lisbon, twentieth century.

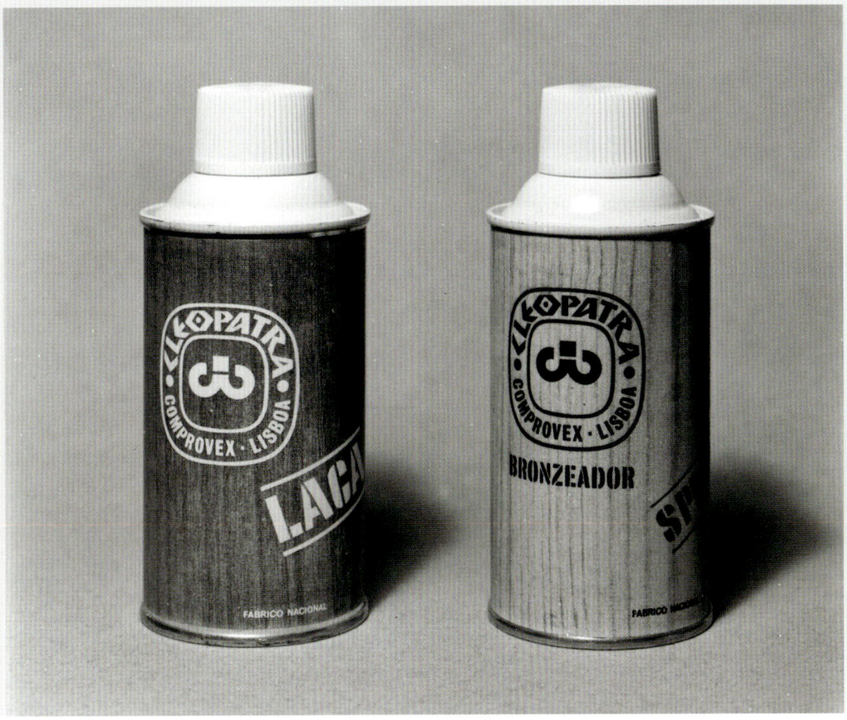

103

LIFE, STRENGTH AND HEALTH

As well as passing on their beauty secrets, the sovereigns also seem to be able to guarantee good health. In 1923, Tutankhamun inspired the creators of 'Rectopanbiline', a treatment for constipation — from which he apparently suffered (cat. 223). But it is Ramesses, once again, who enjoys the largest market share, with the condoms that appeared in his name in 1929 and which are still sold today (cat. 229). A strange choice when we know that he was supposed to have fathered at least a hundred children! But we must remember that the use of condoms as birth control was originally forbidden in some countries and they were restricted to prophylactic use, mainly to protect against venereal diseases. Durability, confidence and excellence, the qualities expected in this type product, were a good fit with the personality of the great pharaoh... Although this did not prevent him boasting: 'How do you think I was able to have 198 kids? Ramses, brought up on Banania!' (advertisement for the chocolate-banana drink, 1988).

The optical field has not been left out: Tutankhamun promoted Titmus contact lenses in 1986, while Nefertiti presided over the destiny of the 'Divine' eyewear collection, created by Cari Zalloni for his German brand Cazal (1992–5).

As for 'medicinal' tobacco, there isn't a single one of our sovereigns who hasn't had his or her own brand of cigarettes (cats. 176 and 179).

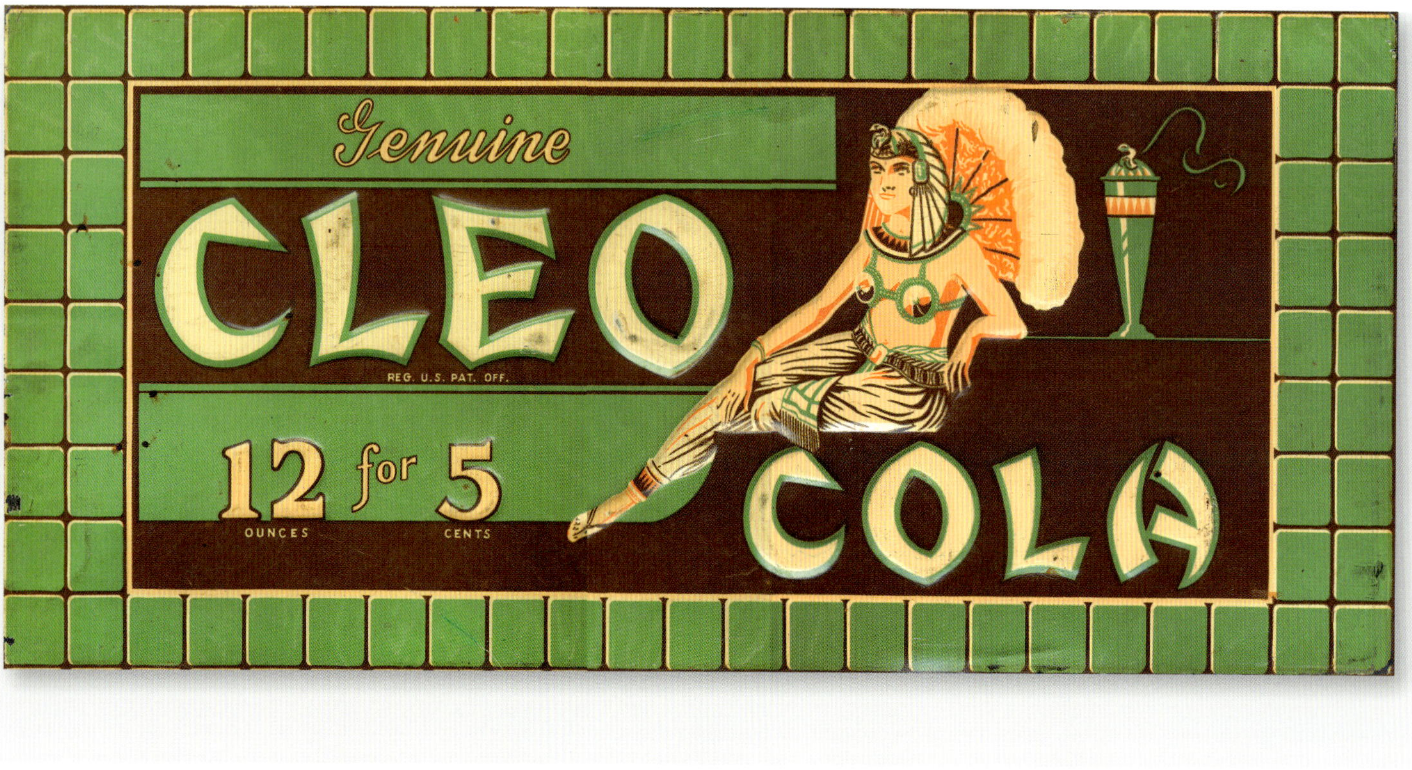

229

Box of condoms,
Ramses brand, USA, 1947.

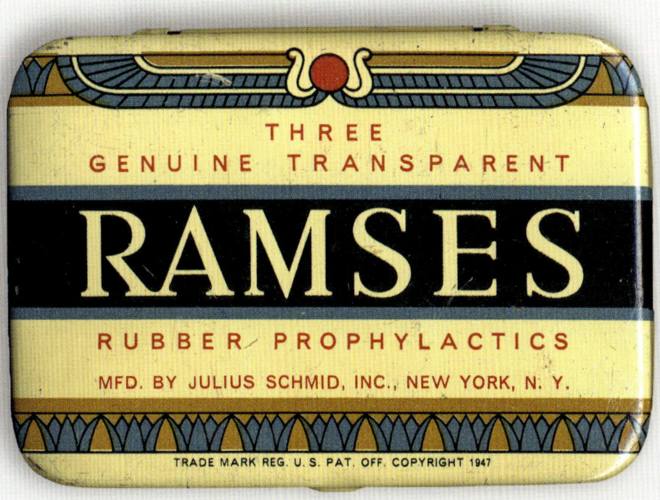

226

Box of Tutenkamen skin care
cream, USA (?), twentieth century.

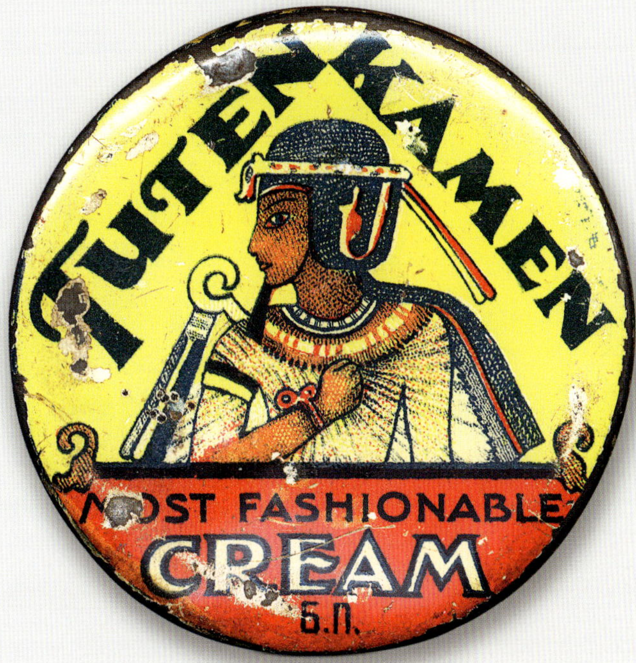

222

Advertising plate for the Cleo
Cola fizzy drink, Cleo Syrup
Corporation, USA, 1935.

ALWAYS AT THE FOREFRONT OF TECHNOLOGY

Technology is another field in which the ancient Egyptians excel. Because of the symbols of solidity and durability that attach to ancient Egypt, construction and real estate sectors are enthusiastic users of Egyptian imagery. And while the Belgian company Djoser has a pyramid under construction as its logo, it is above all Khufu (spelt in several different ways) who has attracted the lion's share of companies specialising in construction or security. His name has even been attached to various nightclubs, discotheques and cafes. Khafre (or Khephren), for his part, has had to make do with some small pyramid-shaped fireplaces (the Arkiane company).

There are some novelties too: Tutankhamun was asked to sing the praises of Robbialac cold enamel paint. Nefertiti followed in his footsteps and appeared wearing a pot of La Seigneurie paint on her head in 1989, for the Eiffel Tower's centenary (cat. 233). It was also Nefertiti who was the reference point when the Lo Tone Wood Conversion Company (Saint Paul, Minnesota) was developing a system of suspended ceilings (1965). And it was she again who made a star appearance when, in a play of words worthy of a comic book, quality and price were associated in the slogan 'Néfer-ti-prix' (Darty chain of shops, 1986). In the 1980s, when information technology was seeing rapid growth, many companies appealed to the Egyptian sovereigns to help inspire confidence in their new products.

To round off this far from exhaustive survey, we should remember that all the sovereigns have their own board games; that the band ZZ Top used an image of Tutankhamun for their shaped picture disc *Sleeping Bag* (cat. 206); and that the pharaohs' names are up in lights in many theme park attractions: for example *Ramses, The Awakening* (Gardaland theme park, Italy, 1987), and the *Challenge of Tutankhamun* (Walibi theme park, Belgium, 2003).

Finally, we may ask ourselves why there are so many cats called 'Ramses'. Evidence for this exists, for example, in the famous pets' cemetery at Asnières outside Paris... Does this stem from the 1990 publicity campaign for Fido cat food? Or is it the simple distinction of a short name whose 'R' sound is a bit like purring?

As surprising as it may seem, in a way these kings and pharaohs have mutated into generic names and all the dates mentioned in this essay are no longer theirs but ours. They have somehow become our perfect contemporaries, sharing our everyday concerns as purchasers. And yet, despite everything we have made them suffer, they retain a semblance of dignity: we may sometimes make fun of them, but always with affection! Who can forget the publicity campaigns that blossomed at the time of the first Tutankhamun exhibition in Paris (1967) (cats. 159, 160 and 161): Trigano motorhome company's slogan 'Tout-en-campant' ('keep on camping'), the truck manufacturers Toutankamion, or the Caisse d'Épargne bank's slogan 'Tout-en-épargnant' ('keep on saving')?

But what about eternal life?

It can thus be seen that our world has appropriated the names of some of ancient Egypt's most distinguished pharaohs and queens. Now, according to the principles of eternal life, as understood by the ancient Egyptians, speaking the names of the dead prolongs their existence. Nevertheless, we may ask ourselves whether these sovereigns would be happy with the way Egyptomania continues to speak their names, for purposes that are mostly not very laudable? It is true that as a result they will benefit from thousands of extra years of afterlife… But will those years be all that enviable? And is the price to pay not a little too high?

BEYOND TUTANKHAMUN: HOWARD CARTER AND THE MAKING OF THE GULBENKIAN COLLECTION OF EGYPTIAN ANTIQUITIES

JOÃO CARVALHO DIAS

It would have been almost impossible for collector Calouste Sarkis Gulbenkian[1] and Egyptologist and 'gentleman dealer'[2] Howard Carter not to cross paths, although Carter's involvement with Gulbenkian as his adviser, helping him to acquire Egyptian antiquities, did not begin in earnest until the sale of Reverend William MacGregor's collection in London from 26 June to 6 July 1922. In the 1920s, more than fifteen years after making his first acquisitions, Gulbenkian's name was sufficiently well-known in the Paris and London art trade for it to be recognised by Carter.[3] The collection, which covers multiple artistic categories,

1 For the most recent biography of Gulbenkian, see Conlin, 2019. On his role as a collector, see the seminal work by José de Azeredo Perdigão [Azeredo Perdigão, 2006 (1969)], and Carvalho Dias, 2006.

2 Expression used by T.G.H. James, *in* James, 2000 (1992), p. 447.

3 See Vassallo e Silva, 2006, pp. 37–47, and Carvalho Dias, 2014, p. 100.

↓ FIG. 1
Gulbenkian at the Temple of the god Horus, Edfu, Egypt, 1934.

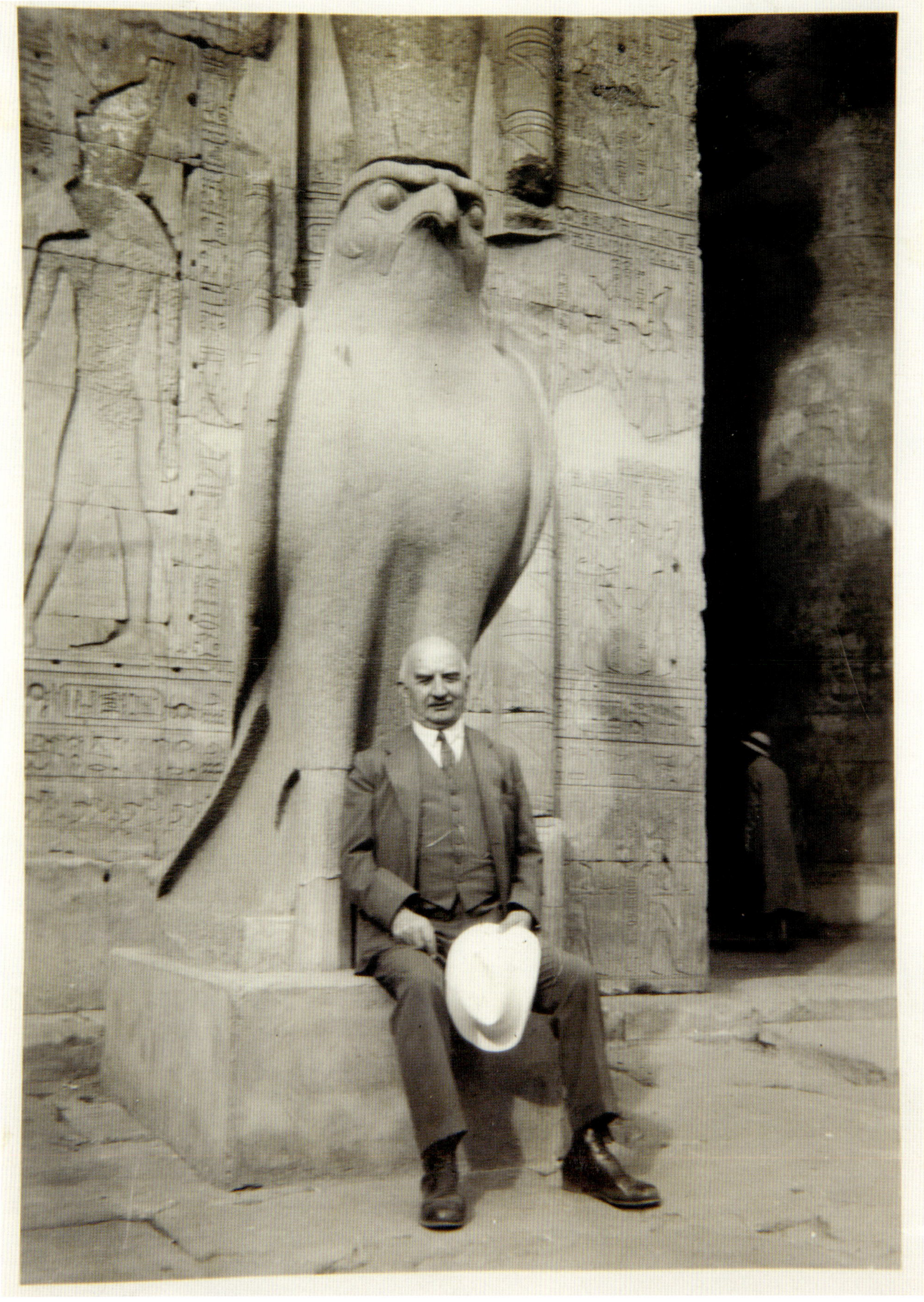

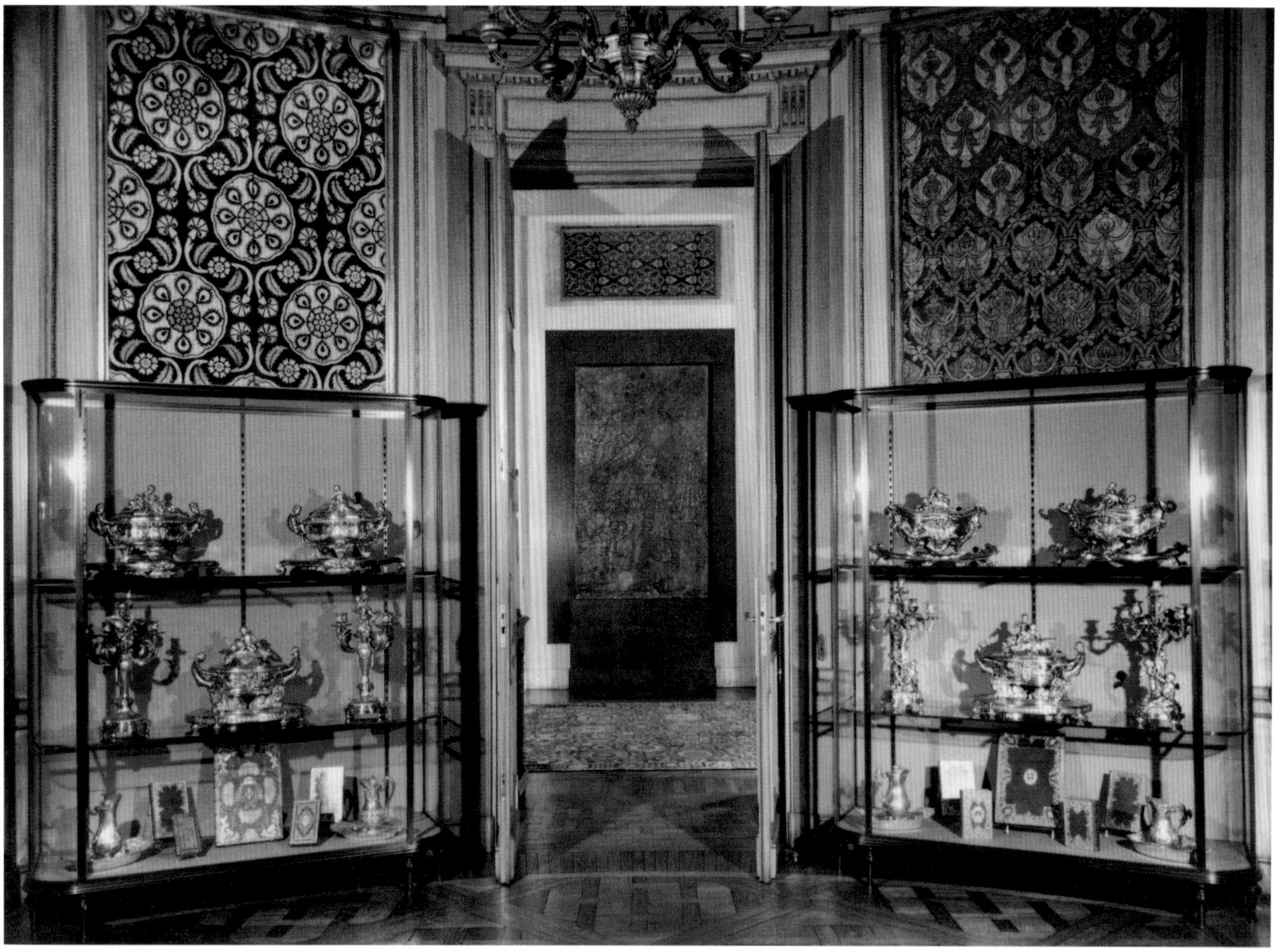

↑ FIG. 2
Entrance to the Assyrian Room, 51 Avenue d'Iéna, Gulbenkian's house in Paris.

↗ FIG. 3
The Head of Senwosret III (right) in a showcase with objects from the Gulbenkian collection of Egyptian antiquities at the National Gallery of Art, Washington, 1949.

chronologies and geographies, was well-established and did not yet include the important acquisitions from the Hermitage Museum in Saint Petersburg (1929–30), which would make Gulbenkian one of the most prominent private collectors in Europe.[4] Gulbenkian continued to build his diverse collection right up to the time of his death in Lisbon in 1955. This extraordinary set of objects has been on permanent display at the Calouste Gulbenkian Museum since 1969.

The Egyptian antiquities occupy a special place within Gulbenkian's wider collection. The pieces were housed in several of the Collector's residences as they were purchased, including Hyde Park Gardens in London, and Quai d'Orsay and Avenue d'Iéna in Paris.[5] The keeper of Gulbenkian's collections, Mme Marcelle Chanet, described the room containing the collection of Egyptian antiquities as 'the most important in the house'.[6] It was in the 'Assyrian Room' (fig. 2), 'where the silhouettes and enigmatic faces of deities and figures from the Egypt of the pharaohs stood out',[7] that this exceptional collection was displayed before finding new homes. The long-term loan made by Gulbenkian to the British Museum in London (1936–49) allowed the collection to be studied

[4] On the acquisitions from the Hermitage, see Conlin, 2019, pp. 185–90. See also Azeredo Perdigão, 2006 (1969), pp. 109–31, and Vassallo e Silva, 2006, pp. 49–57.
[5] See *L'Hôtel Gulbenkian*..., 2011–12.
[6] *C.S. Gulbenkian par Marcelle Chanet*, typewritten pages, p. 109. Gulbenkian Archives, MCG 03615.00001.
[7] *Ibidem.*

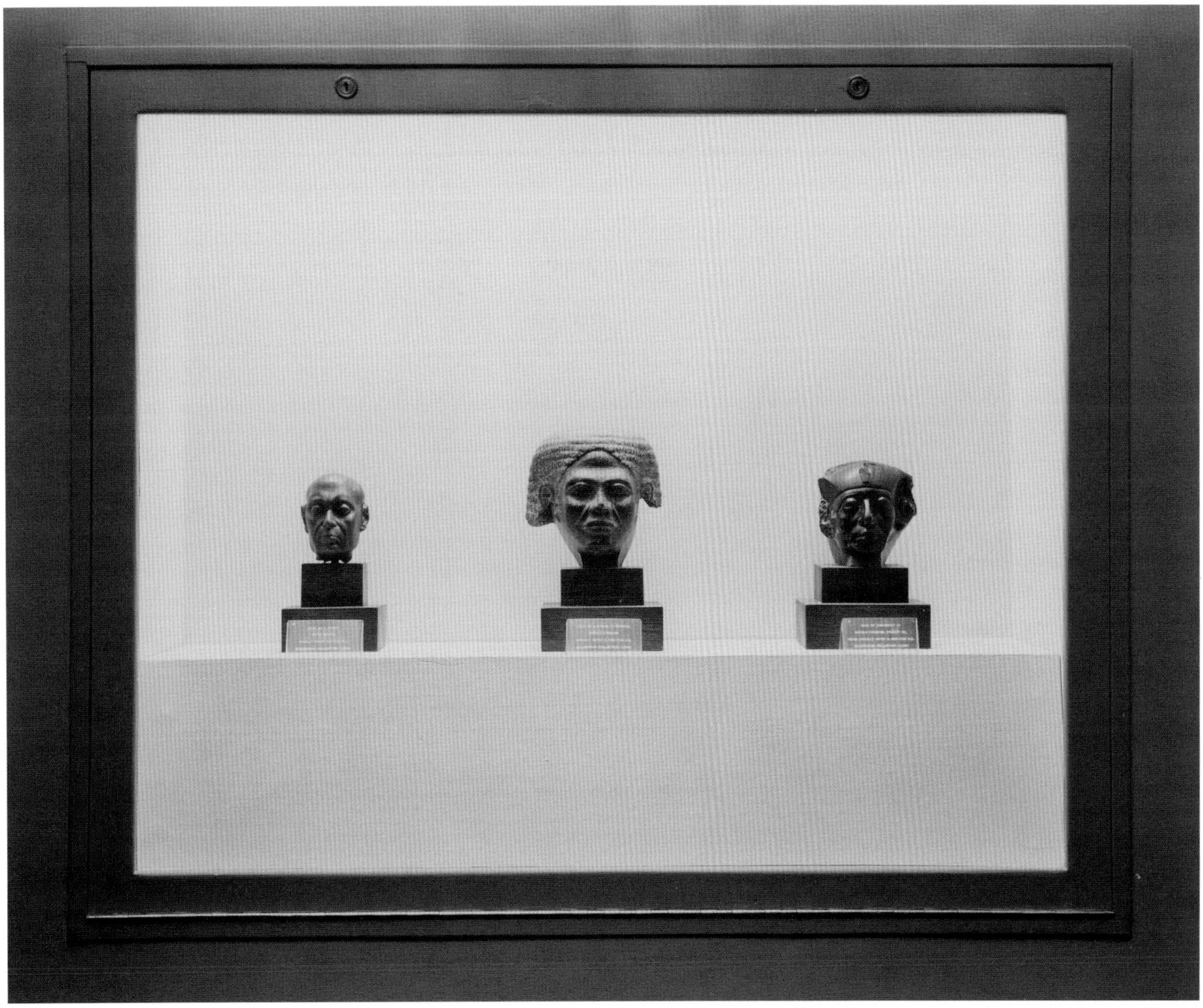

by some of the most reputed Egyptologists, the hieroglyphic inscriptions to be translated and a catalogue to be published, under Gulbenkian's patronage, containing high-quality photographs of the exhibits.[8] This part of the collection was later loaned to the National Gallery in Washington (1949–60),[9] where, to the Collector's great delight, it could be admired by large numbers of visitors. Alexis Leger (aka Saint-John Perse), winner of the Nobel Prize in Literature (1960) and a friend of Gulbenkian, who was living in self-imposed exile in the United States, reported back to the collector on his lengthy 'meditations before the head of Amenemhat III – the "Macgregor head"'[10] (fig. 3 and cat. 22). The collection finally came to rest in Lisbon in the museum that Calouste Gulbenkian did not live to see.[11]

8 *Ancient Egyptian...*, 1937.

9 See Carvalho Dias, 2018, pp. 63–78.

10 Letter from Alexis Leger to Calouste S. Gulbenkian (csg), 1 September 1949, in *Saint-John Perse...*, 2013, p. 71. Belonging to Reverend William MacGregor's collection, the head was initially believed to be a portrait of Amenemhat III but was later recognised as Senwosret III (r. approx. 1878–1841 BCE). Calouste Gulbenkian Museum (CGM), inv. 138.

11 He expressed the wish for his collection to be together on many occasions and was particularly explicit in a letter sent to John Walker, Chief Curator of the National Gallery in Washington, who he trusted deeply. An attempt to negotiate the 'offer' of Gulbenkian's collection with Walker failed as the Collector would never agree to the collection being 'broken up'. csg to John Walker, 10 February 1953. Gulbenkian Archives, MCG 0232. See also Carvalho Dias, 2018, pp. 63–78.

Amassing the Egyptian collection: first steps

Calouste Gulbenkian acquired his first Egyptian piece in 1907: a bowl made from black and yellowish-white breccia from the Ptolemaic dynasty (305–30 BCE).[12] The circumstances that led to this particular acquisition are unclear, but an invoice kept by Gulbenkian from the firm Agnew & Sons with headquarters in Old Bond Street dated January 1908 confirms his method and his eclecticism. The items listed on the invoice include European drawings, engravings and paintings, Persian ceramics and payment of the installation of engravings and other works 'in transit to Paris'. The invoice also shows the inventory numbers assigned to some of the pieces, their location ('in Paris') or simply a question mark (?) indicating the pieces that Gulbenkian decided not to include in his collection.[13]

From 1907 to 1922, Gulbenkian continued to purchase Egyptian antiquities, some of which were truly exceptional, from important collections. He did not call on experts for help in this task, but instead used his regular brokers, Graat & Madoulé,[14] M.K. Gudenian,[15] Spink & Son,[16] Colnaghi,[17] Kalebdjian Frères,[18] and the Duveen Brothers (cat. 52),[19] who bought the pieces at public auctions. Gulbenkian followed the acquisition process closely, requesting additional information and opinions when he was uncertain. He also sought to confirm the legitimacy of the acquisitions. One of the pieces he acquired was the statue of Lady Shepes (*Femme en marche*); several months after it was purchased, Gulbenkian deposited the piece at the Louvre via Graat & Madoulé.[20] Georges Bénédite, curator of Egyptian antiquities, expressed his delight: 'I would like to extend my personal thanks to you for this important deposit'.[21]

Gulbenkian was thus assured that his piece was worthy of display in one of the most eminent museums in the world: 'we cleaned [the piece] [...] which confirmed its good condition [...] I want to express our great interest in the piece, which will be exhibited as soon as we have an adequate display case'.[22]

Gulbenkian's concern for confirming the origin of the objects he acquired in order to legitimate their authenticity was present throughout his life. As well as collecting catalogues and ordering the descriptions of the pieces to be copied, Gulbenkian also sought to inform himself using specialist literature, as confirmed by the contents of his personal library.[23] Around a week before bidding via M. K. Gudenian for six lots from the major sale of the Thomas Hope Collection, two of which contained Egyptian objects,[24] Hagop Kevorkian, an art dealer with offices in Paris and New York, acquired a number of books, on behalf of Gulbenkian, including a copy of *Household Furniture and Interior Decoration / Executed from the Designs by Thomas Hope* (London, 1807).[25] Kevorkian reported back to the Collector: 'the number you have [your copy] contains outlined drawings of the lion, satyr's head, and Apollo [from the Hope Collection]'.[26] The illustrations in the catalogue show three of the six

[12] CGM, inv. 1064. Rane Collection, sold at Christie's, London, 18 December 1907 (lot 7).
[13] Gulbenkian Archives, MCG 00634.
[14] CGM, inv. 400. Dr. Eddé Collection, Alexandria, sold at Hôtel Drouot, Paris, 2 June 1911 (lot 447); CGM, inv. nos. 46, 48, 49 and 411. Daniel Marie Fouquet Collection, established in Cairo, sold at Hôtel Drouot, Paris, 2 June 1922 (lots 19, 38, 114 and 42).
[15] CGM, inv. 403, MNAA 40 (donated to the National Museum of Ancient Art, Lisbon). Thomas Hope Collection, sold at Christie's, London, 24 July 1917 (lots 173 and 176). For the invoice, see Gulbenkian Archives, MCG 00739.
[16] CGM, inv. 129. Grenfell Collection, sold at Christie's, London, 14 November 1917 (lot 51). Gulbenkian Archives, MCG 01568.
[17] CGM, inv. 121A/B. Amherst Collection, sold at Sotheby's, London, 24 June 1921 (lots 384 and 385). Gulbenkian Archives, MCG 00796.
[18] CGM, inv. 402. Amherst Collection, sold at Sotheby's, London, 24 June 1921 (lot 268). Gulbenkian Archives, MCG 00483.
[19] CGM, inv. 52. Count Grigory Sergeievich Stroganoff Collection, Rome, sold at Frederick Muller & Cie., Amsterdam, 13 December 1921 (lot 612). Gulbenkian Archives, MCG 00141.
[20] CGM, inv. 400, see note 14.
[21] Letter from Georges Bénédite to CSG, Paris, 9 September 1911. Gulbenkian Archives, MCG 00323.
[22] *Ibidem.*
[23] Twenty-seven books about Egypt are currently housed in the Art Library, at the Calouste Gulbenkian Foundation, Lisbon.
[24] See note 15. The lion, MNAA inv. 760, and the statue of Djedhor, CGM, inv. 403.
[25] Calouste Gulbenkian Foundation, Art Library. FCG-BA, E-ML1.
[26] Letter from H. Kevorkian to CSG, 30 July 1917. Gulbenkian Archives, MCG 01471.

pieces acquired at the Hope sale. According to the auction catalogue, the lion, made from basalt on a porphyry plinth, had been dated to the Ptolemaic period (323–30 BCE) and had been 'found at the palace of Emperor Tiberius in Capri... purchased by Mr Hope in Italy in the late 18th century...'.[27]

The Amherst Collection

Using correspondence and archive material, it is possible to trace Gulbenkian's quest for Egyptian antiquities confirming that until 1921 there was no clear pattern to his selections, although his acquisitions were all of a very high quality. Between 1921 and the end of June 1922, several important auctions took place where Gulbenkian bid through his usual brokers. Of the auctions held during this period — immediately prior to the MacGregor sale, which was a pivotal moment in the construction of Gulbenkian's Egyptian collection — only the auction of the large collection belonging to Lord Amherst of Hackney[28] is linked to Howard Carter. William Thyssen-Amherst, a British member of parliament who became a baron in 1892, was an amateur Egyptologist and a key figure in Howard Carter's training, inspiring an interest in Egyptian antiquities in him as a young man. Carter frequented Didlington Hall in Norfolk, the ancestral home of the Amherst family, with his father, painter Samuel John Carter, who produced several portraits for the family. It was through Amherst that Carter was able to travel to Egypt in 1891 as a draughtsman, marking the start of a career spanning more than thirty years associated to the archaeological excavations in the country. Carter knew the Amherst Collection inside out and played a central role in preparing its catalogue.[29]

27 https://archive.org/details/catalogueofceleb00chririch/page/n41 (consulted 11 February 2022).

28 For reference of the pieces acquired at the auction of the Amherst Collection, see notes 17 and 18.

29 Catalogue of the Amherst Collection..., 1921.

The sale of the MacGregor Collection: a turning point

Although Howard Carter played a role at the auction of the Amherst Collection, there seems to be no association between the archaeologist and Calouste Gulbenkian at that time, we can assume that the Collector was aware of Carter's merits. Meanwhile, it was Ernest Duveen who put Carter on Gulbenkian's path, for knowing the MacGregor Collection 'very well' and for being one of the 'greatest authorities on Egyptian art'.[30] It was not until the MacGregor auction held in London from 26 June to 6 July 1922[31] that the Collector began to collaborate with Carter, who pointed out new directions and suggested Egyptian antiquities, among other advice. Nevertheless, Gulbenkian continued to purchase only what he liked and what was of genuine interest to him. His correspondence with Carter during this period suggests a degree of caution on Gulbenkian's part, as he sought to build a relationship based on mutual trust. An indication of this attitude lies in the fact that, of the thirteen lots acquired at the MacGregor auction, eleven were obtained by Howard Carter and the remaining two, which included the most important, valuable piece among the one thousand eight hundred lots at auction – the head of the Pharaoh Senwosret III[32] (cat. 22) – were purchased by H. Kehyaian, an Armenian dealer who bid under the name of 'Harris'.[33] Among the many telegrams sent by Howard Carter to Gulbenkian to report on the lots he had acquired, there is a message sent the day after the auction ended: 'Head went for ten thousand to a certain Harris'.[34]

In order to understand Gulbenkian's interest in the MacGregor Collection, which was considered one of the most noteworthy collections of Egyptian art ever compiled by a private individual, we must step back another year in time. Reverend William MacGregor (1848–1937) was a patron of archaeological excavations in Egypt and a member of the Egypt Exploration Society and the Institute of Archaeology at the University of Liverpool. His important collection was stored at his home, Bolehall Manor in Tamworth. His intention to hold a public auction of the items in his collection was known, and Gulbenkian wanted to get ahead of the race by establishing the pieces of interest to him in advance:

> 'I have heard that you are interested in the MacGregor Collection [...] overtures have been made to me from another direction and my information is that you are also in the field. I would like to know your intentions, for I am sure you would not do anything to prejudice [*sic*] me and on the other hand I would like to do business with you, but we must work in the proper way. I am especially interested in one or two things — as for instance the Head — and I am told that the Metropolitan Museum is also interested. Do you know if this is a fact? *I must rely on you*'.[35]

30 Letter from Ernest Duveen to CSG, 3 March 1922. Gulbenkian Archives, LDN 00456.

31 *Catalogue of...*, 1922.

32 *Head of the Pharaoh Senwosret III*, c. 1860 BCE. CGM, inv. 138.

33 Invoice from Kehyaian & Co., 6 July 1922, relating to the purchase of the head of Amenhotep III in blue glass for £520 (Fl. 5980), 30 June 1922 (lot 919), CGM, inv. 139; and the head of Senwosret III in obsidian for £10,000 (Fl. 115.000), 6 July 1922 (lot 1676), 'in the name of Harris' [*sic*], MCG, inv. 138. Gulbenkian Archives, MCG 00515.

34 Telegram from Howard Carter (HC) to CSG, 7 June 1922. Gulbenkian Archives, LDN 00456. See also the invoice dated 6 July 'In the name of Harris'. Gulbenkian Archives, MCG 00515.

35 Letter from CSG to Joseph Duveen, Hotel Normandy, Deauville, 2 August 1921. Gulbenkian Archives, LDN 0167.

Joseph Duveen, head of the reputed firm Duveen Brothers, replied several days later, confirming that he had visited the collection at Burlington Fine Arts Club in London[36]: 'and I must tell you that the only object which impressed me there was the Head, together with some of Lord Carnarvon's fine things. The collection was offered to me, but I turned it down [...] I must confess that I know very little about Egyptian antiquities, but I really would like to own the head in question'.[37] Duveen reassured Gulbenkian that neither he nor the Metropolitan Museum of Art in New York would be bidding. Gulbenkian went on to ask Duveen to purchase the 'Head' and several pieces from Lord Carnarvon's collection if the opportunity arose.[38] Although Duveen considered the possibility, he was wary of the prices: 'I will naturally be delighted to give you the preference [...] I repeat, however, that the price they mentioned was quite ridiculous'.[39]

The company Spink & Son from Piccadilly, which Gulbenkian knew well, had acquired the set of Egyptian antiquities from the MacGregor Collection in a direct sale by the owner; however, Spink & Son were not responsible for selling the one thousand eight hundred lots comprising almost nine thousand objects.[40] This responsibility fell to Sotheby's, which organised the auction. It was a unique opportunity for Gulbenkian, who went on to purchase a significant set of objects and made direct contact with Howard Carter.

As noted above, Carter did not make the purchase of the two lots that included the hugely valuable obsidian pharaoh's head. However, the Egyptologist was in close contact with Gulbenkian:

> 'For your private information – as far as I have been able to ascertain, Viscount Cowdray [owner of Pearson & Co., a major British construction company] will possibly [...] purchase at the sale the obsidian head and will pay a sum somewhat about £6,000 to £8,000. Also [William] Permain of King Street [collector] will bid for [William Randolph] Hearst [a leading North American businessman in the publishing industry] [...] The N.Y. Metro Mus. [Metropolitan Museum of Art] are not bidding at all'.[41]

Once the auction had ended, Howard Carter sent a statement showing the lots purchased, (fig. 4) agreeing to send the descriptions for the catalogue but expressing his disappointment that Gulbenkian had not acquired the most significant piece at the MacGregor auction (or so he thought):

> 'I am sorry you did not allow me to purchase an outstanding piece as the obsidian head of Amenemhat III. The information you received regarding my proposed purchasing it for Lord Carnarvon had not a vestige of truth [...] after the second day of the sale I had practically the command of the bidding and with rare exceptions was able to obtain lots at a low value'.[42]

In his response to the letter, Gulbenkian ignored the matter of the 'head' and focused instead on the need for Carter to supply 'a full descriptive statement from the catalogue for future reference' for all the

36 The exhibition in question was entitled *Ancient Egyptian Art* and held at Burlington Fine Arts Club in summer 1921. MacGregor was part of the organising subcommittee, having been made an honorary member of the club for the duration of the exhibition. See Pierson, 2017, pp. 116–17. The exhibition catalogue is held at the Calouste Gulbenkian document library. Art Library, AHP 5407.

37 Letter from Joseph Duveen to CSG, 4 August 1921. The Getty Research Institute, Duveen Brothers Records, 960015_b461_f001_049.

38 Letter from CSG to Joseph Duveen, 6 August 1921. Gulbenkian Archives, LDN 0167.

39 Letter from Joseph Duveen to CSG, 8 August 1921. The Getty Research Institute, Duveen Brothers Records, 960015_b461_f001_049.

40 See Hardwick, 2020.

41 Telegram from HC to CSG, 29 June 1922. Gulbenkian Archives, LDN 00456.

42 Letter from HC to CSG, 8 July 1922. Gulbenkian Archives, MCG 00070.

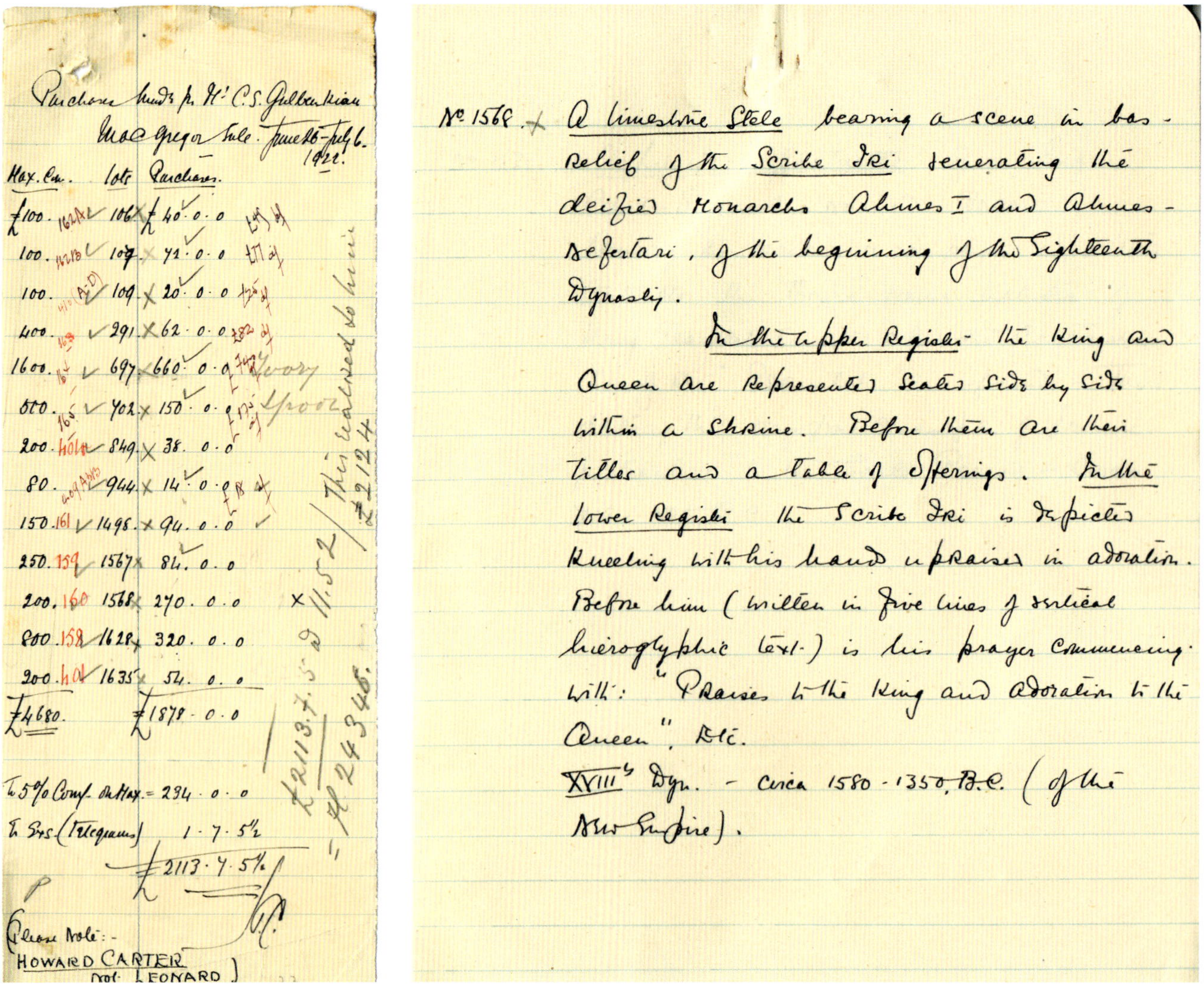

Purchases made for Mr C. S. Gulbenkian
MacGregor Sale. June 26–July 6. 1922.

Max. Com.	Lots	Purchases
£100	106	£40.0.0
100	107	72.0.0
100	109	20.0.0
400	291	62.0.0
1600	697	660.0.0
500	702	150.0.0
200	849	38.0.0
80	944	14.0.0
150	1495	94.0.0
250	1567	84.0.0
200	1568	270.0.0
800	1628	320.0.0
200	1635	54.0.0
£4680		£1878.0.0

To 5% Comm. on Max. = 234.0.0
To Exps (Telegrams) 1.7.5½
£2113.7.5½

Please Note:- HOWARD CARTER not LEONARD

No 1568. A limestone Stele bearing a scene in bas-relief of the Scribe Iri venerating the deified monarchs Ahmes I and Ahmes-Nefertari, of the beginning of the Eighteenth Dynasty.

In the Upper Register the King and Queen are represented seated side by side within a shrine. Before them are their titles and a table of offerings. In the lower Register the Scribe Iri is depicted kneeling with his hands upraised in adoration. Before him (written in five lines of vertical hieroglyphic text.) is his prayer commencing with: "Praise to the King and adoration to the Queen", etc.

XVIIIth Dyn. – circa 1580–1350 B.C. (of the New Empire).

↑ FIG. 4
Note from Howard Carter, acting as Gulbenkian's agent, relating to the purchase of items from the MacGregor sale, together with a description of the 'Stele of the Scribe Iry'. Gulbenkian Archives, MCG 00070.

pieces acquired at the auction.[43] Carter sent all the documents for the lots, including handwritten descriptions of the pieces with notes and pages from the auction catalogue, which can be viewed in the Gulbenkian Archives.[44]

Howard Carter did not know who had purchased the piece and the collector did not provide any further clarification on the matter; on the contrary, he continued to try to obtain information about the fairness of the price:

> '[I] now hear from very reliable source there will be a boni-fide [*sic*] of 10,000£ for the obsidian head. You asked me on the phone this morning if that was not too high a price. In the case of such a unique object, undoubtedly the finest work of art that has ever left Egypt — it is impossible to name a price, and as I have also ascertained that Spink & Son will not let it go for less than 10,000£, it becomes evidence that this is the minimum. This head is causing an immense sensation in the artistic world […]. Under the circumstances I consider that whoever buys it will be fortunate if he acquires it for less than 15,000£'[45].

[43] Letter from CSG to HC, 14 July 1922. Gulbenkian Archives, MCG 00070.

[44] Note from 26 July 1922. Gulbenkian Archives, MCG 00070.

[45] Letter from HC to CSG, 18 July 1922. Gulbenkian Archives, LDN 00456.

[46] Letter from HC to CSG, 21 July 1922. Gulbenkian Archives, LDN 00456.
[47] Letter from HC to CSG, 19 September 1922. Gulbenkian Archives, LDN 00456

Indeed, Gulbenkian was fortunate to have succeeded in acquiring the most valuable item at the auction for the minimum price of £10,000, although this was still a considerable sum of money given that the total value of the remaining pieces he bought was just £2,398. Carter's words matched Gulbenkian's expectations, confirming that he had made an 'exceptional' purchase by all accounts — he would never again spend such a sum on a single Egyptian art piece — and that he had negotiated a price far lower than the maximum estimated value for that item in particular.

It would have been very difficult to continue to hide the name of the true owner of the 'obsidian head' from Carter, especially given that the Egyptologist, who was temporarily in London while waiting to return to Luxor, had an extensive network of contacts who had almost certainly informed him: 'Everyone [...] tell me that you were the purchaser of the obsidian head, but I imagine this is only "Town talk" of the mystery'.[46]

It is likely that Gulbenkian satisfied the Egyptologist's curiosity on the telephone during summer 1922 when he was in St Moritz, or even in person in Paris, where Carter planned to go at the end of September to meet the Collector.[47] In any case, the matter was definitely clarified before Carter returned to Egypt to begin a new season of excavations. Howard Carter could not have foreseen that he was about to make his mark on the history of Egyptology and that his name would be forever associated with one of the great archaeological findings. On 4 November 1922, he made the extraordinary discovery of the almost untouched tomb of the pharaoh Tutankhamun and its magnificent treasures — the famous KV62 —, an excavation sponsored by another collector and amateur archaeologist, Lord Carnarvon.

Howard Carter becoming adviser and agent

The acquisitions from the MacGregor Collection represent something of a turning point, given Howard Carter's presence as an agent for Gulbenkian. Although Carter did not succeed in obtaining the most important piece in the collection, he eventually gained Gulbenkian's trust. The Collector began to call upon him for advice and to be receptive to his proposals, provided that they reflected his personal taste.

From 1922 to the end of that decade, Howard Carter played a very significant role in consolidating the collection's status. Between 1923 and 1929, almost all of Gulbenkian's purchases, with only one exception, went through Howard Carter: the Egyptologist brokered seven acquisitions and sold three pieces directly to the collector.

The first piece acquired after the MacGregor auction was purchased from Carter directly and was a seated bronze cat, 'symbolical of the goddess Bast, from Bubastis in Lower Egypt. A fine specimen in perfect condition (small dirt on shoulders) of the Saite Period, 718–525 BC purchased in Cairo'.[48] The piece was most likely given as a gift to Hélène Constance Linden Berthelot,[49] the wife of diplomat Philippe Berthelot, Secretary-General of the French Ministry of Foreign Affairs. Calouste Gulbenkian was a friend of the couple and handled their investment portfolio.[50]

Gulbenkian frequently consulted Carter to confirm the authenticity of the acquisitions he had made in previous years. When Gulbenkian charged his son Nubar with dealing directly with Carter to arrange delivery of the pieces acquired at the MacGregor auction to his London residence, the Collector asked for him to be granted access to the objects he had acquired in London in 1917: 'especially the LION, and let me know your opinion of them, and whether you think I ought to keep the Lion or dispose of it on a suitable occasion. I bought it at the Hope Sale some time ago'.[51]

No information is available regarding Carter's assessment, but Gulbenkian kept the basalt lion until 1951, when it was transferred to the Portuguese Embassy in Paris and later to Lisbon.[52] The dating of the piece continues to be debated to this day.[53]

When Gulbenkian recommended that Carter visit the Champollion centennial exhibition at the Louvre (opened 12 July 1922), for which he had loaned an ebony statue purchased from Paul Mallon in 1920,[54] (fig. 5) he almost certainly wanted to know the expert's opinion on his piece and clear up his own doubts.[55] The matter had given rise to heated controversy at the time of the purchase, when the authenticity of the piece was called into question.[56] Indeed, when Gulbenkian wrote to Mallon in 1920, the subject was still very much in the air: 'By coincidence, I met a colleague of yours [Kelekian][57] who knows you very well here [Monte Carlo]. Without any invitation to speak on my part, he began to energetically criticise your Egyptian objects, including those that you sold me'.[58]

Through Paul Mallon, Gulbenkian had obtained opinions from prominent Egyptologists such as Flinders Petrie, mentor to the young Howard Carter when he arrived in Egypt for the first time, and Gaston Migeon, curator at the Louvre, who described the piece in the catalogue for the Paul Mallon Collection. Both experts confirmed the authenticity of the Egyptian statue.[59]

In 1921, Georges Bénédite, curator of Egyptian antiquities at the Louvre, used the debate surrounding the Malon piece as a pretext for writing to his American Egyptologist colleague Herbert Eustis Winlock at the Metropolitan Museum of Art, New York, to clarify his stance, which appeared rather uncertain.[60] Bénédite's view on the position adopted by Howard Carter, whose questioning of the authenticity of the piece had reached Gulbenkian's ears, is clear, however: 'As for Carter and Lord Carnarvon, they tend to badmouth any deal that is not their own'.[61]

Bénédite accused Mallon of conserving pieces that were manifestly fake and arousing the suspicions of experts and brokers on the antiquities market. However, according to Bénédite, the possibility that Gulbenkian's

[48] Letter from HC to CSG, 16 June 1923. Gulbenkian Archives, MCG 00078.
[49] *Ibidem.* The letter contains the following handwritten description: 'Given to Mme Berthelot'. I am indebted to Jonathan Conlin for the information on the relationship between Calouste Gulbenkian and Philippe and Hélène Constance Berthelot.
[50] See CONLIN, 2019, pp. 136, 168, 284.
[51] Letter from CSG to HC, 11 July 1922. Gulbenkian Archives, LDN 01600.
[52] List of works sent from Paris to Lisbon, 21 November 1951. Gulbenkian Archives, MCG 02861.
[53] See ASHTON, 2008, no. 49, p. 336.
[54] *Funerary statue* (Middle Kingdom, Eleventh Dynasty, c. 2000 BCE), inv. 142. Gulbenkian Archives, MCG 00984. Gulbenkian also loaned another important piece — *Torso of King Pedubast* (inv. 52) — bought the year before (see note 19).
[55] Letter from CSG to HC, 15 August 1922. Gulbenkian Archives, LDN 01464.
[56] See AZEREDO PERDIGÃO, 2006 (1969), p. 64, and ARAÚJO, 2006, p. 64.
[57] Dikran Kelekian, an art dealer with Armenian origins, with headquarters in Paris, who was one of Gulbenkian's suppliers.
[58] Letter from CSG to Paul Mallon, 5 February 1920 (translated from the French). Gulbenkian Archives, LDN 1451.
[59] The letter from Paul Mallon to CSG, 31 January 1920, confirms Gaston Migeon's description, pls. XI, XII and XIII, *Catalogue de la Collection Paul Mallon, fascicule I.* Gulbenkian Archives, MCG 00984. Flinders Petrie describes the piece in his article 'A Mentuhetep Statute', *Ancient Egypt*, part II (1920), which Gulbenkian kept in his archives. Gulbenkian Archives, MCG 00984.
[60] Letter from Georges Bénédite to CSG, 5 September 1921. Gulbenkian Archives, MCG 00984-00985.
[61] *Ibidem.*

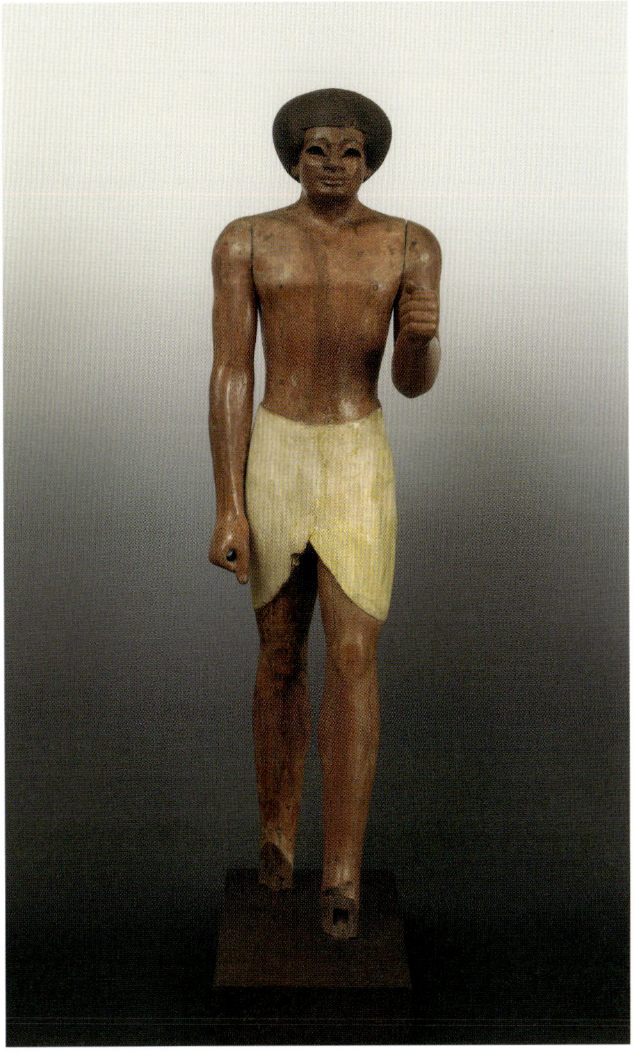

← FIG. 5
Funerary statue acquired from Paul Mallon, Paris, 1920.

piece was fake should be ruled out, as he confirmed in an article published around the same time.[62]

For Gulbenkian, the question of authenticity was of central importance and once doubt had been sown, he attempted at all costs to dispel it. In 1936, when his collection of Egyptian antiquities was loaned on a long-term basis to the British Museum, he wrote to Sir Edgar John Forsdyke to ask for the experts' verdict on the statue that had been 'condemned' by Carter: 'I must state that Mr. Howard Carter did not definitely condemn it but he threw suspicion about it, tantamount condemning it [...] Several of my specimens have been bought through the channel of Howard Carter, but he has nothing to do with this one'.[63]

[62] Bénédite, 1924, pp. 3–11.
[63] Letter from csg to Sir E.J. Forsdyke, 7 September 1936. Gulbenkian Archives, MCG-S010-P0001-D00052. On a previous occasion, Forsdyke had stated that the piece 'is by no means condemned as false by Mr. Howard Carter's opinion'. Letter from Sir E.J. Forsdyke to CSG, 3 September 1936. Gulbenkian Archives, MCG-S010-P0001-D00051.

A foremost collector of Egyptian art

In the month following the discovery of Tutankhamun's tomb, Gulbenkian wrote to Carter, confirming that his intention was to become a great Egyptian art collector:

> 'I had the firm intention of going to Egypt for Christmas, but somehow or other my journey has had to be postponed, and I have now decided not to go this year [...] So I shall look forward to a trip to Egypt next year [...].[64] You know my desire to become a foremost Collector of Egyptian art, and this desire is becoming stronger every day [...] I have been making economies to this end, but statements I have seen in the newspapers to the effect that everything will be taken by the Egyptian Government, have been somewhat disappointing'.[65]

The constraints arising from the new order imposed in Egypt, to which Gulbenkian refers in his letter, limited the export of antiquities; the discovery of Tutankhamun's tomb was also subject to these limitations, posing additional difficulties for Howard Carter. Gulbenkian remained convinced that he could continue to benefit from Carter's privileged position, which derived from his presence in Egypt and his extensive network of contacts, including local and European dealers.

As in other sections of his collection, Gulbenkian was only interested in acquiring pieces of great artistic quality, shying away from archaeological objects. The Collector expressed his reticence upon receiving a proposal from Carter to purchase a granite statue of the famous architect Senenmut, who worked for Hatshepsut (1507–1458 BCE), the female pharaoh. This was a period that Carter knew well, as he had participated in the excavations that uncovered the tombs of Tuthmosis IV (1899) and of Queen Hatshepsut in Deir el-Bahari (1902–3)[66]:

> 'I am sure you will appreciate that, not having seen even a photograph of the Piece you mention, to jump at a decision would be incompatible with the great desire I have to educate myself with the finest specimens only. I shall be only too delighted to be guided by you, and I feel sure that you will make me a very fine collection, and I am quite ready to make the necessary sacrifices to that end [...] as I am more keen [*sic*] than ever on getting the finest pieces of Egyptian art'.[67]

In response to the photographs that Howard Carter sent him, the Collector acknowledged the quality of the piece but expressed doubts:

> 'It is a very fine object of its kind, but more suitable for a museum collection than for me, as it is so much mutilated. [...] I want my collection to be an artistic one rather than of archaeological interest.

[64] Gulbenkian did not visit Egypt until 1934. For his travel journal, see *Calouste Sarkis Gulbenkian...*, 2019.

[65] Letter from csg to hc, 27 December 1922. Gulbenkian Archives, LDN 01581.00001.

[66] See James, 2000 (1992), pp. 135, 170. See also James, 2000 (1992) 2020, p. 343.

[67] Letter from csg to hc, 6 February 1923. Gulbenkian Archives, LDN 01581.

[...] I see from the newspapers that you are re-sealing your tomb for some time. I take this opportunity of renewing the congratulations I expressed in my telegram for the most splendid discoveries you have made'.[68]

Gulbenkian followed Carter and Lord Carnarvon's successful expedition in the press and was quite surprised to learn of the lord's death on 5 April 1923. Lord Carnarvon was a prominent Egyptian art collector and some of the pieces he owned had appeared in the exhibition at Burlington Arts Club,[69] so it was to be expected that Gulbenkian would show an interest in his collection. Indeed, an internal report from Duveen states:

'He [Gulbenkian] telephoned us to-day from Deauville about the Carnarvon things. He is very anxious to know what is going to happen to the Collection. He says that he is interested in the Egyptian things, more especially in the Gold figure and other things which were exhibited at the Burlington Club. We told him you would look after this matter for him as you were very friendly with the family'.[70]

Gulbenkian did not ultimately purchase any of the Egyptian pieces in the Carnarvon Collection, which was instead acquired by the Metropolitan Museum of Art in New York, to the detriment of the British Museum.[71]

[68] Letter from CSG to HC, 24 February 1923. Gulbenkian Archives, LDN 01580.00002.

[69] *Catalogue of...*, 1922. Copy in CSG's document library. Art Library, AHP 5407.

[70] Internal report by the firm Duveen for Captain Ernest Duveen, London, 6 April 1923. Getty Research Institute, bx. 461, f. 1-2. I am grateful to Dr Vera Mariz, a researcher at ARTIS, University of Lisbon, for alerting me to this exchange of correspondence.

[71] See James, 2000 (1992), pp. 409–11. See also Hardwick, 2020, p. 69.

'to have only the best...'

Although Carter's guidance became a constant fixture from 1922 onwards, this did not stop Gulbenkian from making an acquisition through Graat & Madoulé in 1924 without the archaeologist's intervention. The item in question was a cat sarcophagus[72] from the Durighello Collection, about which very little information is available. It is clear that Graat & Madoulé continued to alert Gulbenkian to important sales, such as that of the items belonging to Durighello, some of which now belong to the British Museum collections.

Gulbenkian continued to pay close attention to the market, sending proposals to Carter so that he could research future possibilities like the collection belonging to Reverend William Frankland Hood, which was auctioned at Sotheby's on 11 November 1924. Carter was familiar with the collection, which had begun to scatter several years earlier through private sales.[73] However, after visiting the exhibition at Sotheby's, Carter rejected the possibility of pursuing any prospective purchases because 'there is [no]thing there of sufficient artistic value for you to consider purchase'.[74] In that same year, Carter brokered the acquisition of a piece of great artistic quality: the *Solar Barque of Djedhor*[75] (fig. 6), expressing his enthusiasm for the successful acquisition:

[72] Saite Period (664-525 BC), bronze, inv. 21. Galerie Georges Petit (cat. 22), 12 June 1924.

[73] Letter from HC to CSG, 24 October 1924. Gulbenkian Archives, LDN 00540.

[74] Letter from HC to CSG, 14 November 1924. Gulbenkian Archives, LD N00540.

[75] Egypt, Late Period, Twenty-sixth – Thirtieth Dynasties (c. 380–343 BCE), bronze, inv. 168. Sotheby's, London, 17 December 1924.

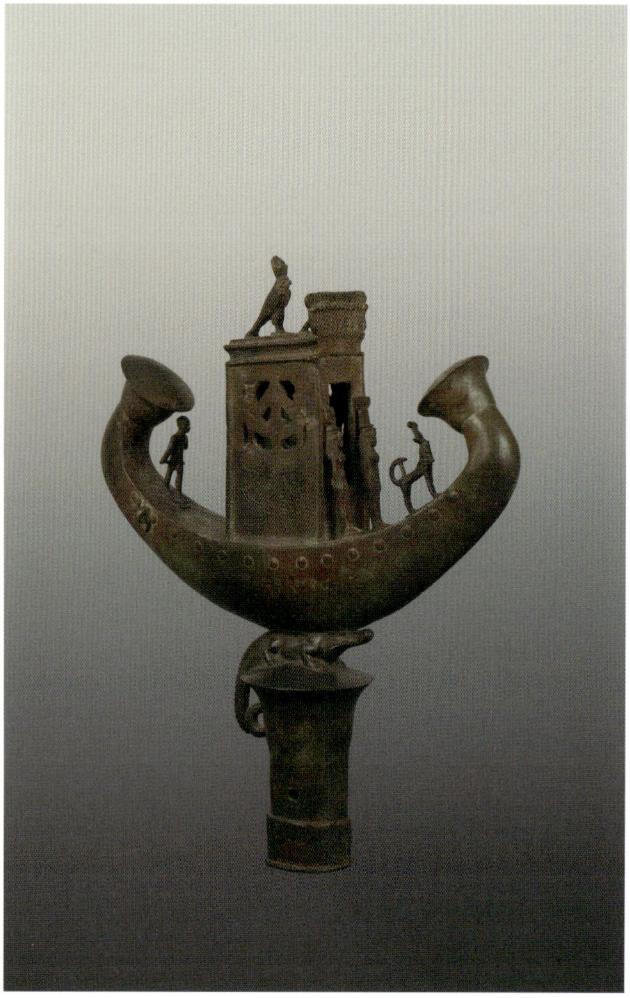

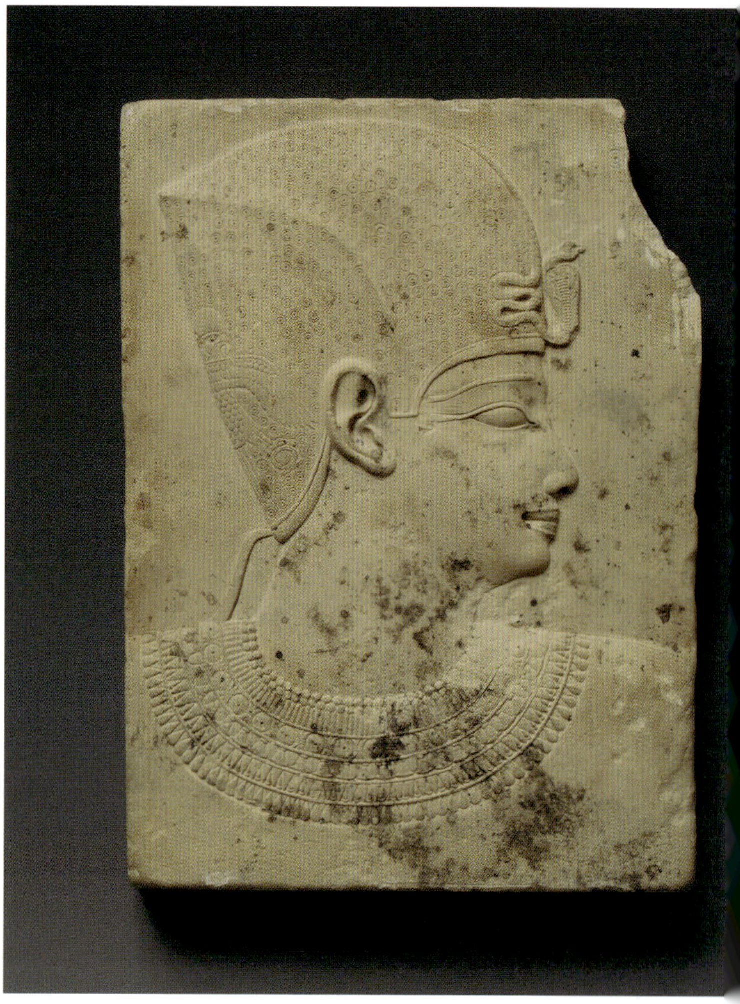

'I was so glad that we were able to obtain the bronze (lot no. 516) for so small a price, and I am grateful to you for your generous thought [250£ plus 50£ for Carter]. Here in Egypt my affairs are progressing slowly but favourably, and soon I hope to go to Luxor to resume my work. In the meantime I have been searching Cairo for material on your behalf with fair success...'[76].

Meanwhile, Carter proposed the acquisition of several pieces, including a *Low-relief of the priest Ameneminet* and 'a fine fragment of a bas-relief of an official of the XIXth Dyn.',[77] from the Khawam Brothers in Cairo. He stepped into his role as dealer, suggesting 'good pieces' to Gulbenkian and sending photographs, which pleased the Collector as it allowed him to obtain an approximate idea of their physical condition and 'artistic quality'. However, Carter did not stop at Egyptian antiquities, proposing other pieces such as Greek art[78] and Celtic amulets[79] to the Collector. As an agent based in Cairo or Luxor, Carter did not make payment directly, instead asking Gulbenkian to do so — 'as I fear I have no current ready cash at hand with all my current exs. [expenses] here'.[80]

[76] Letter from HC to CSG, 2 January 1925. Gulbenkian Archives, LDN 0593.

[77] C. 1320 BCE, limestone fragment, inv. 205. Khawam Brothers, January 1925. Letter from HC to CSG, 2 January 1925, Gulbenkian Archives, LDN 0593.

[78] He referred in particular to a 'gold Greek statuette [...] I am now sure that it is nothing less than a clever forgery'. Letter from HC to CSG, 22 January 1925. Gulbenkian Archives, LDN 0593.

[79] 'They are very well known and published in Joseph Anderson's Scotland in Pagan Times' belonging to Lady Forbes. Letter from HC to CSG, 6 June 1925. Gulbenkian Archives, LDN 06593.

[80] Letter from HC to CSG, 22 January 1925. Gulbenkian Archives, MCG 00072. In this example, he is referring to the acquisition of the low-relief (see note 76).

← FIG. 6
The Solar Barque of Djedhor, one of the many pieces acquired for the collection by Howard Carter, London, 1924.

← FIG. 7
Howard Carter proposed the purchase of the *Low relief of a Pharaoh* from the Khawam Brothers, Cairo, 1926.

Gulbenkian eventually provided Carter with a credit of £5,000 for purchasing artworks. The money could be used on the condition that the pieces were genuine and to the Collector's taste. Gulbenkian viewed this gesture as a demonstration of his trust in the Egyptologist.[81]

Carter's concerns also centred around what he refers to as the 'Tutankhamun affair',[82] or the resumption of work on the tomb, which had been put on hold due to Lord Carnarvon's death and the legal dispute surrounding ownership of the treasure, as well as the increasingly tense relations with the General Manager of the Antiquities Department, the French Egyptologist Pierre Lacau. The tone of the correspondence with Gulbenkian hints at the pressure that Carter was experiencing. His response to a request from Gulbenkian to host his friend Chester Beatty is one such example: 'I am calling upon him [Chester Beatty] at his boat on the Nile at Luxor [...] I am up to my eyes in work and am inundated with all kinds of applications and visits'.[83]

In 1925 and 1926, as well as the aforementioned *Low-relief of the priest Ameneminet*, and a *Low-Relief of a Pharaoh*[84] (fig. 7) acquired from the Khawam Brothers in Cairo and the small scarab amulet purchased directly from Carter by Gulbenkian,[85] two bronze pieces from the Carmichael Collection are of particular interest.[86] Sir Thomas David Gibson, 1st Baron Carmichael of Skirling (Scotland), a liberal, who had been the governor of Victoria (Australia), Madras and Bengal (India), died in 1926 and his diverse collections of Egyptian antiquities, Greek and Roman objects and other European pieces were auctioned individually at Sotheby's on 8 June that year. Gulbenkian expressed his interest in a set of lots from the Carmichael Collection to Ernest Duveen and Howard Carter, explaining that he was looking, above all, for 'transcendent works'.[87] Carter bid for and won two lots: the cat, and the ushabti, which drew the collector's attention immediately and earned the Egyptologist his praise: 'A [*very*, word erased] fine and rare specimen [...] probably of the time of Amen.hetep III or a little later'.[88]

The acquisition of the works from the Carmichael Collection clearly demonstrates Gulbenkian's proactive participation in searching for objects of interest to him, as well as his need for Carter's knowledge to confirm their authenticity. The media attention surrounding the discovery of Tutankhamun's tomb is likely to have contributed to Gulbenkian's confidence in his adviser's expertise. Meanwhile, Carter continued to encourage Gulbenkian to visit Egypt, although his plans were constantly postponed,[89] fuelling this fantasy with notes on his archaeological discoveries: 'the store-room of the tomb to Tut Ankh Amon [*sic*] is producing most beautiful and interesting material, number of fine statuettes of the king and lots of fine jewellery'.[90]

From 1928 to 1929, Gulbenkian made his final acquisitions with Carter as agent, although representatives of the Khawam Brothers continued to present him with proposals, including Greek and Egyptian antiquities, which the collector did not follow up on out of distrust.[91]

In 1928, Gulbenkian's attention was drawn to a mummy mask[92] from the collection belonging to Sir John Maxwell, a general and amateur Egyptologist who had been a personal friend of both Lord Carnarvon and Howard Carter (fig. 8). The piece was bought for £3000 and Gulbenkian expressed his gratitude for the price he had paid: 'I thank you for the

81 Gulbenkian's letter is akin to a genuine contract. Letter from CSG to HC, 1 May 1925. Gulbenkian Archives, LDN 0593.
82 'I have been fortunate enough to settle the Tut.ankh.Amen affair, and shall start work this coming week'. Signed extract, letter from HC to CSG, 22 January 1925. Gulbenkian Archives, MCG 00072.
83 Letter from HC to CSG, 17 February 1925. Gulbenkian Archives, LDN 0593.
84 Early Ptolemaic dynasty (c. 300–250 BCE), inv. 167.
85 Blue faience scarab, Late Period, Twenty-sixth Dynasty (?), inv. 412.
86 *Funerary figurine (ushabti)* of Hesmeref, New Kingdom, Eighteenth Dynasty (c. 1400–1340 BCE), inv. 166 and *Statuette of a cat*, Late Period, Twenty-sixth Dynasty, inv. 399 (lots 255 and 259).
87 Letter from CSG to Ernest Duveen, 28 May and 2 June 1926. Gulbenkian Archives, LDN01592; letter from CSG to HC, 3 June 1926, LDN 01592.
88 Letter from HC to CSG, 15 June 1926. Gulbenkian Archives, MCG 00071.
89 'It is such a pity that year after year I am prevented from going to Egypt – and I don't see any possibility of going out this season'. Letter from CSG to HC, 18 December 1926. Gulbenkian Archives, MCG 00541. See also note 64.
90 Letter from HC to CSG, Luxor, 17 November 1926. Gulbenkian Archives, MCG 00541.
91 A series of letters dating back to 1928 confirm their direct contact with CSG. Gulbenkian Archives, MCG 002409.
92 *Mummy mask*, Late Period, Thirtieth Dynasty (380–343 BCE), gilt silver, inv. 62. Sotheby's, London, 12 June 1928 (lot 279).

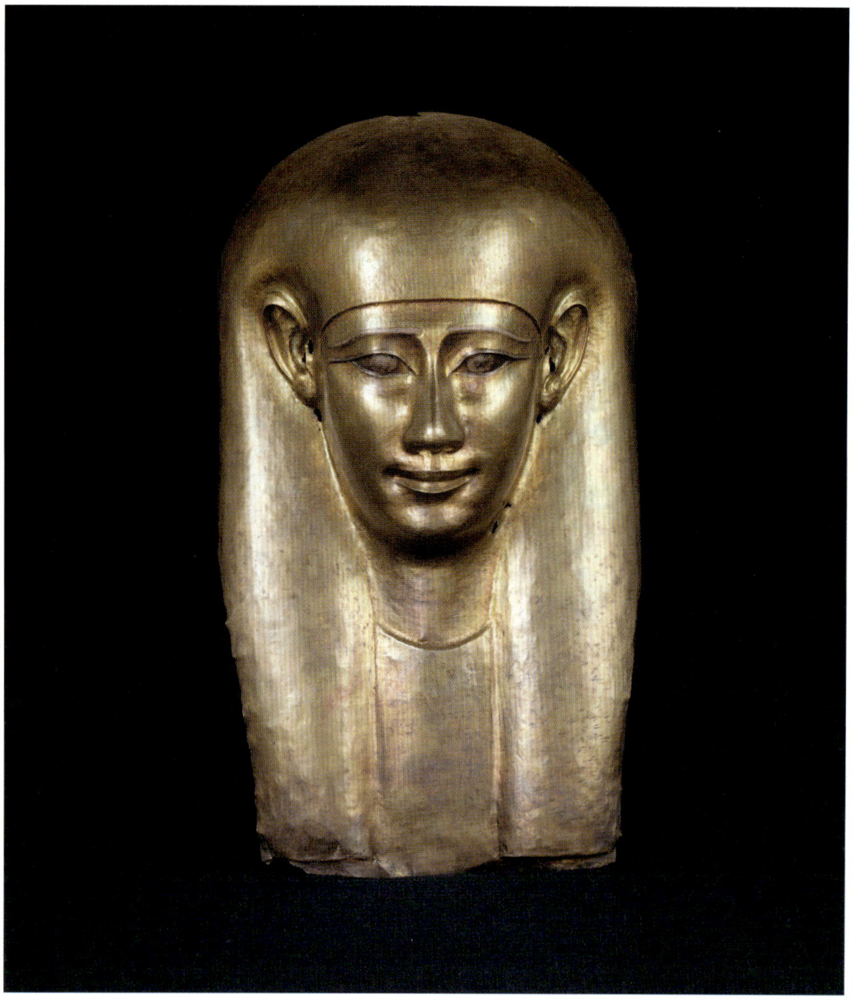

← FIG. 8
Gulbenkian devoted special care to the presentation of the *Funerary mask*, and had a showcase specially built for the purpose. It fell to Howard Carter to supervise its installation, of which no photographic records exist.

care you have taken to get it as cheaply as possible'.[93] To exhibit the mask, a special stand with a glass case was made[94] and installed at Gulbenkian's residence in Avenue d'Iéna under Carter's supervision.[95] The collector was very enthusiastic about his purchase: 'I am looking forward with great interest regarding the mask and the arranging of the whole collection which will give me great pleasure and I am very much obliged to you for your kindness in consenting to do so [...] I am now very keen and very jealous to have only the best'.[96]

[93] Letter from CSG to HC, 13 June 1928. Gulbenkian Archives, PRS 00009.

[94] The item description on the invoice from Spink & Son, Ltd., 23 August 1928, includes clear specifications for the stand: 'cemented glass case with mahogany base covered velvet with interior fitting for gold mask and panel covered with red silk'. Gulbenkian Archives, MCG 01157.

[95] Gulbenkian asked Carter to install his collection in the purpose designed showcases: 'I have left instructions that any morning you would like to come the 'vitrines' are to be placed at your disposal [...] We shall have lunch together I hope you are not engaged'. Letter from CSG to HC, 31 August 1928. Gulbenkian Archives, PRS 00015.

[96] Letter from CSG to HC, 31 July 1928. Gulbenkian Archives, PRS 00009.

Last acquisitions

In summer 1928, new horizons opened up to Gulbenkian, marking the beginning of a process of complex negotiations with the Soviet authorities, which would lead to the acquisition of a prestigious set of artworks. These works came from the Hermitage Museum in Leningrad (now Saint Petersburg), which opened up its collections for Gulbenkian's perusal and purchase. From 1928 to 1930, the Collector obtained paintings by Rembrandt, Rubens and Hubert Robert, silverwork by François-Thomas Germain, furniture by Riesener and Houdon's *Diana* sculpture, among other pieces.[97]

Gulbenkian's interests were diverse and Carter was able to assess the extent to which the collection of Egyptian antiquities held at the Soviet Museum might be of interest to the Collector. The Egyptologist informed Gulbenkian: 'I am also making enquiries re the Hermitage coll.; but have not yet been able to trace an illustrated catalogue'.[98] For Gulbenkian, this represented a further opportunity for new acquisitions: 'I am anxiously awaiting news from you regarding the Hermitage Collection; also I should be very much obliged to you if you could send me photographs of all these objects that are in Russia.'[99]

The Egyptian collection at the Hermitage dated back to the mid-nineteenth century and had been gradually enriched by acquisitions, including the Francesco Castiglione Collection, purchased by the Academy of Sciences in 1825, which contained around one thousand and two hundred objects.

The inventory of the collection was drawn up by Vladimir Golenischev,[100] who is believed to be Russia's first Egyptologist and was responsible for acquiring a very significant set of pieces in Egypt, where he funded excavations and promoted the sale of the archaeological discoveries. Golenischev was also responsible for creating the Egyptology department at the University of Cairo (1923–29). While he was in Cairo, Howard Carter informed Gulbenkian that Golenischev was on leave and that he had been unable to speak to him in person; he ruled out the possibility of writing to him, as he did not consider it 'politic' to do so.[101] Carter's stance with regard to Golenischev is understandable and reflects the secrecy with which Gulbenkian dealt with his purchases from the Hermitage, which began in October 1928.[102] The Collector continued to hope that, when Golenischev returned to Cairo, he would provide him with photographs of the Egyptian pieces to allow him to make his own choice, as the timing was particularly auspicious.

We know now that Gulbenkian did not acquire any Egyptian antiquities from the collections at the Hermitage, but the correspondence that he exchanged with Carter on the matter shows that he was willing to continue to work with the Egyptologist: 'I am glad that this time we understand each other very much better and that you know what I want and I shall be very pleased to see my collection increased through your good services.'[103]

In 1929, the last documented transaction involving Howard Carter took place, resulting in the purchase of three objects: '1) Half-life size

[97] See note 4.
[98] Letter from HC to CSG, 8 September 1928. Gulbenkian Archives, MCG 00015.
[99] Letter from CSG to HC, 10 September 1928. Gulbenkian Archives, PRS 00011.
[100] *Ermitage imperial...*, 1891.
[101] Letter from HC to CSG, 2 October 1928. Gulbenkian Archives, MCG 00015.
[102] Letter from Marcel Aucoc to CSG, 30 October 1928. Gulbenkian Archives, MCG 01134.
[103] Letter from CSG to HC, 25 October 1928. Gulbenkian Archives, PRS 00015.

Egyptian head in black granite, being a portrait of a Nubian official […] 2) A small bronze figure of a cat' and a ceramic lamp from Kütahya.[104] There is little information about the Egyptian pieces in the archive and their origin prior to Carter's purchase is unknown. The ceramic lamp was bought from Boghos K. Ispenian at the Muslim Art Gallery in Cairo by Carter. The descriptions sent by Gulbenkian follow the Collector's usual request regarding the inventory of the collection: 'I myself can describe the lamp but the description and the period of the Head and the Cat are rather beyond my capacity'.[105]

Curiously, the letter describing the pieces contains a proposal from Carter to the Collector in a postscript, 'a very fine French Gothic dressor [*sic*] of the 14th – 15th centuries',[106] although this proposal did not lead to a purchase.

Howard Carter also suggested the acquisition of a piece that was particularly exceptional and called for the utmost secrecy on the matter:

> 'a very fine Falcon in Green Basalt […] with small and charming figures of the king — Nekhthorheb — between its feet, is 70 centimetres in height, a magnificent piece of work: the finest specimen of its kind hitherto discovered. It bears the name of the last Pharaoh of Egypt […] Let me know your own opinion'.[107]

Carter's description corresponds to the piece 'falcon of Nectanebo' or 'the god Horus protecting the pharaoh Nectanebo', which was purchased by the Metropolitan Museum of Art in New York in 1934 through Eustache de Lorey, Carter's agent in Paris[108] (fig. 9).

In the 1930s, correspondence between the Collector and Howard Carter became less frequent, although Gulbenkian finally made his long-postponed trip to Egypt in 1934[109] (fig. 1). In an entry in his travel journal on 18 January, he records his impression of the 'treasures of Tutankhamun' at the Egyptian Museum in Cairo: 'My reading had led me to expect to see superb things, but my imagination could never have conceived of such beauty, such civilisation. If I had to choose, I would take the caskets and the bust'[110] (cat. 150). Two years later, he loaned his collection of Egyptian antiquities to the British Museum, as noted above.[111]

Alerted perhaps by this important loan by Calouste Gulbenkian, Ernest Duveen drew the Collector's attention to an extraordinary piece that was sure to be to Gulbenkian's taste. It was a sphinx 'in the finest and loveliest Egyptian turquoise blue faience'.[112] Duveen learned that the object had become available through Howard Carter and it is curious that Carter did not propose the item to Gulbenkian directly. The matter was clarified by Duveen himself in the same letter:

> 'in the course of conversation [with Carter] he told me about this Sphinx, and I asked him immediately whether he would have any objection to my writing to you about it. He said he had no objection, as long as I impressed on you that if you were not interested that you would not, of any account, mention it to any one […] Carter himself considers this Sphinx one of the greatest pieces of Egyptian Art. I should say that it is absolutely perfect'.[113]

[104] *Head of a Nubian* (?), New Kingdom, Eighteenth Dynasty (c. 1500–1300 BCE), inv. 218; *Statuette of a cat*, Late Period, Twenty-sixth Dynasty (664–525 BCE), inv. 219. *Ceramic lamp*, Kütahya, eighteenth century, inv. 220. Letter from HC to CSG, 17 June 1929. Gulbenkian Archives, MCG 00074.

[105] Letter from CSG to HC, 12 June 1929. Gulbenkian Archives, LDN 0796.

[106] Letter from HC to CSG, 17 June 1929. Gulbenkian Archives, MCG 00074.

[107] Letter from HC to CSG, 26 October 1929. Gulbenkian Archives, MCG 01239.

[108] Quoted by Reeves, 2009 (1997), pp. 242–50, note 3, p. 246. See also *God-Horus Protecting King Nectanebo II*, 360-43 BC, purchased from Eustache de Lorey, Paris, 1934. Metropolitan Museum of Art, New York, inv. 34.2.1 — https://www.metmuseum.org/art/collection/search/544887 (consulted 8 March 2022).

[109] See notes 64 and 89.

[110] Travel journal: Calouste Sarkis *Gulbenkian…*, 2019, p. 11 (translated from the French), Gulbenkian Archives, PT FCG CSGP-S046-D600076. Gulbenkian added several illustrated postcards and photographs of the places he had visited to his travel journal, including images of the bust and sarcophagus of Tutankhamun.

[111] In the same year, an important set of paintings was loaned to the National Gallery in London (1936–50), with the mediation of Sir Kenneth Clark.

[112] Letter from Ernest Duveen (Duveen & Walker Ltd.) to CSG, 18 May 1936. Gulbenkian Archives, MCG 02323.

[113] *Ibidem*.

→ FIG. 9
The God Horus Protecting the Pharaoh Nectanebo II, Egypt, Late Period, 360–343 BCE, metagreywacke, 72 x 20 x 46.5 cm. The Metropolitan Museum of Art, New York. Rogers Fund, 1934, accession no. 34.21.

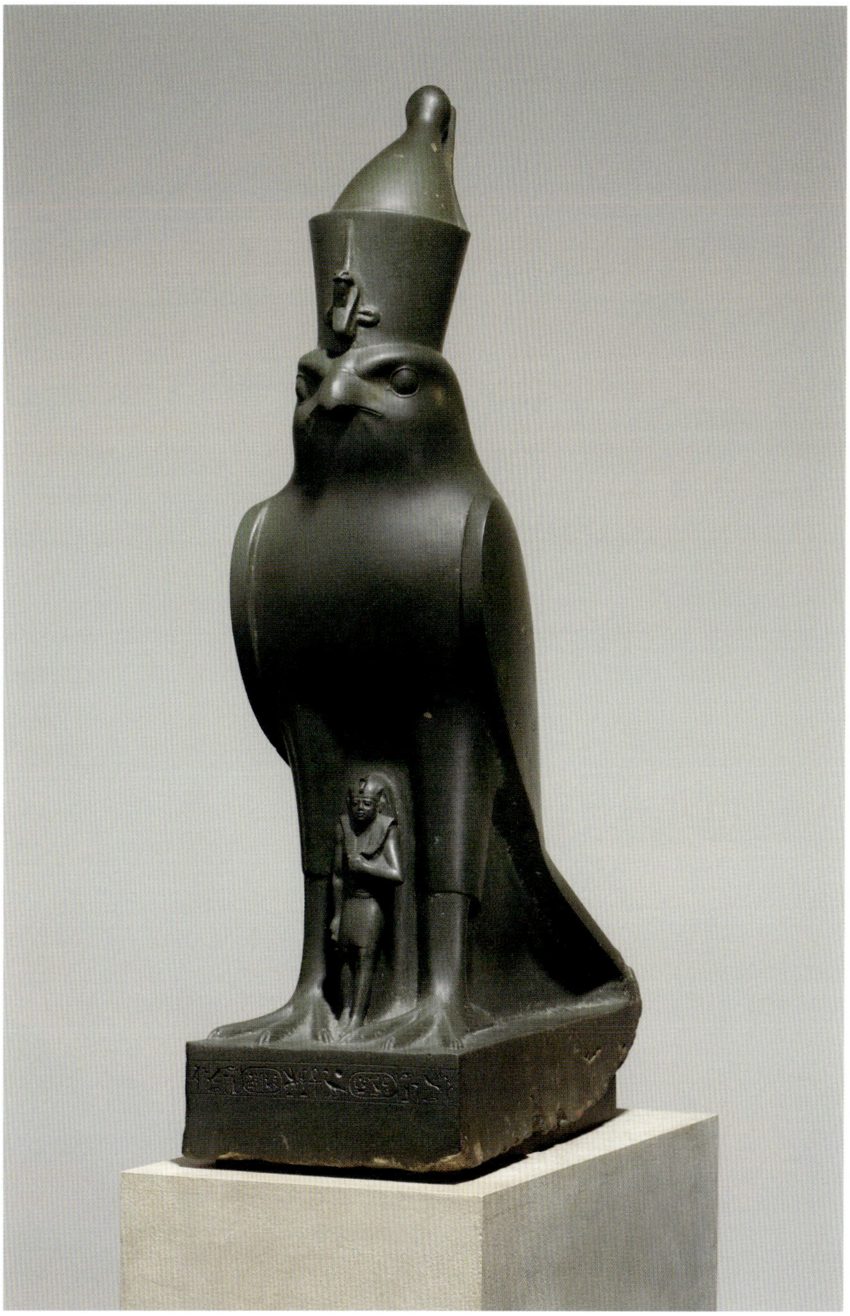

Ernest Duveen knew Gulbenkian well and was aware that he always tried to view the pieces he wished to purchase in person before making a decision or requested photographs if this was not possible. Duveen confirmed the artistic quality, the historical relevance and the excellent condition of the object and offered to arrange a visit to the piece by the Collector with Carter the next time he was in London. Today, we might question why Howard Carter did not offer the piece to Gulbenkian directly. Was there a dispute between them? The matter of Carter's doubts over the figurine acquired from Paul Mallon was still hanging in the air and Gulbenkian was in the process of loaning the piece to the British Museum and seeking guarantees of its authenticity. Their relationship was almost certainly clouded by this incident, although no explicit declaration to this effect appears to have been made.

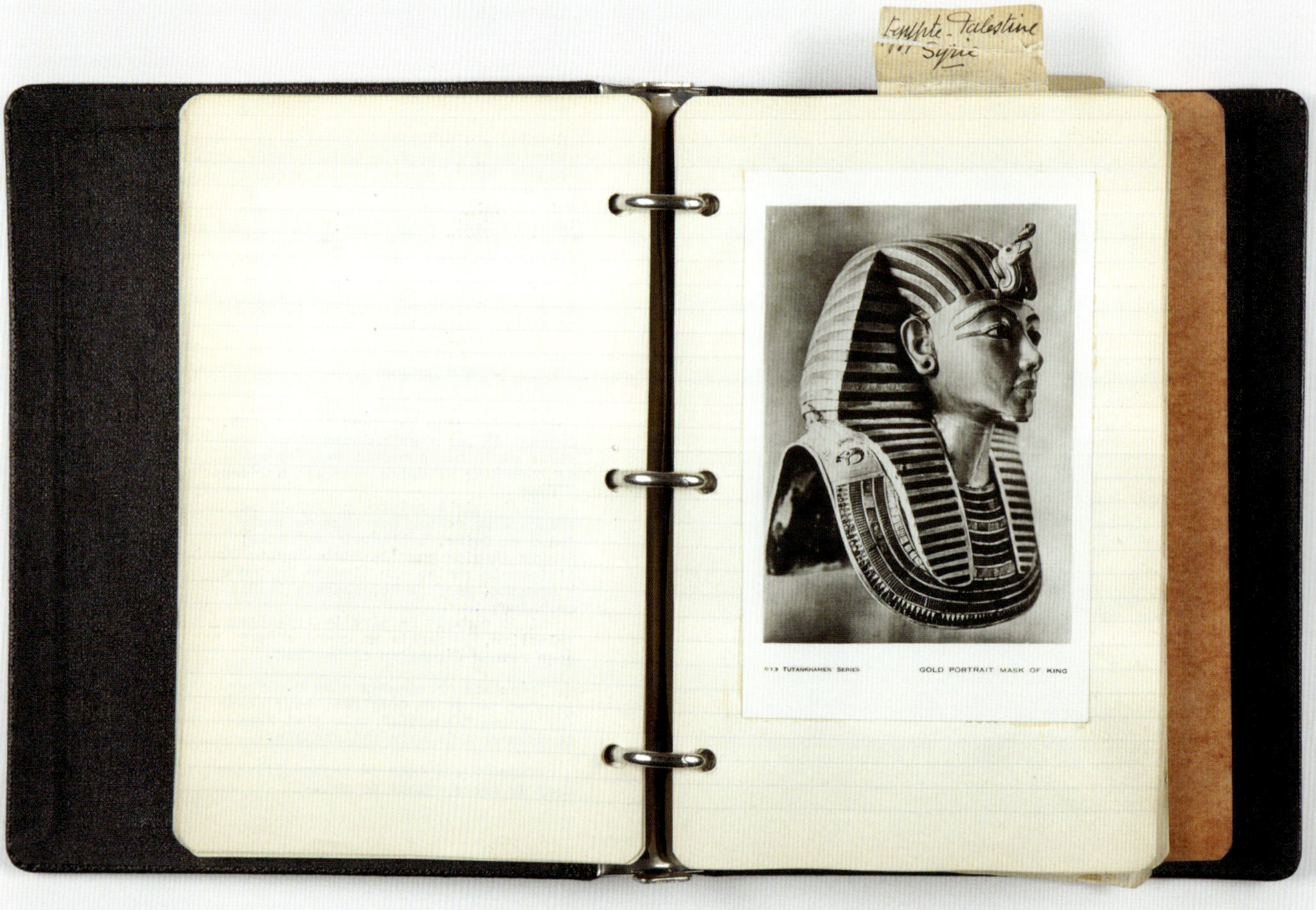

150

The pieces recovered from Tutankhamun's tomb deserved the Collector's special attention, as recorded in the diary of his visit to the Egyptian Museum in Cairo, in which he included several postcards, including one of the bust of the Pharaoh.

Gulbenkian's reply to Ernest Duveen was written the next day and helps to clarify the dissonance that emerged from time to time between Carter and the Collector, who was always interested in high-quality artworks:

> 'Egyptian art interests me very much, but being neither an expert nor a savant, I only take interest in such objects that appeal to me. I have very high esteem for Howard Carter, but between us confidentially when he shows me an object and I am not interested, he seems somewhat peculiarly disappointed'.[114]

Gulbenkian suggested that he would examine the object during his next trip to London, if it had not already been sold, but added: 'I shall certainly be pleased to meet our mutual friend Howard Carter, but please keep to yourself what I have written above, and I should also like to see the object with you alone, if possible, so as to avoid any discontentment'.[115]

A week later, Gulbenkian wrote to Howard Carter in a cordial tone, informing him that he had heard of an auction to be held at Sotheby's on 8 June that included 'Egyptian Works of Art' and wanted to be informed about pieces that might be of interest.[116] No subsequent correspondence is available to confirm Carter's response, although we know that the piece remained in the Egyptologist's possession until his death in London on 2 March 1939.[117] Upon the Collector's request, Gulbenkian's secretary contacted Harry Burton, the photographer from the Metropolitan Museum of Art, who worked with Carter in Egypt, to obtain information about the deceased Egyptologist's collection and request photographs.[118] Despite the proximity between the two men as a result of Burton's central role in documenting the discovery of Tutankhamun's tomb in photographs, his selection as one of the executors of Carter's will was rather surprising.[119] Burton suggests 'a very beautiful blue faience Sphinx [...] quite unique and in perfect condition [...] I am enclosing a list of the outstanding objects, none of the remaining articles, I consider quite up to the standard of Mr. Gulbenkian's Egyptian collection' .[120]

The sphinx was purchased in 1939 by the patrons of the Academy of Art, Bloomfield Hills, Michigan, and has been part of the collection at the Metropolitan Museum of Art, New York, since 1972, following the Sotheby's auction held at Park Bernet, New York[121] (fig 10).

[114] Letter from CSG to Ernest Duveen, 19 May 1936. Gulbenkian Archives, PRS 00078 (letter 116).

[115] *Ibidem*.

[116] Letter from CSG to HC, 28 May 1936. Gulbenkian Archives, PRS 00078 (letter 399). There is no record at Sotheby's of an auction of Egyptian artworks on 8 June 1936. I am grateful to João Magalhães, Director, Senior Specialist European Furniture, and in particular to Richard M. Keresey, Worldwide Director, Egyptian, Classical and Western Asiatic Antiquities at Sotheby's, for the highly relevant information they provided regarding this piece.

[117] The so-called 'Spink list' (Spink & Son Ltd) records the classical and Egyptian antiquities that the dealers decided to catalogue. See REEVES, 2009 (1997), pp. 242–50, pp. 244–5.

[118] Letter from CSG's secretary to Harry Burton, 17 August 1939. Gulbenkian Archives, MCG 02247.

[119] Howard Carter's heir was his niece Phyllis Walker, and the other executor besides Harry Burton was Bruce Ingram, editor of the *Illustrated London News*, who published drawings and watercolours by Howard Carter in his magazine.

[120] Letter from Harry Burton to Mr J. Berthelot, 22 August 1939. Gulbenkian Archives, MCG 02247.

[121] Sphinx of Amenhotep III, possibly from a temple, c. 1390–1352 BCE, accession no. 1972.125. https://www.metmuseum.org/art/collection/search/544498 (consulted 8 March 2022).

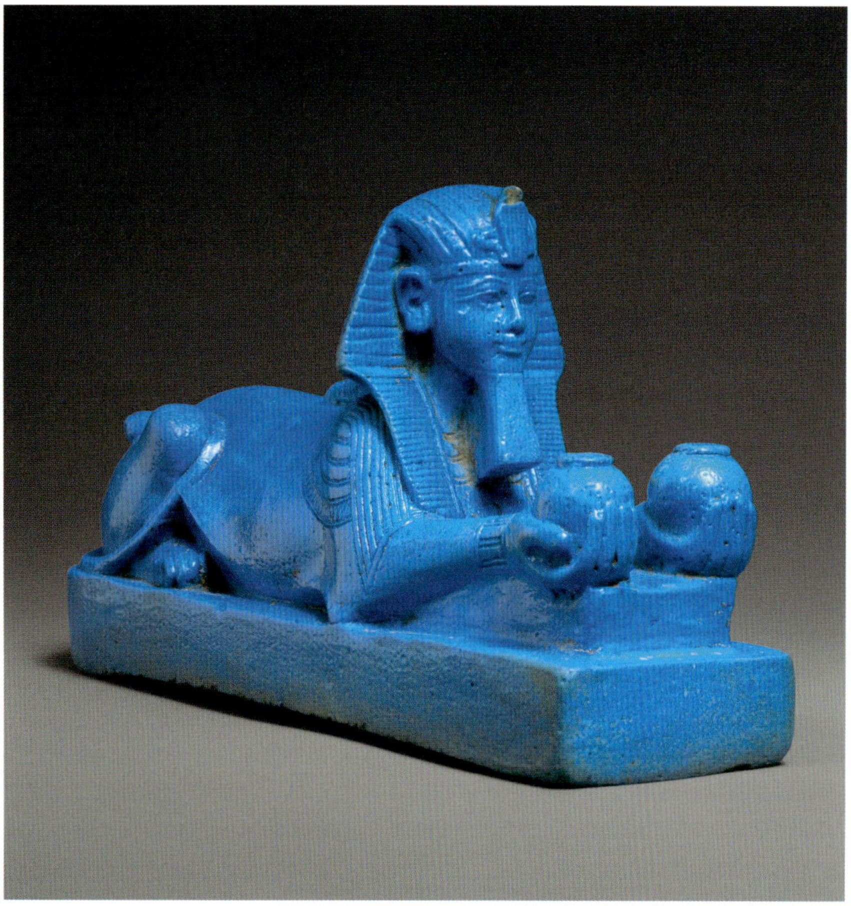

← FIG. 10
Sphinx of Amenhotep III, Egypt, New Kingdom, c. 1390–1352 BCE, faience, remains of a travertine (Egyptian alabaster) tenon, 13.3 x 13.3 x 25.1 cm. The Metropolitan Museum of Art, New York. Purchase, Lila Acheson Wallace Gift, 1972, accession no. 1972.125.

Epilogue

The fifty-four catalogue entries corresponding to the Egyptian antiquities that make up Calouste Gulbenkian's collection were purchased between 1907 and 1942. Following Howard Carter's death, Gulbenkian acquired just two more pieces: two limestone statuettes from the Viscount Rothermere Collection in 1942, in a transaction brokered by Knoedler.[122] Before completing the purchase, as it was no longer possible to consult Howard Carter to confirm the authenticity of the pieces, the Collector contacted the director of the British Museum, Sir Edgar John Forsdyke, who replied:

> 'I am very glad to hear from you and to know that you are safely out of France [123]. I know a great deal about the two Egyptian statuettes and can say that we are greatly disappointed by our inability to acquire them [...] I am not expert in Egyptian antiquities, but [Sidney] Smith and [Stephen] Glanville (Professor of Egyptology in London and a former member of our staff) have no doubts about their genuineness and good condition and fine artistic quality'.[124]

[122] The two figures of officials were dated to the Old Kingdom, Sixth Dynasty (?) (c. 2325–c. 2150 BCE). Acquired by Calouste Gulbenkian through Knoedler Ltd., Sotheby's, London, 16 October 1942 (lots 65–6).

[123] In 1942, Gulbenkian left France, which was occupied by Nazi troops, and settled in Lisbon, the capital of a neutral country that would be positioned in World War II as a key entry point to the American continent. Gulbenkian lived in Lisbon until his death in 1955, making annual trips to Paris and to Deauville in Normandy to visit his 'garden', Les Enclos. See Carvalho Dias, 2014, pp. 99–107. See also Conlin, 2019, pp. 220–23.

[124] Letter from Sir E. J. Forsdyke to csg, 1 October 1942. Gulbenkian Archives, MCG 02431.

[125] The most relevant aspects are described by Araújo, 2006, cats. 65 and 66, invs. 2366 and 2365, pp. 166–8; for more details, see also Azeredo Perdigão, 2006 (1969), pp. 162–8.

The reply appears to provide the perfect reassurance to Gulbenkian's usual concerns, but, like the statuette purchased from Paul Mallon, the authenticity of the Rothermere pieces was called into question, this time by William Smith, an Egyptologist from the Museum of Fine Arts, Boston, and professor at the University of Harvard.[125]

Throughout his life, Gulbenkian's knowledge and resources allowed him to access information from the most reputed experts to confirm the wisdom of his purchases. However, with rare exceptions, he purchased mostly what he liked and based his decisions on his own taste, which he honed over the course of his life through study and intuition, legitimated by the artistic quality, condition and origin of the pieces.

The importance of the contribution made by advisers, agents, scholars and art dealers cannot be overstated, although the final decision was always made by the Collector himself, who did not always share the opinion of his interlocutors. This is evident in the relationship between Gulbenkian and Howard Carter. Whereas contact between the Collector and the Egyptologist was initially cautious, the two men developed a close relationship of mutual respect, which culminated in prudent caution on the part of the Collector. Although Gulbenkian rejected many of Carter's proposals, especially pieces that he viewed as 'archaeological', he called on him to act as agent in most of his acquisitions of Egyptian art, among which the sale of the MacGregor Collection was a particular highlight.

We might ask ourselves, then, what would be of the Gulbenkian collection of Egyptian antiquities without Carter's guidance and suggestions? However, any attempt to answer that question would be merely speculative.

THE IMMORTALS

THREE THOUSAND YEARS OF HISTORY AND A FEW MEMORABLE REIGNS

1

WORSHIPPING THE GODS AND DEFENDING EGYPT: HOW TO BE A GOOD PHARAOH

Of all the pharaohs reigning on the banks of the Nile, who succeeded each other for more than three thousand years, a few became famous from the time of their death. *Superstar Pharaohs* begins by constructing a sort of composite portrait of the ideal monarch, by describing the means pharaohs used to make an impression on minds and overcome oblivion.

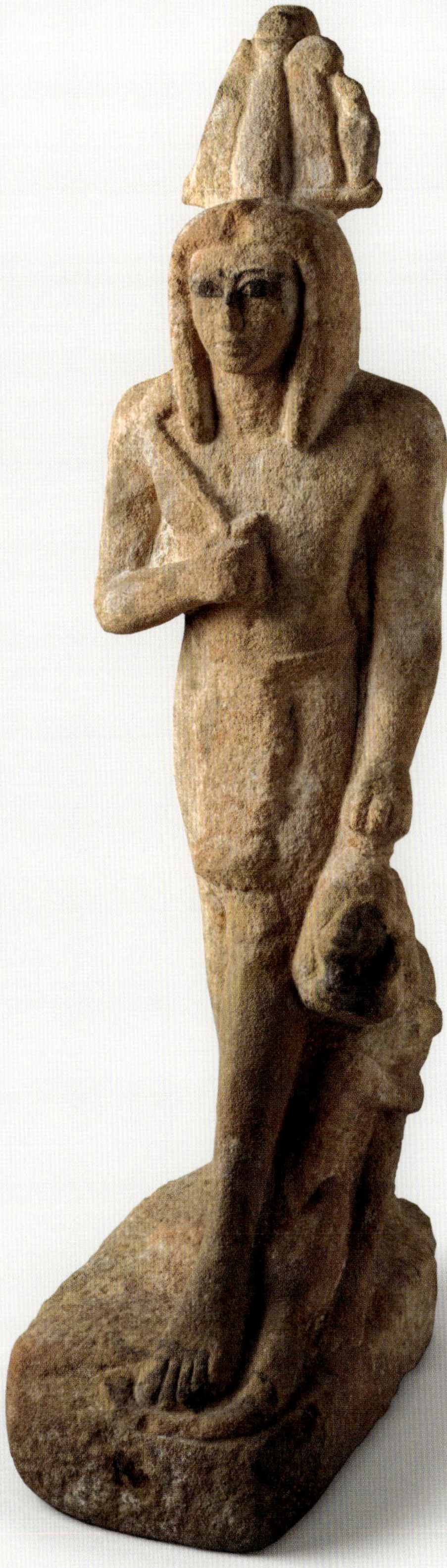

18

Statue of a pharaoh holding a foreigner captive, unknown provenance, second half of the Twentieth Dynasty (mid-twelfth to early eleventh century BCE).

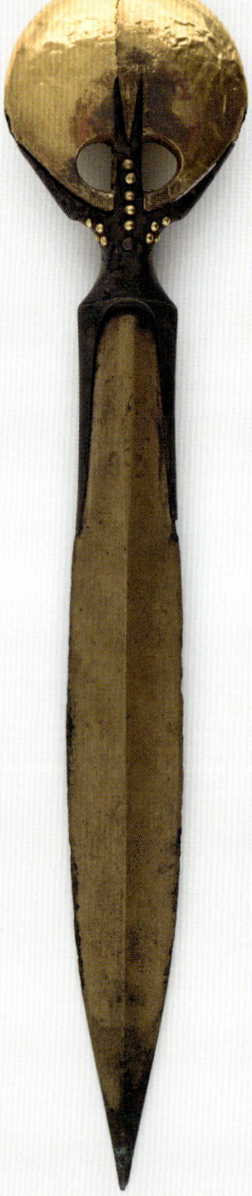

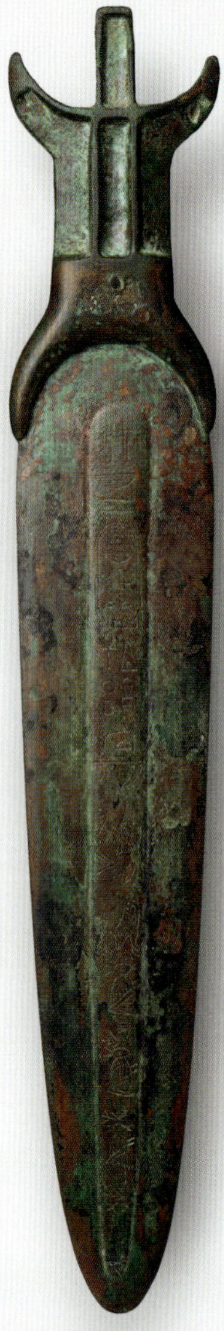

21

Dagger found in the tomb of the pharaoh Kamose, who waged war on the concurrent Hyksos dynasty, Dra Abu el-Naga, Egypt, late Seventeenth Dynasty (c. 1540 BCE).

20

Dagger bearing the name of the pharaoh Ahmose, Egypt, reign of Ahmose (c. 1539–1514 BCE).

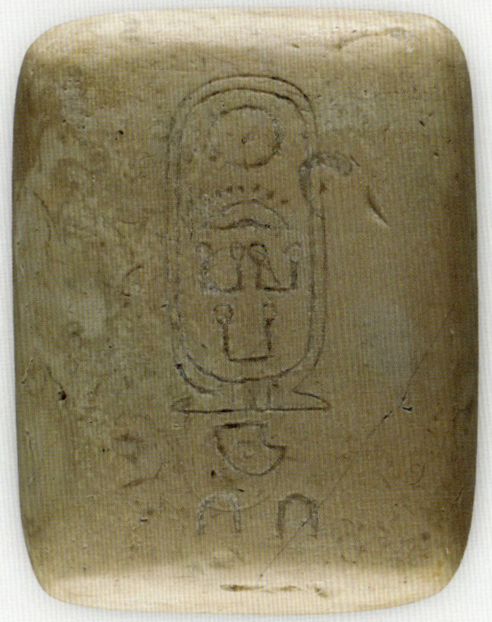

28

Weight for weighing copper,
with the cartouche of Senwosret III,
Mirgissa, Sudan, reign of
Senwosret III (c. 1856–1838 BCE).

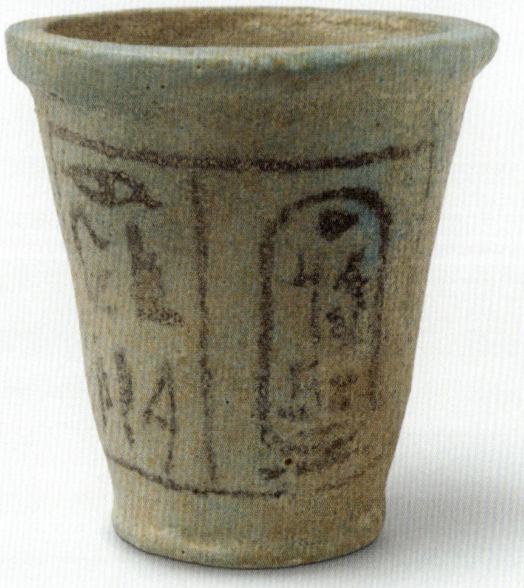

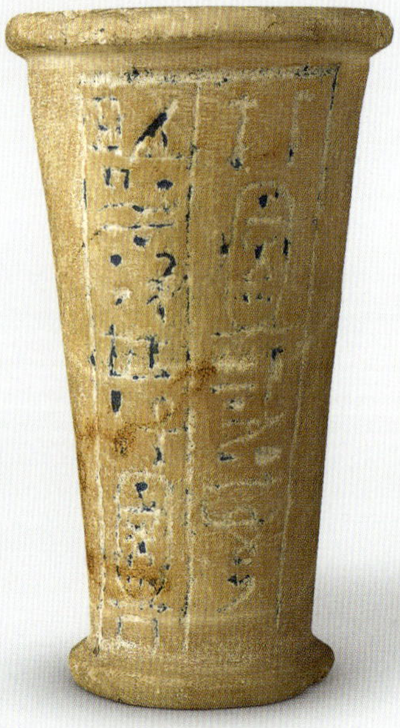

12

Miniature vase from the foundations of a temple dedicated to the god Osiris by Ramesses II, Egypt, reign of Ramesses II (c. 1279–1212 BCE).

13

Miniature vase placed in the foundations of a memorial temple of Thutmose IV, Egypt, reign of Thutmose IV (c. 1398–1388 BCE).

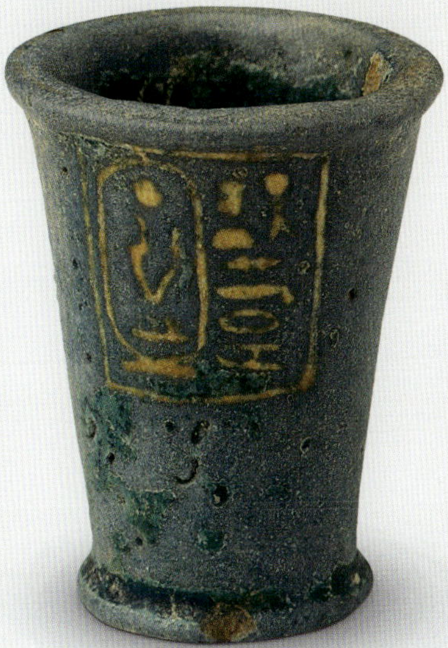

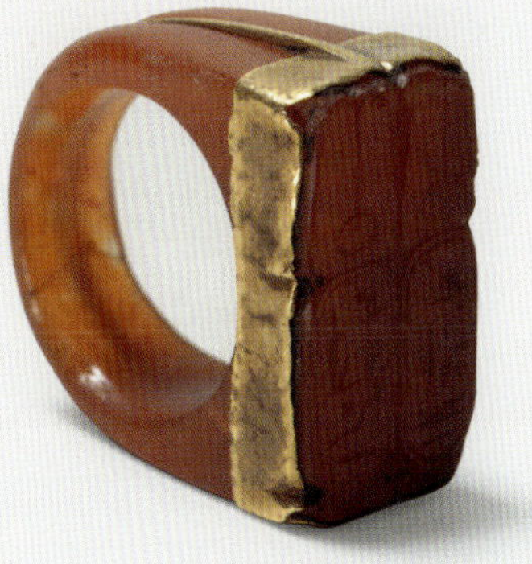

139

14

Miniature vase placed in the foundations of a temple dedicated to the god Ptah-Sokar by Seti I, Egypt, reign of Seti I (c. 1294–1279 BCE).

24

Ring with the cartouches of Ramesses II and his wife Nefertari, Egypt, reign of Ramesses II (c. 1279–1212 BCE).

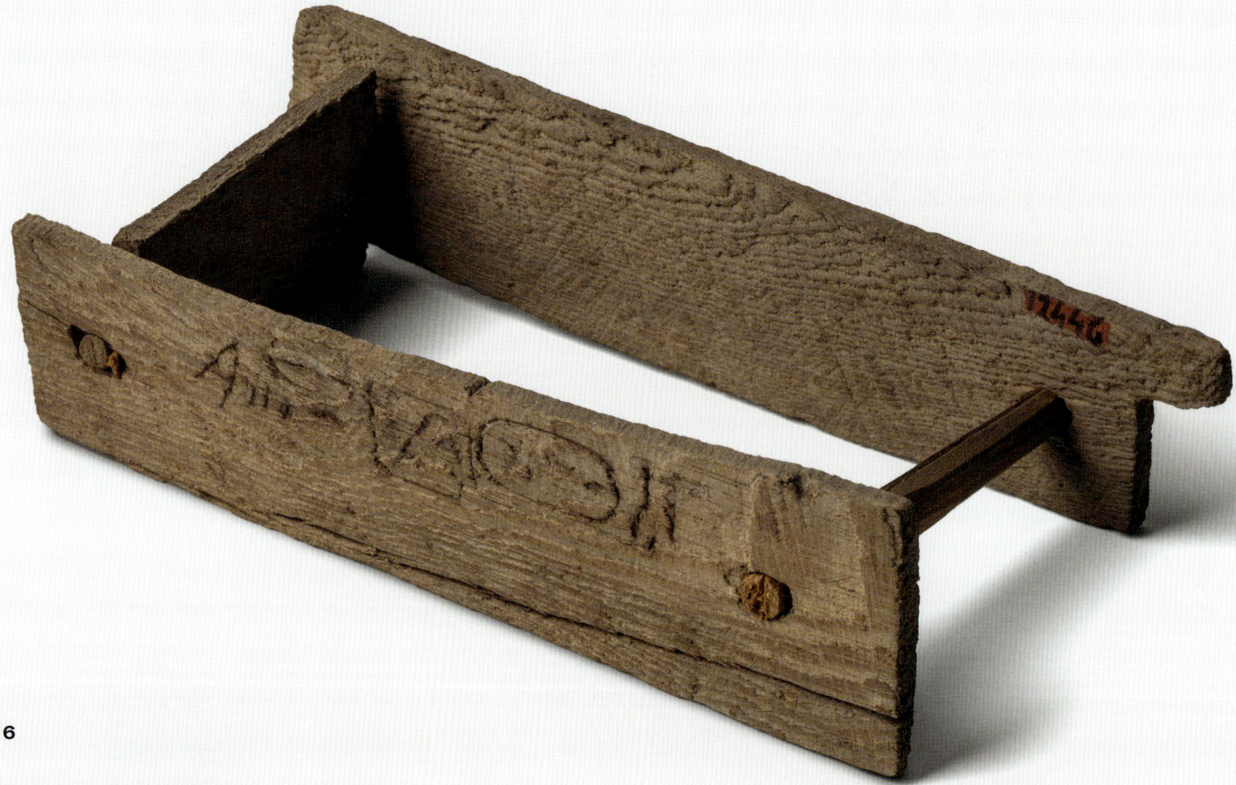

16

Miniature replica of a brick mould, buried in the foundations of a temple built by Thutmose III to provide magical assurance of its stability, Gebelein, Egypt, reign of Thutmose III (c. 1479–1425 BCE).

War and the protection — or extension — of Egyptian territory was one of the pharaoh's fundamental roles and he drew his strength and his power from the gods he worshipped. Military expeditions meant that troops could secure the trade routes and bring raw materials, booty and wealth back to Egypt (cats. 18 and 28). This not only improved people's living conditions, but enabled temples to be built and endowed with offerings, including statues and precious furniture, which archaeologists have found in their thousands. Some pharaohs, warriors and servants of their gods, were renowned in antiquity. These were Sneferu, Senwosret I and Senwosret III, Amenemhat III, Amenhotep III, Thutmose III (cats. 5 and 9) and Ramesses II (cat. 24). Alongside archaeological images and objects alluding to the pharaoh's military

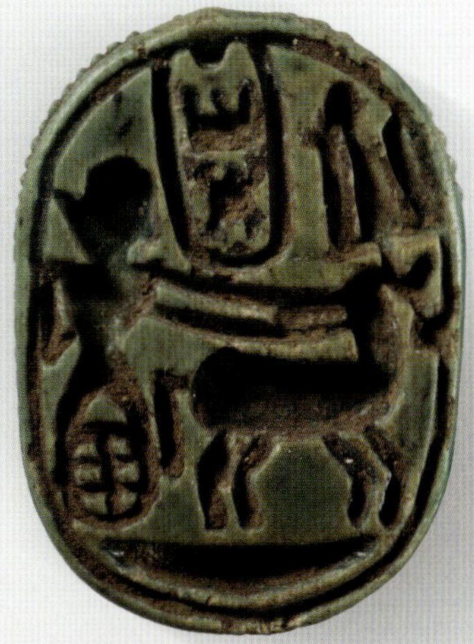

5

Scarab amulet with the image and cartouche of the esteemed King Thutmose III, Egypt, Nineteenth–Twentieth Dynasty (c. 1295–1069 BCE).

9

Scarab mounted on a ring, with the cartouche of King Thutmose III, discovered in the necropolis of Herdade do Gaio, Portugal, seventh century BCE.

This amulet, probably of Phoenician production, uses the name of the great pharaoh as a protective image, at a time when he was still celebrated in Egypt.

function (cats. 20 and 21), together with pieces that demonstrate his role as a provider of temples (cats. 12, 13, 14 and 16), the exhibition presents a few small memorials to the posthumous glory of some of these enterprising kings, known for being builders and for bringing prosperity.

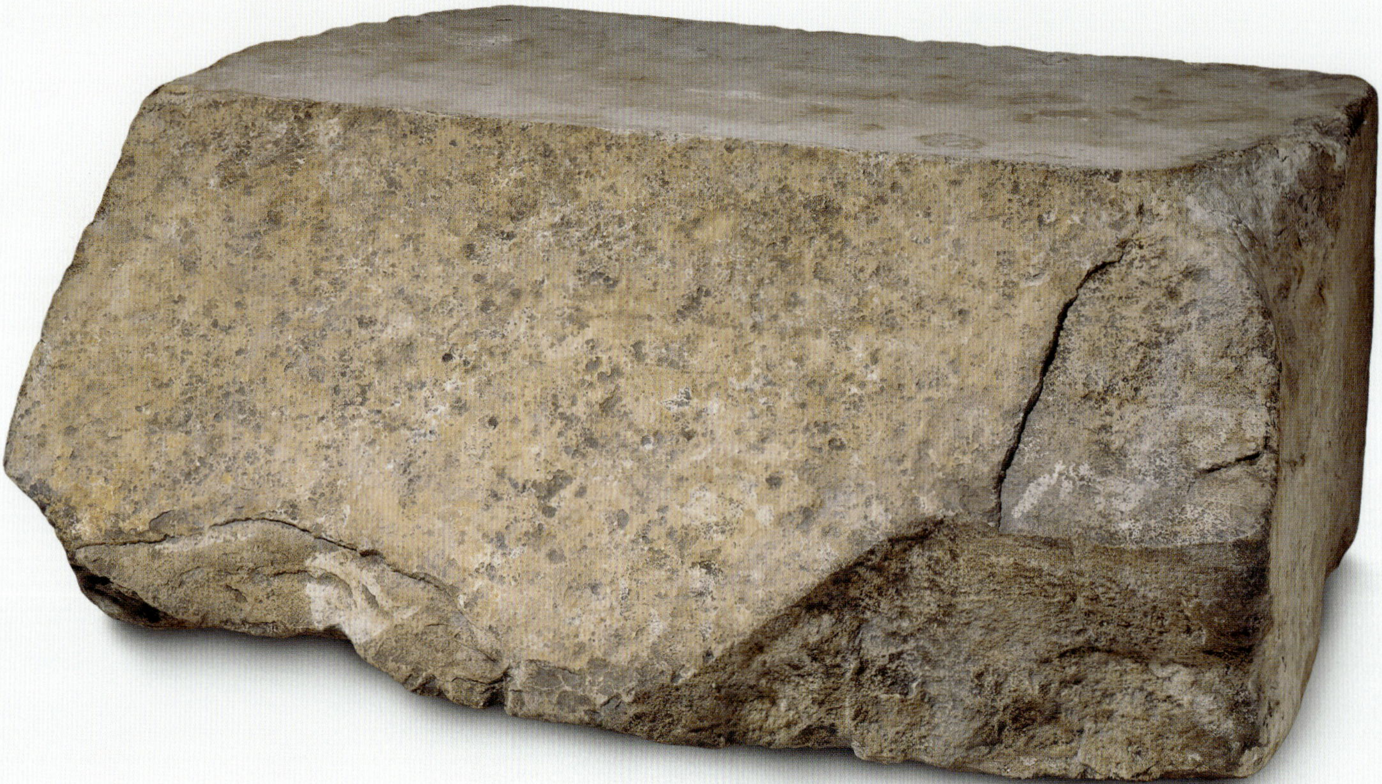

32

Fragment of a block used for casing the pyramid of Khufu, Giza, Egypt, reign of Khufu (c. 2636–2605 BCE).

The polished white limestone casing of the Great Pyramid was intended to reflect the light so that the monument became a mountain shining on the horizon.

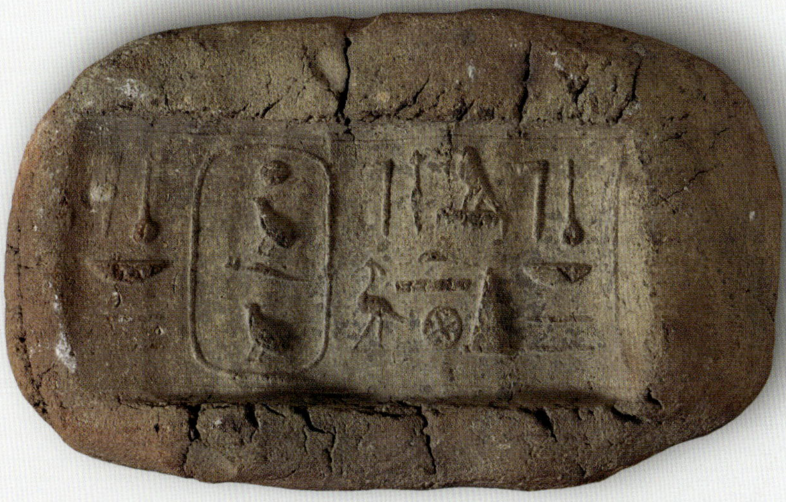

33

Seal imprint from the funerary complex of Khufu, Giza, Egypt, Late Period (c. 664–332 BCE).

This seal imprint probably indicates activity in the funerary temple two thousand years after the pharaoh's death.

MONUMENTS ON THE HORIZON

Throughout Egyptian history, making an impression on the minds and memories of his people seems to have been the pharaoh's constant aspiration. From the time of the Old Kingdom, one of the ways of satisfying this desire to be eternal, in the afterlife as well as on Earth, was to build oneself a pyramid in the desert, close to the Nile and populated areas, as somewhere to reside after death and host a funerary cult appropriate to the pharaoh. Today, travellers along the road from Giza to Faiyum will still pass by an area built with around forty pyramids, covering eighty kilometres. The best-preserved of these stand out on the horizon, creating a formidable impression, which would have been experienced equally by local people in antiquity. Although archaeologists have only unearthed a very small statuette of Khufu (cats. 32–33), no more than seven centimetres tall, they have found colossal statues of later pharaohs distributed among the temple ruins: intact or fragmentary, these reflect the urge to build on a giant scale whose impression would not be forgotten, keeping alive the memory of builder pharaohs such as Amenemhat III (cat. 39) and Ramesses II.

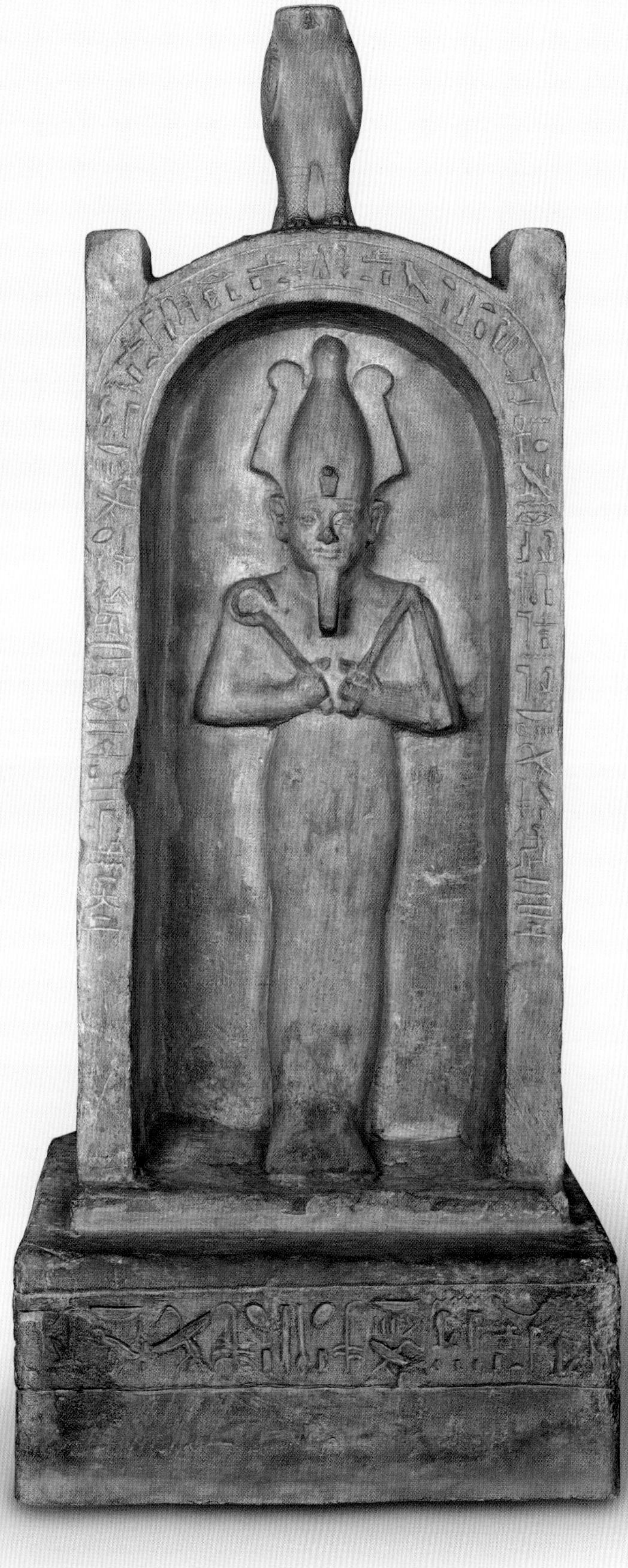

39

Miniature sanctuary dedicated to the god Osiris, Egypt, New Kingdom (c. 1539–1069 BCE).

The throne name of Amenemhat III, Ny-maat-re, is inscribed in a cartouche on the roof of this private votive monument, made more than seven centuries after his reign.

53

Sphinx of Nectanebo I,
Egypt, reign of Nectanebo I
(380–361 BCE).

The inscription on the base bears both Nectanebo's birth name and his throne name, Kheper-Ka-re, which he took from Senwosret I.

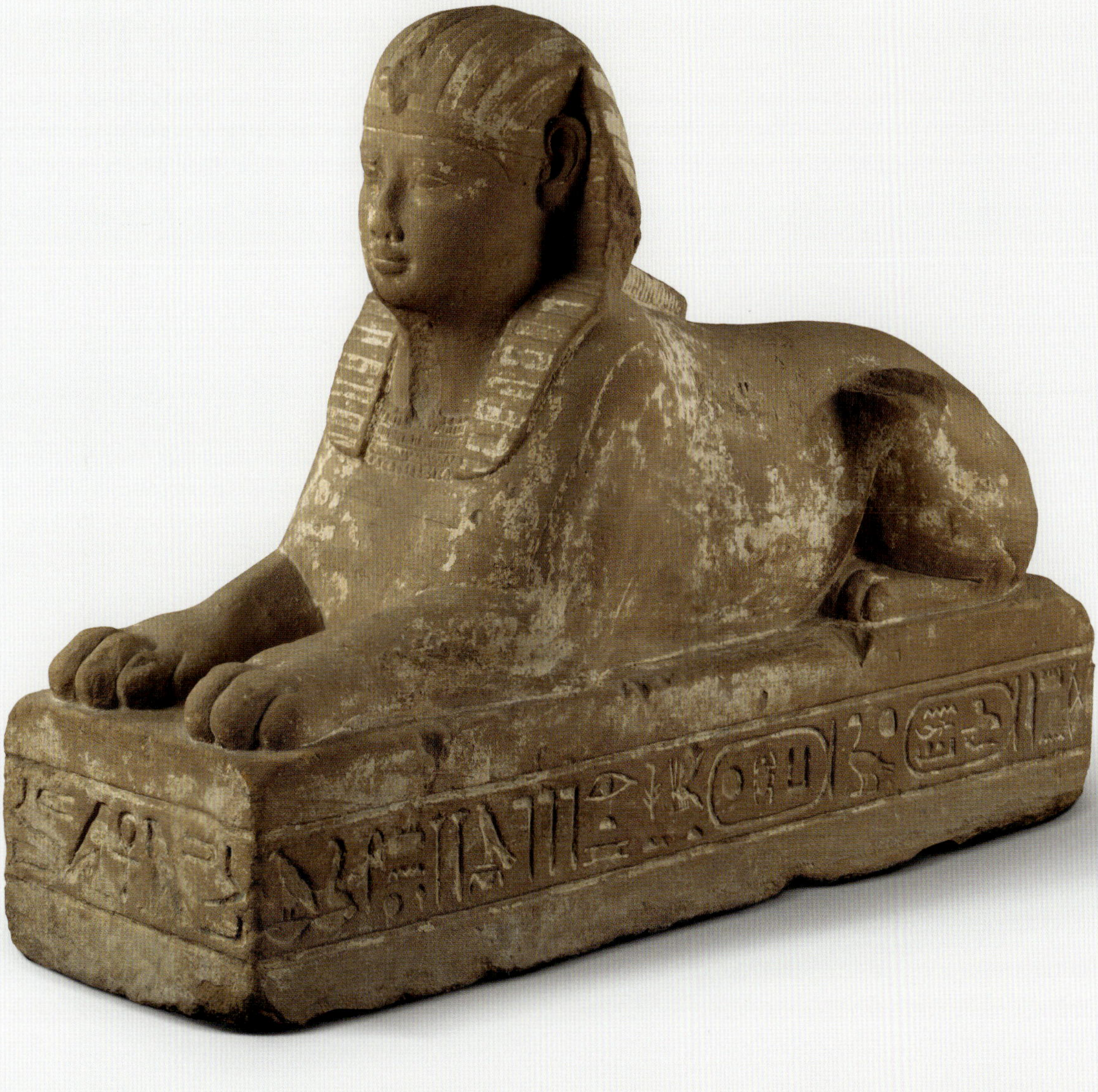

KEEPING THE FLAME ALIGHT

Pharaonic monarchy was based on the principle of continuity of power from the first mythical era. For the kings, it was therefore important to emphasize the links binding them to their predecessors, by dedicating to them – centuries later – monuments, statues or 'ancestral chambers' in the great temples. In this exhibition, several sculptures are related to these royal cults. The great pharaoh Senwosret III held such sway over his successors at the end of the Twelfth Dynasty and during the Thirteenth Dynasty that they even sought to replicate the distinguishing features of his portraits in their own images (cats. 11 and 22). Sometimes, the sovereign would adopt the throne name of a famous predecessor: thus Nectanebo I — one thousand five hundred and twenty years later – took the name of Senwosret I, as the inscription on the Louvre sphinx testifies (cat. 53).
The memorial cults of deceased kings, mostly financed by the Crown since the Old Kingdom, were served by large numbers of dedicated clergy, to the extent that a substantial portion of the Egyptian population was employed in keeping alive the posthumous memory of a few pharaohs. Many statues and bas-reliefs attest to this, bringing to our attention a few individuals who were active in the administration and rituals of temples dedicated to kings who had been dead for several centuries (Senedj, Teti, Thutmose III).
Pharaonic literature, written and preserved on papyri and *ostraca*,[1] regularly names and features former rulers. Generation after generation, apprentice scribes and scholars copied the great literary classics over and over again, preserving the memory of deceased kings in their own way. Texts such as 'Sneferu and the Oarswomen' in the Papyrus Westcar, the 'Instruction of Amenemhat', the 'Tale of Sinuhe' and the 'Inebriation of Amasis' describe kings in situations that are far removed from the dignity conferred upon them by their supreme function (Sneferu and Amasis) or, conversely, eulogize them (Amenemhat I and Senwosret I).

[1] *Ostracon*, plur. *ostraca*: a Greek word meaning a sliver of limestone or a pottery shard used as a support for writing or drawing.

THE EXEMPLARY CASE OF THE FOUNDERS OF THE NEW KINGDOM

The Egyptians, conscious of the historical role played by some of their rulers, particularly venerated those responsible for great periods of prosperity. The first sovereigns of the New Kingdom, Ahmose and his wife Ahmose-Nefertari, were seen as the country's benefactors, having repulsed invasions by their enemies, the Hyksos. Later, under the Ramesses dynasty, in the Theban region, their son Amenhotep I became, like his parents, a local patron saint of everyday life and the afterlife. This is an exemplary case, because the abundance of available sources concerning these specific circumstances allows us to examine the detail of practices linked to many posthumous monuments and objects, all of which reveal deep devotion and confidence in the sovereigns' power.

THE DOOMED KINGS

From antiquity onwards, *damnatio memoriae* attached to the memory of some kings, as well as to some members of civil society. The most effective way of achieving it was to supress their images and erase their names, thus directly attacking the material supports of the shunned souls.
The sculptor would deface or destroy these elements, obliterating the being who was portrayed or named.
The reign of Queen Hatshepsut was very quickly erased from memory by her successor Thutmose III in the fifteenth century BCE. This exceptional female pharaoh was ambitious and a good strategist, but badly upset the patrilinear monarchy: the royal *uraeus* (a rearing cobra), which decorated her forehead on statues, was erased, while her name on her monuments was chiselled away and replaced by that of her predecessor or successor. The same treatment was meted out to the memory of the most famous ill-fated sovereigns, the reformers Akhenaten and Nefertiti (fourteenth century BCE), who attempted to introduce a different political agenda and the almost exclusive worship of the solar disc Aten. It was not long before they were seen as destabilizing the kingdom and insulting the gods. Their images were mutilated, their names erased, their statues broken. Tutankhamun, heir to the disgraced couple, was associated by his successors with this discredited royal episode. And in fact Hatshepsut, Akhenaten and Tutankhamun no longer appeared in the king lists compiled during the Ramesses dynasty, in the thirteenth century BCE. The irony of history is that some of these individuals are now superstars. **GA-L/FM**

MONUMENTS ON THE HORIZON

'Make many monuments for god, because it means the perpetuation of the name of the one who does so'. The 'Instruction for Merikare' — a collection of the pharaoh Kheti's advice to his son — thus emphasizes the importance of erecting temples and statues for the deity, not only to obtain his favour, but to be remembered and so attain a form of eternal life. It is notable that the rulers who have been remembered for longest were builders. The great pyramids of the Old Kingdom are like artificial mountains: for thousands of years they have dominated the very flat horizon in the vicinity of Memphis, close to the present day Cairo, daily making their mark on the landscape for countless generations living locally (cat. 30). So, for instance, in the necropolis of Abusir, during the reign of Ramesses II, a scribe who came with his father to worship

31

Lee Miller, *The Shadow of the Great Pyramid*, Giza, Egypt, c. 1937.

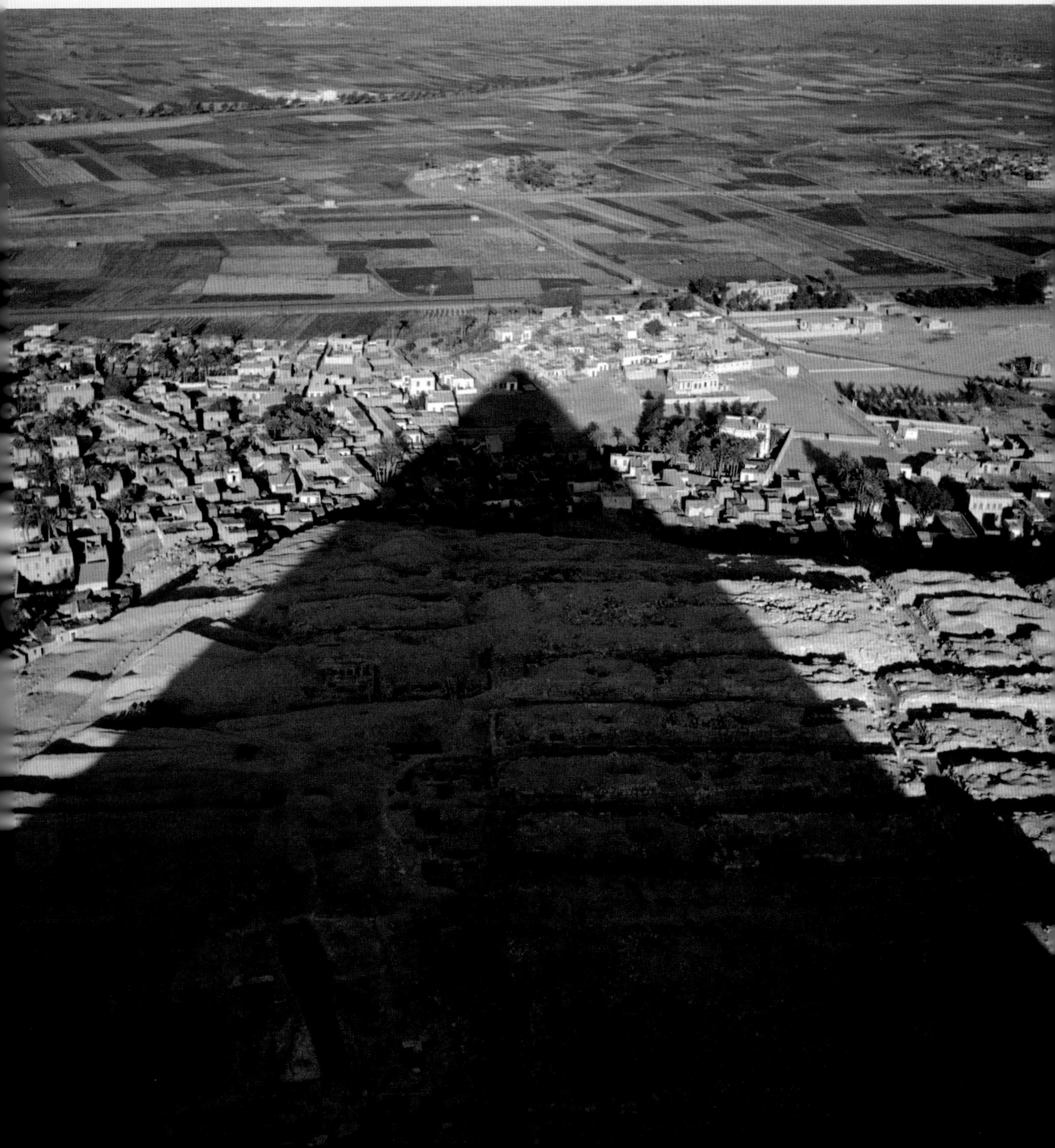

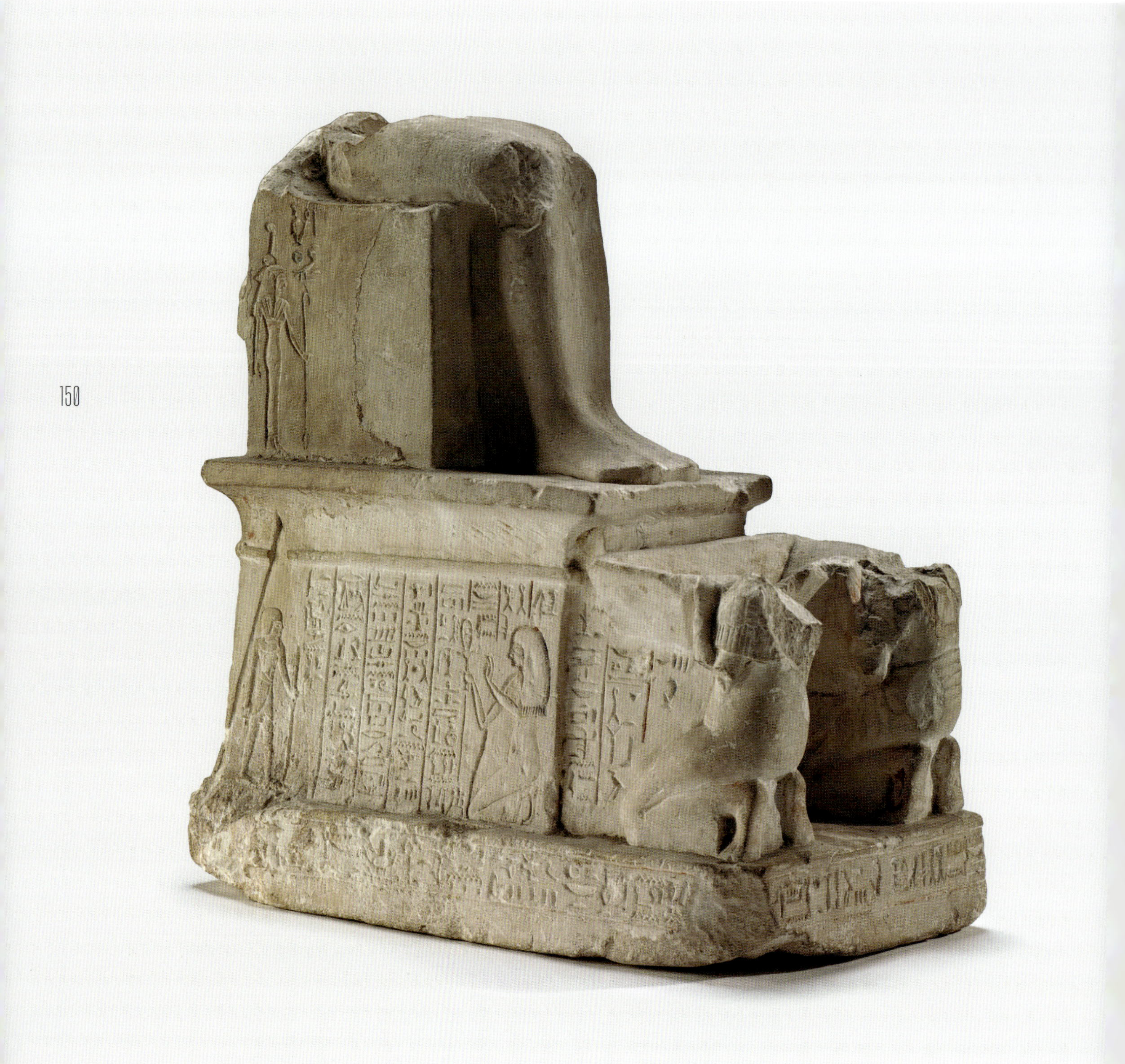

an image of the goddess Sekhmet in the funerary temple of King Sahure left graffiti asserting that he liked to 'contemplate the shadow of the pyramids' built more than a thousand years earlier. As it happens, he was living at a time when ancient monuments were being studied and restored, under the aegis of the pharaoh and his son Khaemweset. In this period too, the Serapeum — the necropolis of the sacred Apis bulls at Saqqara — was much visited by people living in the area. To reach it, they had to pass close by the pyramid of Teti, which had stood there for more than eleven centuries, and probably the pyramid of Menkauhor as well, which was even older but is now entirely destroyed. This is no doubt why these two pharaohs are locally documented among the deities of the necropolis. A small statue group, dedicated to Osiris by a couple of private individuals, shows Teti standing inside his pyramid — one of the very rare ancient depictions of a royal tomb (cat. 35). The deceased ruler, venerated by the man and the woman, one on each side of the sculpture's base, is positioned as an intercessor between them and the great god of the dead seated above them. Similarly, on a contemporary stela found in the Serapeum, Teti is presenting flowers to Osiris on behalf of the dedicant shown in the lower register (cat. 36).

The presence of a pyramid thus prolongs the name of the sovereign buried beneath it — but not in perpetuity: in the first century BCE, when Diodorus Siculus visited Egypt, the identity of the pyramids' builders was debated (*Bibliotheca historica*, I, 64). The pyramid of Khufu, the tallest and most imposing, nevertheless preserved the memory of the king throughout the pharaonic civilization and brought him his present fame. In the fifth century BCE, despite the fact that the official posthumous cult of this pharaoh was then being financed and maintained (cat. 34), Herodotus revived a historical fable, emanating from a doubtless ancient tradition, which paints an incriminating portrait of the Great Pyramid's builder: for its construction he supposedly ruined the country, embezzled the temples' riches and prostituted his daughter (*Histories*, II, 124–6).

35

Votive monument dedicated to the god Osiris and the pharaoh Teti, Saqqara, Egypt, late Eighteenth to early Nineteenth Dynasty (c. 1388–1280 BCE).

30

Émile Burdet, view of Khufu's pyramid reflected in the Nile, Giza, Egypt, late nineteenth to early twentieth century.

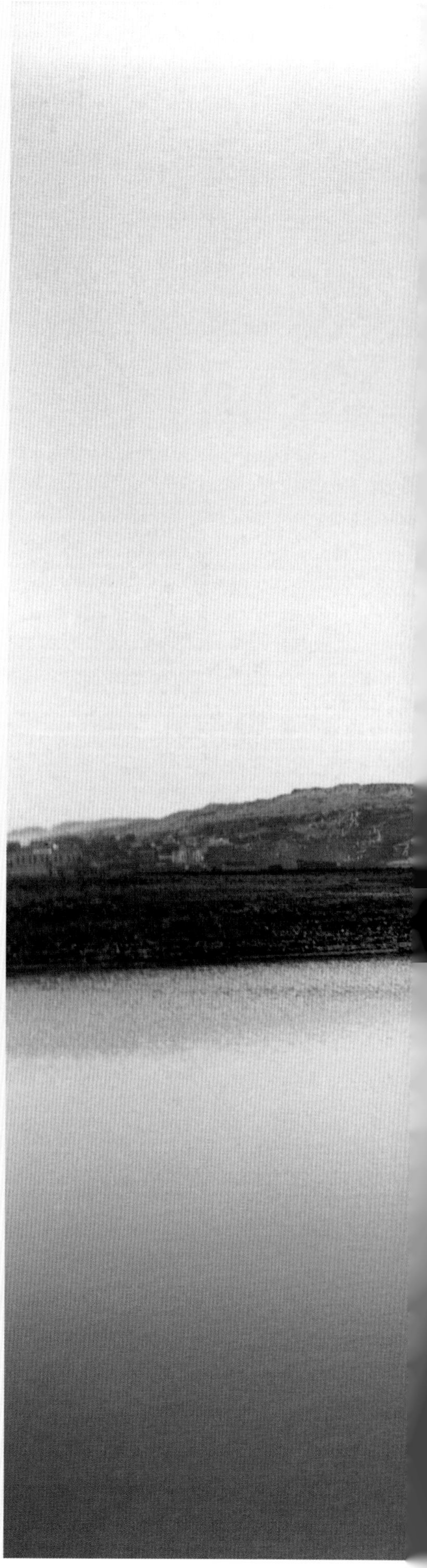

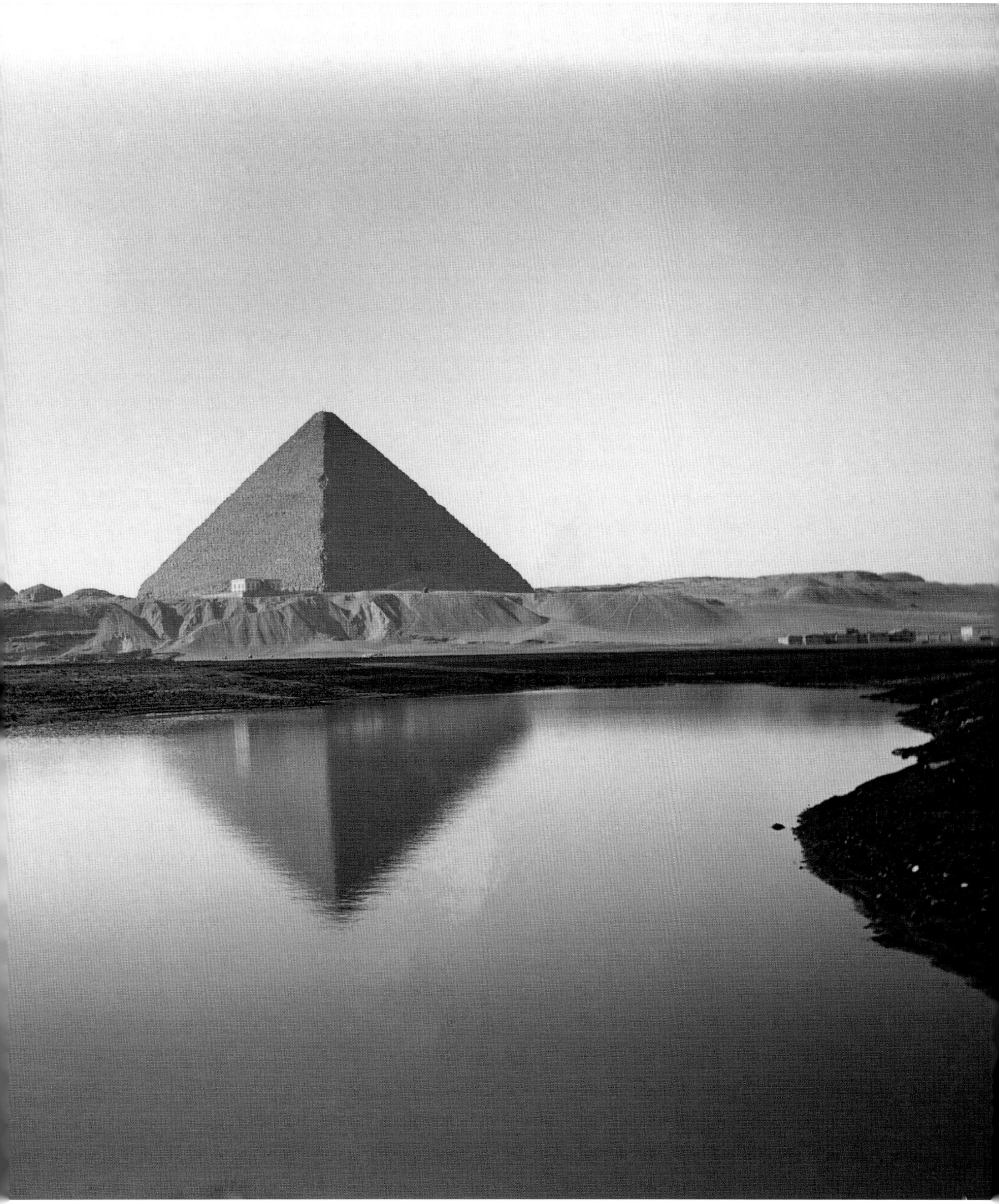

34

Stela mentioning priests serving the cult of Khufu, Khafre and Djedefre two thousand years after these pharaohs reigned, Serapeum of Saqqara, Egypt, 487 BCE.

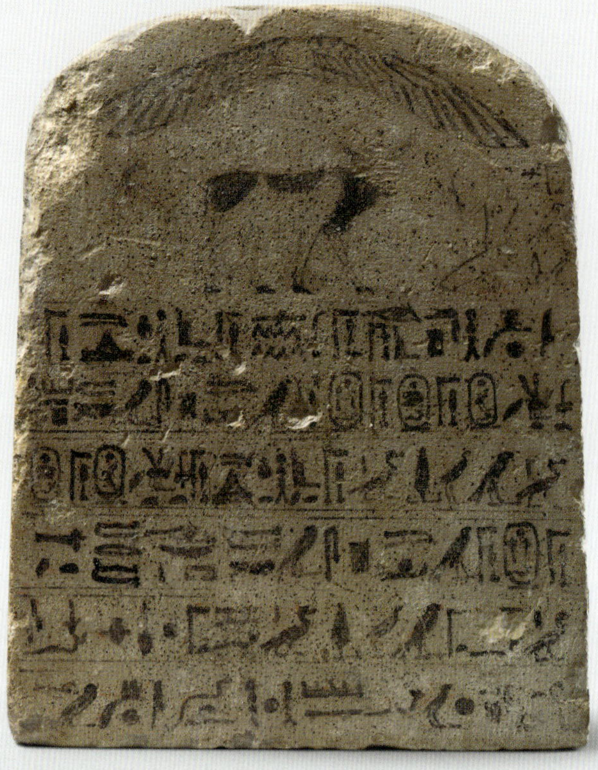

Effigies that have survived for centuries also preserve the memories of those they portray. Herodotus' Egyptian informants could reconstruct a genealogy covering 345 generations from colossi in a temple (*Histories*, II, 143). Like the pyramids, these gigantic statues made their mark on the Egyptian landscape with their height and their siting. Amenemhat III commissioned the building of two colossi, showing him seated on the shores of Lake Qarun, in Faiyum, which must have appeared to be rising out of the waves like the creator god when the waters were high. These monuments, more than eleven metres tall, were visible from afar for a very long time and certainly contributed to the pharaoh's posthumous renown (cat. 38). More usually placed in front of temple gates or in their courtyards — the only spaces accessible to ordinary mortals — colossi could be venerated as intermediaries between the faithful and the god concealed inside the sanctuary. Examples include the images of Amenhotep III in front of his funerary temple at Luxor, now known as the 'Colossi of Memnon'. There is even more surviving evidence of a cult devoted to images of Ramesses II, masterminded by the pharaoh himself (cat. 45). The many statues bearing the name of this pharaoh, whether he commissioned them himself or expropriated them, significantly added

36

Stela dedicated to the gods Osiris and Apis, Serapeum of Saqqara, Egypt, late Eighteenth to early Nineteenth Dynasty (c. 1388–1089 BCE).

More than a thousand years after his reign, Teti is here shown interceding with Osiris, in the context of the funerary cult of the sacred bull Apis.

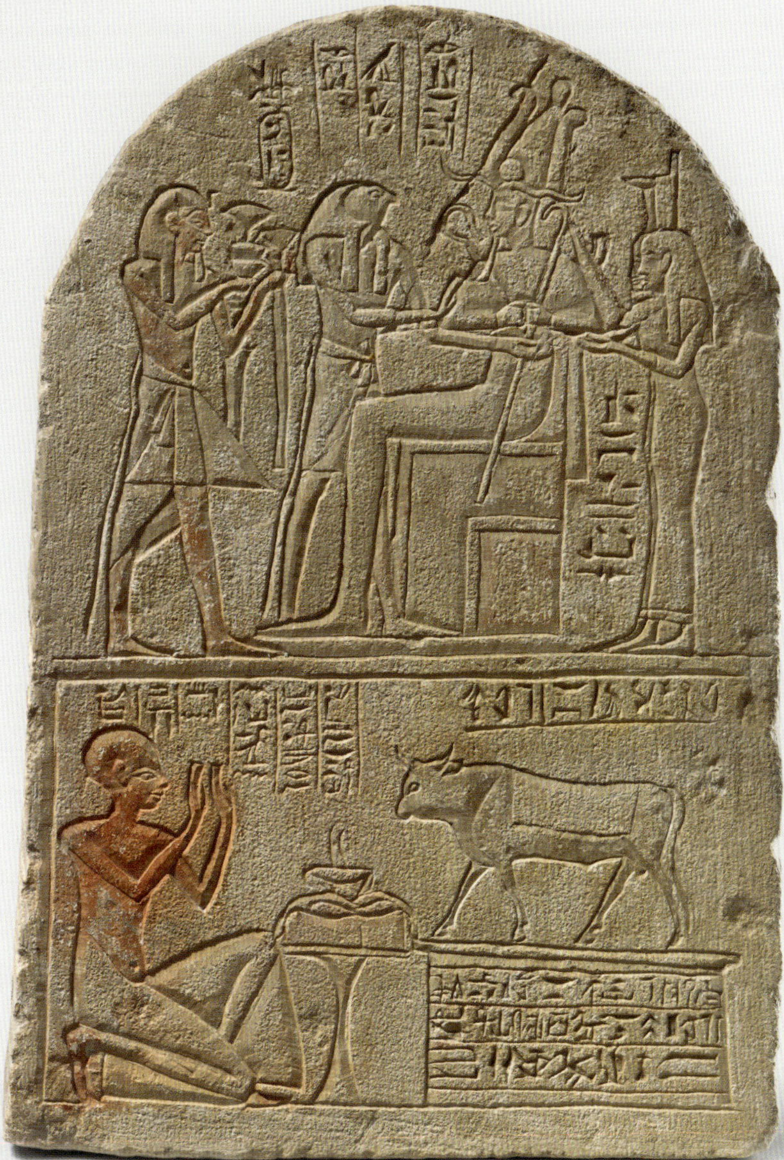

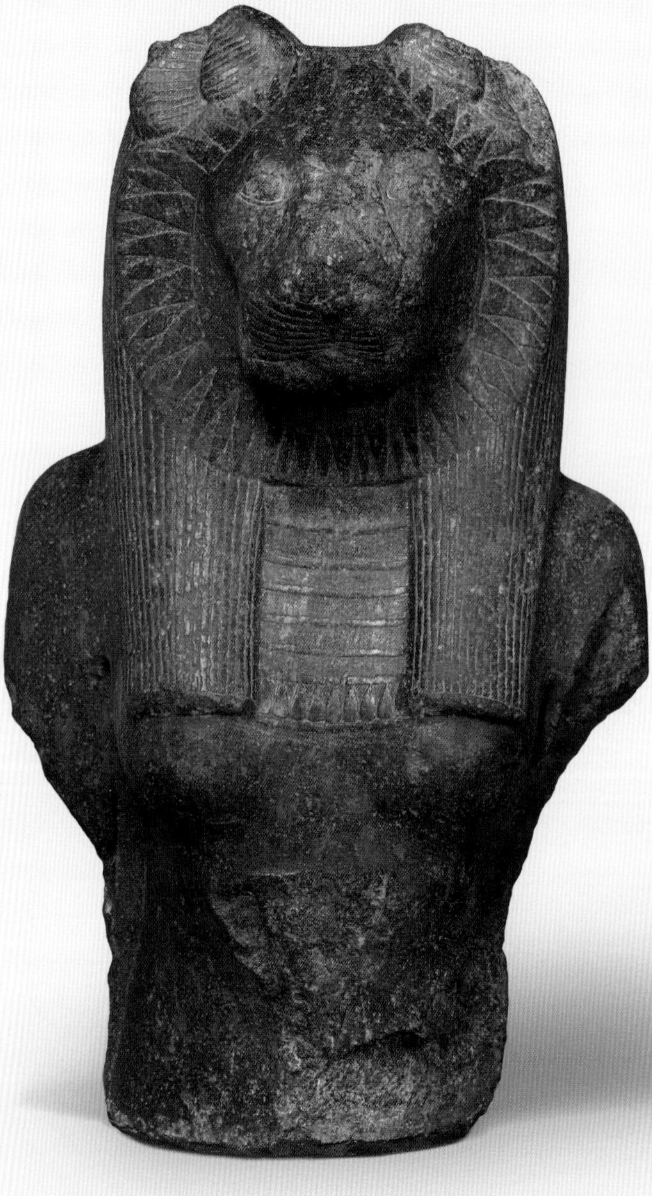

47

Bust of a statue of the goddess Sekhmet, Egypt, reigns of Amenhotep III (c. 1388–1349 BCE) and Ramesses II (c. 1279–1212 BCE).

The statue was carved for Amenhotep III, but the cartouche of Ramesses II was added on the back pillar.

to his celebrity in antiquity and since his rediscovery in the nineteenth century (cat. 47). His memory has long been perpetuated through them, even when legend attributed them to Sesostris or Ozymandias — a Hellenized version of Ramesses' throne name Usermaatre — whose ruined colossus inspired Percy B. Shelley to write a sonnet on the impermanence of power (1817). And it is not by chance that Nasser, in 1955, installed a colossus of Ramesses in front of Cairo station, in Ramses Square (Midan Ramsis), so as to give a splendid welcome to travellers arriving in the capital of his new republic. **FM**

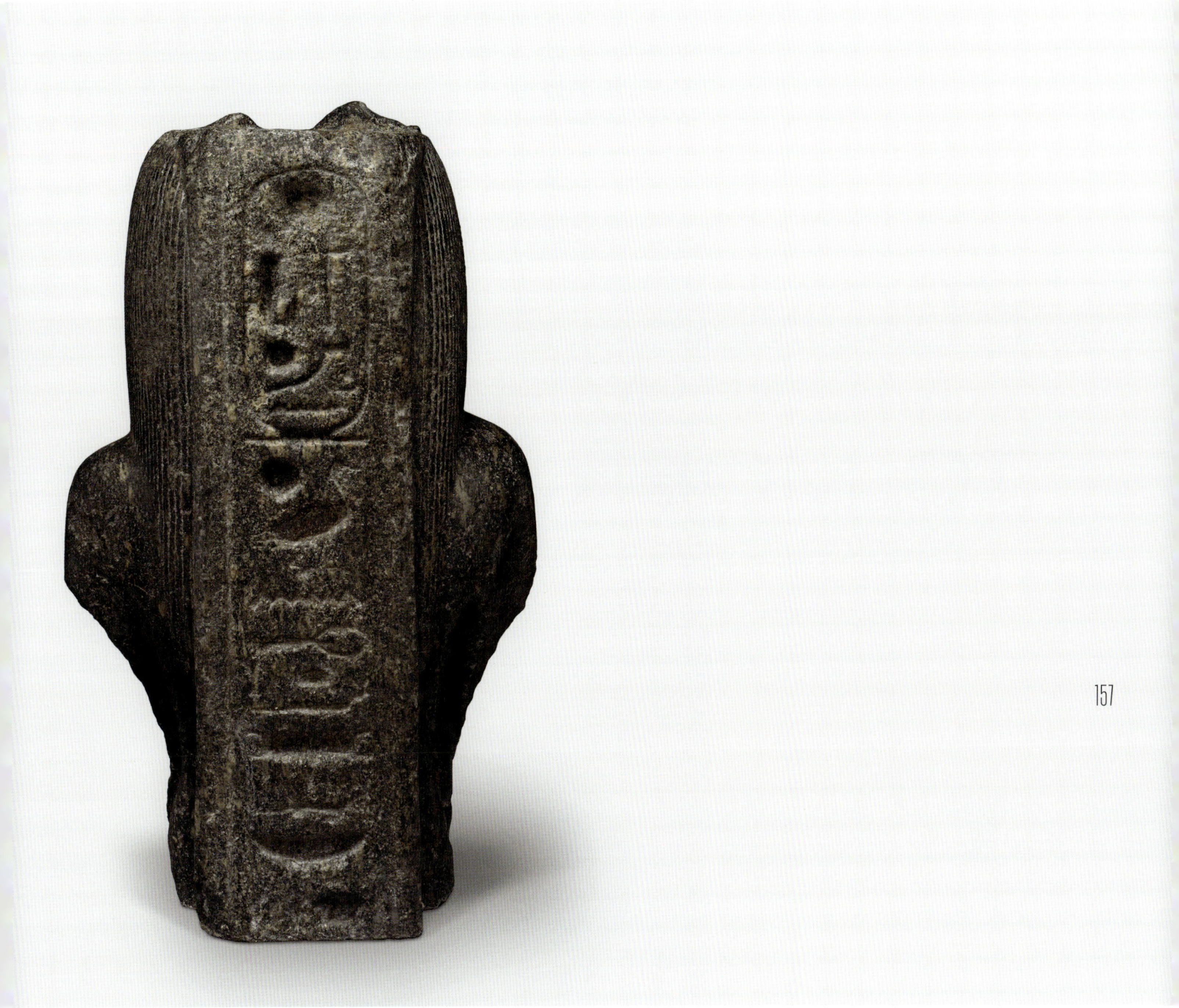

BERLANDINI-GRENIER, J., 'Varia Memphitica I', in *BIFAO* 76, Cairo, 1976, pp. 301–16.

PRICE, C., 'Ramesses, 'King of Kings': On the Context and Interpretation of Royal Colossi', in COLLIER, M., SNAPE, S., *Ramesside Studies in Honour of K. A. Kitchen*, Bolton, 2011, pp. 403–11.

RYHOLT, K., 'Egyptian Historical Literature from the Greco-Roman Period', in FITZENREITER, M. (ed.), *Das Ereignis Geschichtsschreibung zwischen Vorfall und Befund*, in *IBAES X*, London, 2009, pp. 231–8.

FROM AMENEMHAT TO MOERIS

Phamarres, Premarres, Preamarres, Poramarres in documents from Egypt written in Greek; Lamares, Lamaris or Lampares in the writings of Manetho; Moeris, Moteris, Marros, Mendes, Menas, Ismandes in texts by Greek authors... The reason these names seem strange is that they are adaptations made to fit a script that was foreign to Egypt — the Greek that was used under Ptolemaic rule by the successors of Alexander the Great. Yet behind them all are the hieroglyphs *Per-aâ-Maâ-Rê*, 'the pharaoh Maât-Rê', deriving from Nymaatre, the throne name of Amenemhat III, a Middle Kingdom sovereign who had lived some 1,500 years earlier (cat. 26). All these different forms tell us about the difficulty of using the Greek alphabet to transcribe Egyptian pronunciation in a single way, but also about the need to preserve the memory of the pharaoh, since tradition had deified him and made him a 'saint' of Faiyum. There was indeed every reason to ensure his sanctified memory endured, since the activities of this enlightened monarch had left their stamp permanently on the province: the land had been improved, with marshes transformed into irrigated and cultivable fields; colossi had been erected in his image at the place called Biahmu (cats. 38 and 38A); a sumptuous pyramid had been built at Hawara, flanked by a mortuary temple the like of which had never been seen and an immense temple dedicated to the myriad forms of the crocodile god Sobek. The British Museum stela (cat. 41) comes

41

Stela dedicated to the deified Amenemhat III, Hawara, Egypt, Ptolemaic period (240–200 BCE).

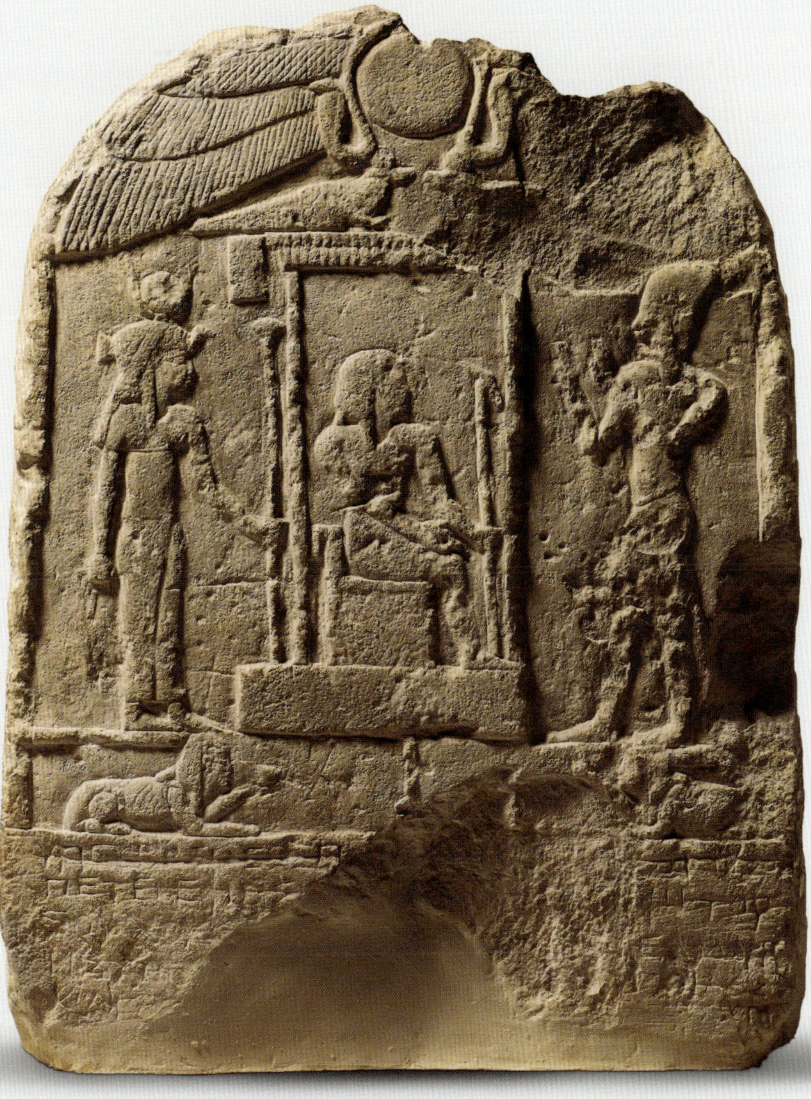

26

Head of a sphinx of Amenemhat III, Egypt, reign of Amenemhat III (c. 1838–1794 BCE).

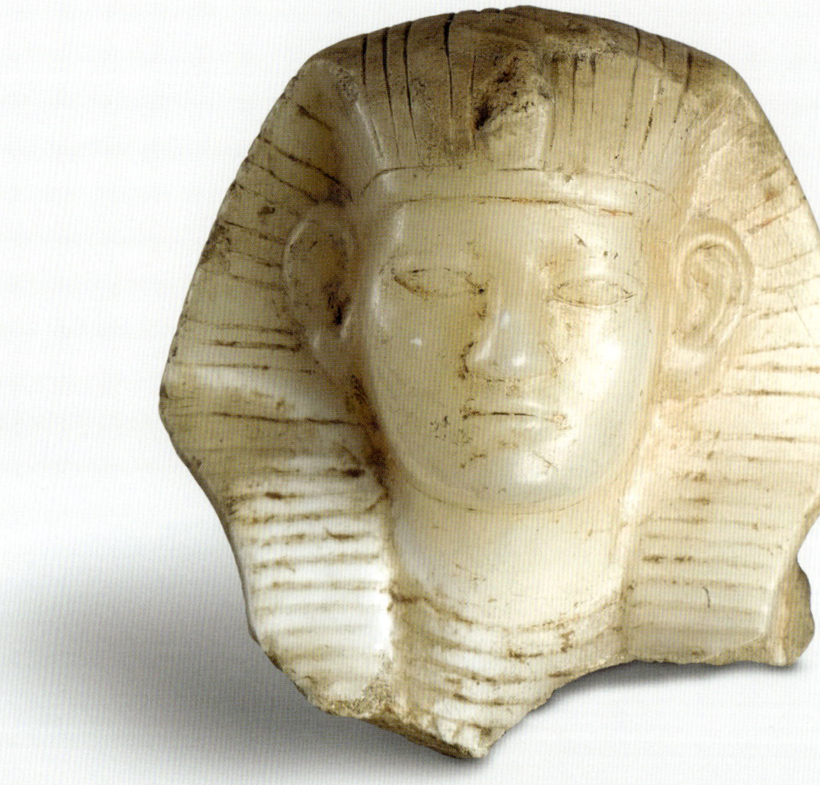

from this site. There is no hieroglyph naming the figures in this scene. And yet it easy to recognize on the right a Ptolemaic king praying to Pramares — the deified Amenemhat III — in the inner sanctum of his chapel, with two crocodiles above, and clearly identified by the *nemes* (a striped headcloth) that he wears; behind him there is a standing goddess, probably Isis. Reality — re-established and proven by archaeology — soon gave way to fantasy: Amenemhat III was credited with the model for the Labyrinth designed by Daedalus for the Minotaur. After seeing it, Herodotus said that it 'surpassed the pyramids' and one of Amenemhat's names, Moeris, was given to the salt lake on the edge of the Faiyum basin, which was reputed to have been dug by divine hands.

Like Senwosret III, his father, Amenemhat III embodied the perfection demanded of the pharaoh, who was expected to assure the divine order that regulated the world: both in the vigour of youth, when he had to defend the country against real or mythical enemies (cat. 40), and with the wisdom of maturity which brought the moderation and justice appropriate to perfect government.

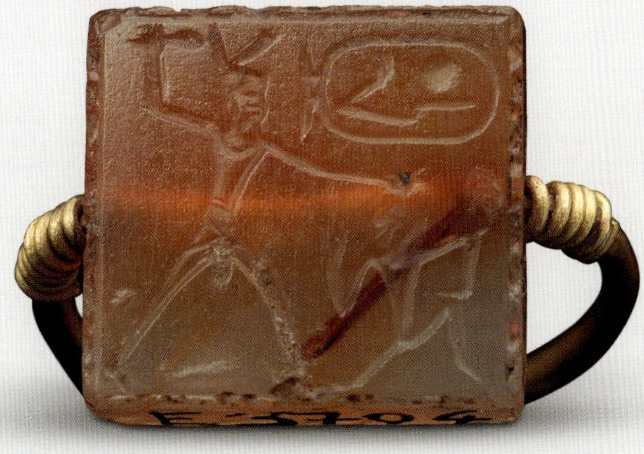

40

Ring decorated with an image of Amenemhat III killing an enemy, Egypt, Late Period (c. 664–332 BCE).

This jewel, worn as an amulet, was intended to attract the protection of the revered king who had died a thousand years earlier.

There are several known instances of a canonical iconography representing the meeting between two deities: Pramarres and Sobek-Re, the principal god of Faiyum. The scene shows the face to face encounter between the god — importantly identified as a solar figure — and the pharaoh saint who is recognizable from his *nemes*, the very distinctive headcloth worn specifically by sovereigns: it can be seen on the sphinx at Giza as well as on the mask of Tutankhamun, the colossi of Abu Simbel and the statue of Amenemhat III. Both are raising their right hands in greeting, son to father and father to son, since the pharaoh was, as his titulary indicates, 'son of Ra'. These images are datable to the second century CE, the period when Egypt was a province of the Roman Empire, ruled by the emperor of Rome, who was crowned pharaoh in accordance with ancient protocols. At this time, however, iconographic conventions had radically changed: it had been decided that the Egyptian gods could no longer be portrayed in accordance with the pharaonic canon but must, from that moment on, conform to the canon of Hellenism as diffused throughout the Empire. It was the end of the 'Egyptian profile', which

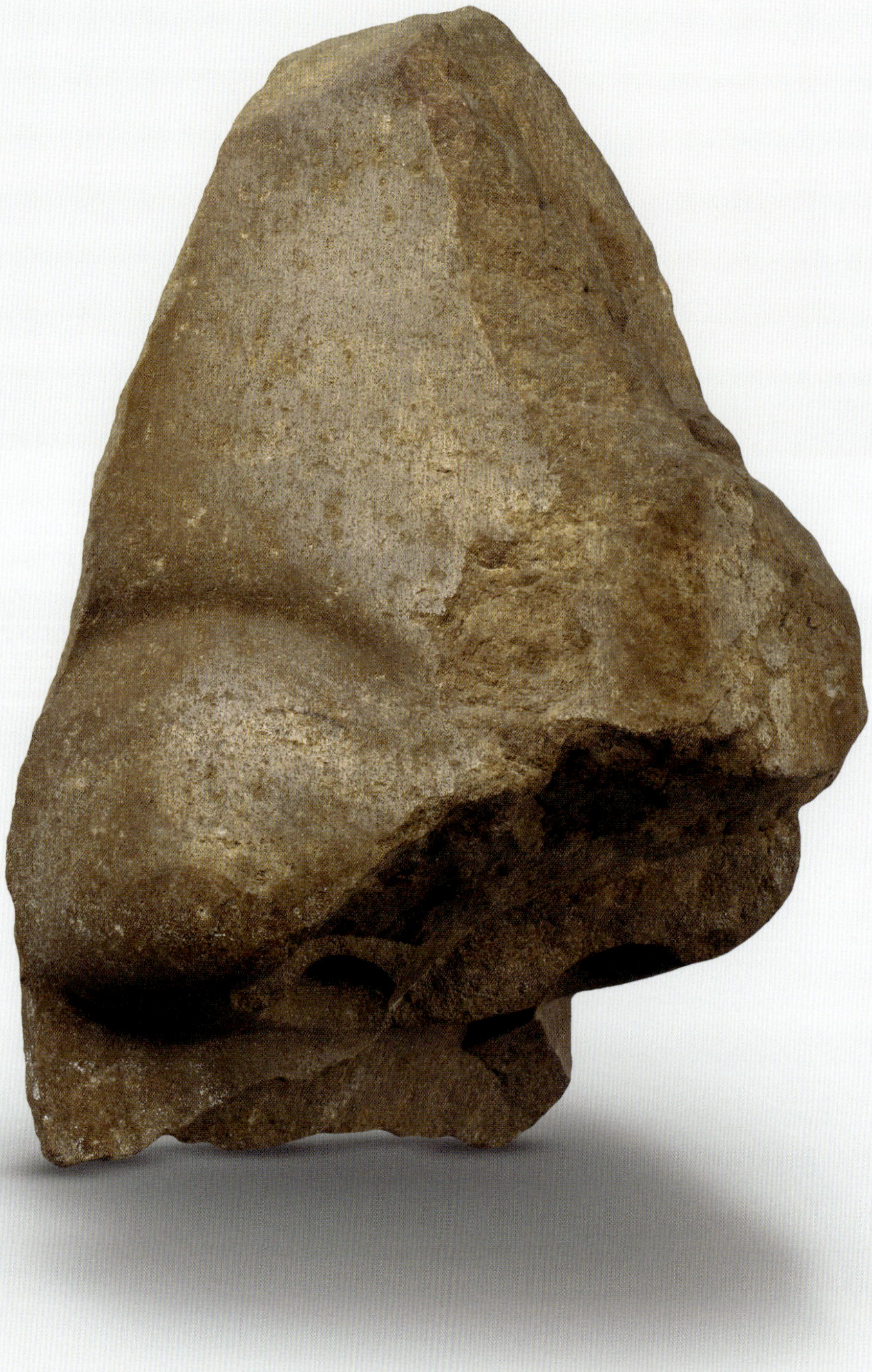

38

Nose of a colossus
of Amenemhat III, Biahmu,
Egypt, reign of Amenemhat III
(c. 1838–1794 BCE).

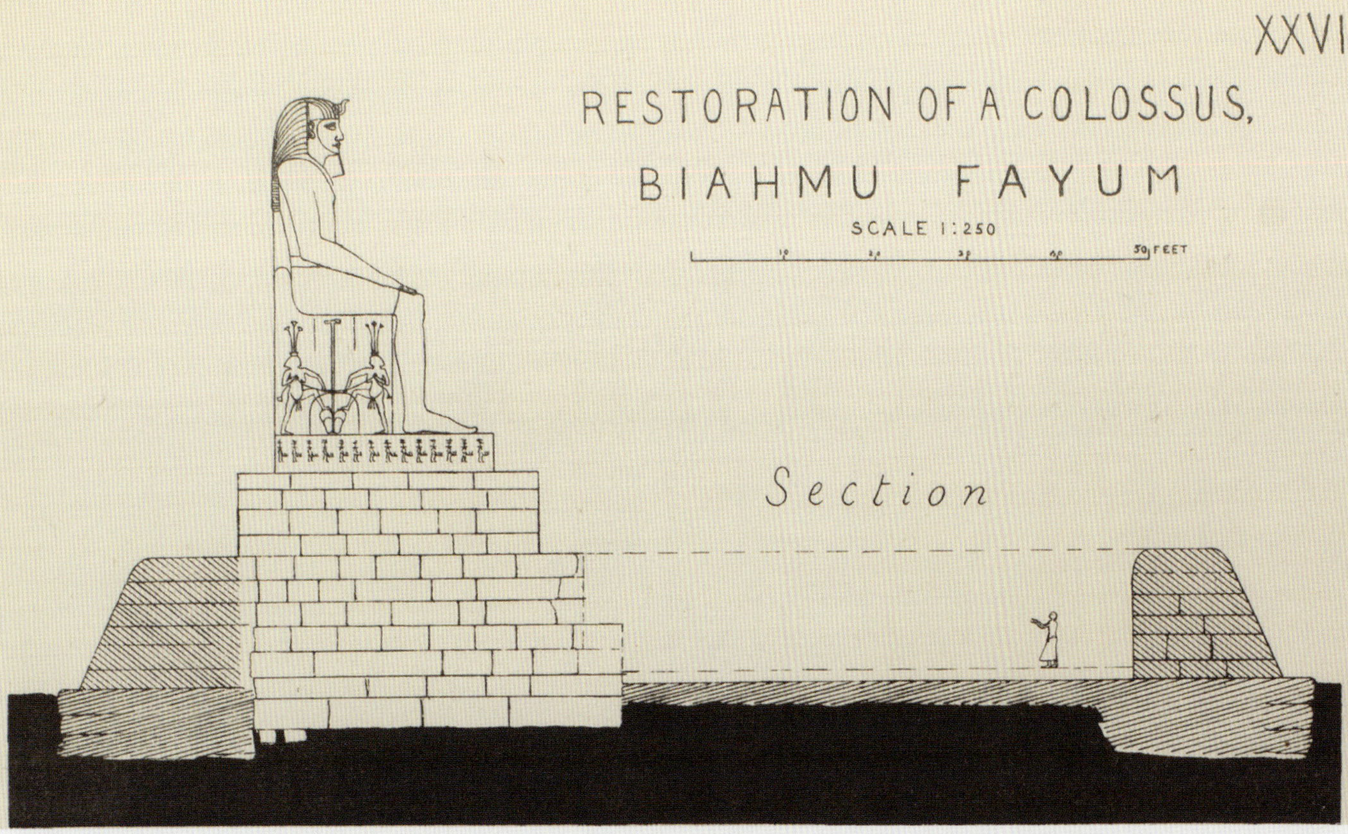

38A

Hypothetical reconstruction of a colossus of Amenemhat III at Biahmu by William Flinders Petrie, in *Hawara, Biahmu and Arsinoe*, 1889.

gave way to the contrapposto, the swaying stance of classical statuary; and the end of the crocodile's head attached to a man's body: Sobek became entirely human, a handsome young man wearing the Greek chiton and himation, his long hair nimbed with the rays of the sun like the Roman god Sol. Yet it was still essential that Sobek could be recognized in this exclusively human male body: the solution was to have him carry a small crocodile, like a pet, just as Jupiter carries his thunderbolt. Facing him, the pharaoh Nimaatre retains his *nemes*, so that he can still be recognized as a pharaoh, and wears a robe covered with the fringed shawl proper to deified figures. So it was that for several more centuries, until the end of paganism, the crocodile god known since the Old Kingdom and the pharaoh in his Middle Kingdom guise continued to be venerated, though now depicted just like Greek gods. **VR**

RONDOT, V., VASSILIEVA, O., 'Sobek-Rê et Pramarrès au musée Pouchkine', in GASSE, A., SERVAJEAN, Fr., THIERS, Chr. (eds), *Et in Ægypto et ad Ægyptum. Recueil d'études dédiées à Jean-Claude Grenier* IV, CENIM 5, Montpellier, 2012, pp. 667–74.

WIDMER, G., 'Pharaoh Maâ-Rê, Pharaoh Amenemhat and Sesostris: Three Figures from Egypt's Past as Seen in Sources of the Graeco-Roman Period', in RYHOLT, K. (ed.), *Acts of the Seventh International Conference of Demotic Studies*. Copenhagen, 23–7 August 1999, CNIP 27, Copenhagen, 2002, pp. 377–93.

THE FOUNDERS OF THE NEW KINGDOM

It is a cliché that Egypt's pharaonic history appears to have survived for more than three thousand years without a hitch, without any social or political disruption — but it is a cliché that must be qualified. Historians use the expression 'intermediate periods' to describe upheavals that destabilized and weakened the country, or invasions that it experienced. Just after the Second Intermediate Period, the New Kingdom was launched with the reigns of Ahmose, his wife Ahmose-Nefertari and their son Amenhotep I. Ahmose, who came from Thebes in Upper Egypt, expelled the Hyksos from the north-east of the Delta and led his reunified kingdom into a new, glorious and victorious era, giving back his country its unity and greatness. In later king lists, like the procession of statues of ancestor kings in the temple of Ramesses III at Medinet Habu more than three hundred years later, he appears as the founder of the New Kingdom next to the first pharaoh of the Middle Kingdom, Mentuhotep II. His military victories, as much in Nubia as in the Near East where the Hyksos came from, went hand in hand with a wide-ranging policy of restoration: he reopened mines and quarries, relaunched commercial and international relations, resumed levying taxes, reorganized temple foundations and planned monumental building works, principally in the Theban area.

60

Stela of the scribe Iry, dedicated to Ahmose and Ahmose-Nefertari, Egypt, late Eighteenth Dynasty (c. 1300 BCE).

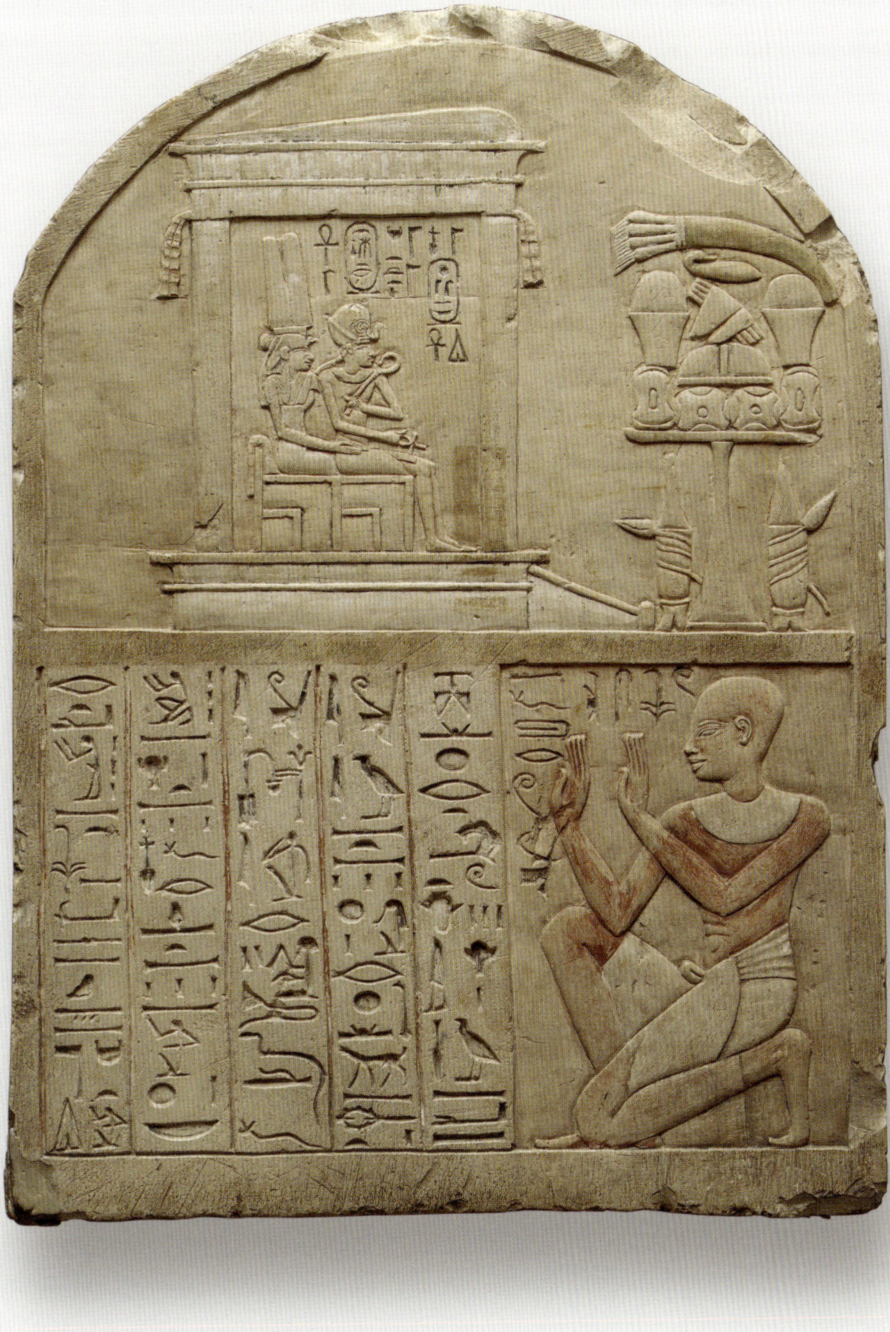

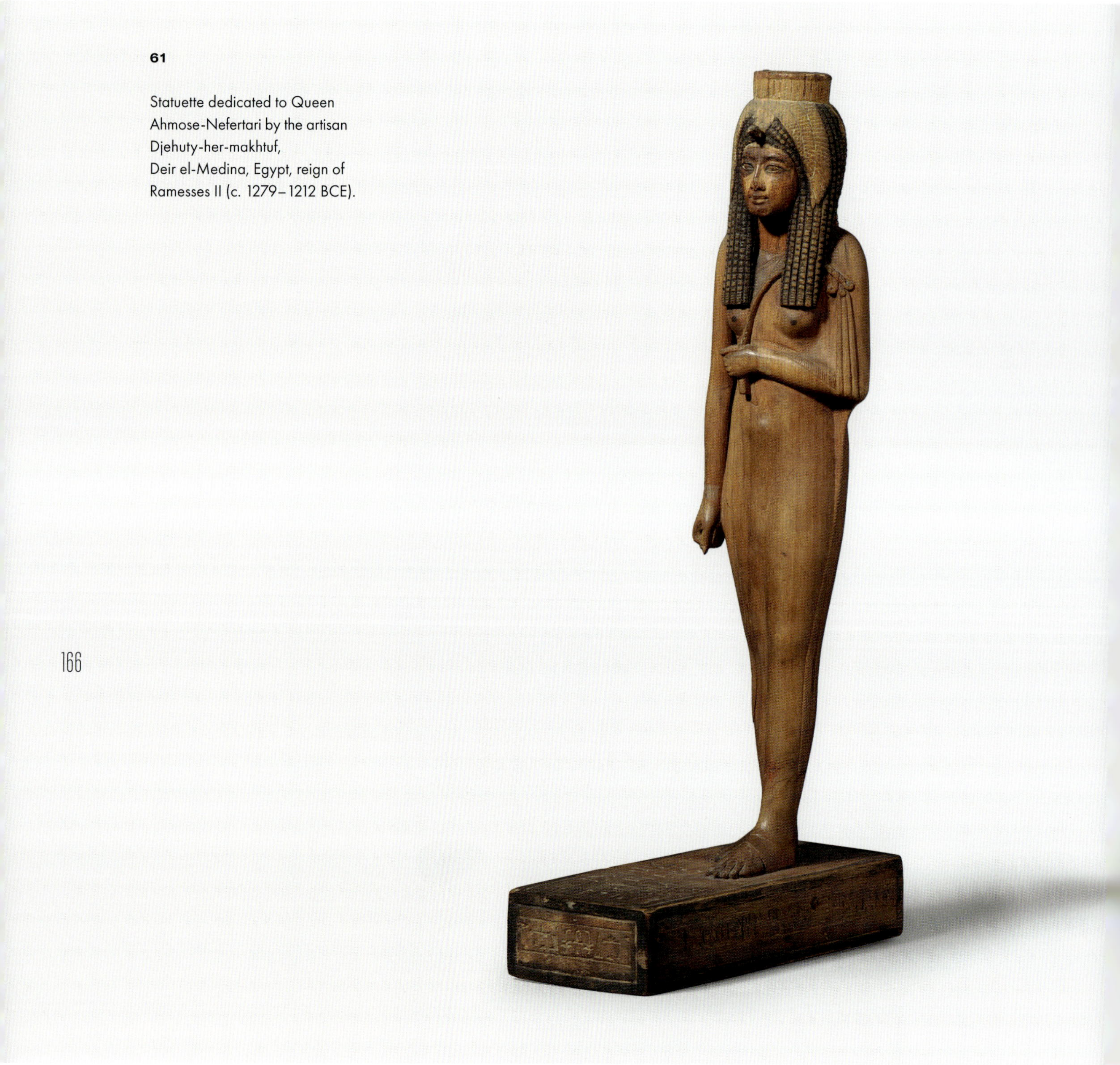

61

Statuette dedicated to Queen Ahmose-Nefertari by the artisan Djehuty-her-makhtuf, Deir el-Medina, Egypt, reign of Ramesses II (c. 1279–1212 BCE).

It seems that Ahmose was markedly influenced by the exploits, conquests and ambitions of the pharaoh Senwosret III, who reigned three centuries before him but whose memory and posthumous cult was still alive at the beginning of the New Kingdom. His fascination for his illustrious predecessor was manifested in architectural projects in Abydos, where Sesostris' tomb and mortuary temple inspired Ahmose also to build a monumental complex there. Ahmose was later the object of a posthumous cult and became a local patron saint.

62

Statuette dedicated to Queen Ahmose-Nefertari by the artisan Uadjmes, Deir el-Medina, Egypt, reign of Ramesses II (c. 1250 BCE).

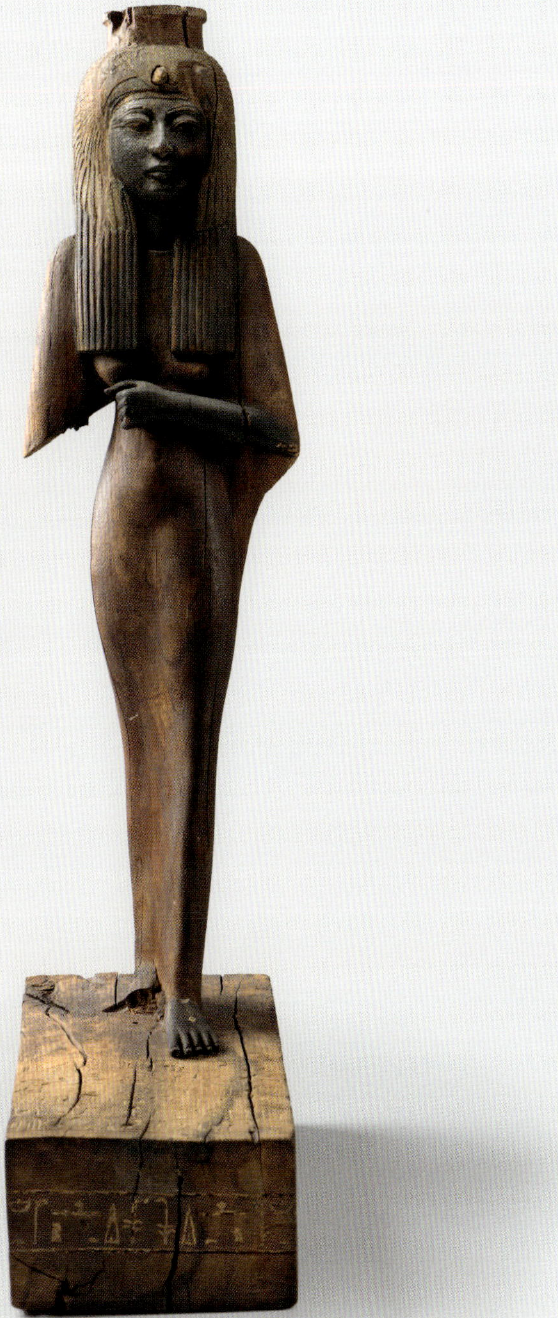

Much later, in our own twentieth century, Ahmose was once again remembered by the Egyptians as a hero of antiquity and featured in the school curriculum, commemorated as his country's liberator. The Egyptian writer Naguib Mahfouz wrote a novel about him in 1944, *Kifâh Tîba* (Thebes at War), in which the Hyksos who were to be expelled had all the characteristics of contemporary British colonisers (cat. 99).

In the early days of the New Kingdom, queens had a distinctive role alongside Ahmose. His wife Ahmose-Nefertari contributed to the family's

63

Stela offered to the deified Amenhotep I by the priest Aapanefu, Deir el-Medina, Egypt, Nineteenth or Twentieth Dynasty (thirteenth to twelfth century BCE).

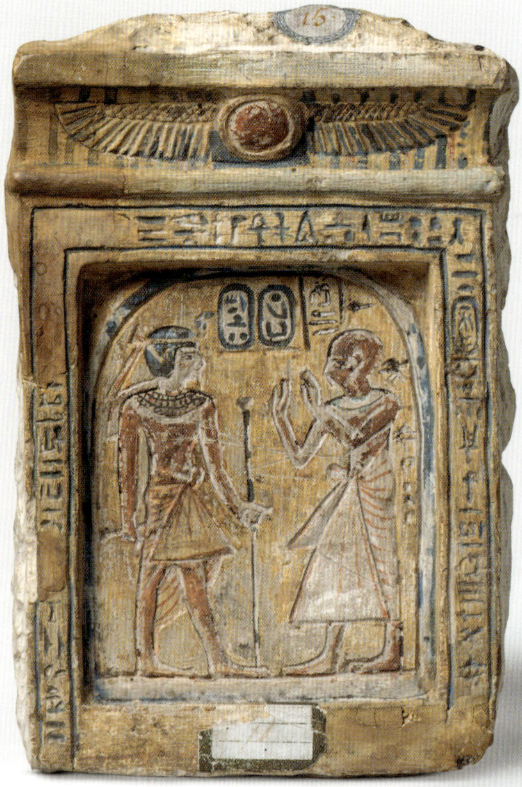

efforts to take the country in hand. As the first queen of Egypt to bear the title Divine Bride, she was given key priestly responsibilities in the great temple complex of the god Amun at Karnak. On the death of her husband, she became regent for her son, the pharaoh Amenhotep I, during his minority. Amenhotep carried on his parents' work and built many sanctuaries in the Theban region, where he was venerated long after his death.

From the reign of Amenhotep III (a century later), and more especially under Ramesses, several decades after that, the queen and her son became the objects of an exceptional posthumous cult, as protecting ancestors and esteemed Egyptian heroes. In a collective impulse, the Theban population placed itself under the auspices of this cult twosome. Countless votive objects (statuettes, bas-reliefs, ex-votos, stelae (cats. 61, 62 and 63) reveal the strength of devotion to them, particularly in Deir el-Medina (on the west bank of Thebes), where a community of craftworkers was engaged in building and decorating tombs in the Valley of the Kings and the Valley of the Queens. Devout practice inspired by the queen and her son was local and often private, confined to the family circle. Here, sympathetic ancestors were venerated, those who knew how to listen and answer prayers. Objects in the exhibition include the beautiful, very finely made stela dedicated by the scribe Iry to Ahmose and his queen Ahmose-Nefertari some two hundred years after their

71

Djedmut's shroud, with Amenhotep I replacing the god Osiris, Luxor, Egypt, Twenty-first Dynasty (c. 1069–943 BCE).

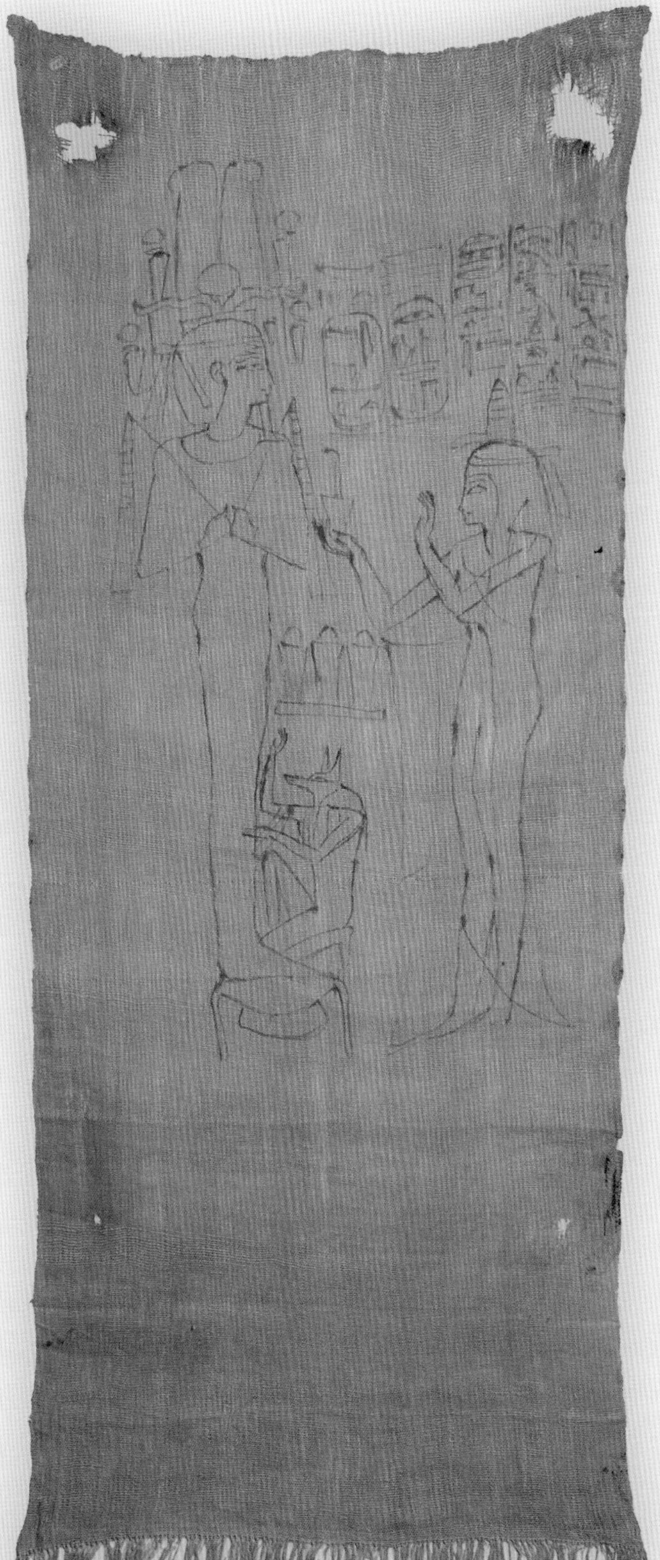

67

Fragment of a stela depicting the procession of a statue of Amenhotep I, Deir el-Medina, Egypt, Twentieth Dynasty (c. 1150 BCE).

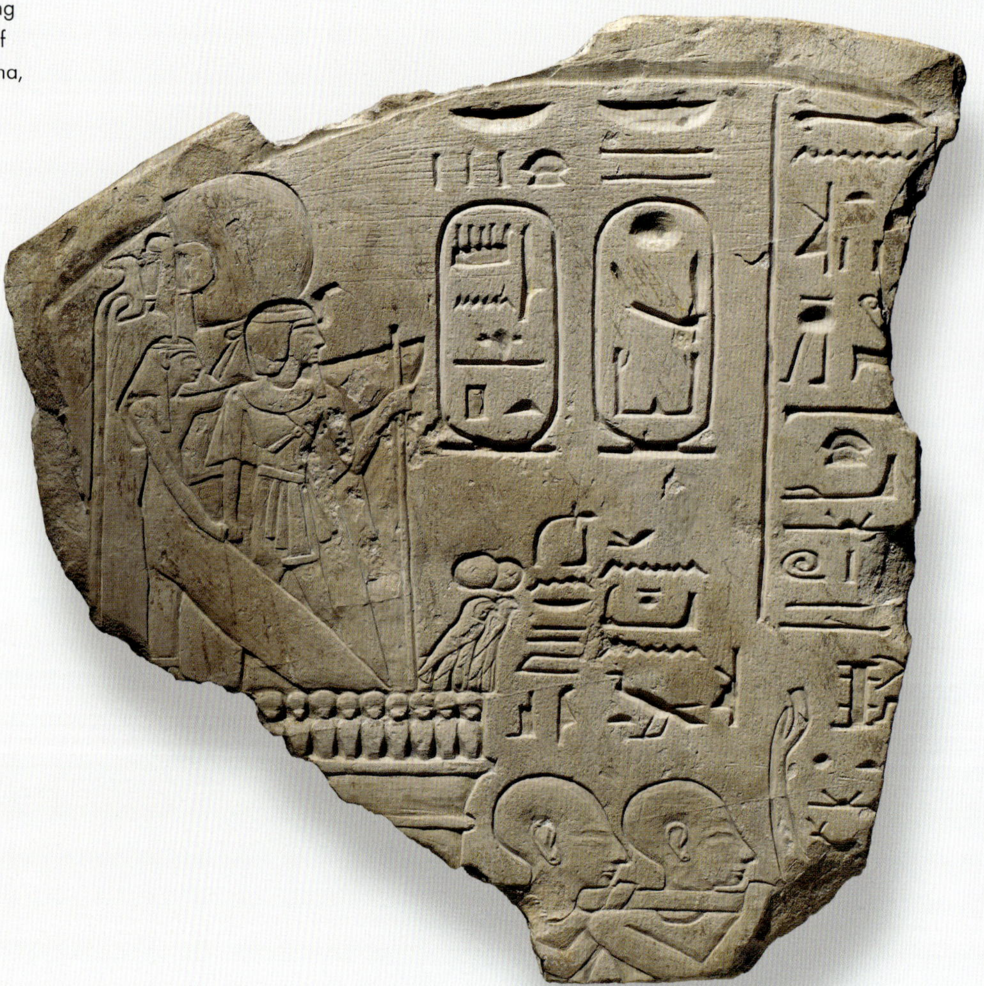

reign (cat. 60). The pair are shown in a chapel, seated in front of offerings. Below, Iry sets out his prayer, asking them to intervene with Ra 'who knows what is in the body, who judges the state of hearts, who responds to the voice of one calling to him and who is well-disposed to one who follows him'. This text expresses Iry's fear of Ra's judgement and his hope that the venerated pair will listen to him. This capacity for being sympathetic to requests and settling internal disagreements in the village is attested by the many 'questions to the oracles' asked of Amenhotep I's statue, carried in procession every year, and by the presence of carved ears on stelae, or even placed as votive objects at the foot of shrines (cats. 64, 67, 68 and 69). Festivals devoted to the deified king and his mother were so important in Thebes that from the thirteenth century BCE, the seventh month of the year was called 'that of Amenhotep' — a name that has been preserved in the Coptic calendar as Phamenoth.

One of the enigmas that attach to the portrayal of Ahmose-Nefertari is that she is sometimes shown as having a black skin (cat. 62). This may

64

Votive ears, Egypt, New Kingdom (c. 1539–1069 BCE).

Objects such as this were placed close to images of the gods to enhance their ability to hear prayers.

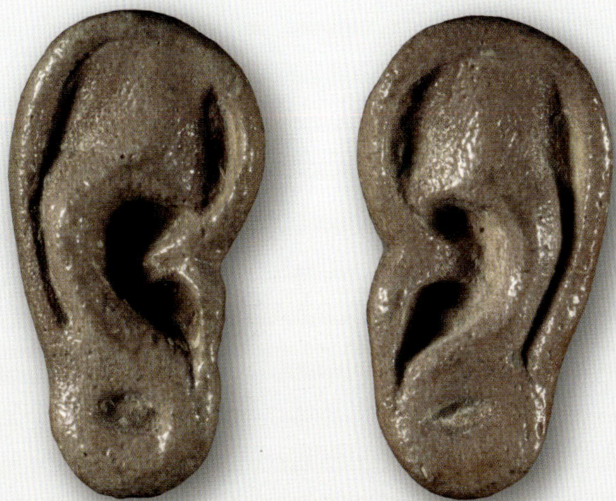

68–69

Two ostraca with questions for the oracle of Amenhotep I: 'Should I really write about them?' (above) and 'Will a paper knife be given to the two scribes?' (below), Deir el-Medina, Egypt, Nineteenth to Twentieth Dynasty (c. 1295–1069 BCE).

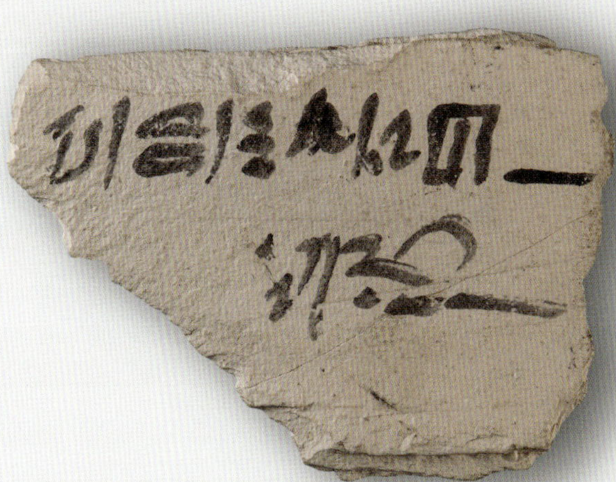

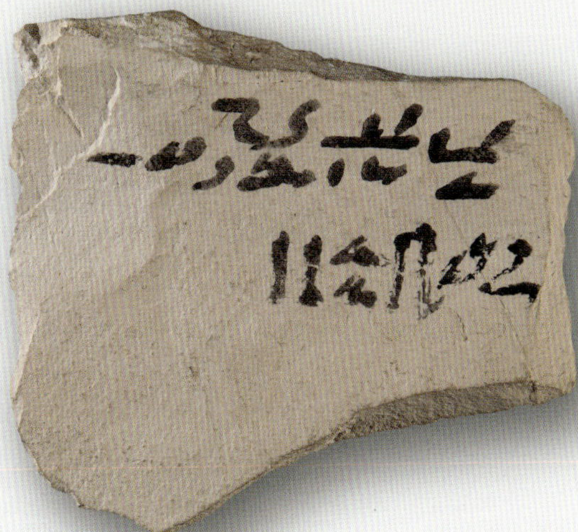

allude to the votive festivals dedicated to the queen, during which a statue was brought out, carved in a very dark bituminized wood. In pharaonic art, black skin — the colour of fertile silt — was usually a symbol of fertility. The mother of Amenhotep I is thus shown as the matriarch of the whole dynasty and of the New Kingdom.

Deities of everyday life, the sovereigns were also associated with the gods of the funerary world, welcoming the deceased into the afterlife (cat. 70). Evidence of this can be seen in the shroud of Djedmut, which shows Amenhotep I identified with Osiris, some five hundred years after his reign (cat. 71). **GA-L**

ANDREU, G., *La Statuette d'Ahmès Néfertari*, coll. 'Solo', RMN-Musée du Louvre, Paris, 1997.

BARBOTIN, C., *Âhmosis et le début de la XVIIIe dynastie*, coll. 'Les Grands Pharaons', Pygmalion, Paris, 2008.

EL SHAZLY, Y., *Royal Ancestor Worship in Deir el-Medina during the New Kingdom*, Abercromby Press, Wallasey, 2015.

HOLLENDER, G., *Amenophis I. und Ahmes Nefertari: Untersuchungen zur Entwicklung ihres posthumen Kultesanhand der Privatgräber der thebanischen Nekropole*, SDAIK 23, 2009.

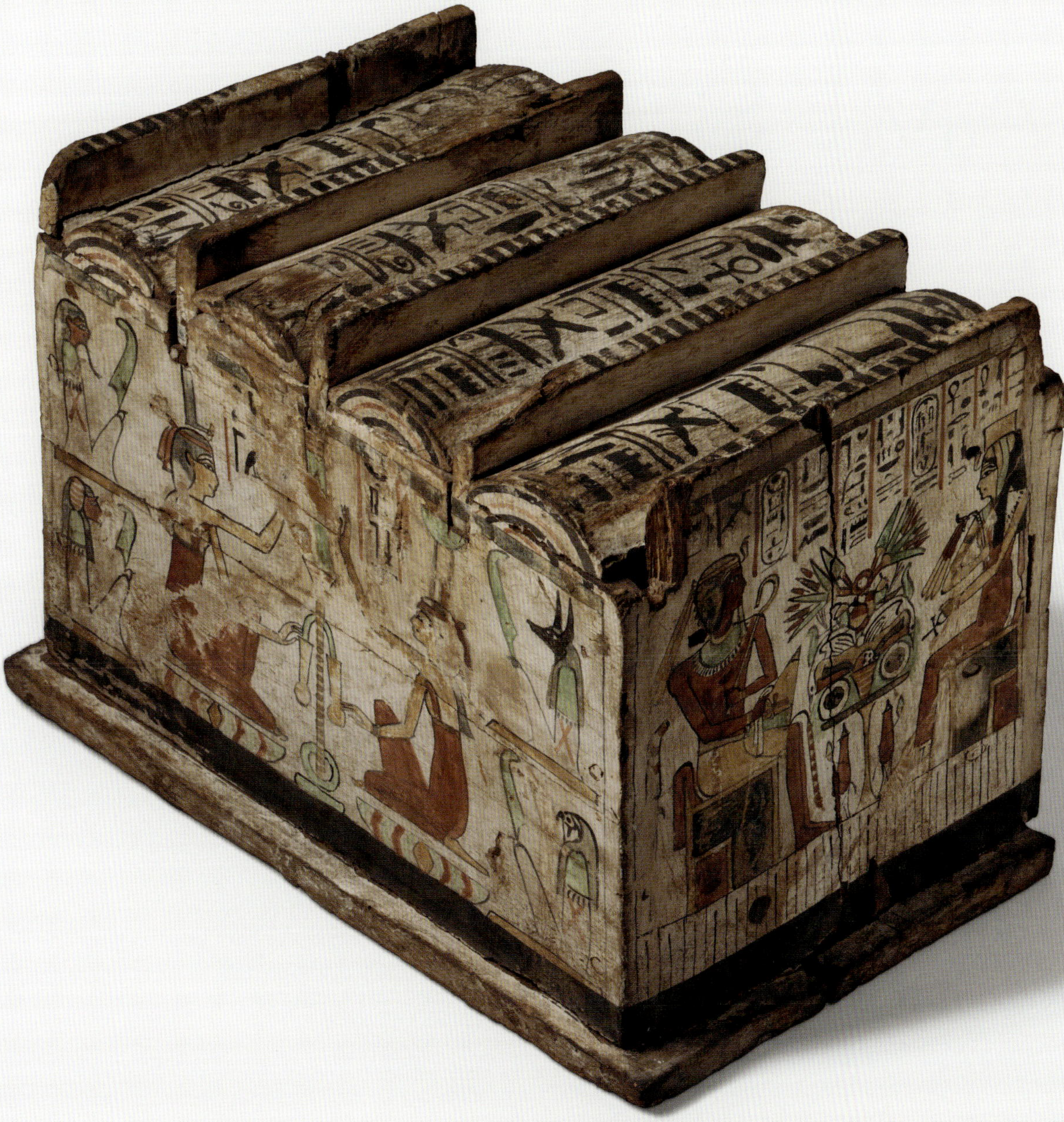

71

Box with funerary figures decorated with images of the deified Amenhotep I and Ahmose-Nefertari, Egypt, Twenty-first to Twenty-second Dynasty (c. 1069–735 BCE).

RAMESSES THE GREAT

Ramesses II was quite justified in calling himself 'Ramesses the Great' and in being compared to Louis XIV. Everything about this ruler was colossal, immeasurable, monumental and excessive: his reign could be described as 'pharaonic' in the sense that the adjective can be used to mean something impressively huge.

Ramesses came from a military family in the eastern Delta and became the most brilliant pharaoh of the Nineteenth Dynasty. His conquests and exploits have led Egyptologists to refer to this period as the 'Ramesside Period' and sometimes to describe it as 'Egypt of the conquering kings'. His long reign (sixty-seven years), the large number of women in his harem and the numerous children — a hundred or so — that he is known to have fathered are all reflections of this spectacular reign.

The historical and cultural schism created by the reign of Akhenaten some sixty years earlier was already in the past when Ramesses II ascended the throne in 1279 BCE: orthodoxy had been re-established and the political landscape, both internal and external, had changed. Ramesses' vast achievements took numerous forms. For many years, as a war leader, Ramesses launched raids against the Hittites, drove the Bedouins from the Delta, controlled the Libyan hordes and built a line of fortresses on the eastern frontier. In the south, the borders were held by viceroys, who ensured the stability of Egyptian colonisation.

126

Edition of *Life* magazine, 29 October 1965, concerning the relocation of the Abu Simbel temples, USA.

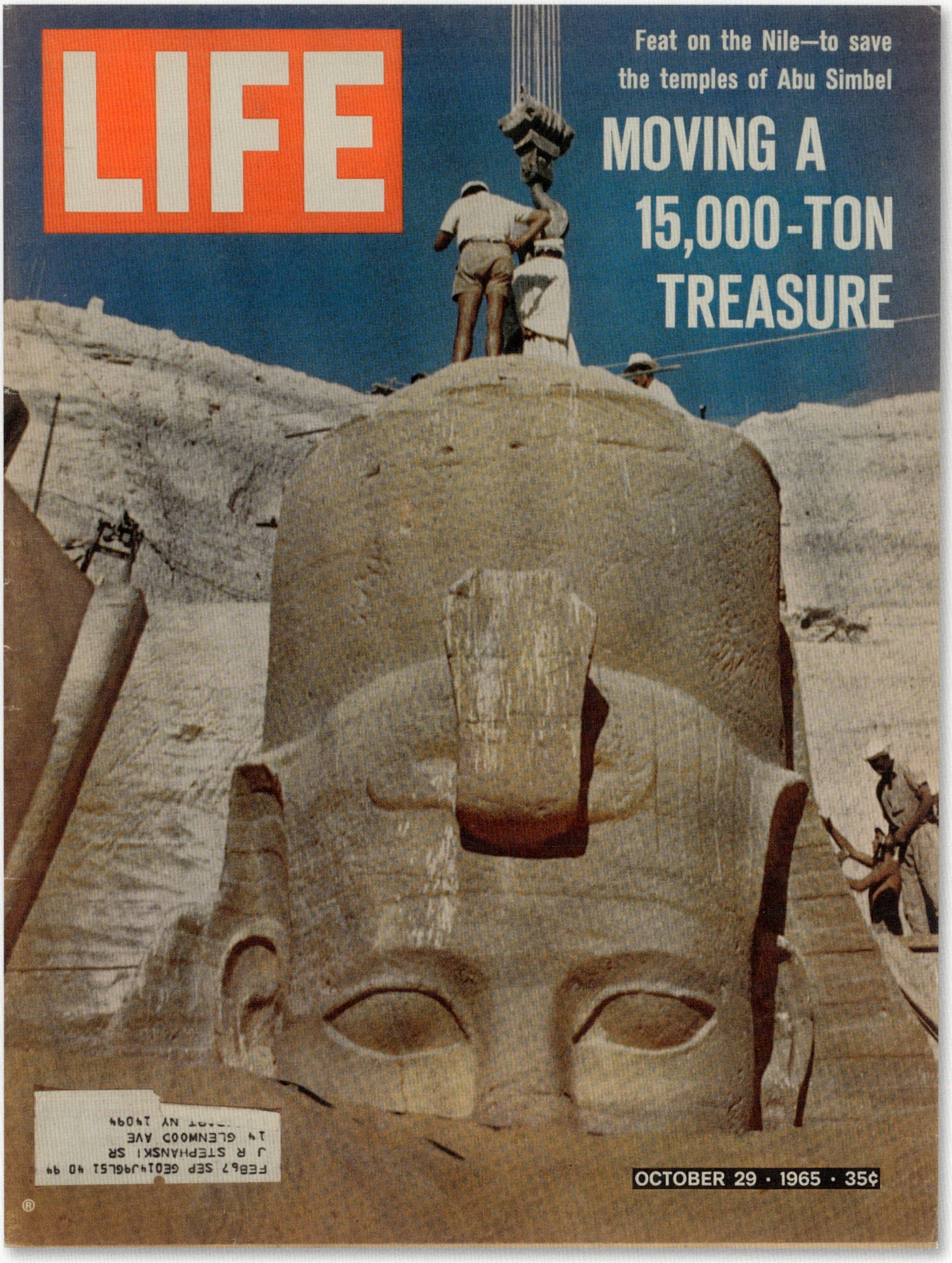

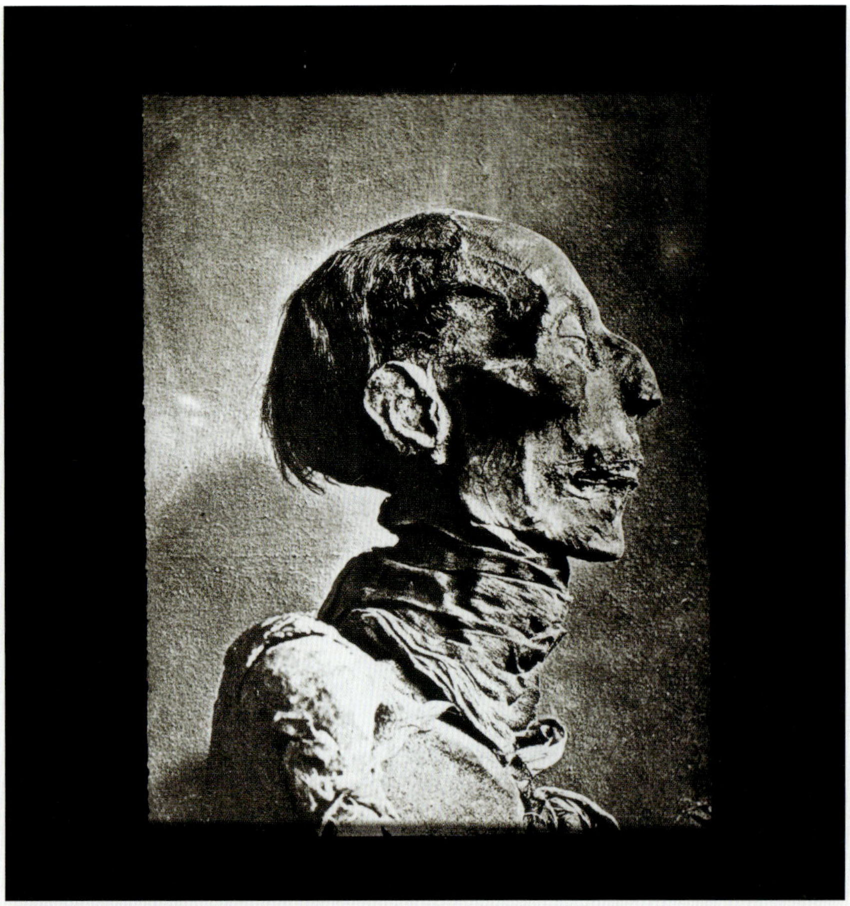

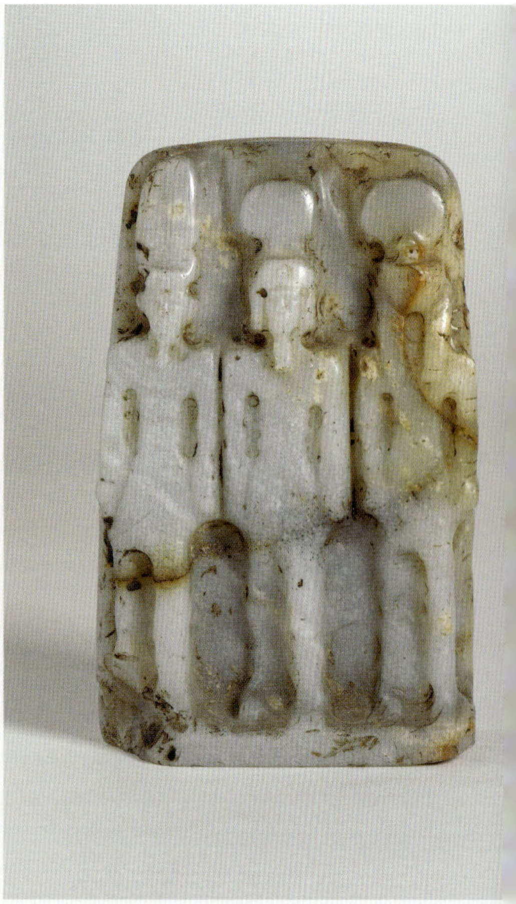

123

Emil Brugsch (?), mummy of Ramesses II labelled as 'Sesostris', glass slide from the photographic laboratory of the Musée de l'Homme, Cairo and Paris, 1886–94.

46

Triad depicting Ramesses II as the sun god Shu, between Amun-Ra and Horakhty, Egypt, reign of Ramesses II (c. 1279–1212 BCE).

In large part, Ramesses II's fame stemmed from the countless monuments and colossi (cat. 43) he scattered around his empire, paying homage to the dynastic gods and to his own glory. From Byblos to Napata (Sudan), there are buildings that bear his mark, his cartouches and his style, 'harmonious in their vastness' (J. Yoyotte). The high walls of the temples are carved in sunken relief, the columns are simple shafts, the statues are colossal, the pylons are massive and the impression created by the architecture is one of disproportionate grandeur. His best-known monuments are the Ramesseum, in the necropolis of Thebes opposite Luxor, and especially the temples of Abu Simbel, south of Aswan.
In the Valley of the Kings, he had a large tomb built for himself and commissioned another immense tomb for his children. But the most

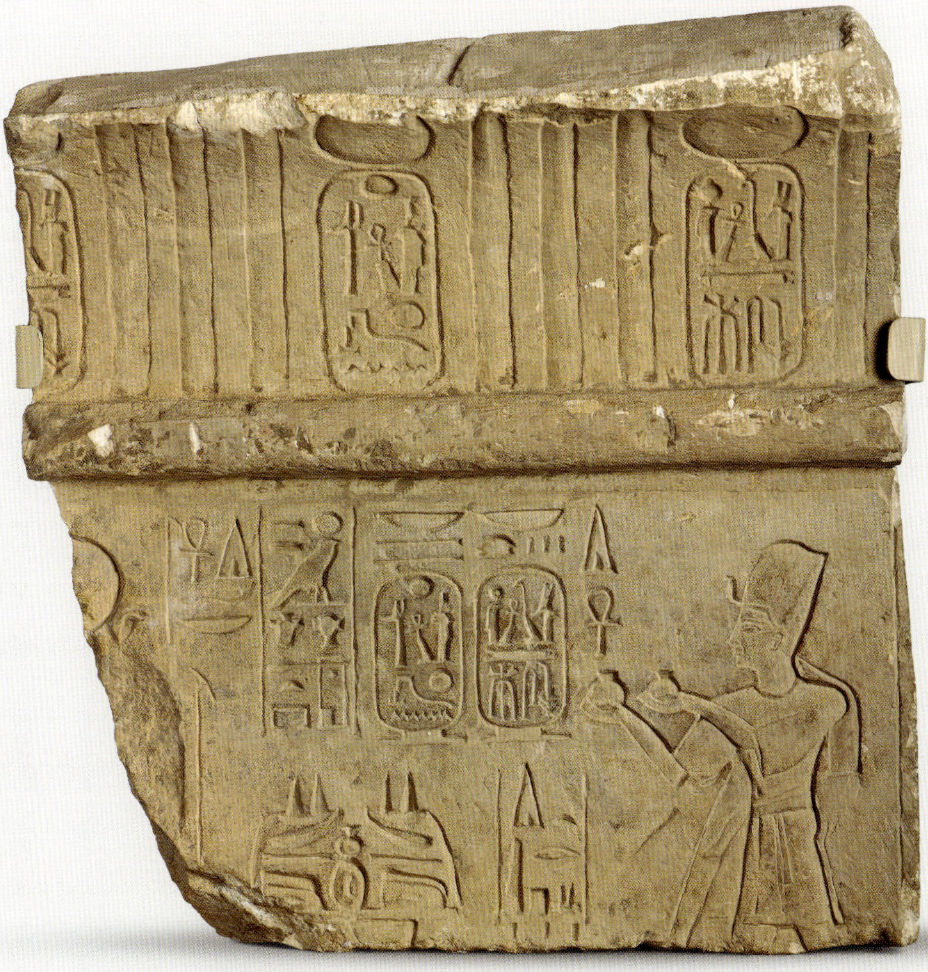

17

Fragment of the wall of a temple of Ramesses II showing the pharaoh presenting an offering of wine to the sun god Ra-Horakhty, Egypt, reign of Ramesses II (c. 1279–1212 BCE).

29

Fragment of an obelisk dedicated by Ramesses II to the god Ra, Tanis, Egypt, reign of Ramesses II (c. 1279–1212 BCE).

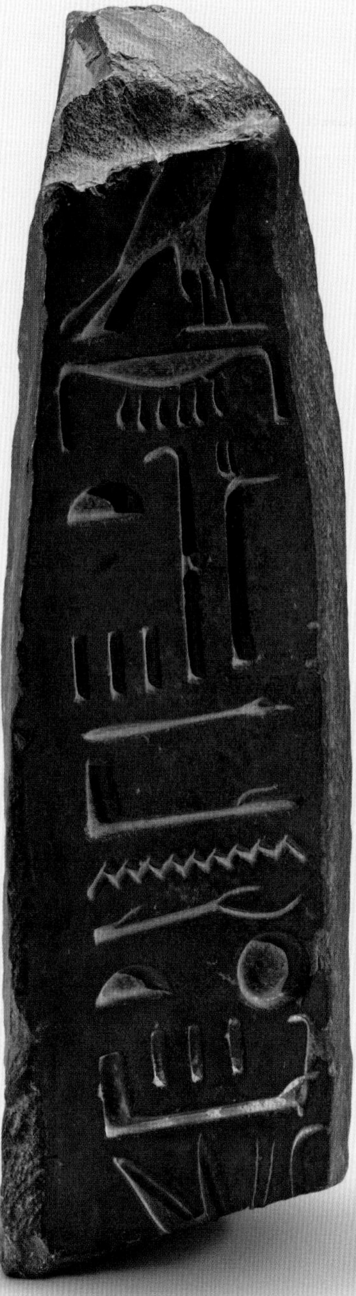

beautiful tomb was in the Valley of the Queens, dedicated to the Great Royal Wife, Queen Nefertari (cat. 166).

One of Ramesses II's strokes of genius was to organize his own cult while he was still alive, deifying himself on votive monuments, remains of which can be found throughout the Nile Valley. Some of these — mostly stelae — show priests or important figures worshipping the reigning pharaoh or his statue (cat. 44). Others seek to ensure a long-lasting

45

Stela portraying Ramesses II presenting an offering to his own colossus, Egypt, reign of Ramesses II (c. 1279–1212 BCE).

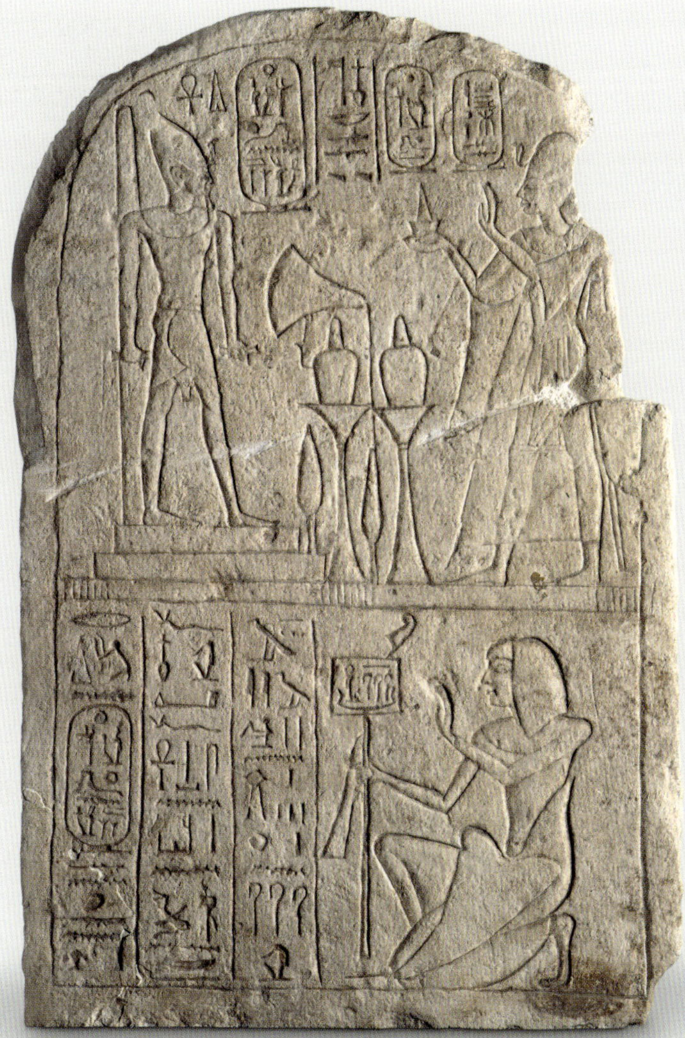

posthumous memory for the sovereign, depicted praying before his own colossus (cat. 45). Many temple scenes and small votive objects portray him majestically seated, ranked alongside the most important gods of the Egyptian pantheon. The small triad in the exhibition, in which Ramesses is flanked by Amun-Ra and Ra-Horakhty, is a perfect example of this (cat. 46).

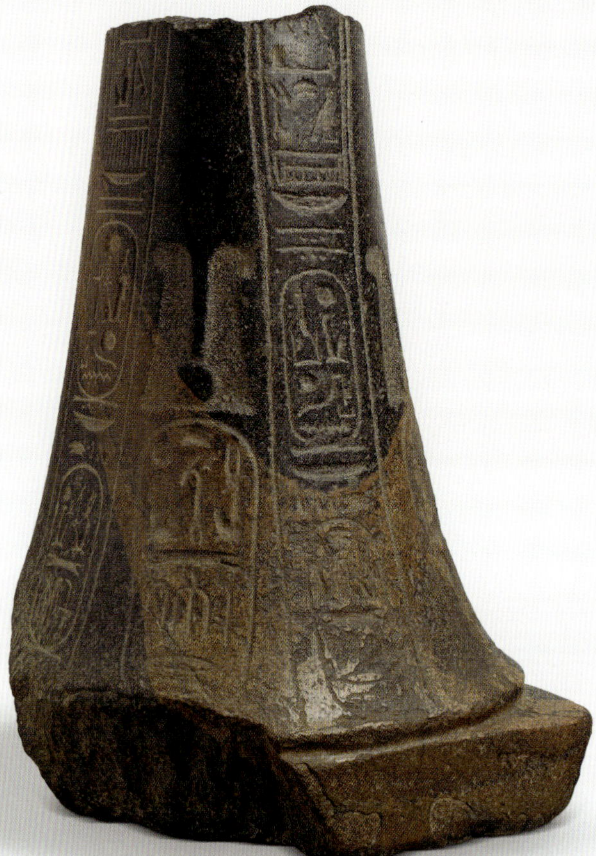

51

Base of an altar dedicated by Ramesses II, reused by Ramesses III, Ramesses VII, Ramesses IX and Ramesses XI, Mit-Rahina, Egypt, (13th-11th centuries BCE).

His reign left an impression on his successors, who tried — to no avail — to amass the same sort of glory and fame. From Ramesses III to Ramesses XI, all pharaohs called themselves 'Ramesses', thus invoking the patronage of the great Ramesses (cats. 29 and 17). An altar base in the exhibition (cat. 51), carved and engraved in a fine black granite, has columns of text that include the cartouches of Ramesses II, Ramesses III, Ramesses VII and finally Ramesses IX, an inconsequential king who had his cartouches engraved in several places on this object.

In the fifth century BCE, the Greek writer Herodotus wrote of Ramesses II but called him Sesostris, thus sparking a confusion that blighted the memory of the great Ramesses (cat. 123). This confusion continued until Champollion succeeded in deciphering hieroglyphs in 1822: Ramesses' exceptional role in the history of the pharaohs could now be re-established. In the 1960s, the rescue of the Abu Simbel temples

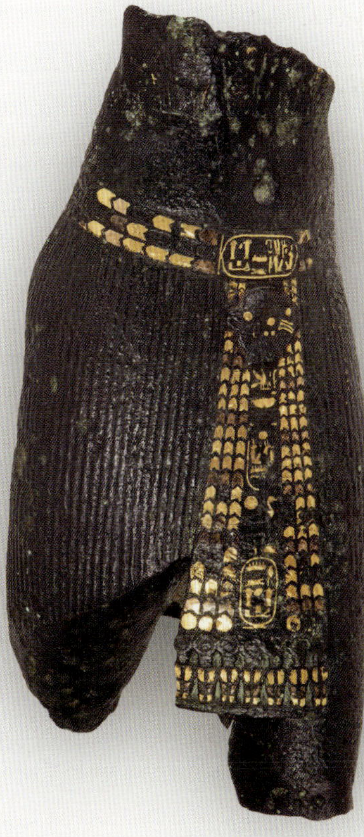

52

Torso of King Pedubast I, Egypt, Third Intermediate Period, Twenty-third Dynasty (c. 818–793 BCE).

The throne name chosen by this king, Usermaatre-Setepenimen, legible on the buckle of his belt, is a homage to that of the glorious Ramesses II, Usermaatre-Setepenre (c. 1279–1212 BCE).

(cat. 126), carved out of the Nubian rockface on the banks of the Nile by and for Ramesses II and his wife Nefertari, shone a dazzling light on the great pharaoh and tourists flocked to this important site. Then, in 1976, the exhibition *Ramesses the Great* in Paris completed the rehabilitation of this illustrious pharaoh, who was altogether unique in the history of ancient Egypt. Because of his glowing reputation for power and vigour, the name Ramesses was adopted in our own twentieth century by marketing professionals (cat. 229). The first car manufactured in Egypt in the 1960s, intended to reflect the modernization of Egyptian society to which President Nasser aspired, was called 'Ramses' (cat. 174). His name was also used to sell a popular chocolate drink and cat food — the ultimate irony for a pharaoh who saw himself as a god. **GA-L**

BARBOTIN, C., FAROUT, D., 'Le Poème de Qadech', *Égypte, Afrique et Orient* 93, 2019, pp. 22–32.

JAMES, T. G. H., *Ramsès II*, Gründ, Paris, 2002.

OBSOMER, C., *Ramsès II*, coll. 'Les Grands Pharaons', Pygmalion, Paris, 2012.

RAMSÈS le Grand, exh. cat., ed. by C. Desroches Noblecourt, Galeries Nationales du Grand Palais, Paris, 1976.

WHAT REMAINS OF THE PHARAOHS? HISTORY AND LEGENDS

2

From the moment in the seventh century BCE when Hellenic populations established lasting contacts with Egypt, and especially when the Nile Valley was incorporated into the Hellenistic kingdom of the Ptolemies and later into the Roman Empire, knowledge of the civilization of the pharaohs increased and became more clearly understood in Europe. However, the closing of the polytheist temples in the fourth century CE and the gradual Christianization of the country signalled the end of the pharaonic civilization, whose earliest history was slowly forgotten. From the Middle Ages to the nineteenth century, Europe and the Arabized world only preserved the memory of the pharaohs mentioned by Greek and Latin historians: Herodotus (fifth century BCE), Manetho (third century BCE), Diodorus Siculus (first century BCE), Strabo (first century BCE to first century CE), Plutarch (first to second century CE), Aelian (second to third century CE) and so on. As was also true for biblical

Jean-Baptiste Tillard or Tilliard, after Charles Monnet, 'La mort du grand roi Sesostris' (The death of the great King Sesostris), in François Fénelon, *Les Aventures de Télémaque, fils d'Ulysse* (The adventures of Telemachus, son of Ulysses) published by François Ambroise Didot, Paris, France, 1783.

In this didactic novel inspired by the epics of antiquity and addressed to the grandson of Louis XIV of France, Sesostris is presented as a wise king and an example to follow, whose death plunges his subjects into despair.

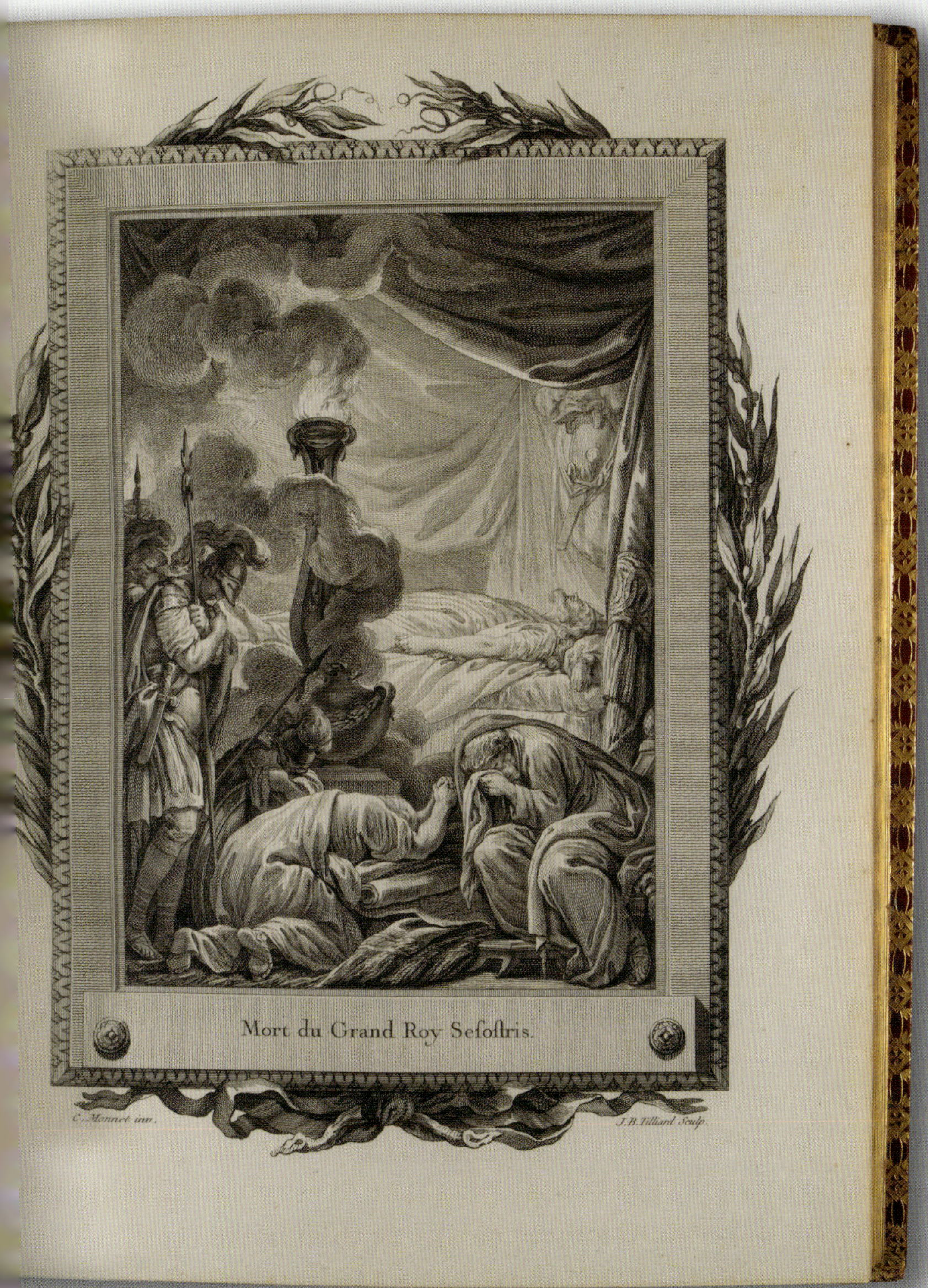

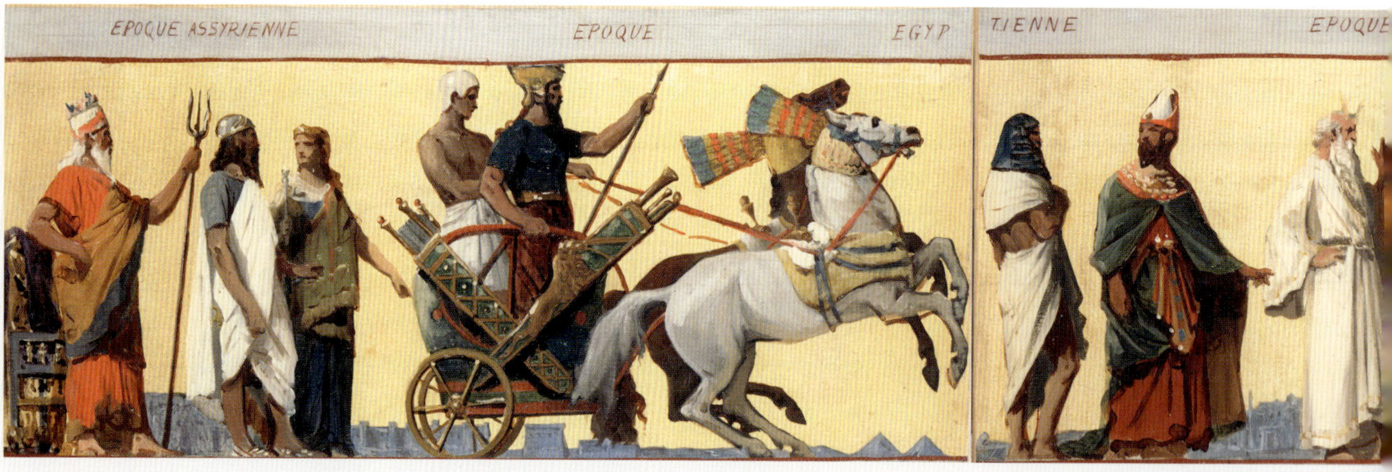

84

Joseph Jean-Félix Aubert, sketch for the decoration of the drawing class in the boys' school in Rue Dombasle, Paris, c. 1879.

and qur'anic traditions, these authors drew from Egypt and Mediterranean literature a distorted memory of the ancient kings, who thus became semi-historical and semi-legendary figures.

From the Amasis described by Greek historians to the legendary sovereign Sesostris, not forgetting the much romanticized Cleopatra and the mysterious Pharaoh of the Bible, *Superstar Pharaohs* presents a gallery of portraits that gradually shift from history to myth. There are fewer works in this section, reflecting the relative disappearance of the pharaohs from Western and Eastern consciousness between the end of antiquity and the nineteenth century — a gap of more than one thousand and three hundred years.

Throughout this period, scholars in the Arab world and in Europe, who had access to Greco-Roman sources for the ancient history of Egypt, perpetuated the names of a few pharaohs. The *Chronology of Ancient Nations* by the Persian historian Al-Biruni (tenth century) contains a list of 'Coptic kings' (meaning here Egyptian), taken from the historical works of Manetho written in the third century BCE (cat. 82). At the end of the nineteenth century, when Joseph Jean-Félix Aubert presented his plans for the decoration of the drawing class in the boys' school in Rue Dombasle in Paris, he came up with a succession of figures representing the great periods of ancient art history: alongside the Greeks, the Hebrews and the Assyrians, Egypt is represented by Psamtik and Sesostris, two pharaohs unknown to the wider public today (cat. 84).

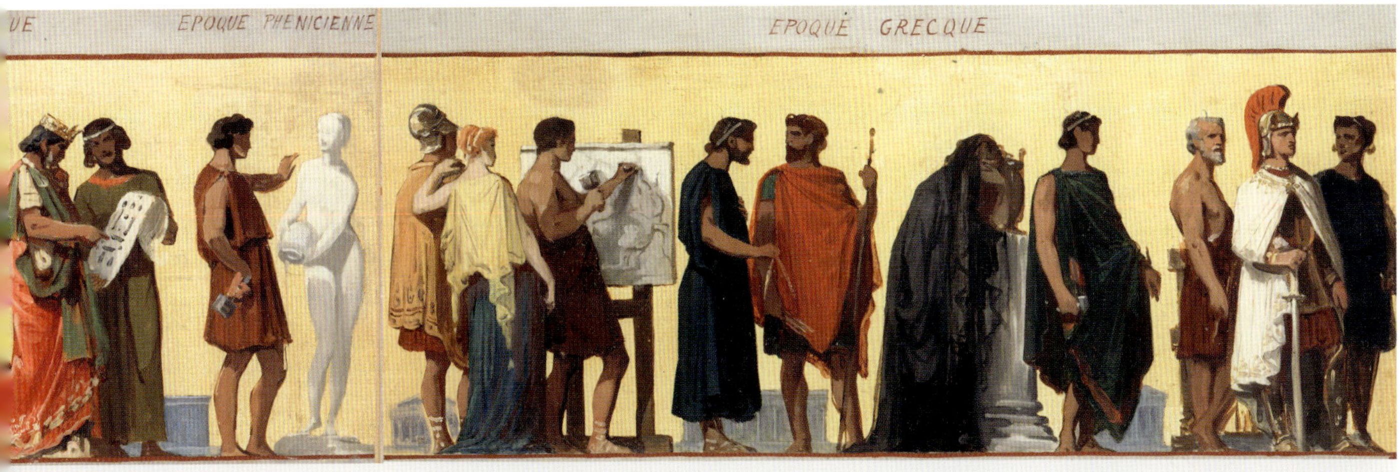

AMASIS AND PSAMTIK, THE KINGS WHO LOVED THE GREEKS

Because they enjoyed sustained relations with the Greeks, the pharaohs of the seventh and sixth centuries BCE are often mentioned in classical literature. Psamtik I employed Carian and Ionian mercenaries to control Egypt, while Amasis accorded significant benefits to merchants from the Aegean established in the Delta, in the Greek trading post of Naucratis. Many products from Asia Minor and Egypt provide evidence of economic and cultural exchanges between the Nile Valley and the Greek world at this time (cat. 85). Some of them bear the cartouche of those pharaohs who were thought of as 'philhellene', for example *aryballoi*, flasks containing precious essences, the most remarkable of which are shaped like a Greek warrior's head (cats. 86 and 87). Texts written by Greek historians describing the reigns of these kings inspired European artists from the Renaissance onwards (in drawing, painting, music, theatre and literature). Particularly popular were illustrations of Amasis taking the throne of Egypt, as well as a few anecdotal stories in which Psamtik was the hero.

NECTANEBO, FATHER OF ALEXANDER THE GREAT

Another king now completely forgotten was Nectanebo II, the last pharaoh of the last Egyptian dynasty (360–342 BCE). He became a legendary figure: a magician, seducer, and supposedly Alexander the Great's father. His reputation followed him into the modern era, in the wake of memories of the celebrated conquering hero. Alongside ancient written and archaeological sources which anchor this story in history, many medieval illuminated manuscripts show how his legend survived (cats. 95 and 96).

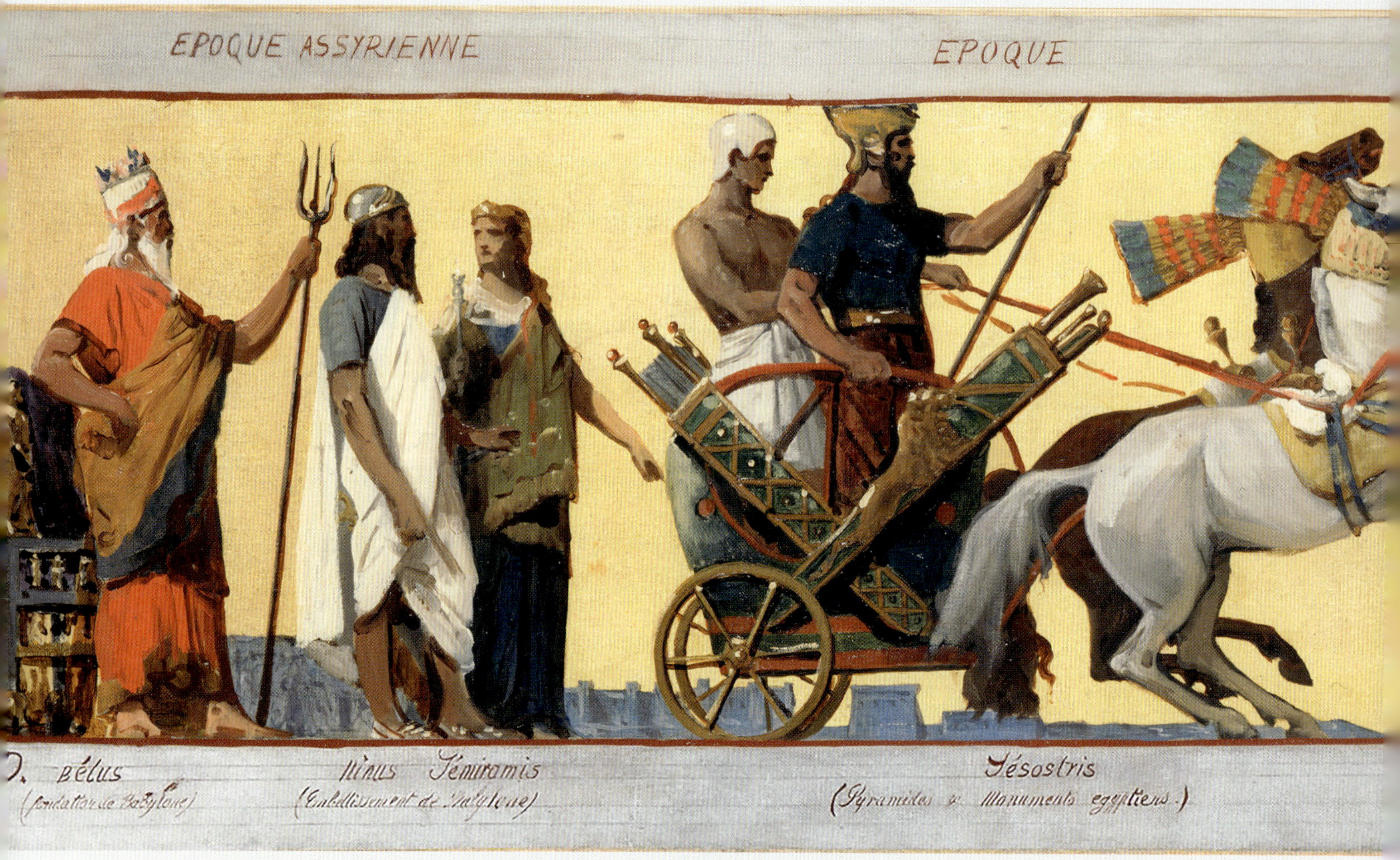
EPOQUE ASSYRIENNE
EPOQUE
Bélus
(fondateur de Babylone)
Ninus Sémiramis
(Embellissement de Babylone)
Sésostris
(Pyramides & Monuments égyptiens.)

84 (detail)

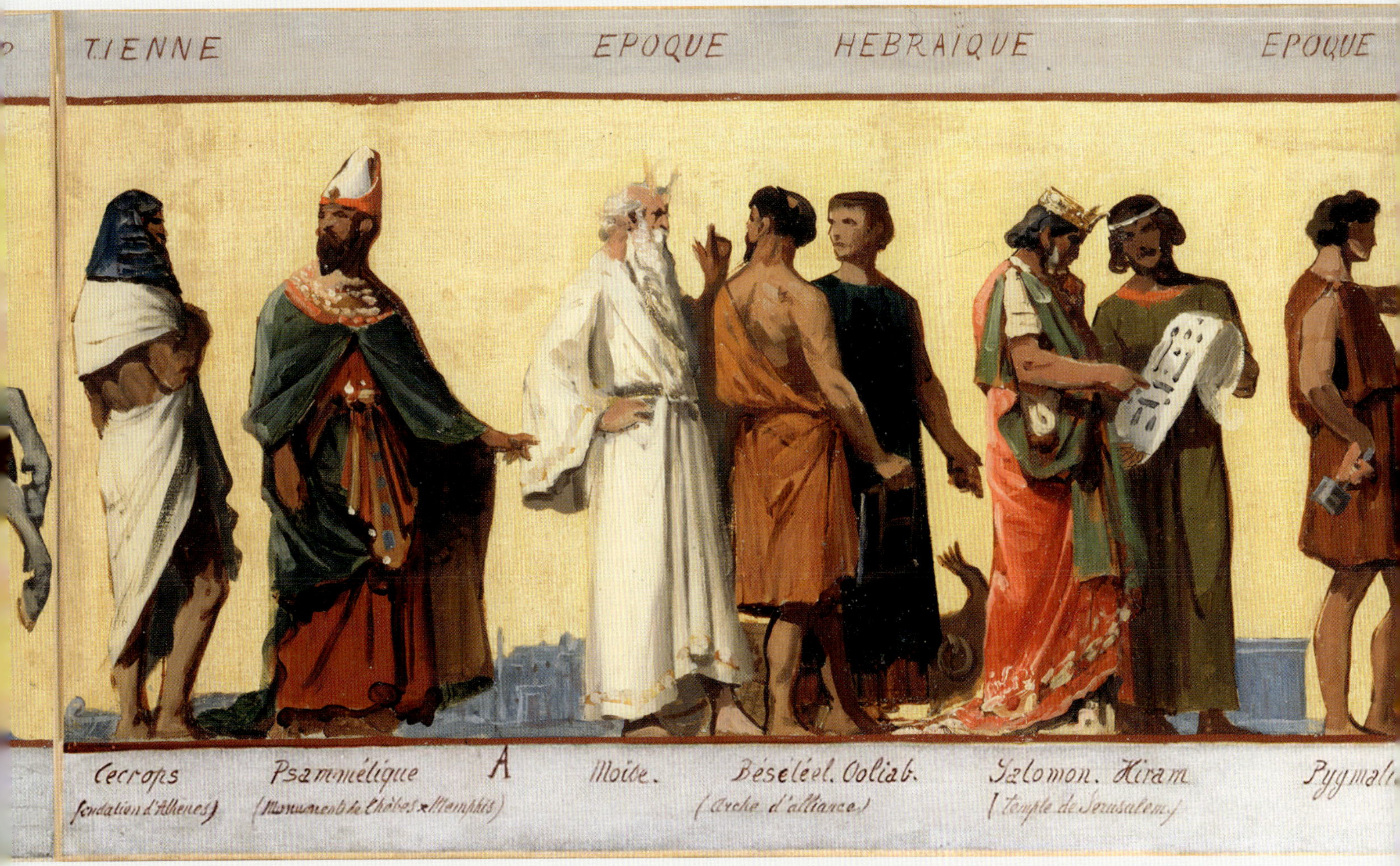
T.IENNE
EPOQUE HEBRAÏQUE
EPOQUE
Cecrops
fondation d'Athènes
Psammétique
(Monuments de Thèbes et Memphis)
A
Moïse.
Béséléel. Ooliab.
(Arche d'alliance)
Salomon. Hiram
(Temple de Jérusalem)
Pygmali

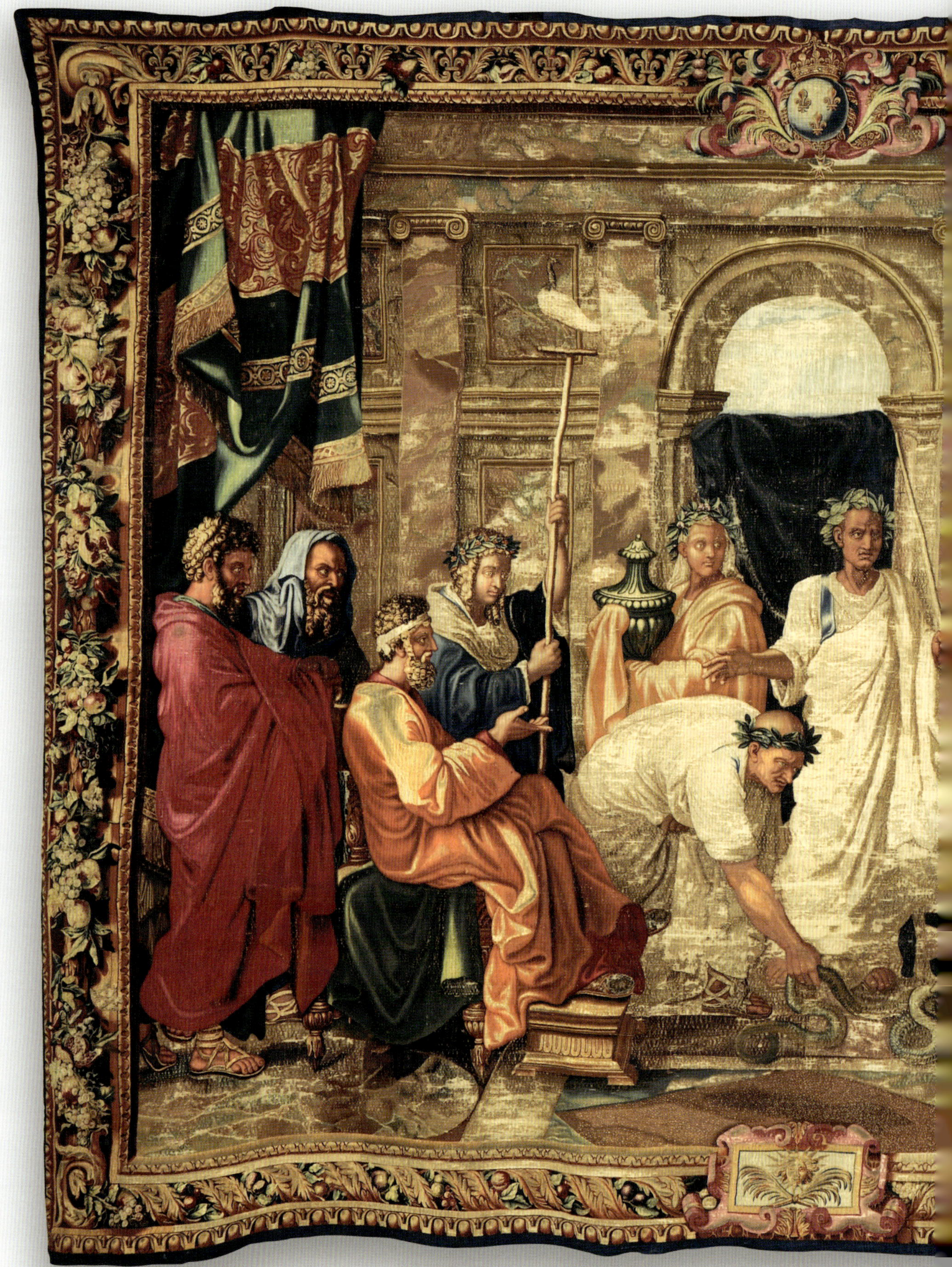

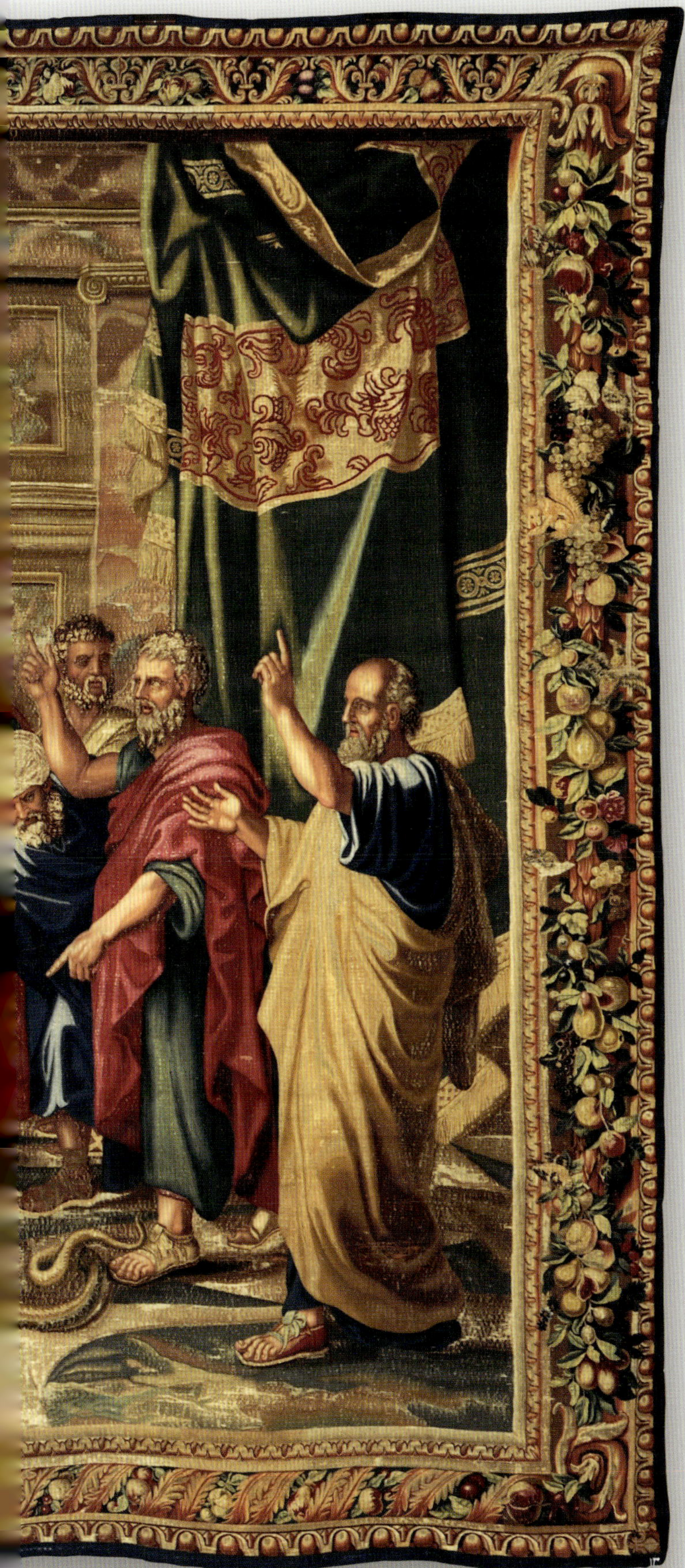

116

Gobelins Manufactory, after Nicolas Poussin, tapestry depicting the story of Moses: *The Rod Turned into a Serpent*, Paris, France, 1683.

To demonstrate his power to Pharaoh, God transforms the staff of Aaron, brother of Moses, into a serpent more powerful than those produced by the Egyptian magicians.

CLEOPATRA, *FEMME FATALE* OR WISE QUEEN

In the world of historical and mythical pharaohs, Cleopatra (cat. 97) certainly occupies the prime position, and it is not going to be taken away from her any time soon. Roman historians presented her as a sensual and manipulative seductress, embodying the dangerous charms of the East, but in the classical Arab world she was considered a wise queen and a great builder of monuments.

Cleopatra's legendary suicide by means of a serpent's bite was a huge source of inspiration to European artists from the Renaissance onwards. Innumerable works from the early sixteenth to the end of the nineteenth century demonstrate the longevity of Cleopatra's exceptional popularity. On the other hand, it is less common to find works referring to her exalted posthumous memory in the Arab world, apart from in ancient manuscripts or works illustrating the monuments which — according to legend — she built in Egypt.

97

Bust of a statue considered to be that of Cleopatra VII, Egypt, late Ptolemaic period (c. 100–31 BCE).

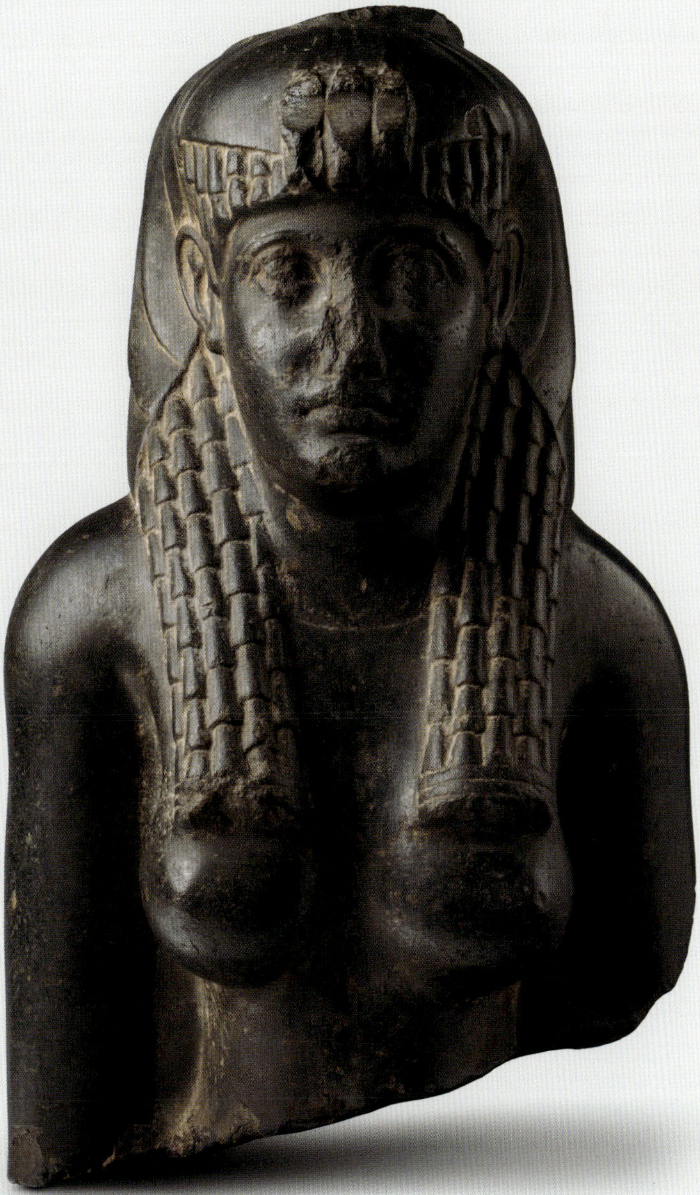

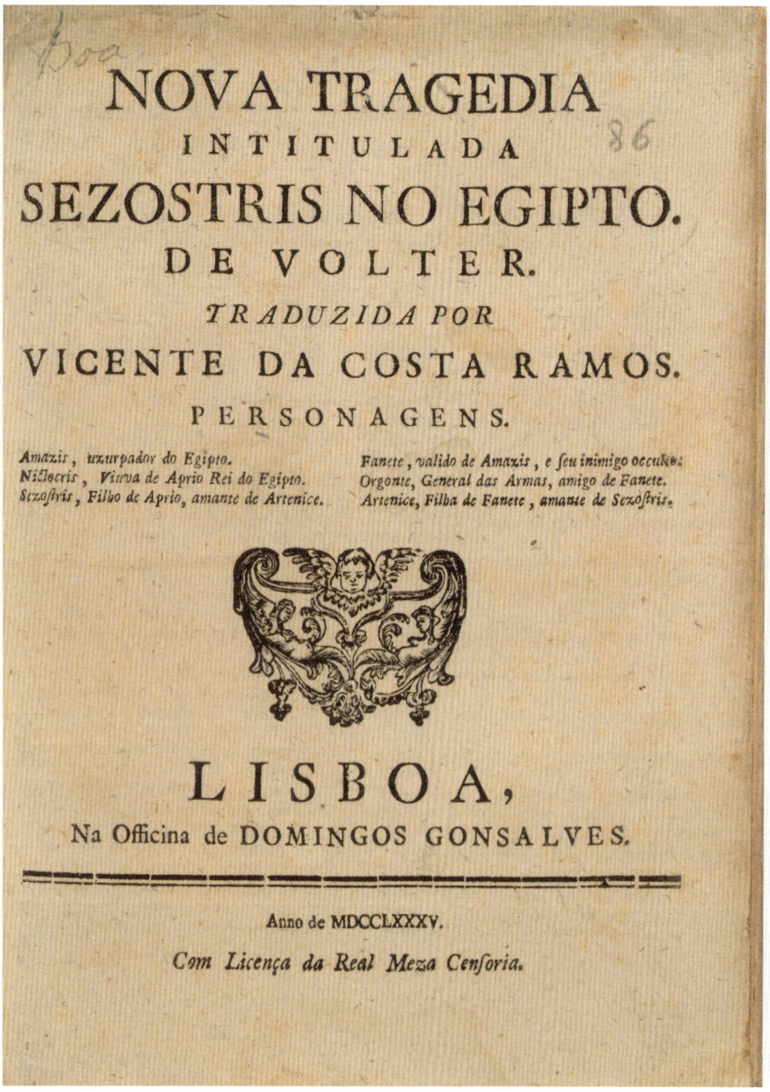
NOVA TRAGEDIA
INTITULADA
SEZOSTRIS NO EGIPTO.
DE VOLTER.
TRADUZIDA POR
VICENTE DA COSTA RAMOS.
PERSONAGENS.

Amazis, uzurpador do Egipto.
Nitocris, Viuva de Aprio Rei do Egipto.
Sezostris, Filho de Aprio, amante de Artenice.
Fanete, valido de Amazis, e seu inimigo occulto.
Orgonte, General das Armas, amigo de Fanete.
Artenice, Filha de Fanete, amante de Sezostris.

LISBOA,
Na Officina de DOMINGOS GONSALVES.
Anno de MDCCLXXXV.
Com Licença da Real Meza Censoria.

110

Voltaire, *Nova Tragedia intitulada Sezostris no Egipto* (A New Tragedy Titled Sesostris in Egypt), translated by Vicente da Costa Ramos, published by Domingos Gonçalves, Lisbon, 1785.

117

Moses Confronts Pharaoh, in a Haggadah of Passover by Yehuda Lajb Ben Betsalel, published by Jacob Zvi Hirsch, Metz, France, 1767.

A Haggadah is a book explaining the origins of the traditions of Passover, the Jewish holiday commemorating the Israelites' Exodus from Egypt.

SESOSTRIS, QUINTESSENTIAL KING OF EGYPT

Sesostris was a mythical pharaoh largely inspired by various powerful sovereigns in Egyptian history. He appears as the archetypal Egyptian king in Greek sources, which shaped the views of the first Western travellers and historians. This hybrid figure has been attributed with imaginary exploits, including great victories over his enemies, as well as with statues and colossuses which archaeology later reassigned to historical figures.
The exhibition has on display several documents and works illustrating the legendary Sesostris' astonishing power, as well as his name's renown in classical culture (cat. 110).

PHARAOH IN THE BIBLE, FIRAUN IN THE QUR'AN

Genesis and Exodus gave the name 'Pharaoh' to the rulers of Egypt who had dealings with the patriarchs, while the Qur'an uses the name 'Firaun', the Arabic equivalent. In the holy texts, Pharaoh is both a title and a name, attached to mythical kings. Since the end of antiquity, these mythical sovereigns, whose name appears throughout Christianity and Islam and of course in Judaism (cat. 117), have probably been the best-known Egyptian rulers.
In the Christian and Islamic worlds, literature and the plastic arts have seized upon these stories, beginning with that of Joseph/Yusuf, who was promoted to the rank of minister by the Egyptian king (cats. 111 and 113).

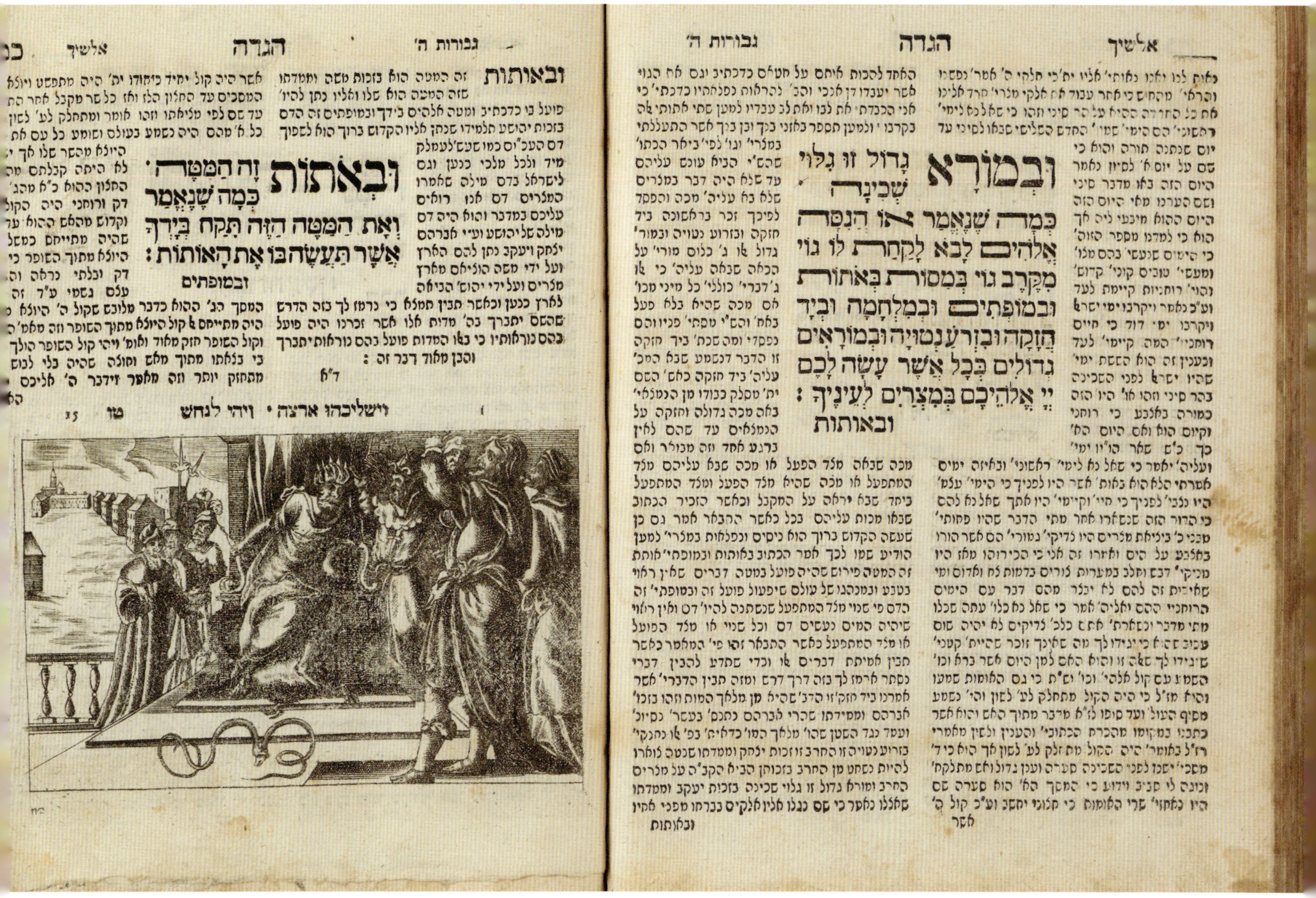

Meanwhile, Moses' adversary symbolizes for posterity the arbitrary, unjust and impious tyranny long associated with the name of Pharaoh, especially in Islam. The phases of Moses' life in Egypt, his adoption by Pharaoh's daughter and Pharoah's eventual punishment, swallowed up by the sea, also supplied subject matter for various artistic works: the exhibition has gathered together a few of them, from the seventeenth to the twentieth century (cat. 116). **GA-L/FM**

NECTANEBO, SUPREME SEDUCER AND FATHER OF ALEXANDER THE GREAT

'Most people are mistaken when they claim that he [Alexander] was the son of King Philip. This is not true. He was not Philip's son, but — according to the wisest Egyptians — he was the son of Nectanebo, after the latter ceased to be king'.

This historical fabrication comes at the beginning of the *Alexander Romance,* a romanticized biography that glorifies the Macedonian hero. Originally written in Greek in the late second or early third century CE, in the cosmopolitan milieu of Alexandrian scholars, the work has been copied and adapted many times — the latest versions date to the sixteenth century — in a wide range of languages: Latin, Armenian, Coptic, Arabic, Hebrew and even, via Persian, in Thai and Mongolian. The dodecasyllables in which it was set to verse in twelfth century French are what we now call 'alexandrines'.

In medieval illuminated manuscripts, where text and images are linked, the scribes chose to reproduce the most striking moments in the story of Alexander's conception as the son of Nectanebo — that is to say Nectanebo II, the third and last pharaoh of the Thirtieth Dynasty (cat. 91), after whose time the throne of Egypt was occupied by foreign rulers, first Persians and then Macedonians.

91

Funerary figurine of Nectanebo II, Egypt, reign of Nectanebo II (360–342 BCE).

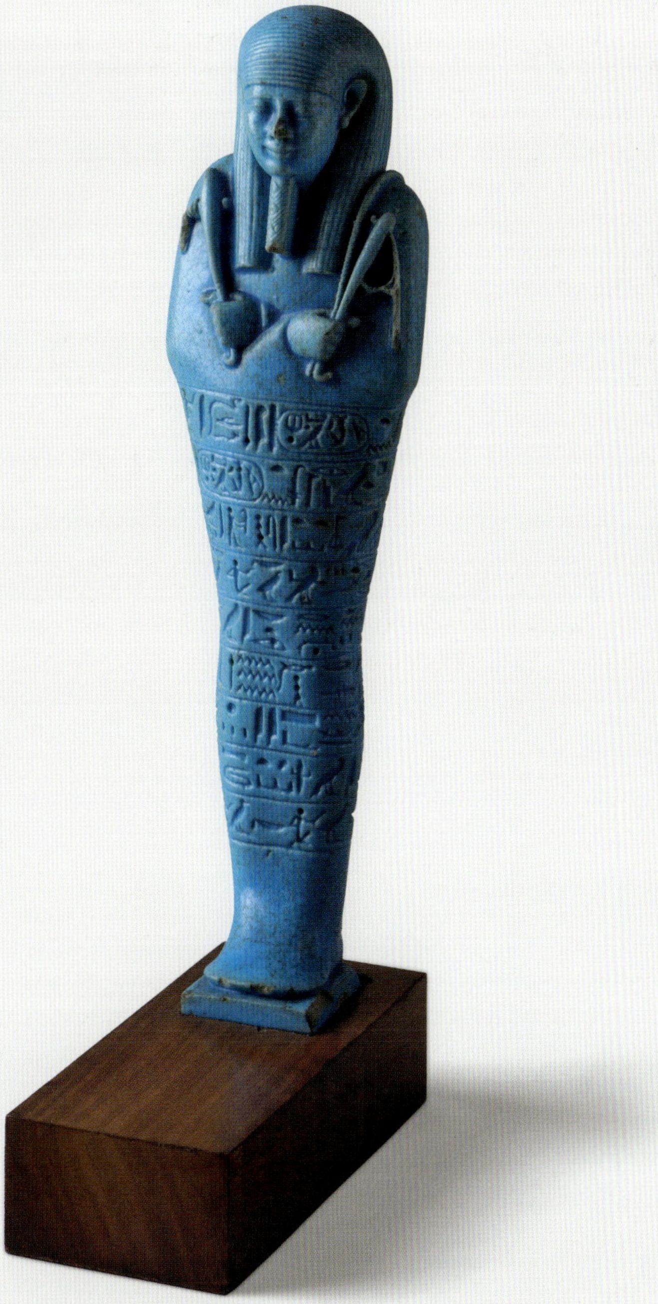

92–93–94

Medals depicting the deified Alexander the Great, Abu Qir, Egypt, third century.

The curved horn visible on the hero's temple assimilates him with Ammon, the Libyan-Egyptian god that Nectanebo pretended to embody in order to seduce Olympias in the *Alexander Romance*.

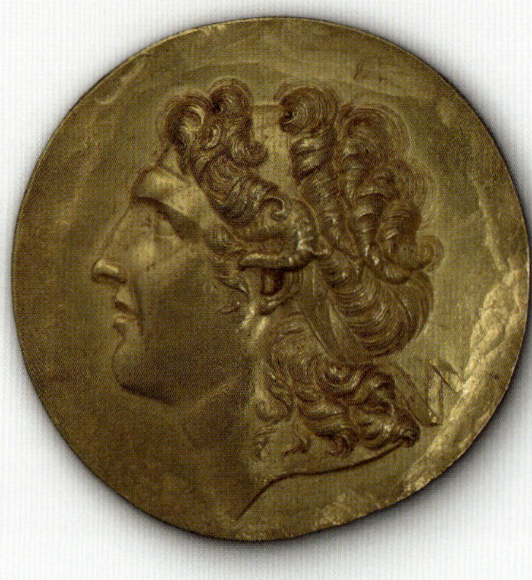

The pharaoh is portrayed as a figure fixated with sorcery, who prefers to resort to divination rather than fight against the invading army of Artaxerxes III. After reading in his magic bowl that 'the last days of the Egyptian kingdom are approaching', the sovereign disguises himself as a priest and flees to Macedonia, having 'hidden much gold about his person'. Once there, he takes advantage of the fact that Philip is away at war, using subterfuge to seduce the king's wife, Queen Olympias: he disguises himself as the ram of Ammon, his body covered with 'a very soft fleece of sheep's wool, with horns on the temples, the whole seeming to be of gold'. Then he lies with the queen, promising that their lovemaking will result in the birth of 'a male child' who will become 'king of the whole inhabited universe and ruler of the world' (cat. 95). Olympias, not at all averse to this nocturnal liaison, asks in the morning: 'Will this god come to me again? For he gave me pleasure!' So Nectanebo 'goes to Olympias's room whenever she wants and she assumes he is the god Ammon'.

This fictionalized account of history, giving the son of Philip and Olympias an Egyptian ancestry, was the pretext for a parodic fable likely

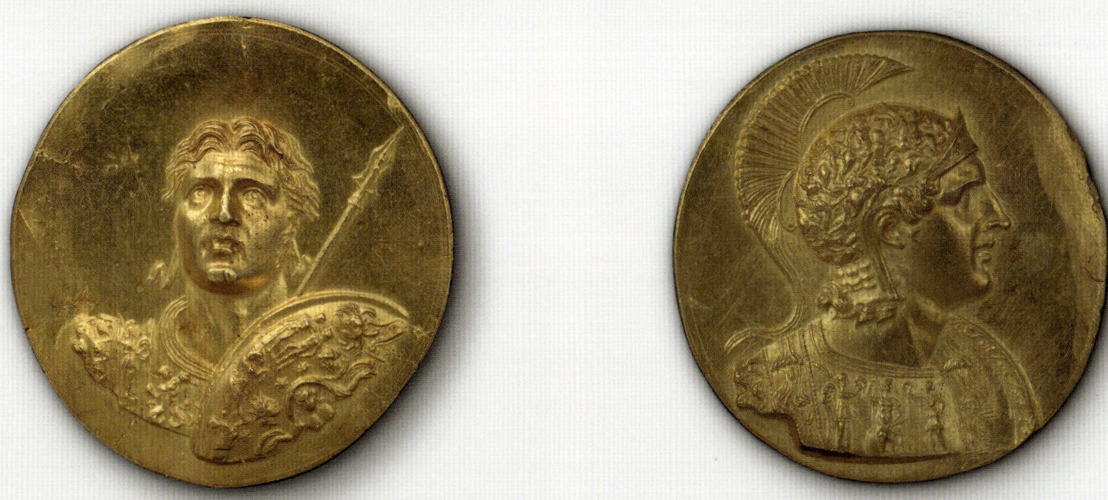

to appeal to a Greek-speaking readership fond of mythological tales, in which gods and humans rub shoulders and express themselves in a common language. It was not, however, without purpose: it aimed to establish that the pretensions of Alexander and his successors to the pharaonic heritage were legitimate (cat. 96). It is also a crude fictional rendering of the dogma that asserted the Egyptian monarchy's divine nature. During the New Kingdom, this was illustrated in cycles depicting the ritual of the king's divine birth, in which the dynastic god Amun, appearing as the reigning monarch, begets the future holder of the crown. In a similar vein, as soon as he had conquered Egypt, Alexander braved innumerable dangers by taking himself off to the distant Siwa oasis, seeking recognition as 'son of the god'. In this case, the god was Ammon of Libya, whose sacred animal was a ram, in whose guise the Nectanebo of the *Alexander Romance* had seduced Olympias. A political act on one hand, a literary pastiche on the other: both signs of the enduring quality of ancient Egypt's cultural legacy. **AF**

95

Nectanebo seduces Queen Olympias in the *Speculum historiale* by Vincent de Beauvais, illuminated by the Master of Jouvenel des Ursins, France, [1401–1425], fol. 89r.

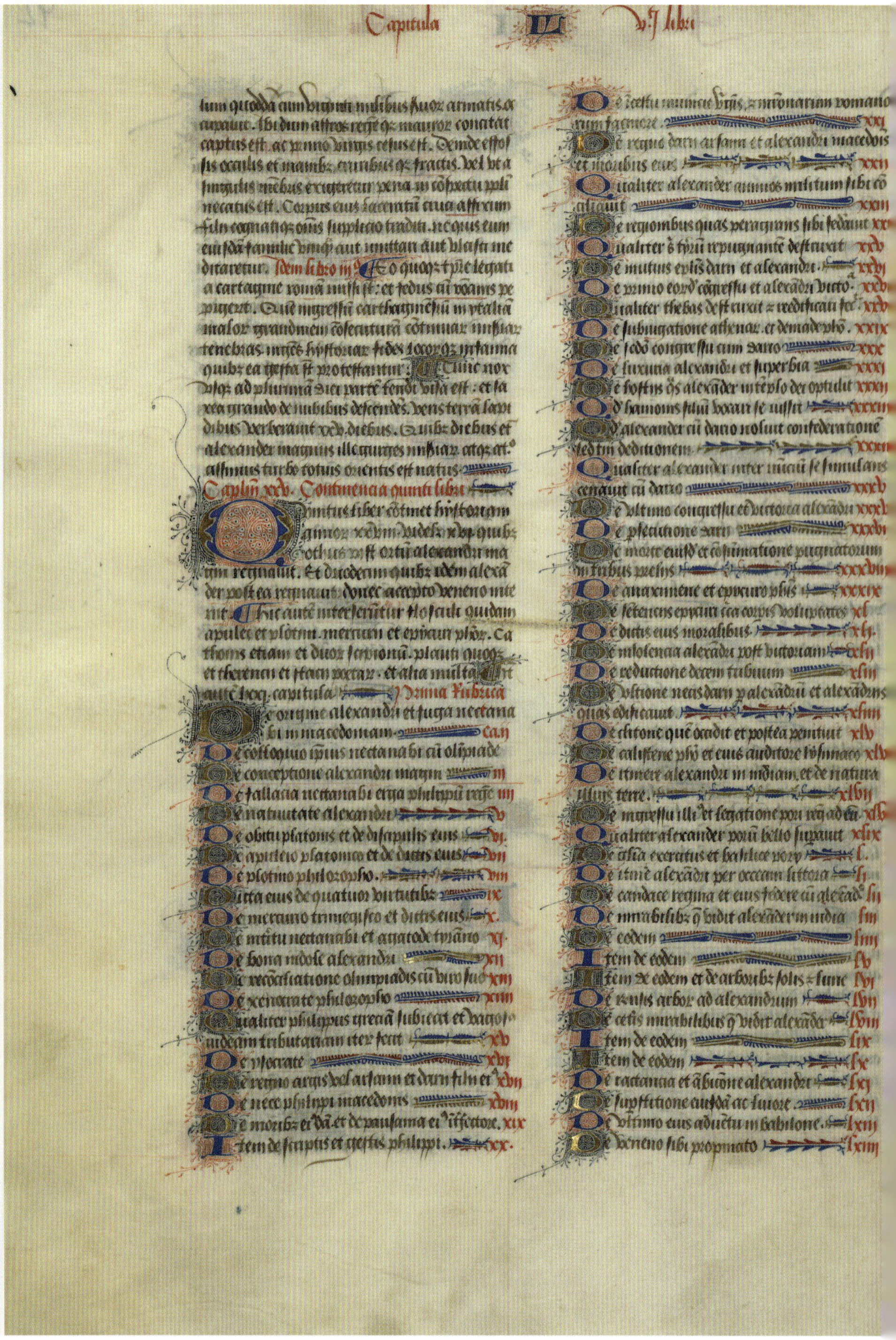

ANONYMOUS, *The Greek Alexander Romance*, trans. Richard Stoneman, Penguin, London and New York, 1991.

BOUNOURE, G., SERRET, B., *Pseudo-Callisthène, Le Roman d'Alexandre. La vie et les hauts faits d'Alexandre de Macédoine*, coll. 'La roue à livres', Les Belles Lettres, Paris, 1992.

FORGEAU, A., *Nectanébo. La dernière dynastie égyptienne*, ch. 1.4, 'La littérature mémorielle', Éditions Khéops, Paris, 2018, pp. 40–7.

MATTHEY, P., *Pharaon, magicien et filou: Nectanébo II entre l'histoire et la légende*, doctoral thesis presented at the University of Geneva on 10 June 2012, available online at https://archive-ouverte.unige.ch/unige:24160 (accessed 7 June 2020).

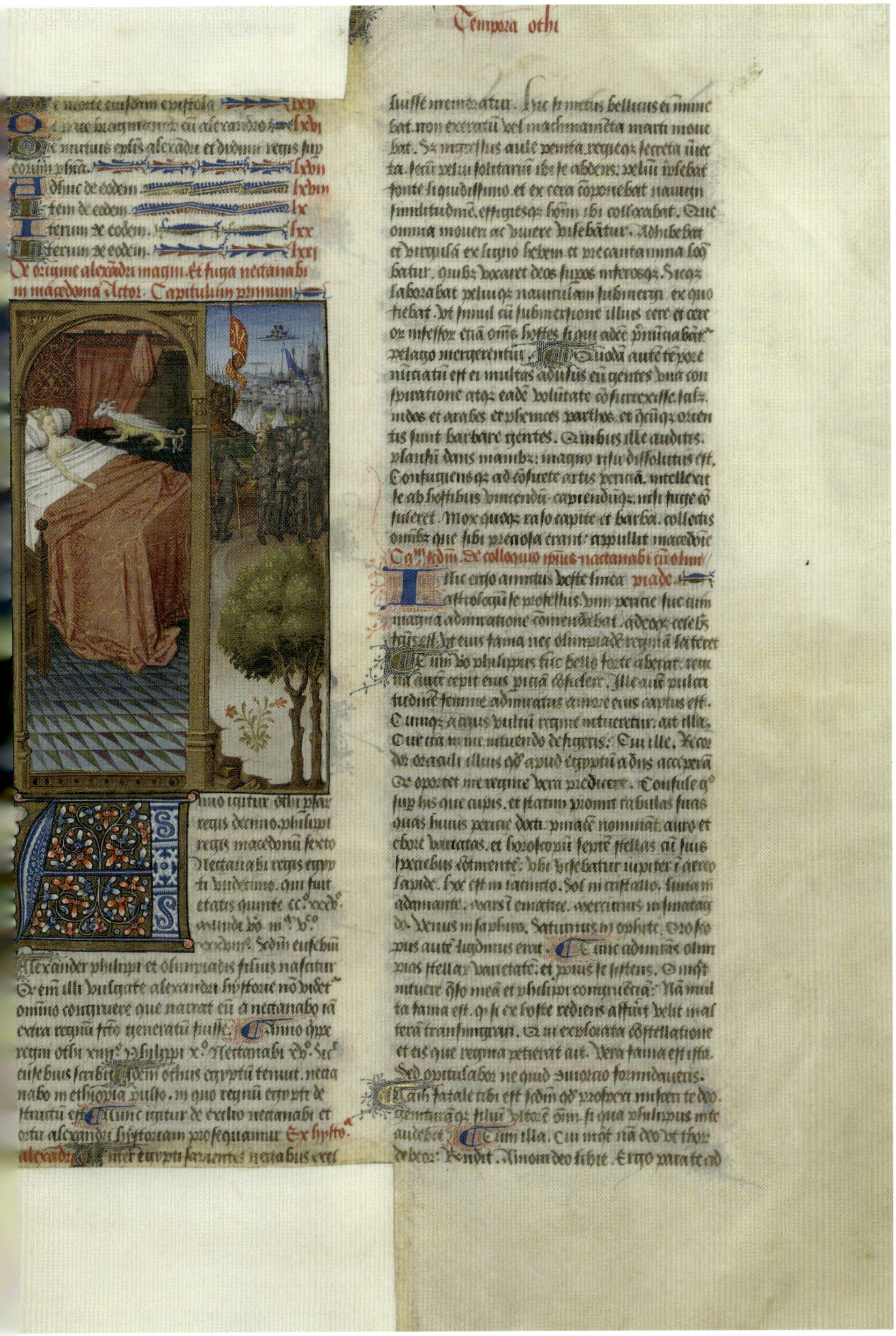

96

Alexander the Great, his parents and successors in the *Liber chronicarum,* (known in English as the *Nuremberg Chronicle*) by Hartmann Schedel, published by Anton Koberger, Nuremberg, Germany, 1493, fol. LXXVI.

The branch joining the hero to his parents passes in front of Philip of Macedonia, so as to link Queen Olympias and 'the magus Nectanebo, father of Alexander'.

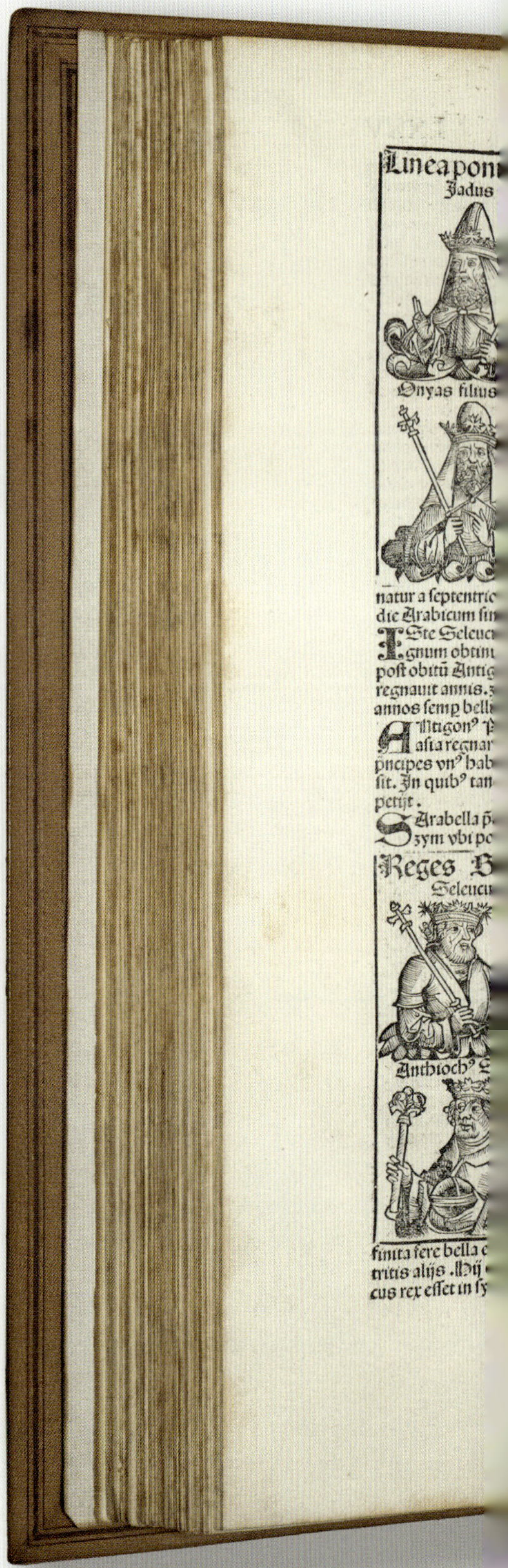

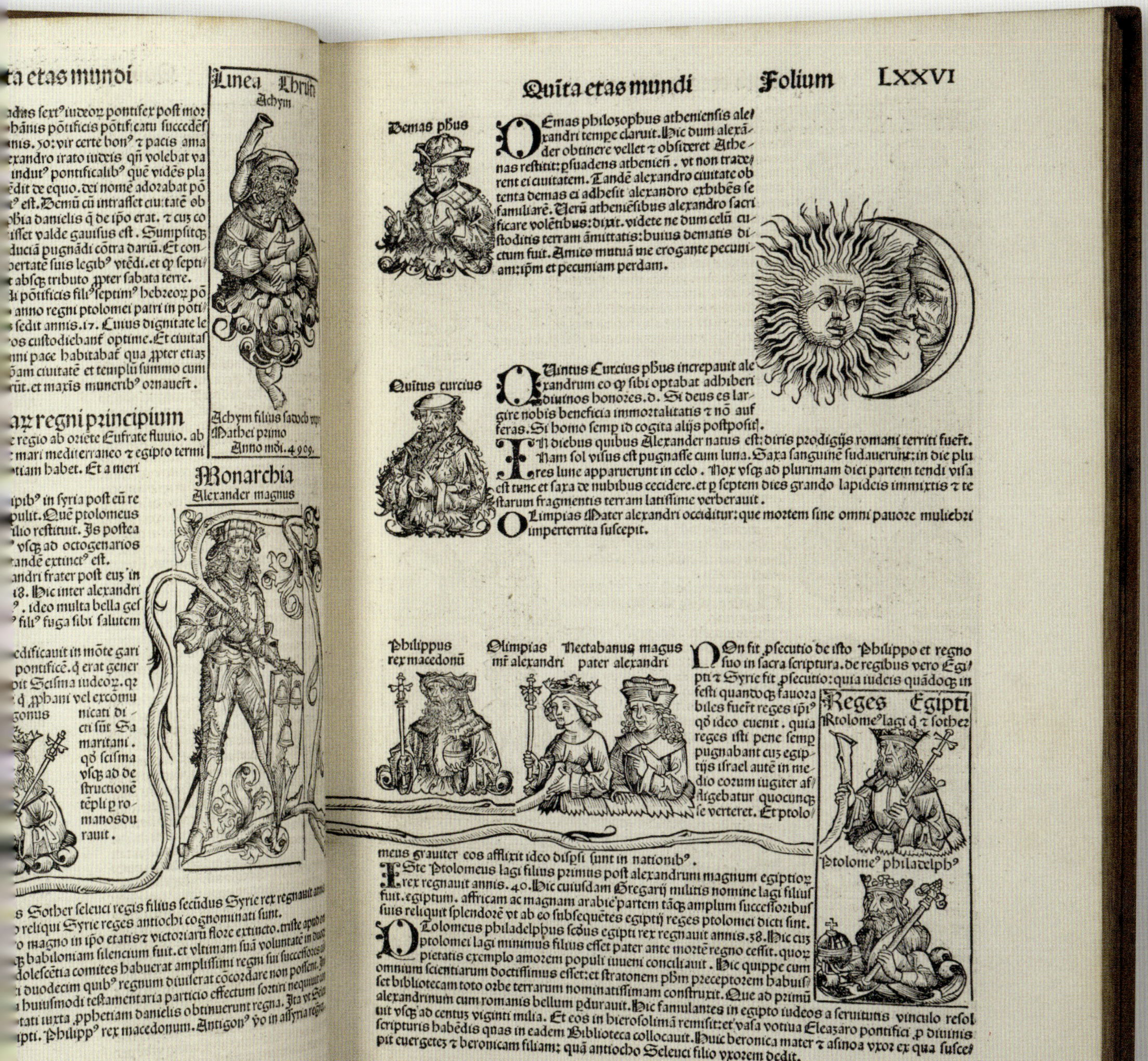

Quita etas mundi Folium LXXVI

Demas phus

Demas philozophus atheniensis alexandri tempe claruit. Hic dum alexāder obtinere vellet τ obsideret Athenas restitit: psuadens athenieñ. vt non traderent ei ciuitatem. Tandē alexandro ciuitate obtenta demas ei adhesit alexandro exhibēs se familiarē. Verū atheniēsibus alexandro sacrificare volētibus: dixit. videte ne dum celū custoditis terram āmittatis: huius dematis dictum fuit. Amico mutuā me erogante pecuniam: ipm et pecuniam perdam.

Quitus curcius

Quintus Curcius phus increpauit alexandrum eo q sibi optabat adhiberi diuinos honores. d. Si deus es largire nobis beneficia immortalitatis τ nō aufferas. Si homo semp id cogita alijs postpositis.

In diebus quibus Alexander natus est: diris prodigijs romani territi fuerūt. Nam sol visus est pugnasse cum luna. Saxa sanguinē sudauerunt: in die plures lune apparuerunt in celo. Nox vsq ad plurimam diei partem tendi visa est tunc et saxa de nubibus cecidere. et p septem dies grando lapideis immixtis τ testarum fragmentis terram latissime verberauit.

Olimpias Mater alexandri occiditur: que mortem sine omni pauore muliebri imperterrita suscepit.

Philippus rex macedonū — Olimpias mr̄ alexandri — Nectabanus magus pater alexandri

Non fit psecutio de isto Philippo et regno suo in sacra scriptura. de regibus vero Egipti τ Syrie fit psecutio: quia iudeis quādoq infesti quandoq fauorabiles fuerūt reges ipi⁹ qd ideo euenit. quia reges isti pene semp pugnabant cū egiptijs israel autē in medio eorum iugiter affligebatur quocunq se verteret. Et ptolomeus grauiter eos afflixit ideo dispsi sunt in nationib⁹.

Reges Egipti

Ptolome⁹ lagi q̄ τ sother

Ptolome⁹ philadelph⁹

Iste Ptolomeus lagi filius primus post alexandrum magnum egiptiorū rex regnauit annis. 40. Hic cuiusdam Gregarij militis nomine lagi filius fuit. egiptum. affricam ac magnam arabie partem tāq amplum successoribus suis reliquit splendorē vt ab eo subsequētes egiptij reges ptolomei dicti sint.

Ptolomeus philadelphus scd̄us egipti rex regnauit annis. 38. Hic cū ptolomei lagi minimus filius esset pater ante mortē regno cessit. quorū pietatis exemplo amorem populi iuueni conciliauit. Hic quippe cum omnium scientiarum doctissimus esset: et stratonem phm preceptorem habuisset bibliotecam toto orbe terrarum nominatissimam construxit. Que ad primū alexandrinum cum romanis bellum pdurauit. Hic famulantes in egipto iudeos a seruitutis vinculo resoluit vsq ad centū viginti milia. Et eos in hierosolimā remisit: et vasa votiua Elezaro pontifici p diuinis scripturis habēdis quas in eadem Bibliotheca collocauit. Huic beronica mater τ asinoa vxor ex qua suscepit euergetē τ beronicam filiam: quā antiocho Seleuci filio vxorem dedit.

201

CLEOPATRA, *FEMME FATALE* OR WISE QUEEN

Cleopatra VII (51–30 BCE) was the last representative of the Ptolemies, an originally Macedonian dynasty. For two thousand years, she has remained unquestionably the best-known and most romanticized queen of Egypt, to the extent that her image appears reproduced in countless formats, from the far west to the far east (cats. 230 and 217).

Because Cleopatra collided with Octavian head-on — after turning the heads of Julius Caesar and Anthony — thereby disrupting geopolitical calculations concerning the dying republic, Roman propaganda created a deplorable reputation for the Greco-Egyptian queen. In the West, later generations derived their image of her from Latin authors, as a libidinous and immoral seductress and as a cruel, excessively ambitious sovereign. The imagination of artists was particularly excited by the legendary episode of her suicide, after being defeated by Octavian, when she chose death by snakebite in preference to captivity in the conqueror's triumphal cortege (cat. 100).

98

Unknown artist, after Domenico di Puligo, *The Death of Cleopatra*, mid-sixteenth century.

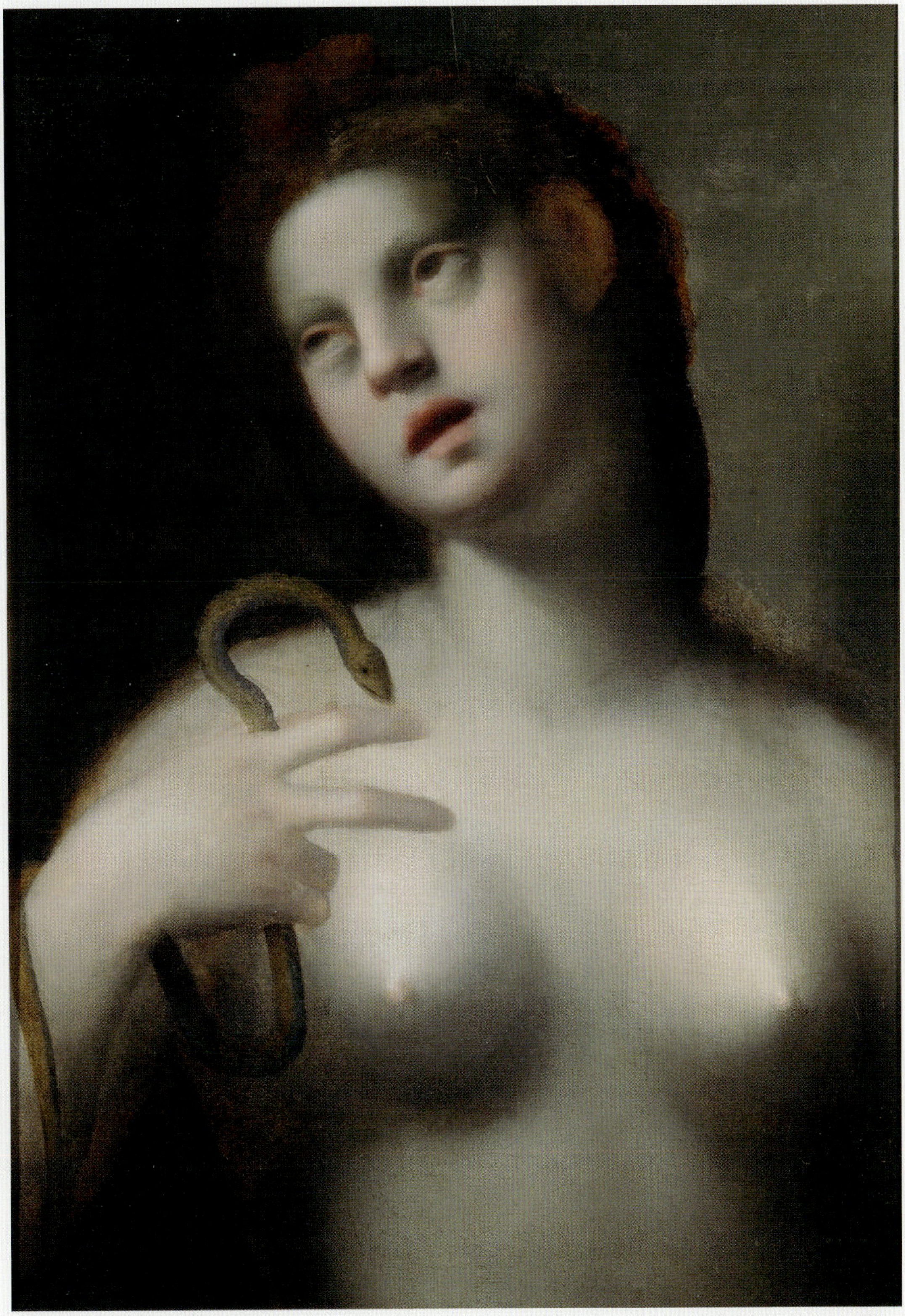

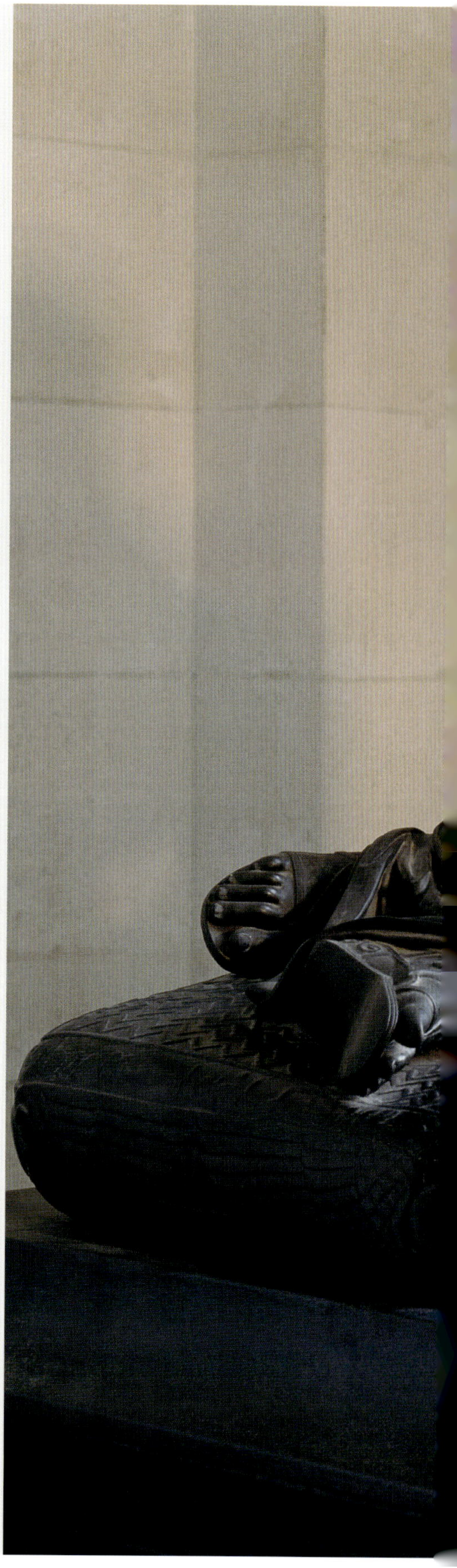

102

Henri Ducommun du Locle,
Cleopatra, France, 1852–3.

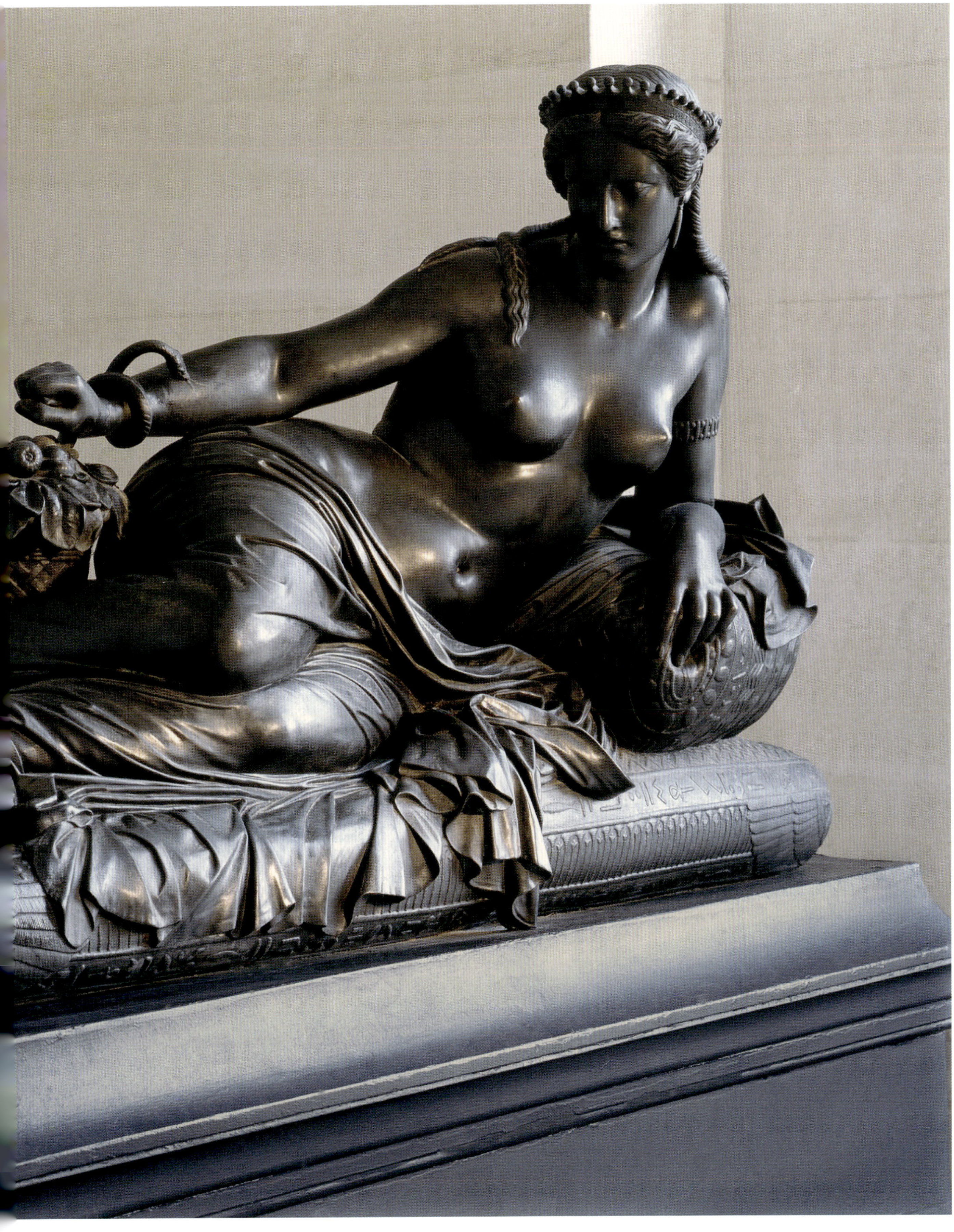

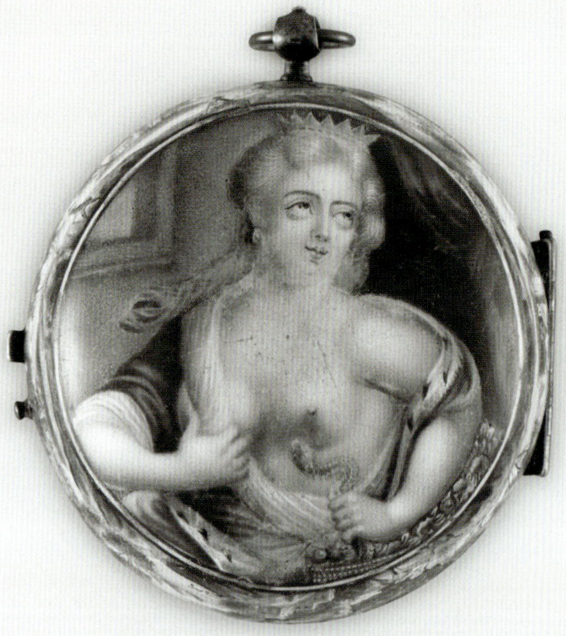

99

Isaac Thuret, watch depicting the death of Cleopatra, Paris, late seventeenth century.

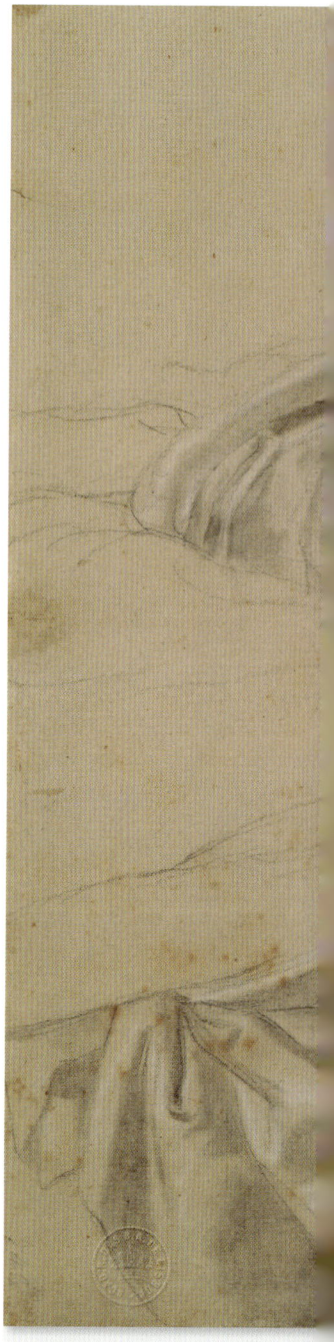

In artworks of the early Renaissance, the queen is shown naked at the exact moment the snake bites her, sometimes in a garden. This iconography connects her with Eve, the first sinner (cat. 98). Artists took pains to depict the dying woman's ambiguous pose, with her head thrown back, her eyes rolling inwards and her mouth half open — all signs of a rapture that hovers between death and orgasm, comparable to Baroque depictions of Mary Magdalene in ecstasy (cat. 101). Cleopatra's nudity and her sensual agony invite viewers to deplore the sins of the flesh, while allowing them to experience a voyeuristic frisson given legitimacy by a respectable subject drawn from antiquity (cat. 99). In the second half of the seventeenth century, there was an interlude when the eroticism was toned down: Cleopatra's political role and the heroism of her last act were given more prominence, conveyed especially through historical

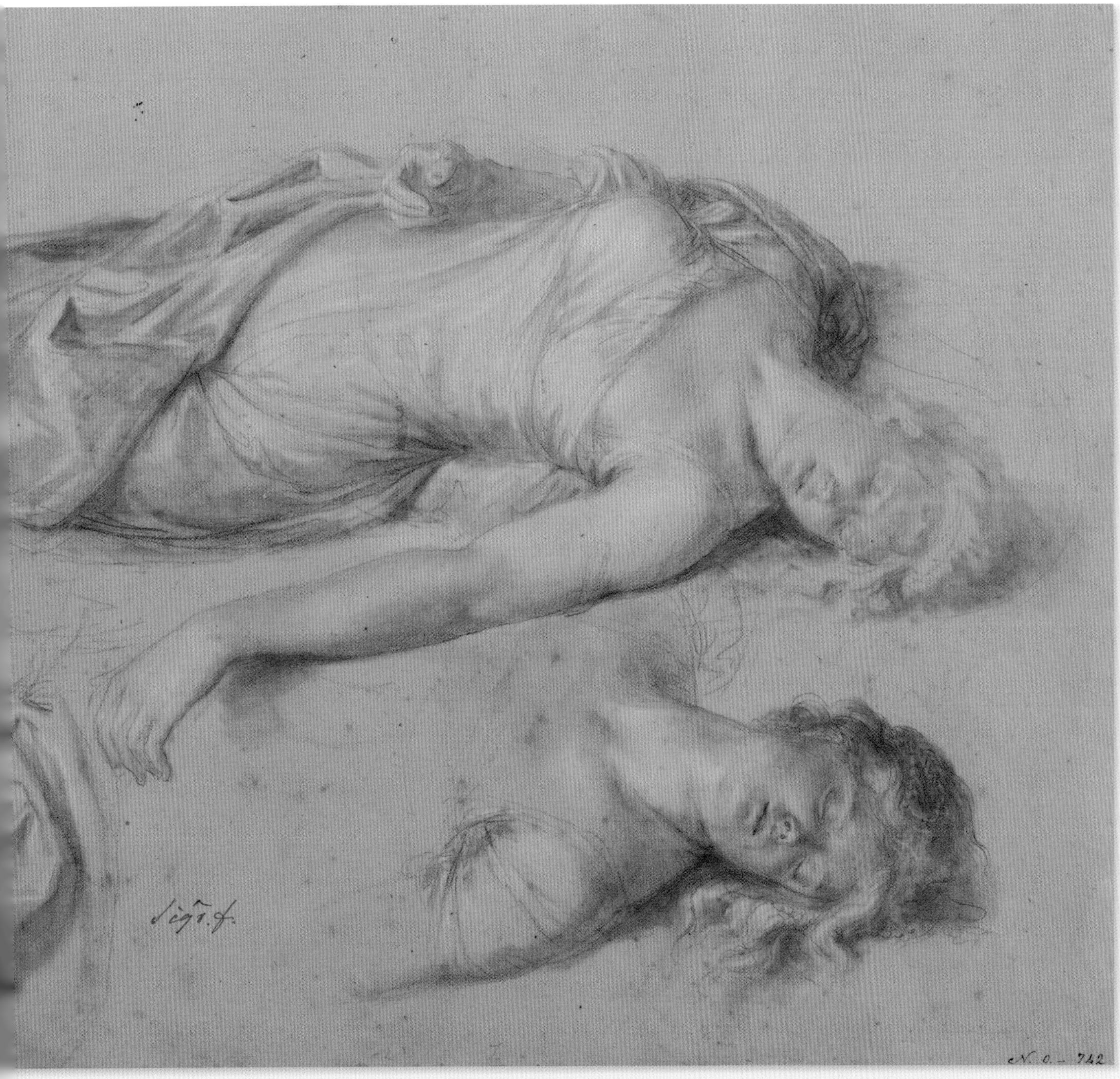

100

Domingos António de Sequeira, *Estudo Preparatório para «A Morte de Cleópatra»* (Preparatory Study for 'The Death of Cleopatra'), Rome, c. 1791.

104

Isabelle Van Berchem, *née* Naville, *The Baths of Cleopatra*, Aswan, 1893.

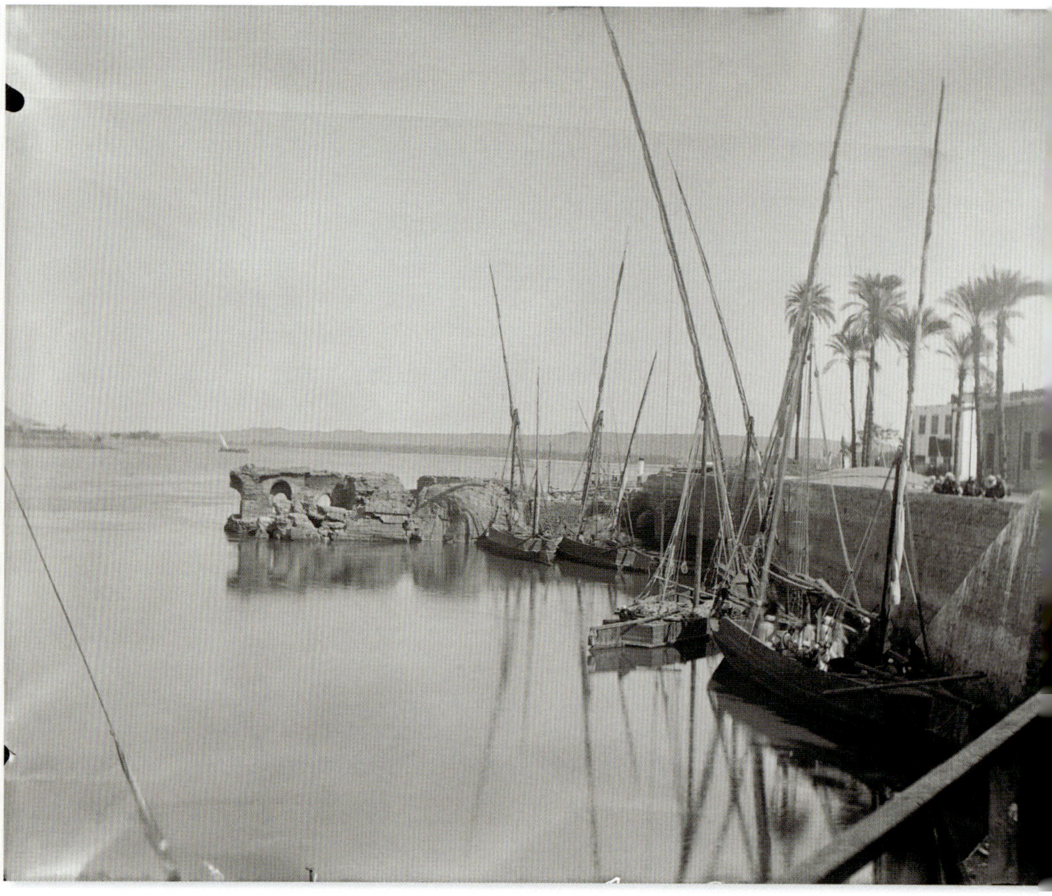

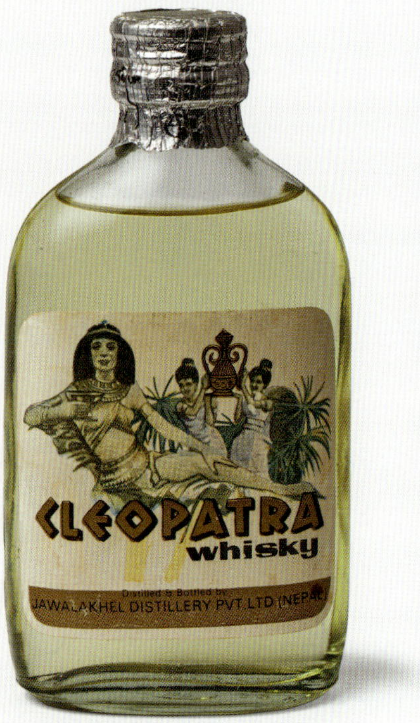

230

Cleopatra whisky bottle, Nepal, second half of the twentieth century.

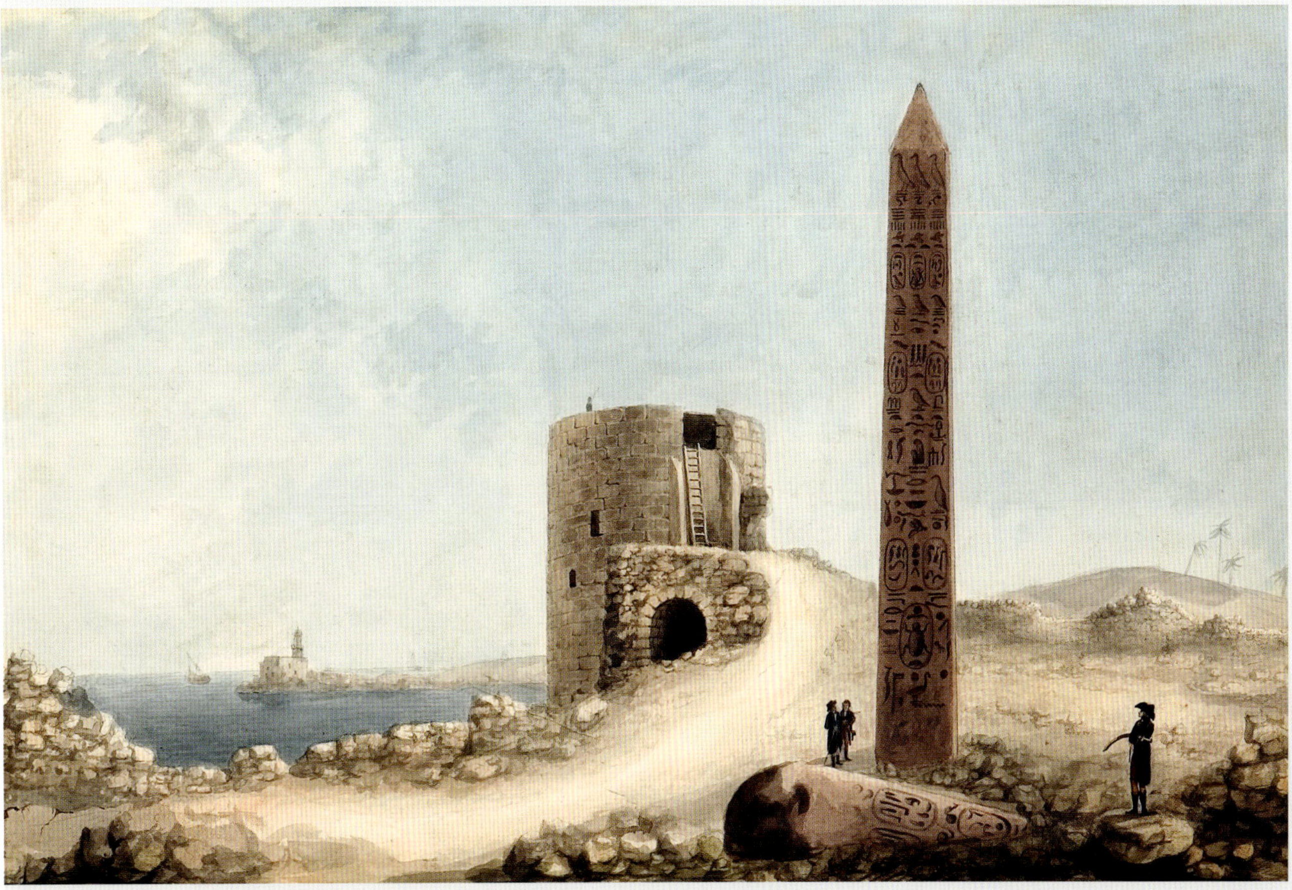

103

Nicolas-Jacques Conté, obelisk known as 'Cleopatra's Needle', Alexandria, 1798–1800.

101

Claude Bertin, *Cleopatra*, before 1697.

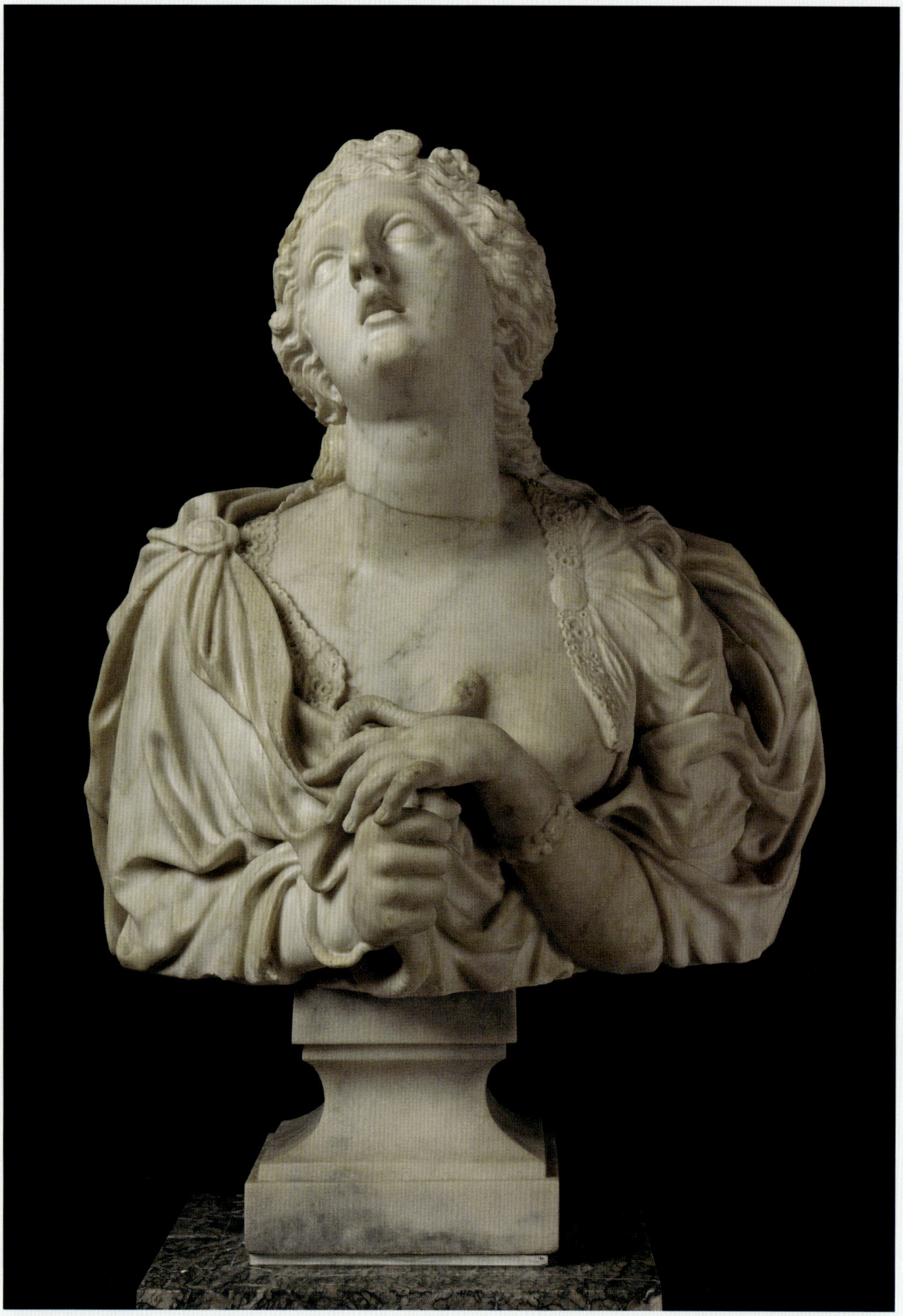

217

Luís Jardim Portela, *Cleopatra*, 1963.

This caricature was drawn in the year that Elizabeth Taylor brought new popularity to the seductive figure of Cleopatra in the film by Joseph L. Mankiewicz.

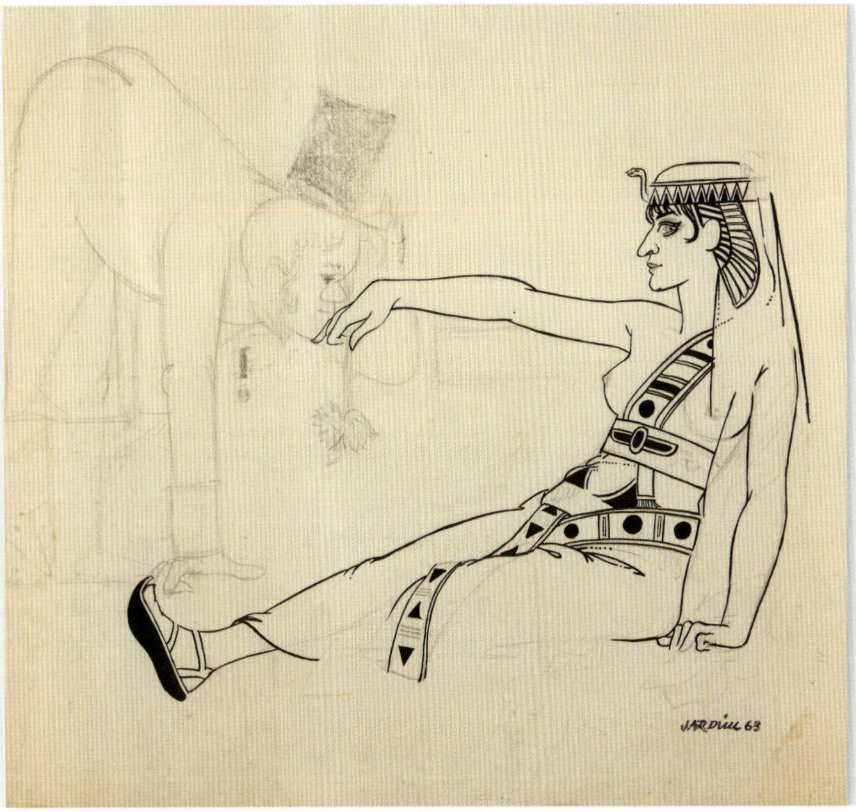

details such as the basket of figs in which the fatal reptile was hidden. The nineteenth century reverted to a very sexualized image of Cleopatra: an erotic appeal to the male gaze mixed with colonial exoticism (cat. 102), a stereotype that has prevailed until today in general culture. In parallel, a more scholarly rehabilitation of the Greek stateswoman portrayed her as shrewd and cultured.

While the West blindly accepted the tarnished legend fabricated by Rome and Christian morality, premodern Arab historians promoted a much more flattering image of Cleopatra as a skilled administrator committed to the defence of her kingdom, equally capable of debating science and philosophy, fascinated by alchemy, and the author of treatises on toxicology and mathematics. They fancifully attributed her with fabulous monuments, such as a gigantic wall around Egypt, the famous lighthouse of Alexandria and a palace with adjoining obelisks known as 'Cleopatra's needles' (cat. 103). Finally, the toponymy of Egypt and its surrounding oases, especially various managed springs and creeks known as the 'Baths of Cleopatra' (cat. 104), have still left a few traces of the legendary queen. **FM**

De Callataÿ, F., *Cléopâtre, usages et mésusages de son image*, Académie royale de Belgique, Brussels, 2015.

El-Daly, O., *Egyptology: The Missing Millennium. Ancient Egypt in Medieval Arabic Writings*, Routledge, New York and London, 2005, pp. 131–7.

SENWOSRET/ SESOSTRIS, MODEL PHARAOHS

Although the name Senwosret is not as famous as that of Tutankhamun, it is nevertheless attached to a dynasty of exceptional and exemplary pharaohs, despite the vagaries of collective memory which have seen some important sovereigns fall into oblivion. According to the eyes of historians, Senwosret I and Senwosret III — members of the dynasty who turned Egypt in the Middle Kingdom, at the beginning of the second millennium BCE, into an all-powerful state — remain supreme models for their successors.

Key figures in the Twelfth Dynasty, just like Amenemhat III, these sovereigns colonized Nubia, south of Egypt (cat. 2). They developed the province of Faiyum, at the junction between Upper and Lower Egypt, and established their capital and their pyramids there. They introduced radical administrative reforms, built temples to the dynastic gods and sent expeditions into mines and quarries, some of which comprised more than fifteen thousand men.

Senwosret III, who reigned for thirty-four years, is the best-known of the line, familiar from both texts and images of him that have been found (cat. 11 and 22). There are numerous portraits of him — mostly statues — expressing the authoritarian and implacable character of one who could also show himself to be merciful and considerate to his people.

Jean-Baptiste Thiébault, engraver, after François Georgin, *Apothéose de Napoléon* (Apotheosis of Napoleon), published by Pellerin, Épinal, France, after 1837.

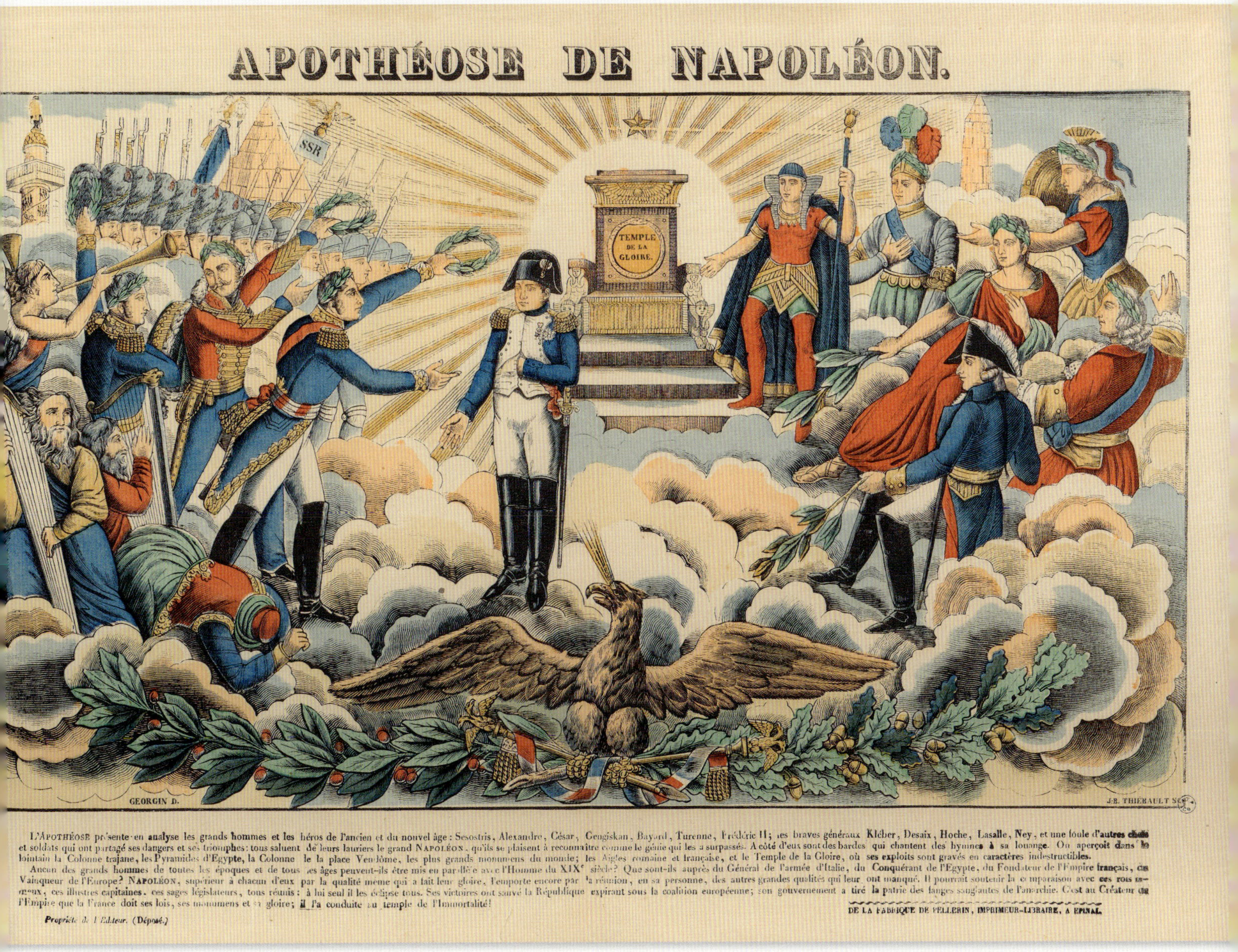

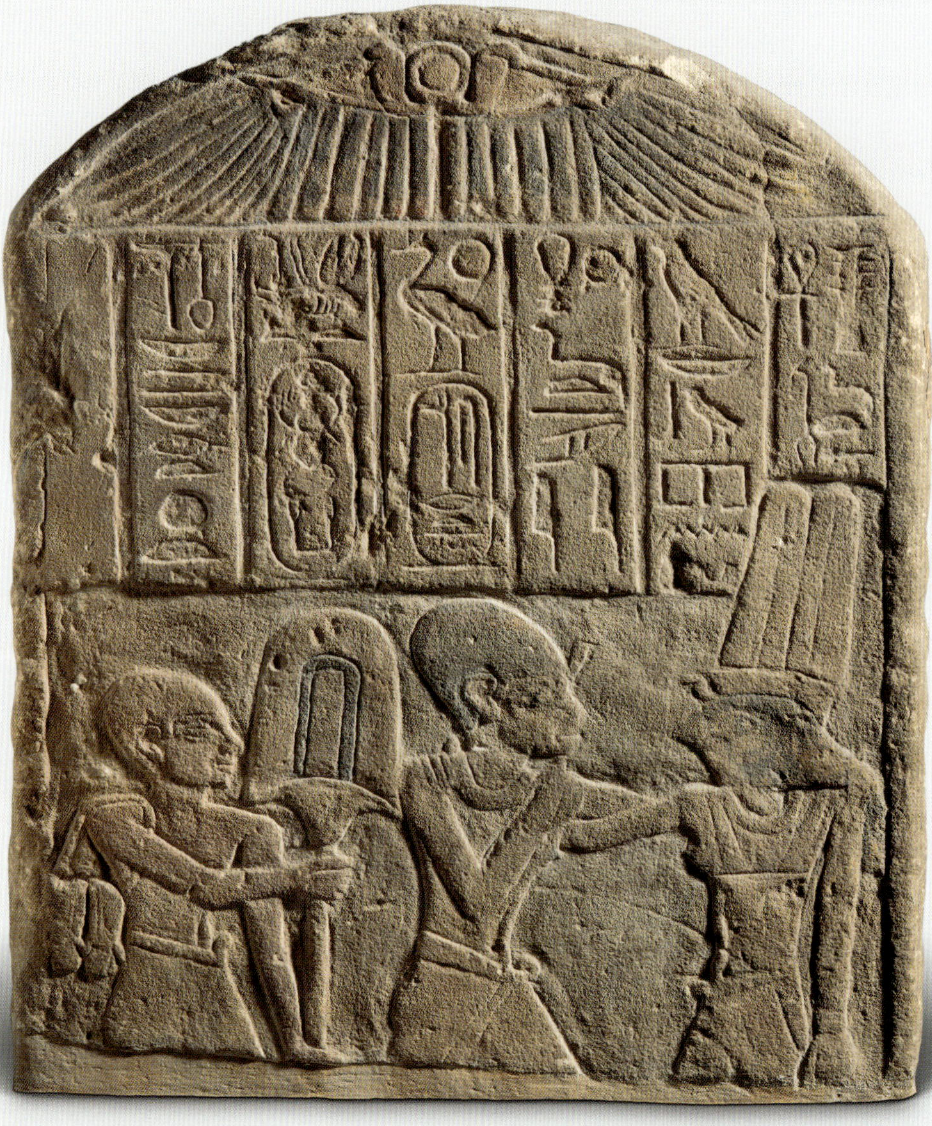

2

Stela depicting the ancient King Senwosret I embracing the god Horus of Buhen, fortress of Buhen, Sudan, Thirteenth to Seventeenth Dynasty (c. 1781–1539 BCE).

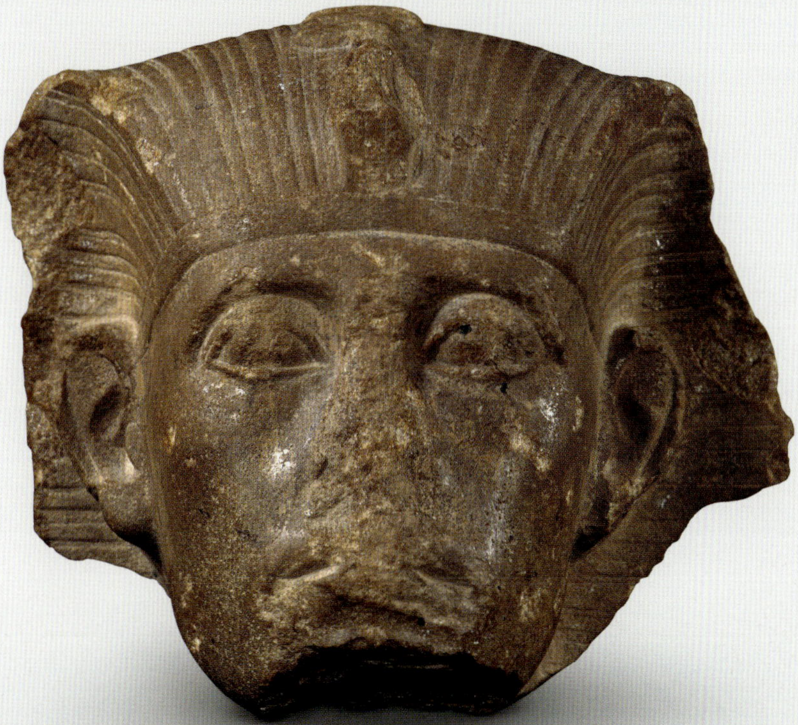

11

Head of a sphinx of Senwosret III, Egypt, reign of Senwosret III (c. 1856–1838 BCE).

107

Émile Béchard, *Vue d'ensemble avec la palmeraie. Statue de Sésostris renversée* (General view with palm grove and toppled statue of Sesostris), Mit Rahina, Egypt, between 1868 and 1880.

This colossus was in reality one of the statues of Ramesses II which had stood in front of the temple of Ptah at Memphis.

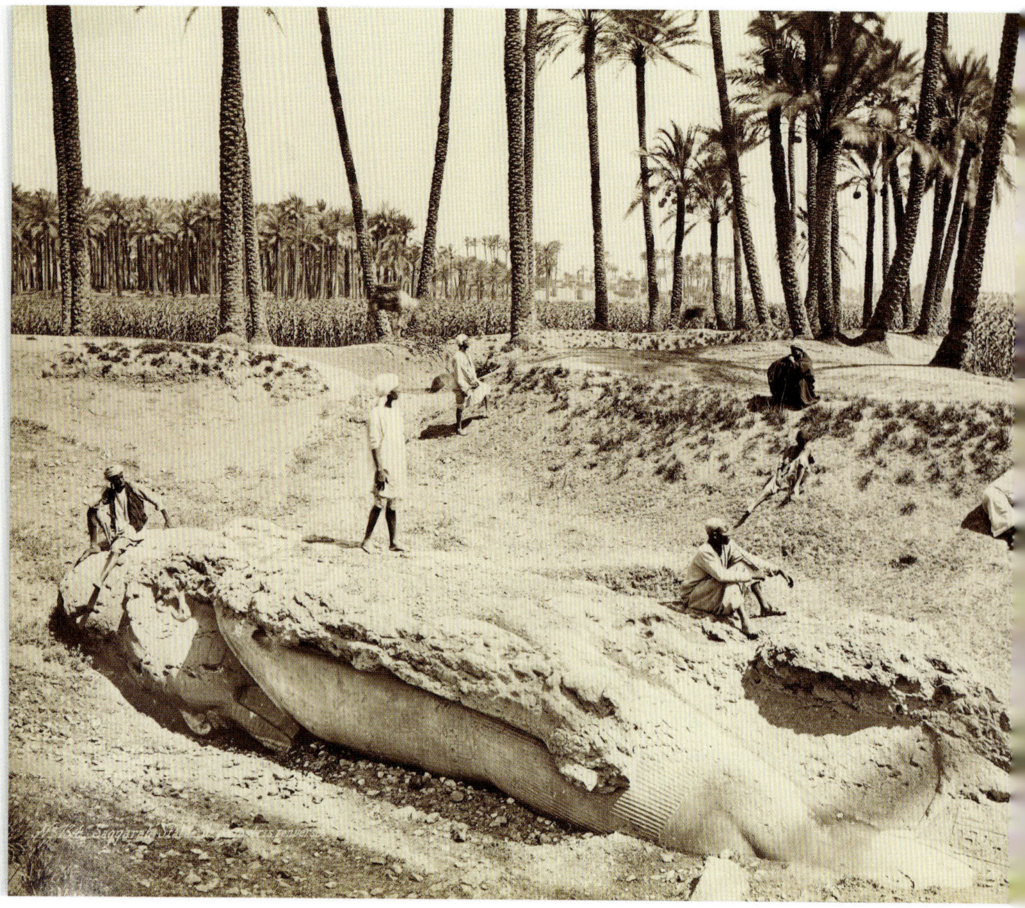

After his death, he was seen as the equal of the gods. It is in Nubia that there is most evidence of a posthumous cult in his name, giving him the status of a local god. Three centuries later, his deification reached its peak under Thutmose III, the glorious pharaoh of the New Kingdom, who legitimized his ambitions for Nubia by invoking the conquests of Senwosret, his predecessor. And twelve centuries after his death, the Nubian pharaoh Taharqa honoured the deified pharaoh Senwosret on an altar in the fortress of Semna.

The posthumous glory of the Senwosret dynasty, whose name has been distorted by time and translations, sparked many legends in Egypt in the Late Period. Greek and demotic literature eagerly recounts the adventures of a king called Sesostris, Sesoösis or even Sesonchosis: in the fifth century BCE, the Greek writer Herodotus made him an Egyptian hero, combining the exploits and qualities of Senwosret I and Senwosret III, and mixing in elements of Ramesses II, Shoshenq and Alexander the Great. Little by little, in the writing of authors such as Aristotle, Diodorus, Strabo, Pliny the Elder and Clement of Alexandria, this mythical Sesostris became the paragon of Egyptian monarchy, described as powerful and brave, but also as a cruel, merciless tyrant. This legendary pharaoh has left his mark across the centuries: a map

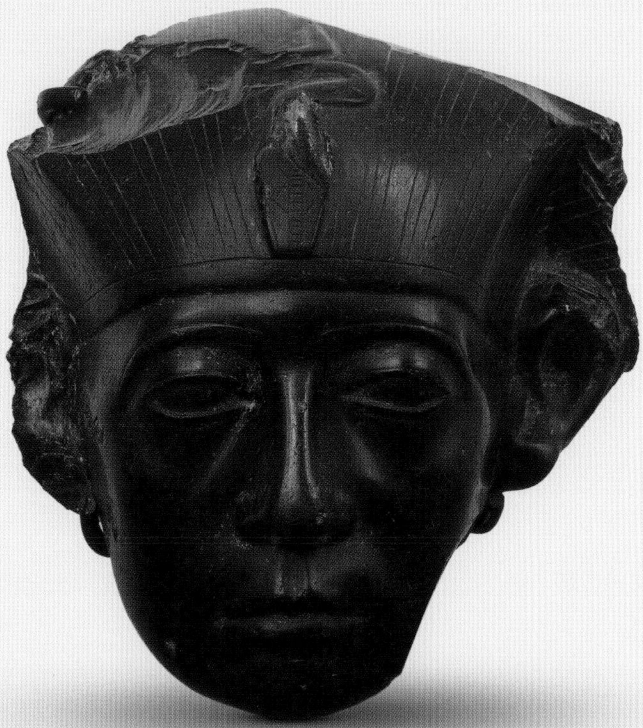

22

Head of Senwosret III, Egypt,
Twelfth Dynasty (c. 1860 BCE)

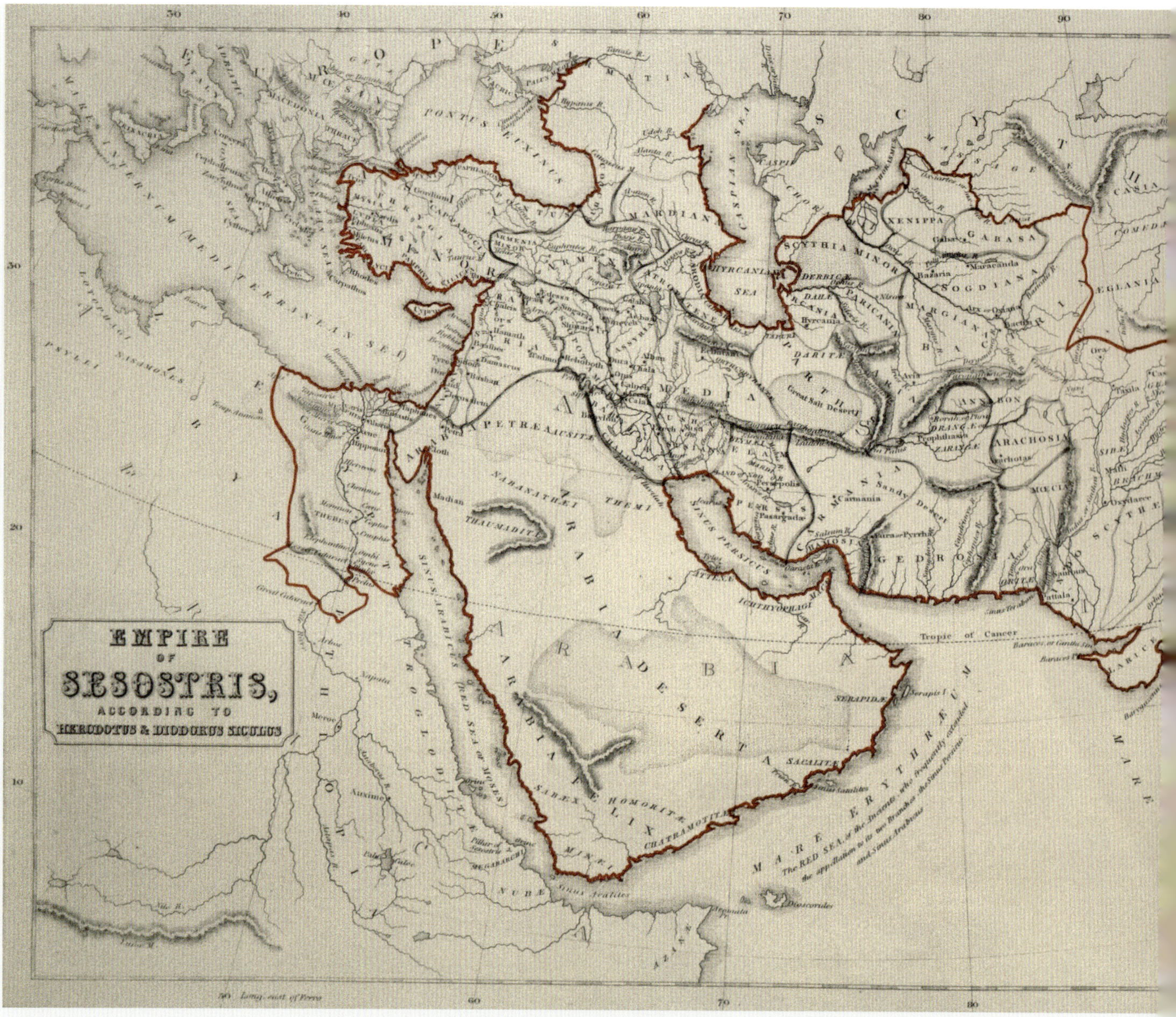

106

The Empire of Sesostris in *Monumenta Cartographica Africae et Aegypti*, Yusuf Kamal, publisher, Cairo, 1933.

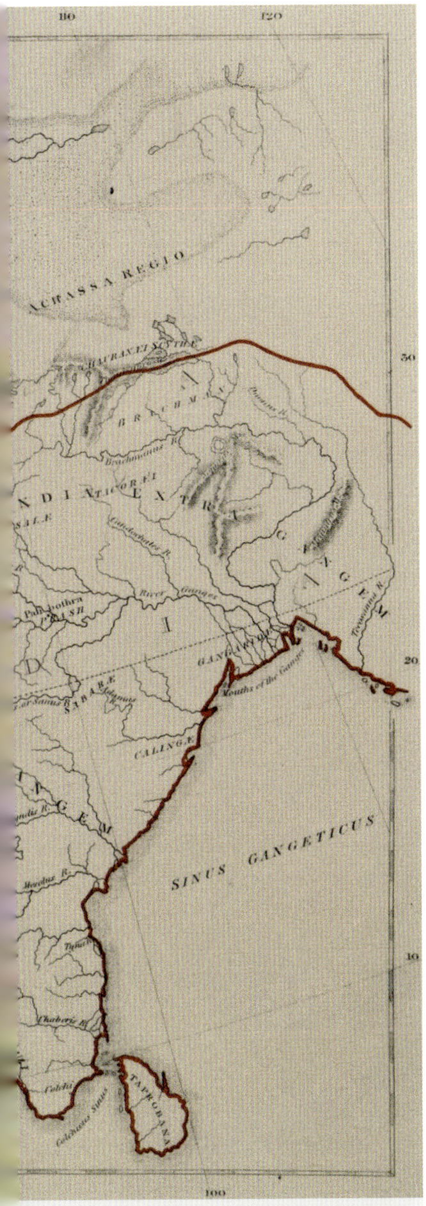

of his conquests, with the legend 'Imperium Sesostris', created in the early eighteenth century by Johann Matthias Hase (1684–1742), attributes him with a vast territory, covering Egypt, Nubia, Asia Minor and the Levant, reaching as far as Afghanistan (In 1933 the Egyptian prince and geographer Yusuf Kamal drew a very similar map of this legendary empire, cat. 106).

This phenomenal figure has also featured in novels, tragedies and operas by European artists, especially in the eighteenth and nineteenth centuries. The name 'Sesostris' was given to a species of butterfly in 1779 (cat. 109) and to a ship of the French marine postal service in the Levant in the nineteenth century. Not until hieroglyphs were deciphered in 1822 did it become apparent that many monuments attributed by travellers and historians to Sesostris were in fact the work of the great Ramesses (cat. 107), who was at last able to find his place among the 'superstar pharaohs', no longer under the shadow of Sesostris, whose fame today is now restricted to the world of Egyptologists. **GA-L**

El-Enany, Kh., 'Le "dieu" nubien Sésostris III', in *BIFAO* 104, 2004, Cairo, pp. 207–13.

Favry, N. *Sésostris Ier et les débuts de la XIIe dynastie*, coll. 'Les Grands pharaons', Pygmalion, Paris, 2009.

Morfoisse, F., Andreu-Lanoë, G., eds., *Sésostris III, pharaon de légende*, exh. cat., Palais des Beaux-arts, Lille, Snoeck, 2014.

Tallet, P., *Sésostris III et la fin du Moyen Empire*, coll. 'Les Grands pharaons', Pygmalion, Paris, 2015.

PHARAOH IN THE BIBLE, *FIRAUN* IN THE QUR'AN

The best-known kings of Egypt, throughout the Middle Ages and up to the present day, have perhaps been those that the holy books simply refer to as 'Pharaoh'. This word, which comes from the Egyptian expression for the royal palace, is the title given to Egyptian sovereigns from the Eighteenth Dynasty onwards, in the same way that the Roman emperors were named 'Augustus'. During the first millennium BCE, the term began to be used on its own, without specifying a personal name, both in Egyptian sources and in biblical texts. In Bible translations and commentaries, Pharaoh began to be used as a first name as much as a title. An ambiguous 'Pharaoh' or 'Pharaoh, King of Egypt' is found in Western literature and iconography to this day (cat. 112). This confusion also exists in several surahs in the Qur'an as well as in Arab literature: the name 'Firaun' is given to the kings who had some interaction with the patriarchs Abraham, Joseph and Moses, just as in Genesis and Exodus. The Qur'an itself mentions Firaun no less than seventy-four times.

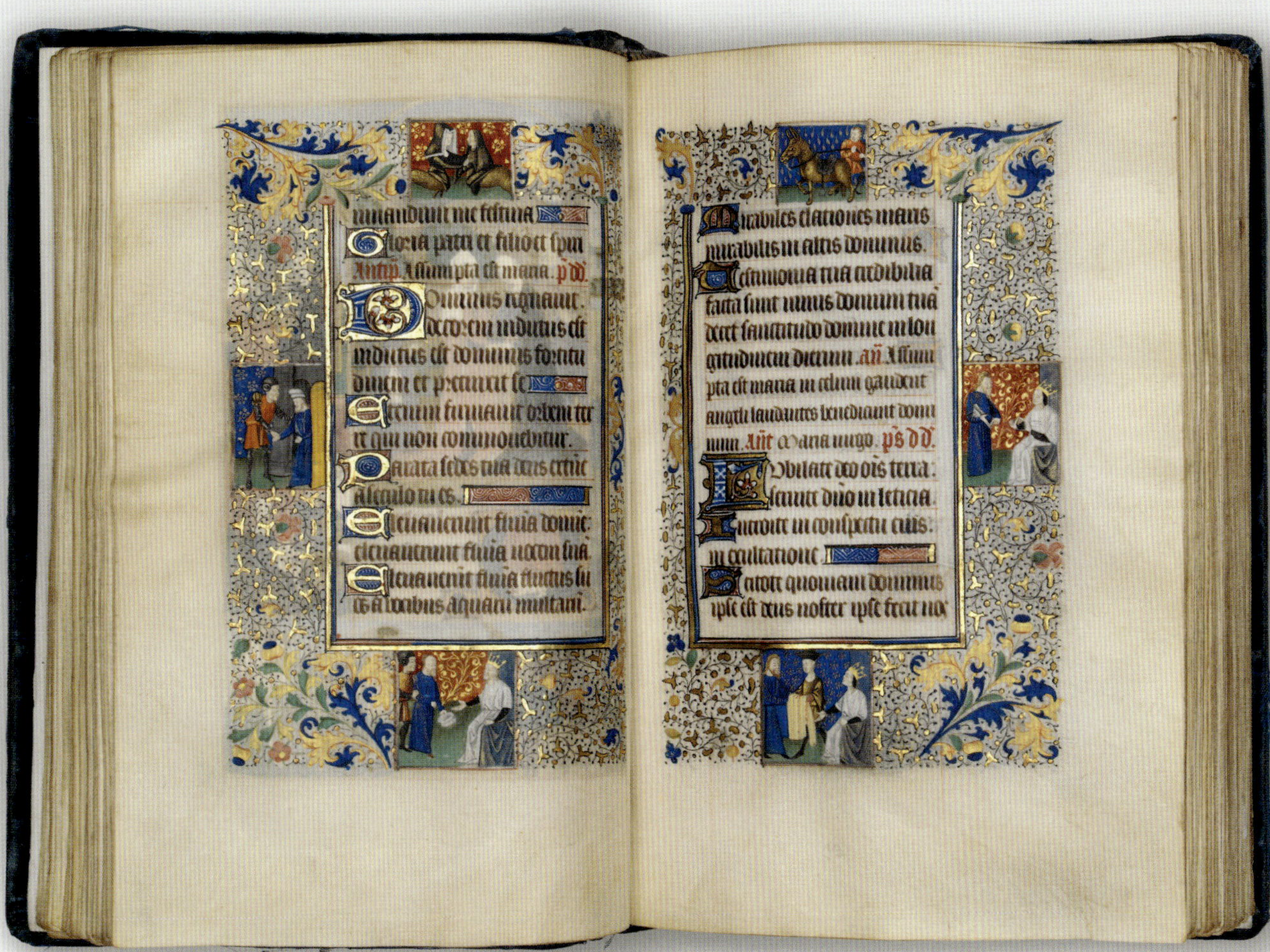

111

Scenes depicting *Joseph and Pharaoh* in a Book of Hours: illuminations by two followers of the Master of Adelaide of Savoy, by an illuminator of the circle of the Master of Jouvenel and by an artist from Tours in the style of Jean Fouquet, Poitiers and/or Tours, France, c. 1460–70, fols. 32–33r.

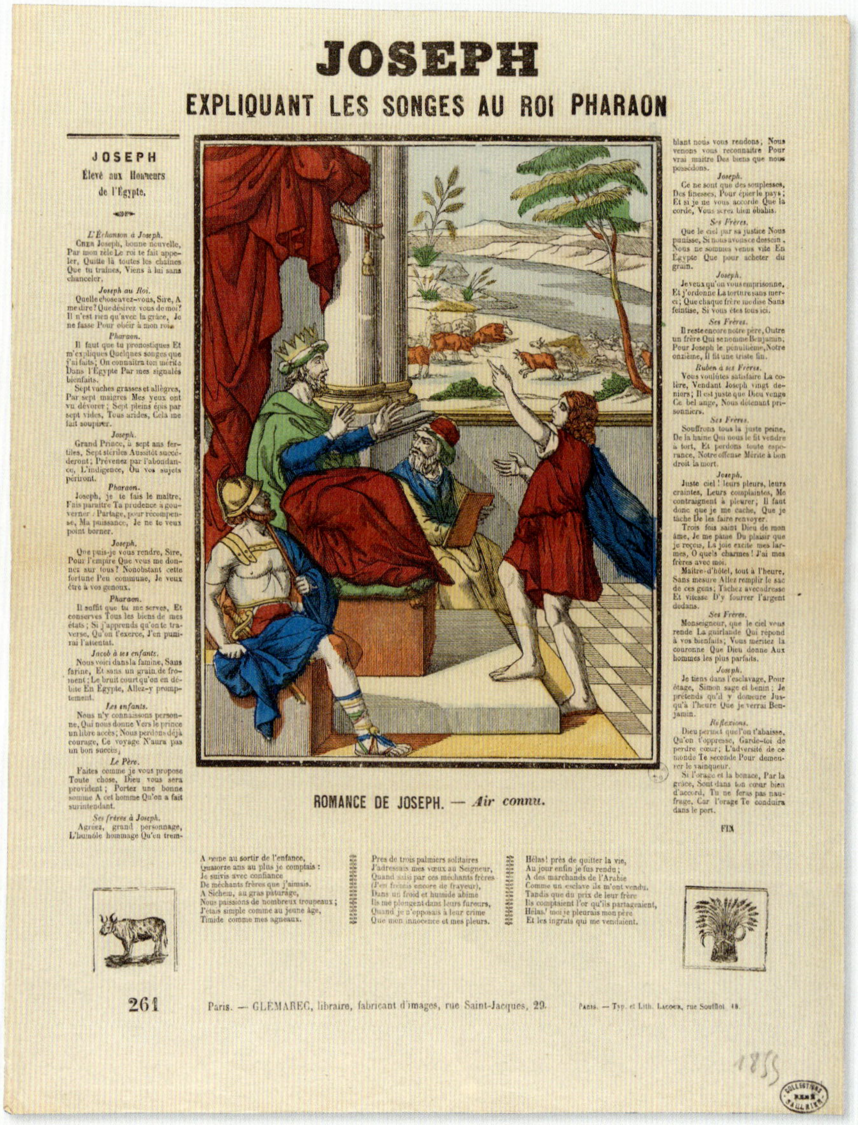

112

François Lacour, *Joseph expliquant les songes du roi Pharaon* (Joseph explaining King Pharaoh's dreams), Charles-Eugène Glémarec, publisher, Paris, between 1858 and 1860.

For the sacred texts' innumerable readers and listeners, these different 'Pharaohs' express contrasting images of ancient Egypt. In particular, in the story of Joseph, the king raises the hero to an almost royal rank (cats. 113 and 114), symbolizing the legendary hospitality of his country towards foreigners, beginning with the Jews of the diaspora. Conversely, as the adversary of Moses, Pharaoh is clearly an oppressor and tyrant. Arbitrary, cruel, wondering whether to have the young Moses killed for fear of being overthrown by him (cat. 115), he is the antithesis of God and his law, the brightly shining fires of freedom awaited by the Hebrew people. Fortunately and inevitably, Pharaoh is humiliated by God through his miracles, which are mediated by Moses (cat. 117), and eventually exterminated (cat. 118). This image of a tyrant reminded of God's law served as a political lesson in Christian kingdoms (cat. 116) and it is this same image that in Christianity is primarily associated with the name of Pharaoh, especially in the Protestant world. It is even more marked in Islam, where Pharaoh is a synonym for ungodly otherness

113

Léonce Schérer, *Délivrance et élévation de Joseph* [The saving and elevation of Joseph), Imprimerie Pellerin, Épinal, France, c. 1877.

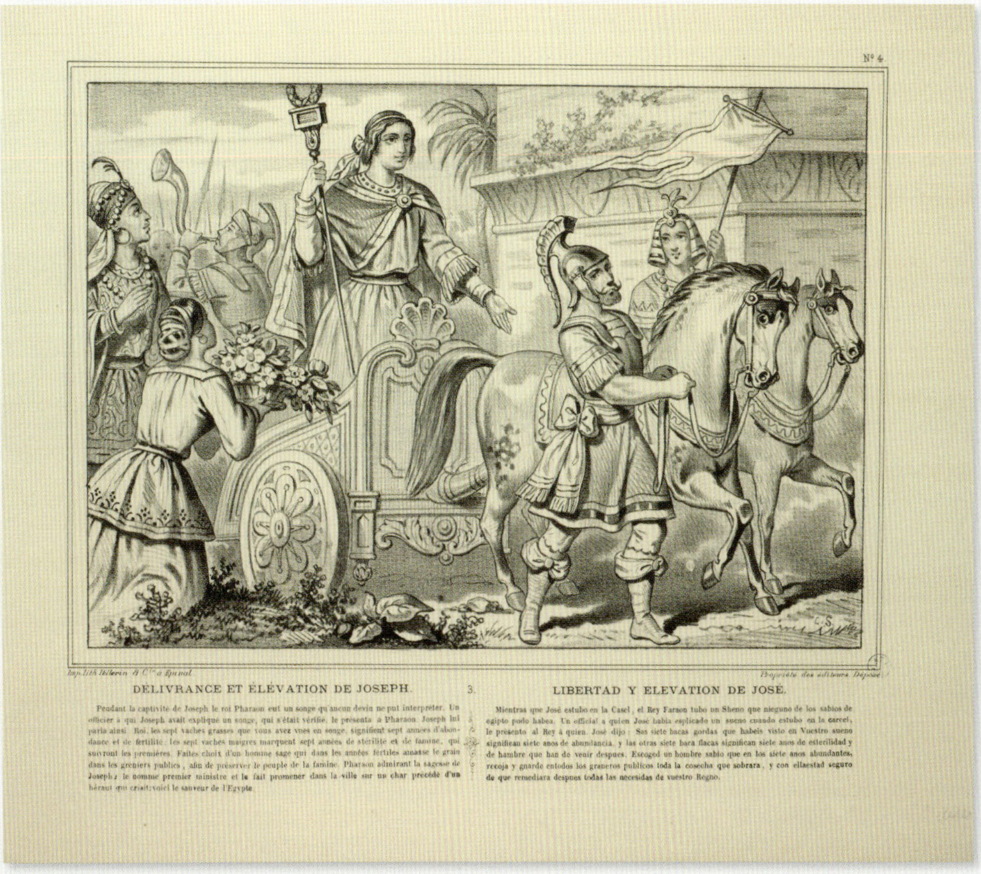

114

Yusuf/Joseph becomes minister for Pharaoh and receives a shining mirror as a gift, in *Tuhfat al-Ahrar* (Gift of the Free) by ʻAbd al-Rahman ibn Ahmad Jami, possibly Bukhara, Uzbekistan, 1554–5 (dated AH 962).

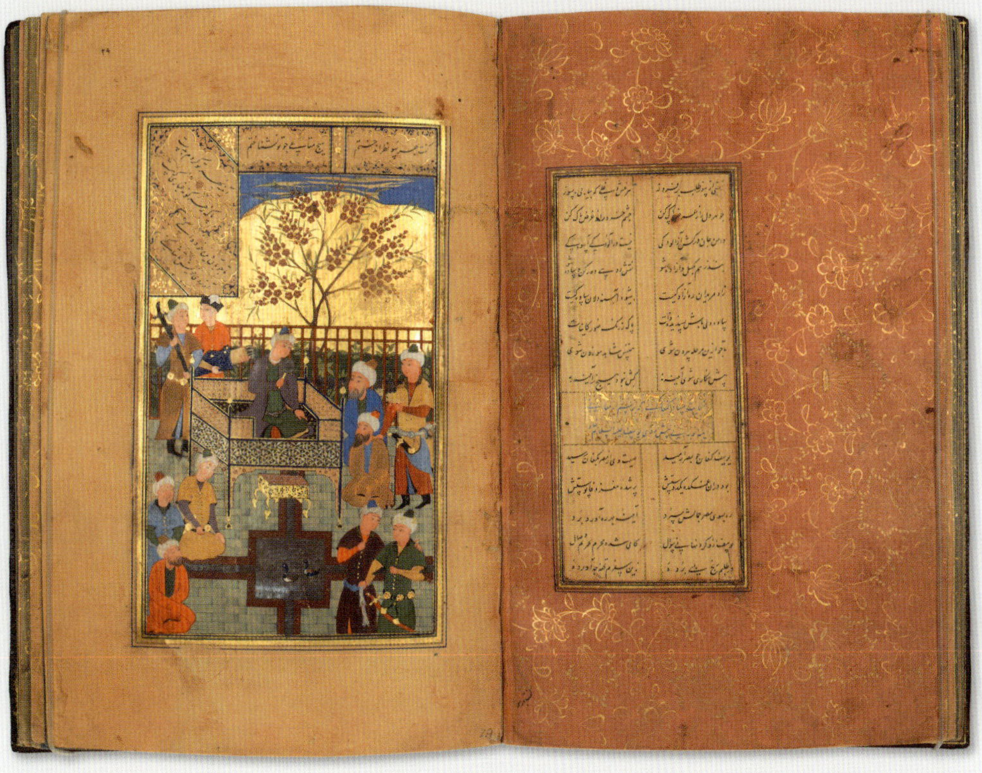

and injustice. Even in today's Egypt, people who are domineering or abuse their power are called 'Firaun', as could be heard when the former president Hosni Mubarak was jeered during the 2011 revolution. Islamic tradition most often refers to the fall of Firaun as a paradigm for enemies of the religion who are overthrown by Allah (Qur'an, 69, 9) (cat. 119). His body is said to have been preserved as a testament for human edification (Qur'an, 10, 90–2); according to the most devout, it should therefore be possible to identify his corpse among the mummies preserved in Cairo. His identity has been debated since the Middle Ages. And although the villain of Exodus has been given various names, derived from the works of Greco-Roman historians, since the nineteenth century the glorious Ramesses II and his son Merneptah have been the favoured candidates, as acceptable and prestigious adversaries for God and Moses. However, the most recent philological studies have demonstrated that the 'Pharaohs' of the Bible are literary figures, reconstructed from a mixture of memories of ancient rulers, in particular Ahmose, Akhenaten, and members of the Ramesses dynasty. **FM**

CANNUYER, CH., 'Les pharaons dans les traditions coptes et musulmanes: entre oubli, anathème et mémoire merveilleuse', in *Égypte* 97, March to May 2020, pp. 37–50.

VOLOKHINE, Y., 'L'image de Pharaon dans la Bible', in *Pharaons. L'héritage en questions, Le Monde de la Bible* 229, June to August 2019, pp. 56–61.

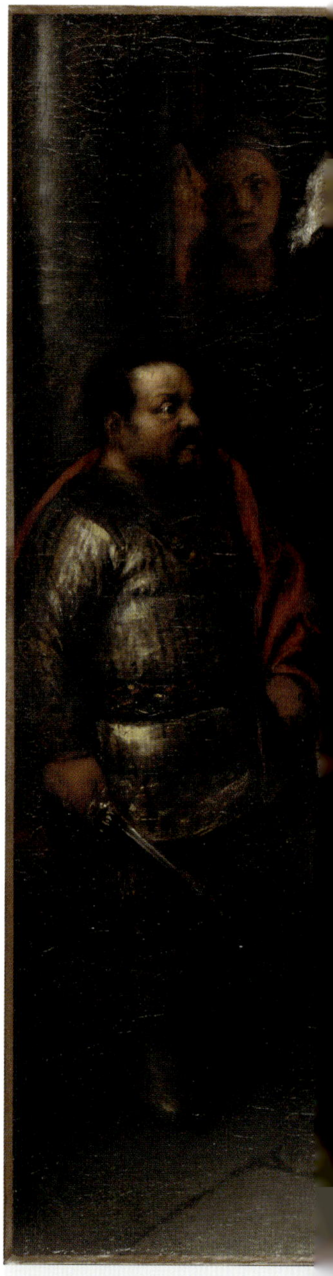

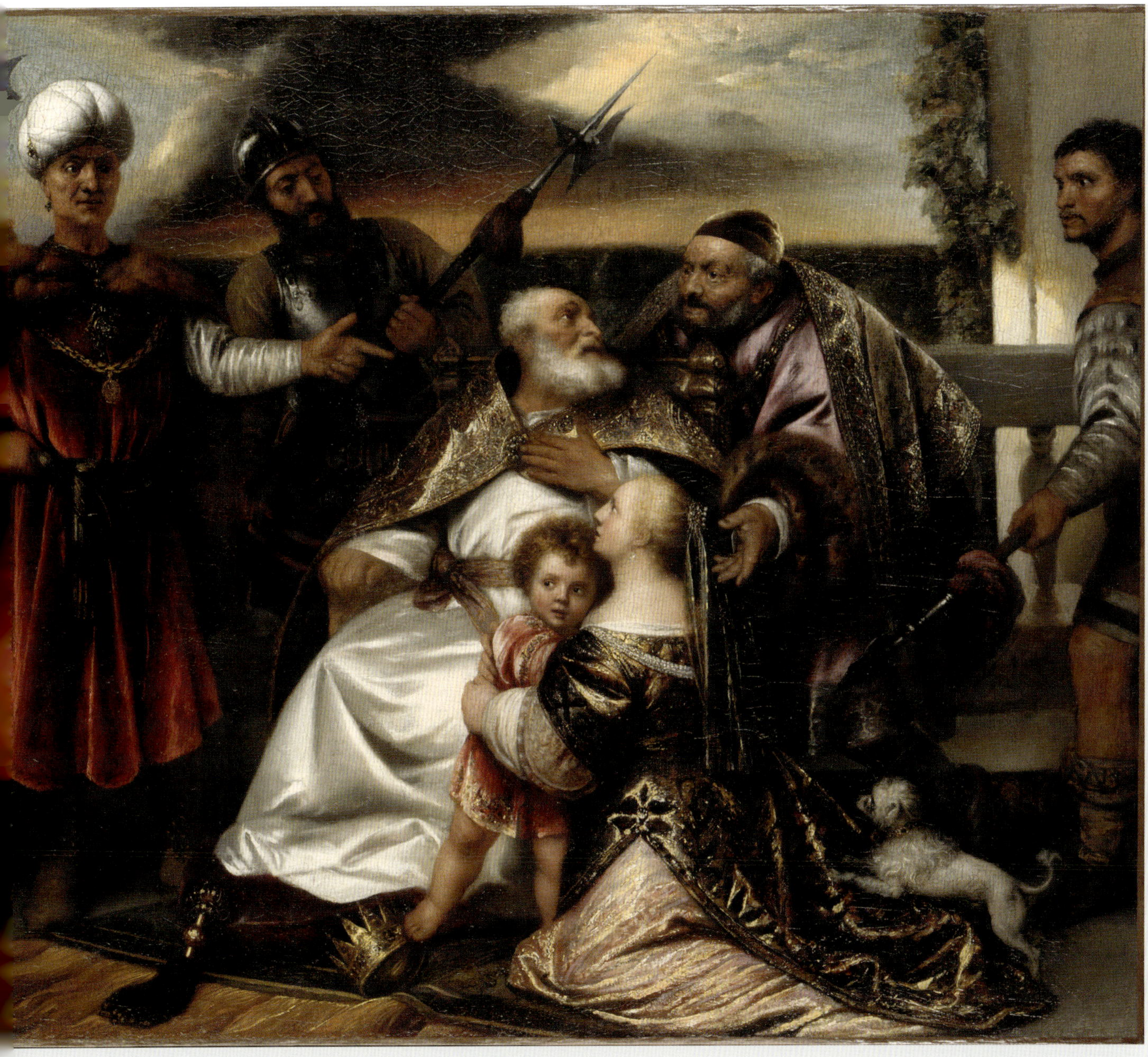

115

Jan Lievens the Elder, *The Infant Moses Trampling Pharaoh's Crown*, The Netherlands, 1630.

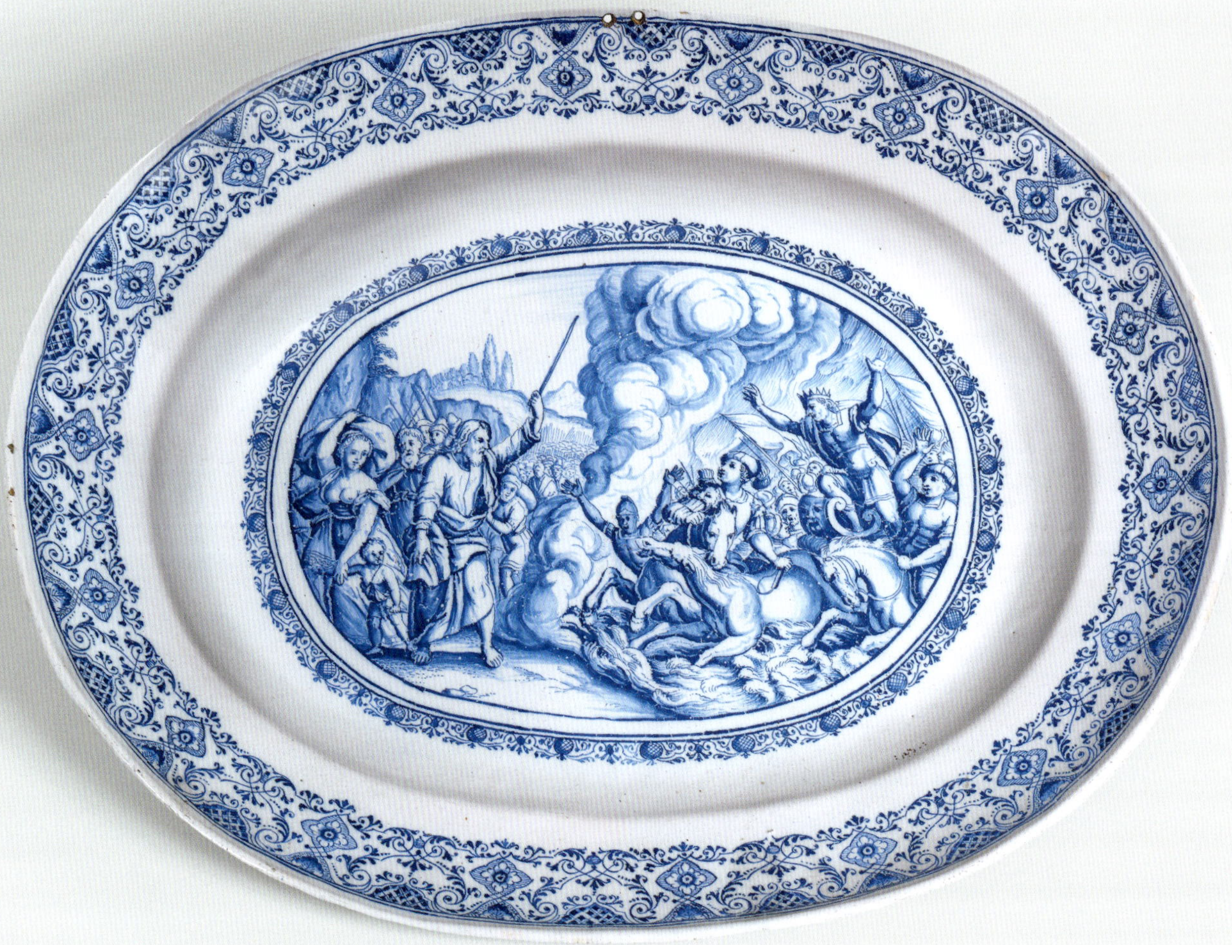

118

Dish showing Moses making the sea swallow Pharaoh's army, Ateliers Clérissy, after an engraving by Pierre Mariette, Moustiers-Sainte-Marie, France, first quarter of the eighteenth century.

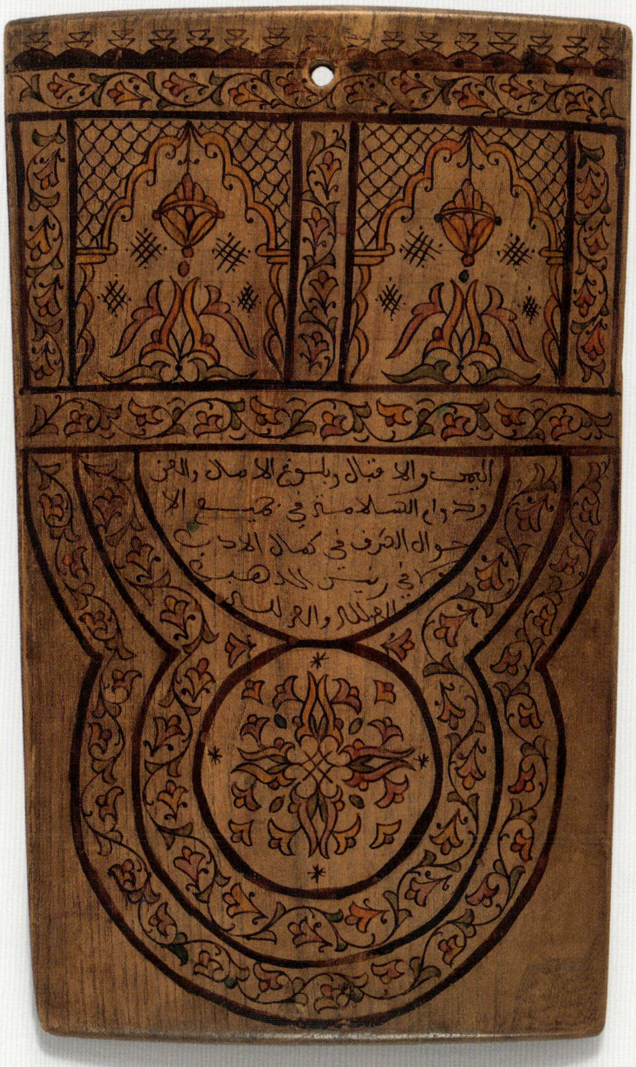

119

Tablet belonging to a Quranic schoolboy, Marrakesh, first half of the twentieth century.

RETURN OF THE PHARAOHS

3

DISCOVERIES THAT CHANGED EVERYTHING

The third and last section of *Superstar Pharaohs* shows how, over two centuries, our knowledge in the field of Egyptology, running alongside the continuing growth of archaeology, tourism, media and exhibitions, transformed and sometimes corrected the image of many pharaohs. Some at last saw the light of day, while others, who had been remembered since the Middle Ages, fell into relative obscurity as far as the public was concerned. A list of royal cartouches, copied by Jean-François Champollion (1790–1832) in his *Grammaire égyptienne* (cat. 120), introduces this last section and marks the birth of Egyptology. Champollion set out the principles behind the writing of hieroglyphs and explained how they transcribed the language of the ancient Egyptians, in this case the names of some of the best-known pharaohs: Menes, the mythical founder of the monarchy, Thutmose and Ramesses, Shoshenq, who is mentioned in the Bible (as Shishak), Ahmose or Amasis, and Psamtik.

246

Madame Yevonde, *Still Life with the Head of Nefertiti*, 1938.

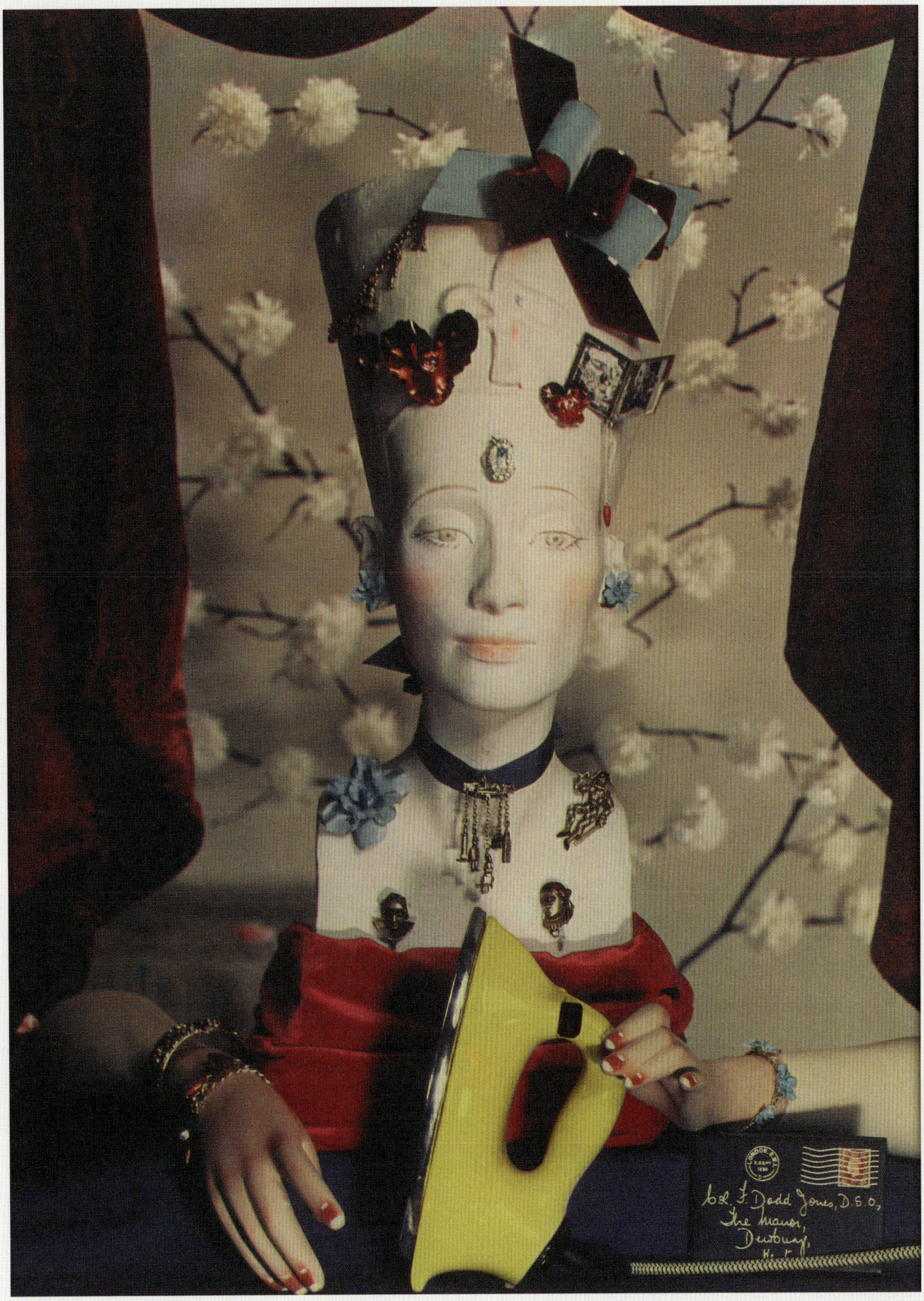

120

Jean-François Champollion, *Grammaire égyptienne, ou principes généraux de l'écriture sacrée égyptienne appliquée à la représentation de la langue parlée* (Egyptian grammar, or general principles of sacred Egyptian writing applied to the representation of the spoken language), published by Jacques-Joseph Champollion, Paris: Firmin Didot Frères, 1836–41.

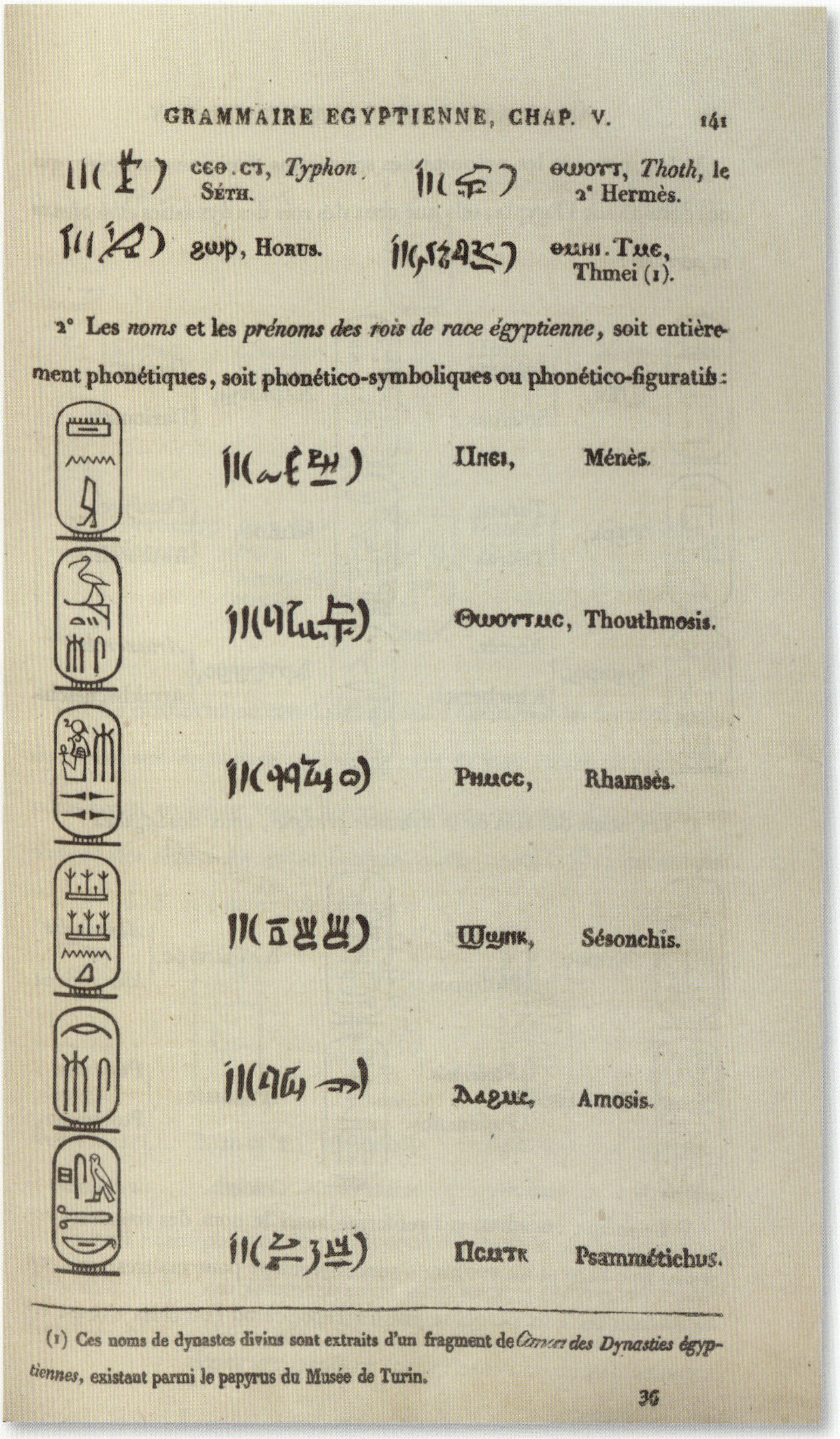

GRAMMAIRE EGYPTIENNE, CHAP. V. 141

ⲥⲉⲑ.ⲥⲧ, *Typhon*, Séth. — ⲑⲱⲟⲩⲧ, *Thoth*, le 2ᵉ Hermès.

ϩⲱⲣ, Horus. — ⲑⲙⲏⲓ.Ⲧⲙⲉ, Thmei (1).

2° Les *noms* et les *prénoms des rois de race égyptienne*, soit entièrement phonétiques, soit phonético-symboliques ou phonético-figuratifs :

Ⲙⲛⲏⲓ,	Ménès.
Ⲑⲱⲟⲩⲧⲙⲥ,	Thouthmosis.
Ⲣⲙⲥⲥ,	Rhamsès.
Ϣϣⲛⲕ,	Sésonchis.
Ⲁϩⲙⲥ,	Amosis.
Ⲡⲥⲙⲧⲕ	Psammétichus.

(1) Ces noms de dynastes divins sont extraits d'un fragment de *Canon des Dynasties égyptiennes*, existant parmi le papyrus du Musée de Turin.

36

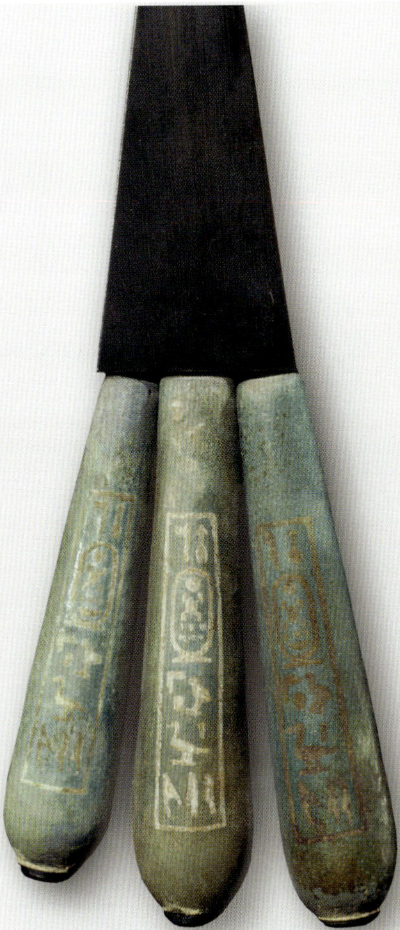

139

Three beads from a sceptre with the cartouche of Tutankhamun, Serapeum of Saqqara, Egypt, reign of Tutankhamun (c. 1330–1320 BCE).

Found by the archaeologist Auguste Mariette in 1851, these beads are among the very few objects bearing the name of this pharaoh that were known before the discovery of his tomb.

It was in particular the cartouches of the prolific Thutmose III, which he translated in Coptic as 'born from Thoth' and of Ramesses II — 'born from Ra' — that led to Champollion's flash of intuition: he realized that hieroglyphs had a double nature, as both phonograms and ideograms. The Rosetta Stone, a large block of stone engraved with a decree issued in Memphis in 196 BCE and transcribed in three scripts — Greek, Demotic and hieroglyphics — enabled him to confirm his intuition: it appeared plausible that the Greek text was a translation of the two Egyptian scripts and that comparing them would help him to decipher the hieroglyphics. The presence of cartouches on this stone and on an obelisk from Philae gave Champollion the key to reading the names Cleopatra and Ptolemy and allowed him to apply what he had understood to other hieroglyphic inscriptions.

THE REVENGE OF RAMESSES

Excavations multiplied in Egypt throughout the nineteenth century, bringing back antiquities that enriched Western museums and prompted new studies. Texts were deciphered and pharaohs were assigned their true names and achievements. Ramesses II, who sowed the seeds for his own fame throughout his reign, was recognized as one of the greatest builders and war leaders, becoming the reference point for pharaohs in modern times. In the painting *Ramesses in his Harem* by Lecomte du Noüy (1885), the sovereign — now finally emerging from Sesostris' shadow — is the incarnation of the quintessential pharaoh, in a work that typifies Orientalism and Egyptomania (cat. 127). The twentieth century confirmed his celebrity: for a long time, the epic film *The Ten Commandments*, by Cecil B. DeMille (1956) (cat. 128), enshrined the idea in popular culture that he was the Pharaoh of Exodus.

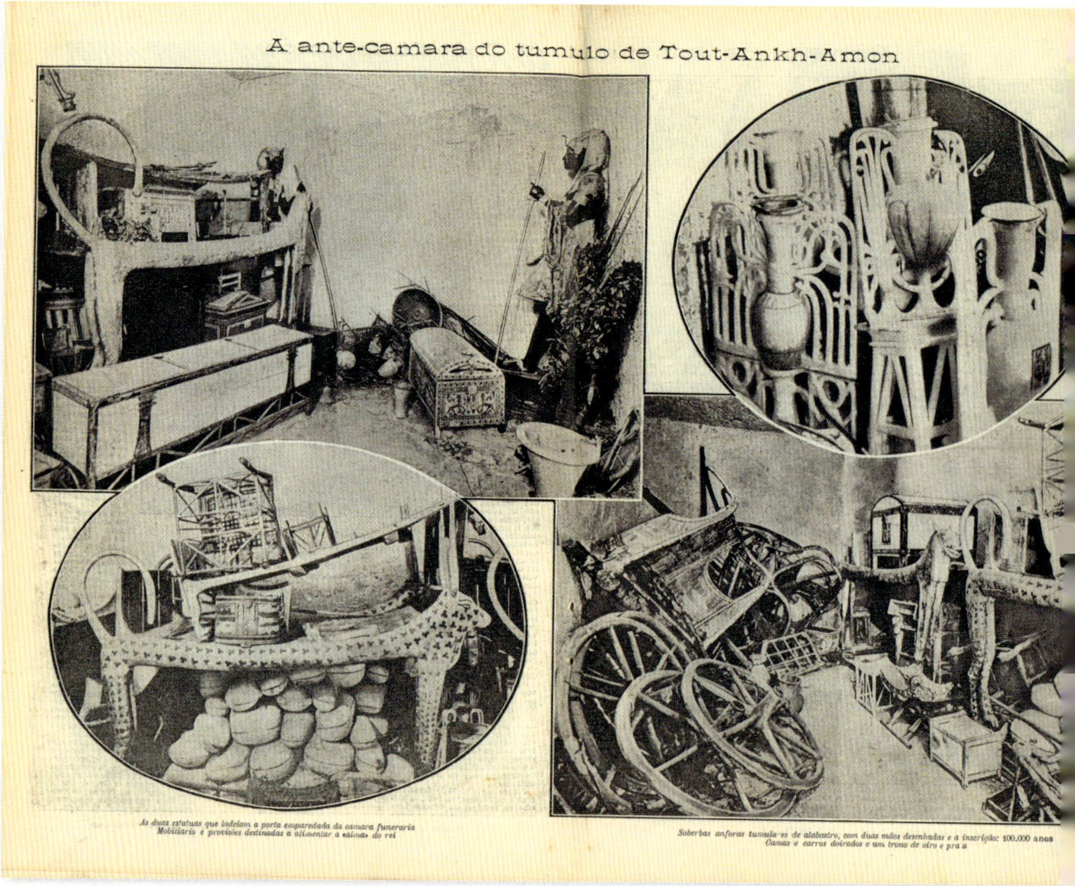
A ante-camara do tumulo de Tout-Ankh-Amon

As duas estatuas que ladeiam a porta emparedada da camara funeraria
Mobiliario e provisões destinadas a alimentar a «alma» do rei

Soberbas anforas tumula-es de alabastro, com duas mãos desenhadas e a inscrição: 100.000 anos
Camas e carros doirados e um trono de oiro e pra a

153

José Joubert Chaves, 'Os Tesouros de Tout-Ankh-Amon' (The treasures of Tutankhamun), in *Ilustração Portuguesa*, 10 March 1923.

Photographs for this article were taken by the excavation's official photographer, Harry Burton: his were the only images of the tomb's interior available to the press at this time, since the dig's patron, Lord Carnarvon, had a monopoly over all information relating to the tomb's investigation.

THE MESMERIZING POWER OF AKHENATEN, NEFERTITI AND TUTANKAHMUN

From the end of the nineteenth century, there were some archaeological discoveries that turned history, art history and the art market upside down. Historians of religion seized upon these discoveries, notably coming to the view that Akhenaten and Nefertiti were precursors of a form of monotheism, dedicated to Aten, the disc of the sun. In 1912, German excavations at Amarna brought to light striking evidence of the beauty and singularity of the pharaoh and his wife. From that moment on, the bust of the queen was destined to be an icon, and it is still making its mark to this day. However, it was their presumed son Tutankhamun who became the greatest star in this pantheon (cat. 139). In 1922, the archaeologist Howard Carter and his patron Lord Carnarvon discovered his tomb, which had not been looted: it caused a worldwide sensation. Films, newspapers, photographs and correspondence all show how much Tutankhamun's fame owed to the media (cats. 153 and 156), which was flourishing in the early twentieth century — although Carter's work was made complicated by the presence of the press and official visitors. The beauty of Tutankhamun's treasure also awed the public: exhibitions proliferated in the West and in Asia, with record numbers of visitors.

THEIR ANCESTORS THE PHARAOHS

From the 1920s, the Egyptians' nationalist aspirations led them to enthusiastically borrow the ancient Egyptian pharaohs as reference points and symbols that would bind their claims to their country's earliest history. A 'pharaonic' fashion permeated the arts and animated the work of the sculptor Mahmoud Mokhtar, who in about 1929 produced the charming statue *Arous el-Nil* (The Bride of the Nile) (cat. 172), a fine example of the work of this artist, whose training in modern art did not

156

Press cuttings from Portuguese newspapers (*Diário de Lisboa* and *A Capital*) covering the 'curse of Tutankhamun', 1923.

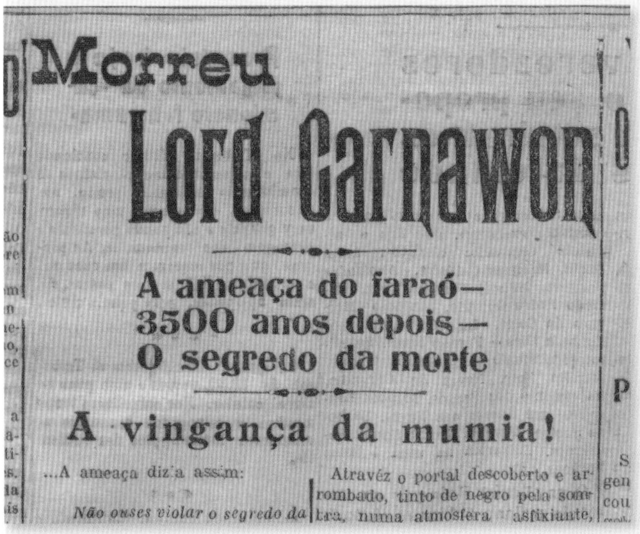

Morreu

Lord Carnawon

A ameaça do faraó— 3500 anos depois— O segredo da morte

A vingança da mumia!

...A ameaça diz a assim:

Não ouses violar o segredo da

Atravéz o portal descoberto e arrombado, tinto de negro pela sombra, numa atmosfera asfixiante,

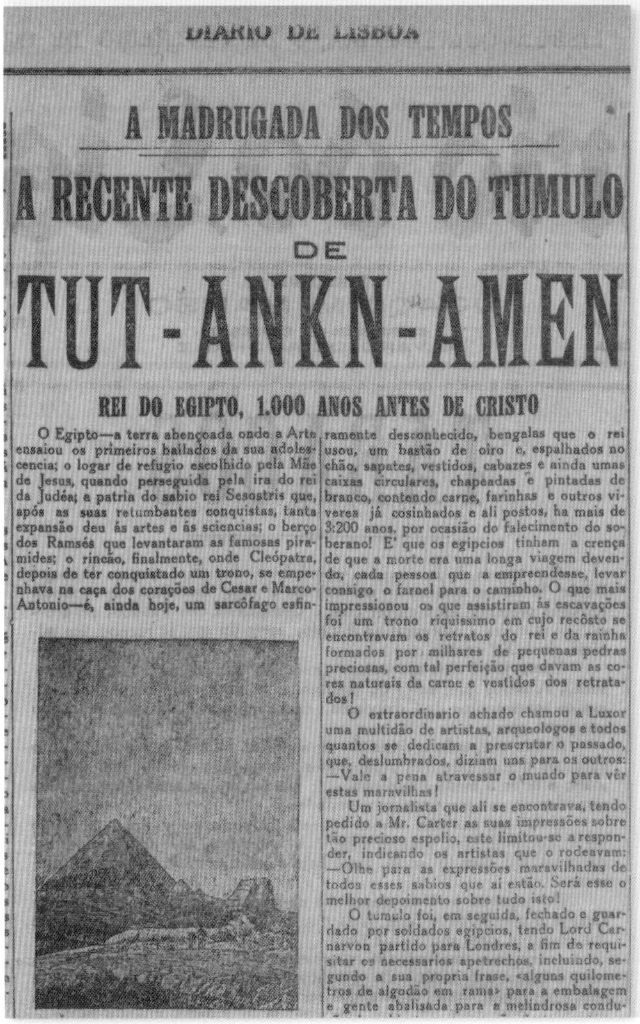

DIARIO DE LISBOA

A MADRUGADA DOS TEMPOS

A RECENTE DESCOBERTA DO TUMULO DE

TUT-ANKN-AMEN

REI DO EGIPTO, 1.000 ANOS ANTES DE CRISTO

O Egipto—a terra abençoada onde a Arte ensaiou os primeiros bailados da sua adolescencia; o logar de refugio escolhido pela Mãe de Jesus, quando perseguida pela ira do rei da Judéa; a patria do sabio rei Sesostris que, após as suas retumbantes conquistas, tanta expansão deu ás artes e ás sciencias; o berço dos Ramsés que levantaram as famosas piramides; o rincão, finalmente, onde Cleópatra, depois de têr conquistado um trono, se empenhava na caça dos corações de Cesar e Marco-Antonio—é, ainda hoje, um sarcôfago esfin-

ramente desconhecido, bengalas que o rei usou, um bastão de oiro e, espalhados no chão, sapatos, vestidos, cabazes e ainda umas caixas circulares, chapeadas e pintadas de branco, contendo carne, farinhas e outros viveres já cosinhados e ali postos, ha mais de 3:200 anos, por ocasião do falecimento do soberano! E' que os egipcios tinham a crença de que a morte era uma longa viagem devendo, cada pessoa que a empreendesse, levar consigo o farnel para o caminho. O que mais impressionou os que assistiram ás escavações foi um trono riquissimo em cujo recôsto se encontravam os retratos do rei e da rainha formados por milhares de pequenas pedras preciosas, com tal perfeição que davam as cores naturais da carne e vestidos dos retratados!

O extraordinario achado chamou a Luxor uma multidão de artistas, arqueologos e todos quantos se dedicam a prescrutar o passado, que, deslumbrados, diziam uns para os outros:

—Vale a pena atravessar o mundo para vêr estas maravilhas!

Um jornalista que ali se encontrava, tendo pedido a Mr. Carter as suas impressões sobre tão precioso espolio, este limitou-se a responder, indicando os artistas que o rodeavam:

—Olhe para as expressões maravilhadas de todos esses sabios que aí estão. Será esse o melhor depoimento sobre tudo isto!

O tumulo foi, em seguida, fechado e guardado por soldados egipcios, tendo Lord Carnarvon partido para Londres, a fim de requisitar os necessarios apetrechos, incluindo, segundo a sua propria frase, «alguns quilometros de algodão em rama» para a embalagem e gente abalisada para a melindrosa condu-

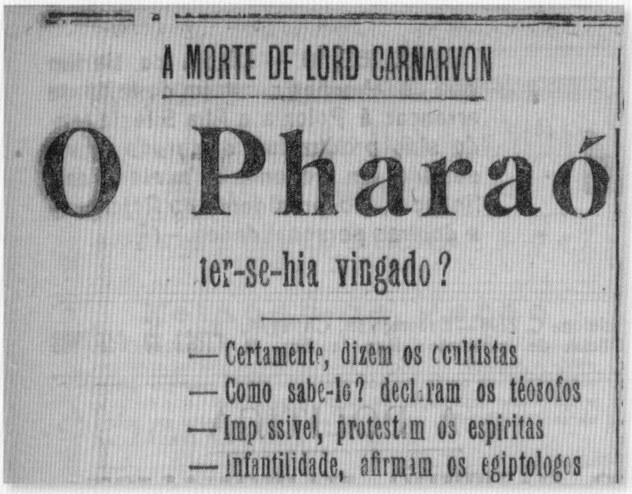

A MORTE DE LORD CARNARVON

O Pharaó

ter-se-hia vingado?

— Certamente, dizem os ocultistas
— Como sabe-lo? declaram os téosofos
— Impossivel, protestam os espiritas
— Infantilidade, afirmam os egiptologos

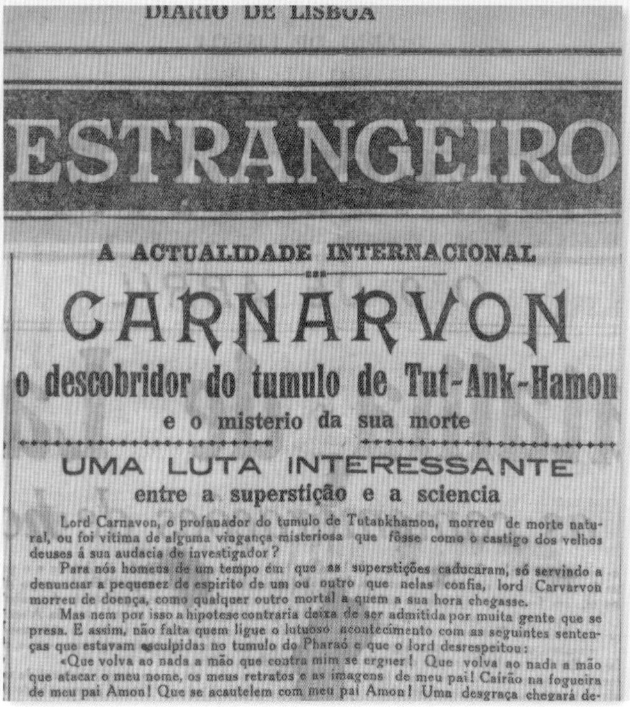

DIARIO DE LISBOA

ESTRANGEIRO

A ACTUALIDADE INTERNACIONAL

CARNARVON

o descobridor do tumulo de Tut-Ank-Hamon e o misterio da sua morte

UMA LUTA INTERESSANTE entre a superstição e a sciencia

Lord Carnavon, o profanador do tumulo de Tutankhamon, morreu de morte natural, ou foi vitima de alguma vingança misteriosa que fôsse como o castigo dos velhos deuses á sua audacia de investigador?

Para nós homens de um tempo em que as superstições caducaram, só servindo a denunciar a pequenez de espirito de um ou outro que nelas confia, lord Carvarvon morreu de doença, como qualquer outro mortal a quem a sua hora chegasse.

Mas nem por isso a hipotese contraria deixa de ser admitida por muita gente que se presa. E assim, não falta quem ligue o lutuoso acontecimento com as seguintes sentenças que estavam esculpidas no tumulo do Pharaó e que o lord desrespeitou:

«Que volva ao nada a mão que contra mim se erguer! Que volva ao nada a mão que atacar o meu nome, os meus retratos e as imagens de meu pai! Cairão na fogueira de meu pai Amon! Que se acautelem com meu pai Amon! Uma desgraça chegará de-

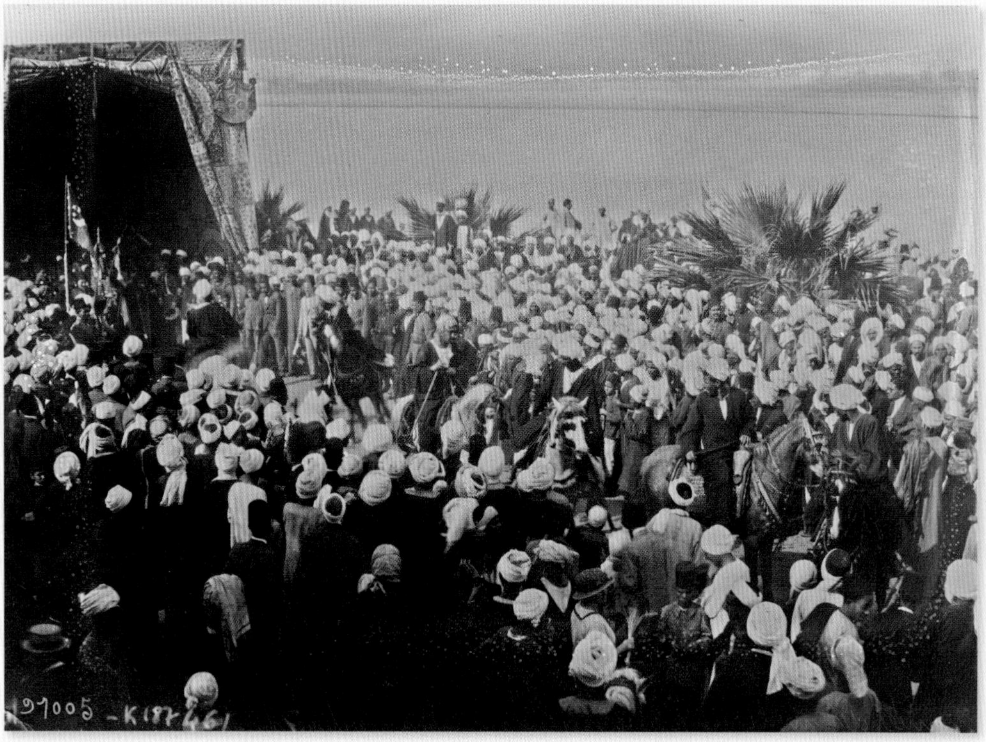

167

Arrival of guests of the Egyptian government at the official opening of Tutankhamun's tomb, Rol press agency, Luxor, Egypt, early March 1924.

prevent him applying traditional pharaonic codes to it: frontality and profile, a kneeling figure, a rectangular base and, in this case, royal jewels. In the 1950s and 1960s, the names of the iconic pharaohs, especially Cleopatra and Ramesses, were regularly used to promote the products of Nasser's Egypt, and featured frequently in commercials.

Superstar Pharaohs will provide food for thought as regards the perception of pharaonic antiquity by contemporary Egyptians. Since the early twentieth century, they seem to have been promoting their heritage, especially to foreigners, tourists and investors (cat. 167). There is an allusion to this in the *Temples* series by the photographer Olivier Cablat (cats. 189 to 194): a succession of souvenir shop fronts, which until the 2000s Luxor shopkeepers were in the habit of decorating with pharaonic scenes. However, the question of the adoption of the pharaonic heritage by today's Egyptians can be articulated by comparing two very different films. In the first, the historical drama *Al Mummia* (or The Mummy, 1969) (cat. 195), the Egyptian director Shadi Abdessalam makes the case for his compatriots claiming and defending the heritage of the pharaohs. The second, *A God Passing* by the French artist David G. Tretiakoff (2008) (cat. 196), shot with a handheld camera in the streets of Cairo, shows that the legacy of the great Ramesses has not been uniformly assimilated by all Egyptians. It is easy to see how sensitive this theme is and to understand that no theory reflects unanimity, no generalization can convey the complex feelings of a whole nation.

However, as Fayza Haikal has described above, pharaonic icons remain the best equipped to unite Egyptians, as much in political crises as in football matches — after all, the national team is known as 'The Pharaohs' (cat. 203).

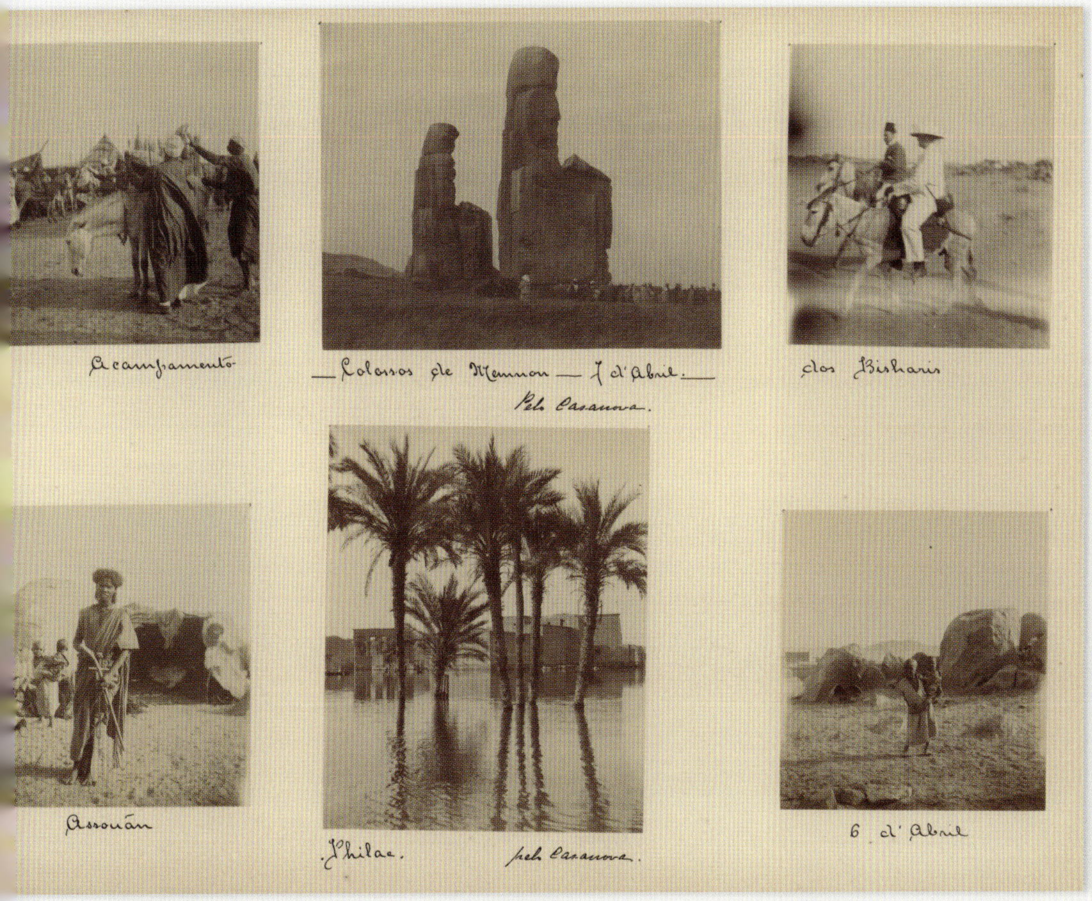

121

Photograph album from a trip to Egypt made by the Portuguese queen, Dona Amélia, April 1903: views of a Bishari encampment, the colossi of Memnon and the submerged temple of Philae.

GLOBAL POPULAR ICONS AND EGYPTOMANIA

The evocative power that the country of the pharaohs exerts beyond the borders of Egypt is easy to understand: longevity, the strong rule of monarchy, a fascination for death and resurrection, biblical references, mysteries, precious materials, exoticism, a torrid climate... It is therefore unsurprising that these highly marketable qualities have been so effectively incarnated by the pharaohs. The rulers revealed by archaeology thus became icons, clear and vivid reference points for everyone (cats. 121 and 124), capable of thrilling an audience or beguiling a consumer. They are now superstars in merchandising, advertising and the leisure industry: film, music, games and graphic novels...

From the end of the nineteenth century, and particularly from the moment Tutankhamun's tomb was discovered, these famous kings became the stuff of dreams, adored by children and adults alike. They were made to sell all sorts of things, sometimes without much logical basis, with only a tenuous link between the pharaoh's status and attributes and the object being offered to the consumer. This is illustrated by the Keops motorbike (1926) (cat. 236), which borrowed its name from the pharaoh famed for his building projects (now known as Khufu), in the hope that this would suggest the eternal qualities of the Great Pyramid. In the waves of Egyptomania that followed, irony and humour is rarely absent.

The world of entertainment also called upon pharaonic star attractions, whose virtues and vices inspired writers and whose fame attracted the public. Theatre and opera, soon followed by operettas and popular music, then cinema in its early days and finally television, all have provided numerous examples featuring Egyptian sovereigns as protagonists or as their adversaries (cats. 205 and 206).

205

Ags Czabo, artist, sheet music for *Old King Tut* by William Jerome and Harry Von Tilzer, published by Harry Von Tilzer Music Pub. Co, New York, 1923.

This song came out at the height of 'Tut-mania', while the excavation of the tomb was still under way. Since Tutankhamun's mummy had not yet been revealed, the dead pharaoh, who died prematurely, could still be described as 'Old King Tut'.

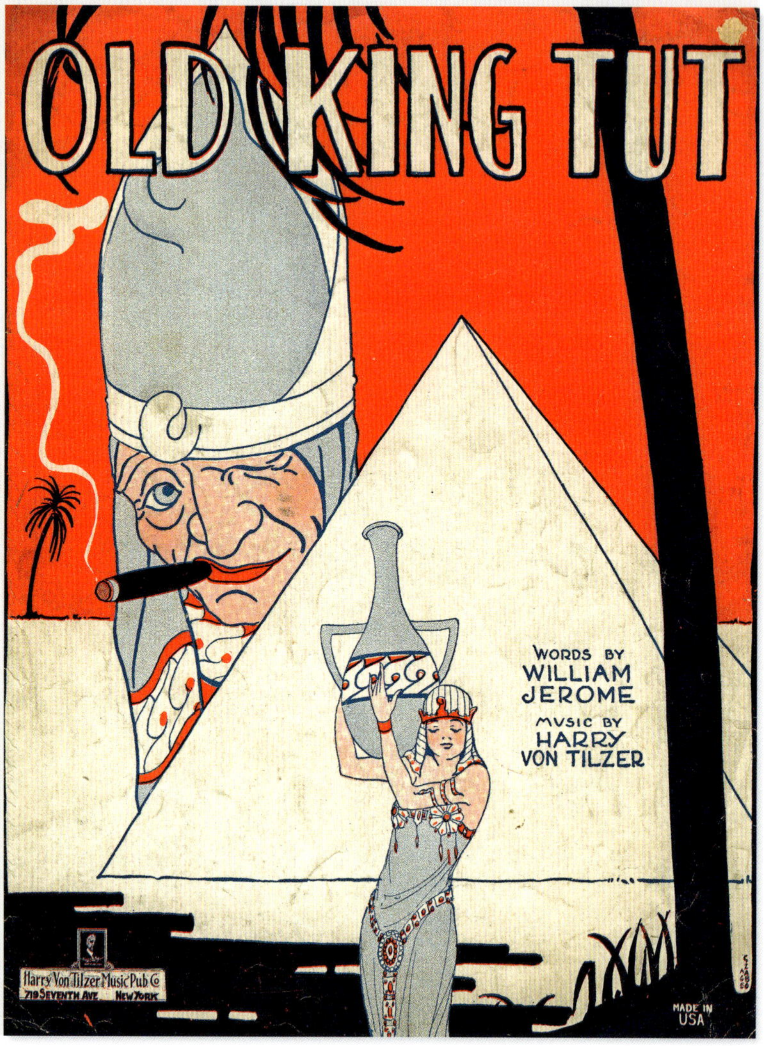

It is worth underlining a more specific aspect concerning these ancient icons, turned into stars by popular culture. Since they were rediscovered, Egyptian pharaohs have inspired writers, artists and political movements, emphasizing the fact that Egypt is in Africa (cats. 238 and 239). Adopted as standards of Blackness by Africans and African diasporas, these pharaohs, some of whom were indeed Black, are regularly referenced in popular music and cinema (cats. 240 and 241).
With its 'Gallery of Nefertitis', which brings together several doctored representations of the famous bust of the queen, *Superstar Pharaohs* gives the last word to contemporary creators who have also, in their turn, appropriated this iconic figure of Egyptian origin, now unequivocally timeless and universal (cats. 244, 245, 246, 247, 249 and 250). **GA-L/FM**

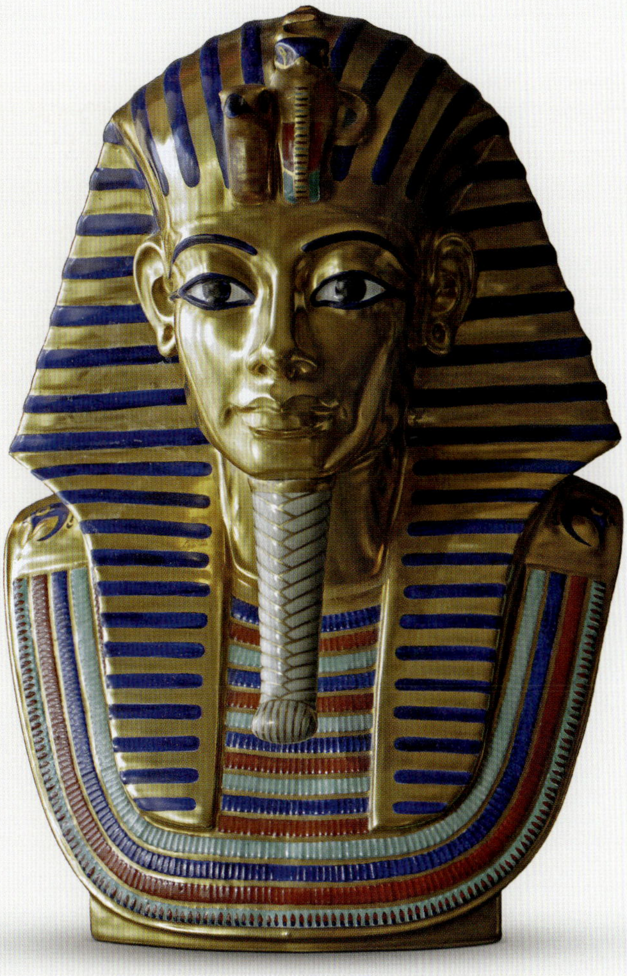

204

Jean Goy, Manufacture Raynaud, interpretation of Tutankhamun's funerary mask, Limoges, France, c. 1970.

COPIES AND FAKES: THE PRICE OF FAME

In 1912, the discovery of Queen Nefertiti's bust in Amarna by German archaeologists (cats. 134 and 135), found in the debris of the workshop belonging to the sculptor Thutmose, very quickly had a considerable impact on the history of Egyptian art and then, in turn, on the trade in so-called Amarnian art. For the first time, Westerners could gaze upon reproductions of the portrait of a woman whose harmonious grace was dazzling, with perfect facial features, elegantly made up, matching the contemporary world's ideal of feminine beauty. For several decades, sculptures and bas-reliefs emerged from the excavations at Amarna, bringing to light images of the husband and wife Akhenaten and Nefertiti, who shared a distinctive appearance: an elongated skull, a fleshy mouth, a prominent chin, a long, slender neck, a narrow bust, skinny arms, very long hands, a pot belly, plump thighs and rounded buttocks (cat. 129). Their daughters, who were often depicted with them in charming scenes of filial affection, also had these same physical characteristics: these intimate groups created a new point of reference for royal iconography.

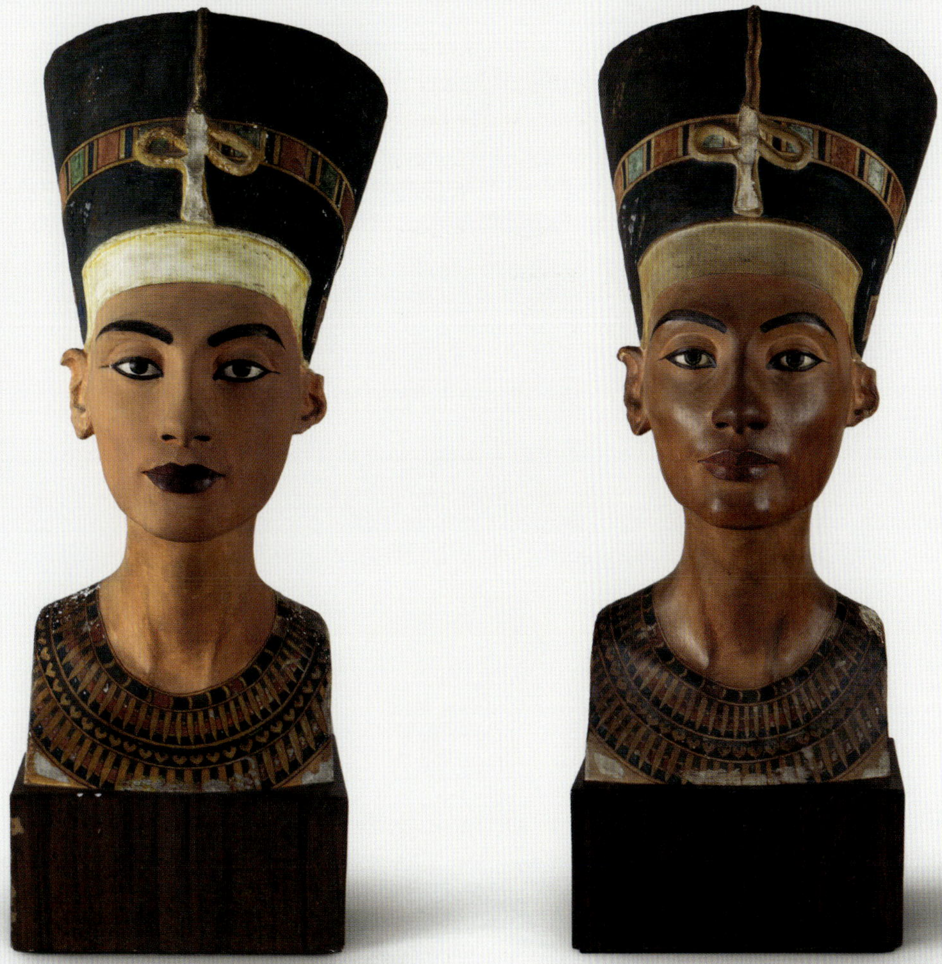

134–135

Replicas of the bust of Nefertiti made by the Berlin Museums plaster casting workshop, 1933.

129

Fragment of a column depicting Nefertiti, Amarna, Egypt, reign of Akhenaten (c. 1349–1333 BCE).

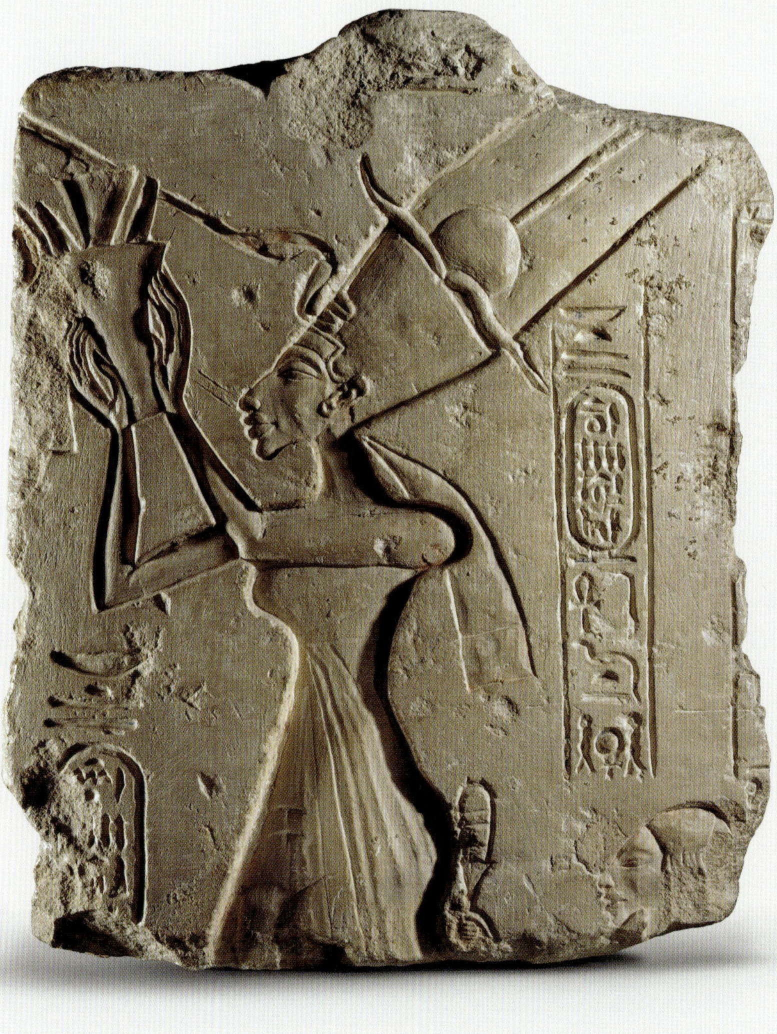

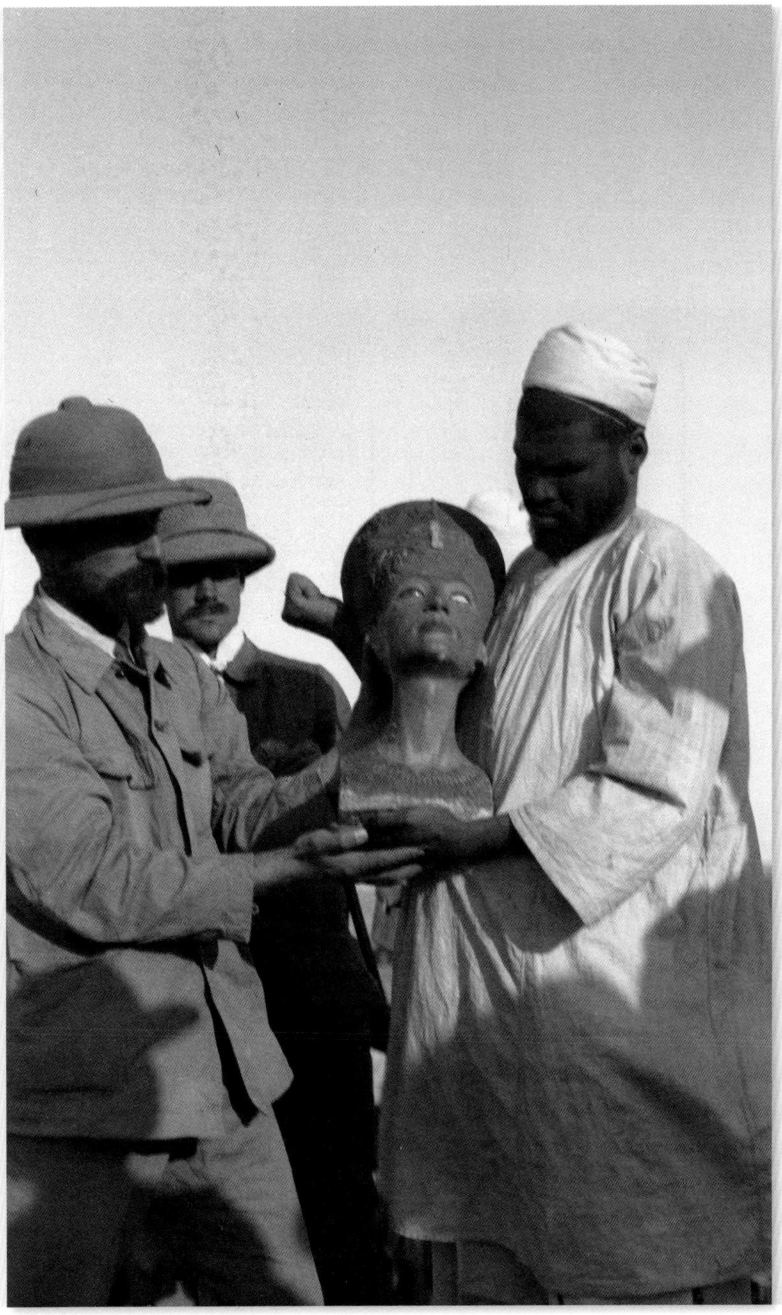

131

Johann Georg of Saxony, discovery of the bust of Nefertiti. In the photo: Hermann Ranke, Paul Hollander and Mohamed es-Senussi, Amarna, Egypt, 1912.

When the bust of Nefertiti went on display in Berlin in 1924, it triggered a frenzied enthusiasm for this Amarnian art, and both museum curators and collectors were anxious to acquire examples. However, only a very limited amount of art from Amarna existed: no works reached the art market. There were two solutions to this problem: replicas based on the originals, which were mostly in Berlin – and fakes. From the 1920s, the Berlin museum's plaster casting workshop could produce series of replicas for sale (cat. 133). And in the wake of this, museums started acquiring replicas of the famous bust, including the Musées royaux d'Art et d'Histoire in Brussels in the 1930s (cats. 134 and 135).

It was also a golden age for fakers. The risks were small: authentic pieces were so rare that comparing their products with originals was

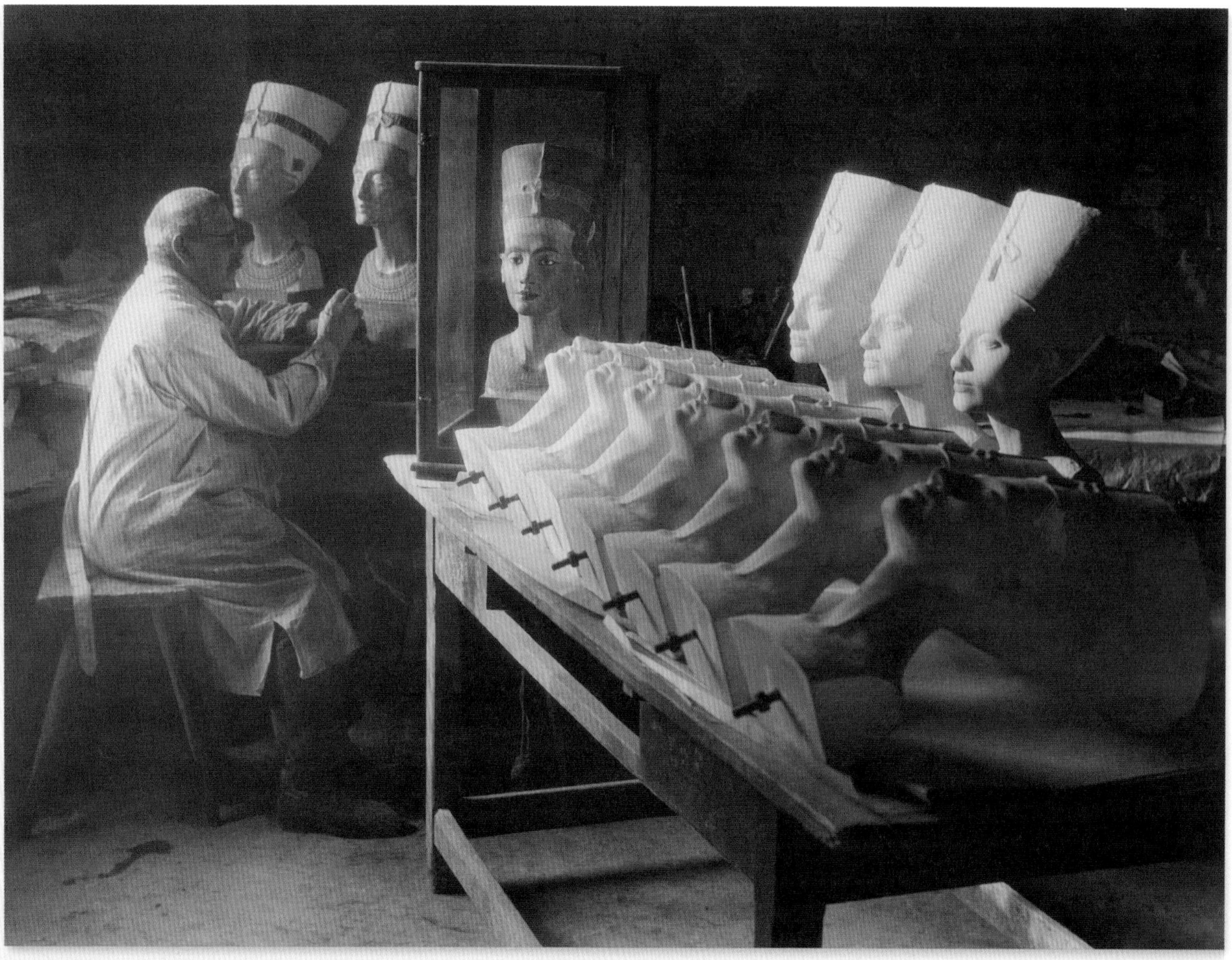

133

Fritz Zielesch, Berlin Museums plaster casting workshop, 1930.

virtually impossible. And it has to be admitted that the Amarnian fakes were often appealing, even irresistible. The Musée du Louvre succumbed to this temptation: until the 1980s it had on display two fakes that were thought to be masterpieces of Amarnian art.

Added to the national collections in 1932, the 'harp head' (thought to be an element decorating a musical instrument; cat. 136) is carved from a dark wood and was featured in art history publications until the mid-twentieth century, when experts began to express doubts about its authenticity. The wood was identified as rengas, a species unknown in Egypt; in 1986, a carbon-14 analysis determined that the wood was 'one to four centuries old'. It was therefore a fake.

136

The 'Harp-head', a fake imitating portraits of Nefertiti and Akhenaten, bought in Paris in 1932.

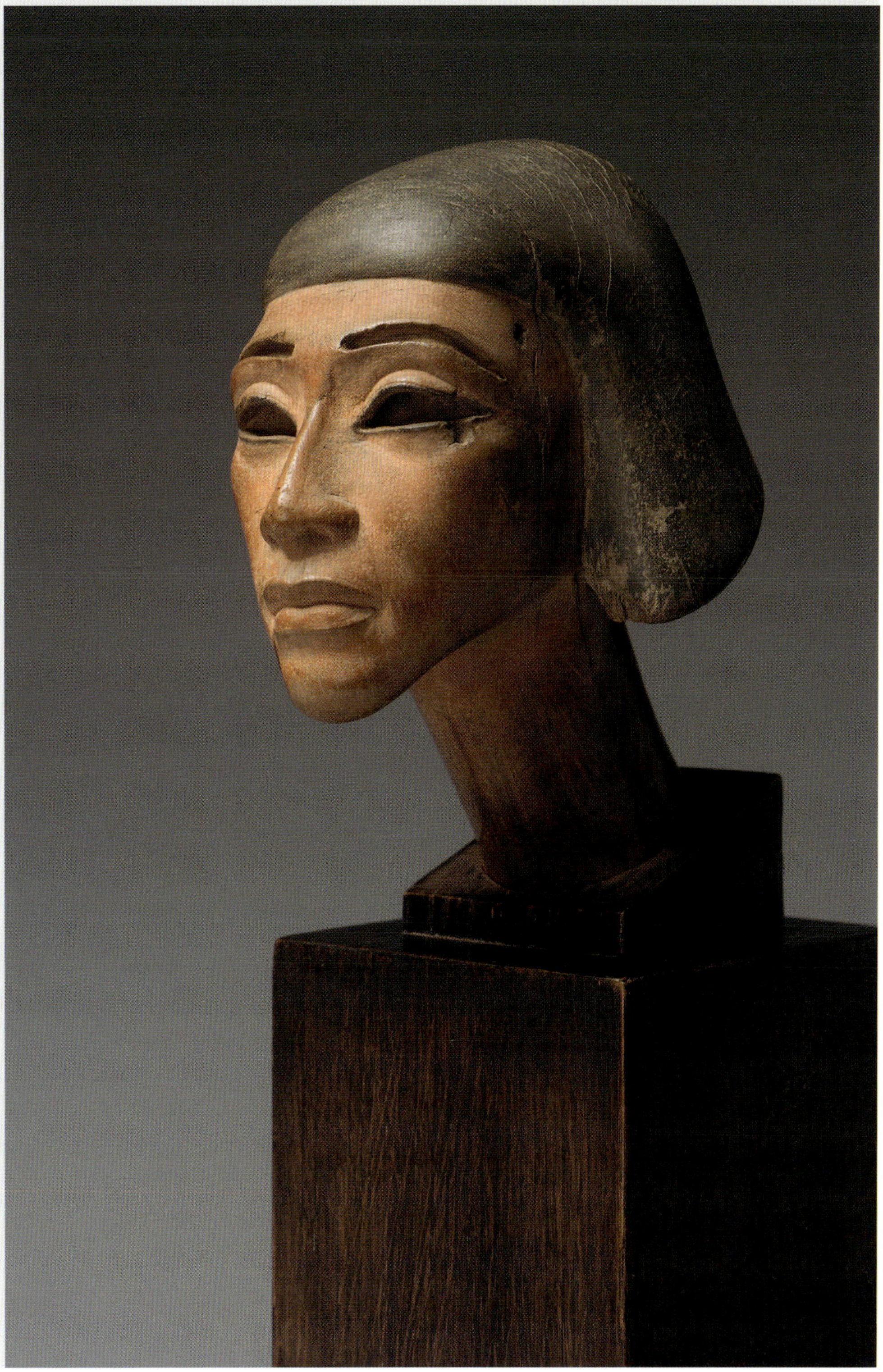

The other 'Amarnian masterpiece' was a charming little blue glass head (cat. 137). Acquired in 1923, it intrigued experts from early on. It was necessary to await developments in archaeometry (in this case, the chemical analysis of glass) before it became clear that the material and techniques used to make this work were modern. With its helmet-shaped wig, the Louvre's 'blue head' became a good example of the Egyptomania of the 1920s. **GA-L**

Cénival, J.-L. de, Arnold, M., Valladas, H., 'La fin de la tête de harpe', in *Revue du Louvre-La revue des musées de France*, 1991, pp. 6–7.

Fiechter, J.-J., *Faussaires d'Égypte*, chap. VII, 'Une nouvelle source d'inspiration pour les faussaires, la redécouverte de l'art amarnien', Flammarion, Paris, 2009, pp. 124–35.

Gaber, H., Grimal, N., Perdu, O. (ed.), *Imitations, copies et faux dans les domaines pharaonique et de l'Orient ancien*. Actes du colloque Collège de France – Académie des Inscriptions et Belles-lettres, (Paris, 14–15 January 2016), Académie des inscriptions et belles-lettres/Soleb, 2018.

Pierrat-Bonnefois, G., Biron, I., 'La tête égyptienne en verre bleu: la conclusion d'une enquête', in *Revue du Louvre-La revue des musées de France*, 2003, pp. 27–35.

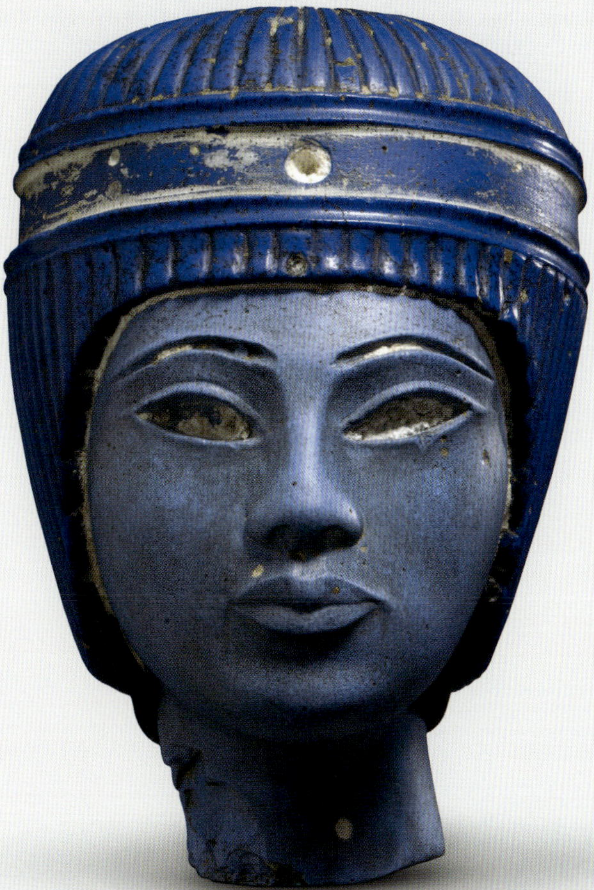

137

The 'Blue-head', a fake imitating portraits of Nefertiti and Tutankhamun, bought in Paris in 1923.

TUTANKHAMUN'S AMAZING DESTINY

The undamaged tomb of the young Tutankhamun, which came to light in the Valley of the Kings in 1922, remains — a century later — the most sensational archaeological discovery ever. It was a unique, unmatched event and Howard Carter (cat. 146), who found it, managed its exploitation across all fields. The archaeological domain was of course his preserve: he had the heavy responsibility for organizing the extraction from the tomb of five thousand three hundred and ninety-six intact works of art, covered in gold and semi-precious stones, which he discovered as he moved through the tomb chambers. But at the same time, he was faced with problems that he would not have experienced a few decades earlier: as soon as it was announced, the discovery became a hot topic for the international written press, as well as for photographers and film makers, who captured images and made movies of this spectacular news story (cat. 145). In the 1920s, the term 'mediatization' was not yet in use, but with the discovery of Tutankhamun's tomb and the enthusiasm it engendered in the media and their public, it is not unreasonable to suggest that this was one of the first global manifestations of this type of communication.

146

Howard Carter shows the press a silver staff from Tutankhamun's tomb, Meurisse press agency, Valley of the Kings, Egypt, 1925.

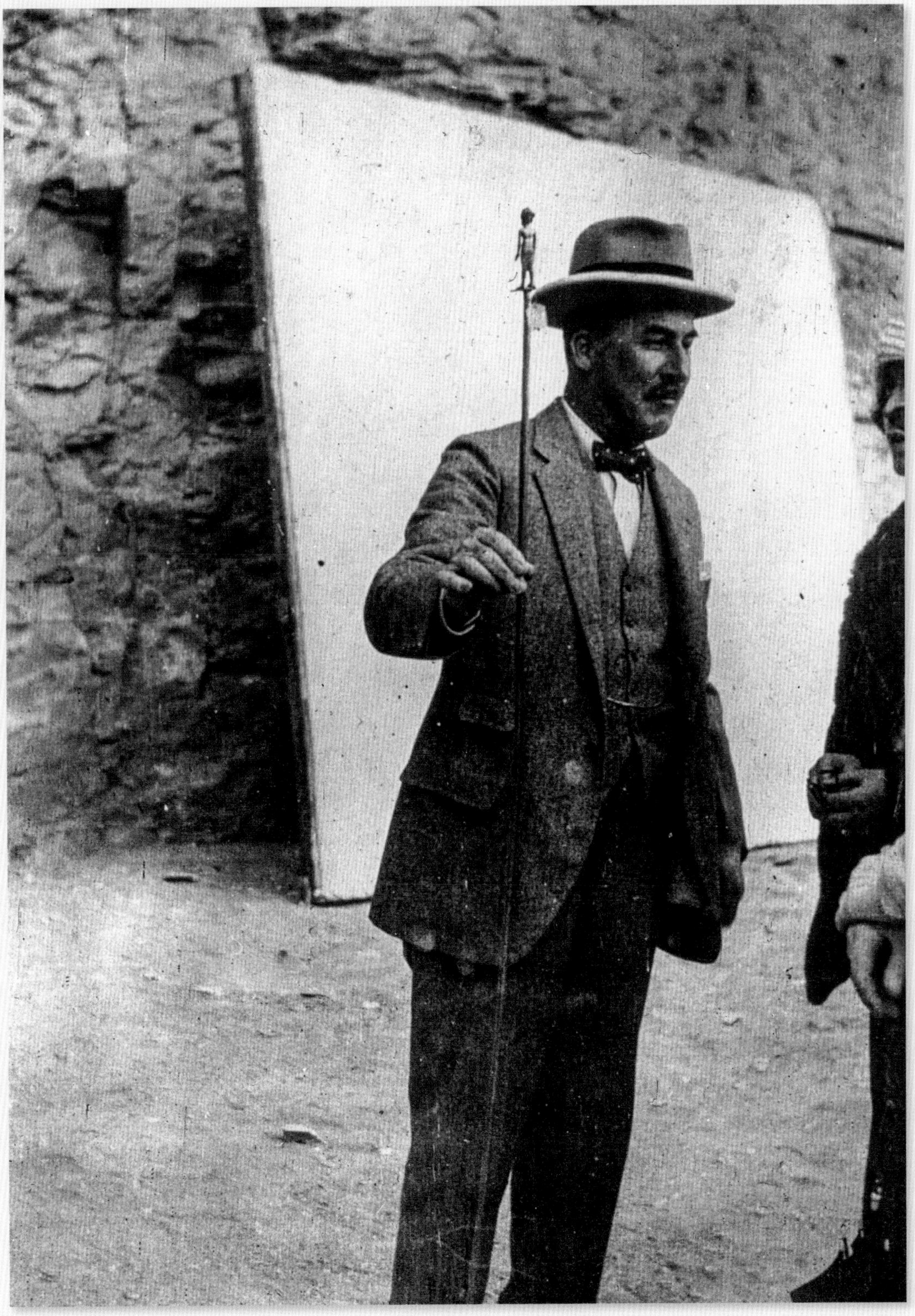

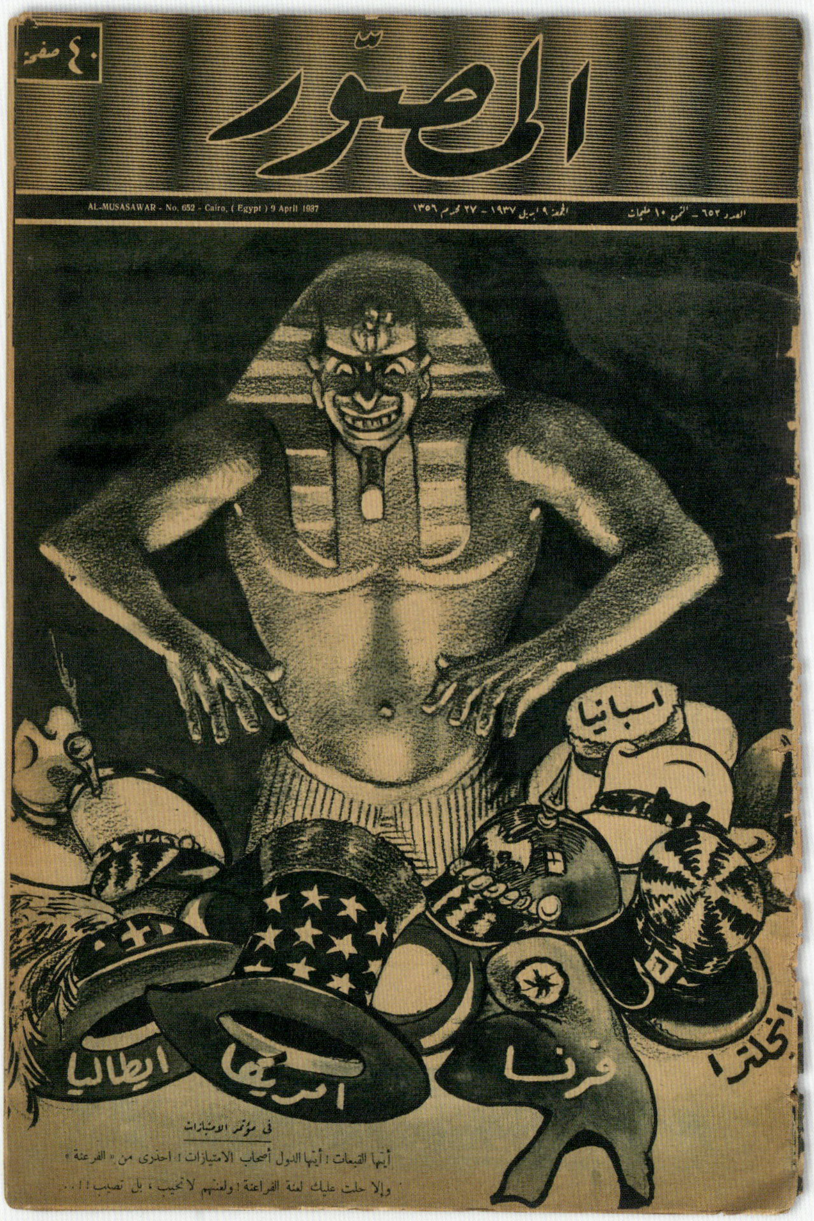

155

Edition of *Al-Musawar*, 9 April 1937, alluding to 'the curse of the pharaohs', Dar Al-Hilal (publisher), Cairo.

Several elements were behind this media hype and the general enthusiasm it triggered. Firstly, it goes without saying, the beauty of the treasures brought out from the little chambers met with immediate admiration, helped along by the pioneering role of photography, which newspapers were using more and more. Each week, as part of an agreement reached with *The Times*, the field photographer Harry Burton sent the newspaper images of the discovery as though it were a soap opera: the public at large breathlessly waited every instalment. Other photographers and film makers soon started recording the event too, greatly hindering Carter's work and irritating the Egyptians, who felt they were being left out of this extraordinary discovery (cats. 141, 142 and 143). Cinema had been born, and flexible film was now used in film cameras and increasingly in photographic cameras, which were getting

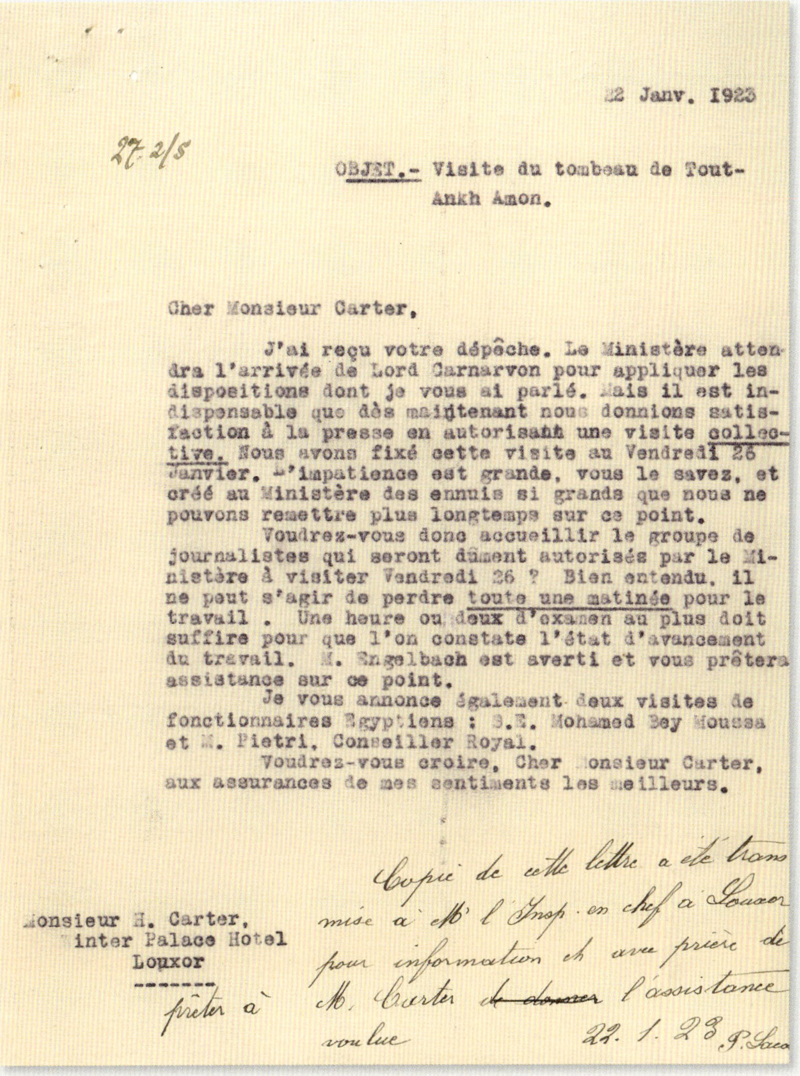

22 Janv. 1923

27-2/8

OBJET.- Visite du tombeau de Tout-Ankh Amon.

Cher Monsieur Carter,

J'ai reçu votre dépêche. Le Ministère attendra l'arrivée de Lord Carnarvon pour appliquer les dispositions dont je vous ai parlé. Mais il est indispensable que dès maintenant nous donnions satisfaction à la presse en autorisant une visite collective. Nous avons fixé cette visite au Vendredi 26 Janvier. L'impatience est grande, vous le savez, et créé au Ministère des ennuis si grands que nous ne pouvons remettre plus longtemps sur ce point.

Voudrez-vous donc accueillir le groupe de journalistes qui seront dûment autorisés par le Ministère à visiter Vendredi 26 ? Bien entendu, il ne peut s'agir de perdre toute une matinée pour le travail . Une heure ou deux d'examen au plus doit suffire pour que l'on constate l'état d'avancement du travail. M. Engelbach est averti et vous prêtera assistance sur ce point.

Je vous annonce également deux visites de fonctionnaires Egyptiens : S.E. Mohamed Bey Moussa et M. Pietri, Conseiller Royal.

Voudrez-vous croire, Cher Monsieur Carter, aux assurances de mes sentiments les meilleurs.

Monsieur H. Carter,
Winter Palace Hotel
Louxor

Copie de cette lettre a été transmise à M. l'Insp. en chef à Louxor pour information et avec prière de prêter à M. Carter ~~de donner~~ l'assistance voulue 22. 1. 23 P. Lacau

141

Letter from Pierre Lacau, Director of the Antiquities Service, to Howard Carter about arrangements for the press to visit the tomb, Luxor, Egypt, 22 January 1923.

249

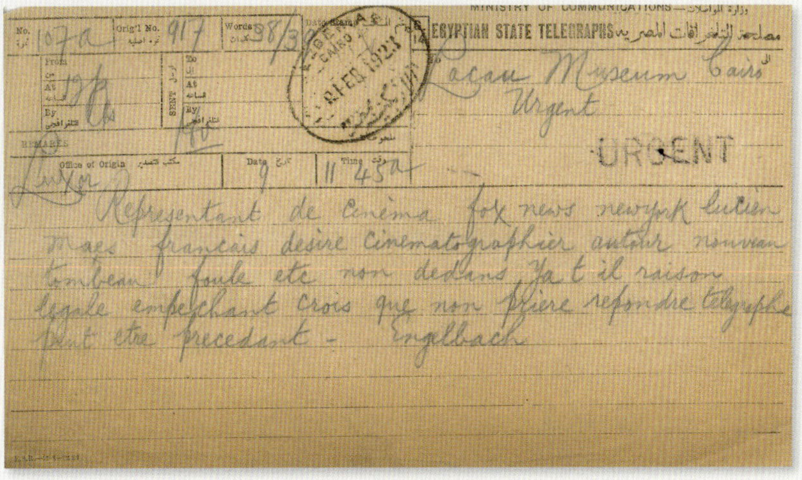

MINISTRY OF COMMUNICATIONS
EGYPTIAN STATE TELEGRAPHS

Lacau Museum Cairo
Urgent

URGENT

Luxor

Representant de cinema fox news newyork lucien maes français desire cinematographier autour nouveau tombeau foule ete non dedans Ya t il raison legale empechant crois que non prière repondre telegraphe peut etre precedant - Englbach

142

Telegram from Reginald Engelbach, Inspector of Antiquities in Luxor, to Pierre Lacau, Director of Egypt's Antiquities Service, Luxor, Egypt, 9 February 1923.

The inspector was urgently seeking permission from his superior for a Fox News reporter to film the crowd around Tutankhamun's tomb.

143

Reginald Engelbach, diagram of the tomb's layout, made for the visit of officials at its inauguration by the Egyptian government, Luxor, Egypt, 2 March 1924.

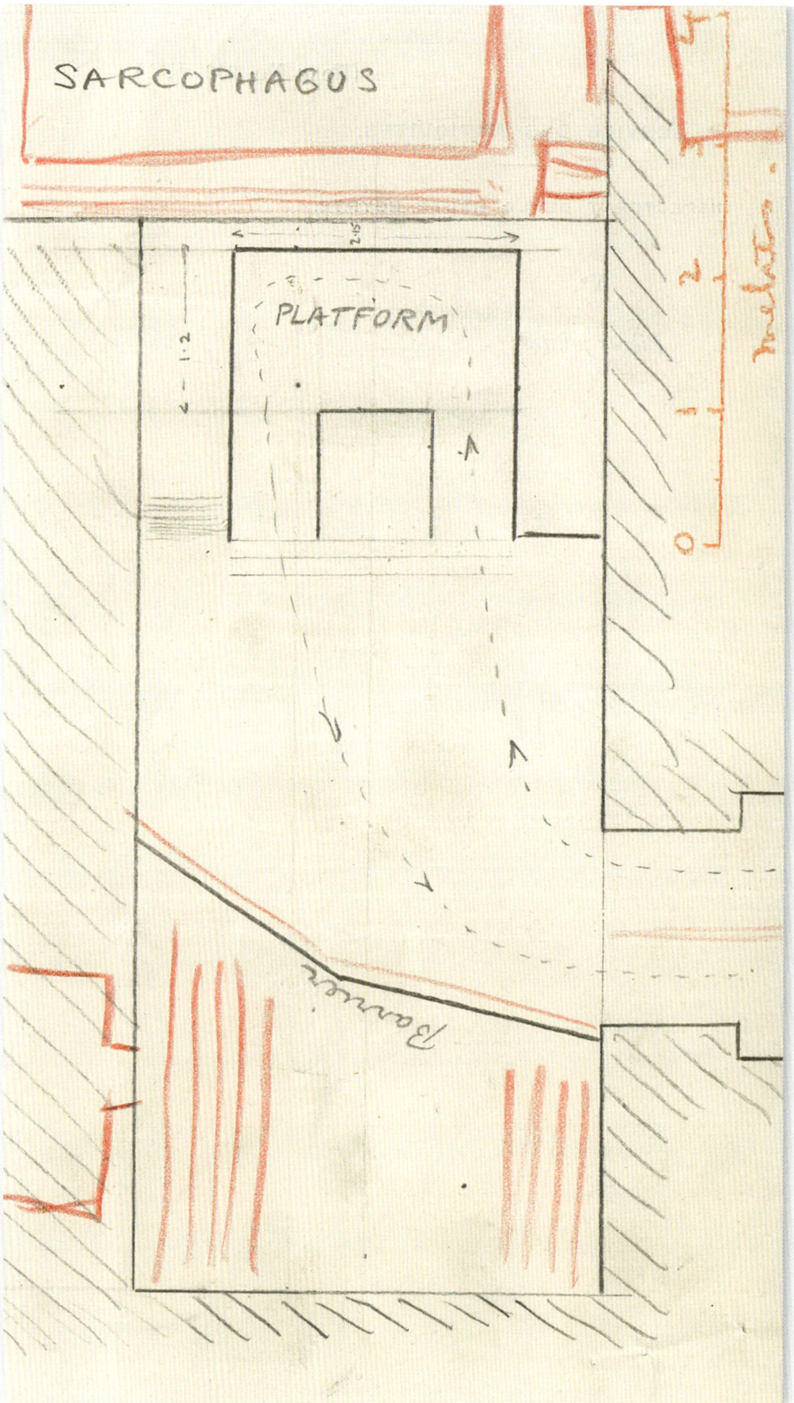

smaller and lighter. Howard Carter, who had arrived in Egypt in 1891, gave many lectures (especially in America) illustrated with his own slides, which were still made from medium-sized glass plates, some of which were hand-coloured (cat. 144). In 1923, the death of Lord Carnarvon, the dig's patron, started a persistent rumour, according to which about ten people associated with the tomb's discovery, on site or from afar, died between 1923 and 1927. The 'curse of Tutankhamun' was a boon to both the Egyptian and the international press, which talked up deaths that were perfectly natural into something more dramatic (cat. 155).

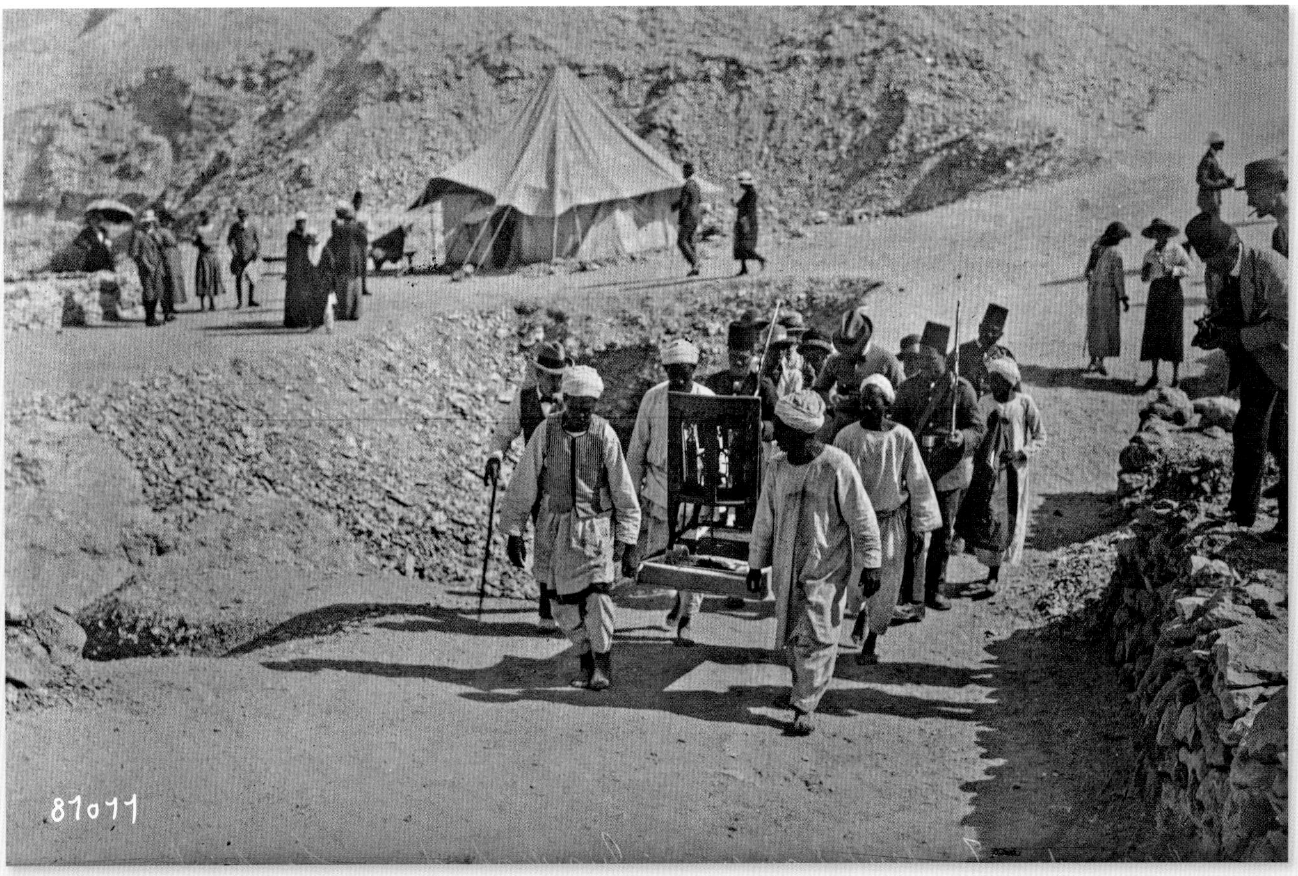

145

Transporting an armchair from Tutankhamun's tomb under the photographers' lenses, Rol press agency, Valley of the Kings, Egypt, January 1923.

From the 1960s, Tutankhamun's popularity was boosted again by the numerous Tutankhamun exhibitions — ten in all — which took place in sixty cities in Europe, North America (cats. 159, 161 and 162), Japan and Australia. All of these displayed works of art brought from Cairo. Paris was not to be outdone: nearly one million two hundred and fifty thousand visitors rushed to the Petit Palais in 1967. In 2019, the Grande Halle de la Villette, also in Paris, welcomed almost one million and five hundred thousand visitors, who were full of admiration for these fabulous treasures. And the tour is not yet over... **GA-L**

144

The third sarcophagus of Tutankhamun at the moment of its discovery; reproduction after original glass slides used by Howard Carter in his lectures, from a photograph by Harry Burton, 1925.

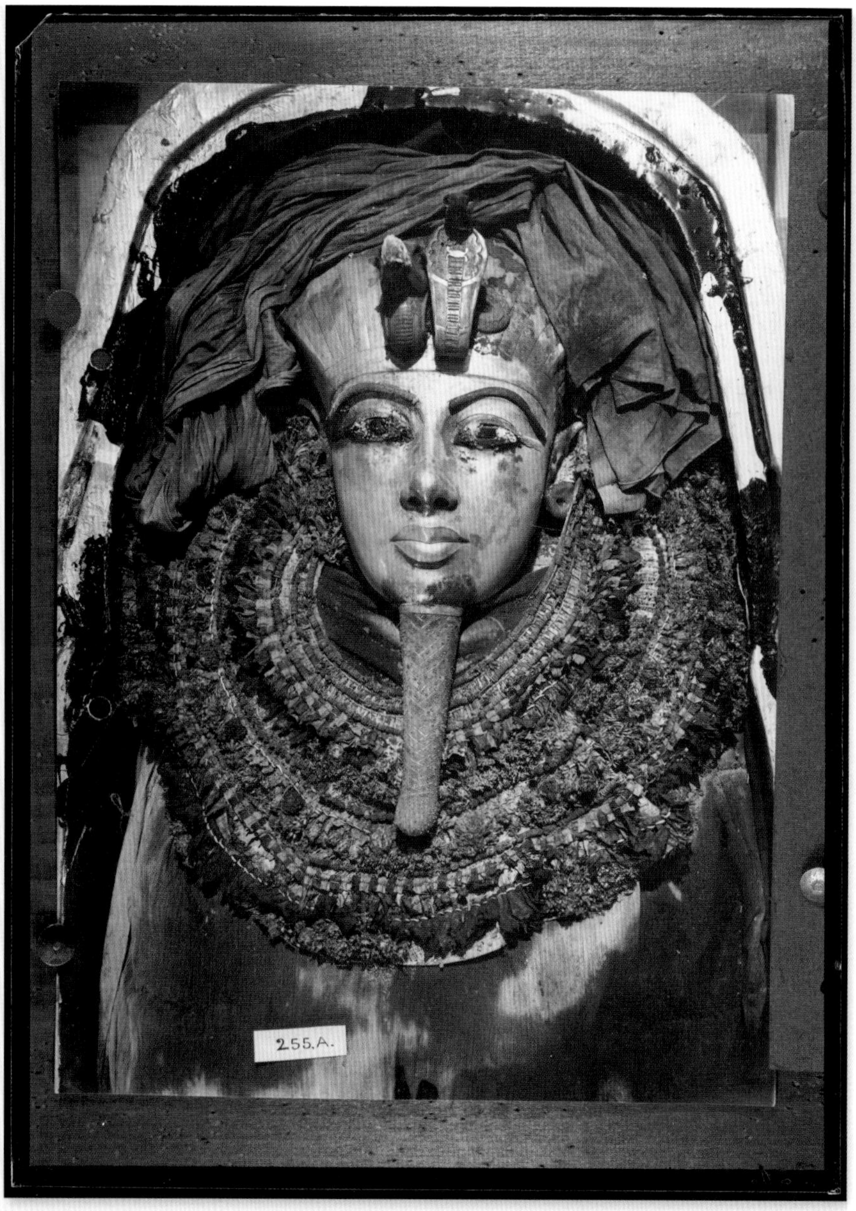

GABOLDE, M., *Toutankhamon*, coll. 'Les Grands Pharaons', Pygmalion, Paris, 2015.

HAWASS, Z., *Toutankhamon, Trésors du pharaon doré, le centième anniversaire*, exh. cat., Grande Halle de la Villette, Paris, 2019.

RIGGS, CHR., 'La photographie et les médias dans la tombe de Toutankhamon', in *Toutankhamon, à la découverte du pharaon oublié*, exh. cat., ed. by S. Connor and D. Laboury, Liège, 2019, pp. 52–61.

TOUTANKHAMON et son temps, exh. cat., ed. by C. Desroches Noblecourt, Petit Palais, Paris, 1967.

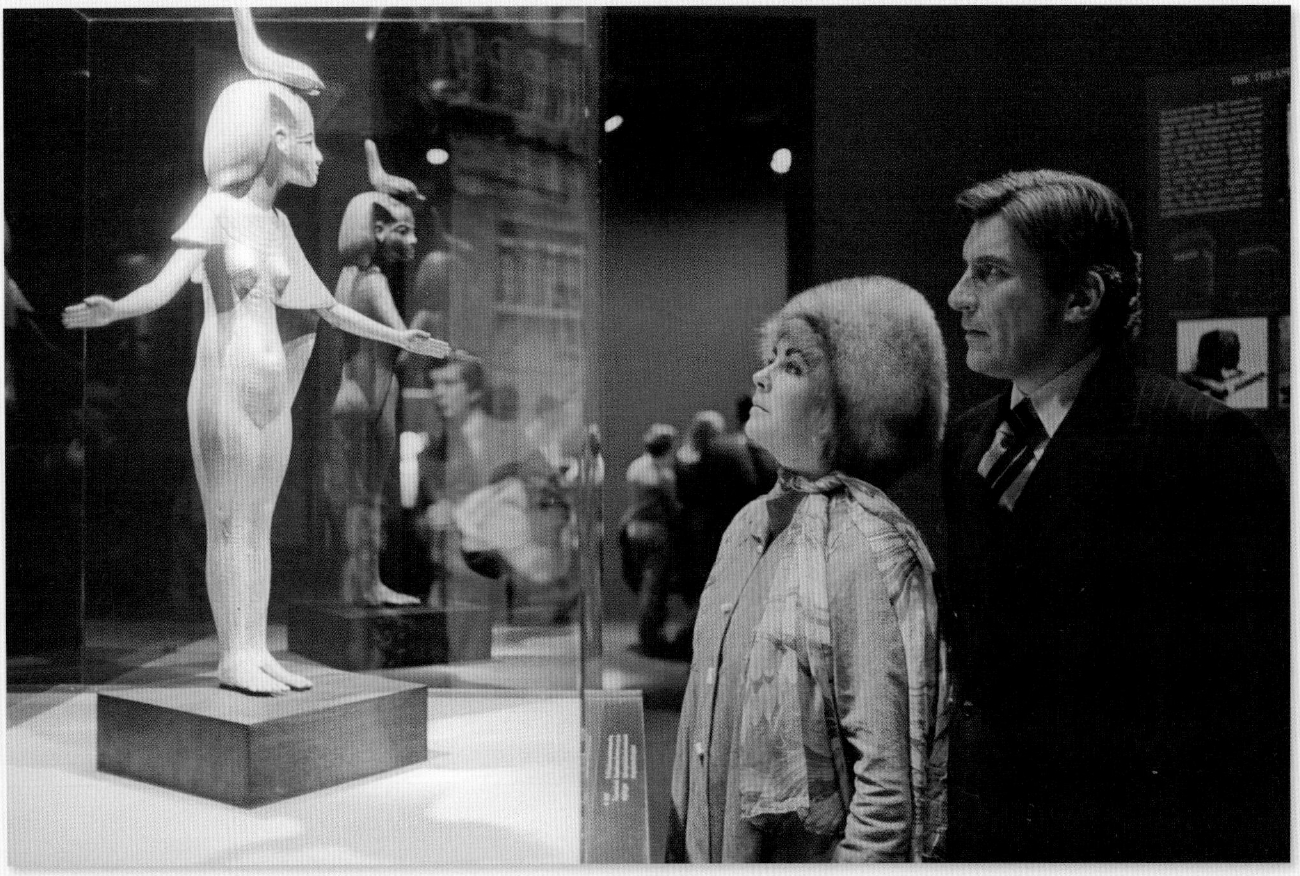

162

Elizabeth Taylor and her husband John Warner visiting the exhibition *The Treasures of Tutankhamun* at the National Gallery of Art, Washington, 1976 (unknown photographer).

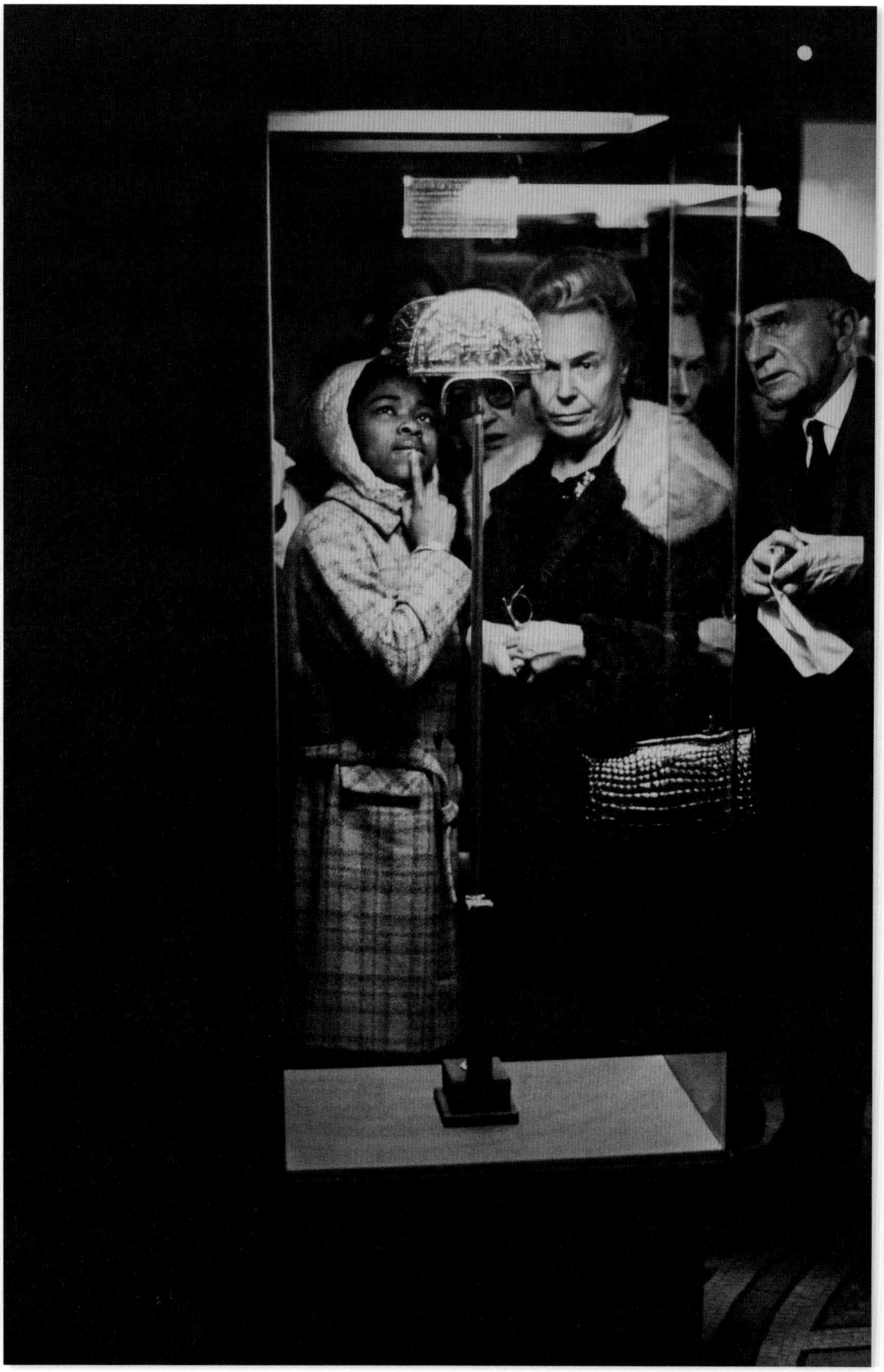

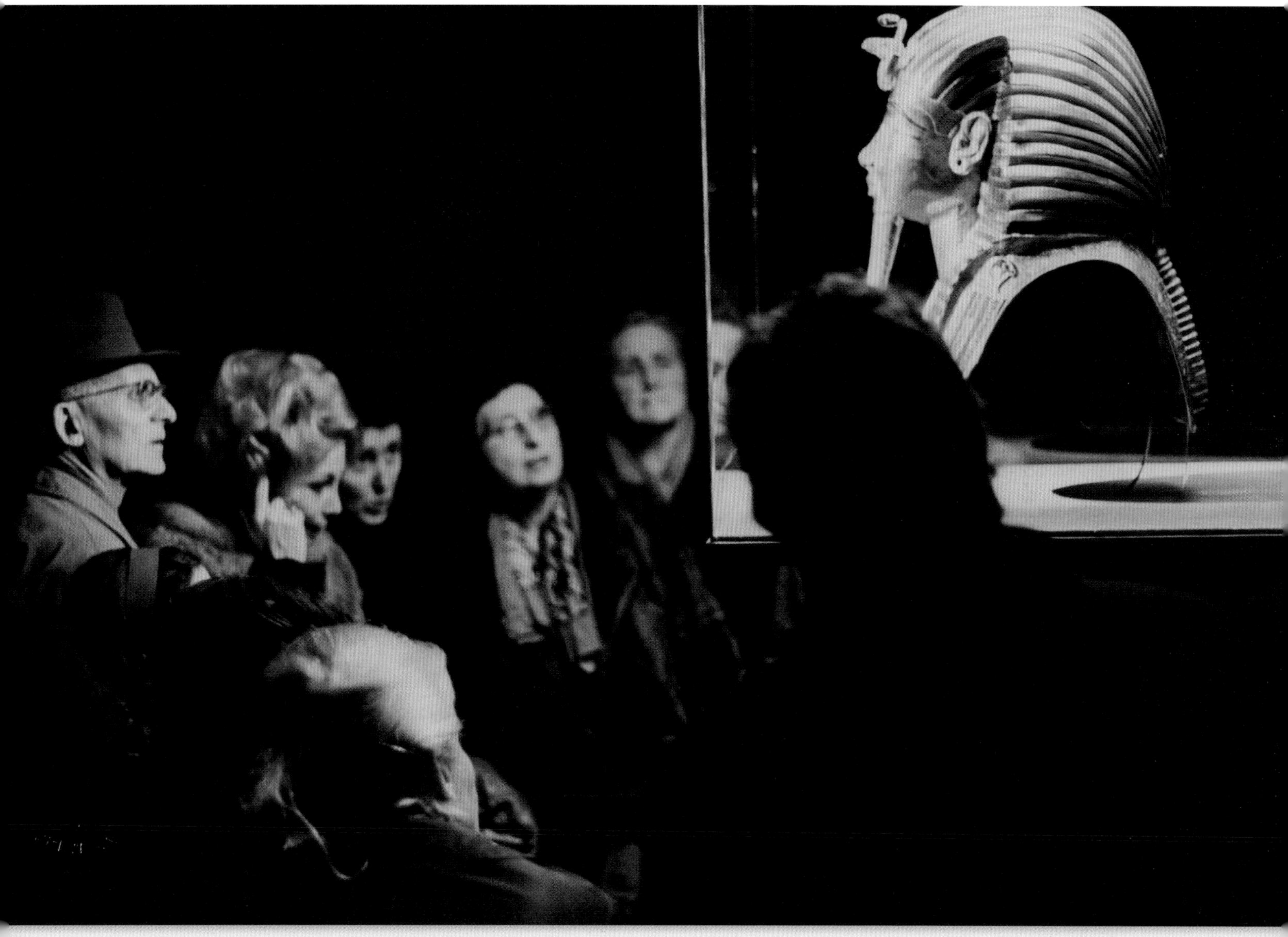

161–160

Jean Marquis, views of the exhibition *Tutankhamun et son temps* (Tutankhamun and his time) at the Petit Palais, Paris, 1967.

THE PHARAOHS WORKING FOR NATIONAL INDUSTRY

When he became leader of the new Arab Republic of Egypt in 1954, Gamal Abdel Nasser launched a wide-ranging policy of nationalization, encompassing both resources and means of production. Seeking to break free from the former colonial administration and to make Egypt a spearhead of non-aligned countries, Nasser set an objective for agricultural and industrial autonomy: Egypt must make everything, 'from the needle to the rocket'. Nationalized factories produced consumer goods intended to create a modern society that would not be inferior to the great powers in terms of its standard of living. To promote these Egyptian products, the government often chose pharaonic names and logos for them.

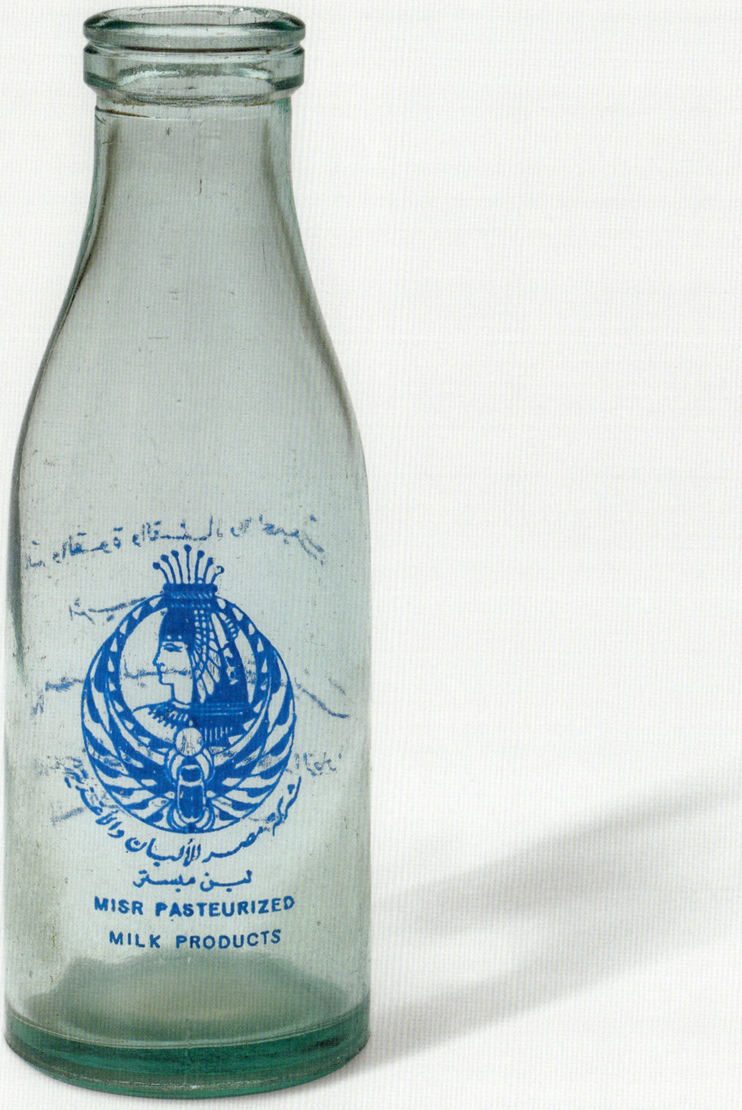

175

Bottle of milk from the Misr dairies, Egypt, second half of the twentieth century.

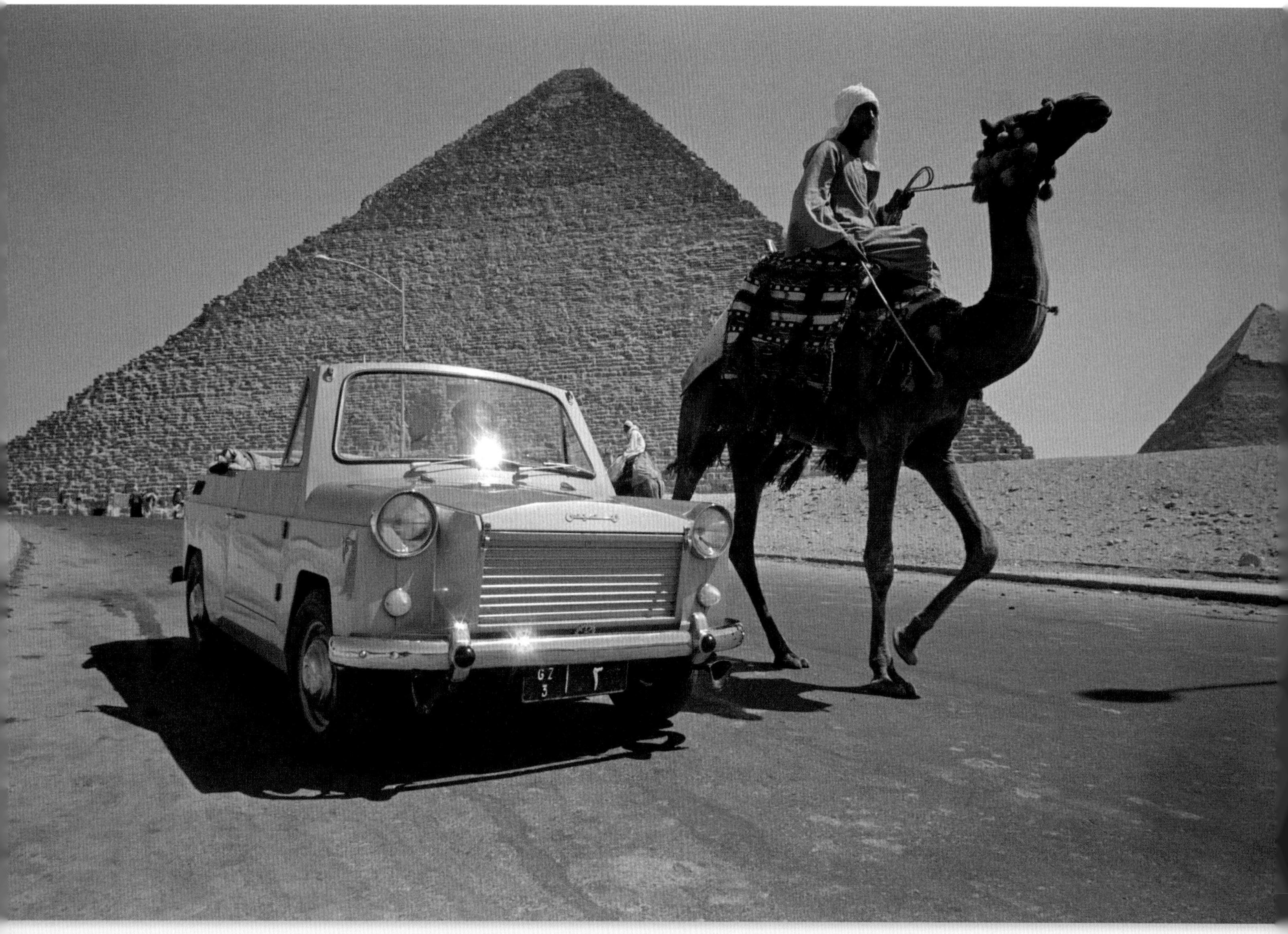

174

René Burri, *Voiture Ramses, Égypte, 1962* (Ramesses Car, Egypt, 1962).

176

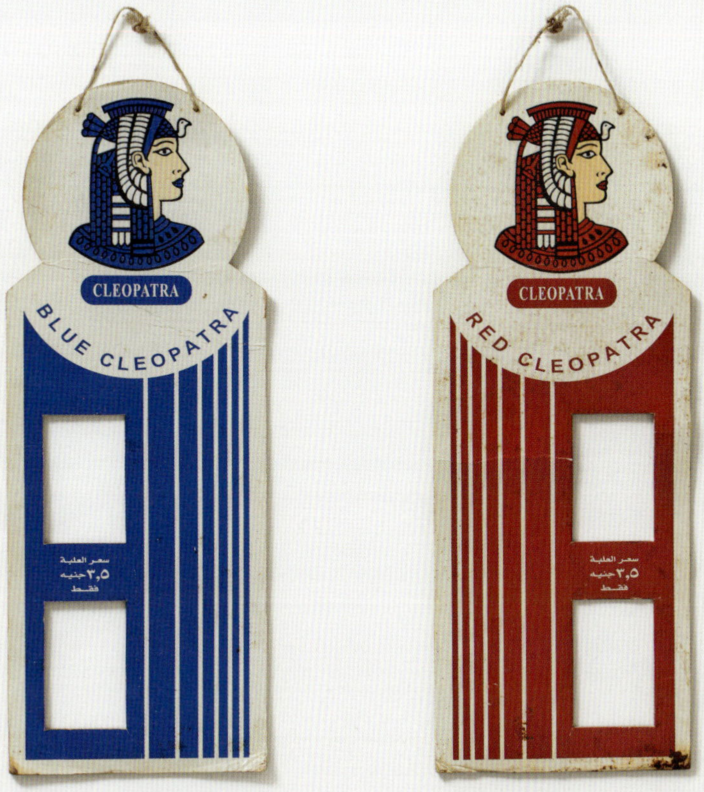

Display stand for *Cleopatra* cigarettes, Egypt, second half of the twentieth century (front and back).

From 1958 onwards, military factories for the production of civilian goods came up with the Nefertiti sewing machine (cat. 180). Operated manually or connected to a motor like the previously common Singer sewing machine, the Nefertiti was widely used in homes and workshops. By applying this familiar name, written solely in Arabic, and the image of the bust which had been a patriotic icon since the 1920s (despite being in Berlin), the authorities were banking on the queen's powers of seduction over citizen-consumers. The same strategy was used in 1959 for the Ramses car (cat. 174), the first vehicle that was supposedly entirely Egyptian. In fact, the body was an Italian model and the engine was imported from Germany, but it was assembled in Egypt. Something similar probably occurred with the sewing machine, which resembles models made in Asia to which large European firms simply apply their branding. The Nasr national factories also produced a range of pencils called Ramses: tools for the school student, the artist and the engineer,

underpinning the regime's social and economic project. The great pharaoh also featured in a commercial for ice creams produced by dairies called Misr ('Egypt' in Arabic) which, from 1956 until the 1990s, collected, processed and distributed milk following a modern agro-industrial model (cat. 175). This operation was part of a consortium linked to the Misr bank, created in 1919 in a first nationalist wave, and shares its pharaonic logo: a female profile surmounted by the vulture crown worn by goddesses and queens and a stand of papyrus, surrounded by plant stalks or scarab wings. This ancient image appears everywhere on the bank's branch signs as well as on the many products produced by Misr companies. It has become a popular motif, reproduced on the seats of café chairs (cat. 182), where people might well sit to smoke a Cleopatra cigarette (cat. 176).
It was apparently Nasser himself who commissioned the brand from the Eastern Tobacco Company in 1961, as an Egyptian equivalent of American Kent cigarettes, which he couldn't be seen to smoke in public. The queen of antiquity, turned into a global star in 1963 in the guise of Elizabeth Taylor, and the initial intervention of the *rais* (president) helped to give the cigarettes an excellent start, and they are still the most smoked cigarettes in Egypt today. Although other products with pharaonic names have not known the same longevity, they nonetheless made their mark on several generations, both illustrating and bolstering the popularity of the great kings and queens who are the Egyptians' pride. **FM**

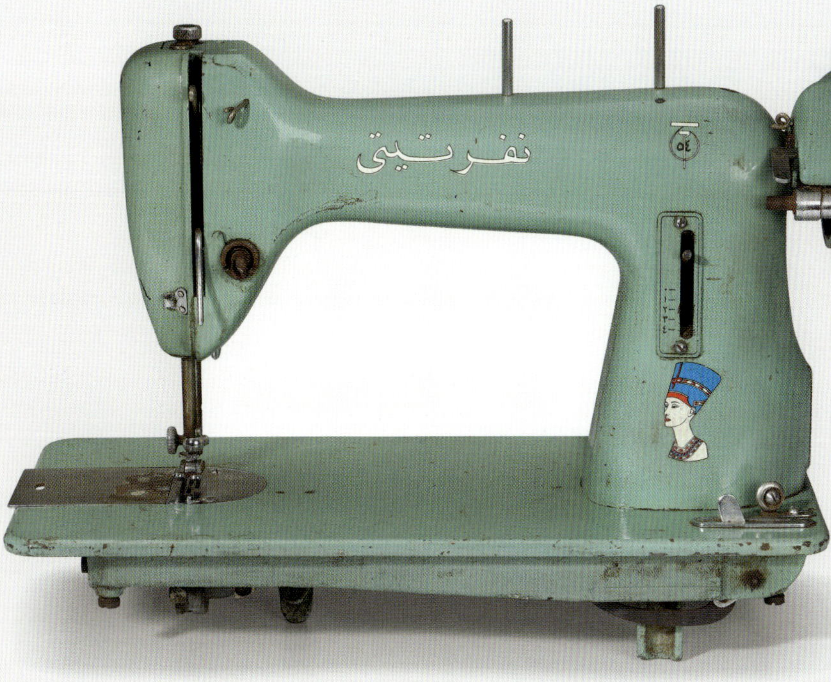

180

Nefertiti sewing machine, made by military factories for the production of civilian goods, Helwan, Egypt, late 1950s–1960s.

BLACK PHARAOHS, BLACK ICONS

Egypt is of course located in what we know as Africa and Egyptologists — mostly Europeans and Americans — have not tended to make much of this, but African intellectuals, and those from the African diaspora, have sought to underline the kinship between the pharaonic civilization and other peoples of the continent. The American George W. Parker was one of the first to do so in *The Children of the Sun* (1918), but in the French-speaking world it is the works of the Senegalese scholar Cheikh Anta Diop that have had the most resounding impact. In his works *Nations nègres et culture* (1954) and *Antériorité des civilisations nègres* (1967), he sought to 'reconcile African civilizations with history.'

241

Poster for the film *Cleopatra Jones* by Jack Starrett, Lithographers' and Photoengravers' International Union, USA, 1973.

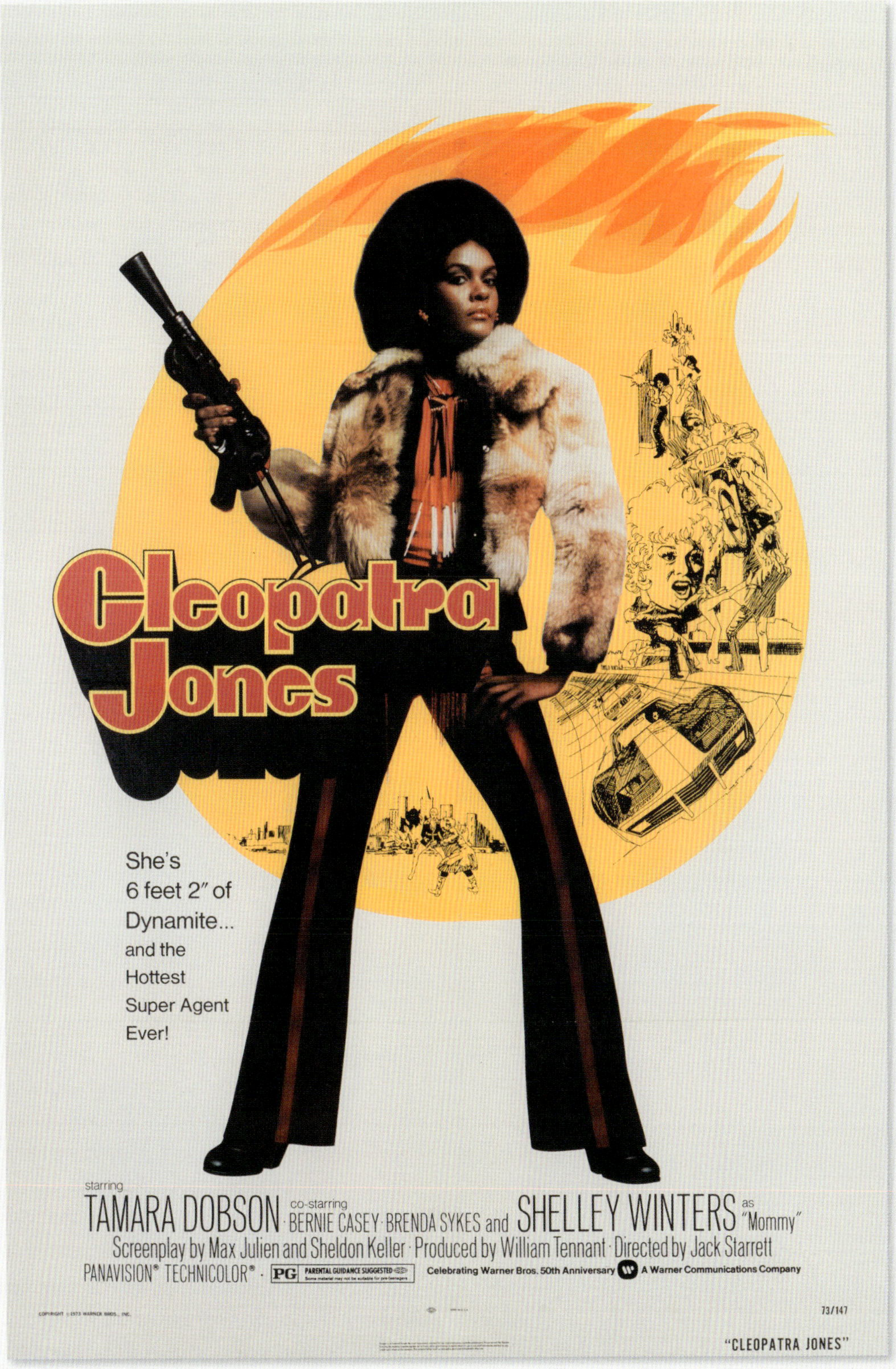

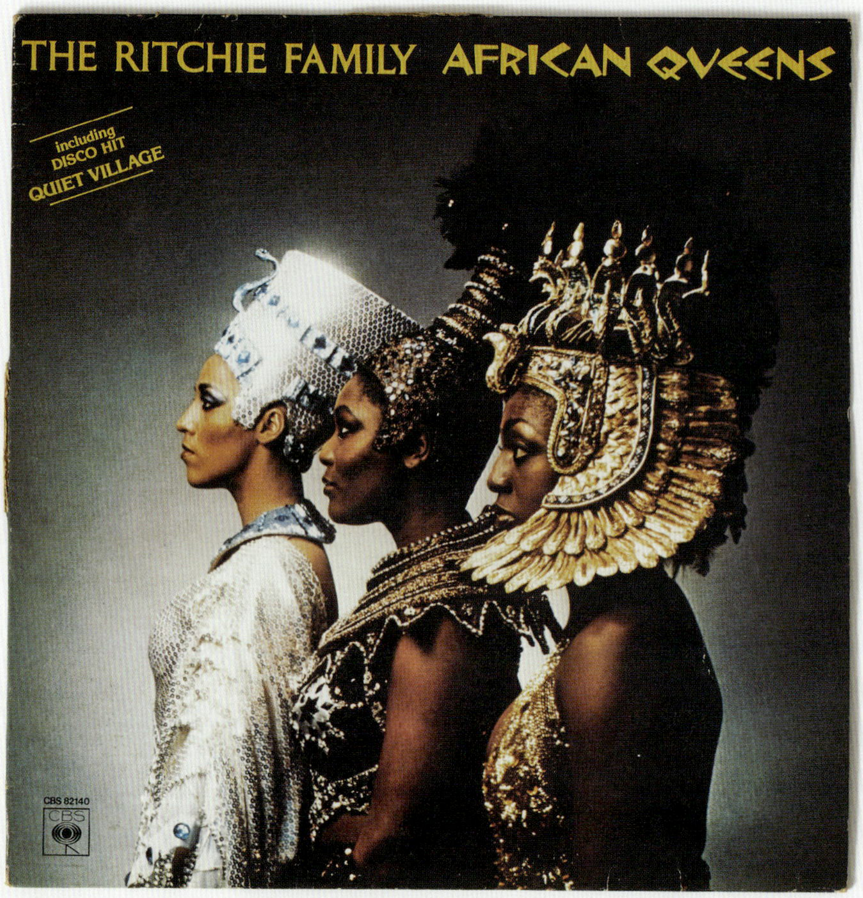

240

Record sleeve for *African Queens* by The Ritchie Family, CBS, USA, 1977.

Whether or not his theories were well-founded, many Africans or descendants of Africans have been inspired by them to consider the pharaohs as guardians of their Black identity. His ideas were first taken up by African Americans fighting for their civil rights, who thought that Cleopatra, who preferred death to slavery, could be a model for Black emancipation. The idea of African pharaohs has also appealed to Black people the world over (cat. 241), who believe that the historical importance of African peoples has been denied through white imperialism, the slave trade and colonialization. This is reflected in onomastics, especially in West Africa and the USA, where the first names Nefertiti, Ramses and Pharaoh are not uncommon. It is primarily in the context of hip-hop, rap and R&B that we see a proliferation of references connecting Black Africa with pharaonic Egypt. For example, in 1983, the bravura track *The Crown*, composed by 'Imhotep' Gary Byrd

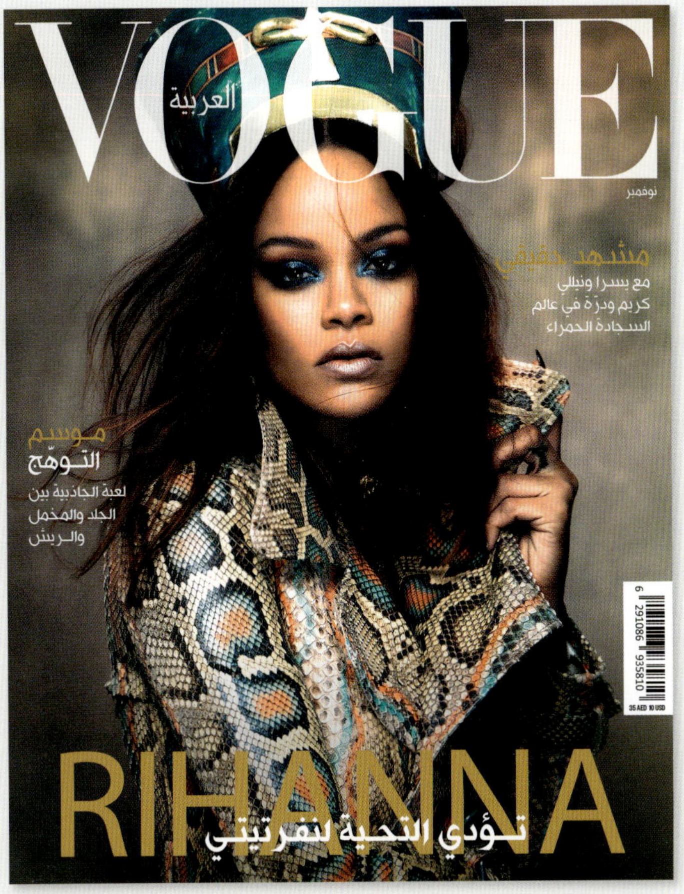

242

Edition of *Vogue Arabia*, November 2017: 'Rihanna pays homage to Nefertiti', photography: Greg Kadel; styling: Konca Aykan.

and Stevie Wonder, is a long African American history lesson, as strong on rhythm as it is on partiality, which mentions Akhenaten, Nefertiti, and Tutankhamun among the ancestors of those listening or dancing to the music. Female singers have mostly been drawn to the figure of Nefertiti, easily identified by her crown's truncated cone shape — perhaps because Cleopatra suffered from a reputation that was too scandalous or because her European origins ruled her out. Examples include the outfit worn by one of the Ritchie Family singers on the *African Queens* album cover (cat. 240) and Rihanna's famous fondness for Nefertiti, whose crown she wore for *Vogue Arabia* in 2017 (cat. 242). Even more significant is Beyoncé's use of the queen's image. Several costumes for her massive set at the 2018 Coachella festival bore an emblem mimicking those of university fraternities: a bee, a sort of hieroglyph for her nickname Queen B(ee), a raised, black fist and the head of a black panther,

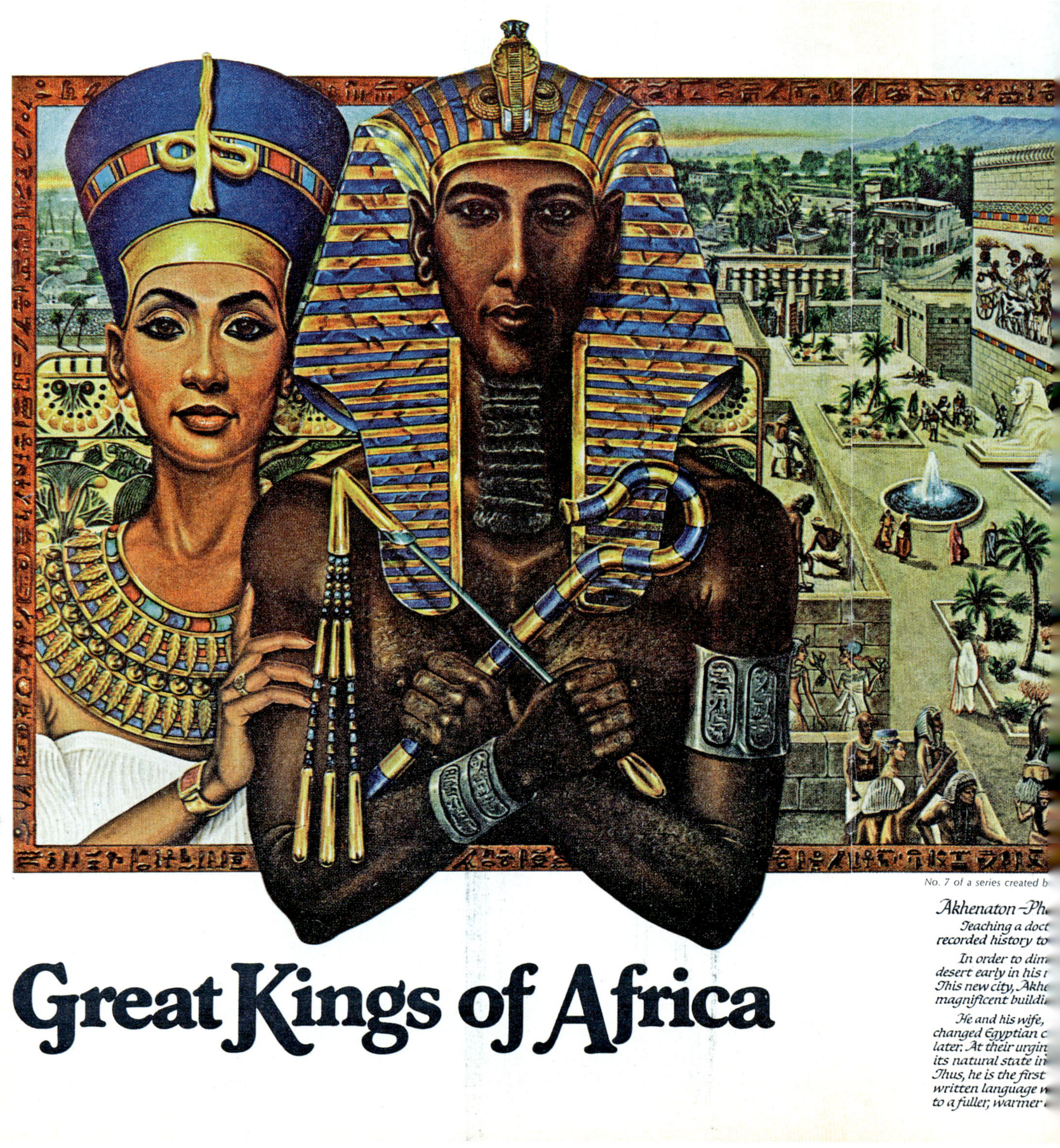

emblems of the Black Panthers, and a bust of Nefertiti with African features. The queen universally lauded for her beauty thus becomes an icon for African American pride and Black feminism — which has a certain irony given that the 1930s press debated whether or not she was 'Aryan'. **FM**

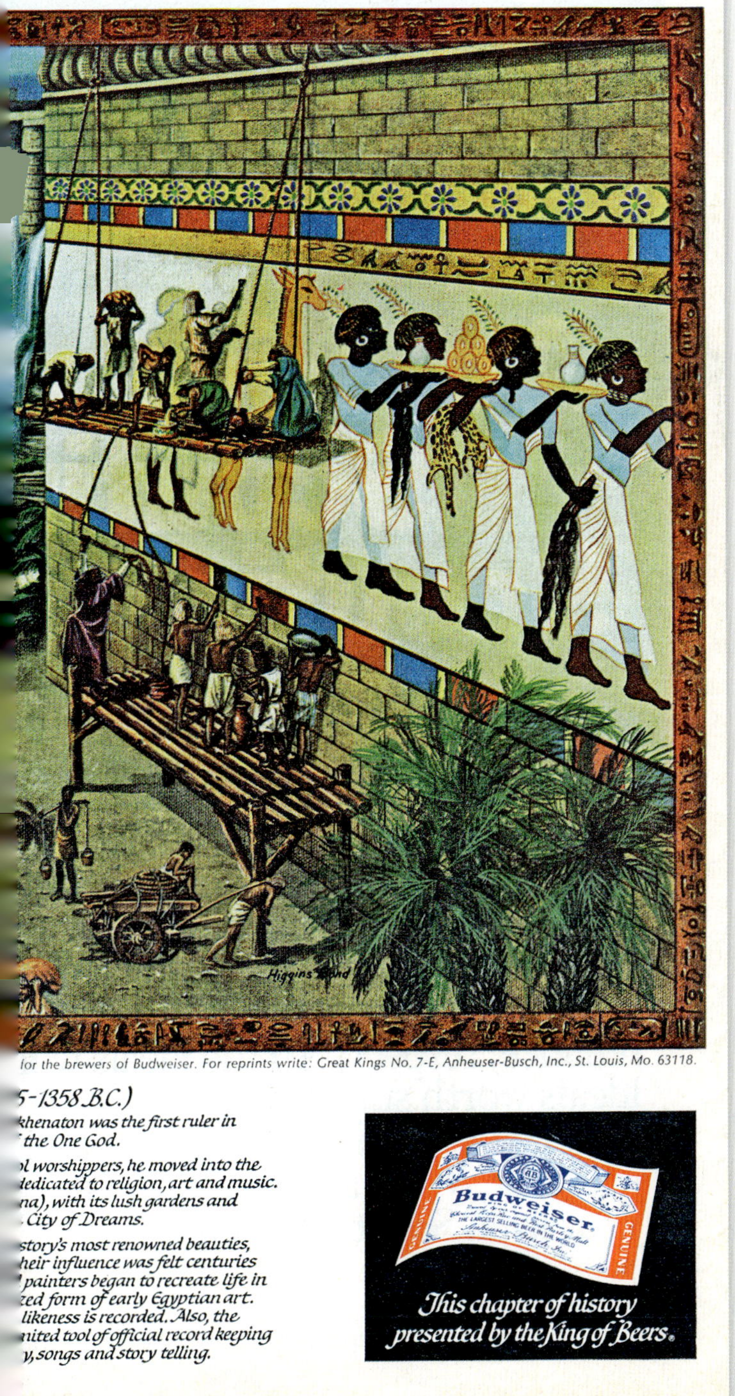

239

Advertisement for Budweiser beer, original painting by Barbara Higgins Bond, USA, 1978.

Bièvre-Perrin, F., 'Rihanna et l'Antique: de Néfertiti à Méduse', in Bièvre-Perrin, F. (ed.), *Antiquipop*, Lyon, 17 December 2017, available online.

Bièvre -Perrin, F., 'L'Égypte antique convoquée à Coachella par Beyoncé : pourquoi Toutankhamon et Néfertiti?', in Bièvre -Perrin, F. (ed.), *Antiquipop*, Lyon, 16 April 2018, available online.

Cachin, O., 'L'Égypte mythique de la rap generation', in Quentin, F. (ed.), *Le Livre des Égyptes*, Robert Laffont, Paris, 2014, pp. 790–93.

O'Connor, D., Reid, A., *Ancient Egypt in Africa*, UCL Press, London, 2003.

NEFERTITI, QUEEN OF CONTEMPORARY ART

From the moment it went on display at the Berlin museum in 1924, with the inventory number ÄM 21300, the official portrait of Nefertiti by the sculptor Thutmose became one of the most famous works of art in the world. Reproduced millions of times over in two and three dimensions, especially in advertising as well as tourist souvenirs in both Egypt and Berlin, this image resurfaces every time there is mention of ancient Egypt or the ideal of female beauty, which Nefertiti supposedly embodies (cat. 245). Artists have been influenced by this icon perhaps more than any other viewers or consumers: it must arouse their aesthetic sensibilities, reawaken memories of art history courses and books, and sometimes stimulate or grate on their political convictions. This ancient sculpture has inspired modern art by providing a metaphor that most people can easily absorb, evoking values and attitudes that characterize contemporary art. The extensive production of the Berlin museums' plaster casting workshop, over almost a century, has also provided artists with faithful copies that can be replicated in large numbers. Like the Venus de Milo and the Mona Lisa, the royal bust is often manipulated by iconoclastic creative artists seeking to topple from their pedestals old idols venerated by scholars and museums, although in truth their irony does not obscure the tribute paid to the masterpiece. No doubt playing on the publicity, some female artists have turned the queen's portrait into a wry comment on the condition of women and the demands for perfection that such a model imposes (cat. 247). Madame Yevonde's 1938 photograph *Still Life with the Head of Nefertiti* shows a white bust,

249

Mehdi-Georges Lahlou,
I used to be Nefertiti, 2014.

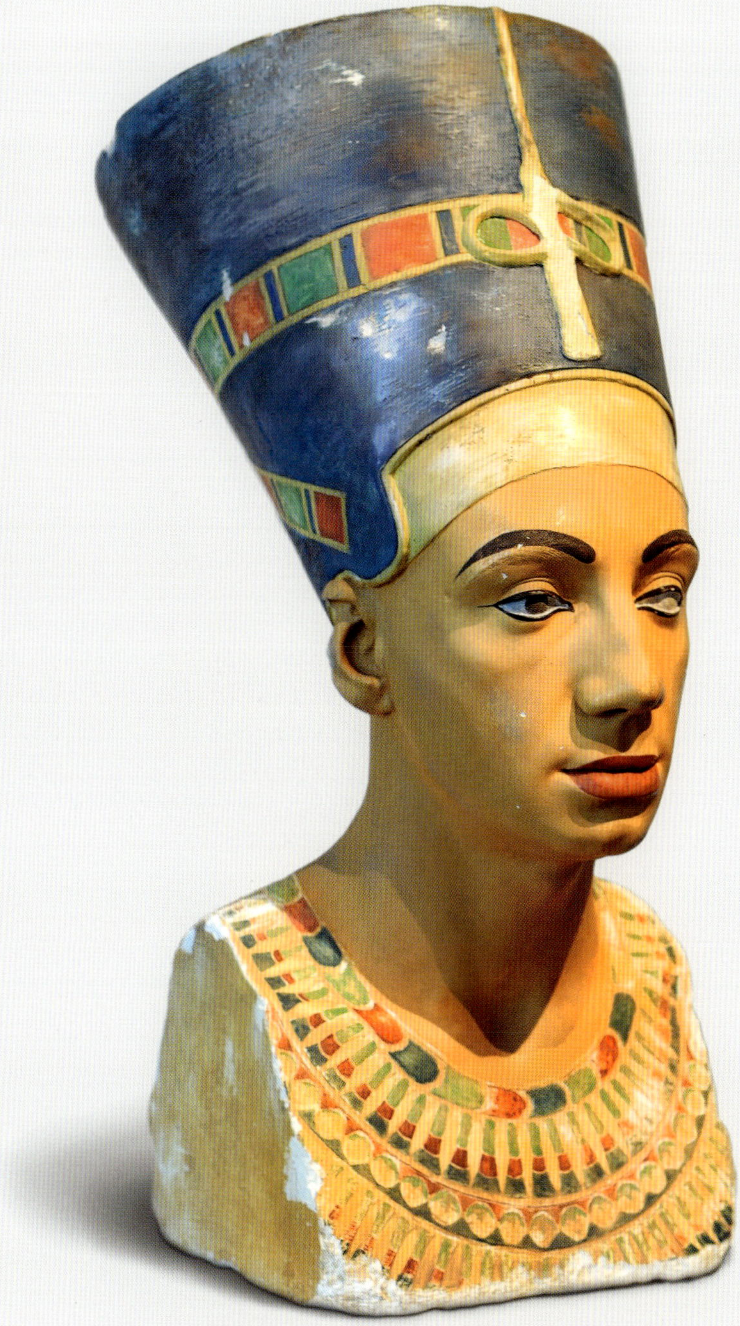

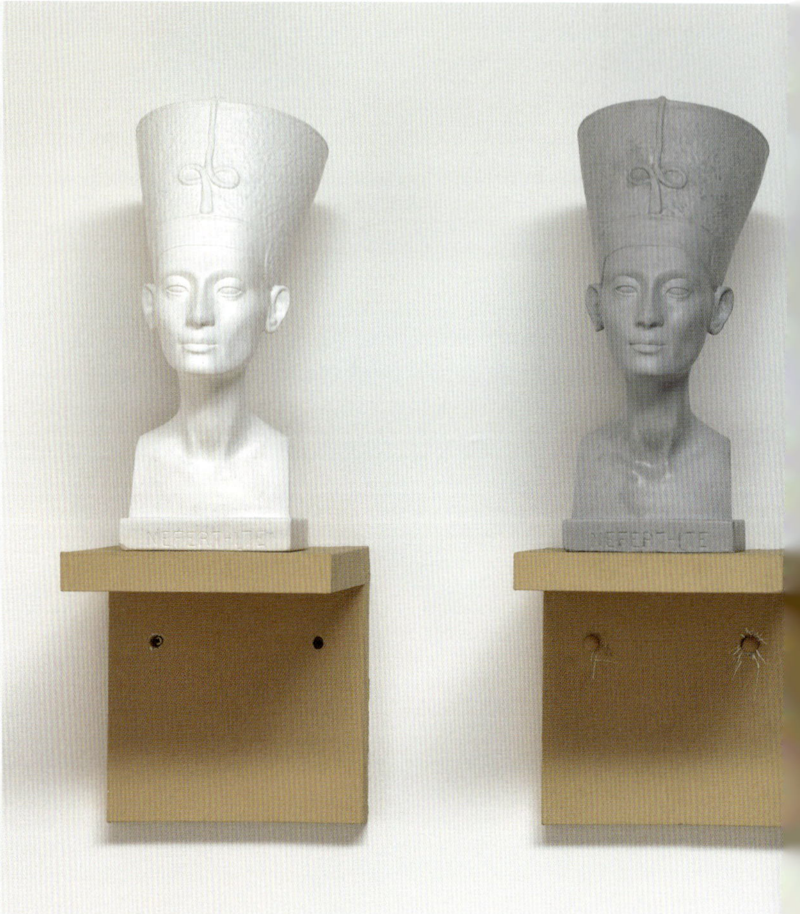

244

Fred Wilson, *Grey Area*, 1993.

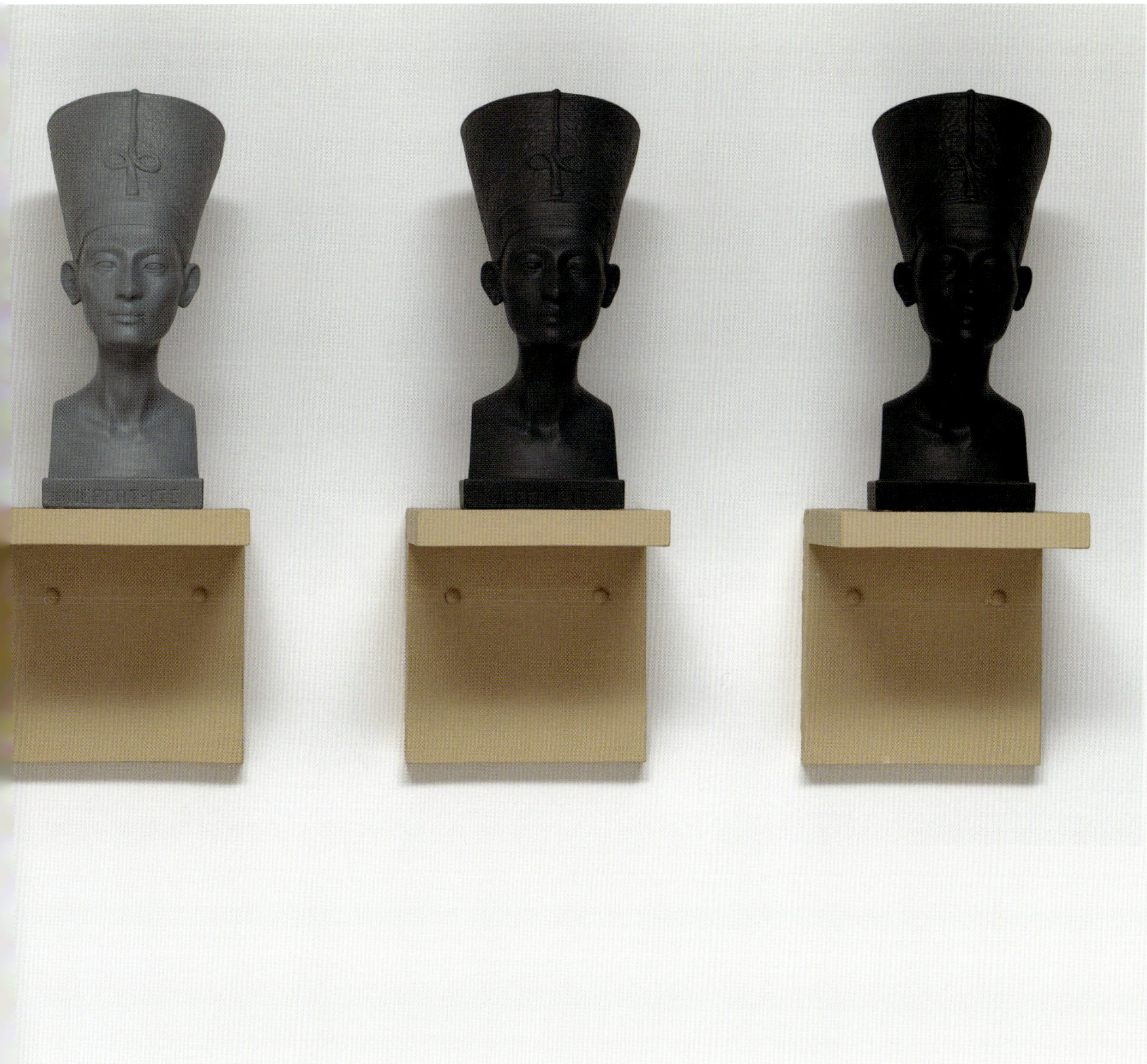

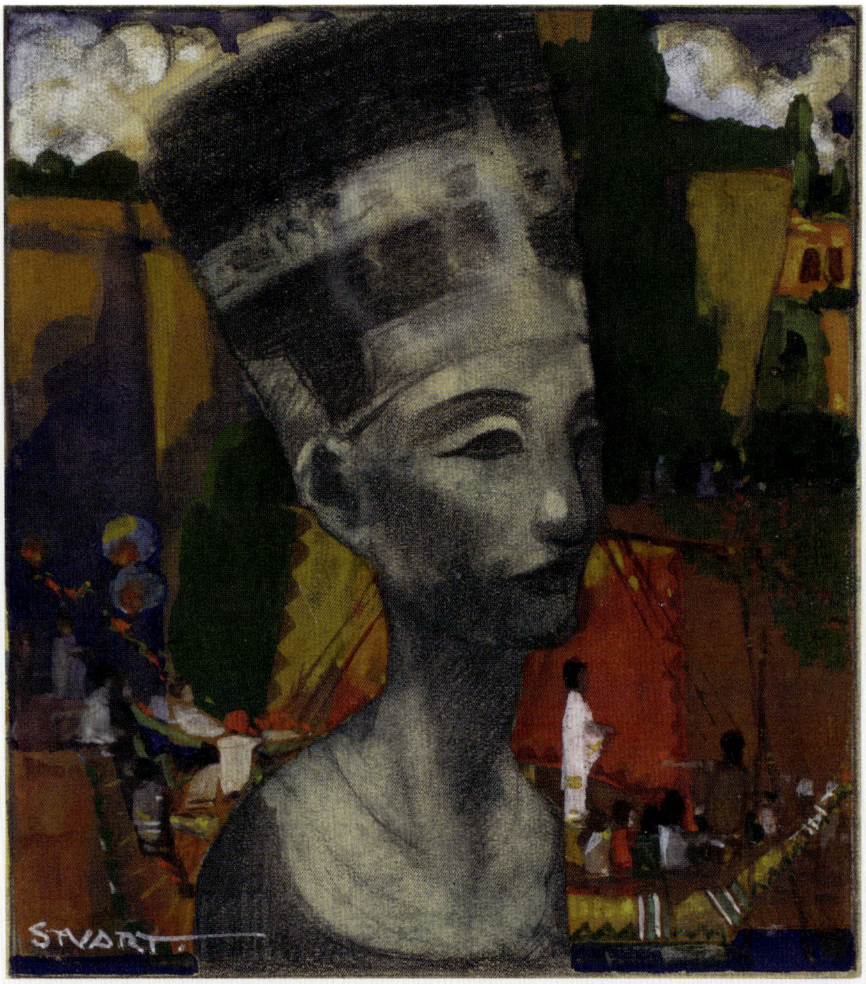

245

Stuart Carvalhais, *Nefertiti*, n.d.

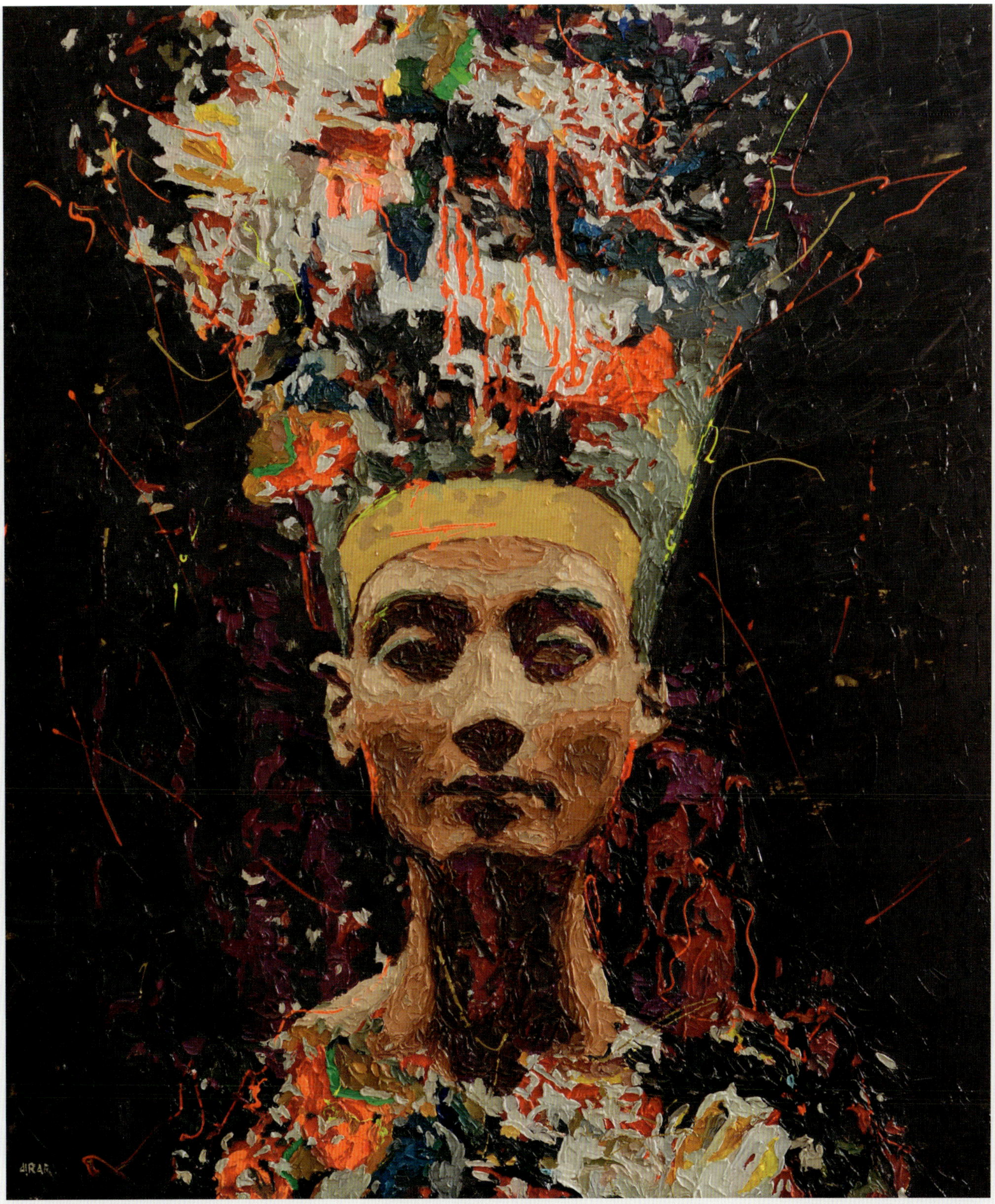

250

Hossam Dirar, *Nefertiti*, 2018.

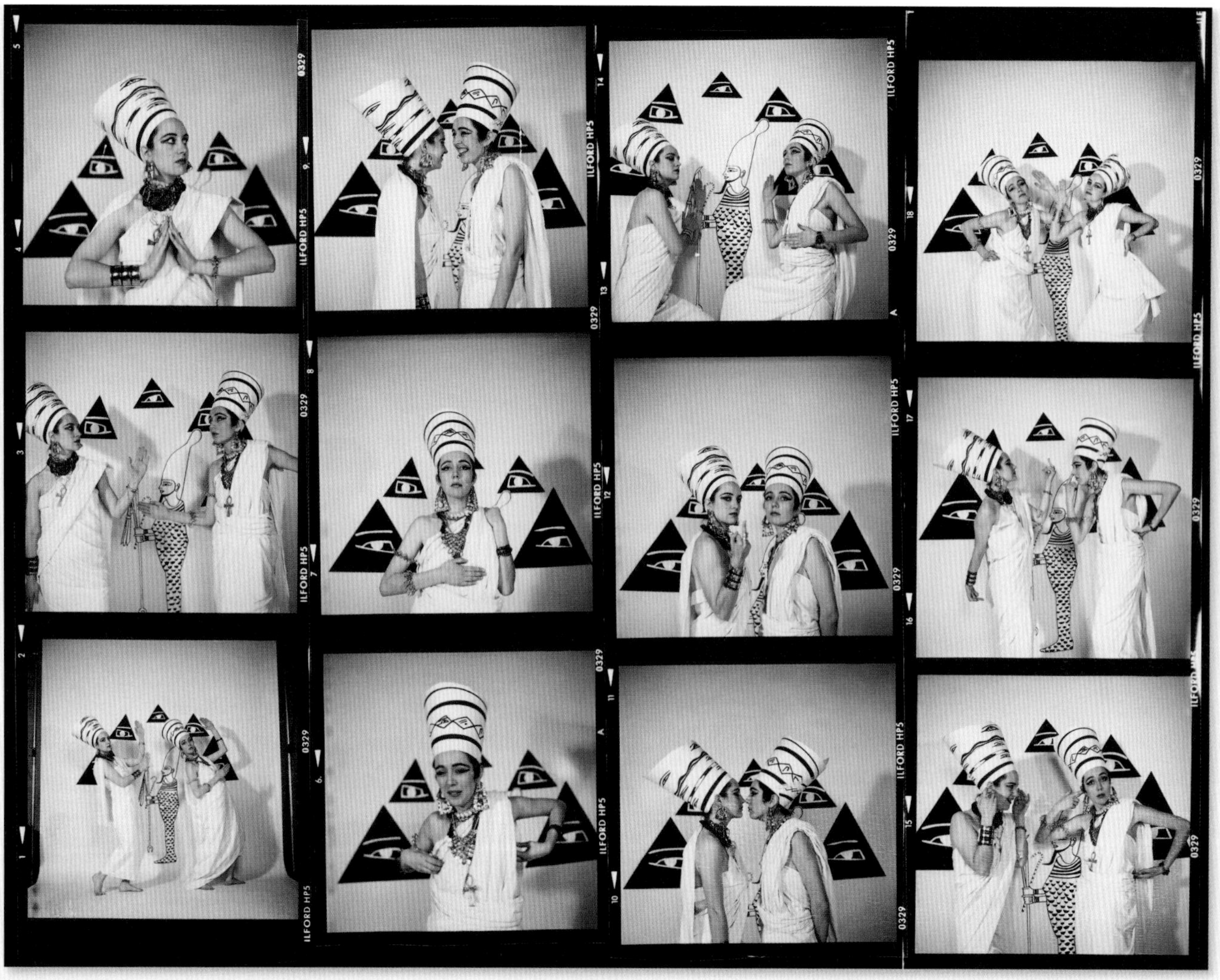

247

Les Rouquines, *Pharaonas* series, Marseille, 1992.

wearing make-up and finery, her fingernails varnished, holding an iron against a background of flowering branches. In the hands of African American artists such as Fred Wilson and his brown and black versions of *Grey Area* (cat. 244), the bust also becomes the repository for questions about race and identity. With the exception of some works evoking the historical figure, such as the series by Hossam Dirar (cat. 250) — a homage to Egyptian women and an encouragement to them to reclaim the freedom that the wife of Akhenaten would have enjoyed — the queen and the real woman have disappeared behind the stereotyped bust, which for a long time has not been her own. **FM**

Bardaouil, S., Fellrath, T., *Le Théorème de Néfertiti. Itinéraire de l'œuvre d'art: la création des icônes*, Skira and Institut du Monde Arabe, Paris, 2013.

Tyldesley, J., *Nefertiti's Face. The Creation of an icon*, Profile Books, London, 2018.

TEMPLES

OLIVIER CABLAT

189–194

The *Temples* series consists of multiple examples of architecture inspired by pharaonic art, including many souvenir shop façades aimed at tourists.

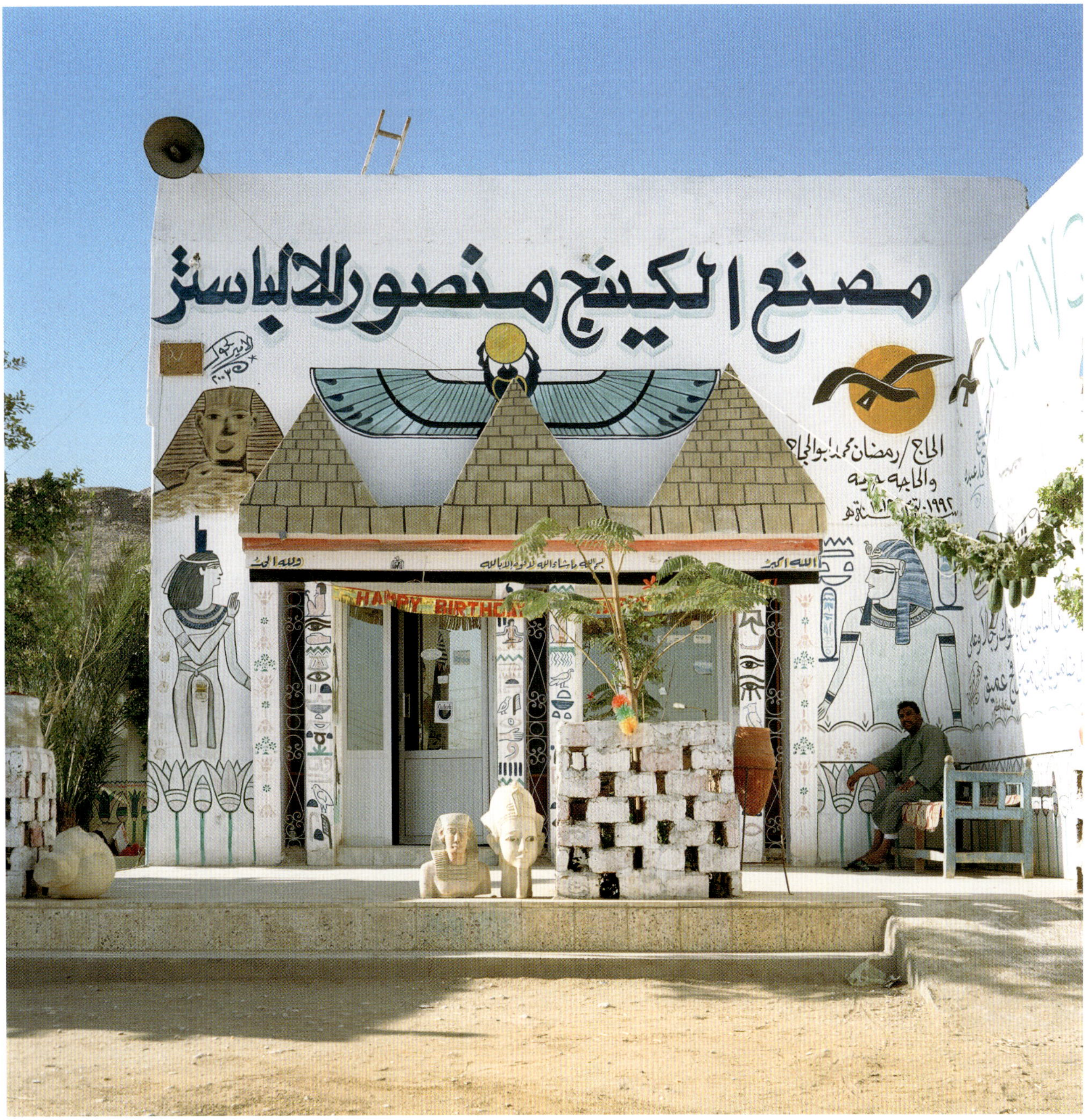
مصنع الكينج منصور للالباستر

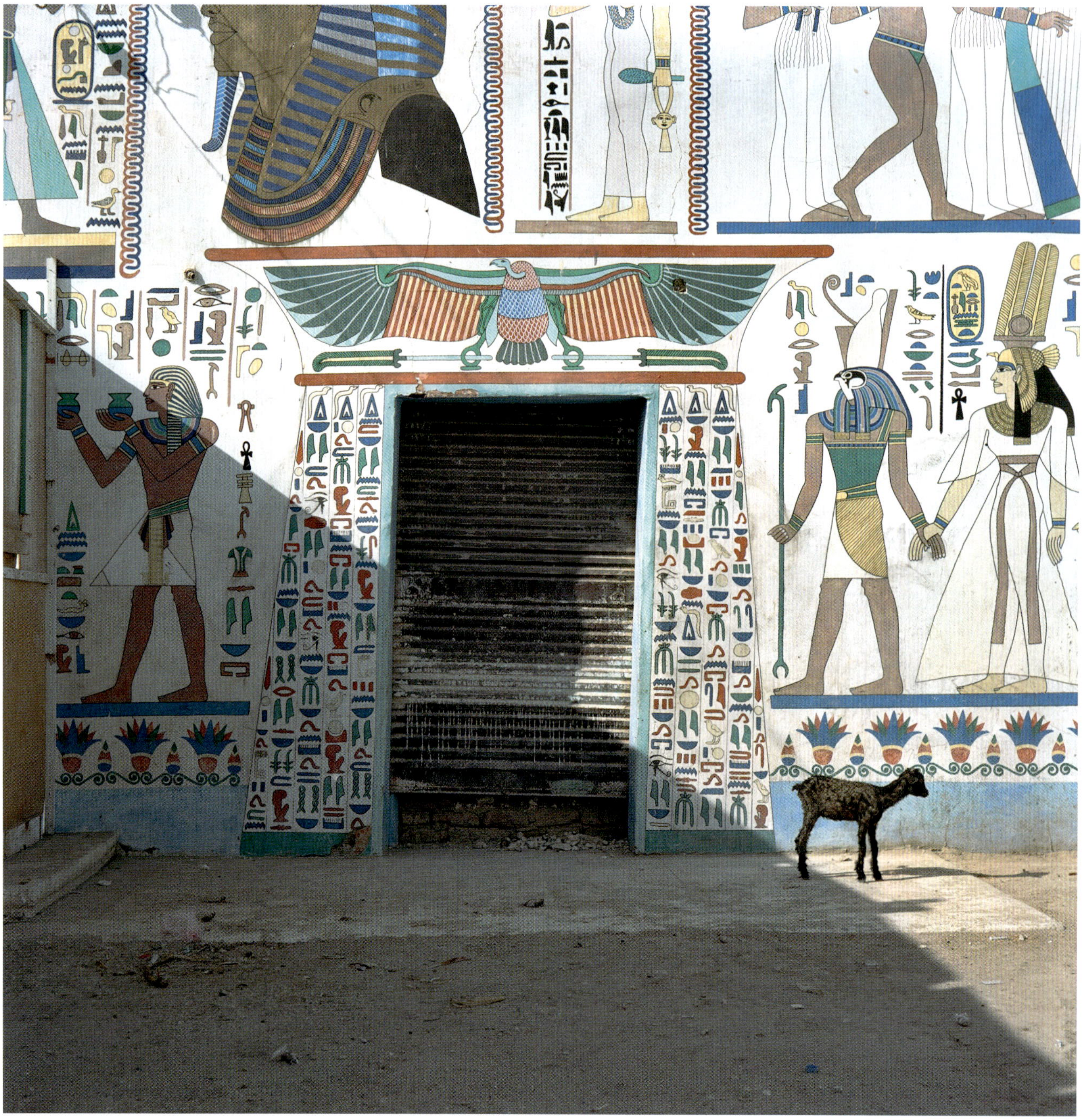

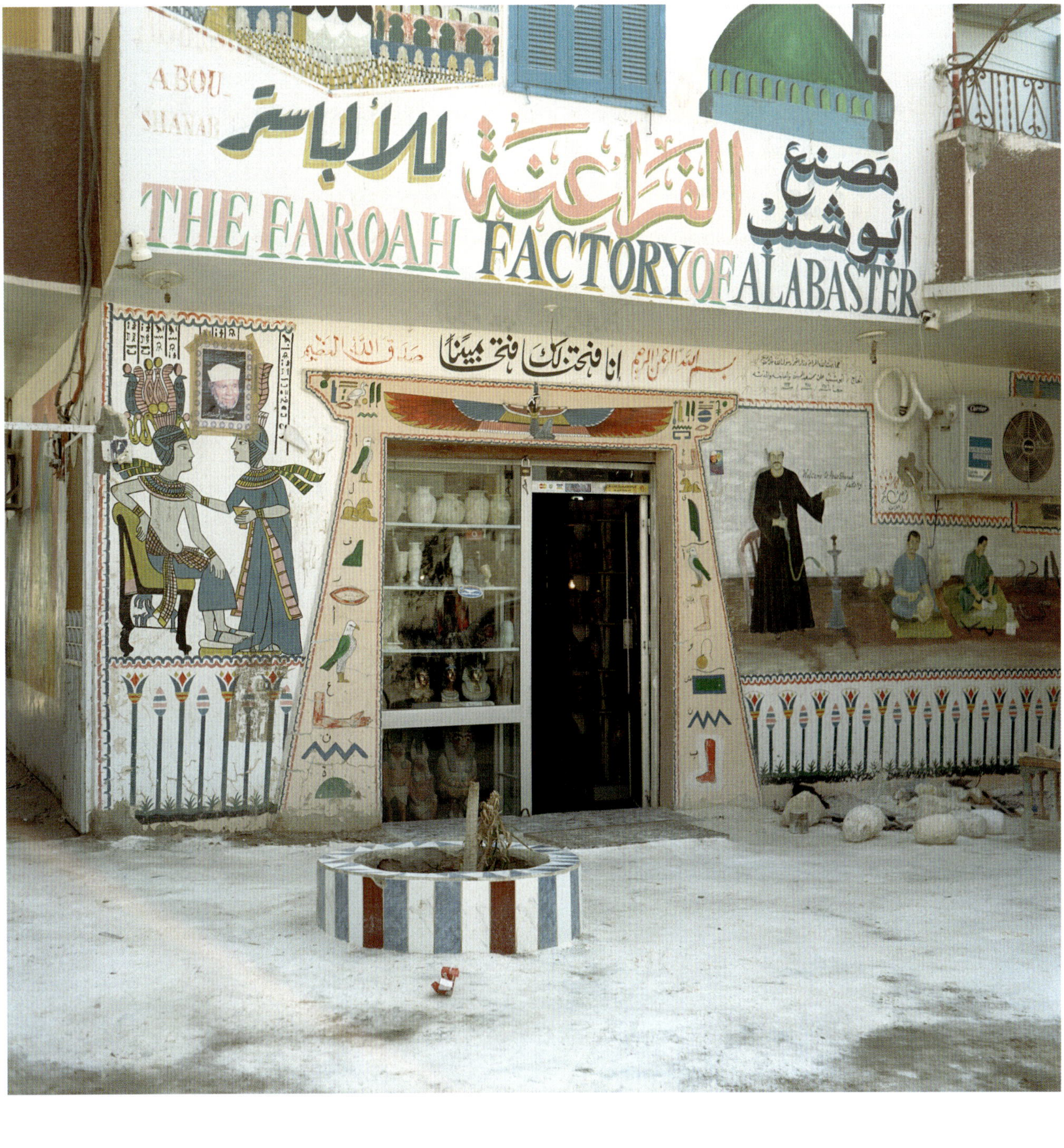
ABOU-
SHANAB
مصنع الفراعنة للألباستر
أبوشنب
THE FAROAH FACTORY OF ALABASTER
انا فتحنا لك فتحا مبينا

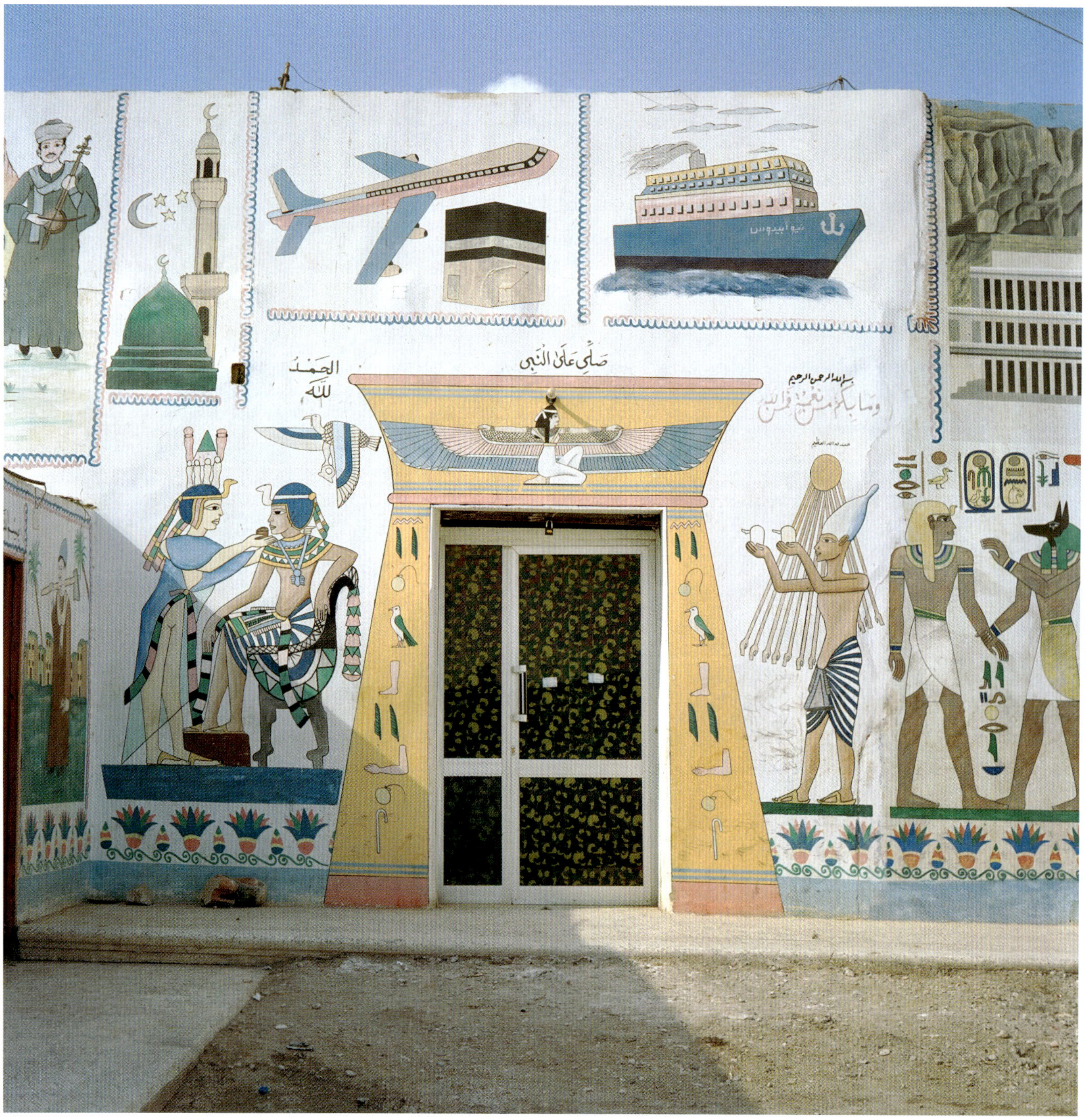
صلي على النبي
الحمد لله

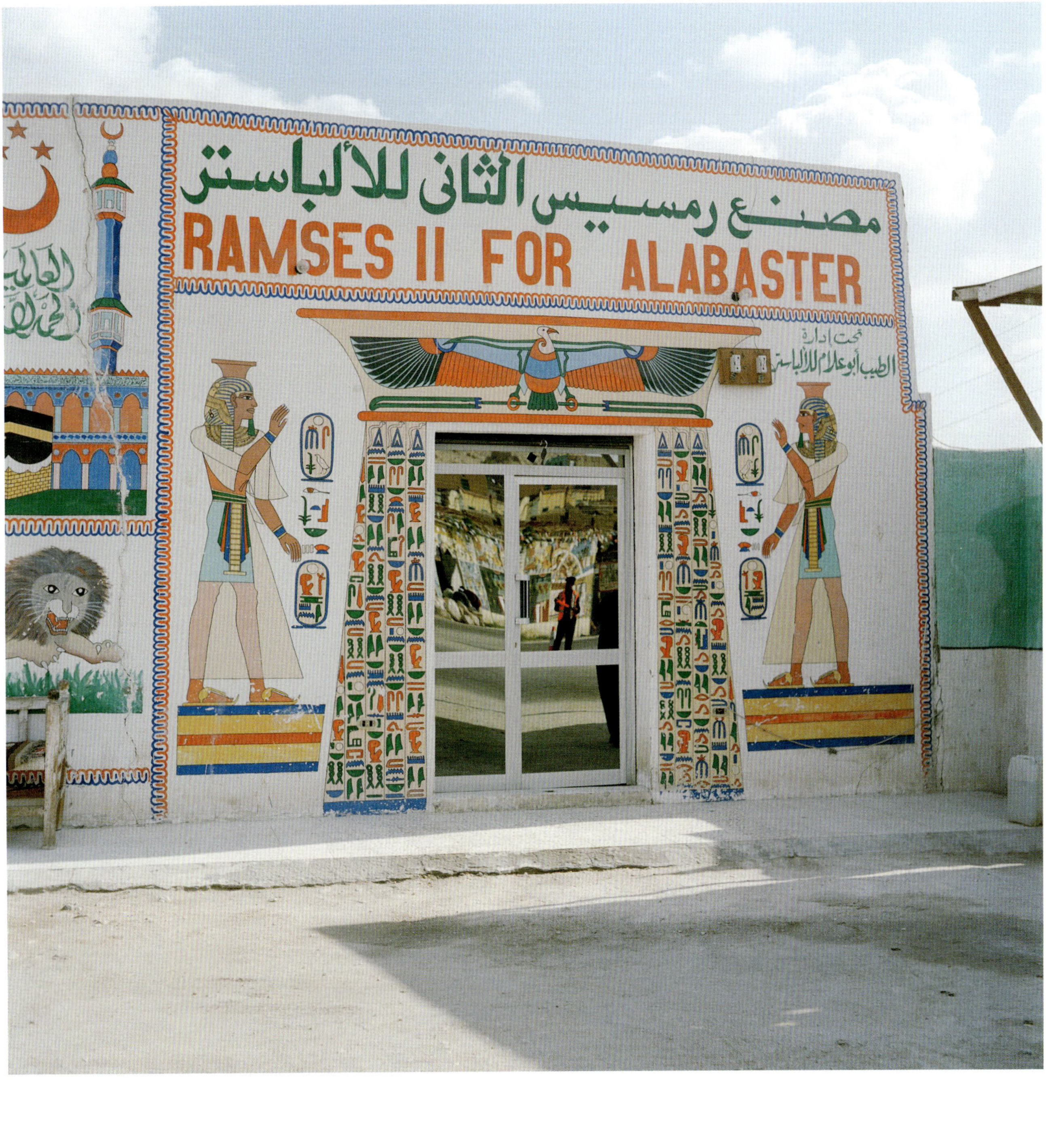
مصنع رمسيس الثانى للألباستر
RAMSES II FOR ALABASTER

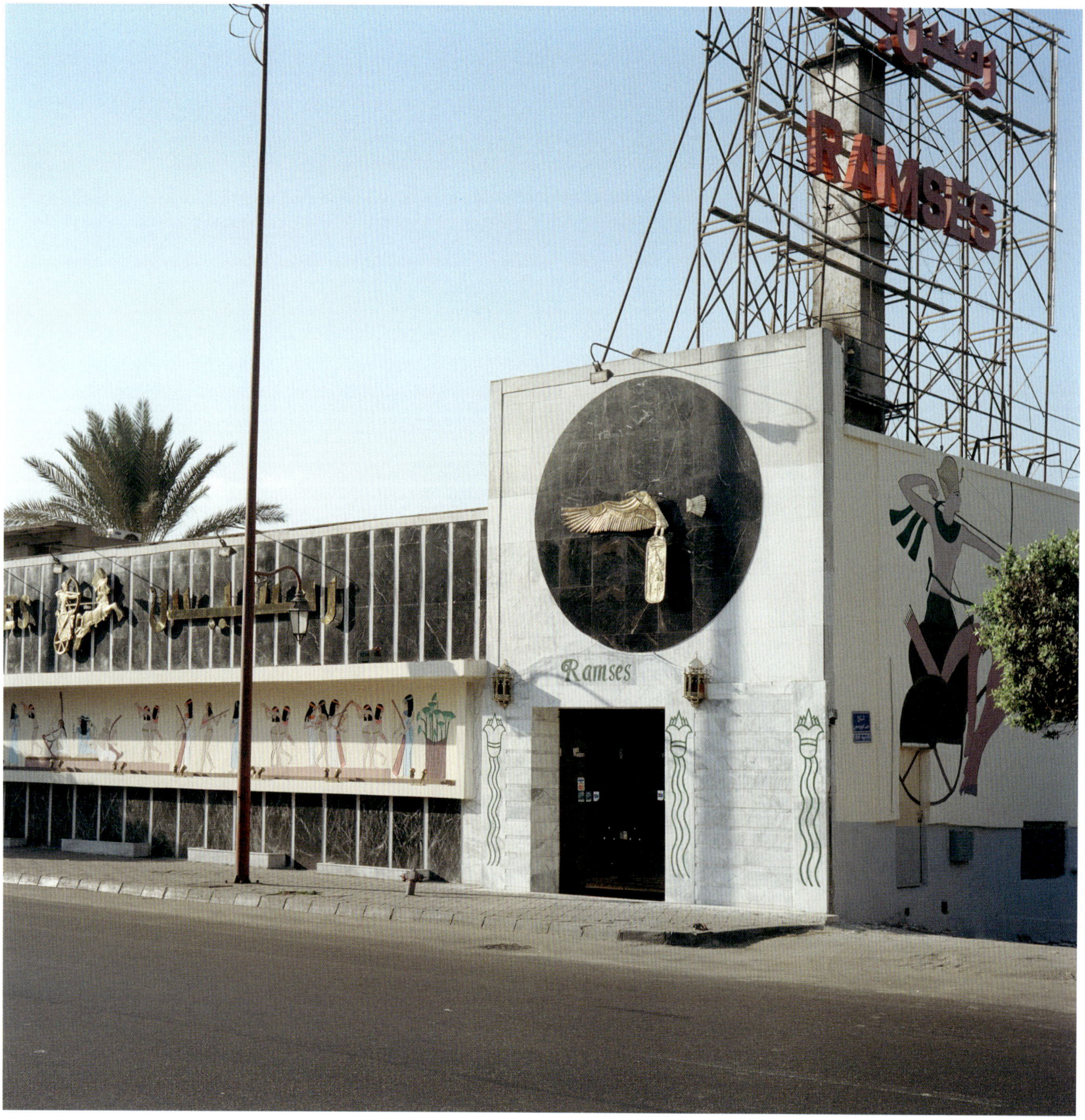
RAMSES
Ramses

List of works in the exhibition

THREE THOUSAND YEARS OF HISTORY AND A FEW MEMORABLE REIGNS

1
Offering table of Qenherkhepechef, author of the inscriptions, dedicated to sixteen past kings and two queens, Deir el-Medina, Egypt, reigns of Ramesses II and Merenptah (c. 1279–1202 BCE), limestone, 14.5 × 39.5 × 34 cm. Musée d'Archéologie Méditerranéenne, Marseille, inv. 204

WORSHIPPING THE GODS AND DEFENDING EGYPT: HOW TO BE A GOOD PHARAOH

2
Stela depicting the ancient King Senwosret I embracing the god Horus of Buhen, fortress of Buhen, Sudan, 13th to 17th Dynasty (c. 1781–1539 BCE), painted sandstone, 44 × 33.8 cm. Ashmolean Museum, University of Oxford, inv. AN1893.175

3
Scarab with the cartouche of Men-kheper-re mounted on a ring, Egypt, 19th Dynasty (c. 1295–1188 BCE), steatite and gold, 1.4 × 1 × 0.6 cm. Musées royaux d'Art et d'Histoire, Brussels, inv. E.8784

4
Scarab with the cartouche of Men-kheper-re mounted on a ring, Egypt, 20th Dynasty (c. 1188–1069 BCE), steatite, 2.9 × 2.1 × 1.3 cm. Musées royaux d'Art et d'Histoire, Brussels, inv. E.5355

5
Scarab amulet with the image and cartouche of the esteemed King Thutmose III (c. 1479–1425 BCE), Egypt, 19th–20th Dynasty (c. 1295–1069 BCE), enamelled siliceous earthenware or glazed steatite, 2.2 × 1.7 × 0.9 cm. Musées royaux d'Art et d'Histoire, Brussels, inv. E.2121

6
Scarab with the cartouche of Men-kheper-re, Egypt, 19th–20th Dynasty (c. 1295–1069 BCE), enamelled siliceous earthenware, 1.8 × 1.3 × 0.8 cm. Musées royaux d'Art et d'Histoire, Brussels, inv. E.5349

7
Scarab with the cartouche of Men-kheper-re, Egypt, 19th–20th Dynasty (c. 1295–1069 BCE), steatite, 2.9 × 2 × 1.1 cm. Musées royaux d'Art et d'Histoire, Brussels, inv. E.7270

8
Amulet with the cartouche of Men-kheper-re, Egypt, 21st Dynasty (c. 1069–943 BCE), enamelled siliceous earthenware, 1.8 × 1.3 × 0.6 cm. Musées royaux d'Art et d'Histoire, Brussels, inv. E.5351
Over a long period, the throne name of Thutmose III was inscribed on amulets as a protective image.

9
Scarab mounted on a ring, with the cartouche of King Thutmose III (1479–1425 BCE), discovered in the necropolis of Herdade do Gaio, Portugal, 7th century BCE, enamelled siliceous earthenware and silver, 2 × 1.4 × 0.8 cm. Câmara Municipal de Sines – Museu de Sines

10
Egyptianising statuette with the cartouche of Thutmose III, unknown provenance, Roman period [1st century BCE–1st century CE (?)], terracotta, h. 13 cm. Musées royaux d'Art et d'Histoire, Brussels
Similar figurines have been found on several archaeological sites of the Hellenistic or Roman period outside Egypt, for example in Croatia and Morocco.

11
Head of a sphinx of Senwosret III, Egypt, reign of Senwosret III (c. 1856–1838 BCE), sandstone, 20.5 × 22.5 × 23.5 cm. Paris, Musée du Louvre, Département des Antiquités égyptiennes, inv. E 25370

12
Miniature vase from the foundations of a temple dedicated to the god Osiris by Ramesses II, Egypt, reign of Ramesses II (c. 1279–1212 BCE), enamelled siliceous earthenware, 4.5 × 4.3 cm. Musée d'Archéologie Méditerranéenne, Marseille, inv. 1996-1-1.

13
Miniature vase placed in the foundations of a memorial temple of Thutmose IV, probably Luxor region, Egypt, reign of Thutmose IV (c. 1398–1388 BCE), calcite, h. 6 cm; diam. 4.6 cm. Museu da Farmácia, Lisbon, inv. 6888

14
Miniature vase placed in the foundations of a temple dedicated to the god Ptah-Sokar by Seti I, Egypt, reign of Seti I (c. 1294–1279 BCE), enamelled siliceous earthenware, h 5.1 cm; diam. 2.4 cm. Museu da Farmácia, Lisbon, inv. 10306

15–16
Miniature replicas of a sculptor's chisel and a brick mould, buried in the foundations of a temple built by Thutmose III to provide magical assurance of its stability, Gebelein, Egypt, reign of Thutmose III (c. 1479–1425 BCE), wood; bronze, 17.4 × 1.8; 4.6 × 19 × 9.3 cm. Turin, Museo Egizio, invs S. 12426; S. 12446.

17
Fragment of the wall of a temple of Ramesses II showing the pharaoh presenting an offering of wine to the sun god Ra-Horakhty, Qantir, Egypt, reign of Ramesses II (c. 1279–1212 BCE), limestone, 72 × 75 × 15 cm. Musée d'Archéologie Méditerranéenne, Marseille, inv. 1990-1-4

18
Statue of a pharaoh holding a foreigner captive, unknown provenance, second half of the 20th Dynasty (mid–12th to early 11th century BCE), sandstone, 58.5 × 15.3 × 20.5 cm. Turin, Museo Egizio, inv. Cat. 1392

19
Votive statuette representing a bound Nubian, fortress of Mirgissa, Sudan, 1st half of the 12th Dynasty (c. 1974–1856 BCE), limestone, 13 × 5.3 × 3.5 cm. Collection HALMA-IPEL, Université de Lille, loan from the government of Sudan, inv. L 2489

20
Dagger bearing the name of the pharaoh Ahmose, Egypt, reign of Ahmose (c. 1539–1514 BCE), copper alloy, 37.2 × 6.15 × 1.9 cm. Paris, Musée du Louvre, Département des Antiquités égyptiennes, inv. E 27218

21
Dagger found in the tomb of the pharaoh Kamose, Dra Abu el-Naga, Egypt, late 17th Dynasty (c. 1540 BCE), copper alloy, silver and gold, 31.8 × 3.1 cm. KBR-Bibliothèque royale de Belgique, Brussels, inv. KBR-Medals-1899-de Hirsch, Kamose

22
Head of Senwosret III, Egypt, Middle Kingdom, 12th Dynasty (c. 1860 BCE), obsidian, 12 × 10 × 10 cm. Calouste Gulbenkian Museum, Lisbon, inv. 138
Provenance: Rev. William MacGregor Collection. Acquired by Calouste Gulbenkian, through H. Kehyaian, at the MacGregor Collection sale, Sotheby, Wilkinson & Hodge, London, 6 July 1922.

23
Ring with the name of Thutmose III, Egypt, reign of Thutmose III (c. 1479–1425 BCE), gold, length: 2.5 cm. Paris, Musée du Louvre, Département des Antiquités égyptiennes, inv. N 729

24
Ring with the cartouches of Ramesses II and his wife Nefertari, Egypt, reign of Ramesses II (c. 1279–1212 BCE), cornelian and gold, 2.3 × 2.1 × 1.3 cm. Paris, Musée du Louvre, Département des Antiquités égyptiennes, inv. E 31890

25
Jewellery depicting a fly, a frog, two vases and perhaps two tortoises, Mirgissa, Sudan, c. 1800–1500 BCE, gold, 1 × 0.5 cm (each). Collection HALMA-IPEL, Université de Lille, on loan to the Palais des Beaux-Arts, Lille, inv. L 942

26
Head of a sphinx of Amenemhat III, Egypt, reign of Amenemhat III (c. 1838–1794 BCE), calcite, 7.5 × 7.3 × 7.9 cm. Paris, Musée du Louvre, Département des Antiquités égyptiennes, inv. E 10938

27
Head of Amenhotep III, Egypt, New Kingdom, 18th Dynasty (c. 1402–1364 BCE), blue glass paste, h. 3.7 cm. Calouste Gulbenkian Museum, Lisbon, inv. 139
Provenance: Rev. William MacGregor Collection. Acquired by Calouste Gulbenkian, through H. Kehyaian, at the MacGregor Collection sale, Sotheby, Wilkinson & Hodge, London, 30 June 1922.

28
Weight for weighing copper, with the cartouche of Senwosret III, fortress of Mirgissa, Sudan, reign of Senwosret III (c. 1856–1838 BCE), limestone, 8 × 6 × 4 cm. Collection HALMA-IPEL, Université de Lille, on loan to the Palais des Beaux-Arts, Lille, inv. L 2382

29
Fragment of an obelisk dedicated by Ramesses II to the god Ra, Tanis, Egypt, reign of Ramesses II (c. 1279–1212 BCE), graywacke, 45 × 22 × 10 cm. Musée d'Archéologie Méditerranéenne, Marseille, inv. 201

MONUMENTS ON THE HORIZON

30
Émile Burdet (1849–1922), *view of Khufu's pyramid reflected in the Nile*, Giza, Egypt, late 19th to early 20th century. MAH Musée d'art et d'histoire, Ville de Genève, inv. A 2006-0029-106, Mucem reproduction

31
Lee Miller (1907–1977), *The Shadow of the Great Pyramid, Giza, Egypt*, c. 1937. Lee Miller Archives, East Sussex, England, inv. E1860

32
Fragment of a block used for casing the pyramid of Khufu, Giza, Egypt, reign of Khufu (c. 2636–2605 BCE), limestone, 30.5 × 64 × 47 cm. British Museum, London, inv. EA490, presented by Colonel R. W. Howard Vyse

33
Seal imprint from the funerary complex of Khufu, Giza, Egypt, Late Period (c. 664–332 BCE), clay, 5.8 × 9.7 × 2.6 cm. Paris, Musée du Louvre, Département des Antiquités égyptiennes, inv. E 22350

34
Stela mentioning priests serving the cult of Khufu, Khafre and Djedefre two thousand years after these pharaohs reigned, Serapeum of Saqqara, Egypt, 487 BCE, painted limestone, 14.9 × 11.7 × 5.2 cm. Paris, Musée du Louvre, Département des Antiquités égyptiennes, inv. N 444/IM 2857

35
Votive monument dedicated to the god Osiris and the pharaoh Teti, Saqqara, Egypt, late 18th to early 19th Dynasty (c. 1388–1280 BCE), painted limestone, 27 × 14.5 × 25 cm. Musée d'Archéologie Méditerranéenne, Marseille, inv. 211

36
Stela depicting the pharaoh Teti offering flowers to Osiris a thousand years after his reign, Serapeum of Saqqara, Egypt, late 18th–19th dynasty (c. 1388–1089 BCE), painted limestone, 43 × 29 × 4 cm. Paris, Musée du Louvre, Département des Antiquités égyptiennes, inv. E 3012/IM 5305

37
Fragment of a tomb wall depicting King Menkauhor a thousand years after his reign, Saqqara, Egypt, late 18th Dynasty (c. 1330–1295 BCE), limestone, 82.5 × 37.5 × 22 cm. Paris, Musée du Louvre, Département des Antiquités égyptiennes, inv. E 3028

38
Nose of a colossus of Amenemhat III, Biahmu, Egypt, reign of Amenemhat III (c. 1838–1794 BCE), quartzite, 35 × 27 × 33 cm. Ashmolean Museum, University of Oxford, inv. AN1888.759A

38A
Hypothetical reconstruction of a colossus of Amenemhat III at Biahmu by William Flinders Petrie, in *Hawara, Biahmu and Arsinoe*, 1889. Courtesy of The Petrie Museum of Egyptian Archaeology, UCL

39
Miniature sanctuary dedicated to the god Osiris, Egypt, New Kingdom (c. 1539–1069 BCE), limestone, 93 × 38.5 × 40 cm. British Museum, London, inv. EA 1135, bought from R. J. Moss & Co

40
Ring decorated with an image of Amenemhat III killing an enemy, Egypt, Late Period (c. 664–332 BCE), gold and cornelian, diam. 1.85 cm. Paris, Musée du Louvre, Département des Antiquités égyptiennes, inv. E 3704

41
Stela dedicated to the deified Amenemhat III, Hawara, Egypt, Ptolemaic period, 240–200 BCE, limestone, 30.5 × 23 cm. British Museum, London, inv. GR 1888,0920.6, presented by Henry Martyn Kennard

42
Oil lamp in Egypto-Roman style in the shape of a sphinx, maybe the deified Amenemhat III, Egypt, Roman period (1st century BCE–1st century CE), painted terracotta, 16.1 × 11.5 × 6.3 cm. Paris, Musée du Louvre, Département des Antiquités égyptiennes, inv. E 20802

43
Left fist from a colossus of Ramesses II, Mit Rahina, Egypt, reign of Ramesses II (c. 1279–1212 BCE), red granite, 73 × 151.5 × 113 cm. British Museum, London, inv. EA 9, presented by King George III.

44
Stela depicting an offering to a colossus of Ramesses II, Qantir (?), Egypt, reign of Ramesses II (c. 1279–1212 BCE), limestone, 26.5 × 17.5 × 6 cm. Musées royaux d'Art et d'Histoire, Brussels, inv. E.3048

45
Stela portraying Ramesses II presenting an offering to his own colossus, Egypt, reign of Ramesses II (c. 1279–1212 BCE), limestone, 44.5 × 29.7 × 6 cm. Paris, Musée du Louvre, Département des Antiquités égyptiennes, inv. E 27222

46
Triad depicting Ramesses II as the sun god Shu between Amun-Ra and Horakhty, Egypt, reign of Ramesses II (c. 1279–1212 BCE), calcedony, 11 × 6.2 × 3.2 cm. Musée d'Archéologie Méditerranéenne, Marseille, inv. 1089

47
Bust of a statue of the goddess Sekhmet, Egypt, reigns of Amenhotep III (c. 1388–1349 BCE) and Ramesses II (c. 1279–1212 BCE), diorite, 62.4 × 37.5 × 34 cm. Paris, Musée du Louvre, Département des Antiquités égyptiennes, inv. A 6/N 6

KEEPING THE FLAME BURNING

48
Fragment of a statue dedicated by Senwosret I to King Sneferu, Serabit el-Khadim, Egypt, reign of Senwosret I (c. 1944–1900 BCE), sandstone, 24.7 × 20.5 × 34.3 cm. Musées royaux d'Art et d'Histoire, Brussels, inv. E.2146

49
Fragment of a statue dedicated by Senwosret I to King Nyuserre, probably Karnak, Egypt, reign of Senwosret I (c. 1944–1900 BCE), granite, 35 × 22 × 38 cm. British Museum, London, inv. EA 870, bought from George Bunsen.
This statue of a pharaoh who had been dead for nearly five hundred years was probably in a 'chamber of ancestors' created by Senwosret I in the temple at Karnak.

50
Statue of a falcon-god protecting a pharaoh, probably Nectanebo II, Egypt, probably reign of Nectanebo II (360–342 BCE), limestone, 50 × 18.2 × 46.2 cm. Paris, Musée du Louvre, Département des Antiquités égyptiennes, inv. E 11152

51
Base of an altar dedicated by Ramesses II, reused by Ramesses III, Ramesses VII, Ramesses IX and Ramesses XI, Mit-Rahina, Egypt, 13th-11th centuries BCE, granite, 57 × 35 × 35 cm. Musée d'Archéologie Méditerranéenne, Marseille, inv. 205

52
Torso of King Pedubast I, Egypt, Third Intermediate Period, 23rd Dynasty (c. 818–793 BCE), bronze inlaid with gold and copper, 28 × 12.5 × 14 cm. Calouste Gulbenkian Museum, Lisbon, inv. 52
Provenance: Collection of Count Gregory Stroganov, Rome. Acquired by Calouste Gulbenkian, through Duveen, at Frederik Müller (auctioneers), Amsterdam, 13 December 1921.

53
Sphinx of Nectanebo I, Egypt, reign of Nectanebo I (380–361 BCE), painted sandstone, 63 × 26 × 89 cm. Paris, Musée du Louvre, Département des Antiquités égyptiennes, inv. A 29/N 29

54
Fragment of a wall from the tomb of Inkef, priest of the funerary cult of King Sened, who had died about two hundred years earlier, Saqqara, Egypt, reign of Khufu (c. 2636–2605 BCE), limestone, 153.5 × 51 × 13 cm. Musée Granet, Ville d'Aix-en-Provence, inv. 821-1-75

55
False-door stela of Isi, administrator of the estates of the pyramid of King Teti, who had died about two hundred years earlier, Memphis region, Egypt, First Intermediate Period (c. 2250–2045 BCE), painted limestone, 76 × 48.3 × 14 cm. Paris, Musée du Louvre, Département des Antiquités égyptiennes, inv. E 6206

56
Low-relief of the priest Ameneminet, Saqqara, Egypt, late 18th Dynasty (c. 1320 BCE), limestone, 66 × 36 cm. Calouste Gulbenkian Museum, Lisbon, inv. 205
Provenance: Acquired by Calouste Gulbenkian, through Howard Carter, from Khawam Brothers, Cairo, January 1925.

57
Animated film: *Kings of the Past in Pharaonic Literature*, directed by Thierry Dejean; executive production: AAA Production, Matthieu Lamotte; story-board and drawings: Christian Ragoust, animation: Gabriel Decarra; sound design and music: Maxwell; voices: Belaïd Boudellal, Laurent-Henry David, Stéphanie Dussine; translation and subtitles by Hands Voice (Portugal); Mucem production, 2020, France.

58
Literary *ostracon*: beginning of the *Instruction of Amenemhat I to his son Senwosret*, Luxor, Egypt, New Kingdom (c. 1539–1069 BCE), terra cotta and pigments, 15 × 12 cm. Musées royaux d'Art et d'Histoire, Brussels, inv. E.6445
This copy of the text is more than four hundred years later than the reign of Amenemhat I.

59
Literary *ostracon*: extract from *Story of Sinuhe*, Deir el-Medina, Egypt, 19th Dynasty (c. 1295–1188 BCE), limestone and pigments, 11.5 × 19.2 × 2.9 cm. Paris, Musée du Louvre, Département des Antiquités égyptiennes, inv. E 33400
The passage describes the death of Amenemhat I, which occurred about seven hundred years before this copy of the text was made.

THE EXAMPLE SET BY THE FOUNDERS OF THE NEW KINGDOM

60
Stela of the scribe Iry, dedicated to Ahmose and Ahmose-Nefertari, Egypt, late 18th Dynasty, c. 1300 BCE, painted limestone, 29 × 21.6 × 3.5 cm. Calouste Gulbenkian Museum, Lisbon, inv. 160
Provenance: Rev. William MacGregor Collection. Acquired by Calouste Gulbenkian, through Howard Carter, at the MacGregor Collection sale, Sotheby, Wilkinson & Hodge, London, June–July 1922.

61
Statuette dedicated to Queen Ahmose-Nefertari by the artisan Djehuty-her-makhtuf, Deir el-Medina, Egypt, reign of Ramesses II (c. 1279–1212 BCE), painted shea wood, 35.1 × 7.9 × 18 cm. Paris, Musée du Louvre, Département des Antiquités égyptiennes, inv. N 470

62
Statuette dedicated to Queen Ahmose-Nefertari by the artisan Uadjmes, Deir el-Medina, Egypt, reign of Ramesses II (c. 1250 BCE), painted wood, 48 × 10.8 × 27 cm. Turin, Museo Egizio, inv. Cat. 1369

63
Stela offered to the deified Amenhotep I by the priest Aapanefu, Deir el-Medina, Egypt, 19th or 20th Dynasty (13th to 12th century BCE), painted limestone, 18 × 12 × 5.5 cm. Turin, Museo Egizio, inv. Cat. 1451

64
Votive ears, Egypt, New Kingdom (c. 1539–1069 BCE), enamelled siliceous earthenware, 5.03 × 2.75 × 1.02 cm. Paris, Musée du Louvre, Département des Antiquités égyptiennes, inv. E 14242

65
Amulet in the shape of a shield with the names of Amenhotep I, Egypt (6th–11th century BCE), painted wood, 6.6 × 5.75 cm. Paris, Musée du Louvre, Département des Antiquités égyptiennes, inv. N 556

66
Amulet in the shape of a shield, showing Amenhotep I striking a lion that he is holding by the tail, Egypt, 20th Dynasty (c. 1188–1069 BCE), painted wood, 7.8 × 6.5 × 3 cm. Turin, Museo Egizio, inv. Provv. 0613

67
Fragment of a stela depicting the procession of a statue of Amenhotep I, Deir el-Medina, Egypt, 20th Dynasty (c. 1150 BCE), limestone, 18.5 × 18 × 3.5 cm. Paris, Musée du Louvre, Département des Antiquités égyptiennes, inv. N 665

68–69
Two *ostraca* with questions for the oracle of Amenhotep I: 'Should I really write about them?' and 'Will a paper knife be given to the two scribes?', Deir el-Medina, Egypt, 19th–20th Dynasty (c. 1295–1069 BCE), limestone and pigments, 5 × 7 × 1 cm; 5.5 × 6 × 1 cm. Paris, Musée du Louvre, Département des Antiquités égyptiennes, invs E 33402; E 33403

70
Box with funerary figures decorated with an image of the deified Amenhotep I and Ahmose-Nefertari, Egypt, 21st–22nd Dynasty (c. 1069–735 BCE), wood and pigments, 35.5 × 55.5 × 34 cm. Turin, Museo Egizio, inv. Cat. 2430

71
Djedmut's shroud, with Amenhotep I replacing the god Osiris, Luxor, Egypt, 21st Dynasty (c. 1069–943 BCE), linen and pigments, 164 × 68 cm. Paris, Musée du Louvre, Département des Antiquités égyptiennes, inv. E 10301

THE CURSED KINGS

72
Stela from which the image and name of the deceased have been erased with chisel blows, Egypt, reign of Amenhotep III (c. 1388–1349 BCE), limestone, 63 × 55 × 7 cm. Paris, Musée du Louvre, Département des Antiquités égyptiennes, inv. C 54/N 208

73
Obelisk from which the names of Hatshepsut have been erased, Qasr Ibrim, Egypt, reigns of Hatshepsut and Thutmose III (c. 1479–1458 BCE), red granite, 166 × 24 × 24 cm. British Museum, London, inv. EA 1834, presented by the Egypt Exploration Society

74
Image of Hatshepsut reallocated with the name of her predecessor, Deir el-Bahari, Egypt, reigns of Hatshepsut and Thutmose III (c. 1479–1425 BCE), painted limestone, 44 × 33.5 cm. Musées royaux d'Art et d'Histoire, Brussels, inv. E. 3044

75
Head of a statue of Hatshepsut, Egypt, reign of Hatshepsut (c. 1479–1458 BCE), red granite and copper alloy, 30 × 19.5 × 23.5 cm. Toulouse, Musée Georges-Labit, inv. 49.282

76
Fragment from the wall of a temple of Akhenaten with chisel marks on the king's image, Karnak, Egypt, reign of Akhenaten (c. 1349–1333 BCE), sandstone, 15.5 × 16 × 5.1 cm. Paris, Musée du Louvre, Département des Antiquités égyptiennes, inv. E 26013

77
Facial fragment from a statue of Akhenaten, Amarna, Egypt, reign of Akhenaton (c. 1349–1333 BCE), crystalline limestone, 15.8 × 11.5 × 15 cm. British Museum, London, inv. EA 1336, presented by John Shae Perring

78
Broken funerary statuette of Akhenaten, probably from Amarna, Egypt, reign of Akhenaten (c. 1349–1333 BCE), quartzite, 9.9 × 7.6 × 6.3 cm. Paris, Musée du Louvre, Département des Antiquités égyptiennes, inv. E 17457

79
Fragmentary statuette of Tutankhamun, usurped by Horemheb, Egypt, reigns of Tutankhamun and Horemheb (1330–1295 BCE), steatite, 30.9 × 14 × 13 cm. British Museum, London, inv. EA 37639, presented by W. McOran Campbell

80
Statue of Amun with Tutankhamun, whose image and names have been destroyed, Karnak or Luxor, Egypt, reign of Tutankhamun (c. 1330–1320 BCE), diorite, 111 × 28.5 × 70 cm. Paris, Musée du Louvre, Département des Antiquités égyptiennes, inv. E 11005

WHAT REMAINS OF THE PHARAOHS? HISTORY AND LEGENDS

81
Card game used to teach about the great figures of antiquity, Netherlands, first half of the 19th century, paper, 32.2 × 50.2 cm. Marseille, Mucem, inv. 1978.40.37.1/10

82
Abu Rayhan Al-Biruni (973–c. 1052), *Chronology of Ancient Nations*, Iran, manuscript dated 1307 (706 A. H.), paper, 31 × 19.5 cm. Centre for Research Collections, University of Edinburgh, inv. Or.MS.161, Mucem reproduction

83
Flavius Josephus (1st century CE), Greek edition of the *Flavii Iosephi Opera* (Antiquities of the Jews), Basel: Froben, 1544; Parisian Morocco binding, 1550, printed on paper, 34 × 23 × 65 cm. Calouste Gulbenkian Museum, Lisbon, inv. LA251
Provenance: Marcus Fugger Collection, Germany, 16th century; Lucius Wilmerding Collection, New York, 20th century. Acquired by Calouste Gulbenkian, through Hans Stiebel, at the Lucius Wilmerding sale, New York, 5 March 1951.

84
Joseph Jean-Félix Aubert (1849–1924), sketch for the decoration of the drawing class in the boys' school in Rue Dombasle, Paris, c. 1879, triptych, oil on canvas, 40.5 × 231 cm. Petit Palais, Musée des Beaux-Arts de la Ville de Paris, inv. PPP3801-PPP3802-PPP3803

AMASIS AND PSAMTIK, THE KINGS WHO LOVED THE GREEKS

85
Neck of a Greek amphora stamped with the cartouche of Amasis, Chios, Greece (found at Tell Dafana, Egypt), reign of Amasis (c. 570–527 BCE), terracotta, clay, plaster, 37 × 27 × 15.7 cm. British Museum, London, inv. EA 22365, presented by the Egypt Exploration Fund

86
Flask in the shape of a Greek soldier's head, with the cartouche of Psamtik I, Egypt or Rhodes (found in Corinth, Greece), reign of Psamtik I (c. 664–610 BCE), terracotta, 6.5 × 4.7 cm. Paris, Musée du Louvre, Département des Antiquités grecques, étrusques et romaines, inv. MNB 1143

87
Flask in the shape of a Greek soldier's head, with the cartouche of Amasis, Egypt, reign of Amasis (c. 570–527 BCE), enamelled siliceous earthenware, 4.5 × 4.5 cm. Musées royaux d'Art et d'Histoire, Brussels, inv. E.3398

88
Adrien Guignet (1816–1854), *Cambyse et Psamménite* (Cambyses and Psammetichus), France, 1841, oil on canvas, 114 × 211 cm. Paris, Musée du Louvre, Département des Peintures, inv. 5255

89
Jean-Baptiste de Monicart (1656–1755), *Versailles immortalisé par les merveilles parlantes*, translated by Romain le Testu, with drawings by Gilbert de Sève (c. 1615–1698), engraved by Marie-Jeanne Renard Bos, Paris: Chez Etienne Ganneau, 1720, 26 × 20 cm. Palácio Nacional de Mafra, inv. BPNM 2-23-6-2/3

90
François-Joseph de La Grange-Chancel (1677–1758), *Amasis, tragédie* (Amasis, a tragedy), in *Œuvres de Monsieur de La Grange-Chancel*, Paris: Compagnie des Libraires associés, 1742, printed on paper, 17 × 10 × 3 cm. Private collection

NECTANEBO, 'FATHER' OF ALEXANDER THE GREAT

91
Funerary figurine of Nectanebo II, Egypt, reign of Nectanebo II (360–342 BCE), enamelled siliceous earthenware, 23 × 6.5 × 4 cm. Turin, Museo Egizio, inv. Cat. 2509

92 to 94
Medallions depicting the deified Alexander the Great, Aboukir, Egypt, 3rd century, gold, diam. 5.5 cm; diam. 5.7 cm; diam. 5.2 cm. Calouste Gulbenkian Museum, Lisbon, invs. 2426, 2430 and 2431 Provenance: Collection Singa, Alexandria; Collection James Loeb (inv. 2426); Collection Eddé, Alexandria; Collection Pierpont Morgan (invs. 2430; 2431).

95
Vincent de Beauvais (1190?–1264), *Speculum Historiale*, illuminated by the Master of Jouvenel des Ursins, France, mid-15th century, manuscript on parchment, 335 fols., 47.7 × 34 × 10 cm. Biblioteca Nacional de Portugal, inv. IL.126

96
Hartmann Schedel (1440–1514), *Liber chronicarum* (known in English as the *Nuremberg Chronicle*) with engraved illustrations by Michael Wolgemut (1434–1519) and Hans Pleydenwurff (d. 1472), Nuremberg: Anton Koberger, 1493, printed on paper, 45 × 35 × 6.5 cm. Museu Nacional de Arte Antiga, Lisbon, inv. LBS RES 730

CLEOPATRA, *FEMME FATALE* OR WISE QUEEN

97
Bust of a statue considered to be that of Cleopatra VII, Egypt, late Ptolemaic period, c. 100–31 BCE, basalt, 44 × 26.7 × 21 cm. Turin, Museo Egizio, inv. Cat. 1385

98
Unknown artist, after Domenico di Puligo (1492–1527), *The Death of Cleopatra*, Tuscany, Italy, mid-16th century, oil on wood, 59 × 43 cm. Paris, Musée de l'Assistance publique – Hôpitaux de Paris, inv. A.P.1538

99
Isaac Thuret (1630–1706), watch depicting the death of Cleopatra, Paris, late 17th century, brass and enamel, 6.2 × 5.8 × 3.8 cm. Paris, Musée du Louvre, Département des Objets d'Art, inv. OA 10076

100
Domingos António de Sequeira (1768–1837), *Estudo Preparatório para «A Morte de Cleópatra»* (Preparatory Study for 'The Death of Cleopatra'), Rome, c. 1791, black pencil, charcoal, crayon and chalk on paper, 24.3 × 34.5 cm. Museu Nacional de Arte Antiga, Lisbon, inv. 742 Des

101
Claude Bertin (1653–1705), *Cleopatra*, Versailles, France, before 1697, marble, 56 × 49.5 × 35 cm. Paris, Musée du Louvre, Département des Sculptures, inv. R.F. 3717

102
Henri Ducommun du Locle (1804–1884), *Cleopatra*, France, 1852–3, bronze, 104.5 × 181 × 83 cm. Marseille, musée des Beaux-Arts, inv. S 8

103
Nicolas Jacques Conté (1755–1805), obelisk known as 'Cleopatra's needle', Alexandria, 1798–1800, watercolour on paper, 38 × 54 cm. Baron Thénard Collection

104
Isabelle Van Berchem, *née* Naville (1874–1962), *The Baths of Cleopatra*, Aswan, 1893. MAH Musées d'art et d'histoire, Ville de Genève, inv. A2006-0030- 209-09, Mucem reproduction

SESOSTRIS, QUINTESSENTIAL KING OF EGYPT

105
Jean-Baptiste Thiébault (1809–1833), after François Georgin (1801–1863), *Apothéose de Napoléon* (Apotheosis of Napoleon), Épinal: Pellerin, after 1837, lithograph on paper, 43.7 × 63 cm. Marseille, Mucem, inv. 1982.3.384

106
Monumenta Cartographica Africae et Aegypti, edited by Yusuf Kamal (1882–1965), Cairo, 1933, 76 × 62.5 × 6 cm. Sociedade de Geografia de Lisboa, inv. CSGL 12-6

107
Émile Béchard (1844–?), *Vue d'ensemble avec la palmeraie. Statue de Sesostris renversée* (General view with palm grove and toppled statue of Sesostris), Mit Rahina, Egypt, between 1868 and 1880. Médiathèque du patrimoine et de la Photographie, Charenton-le-Pont, inv. AP07R00466, Mucem reproduction

108
François Fénelon (1651–1715), *Les Aventures de Télémaque, fils d'Ulysse* (The adventures of Telemachus, son of Ulysses), with illustrations by Charles Monnet (1732–1803), engraved by Jean-Baptiste Tillard or Tilliard (1740–1813), Paris: Imprimerie de François Ambroise Didot, 1783, printed on paper, 29.8 × 23.3 × 5.1 cm. Calouste Gulbenkian Museum, Lisbon, inv. LA44A
Provenance: Acquired by Calouste Gulbenkian from Paul Groupe, Berlin, 25 April 1932.

109
Butterflies of the species *Parides sesostris*, originating from Peru, acquired in Brugge, 2019, 6 × 8.5 cm (each). Private collection

110
Voltaire (1694-1778), *Nova Tragedia intitulada Sezostris no Egipto* (A new tragedy titled Sesostris in Egypt), translation by Vicente da Costa Ramos, published by Domingos Gonçalves, Lisbon, 1785, printed on paper, 22 × 16 cm. Collection Teatro de Cordel, Biblioteca de Arte e Arquivos Gulbenkian, inv. TC 86

PHARAOH IN THE BIBLE, *FIRAUN* IN THE QUR'AN

111
Book of Hours, illuminations by two followers of the Master of Adelaide of Savoy, by an illuminator of the circle of the Master of Jouvenel and by an artist from Tours in the style of Jean Fouquet, Poitiers and/or Tours, c. 1460–70, manuscript on parchment, 172 fols., 24.3 × 16.2 cm. Calouste Gulbenkian Museum, inv. LA135
Provenance: former Chedeau Collection, Saumur; Henri Bordes Collection, Bordeaux; Robert Hoe Collection, New York, 1912; Engel-Gros Collection, Château de Ripaille (Savoie), 1921. Acquired by Calouste Gulbenkian, through Leclerc, in the Engel-Gros Collection sale, Galerie Georges Petit, Paris, 2 June 1921.

112
François Lacour (1808–?), *Joseph expliquant les songes du roi Pharaon* (Joseph explaining King Pharaoh's dreams), Charles-Eugène Glémarec (1820–1896), publisher, Paris, between 1858 and 1860, lithograph on paper, 42 × 33 cm. Marseille, Mucem, inv. 1950.39.696

113
Léonce Schérer (act. 1850–1871), *Délivrance et élévation de Joseph* (The saving and elevation of Joseph), Épinal: Pellerin, c. 1877, lithograph on paper, 29.8 × 45 cm. Marseille, Mucem, inv. 1950.39.706

114
'Abd al-Rahman ibn Ahmad Jami, *Tuhfat al-Ahrar* (Gift of the Free), Bukhara (?), Uzbekistan, 1554–5 (dated AH 962), ink, gold and watercolour on paper, 69 fols., 25 × 19 cm. Calouste Gulbenkian Museum, Lisbon, inv. LA184

Provenance: Claude Anet Collection. Acquired by Calouste Gulbenkian, through M. K. Gudénian, at the Claude Anet Collection sale, London, 4 June 1920.

115
Jan Lievens the Elder (1607–1674), *The Infant Moses Trampling Pharaoh's Crown*, Netherlands, 1630, oil on canvas, 114 × 175 cm. Palais des Beaux-Arts, Lille, inv. P.976

116
Gobelins Manufactory, after Nicolas Poussin (1594–1665), tapestry depicting the story of Moses: *The Rod Turned into a Serpent*, Paris, 1683, silk and gold, 268 × 468 cm. Mobilier national, Paris, inv. GMTT/32/004

117
Yehuda Lajb Ben Betsalel (1525?–1609), Haggadah of Passover, Metz: Jacob Zvi Hirsch, 1767, printed on paper, 22 × 17.4 × 2 cm. Marseille, Mucem, inv. RES 1B REL 484

118
Dish showing Moses making the sea swallow Pharaoh's army, Ateliers of the Clérissys, after an engraving by Pierre Mariette (1694–1774), Moustiers-Sainte-Marie, France, first quarter of the 18th century, stanniferous faience, 47 × 57.2 × 7.5 cm. Marseille, Mucem, inv. 2017.26.1

119
Tablet belonging to a Quranic schoolboy naming *Firaun* among the enemies destroyed by God, Marrakesh, first half of the 20th century, pinewood, 36 × 22.7 × 2.1 cm. Marseille, Mucem, inv. 2003.8.29

RETURN OF THE PHARAOHS

120
Jean-François Champollion (1790–1832), *Grammaire égyptienne, ou principes généraux de l'écriture sacrée égyptienne appliquée à la représentation de la langue parlée* (Egyptian grammar, or general principles of sacred Egyptian writing applied to the representation of the spoken language), published by Jacques-Joseph Champollion, Paris: Firmin Didot Frères, 1836–41, printed on paper, 32.2 × 23 × 4 cm. Biblioteca Nacional de Portugal, inv. L. 361 A.

121
Photograph album from a trip to Egypt made by the Portuguese queen, Dona Amélia, April 1903: views of a Bishari encampment, the colossi of Memnon and the submerged temple of Philae, [38] fols, 230 photographs, with captions, black and white and sepia, 28 × 42.5 × 6 cm. Biblioteca Nacional de Portugal, inv. E.A. 558 V

THE REVENGE OF RAMESSES

122
Francesco Salvolini (1809–1838) Facsimile of the papyrus Sallier III: account of the battle between 'Sesostris Ramesses' (Ramesses II) and the Hittites at Qadesh, Aix-en-Provence, France, 1834, tracing paper, 22.5 × 30 cm. Private collection

123–124
Emil Brugsch (1842–1930) (?), mummy of Ramesses II labelled as 'Sesostris', after the glass slide from the photographic laboratory of the Musée de l'Homme, Cairo and Paris, 1886–94, 8.5 × 10 cm (size of the originals). Musée du quai Branly – Jacques Chirac, Paris, invs. PV0029257 and PV0029258, Mucem reproduction

125
Unidentified photographer, expedition led by the Egyptologist Henry Breasted photographing the colossi of Ramesses at Abu Simbel, Egypt, 1905–6. Courtesy of the Oriental Institute of the University of Chicago, Calouste Gulbenkian Museum reproduction

126
Edition of *Life* magazine, 29 October 1965, concerning the relocation of the Abu Simbel temples, USA, 34.5 × 26.9 × 0.4 cm. Marseille, Bibliothèque du Mucem.

127
Jean Lecomte du Noüy (1842–1923), *Ramsès dans son harem* (Ramesses in his harem), 1885–6, triptych, oil on canvas, gilded wood, 128.1 × 301 cm. Paris, Musée d'Orsay, inv. RF MO P 2015 42

128
Excerpt from the film *The Ten Commandments*, by Cecil B. DeMille (1881–1959), USA, 1956, Courtesy of Paramount Pictures

THE MESMERIZING POWER OF AKHENATEN, NEFERTITI AND TUTANKHAMUN

129
Fragment of a column depicting Nefertiti, Amarna, Egypt, reign of Akhenaten (c. 1349–1333 BCE), limestone, 34 × 30 × 10 cm. Ashmolean Museum, University of Oxford, inv. AN1893.1-41.71

130
Arthur Weigall (1880–1934), *The Life and Times of Akhnaton, Pharaoh of Egypt*, London: William Blackwood and Sons, 1911 (first edition 1910), printed on paper, 22.8 × 16 × 4.5 cm. Private collection

131
Johann Georg de Saxe (1869–1938), discovery of the bust of Nefertiti. In the photo: Hermann Ranke, Paul Hollander and Mohamed es-Senussi, Amarna, Egypt, 1912. Universitätsarchiv Freiburg, inv. C 197/6643, Mucem reproduction

132
Unidentified photographer, view of the Amarna Courtyard in the Neues Museum, containing works from the reign of Akhenaten, Berlin, 1939. Zentralarchiv der Staatlichen Museen zu Berlin, inv. ZA 1.1.3./02938, Mucem reproduction

133
Fritz Zielesch (1894–1971), Berlin Museums plaster casting workshop, 1930. Ullstein bild Dtl./Getty Images, Mucem reproduction

134-5
Replicas of Nefertiti's bust made by the Berlin Museums plaster casting workshop, 1933, painted plaster, 49 × 24.5 × 35 cm. Musées royaux d'Art et d'Histoire, Brussels, inv. EM.1a-b

136
The 'Harp-head', a fake imitating portraits of Nefertiti and Akhenaten, bought in Paris in 1932, rengas wood, 19.7 × 9.2 × 10 cm. Paris, Musée du Louvre, Département des Antiquités égyptiennes, inv. E 14255

137
The 'Blue-head', a fake imitating portraits of Nefertiti and Tutankhamun, bought in Paris in 1923, glass, 9 × 7.6 cm. Paris, Musée du Louvre, Département des Antiquités égyptiennes, inv. E 11658

138
Fake imitating a bas-relief from the reign of Akhenaten and Nefertiti, unknown provenance, 20th century, limestone, 46 × 25.2 × 5.6 cm. Musées royaux d'Art et d'Histoire, Brussels, inv. EF.2
This forgery, showing the royal couple bathed by the sun's rays, is a crude copy of a famous relief found in 1891 in Akhenaten's palace in Amarna, now in the Cairo Museum (registered as 30/10/26/12).

139
Three beads from a sceptre with the cartouche of Tutankhamun, Serapeum of Saqqara, Egypt, reign of Tutankhamun (c. 1330–1320 BCE), enamelled siliceous earthenware, 10.5 × 2.5 cm max. Paris, Musée du Louvre, Département des Antiquités égyptiennes, inv. N 2271 A-C

140
Letter from Howard Carter to Pierre Lacau, Director of Egypt's Antiquities Service, Luxor, Egypt, 6 January 1923, paper, 26 × 20 cm. Paris, EPHE, archives du Centre Wl. Golenischeff, Archives Lacau, EPHE CWG LAC/49

141
Letter from Pierre Lacau, Director of Egypt's Antiquities Service, to Howard Carter, about arrangements for the press to visit Tutankhamun's tomb, Luxor, Egypt, 22 January 1923, paper, 22.4 × 17.8 cm. Paris, EPHE, archives du Centre Wl. Golenischeff, Archives Lacau, EPHE CWG LAC/49

142
Telegram from Reginald Engelbach, Inspector of Antiquities in Luxor, to Pierre Lacau, Director of Egypt's Antiquities Service, Luxor, Egypt, 9 February 1923, paper, 14.9 × 25.5 cm. Paris, EPHE, archives du Centre Wl. Golenischeff, Archives Lacau, EPHE CWG LAC/49

143
Reginald Engelbach, diagram of the tomb's layout made for the visit of officials at its inauguration by the Egyptian government, Luxor, Egypt, 2 March 1924, paper, 21.2 × 12.3 cm. Paris, EPHE, archives du Centre Wl. Golenischeff, Archives Lacau, EPHE CWG LAC/49

144
Photographs of Tutankhamun's tomb used by Howard Carter in his lectures, taken by Harry Burton, colouring by Reginald Malby, Egypt, 1922–6, projection of the reproduction after original glass slides. Griffith Institute, University of Oxford

145
Transporting an armchair from Tutankhamun's tomb under the photographers' lenses, Rol press agency, Valley of the Kings, Egypt, January 1923. Bibliothèque nationale de France, inv. EI-13 (978)/Pho20Rol, Mucem reproduction

146
Howard Carter shows the press a silver staff from Tutankhamun's tomb, Meurisse press agency, Valley of the Kings, Egypt, 1925. Bibliothèque nationale de France, inv. EI-13 (2766)/Meurisse 20319 A, Mucem reproduction

147
'Luxor' portable camera made by Photo-Plait and its case, France, 1930s, metal, glass and leather, 14 × 9.7 × 5.2 cm; 16 × 12.4 × 10.6 cm. Marseille, Mucem, inv. 1976.37.21

148
Letter from Howard Carter to Calouste Gulbenkian about the acquisition of the 'head of Senwosret III', four months before the discovery of Tutankhamun's tomb, Luxor, Egypt, 8 July 1922, paper, 17.8 × 22.4 cm. Biblioteca de Arte e Arquivos Gulbenkian, MCG 00070

149
Letter from Howard Carter to Calouste Gulbenkian about the Ameneminet bas-relief, mentioning his difficulties with the Egyptian authorities after opening Tutankhamun's tomb, Luxor, Egypt, 22 January 1925, paper, 22.1 × 18 cm. Biblioteca de Arte e Arquivos Gulbenkian, MCG 00072

150
Diary kept by Calouste Sarkis Gulbenkian (1869–1955) during his travels to Egypt, Palestine and Syria: *Voyage en Égypte, Palestine et Syrie (Janvier–Février 1934)*, 71 typewritten sheets and 68 photographs, 20.4 × 16.2 × 3.8 cm. Biblioteca de Arte e Arquivos Gulbenkian, I04-055

151–152
Reports on the discovery of Tutankhamun's tomb in *L'Illustration*, Paris, 3 and 10 February 1923, paper, 40.7 × 30 cm. Marseille, Bibliothèque du Mucem

153
Report on the excavations of Tutankhamun's tomb in *Ilustração Portuguesa*, 10 March 1923, Lisbon, José Joubert Chaves, literary editor, photographs by Harry Burton, published by Empreza do Jornal O Século, 28.8 × 18.5 cm. BLX, Hemeroteca Municipal de Lisboa, inv. Res. 33

154
Fernando do Rio de Carvalho Henriques (1897–1962), *A Profecia ou o Mistério da Morte de Tut-Ank-Amon* (The Prophecy, or the mysterious death of Tut-Ank-Amun), Lisbon, 1924, printed on paper, 19 × 13.2 × 2.3 cm. Biblioteca Nacional de Portugal, inv. L. 29863 P.

155
Edition of *Al-Musawar*, 9 April 1937, alluding to 'the curse of the pharaohs', Dar-Al-Hilal (publisher), Cairo, paper, 41.5 × 28 cm. Marseille, Bibliothèque du Mucem

156
Press cuttings from Portuguese newspapers (*Diário de Lisboa* and *A Capital*) covering the 'curse of Tutankhamun', editions of 8 February and 9 April 1923 and editions of 5 and 10 April 1923. BLX, Hemeroteca Municipal de Lisboa, Calouste Gulbenkian Museum reproduction

157
News film: visit to Tutankhamun's tomb by the Belgian queen, Elisabeth de Bavière, the Duke of Brabant and Lord Allenby, British High Commissioner in Egypt, accompanied by the archaeologist Howard Carter and Pierre Lacau, Director of Egypt's Antiquities Service, Valley of the Kings, Egypt, February 1923. Gaumont Pathé Archives, Saint-Ouen-sur-Seine

158
News film: the Duke and Duchess of Aosta take part in the Egyptian government's official opening ceremony of Tutankhamun's tomb, Valley of the Kings, Egypt, March 1924. Gaumont Pathé Archives, Saint-Ouen-sur-Seine

159
Jean Marquis (1926–2019), views of the exhibition *Toutânkhamon et son temps* (Tutankhamun and his time) at the Petit Palais: visitors crowd into the museum, Paris, 1967. Bibliothèque historique de la Ville de Paris, inv. 4-ENA-00161-0002, Mucem reproduction

160
Jean Marquis (1926–2019), view of the exhibition *Toutânkhamon et son temps* (Tutankhamun and his time) at the Petit Palais: visitors admiring the funerary mask, Paris, 1967. Bibliothèque historique de la Ville de Paris, inv. 4-ENA-00161-0004, Mucem reproduction

161
Jean Marquis (1926-2019), view of the exhibition *Toutânkhamon et son temps* (Tutankhamun and his time) at the Petit Palais: visitors admiring the golden fan, Paris, 1967. Bibliothèque historique de la Ville de Paris, inv. 4-ENA-00161-0005, Mucem reproduction

162
Elizabeth Taylor and her husband John Warner visiting the exhibition *The Treasures of Tutankhamun* at the National Gallery of Art, Washington, 1976. Courtesy of National Gallery of Art, Washington, DC, Gallery Archives, Mucem reproduction

163
Gary Fong (1960–), visitors admiring Tutankhamun's funerary mask at the exhibition *The Treasures of Tutankhamun* at the De Young Museum, San Francisco, 1979. Gary Fong/San Francisco Chronicle/Polaris, Mucem reproduction

164
Publication produced for the exhibition *O Túmulo da Rainha Nofretari* (The tomb of Queen Nefertari) at the Calouste Gulbenkian Museum, Américo Silva, graphic design, Lisbon: Fundação Calouste Gulbenkian, 1979, paper, 47 × 31 cm. Calouste Gulbenkian Museum Archives

165
News film: the Egyptologist Christiane Desroches Noblecourt takes André Malraux, Sarwat Okasha and Christian Fouchet around the exhibition *Toutânkhamon et son temps* (Tutankhamun and his time) at the Petit Palais, 1967. Paris, Gaumont Pathé Archives, Saint-Ouen-sur-Seine

166
A report by the television programme *Comarca das Artes* on the exhibition *O Túmulo da Rainha Nofretari* (The tomb of Queen Nefertari) at the Calouste Gulbenkian Museum, Lisbon, 1979. RTP Arquivos

THEIR ANCESTORS THE PHARAOHS

167
Arrival of guests of the Egyptian government at the official opening of Tutankhamun's tomb, Rol press agency, Luxor, Egypt, early March 1924. Bibliothèque nationale de France, Paris, inv. EI-13 (1096)/Pho20Rol, Mucem reproduction

168
Publicity poster for the Messageries Maritimes, Imprimeries Frères Réunies, 1925, Paris, paper, 105 × 74.5 cm. Collections Chambre de Commerce et d'Industrie métropolitaine Aix-Marseille-Provence, inv. QAF02121 The poster shows Thot, the god of scribes, writing King Fuad's name in hieroglyphics in a cartouche.

169
Edition of *Al-Fokkaha* recording the creation of the Egyptian air fleet, Al-Helal (publisher), Cairo, 1932, paper, 28.5 × 21.2 cm. Marseille, Bibliothèque du Mucem, inv. ME2019.6.1

170
Edition of *Al-Kashkoul* reporting the assassination of Sir Lee Stack, British Commander-in-Chief of the Egyptian army, Cairo, 1924, paper, 36 × 25.8 cm. Marseille, Bibliothèque du Mucem, inv. ME2019.6.2

171
Edition of *Al-Musawar*, 14 January 1927: Saad Zaghloul, Egyptian's Prime Minister, visits the building site of *Egypt's Renaissance* by Mahmoud Mokhtar, Dar Al-Hilal (publisher), Cairo, 1927, paper, 33 × 24.1 cm. Marseille, Bibliothèque du Mucem, inv. ME21018.7.1

172
Mahmoud Mokhtar (1891–1934), *Arous-el-Nil. La Fiancée du Nil* (known in English as *The Bride of the Nile*), Cairo, c. 1929, stone, 149 × 60 × 37 cm. Centre Pompidou Paris, Musée national d'Art moderne – Centre de création industrielle. On loan since April 2018 to La Piscine – Musée d'art et d'industrie André Diligent (Roubaix), inv. JP 66 S

173
Edition of *Akher Sa'aa*, 19 December 1979, Cairo, paper, 39 × 27.2 cm. Marseille, Bibliothèque du Mucem, inv. ME2018.7.7

174
René Burri (1933–2014), *Voiture Ramses, Égypte, 1962* (Ramesses Car, Egypt, 1962). Magnum Photos, Paris, Mucem reproduction

175
Bottle of milk from the Misr dairies, Egypt, second half of the 20th century, glass, 21 × 7.5 × 7.5 cm. Marseille, Mucem, inv. 2019.21.3

176
Display stand for Cleopatra cigarettes, Egypt, second half of the 20th century, cardboard, 52.3 × 18 × 0.5 cm. Private collection

177
Ramesses pencils, El-Nasr company, Cairo, 1960s, wood and graphite, 18 × 0.8 cm. Marseille, Mucem, inv. 2019.21.1

178
Cleopatra cigarette lighter, Egypt, second half of the 20th century, metal, 6.25 × 2.25 × 1.2 cm. Marseille, Mucem, inv. 2019.22.4

179
Cleopatra cigarette pack, Egypt, 20th century, paper, plastic, tobacco, 8.5 × 5.5 × 2 cm. G. Andreu-Lanoë Collection

180
Nefertiti sewing machine, made by military factories for the production of civilian goods, Helwan, Egypt, late 1950s–1960s, painted metal, 26.5 × 40.5 × 17.6 cm. Marseille, Mucem, inv. 2018.70.1

181
Café chair decorated with an image of the Misr business logo, sometimes known as 'Cleopatra', burnt into the wood using pyrography, Cairo, 20th–21st centuries, wood, 80 × 40 × 38 cm. Marseille, Mucem, inv. 2019.23.1

182
Shopkeepers' chair decorated with the mask of Tutankhamun, burnt into the wood using pyrography, Cairo, 20th and 21st centuries, wood, 80 × 40 × 38 cm. Marseille, Mucem, inv. 2019.22.5

183-184
Forms for entry into Egypt for Egyptian residents (with the mosque of Cairo's citadel) and foreigners (with Nefertiti), Egypt, 2018, paper, 14.5 × 9.7 cm each. Marseille, Archives du Mucem, invs. 2019. PC25.2; 2019.PC25.3

185
Banknote for 10 Egyptian pounds, Egypt, 1965, 9.5 × 17.9 cm. Marseille, Mucem, inv. 2019.16.3

186
Banknote for 10 Egyptian pounds, Egypt, 1978, 8.8 × 17.9 cm. Marseille, Mucem, inv. 2019.16.4

187
Banknote for 10 Egyptian pounds, Egypt, 2000s, 7 × 15 cm. Private collection

188
İhap Hulusi Görey (1898–1986) and Institut Graphique Égyptien, poster promoting tourism in Egypt, Cairo, 1960, paper, 99 × 71 cm. Collections Chambre de Commerce et d'Industrie métropolitaine Aix-Marseille-Provence, inv. QAF0249

189 to 194
Olivier Cablat (1978–), *Temples* series, Egypt, 2004, prints from the artist's digital photographs. O. Cablat Collection

195
Excerpt from the film *Al Mummia* (The Mummy), by Shadi Abdessalam (1930–1986), Egypt, 1969. Courtesy of Films sans frontières

196
Excerpt from the film *A God Passing* by David G. Tretiakoff (1970–), Cairo, 2008. Courtesy David G. Tretiakoff

197
Naguib Mahfouz (1911–2006), children's edition of *ʿAbaṯ al-aqdār* (Ironies of Fate), adapted by Mohamed Al-Mou'alim, illustrated by Mostafa Hussein, Cairo: Dar Al-Shorouk, 2009, printed on paper, 24.5 × 17.1 cm. Marseille, Bibliothèque du Mucem

198
Naguib Mahfouz (1911–2006), children's edition of *Kifâh Ahmus* (Ahmose at war), adapted by Mohamed Al-Mou'alim, illustrated by Mostafa Hussein, Cairo: Dar Al-Shorouk, 2009, printed on paper, 24.5 × 17.1 cm. Marseille, Bibliothèque du Mucem

199
Naguib Mahfouz (1911–2006), children's edition of *Kifâh Tîba* (Thebes at war), adapted by Mohamed Al-Mou'alim, illustrated by Mostafa Hussein, Cairo: Dar Al-Shorouk (publisher), 2009, printed on paper, 24.5 × 17.1 cm. Marseille, Bibliothèque du Mucem

200
Edition of the magazine *Mickey*, 17 August 1967, Cairo, paper, 26.3 × 18 cm. Marseille, Mucem, inv. ME2018.3.5

201
Marwan Shahin, graffiti of Tutankhamun wearing the Anonymous mask, symbol of the revolution, Marsh Thyson, photographer, Alexandria, 2011, aerosol painting. Mucem reproduction

202
El-Zeft, *Nefertiti*, allegory of the Revolution, Cairo, 2013. Mucem reproduction

203
T-shirt for supporters of the Pharaohs, the Egyptian national football team, distributed by the Coca-Cola company, Egypt, 2018, polyester, 73.5 × 85.5 cm. Private collection

GLOBAL POP ICONS

204
Jean Goy, Manufacture Raynaud, interpretation of Tutankhamun's funerary mask, Limoges, France, c. 1970, painted and gilt porcelain, 42 × 32 × 30 cm. Jean-Marcel Humbert Collection, Paris

205
William Jerome (1865–1932) and Harry Von Tilzer (1872–1946), Sheet music for *Old King Tut*, AGS Szabo, graphic artist, New York: Harry Von Tilzer Music'Pub Co,

1923, printed on paper, 31 × 23.5 cm. Jean-Marcel Humbert Collection, Paris

206
Sleeping Bag picture disc, ZZ Top, Warner Bros Records, UK, 1985, PVC, 28 × 24.5 cm. Jean-Marcel Humbert Collection, Paris

207
Reinhold Conrad Muschler (1882–1957), *Nofretete*, Berlin: Paul Neff, 1935, 19 × 12.2 × 1.3 cm. Private collection

208
Lucien De Gieter (1932–), *La Vengeance des Ramsès* (The Ramesses revenge), Brussels: Dupuis, 1984, 29.9 × 21.8 cm. Private collection

209
L'Œil de Néfertiti (Nefertiti's eye), adult comic, France: Éditions Elvifrance, 1983, 18 × 13 × 1.4 cm. Jean-Marcel Humbert Collection, Paris

210
Lucien De Gieter (1932–), *Toutânkhamon le pharaon assassiné* (Tutankhamun, the assassinated pharaoh), Brussels: Dupuis, 1994, 29.9 × 21.8 cm. Private collection

211
Edition of the historical magazine *Hombres y Héroes* devoted to the curse of Tutankhamun, Mexico: Novedades Editores, 2000, 14.2 × 13 × 0.5 cm. Jean-Marcel Humbert Collection, Paris

212
Excerpt from the film *Cleopatra*, directed by J. Gordon Edwards (1867–1925), USA, 1917
One of the first films devoted to the Egyptian queen, here portrayed by Theda Bara (1885–1955), one of the most popular actresses in silent film.

213
Press coverage of *The Notorious Cleopatra* (1970), by Peter Perry Jr., Portugal, 1970, paper, 44.5 × 29 cm. Cinemateca Portuguesa – Museu do Cinema, IP, inv. PS 11091

214
Excerpt from the play *António e Cleópatra*, directed by Tiago Rodrigues (1977–); script by Tiago Rodrigues with quotations from *Antony and Cleopatra* by William Shakespeare; translated by Rui Carvalho Homem; performed by Sofia Dias and Vítor Roriz; set design by Ângela Rocha; costumes by Ângela Rocha and Magda Bizarro; lighting design by Nuno Meira; artistic collaboration from Maria João Serrão and Thomas Walgrave. TNDM II production based on an original creation by the Mundo Perfeito company, co-produced with Centro Cultural de Belém, Centro Cultural Vila Flôr, Temps d'Images. Premiere on 4 December 2014, Centro Cultural de Belém, Lisbon.

215
Advertising flyer for the risqué entertainment spectacle *Kleopatra!*, Germany, early 20th century, paper, 9.7 × 12.1 cm. Archives du Marseille, Mucem, inv. Af-sou-61-1029

216
Programme for São Jorge cinema, Lisbon, showing the film *Cleopatra* (1934), directed by Cecil B. DeMille (1881–1959), Portugal, 18 August 1955, paper, 23.6 × 11 cm. Cinemateca Portuguesa – Museu do Cinema, IP, inv. PR 10816

217
Luís Jardim Portela (1931–2003), *Cleopatra*, Portugal, 1963, Indian ink and graphite on paper, 43.2 × 46.5 cm. CAM – Centro de Arte Moderna Gulbenkian, Lisbon, inv. DP3329

218
Howard Terpning (1927–), poster for the film *Cleopatra* (1963) by Joseph L. Mankiewicz (1909–1993), Italy, 1965, paper, 70.5 × 33.5 cm. Jean-Marcel Humbert Collection, Paris

219
Tom Chantrell (1916–2001), poster for the film *O.K. Cleo* (1964) by Gerald Thomas (1920–1993), printed by J. Lichtert et Fils, Belgium, 1964, 53.5 × 35.5 cm. Jean-Marcel Humbert Collection, Paris

220
Text by René Goscinny (1926–1977) and illustrations by Albert Uderzo (1927–2020), *Astérix et Cléopâtre*, Paris: Dargaud S.A., 1965, printed on paper, 28.9 × 22.9 cm. G. Andreu-Lanoë Collection

221
Advertisement for Ramsès face powder, in *L'Illustration*, 20 December 1919, Paris, paper, 40.5 × 30.5 cm. Jean-Marcel Humbert Collection, Paris

222
Advertising plate for the Cleo Cola fizzy drink, Cleo Syrup Corporation, USA, 1935, metal, 35 × 73 cm. Jean-Marcel Humbert Collection, Paris

223
Advertisement for Rectopanbaline : 'Rassure- toi impérissable Tut-Ankh-Amon la science moderne, perfectionnant nos anciennes

méthodes, guérira ta constipation… malgré ses 3000 ans', (Don't worry, everlasting Tut-Ankh-Amun, by improving on ancient methods, modern science will cure your constipation… even if you've had it for 3000 years). Henri-Konrad Wagner, graphic artist, printed by G. Deberque, France, 1923, paper, 9 × 13.8 cm. Jean-Marcel Humbert Collection, Paris

224
Card advertising meat extract, from the series 'Au pays des pharaons': *Le roi Ramsès avec ses lions de combat dans la bataille* (In the land of the pharaohs: king Ramesses with his combat lions in battle), Antwerp, Belgium, 1904, cardstock, 7 × 11 cm. Marseille, Mucem, inv. 1995.1.1251.1

225
Card advertising meat extract, from the series 'Les grands conquérants': *Thoutmosis III* (The Great Conquerors: Thutmose III), Antwerp, Belgium, 1903, cardstock, 7.2 × 11.2 cm. Marseille, Mucem, inv. 1995.1.936.1

226
Box of Tutenkamen skin care cream, USA (?), 20th century, metal, diam. 6.5 cm. Jean-Marcel Humbert Collection, Paris

227
Advertising card: *Le Souper de Cléopâtre* (Cleopatra's dinner), Bouillon-Rivoyre, publisher, Paris, between 1877 and 1893, cardstock, 9.7 × 6.7 cm. Marseille, Mucem, inv. 1995.1.3004.3

228
Talcum powder tin, Lady Tut brand, Federal Chemical Co., Boston, USA, 1924, metal, 15.5 × 5.7 × 3.3 cm. Jean-Marcel Humbert Collection, Paris

229
Box of condoms, Ramses brand, USA, 1947, lithographed metal, 5 × 7 cm. Jean-Marcel Humbert Collection, Paris

230
Cleopatra whisky bottle, Nepal, second half of the 20th century, glass, 14.5 × 7.5 × 3.3 cm. G. Andreu-Lanoë Collection

231
Advertisement for Maidenform bras: 'I dreamed I was playing Cleopatra in my Maidenform bra', USA, 1952, paper, 34.7 × 26.5 cm. Jean-Marcel Humbert Collection, Paris

232
Advertisement for the Egyptian Queen girdle, Peter Pan brand, New York, 1954, paper, 34.7 × 25.5 cm. Jean-Marcel Humbert Collection, Paris

233
Poster advertising La Seigneurie paints, inspired by the bust of Nefertiti, agency Saatchi & Saatchi Équipement, France, 1989, paper, 80 × 60 cm. Jean-Marcel Humbert Collection, Paris

234
Prototype labels for Cleopatra hairspray and self-bronzer, by Comprovex, Estúdio Mário Novais, Lisbon, 20th century, Biblioteca de Arte e Arquivos Gulbenkian, Calouste Gulbenkian Museum reproduction

235
Commercials featuring Cleopatra, La Maison de la Pub, DR, Paris: Cleopatra soap, 1986, France (agency Publicis, produced by Tele 2000, directed by Georges Lautner); Sperlari Zanzibar chocolate, 2001, Italy (directed by Riccardo Milani); *Telma* cereal, 2002, Israel; Johnson Terra cleaning product, 2003, France (agency TBWA, produced by Premiers Rendez-Vous); *Voici* Magazine, 2006, France (agency Leo Burnett, directed by Manu Coeman, produced by U Turn Ph); Cruesli cereal, 1991, France (agency Young & Rubicam, directed by Joe Public and Claude Letessier, produced by Quaker Oats Company); Manpower temping agency, 2000, Sweden (agency Lowe Brindfors, produced by Forsberg & Co, directed by Alex Brügge).

236
Kéops motorcycle, Établissements Guinard, Venette, France, 1926, painted metal, rubber, 110 × 200 × 65 cm. Private collection, on loan to the Musée de la moto, Marseille

237
Álvaro Siza Vieira (1933–), *Ramsés* chair, 1993, panga panga wood, 90 × 57 × 44 cm. SPSS. Lda., Vila Nova de Gaia

BLACK PHARAOHS, BLACK ICONS

238
Cheikh Anta Diop (1923–1986), *The African Origin of Civilization*, Chicago: Lawrence Hill Books, 1974, printed on paper, 20.7 × 13.8 × 2.5 cm. Private collection

239
Advertisement for Budweiser beer, original painting by Barbara Higgins Bond, USA, 1978, paper, 33.2 × 50.6 cm. Jean-Marcel Humbert Collection, Paris

240
Record sleeve for *African Queens* by The Ritchie Family, CBS, USA, 1977, cardboard, 31 × 32.5 cm. Private collection

241
Poster for the film *Cleopatra Jones* by Jack Starrett, Lithographers' and Photoengravers' International Union, USA, 1973, paper, 110 × 70 cm. Hubert Cavaniol Collection, Paris

242
Edition of *Vogue Arabia*, November 2017: 'Rihanna pays homage to Nefertiti'; photography: Greg Kadel; styling: Konca Aykan, USA and UAE, paper, 28.5 × 22.2 cm. Marseille, Bibliothèque du Mucem

243
Sweatshirt from Beyoncé's Homecoming collection, after an original idea by Olivier Rousteing for Balmain, USA and Honduras, 2018, cotton and polyester. Marseille, Mucem

THE QUEENS GALLERY

244
Fred Wilson (1954–), *Grey Area*, USA, 1993, plaster, paint and wood, 75 × 116 × 34 cm. Tate, London, inv. T13632, purchased with assistance from the American Patrons of Tate. Courtesy of Pamela Joyner and Reginald Van Lee (2011)

245
Stuart Carvalhais (1887–1961), *Nefertiti*, Portugal, n.d., gouache on paper, 15 × 13.5 cm. Museu Dr. Joaquim Manso, Nazaré, inv. 80 Pint.

246
Madame Yevonde (1893–1975), *Still Life with the Head of Nefertiti*, UK, 1938, taken from the original negative, 50.7 × 40.6 cm. Courtesy of the British Council Collection, London, inv. P7020

247
Les Rouquines, *Pharaonas* series, Marseille, 1992, analogue photography, 20.1 × 30.3 cm. Marseille, Archives du Mucem, inv. 105p82 (facsimile)

248
Ring decorated with Nefertiti's profile, 2014, gold, diamonds and agate, h. 6 cm. Private collection

249
Mehdi-Georges Lahlou (1983–), *I used to be Nefertiti*, 2014, plaster, polystyrene, paint and jesmonite, 60 × 24 × 45 cm. Courtesy of Galerie Transit, Mechelen

250
Hossam Dirar (1978–), *Nefertiti*, 2018, oil on canvas, 140 × 120 cm. Janet Rady Fine Art

251
Joana Vasconcelos (1971–), *Cleópatra* (PA), Lisbon, 2021, faience and crocheted lace from the Azores, 100 × 80 × 135 cm. Artist's own collection, inv. JV01516

Bibliography

FAYZA HAIKAL

DEN DONCKER, A., 'Prélude à une étude de la réception de l'image égyptienne par les anciens Égyptiens', in WARMENBOL, E., ANGENOT, V. (dir.), *Thèbes aux 101 portes. Mélanges à la mémoire de Roland Tefnin, Monumenta Aegyptiaca* XII, Brepols, Turnhout, 2010, pp. 79–89.

EL-DALY, O., *The Missing Millennium. Ancient Egypt in Medieval Arabic Writings*, UCL Institute of Archaeology Publications, London, 2007.

EL-SHOHOUMI, N., *Der Tod im Leben*, Austrian Academy of Sciences Press, 2014.

HAIKAL, F., 'L'égyptomanie des Égyptiens au XXe siècle', in *Faraoni come Dei, Tolemei come Faraoni*, Atti del V Congresso Internazionale Italo-Egiziano, Turin/Palermo, 2003.

HAIKAL, F., 'A Definition of Identity: Neo-Pharaonic Architecture in the XXth Century', in *Bulletin of the American Research Center in Egypt* 185, summer 2004, pp. 1–14.

HAIKAL, F., 'Spiritualité égyptienne', in *BSFE* 168, March 2007, pp. 12–48.

HAIKAL, F., 'Les Égyptes : transmission d'une culture', in QUENTIN, F. (dir.), *Le Livre des Égyptes*, Robert Laffont, Paris, 2014.

HAIKAL, F., *Reflections on Turning Points*, Kadmos, Berlin, 2014.

LEWIS, B., 'The Egyptian Murder Case', in *New York Review of Books*, 31 May 1984.

NUREDDIN, M. A., *La Langue égyptienne ancienne*, Le Caire, 1998 (in arabic).

BERNARD MATHIEU

ALLIOT, M., 'Un nouvel exemple de vizir divinisé dans l'Égypte ancienne', in *BIFAO* 37, 1938, pp. 93–160.

ANDREU-LANOË, G., 'La vie quotidienne à Deir el-Medina sous les Ramsès d'après les sources archéologiques, textuelles et iconographiques', in GABER, H., BAZIN RIZZO, L., SERVAJEAN, Fr. (dir.), *À l'œuvre on connaît l'artisan... de Pharaon! Un siècle de recherches françaises à Deir el-Medina (1917-2017)*, *CENIM* 18, 2017, pp. 31–9.

ASSMANN, J., *Moses the Egyptian. The Memory of Egypt in Western Monotheism*, Harvard University Press, Cambridge (Mass.), 1997.

AUFRÈRE, S. H., 'Les anciens Égyptiens et leur notion de l'antiquité. Une quête archéologique et historiographique du passé', in *Méditerranées* 17, 1998, pp. 11–55.

AUFRÈRE, S. H., 'Manéthôn de Sebennytos et la traduction en grec de l'épistémè sacerdotale de l'Égypte sous le règne de Ptolémée Philadelphe: quelques réflexions', in BAKHOUCHE, B., LE MOIGNE, Ph. (dir.), *"Dieu parle la langue des hommes". Études sur la transmission du texte religieux (Ier millénaire)*, Éditions du Zèbre, Lausanne, 2008, pp. 13–49.

BAINES, J., 'Practical Religion and Piety', in *JEA* 73, 1987, pp. 79–98.

BAUD, M., DOBREV, V., 'De nouvelles annales de l'Ancien Empire égyptien. Une "Pierre de Palerme" pour la VIe dynastie', in *BIFAO* 95, 1995, pp. 23–92.

BAUD, M., DOBREV, V., 'Le verso des annales de la VIe dynastie ("Pierre de Saqqara-Sud")', in *BIFAO* 97, 1997, pp. 35–42.

BAUD, M., GRIMAL, N., 'L'écriture de l'histoire dans les monarchies antiques. Une introduction', in BAUD, M., GRIMAL, N. (dir.), *Événement, récit, histoire officielle, Études d'égyptologie 3*, 2003, pp. 5–11.

BECKERATH, J. von, *Handbuch der ägyptischen Königsnamen*, in *MÄS* 49, 2000.

BERLANDINI, J., 'Varia Memphitica I', in *BIFAO* 76, 1976, pp. 301–16, in particular pp. 313–16 ("Le culte des rois morts").

BERLANDINI, J., 'La pyramide "ruinée" de Sakkara-Nord et le roi Ikaouhor- Menkaouhor', *RdE* 31, 1979, p. 3–28, in particular pp. 16-19.

BÖWE, Chr., 'Vergleichende Datierung der Objekte der Kirche des Isi in Edfu anhand der Objekte der Kirche des Heqaib auf Elephantine', in *GöttMisz* 203, 2004, pp. 11–27.

BOGDANOV, I. V., 'New Relief Fragments from the Tomb of the Seafarer *Jnj*', in *ChronEg* XCIII/186, 2018, pp. 227–47.

ČERNÝ, J., 'Le culte d'Aménophis Ier chez les ouvriers de la Nécropole thébaine', in *BIFAO* 27, 1927, pp. 159–203.

COLLOMBERT, Ph., 'Hout-sekhem et le septième nome de Haute-Égypte. I: La divine Oudjarenes', in *RdE* 46, 1995, pp. 55–79.

COLLOMBERT, Ph., 'Une statue thébaine d'Amenhotep fils de Hapou trouvée à Esna', in *BIFAO* 102, 2002, pp. 137–42.

DAWOOD, K. A., *The Inscribed Stelae of the Herakleopolitan Period from the Memphite Necropolis*, PhD, University of Liverpool, 1998.

DELANGE, É., *Monuments égyptiens du Nouvel Empire. La Chambre des Ancêtres. Les Annales de Thoutmosis III. Le décor de palais de Séthi Ier*, Louvre éditions and éditions Khéops, Paris, 2015.

DEMARÉE, R. J., *The ꜣḫ jqr n Rꜥ-Stelae. On Ancestor Worship in Ancient Egypt, EgUit* 3, 1983.

DONNAT BEAUQUIER, S., *Écrire à ses morts. Enquête sur un usage rituel de l'écrit dans l'Égypte pharaonique*, Éditions Jérôme Millon, Grenoble, 2014.

EDEL, E., 'Inschriften des Alten Reichs. I. Die Biographie des Gaufürsten von Edfu Jzj', in *ZÄS* 79, 1954, pp. 11-17.

EL-ENANY, Kh., 'La vénération post mortem de Sésostris Ier', in *Memnonia* 14, 2003, pp. 129–38.

EL-ENANY, Kh., "Le saint thébain Montouhotep-Nebhéteprê", in *BIFAO* 103, 2003, pp. 167–90.

EL-ENANY, Kh., 'Des pharaons inoubliables', in *Égypte* 74, 2014, pp. 3–12.

EL-ENANY, Kh., 'La divinisation posthume de Sésostris III en Nubie', in MORFOISSE, Fl., ANDREU-LANOË, G. (dir.), *Sésostris III. Pharaon de légende*, exhibition catalogue, Palais des beaux-arts de Lille, Snoeck, Lille, 2014, pp. 228–31.

EL-SHAZLY, Y., *Royal Ancestor Worship in Deir el-Medina during the New Kingdom*, Abercromby Press, Wallasey, 2015.

FAROUT, D., 'Isi, un saint intercesseur à Edfou', in *Égypte* 53, 2009, pp. 3–10.

FISCHER, H. G., 'Biꜣ and the Deified Vizier Mh. W', in *JARCE* 4, 1965, pp. 49–53.

FITZENREITER, M., 'Ancestor Veneration and Ancestor Cult in Pharaonic Egypt', in *Allerhand Kleinigkeiten*, *IBAES* 20, 2018, pp. 53–75.

FRANKE, D., *Das Heiligtum des Heqaib auf Elephantine: Geschichte eines Provinzheiligtums im Mittleren Reich*, in *SAGA* 9, 1994.

GARDINER, A. H., *The Royal Canon of Turin*, Griffith Institute, Oxford, 1959.

GRIMAL, N., 'L'histoire dans la tradition pharaonique', in *Histoire et historiographie dans l'Antiquité*, Cahiers de la Villa Kérylos 11, 2001, pp. 1–12.

HARBOULLÉ, M. d', *La Vénération posthume de Téti*, master's thesis 1, Universidade Paul-Valéry, Montpellier, 2006.

HARRINGTON, N., *Living with the Dead: Ancestor Worship and Mortuary Ritual in Ancient Egypt*, Oxbow Books, Oxford, 2013.

HOLLENDER, G., *Amenophis I. und Ahmes Nefertari: Untersuchungen zur Entwicklung ihres posthumen Kultes anhand der Privatgräber der thebanischen Nekropole*, in *SDAIK* 23, 2009.

HSU, Sh. W., 'The Palermo Stone: the Earliest Royal Inscription from Ancient Egypt', in *ALTORFORSCH* 37, 2010, pp. 68–89.

JAUHIAIENEN, H., *'Do not celebrate your feast without your neighbours'. A Study of References to Feasts and Festivals in Non-Literary Documents from Ramesside Period Deir el-Medina*, Helsinki University Print, Helsinki, 2009.

KEITH, J. L., *Anthropoid Busts of Deir el Medineh and Other Sites and Collections*, in *DFIFAO* 49, 2011.

LEAHY. A., '*Ḥnsw-iy*: A Problem of Late Onomastica', in *GöttMisz* 60, 1982, pp. 67–79.

LEGRAIN, G., 'Au pylône d'Harmhabi à Karnak (X pylône)', in *ASAE* 14, 1914, pp. 13–44.

LEMCHE, N. P., 'Good and Bad in History: The Greek Connection', in MCKENZIE, St. L., RÖMER, Th., (dir.), *Rethinking the Foundations: Historiography in the Ancient World and in the Bible, Essays in Honour of J. Van Seters*, in *BZAW* 294, 2000, pp. 127–40.

MALEK, J., 'The Special Features of the Saqqara King-List', in *JSSEA* 12, 1982, pp. 21–8.

MALEK, J., 'Old-Kingdom Rulers as 'Local Saints' in the Memphite Area During the Middle Kingdom', in BARTA, M., KREJCÍ, J. (dir.), *Abusir and Saqqara in the year 2000*, Archiv Orientalní. Supplementa IX, Prague, 2000, pp. 241–58.

MATHIEU, B., 'Les aventures du pharaon Néferkarê (Pépy II) et du général Siséné', in *Égypte* 7, 1997, p. 9.

MATHIEU, B., 'Les contes du Papyrus Westcar: une interprétation', in *Égypte* 15, 1999, pp. 29–40.

MATHIEU, B., 'La taille de Pharaon. À propos de Diodore, Bibl. hist. I, 44, 4', in GABOLDE, L. (dir.), *Hommages à J.-Cl. Goyon*, BiEtud 143, 2008, pp. 295–300.

MATHIEU, B., 'Réflexions sur le "Fragment Daressy" et ses hommes illustres', in GUERMEUR, I., ZIVIE, Chr. (dir.), *'Parcourir l'éternité'*. Homage to J. Yoyotte II, in *BEHE*, Sciences Religieuses 156, 2012, pp. 819–52.

MEULENAERE, H. De, 'La statue d'un contemporain de Sébekhotep IV', in *BIFAO* 69, 1971, pp. 61–64.

MORALES, A. J., 'Traces of Official and Popular Veneration to Nyuserra Iny at Abusir, Late Fifth Dynasty to the Middle Kingdom', in BARTA, M. *et al.* (dir.), *Abusir and Saqqara in the Year 2005*, Czech Institute of Egyptology, Prague, 2006, pp. 311–41.

MORENO GARCIA, J. C., 'Oracles, Ancestor Cults and Letters to the Dead: The Involvement of the Dead in the Public and Family Affairs in Pharaonic Egypt', in STORCH, A. (dir.), *Perception of the Invisible: Religion, Historical Semantics and the Role of Perceptive Verbs*, *SUGIA* 21, 2010, pp. 133–53.

MORENZ, S., 'Zur Vergöttlichung in Ägypten', in *ZÄS* 84, 1959, pp. 132–43.

MORENZ, S., 'Traditionen um Cheops', in *ZÄS* 97, 1971, pp. 111–18.

MUNRO, P., 'Der Unas-Friedhof Nord- West. 4./5. Vorbericht über die Arbeiten der Gruppe Hannover/ Berlin in Saqqara', in *GöttMisz* 63, 1983, pp. 81–109.

OTTO, E., 'Gehalt und Bedeutung des ägyptischen Heroenglaubens', in *ZÄS* 78, 1942, pp. 28–40.

POSENER, G., *De la divinité du pharaon*, in *CSA* 15, 1960, pp. 70–6.

PREYS, R., 'La fête de Paophi et le culte des ancêtres', in *RdE* 58, 2007, pp. 111–22.

QUAEGEBEUR, J., 'Les saints égyptiens préchrétiens', in *OLP* 8, 1977, pp. 129–43.

RAUE, D., 'Sanctuary of Heqaib', in WENDRICH, W. (dir.), *UCLA Encyclopedia of Egyptology*, Los Angeles, 2014, pp. 1–15 (available on the Internet).

REDFORD, D. B., 'The Historiography of Ancient Egypt', in WEEKS, K. R. (dir.), *Egyptology and the Social Sciences*, American University in Cairo Press, Le Caire, 1979, pp. 3–20.

REDFORD, D. B., *Pharaonic King-Lists, Annals and Day-Books. A Contribution to the Study of the Egyptian Sense of History*, in *SSEAP* IV, 1986.

ROCCATI, A., 'L'onniscienza del faraone, ovvero un caso di meritocrazia', in *Quaderni del Museo del Papiro XV*, Syracuse, 2018, pp. 29–33.

ROMANOVA, O., 'Cults of Local Saints and Texts of Wisdom Literature in Egypt during the Late Old Kingdom and the First Intermediate Period', in *Ukrainsky Istorichny Zbirnyk (Ukrainian Historical Collection)* 13, Kiev, 2010, pp. 6–20 (in ucranian).

ROWE, A., 'Newly-identified Monuments in the Egyptian Museum Showing the Deification of the Dead together with Brief Details of Similar Objects Elsewhere', in *ASAE* 40, 1940, pp. 1–67, 291–9.

RYHOLT, K., 'The Turin King-List or so-called Turin Canon (TC) as source for chronology', in HORNUNG, E., KRAUSS, R., WARBURTON, D. A. (dir.), *Ancient Egyptian Chronology*, HdO 83, 2006, pp. 26-32.

RYHOLT, K., 'The Life of Imhotep (P. Carlsberg 85)', in WIDMER, G., DEVAUCHELLE, D. (dir.), *Actes du IXe Congrès international des études démotiques. 31 août-3 sept. 2005*, BiEtud 147, 2009, pp. 305–16.

SÄVE-SÖDERBERGH, T., *The Old Kingdom Cemetery at Hamra Dom* (El-Qasr wa es-Saiyad), The Royal Academy of Letters, History and Antiquities, Stockholm, 1994.

SCHNEIDER, Th., 'The Old Kingdom Abroad: An Epistemological Perspective with Remarks on the Biography of Iny and the Kingdom of Dugurasu', in MANUELIAN, P. der, SCHNEIDER, Th. (dir.), *Toward a New History for the Egyptian Old Kingdom. Perspectives on the Pyramid Age*, Brill, Leiyden-Boston, 2015, pp. 429–55.

SETHE, K., 'Heroes and Hero-Gods (Egyptian)', in HASTINGS, J. (dir.), *Encyclopaedia of Religion and Ethics* VI, Bloomsbury T&T Clark, Edinburgh, 1913, col. 647–52.

SIMMANCE, E. B., *Amenhotep Son of Hapu: Self-Presentation through Statues and Their Texs in Pursuit of Semi-Divine Intermediary Status*, thesis, University of Birmingham, 2014.

SIMMANCE, E. B., 'The Authority behind Statues and the Authority of Statues: Sistrophores and Intermediaries', in *Birmingham Egyptology Journal Occasional Publication 2, Conference Proceedings*, Birmingham, 2016, pp. 47–66.

STAUDER, A., *Linguistic Dating of Middle Egyptian Literary Texts, Dating Egyptian Literary Texts 2, Lingua Aegyptiaca. Studia Monographica* 12, Widmaier Verlag, Hamburg, 2013, pp. 271–83.

STAUDER-PORCHET, J., *Les autobiographies de l'Ancien Empire égyptien. Étude sur la naissance d'un genre*, in *OLA* 255, 2017, pp. 256–9.

STECKEWEH, H., Steindorff, G., *Die Fürstengräber von Qaw*, Hinrichs, Leipzig, 1936.

TAIT J. (dir.), *'Never Had the Like Occurred': Egypt's View of its Past*, UCL Press, London, 2003.

TATERKA, F., 'Were Ancient Egyptian Kings Literate?', in *SAK* 46, 2017, pp. 267–83.

VERNUS, P., 'Ménès, Achtoès, l'hippopotame et le crocodile – lecture structurale de l'historiographie égyptienne', in VERHOEVEN, U., Graefe, E. (dir.), *Religion und Philosophie im Alten* Ägypten, *Festgabe Ph. Derchain*, in *OLA* 39, 1991, pp. 331–40.

VERNUS, P., *Essai sur la conscience de l'histoire dans l'Égypte pharaonique*, Honoré Champion, Paris, 1995.

VOLOKHINE, Y., 'Les déplacements pieux en Égypte pharaonique : sites et pratiques cultuelles', in FRANKFURTER, D. (dir.), *Pilgrimage and Holy Space in Late Antique Egypt*, *RGRW* 134, 1998, pp. 51–97.

VOLOKHINE, Y., 'Reliques et traces en Égypte ancienne. À propos de la présence sur terre d'écrits et d'objets d'origine divine', in BORGEAUD, Ph.,

VOLOKHINE, Y. (dir.), *Les Objets de la mémoire. Pour une approche comparatiste des reliques et de leur culte*, Peter Lang, Berne, 2005, pp. 47–72.

VON LIEVEN, A., *Heiligenkult und Vergöttlichung im Alten Ägypten*, habilitation thesis, Freie Universität Berlin, 2007.

VON LIEVEN, A., 'Deified Humans', in DIELEMAN, J., WENDRICH, W. (dir.), *UCLA Encyclopedia of Egyptology*, Los Angeles, 2010, pp. 1–6 (available on the Internet).

VON LIEVEN, A., 'Of Choachytes and Saints: Demotic Documentary Texts as Sources for Religious Practices', in JASNOW, R., WIDMER, Gh. (dir.*), Illuminating Osiris. Egyptological Studies in Honor of M. Smith*, *MVCAE* 2, 2017, pp. 239–45.

WEILL, R., 'Le nomarque d'Edfou Isi, de l'Ancien Empire, et le dieu Isi au Moyen Empire', in *RdE* 4, 1940, pp. 215–17.

WILDUNG, D., *Die Rolle ägyptischer Könige im Bewußtsein ihrer Nachwelt* I, in *MÄS* 17, 1969.

WILDUNG, D., *Imhotep und Amenhotep Gottwerdung im alten Ägypten*, in *MÄS* 36, 1977.

WILDUNG, D., *The Egyptian Saints, Deification in Pharaonic Egypt*, New York University Press, New York, 1977.

WILKINSON, T.A.H., *Royal Annals of Ancient Egypt. The Palermo Stone and its associated fragments*, KPI, London/ New York, 2000.

YOYOTTE, J., 'Les pèlerinages dans l'Égypte ancienne', in *SourcOr* 3, 1960, pp. 19–74.

YOYOTTE, J., 'Le dieu Horemheb', in *RdE* 34, 1982-1983, pp. 148–9.

MICHEL CHAUVEAU

AGUT-LABORDÈRE, D., CHAUVEAU, M., *Héros, magiciens et sages oubliés de l'Égypte ancienne. Une anthologie de la littérature en égyptien démotique*, Les Belles Lettres, Paris, 2011.

CHAUVEAU, M., 'Alexandrie et Rhakôtis : le point de vue des Égyptiens', in *Alexandrie: une mégapole cosmopolite*, Cahiers de la Villa Kérylos 9, Paris, 1999, pp. 1–10.

GRANDET, P., *Contes de l'Égypte ancienne*, Hachette, Paris, 1998.

PARYS, L., *Le Récit du Papyrus Westcar. Texte, traduction, interprétation*, Éditions Safran, Brussels, 2017.

POSENER, G., 'Le conte de Neferkarê et du général Siséné (Recherches littéraires IV)', in *RdE* 11, 1957, pp. 119–37.

POSENER, G., *Le Papyrus Vandier*, Institut français d'archéologie orientale, Le Caire, 1985.

QUACK, J., 'Quelques apports récents des études démotiques à la compréhension du livre II d'Hérodote', in COULON, L., GIOVANNELLI-JOUANNA, P., KIMMEL-CLAUZET, F. (dir.), *Hérodote et l'Égypte. Regards croisés sur le Livre II de l'Enquête d'Hérodote*, *MOM* 51, Lyon, 2013, pp. 63–88.

RYHOLT, K., 'Egyptian Historical Literature from the Greco-Roman Period', in FITZENREITER, M. (dir.), *Das Ereignis. Geschichtsschreibung zwischen Vorfall und Befund*, *IBAES* X, London, 2009, pp. 231–8.

RYHOLT, K., 'Late Period Literature', in LLOYD, A. B. (dir.), *A Companion to Ancient Egypt*, Wiley-Blackwell, Chichester, 2010, pp. 709–31.

VERNUS, P., *Sagesses de l'Égypte pharaonique*, Imprimerie Nationale, Paris, 2001.

WINAND, J., 'Le corps du prince – la perception de l'Égypte ancienne', in *Micrologus* XXII, Sismel-Edizioni del Galluzzo, Florence, 2014, pp. 1–9.

SIMON CONNOR

ARNOLD, D., 'The destruction of the statues of Hatshepsut from Deir el-Bahri', in ROEHRIG, C. H., DREYFUS, R., KELLER, C. A. (dir.), *Hatshepsut: From Queen to Pharaoh*, exhibition catalogue, Metropolitan Museum of Art (New York), Yale University Press, New Haven/London, 2005, pp. 270–6.

CONNOR, S., 'Mutiler, tuer, désactiver les images en Égypte pharaonique', in *Perspective* 2018-2, pp. 147–66.

CONNOR, S., 'Killing or 'de-activating' Egyptian statues: who mutilated them, when and why?', in MASSON-BERGHOFF, A. (dir.), *Statues in Context. Production, Meaning and (Re)uses*, British Museum Publications on Egypt and Sudan no 10 (in press).

DUNAND, F., *Corps vivants des dieux : les statues animées dans le monde méditerranéen antique*, Picard, Paris, 2017.

EATON-KRAUSS, M., 'Usurpation', in COONEY, K. M., JASNOW, R. (dir.), *Joyful in Thebes: Material and Visual Culture of Ancient Egypt*, Lockwood Press, Atlanta, 2015, pp. 97–104.

FRANKFURTER, D., 'Iconoclasm and Christianization in Late Antique Egypt: Christian Treatments of Space and Image', in HAHN, J., EMMEL, S., GOTTER, U. (dir.), *From Temple to Church: Destruction and Renewal of Local Cultic Topography in Late Antiquity, Religions in the Graeco-Roman World* 163, Brill, Leiden/Boston, 2008, pp. 135–59.

HANNESTAD, N., 'How Did Rising Christianity Cope with Pagan Sculpture?', in CHRYSOS, E., WOOD, I. (dir.), *East and West: Modes of Communication. Proceedings of the First Plenary Conference at Merida*, Brill, Leiden/Boston, 1999, pp. 173–203.

JAMBON, E., 'La Cachette de Karnak. Étude analytique et essais d'interprétation', in COULON, L. (dir.), *La Cachette de Karnak. Nouvelles perspectives sur les découvertes de G. Legrain*, BiEtud 161, 2016, pp. 131–75.

KRISTENSEN, T. M., *Making and Breaking the Gods: Christian Responses to Pagan Sculpture in Late Antiquity*, Aarhus Universitetsforlag, Aarhus, 2013.

PICARDO, N., '"Semantic Homicide" and the So-called Reserve Heads: The Theme of Decapitation in Egyptian Funerary Religion and some Implications for the Old Kingdom', in *JARCE* 43, 2007, pp. 221–52.

RAEDLER, C., 'Die kosmische Dimension pharaonischer Gunst', in BRÖCKELMANN, D., KLUG, A. (dir.), *In Pharaos Staat: Festschrift für Rolf Gundlach zum 75.* Geburtstag, Harrassowitz Verlag, Wiesbaden, 2006, pp. 145–58.

ROTH, A. M., 'Erasing a Reign', in ROEHRIG, C. H., DREYFUS, R., KELLER, C. A. (dir.), *Hatshepsut: From queen to pharaoh*, exhibition catalogue, Metropolitan Museum of Art (New York), Yale University Press, New Haven/London, 2005, pp. 277–81.

TEFNIN, R., 'La statuaire d'Hatchepsout : une tête d'Hatchepsout-roi au Musée Georges-Labit de Toulouse', in *Égypte* 17, 2000, pp. 33–40.

THOMPSON, K., 'How to destroy an Amarna statue', in *Ancient Egypt* 12/2, Manchester, 2011, pp. 38–44.

VALBELLE, D., 'Statues enterrées, dépôts liturgiques et différentes catégories de favissae', in COULON, L. (dir.), *La Cachette de Karnak. Nouvelles perspectives sur les découvertes de G. Legrain*, BiEtud 161, 2016, pp. 21–33.

JEAN-MARCEL HUMBERT

BARDAOUIL, S., FELLRATH, T. (dir.), *Le Théorème de Néfertiti*, exhibition catalogue, Institut du monde arabe (Paris), Skira, Paris/ Geneva, 2013.

BRONFEN, E., LULIŃSKA, A. dir *Kleopatra. Die Ewige Diva*, exhibition catalogue, Bundeskunsthalle (Bonn), Hirmer Verlag, Munich, 2013.

HUMBERT, J.-M., *L'Égyptomanie dans l'art occidental*, éditions ACR, Paris, 1989.

HUMBERT, J.-M., 'Cléopâtre sur les murs. La publicité à l'égyptienne', in HUMBERT, J.-M. (dir.), *France-Égypte, dialogues de deux cultures*, AFAA, Paris-Musées, Gallimard, *L'Œil*, Paris, 1998, pp. 184–9.

HUMBERT, J.-M., 'Et Cléopâtre ?', in WARMENBOL, E. (dir.), *Beautés d'Egypte, 'Celles que les ans ne peuvent moissonner'*, exhibition catalogue, musée du Malgré-Tout (Treignes), Éditions du Cedarc, 2002, pp. 81–6.

HUMBERT, J.-M., 'Du parfum Ramsès au savon Cléopâtre', in GRASSE, M.-C. (dir.), *L'Égypte, parfums d'histoire*, exhibition catalogue, musée international de la Parfumerie (Grasse), Somogy, Paris, 2003, pp. 173–83.

HUMBERT, J.-M., 'Cléopâtre Superstar', in RITSCHARD, C., MOREHEAD, A. (dir.), *Cléopâtre dans le miroir de l'art occidental*, exhibition catalogue, musée Rath (Geneva), Les Cinq Continents, 2004, pp. 277–92.

HUMBERT, J.-M., 'Cléopâtre reine de nos fantasmes', in LAFONT-COUTURIER, H. (dir.), *Peplum. L'Antiquité spectacle*, exhibition catalogue, Musée gallo-romain (Lyon et Saint-Romain-en-Gal), éditions Fage, Lyon, 2012, pp. 88–93.

HUMBERT, J.-M., 'Titillons Néfertiti : l'égyptomanie, un art éminemment populaire (1880-1980)', in VOLAIT, M., PERRIN, E. (dir.), *Dialogues artistiques avec les passés de l'Égypte. Une perspective transnationale et transmédiale/Fortunes plastiques et politiques de l'art des Anciens Égyptiens*, conference proceedings 'L'Égypte en ses miroirs' (Paris, INHA, 26–27 June 2013), Paris, 2017. Available at http://inha.revues.org/7200.

HUMBERT, J.-M., 'L'Égypte éphémère des parcs d'attraction (1818-2018)', in MAGEN B. (dir.), '... *Denn das Eigentliche Studium der Menschheit ist der Mensch', Festschrift für Alfred Grimm*, Harrassowitz Verlag, Wiesbaden, 2018, pp. 122–39 and 399.

HUMBERT, J.-M., 'King Tut ou la Tut- mania pour tous', in CONNOR, S., LABOURY, D. (dir.), *Toutankhamon, à la découverte du pharaon oublié* (Liège), exhibition catalogue, Presses universitaires de Liège, 2019, pp. 302–9.

HUMBERT, J.-M., 'Plaidoyer pour l'égyptomanie, ou comment s'approprier une Égypte fantasmée', in VERSLUYS, M. J. (dir.), *Beyond Egyptomania, Objects, Style and Agency*, conference proceedings, University of Leiden , 21–22 January 2016, Leiden, 2020, pp. 39–52, 254–7 e 325–32.

HUMBERT, J.-M. (dir.), *L'Égyptomanie à l'épreuve de l'archéologie*, international symposium organized in musée du Louvre (Paris, 1994), musée du Louvre, Paris, Éditions du Gram, Brussels, 1996.

HUMBERT, J.-M. (dir.), *Bonaparte et l'Égypte, feu et lumières*, exhibition catalogue, Institut du monde arabe (Paris), Hazan, Paris 2008.

HUMBERT, J.-M., PANTAZZI, M., ZIEGLER, Ch., *Egyptomania*, exhibition catalogue (Paris, Ottawa and Vienna), Réunion des musées nationaux, Paris, 1994–5.

MONTSERRAT, D., *Akhenaten: History Fantasy and Ancient Egypt*, Routledge, London/New York, 2000.

RESTELLINI, M. (dir.), *Le Mythe Cléopâtre*, exhibition catalogue, Pinacothèque de Paris, Gourcuff Gradenigo, Montreuil, 2014.

SCHNITZLER, B., 'Hijacked Images: Ancient Egypt in French Commercial Advertising', in MACDONALD, S., RICE, M., *Consuming Ancient Egypt*, UCL Press, London, 2003, pp. 144 and pp. 165–73.

WALKER, S., HIGGS, P. (dir.), *Cleopatra of Egypt, from History to Myth*, exhibition catalogue (London, Rome, Chicago), Princeton University Press, 2001.

WESTHEIDER, O., MÜLLER, K. (dir.), *Kleopatra und die Caesaren*, exhibition catalogue, Bucerius Kunst Forum (Hamburg), Hirmer Verlag, Munich, 2006.

JOÃO CARVALHO DIAS

ANCIENT EGYPTIAN Sculpture Lent by C. S. Gulbenkian. Text by Sidney Smith, and Account of Inscriptions by I. E. S. Edwards, London, 1937.

ARAÚJO, Luís Manuel, *Eyptian Art in Calouste Gulbenkian Collection*, Calouste Gulbenkian Museum, Lisbon, 2006.

ASHTON, S-A., in WATKIN, D., HEWAT-JABOOR, P., (eds.), *Thomas Hope, Regency Designer*, exhibition catalogue, New Haven/London, 2008.

AZEREDO PERDIGÃO, José de, *Calouste Gulbenkian Collector*, Calouste Gulbenkian Foundation, Lisbon, 2006 (1969).

BÉNÉDITE, G., 'Vraie ou Fausse ?', in *Revue de l'art*, January-May 1924.

CALOUSTE SARKIS Gulbenkian: Voyage en Egypte, Palestine et Syrie (janvier-février 1934), Calouste Gulbenkian Foundation, Lisbon, 2019.

CARVALHO DIAS, João, 'Calouste S. Gulbenkian. O colecionador que preferiu Portugal 1942-1955', in *ARTIS* (2nd series, no. 3), Caleidoscópio, Lisbon, 2014, pp. 99–107.

CARVALHO DIAS, João, 'A Coleção Gulbenkian e o "exílio americano"', in NETO, Maria João, MALTA, Marize (eds.), *Coleções de Arte em Portugal e Brasil nos Séculos XIX e XX*, Conference Proceedings, Caleidoscópio, Lisbon,2018, pp. 63–78.

CARVALHO DIAS, J. (dir.), *The Collector and his Taste. Calouste S. Gulbenkian 1869-1955*, exhibition catalogue, Calouste Gulbenkian Museum, Lisbon, 2006.

CATALOGUE OF the Amherst Collection of Egyptian & Oriental Antiquities, sale catalogue, London, 13–17 june 1921.

CATALOGUE OF an Exhibition of Ancient Egyptian Art, London, 1922.

CATALOGUE OF the MacGregor Collection of Egyptian Antiquities [....] [sale, London, Sotheby, Wilkinson & Hodge ... 26 June to 3 de July 1922].

CONLIN, J., *Mr Five Per Cent. The Many Lives of Calouste Gulbenkian, the World's Richest Man.* Profile Books, London, 2019.

ERMITAGE IMPERIAL. Inventaire de la collection égyptienne, Leipzig, 1891.

HARDWICK, T., 'The Carter Adventure', in *Tutankhamun: Discovering the Forgotten Pharaoh*, Liège, 2020, pp. 68-71.

HARDWICK, T., 'The Victorian Collectors who Loved Art from Ancient Egypt', in *Apollo*, January 2020. https://www.apollo-magazine.com/bolton-ancient-egypt-museums-collecting/ (accessed February 11, 2022).

JAMES, T. G. H., *Howard Carter. The Path to Tutankhamun*, Cairo Press, 2000 (1992), p. 447.

L'HÔTEL GULBENKIAN. 51, Avenue d'Iéna. Mémoires d'un lieu, exhibition catalogue, Paris, 2011; Lisbon, 2012.

PIERSON, S. J., *Private Collecting, Exhibitions, and the Shaping of Art History in London. The Burlington Fine Arts Club*, New York, 2017, pp. 116-17.

REEVES, N., 'Howard Carter's Collection of Egyptian and Classical Antiquities', in GORING, E., REEVES, N., RUFFLE, J. (eds.), *Chief of Seers. Egyptian Studies in Memory of Cyril Aldred*, London, 2009 (1997), pp. 242-50, note 3, p. 246.

SAINT-JOHN PERSE – Calouste Gulbenkian: Correspondance, 1946-1954, Paris, 2013, p. 71.

VASSALLO E SILVA, Nuno, 'The First Acquisitions', in CARVALHO DIAS, João (dir.), *The Collector and his Taste. Calouste S. Gulbenkian 1869-1955*, exhibition catalogue, Calouste Gulbenkian Museum, Calouste Gulbenkian Foundation, Lisbon, 2006, pp. 36–47.

VASSALLO E SILVA, Nuno, 'The Great Opportunities. The Russian acquisitions', in CARVALHO DIAS, João (dir.), *The Collector and his taste. Calouste S. Gulbenkian 1869-1955*, exhibition catalogue, Calouste Gulbenkian Museum, Calouste Gulbenkian Foundation, Lisbon, 2006, pp. 48–57.

WILKINSON, T., *A World beneath the Sands*, Picador, London, 2020.

Chronological milestones

2636 to 2605 BCE	Khufu.
1974 to 1781 BCE	The Amenemhat and Senwosret line (Twelfth Dynasty).
1539 to 1493 BCE	Ahmose, Ahmose-Nefertari and Amenhotep I.
1349 to 1320 BCE	Akhenaten, Nefertiti and Tutankhamun.
1279 to 1212 BCE	Ramesses II.
664 to 526 BCE	Psamtik and Amasis line (Twenty-sixth Dynasty).
455 to 430 BCE	Herodotus travels to Egypt and writes his *Histories*.
380 to 342 BCE	Nectanebo dynasty, the last Egyptian pharaohs (Thirtieth Dynasty).
331 BCE	Alexander the Great is crowned pharaoh.
30 BCE	Death of Cleopatra VII.
535	The last temple in Philae closes, following the Christianization of Egypt.
642	Egypt is conquered by the Arabs.
1474	Originally written in Greek, Herodotus's work is published in a Latin translation.
1798 a 1801	Napoleon's expedition to Egypt: monuments are surveyed and the Rosetta stone is discovered.

1822	Champollion unravels the hieroglyphic writing system.
1912	Excavations at Amarna and discovery of Nefertiti's bust
1922	Egypt's Independence.
1922	Discovery of Tutankhamun's tomb.
1924	First public exhibition of Nefertiti's bust in Berlin.
1954	Nasser becomes president of the new Egyptian Republic.
1955	Essays by Cheikh Anta Diop proposing that Ancient Egyptians were Black African appear in the publication *Nations nègres et culture*.
1963	The film *Cleopatra* by Joseph L. Mankiewicz is released with Liz Taylor in the title role.
1964	Unesco rescues the temples of Ramesses at Abu Simbel.
1967	Exhibition *Toutânkhamon et son temps* (Tutankhamun and his time) at the Petit Palais in Paris.
2019	The exhibition Toutânkhamon : *Le trésor du pharaon* (Tutankhamun: the pharaoh's treasure) is held at the Grande Halle de la Villette, Paris.

List of pharaohs

Manetho's *Aegyptiaca*

No doubt keen to know about the country he was called upon to govern, the pharaoh Ptolemy II (283–246 BCE), who was originally Macedonian, asked the Egyptian priest Manetho for a history of Egypt since its origins, to be written in Greek. This is the work known as *Aegyptiaca* (About Egypt). Manetho's sources were archives, annals, monumental inscriptions and other accounts of

PREDYNASTIC PERIOD 4500–3100

3200–3100 DYNASTY 0: NAQADA III–A/ B CULTURE

- Iry-Hor
- Ka
- Scorpion (?)

PROTODYNASTIC PERIOD 3100–2750

3100–2900 FIRST DYNASTY: NAQADA III–C CULTURE

About ten kings, including:

- Narmer
- Aha
- Djer
- Djet
- Den
- * Adjib
- Semerkhet
- Qa'a

the past available in temples and their libraries. From these he built up a list of pharaohs going back to mythical times, indicating the duration of each reign. He divided the list into thirty dynasties, corresponding to families or to lineages with the same geographical origins. His work has not survived intact but in fragmentary citations by later historians.

Nevertheless, it provided Egyptology with a basis from which to establish royal succession and chronological bands, before epigraphical and historical studies were able to confirm or correct this 'Manethonian' tradition.

2900–2750
SECOND DYNASTY:
NAQADA III–D CULTURE

About ten kings, including the Horus-kings:

- Hotepsekhemwy
- Raneb
- Ninetjer
- Sekhemib
- * Sened
- Seth-Peribsen
- Horus-Seth Khasekhemwy

OLD KINGDOM
2750–2250

2750–2675
THIRD DYNASTY

- * Horus Netjerikhet (King Djoser)
- Horus Sekhemkhet (King Djoserty)
- Horus Khaba
- * Horus Sanakht (King Nebka)
- Huni

2675–2545
FOURTH DYNASTY

- * Sneferu (2675–2636)
- * Khufu (2636–2605)
- * Djedefre (2605–2597)
- * Khafre (2597–2573)
- Menkaure (2572–2551)
- Shepseskaf (2551–2545)

2544–2413
FIFTH DYNASTY

- Userkaf (2544–2534)
- Sahure (2534–2515)
- Neferirkare Kakai (2515–2501)
- Shepseskare (2501–2495)
- Neferefre (2495–2490)
- * Nyuserre Ini (2490–2478)
- * Menkauhor/Ikauhor (2478–2468)
- Djedkare Isesi (2468–2432)
- * Unas (2432–2413)

2413–2250
SIXTH DYNASTY

* Teti (2413–2394)
Userkare (2394–2393)
Pepi I (2393–2343)
Merenre I (2343–2334)
* Pepi II (2334–2260)
Merenre II (2260–2258)

FIRST INTERMEDIATE PERIOD 2250–2045

2250–2200
SEVENTH AND EIGHTH DYNASTIES

About twenty kings including:
Neferkare Nebi
Qakare Ibi
Neferkauhor

2200–2015
NINTH AND TENTH DYNASTIES (HERACLEOPOLIS)

Eighteen or nineteen kings, including:
Wahkare Khety
Meryibre Khety
Neferkare
Nebkaure Khety
* Merikare Khety

2130–2045
ELEVENTH DYNASTY (THEBES)

Mentuhotep I Tepi-aa (c. 2130)
Intef I (c. 2125–2112)
Intef II (2112–2053)
Intef III (2053–2045)

MIDDLE KINGDOM 2045–1700

2045–1974
ELEVENTH DYNASTY (WHOLE COUNTRY)

* Mentuhotep II (2045–1994; unification in about 2015)
Mentuhotep III (1994–1981)
Mentuhotep IV (1981–1974)

1974–1781
TWELFTH DYNASTY

* Amenemhat I (1974–1944)
* Senwosret I (1944–1900)
Amenemhat II (1900–1865)
Senwosret II (1865–1856)
* Senwosret III (1856–1838)
* Amenemhat III (1838–1794)
Amenemhat IV (1794–1785)
Neferusobek (1785–1781)

1781–1700
THIRTEENTH DYNASTY

About thirty kings based in Itjtawi, including:

Amenemhat-Sobekhotep I

Amenemhat V

Khendjer

Sekhemre-Sewadjtawy Sobekhotep

Neferhotep I

Sahathor

Khaneferre Sobekhotep

Khaankhre Sobekhotep

Ibiau

Ay

SECOND INTERMEDIATE PERIOD 1700–1539

1700–1650
END OF THE THIRTEENTH DYNASTY

About twenty kings based at Itjtawy and Thebes, including:

Neferhotep II

Merkaure Sobekhotep

Dedumose I

1730–1700
FOURTEENTH DYNASTY

About twenty kings at Avaris, including:

Nehesy

1700–1520
FIFTEENTH (HYKSOS) DYNASTY

Six or seven kings based at Avaris, including:

Khyan

Sheshi

Seker-Har

Yaqub-Har

Apepi

Khamudi

1650–1600
SIXTEENTH DYNASTY

About twenty kings at Thebes and/or Abydos, including:

Djehuti

Sekhemre-Seusertawy Sobekhotep

Neferhotep III

Bebiankh

Nebiriau I

Dedumose II

Senebkay

1600–1539
SEVENTEENTH DYNASTY

About fifteen Theban kings, including:

Rahotep

Sobekemsaf I

Sobekemsaf II

Intef V

Intef VI

Intef VII

Ahmose the Elder

Seqenenre Taa

* **Kamose**

NEW KINGDOM
1539–1069

1539–1295
EIGHTEENTH DYNASTY

* Ahmose (1539–1514)
* Amenhotep I (1514–1493)
  Thutmose I (1493–1482)
  Thutmose II (1482–1479)
* Hatshepsut (1479–1458)
* Thutmose III (1479–1425)
  Amenhotep II (1425–1398)
* Thutmose IV (1398–1388)
* Amenhotep III (1388–1349)
* Amenhotep IV/Akhenaten (1349–1333)
  Smenkhkare/Neferneferuaten (1333–1330)
* Tutankhamun (1330–1320)
  Ay (1320–1310)
* Horemheb (1310–1295)

1295–1188
NINETEENTH DYNASTY

  Ramesses I (1295–1294)
* Seti I (1294–1279)
* Ramesses II (1279–1212)
* Merenptah (1212–1202)
  Seti II (1202–1196)
  Rebel ruler: Amenmesse (1201–1198)
  Siptah (1196–1190)
  Tausret (1190–1188)

1188–1069
TWENTIETH DYNASTY

  Setnakht (1188–1184)
* Ramesses III (1184–1153)
  Ramesses IV (1153–1148)
  Ramesses V (1148–1144)
  Ramesses VI (1144–1136)
* Ramesses VII (1136–1128)
  Ramesses VIII (1128–1125)
* Ramesses IX (1125–1106)
  Ramesses X (1106–1103)
* Ramesses XI (1103–1069)

THIRD INTERMEDIATE PERIOD
1069–664

1069–943
TWENTY-FIRST DYNASTY
TANITE KINGS

  Smendes (1069–1043)
  Amenemnesut (1043–1039)
  Psusennes I (1039–989)
  Amenemope (989–980)
  Osorkon the Elder (980–975)
  Siamun (975–956)
  Psusennes II (956–943)

HEBAN HIGH PRIESTS

- Herihor (1073–1064)
- Pinedjem I (1064–1032)
- Masaharta (1054–1046)
- Djedkhonsuefankh (1046?)
- Menkheperre (1045–992)
- Smendes II (992–990)
- Pinedjem II (990–969)
- Psusennes III (958–?)

943–735 TWENTY-SECOND DYNASTY (BUBASTIS)

- Shoshenq I (943–922)
- Osorkon I (922–887)
- Takelot I (887–874)
- Shoshenq II (874–?)
- Tutkheperre Shoshenq (?–?)
- Osorkon II (865–830)
- at Thebes: Harsiesis I (c. 860)

BUBASTITE BRANCH

- Shoshenq III (830–791)
- Shoshenq IV (791–779)
- Pami (779–769)
- Shoshenq V (769–731)

THEBAN BRANCH

- Takelot II (834–809)
- Iuput I (808–796)
- Osorkon III (791–763)
- Takelot III (768–753)
- Rudamun (753–750)

THEBAN USURPERS

- * Pedubast I (824–800)
- Shoshenq VI (800–791)

730–702 TWENTY-THIRD DYNASTY AND LOCAL KINGLETS

- Pedubast II (Tanis) (730–725)
- Osorkon IV (Tanis) (725–715)
- Pami II (Tanis) (c. 712–702)
- Iuput II (Leontopolis) (c. 735–715)
- Peftjaubast (Heracleopolis) (c. 735–720)
- Nimlot (Hermopolis) (c. 730–720)

TWENTY-FOURTH DYNASTY OF SAIS

- * Bakenranef (Bocchoris) (718–712)

C. 770–655 TWENTY-FIFTH (KUSHITE) DYNASTY

- Alara (c. 770)
- Kashta (760?–745)
- Piye (745–713)
- Shebitku (713–705)
- * Shabaqa (705–690)
- Taharqa (690–664)
- Tantamani (664–655)

TWENTY-SIXTH (LOCAL) DYNASTY OF SAIS

- Tefnakht II (680–672)
- Necho I (672–664)

LATE PERIOD
664–332

664–526
TWENTY-SIXTH DYNASTY OF SAÏS (WHOLE COUNTRY)

- * Psamtik I (664–610)
- Necho II (610–595)
- Psamtik II (595–589)
- Apries (589–570)
- * Amasis (570–527)
- Psamtik III (527–526)

526–401
TWENTY-SEVENTH (PERSIAN) DYNASTY

- Cambyses (526–522)
- Darius I (521–486)
- Xerxes (486–466)
- Artaxerxes I (465–424)
- Darius II (424–404/401)

INDIGENOUS KINGLETS

- Pedubast IV (522–521)
- Psamtik IV (c. 486)
- Inaros (c. 464–460)
- Psamtik V (c. 440)

404–399
TWENTY-EIGHTH DYNASTY OF SAÏS

- Amyrtaeus-Psamtik VI (404–399)

399–380
TWENTY-NINTH DYNASTY (MENDES)

- Neferites I (399–393)
- Akoris (393–380)
- Rebel ruler: Psammutis (389–388)
- Neferites II (380)

THIRTIETH DYNASTY (SEBENNYTOS)

- * Nectanebo I (380–362)
- Teos (362–360)
- * Nectanebo II (360–342)

THIRTY-FIRST (PERSIAN) DYNASTY

- Artaxerxes III (Oco) (342–338)
- Artaxerxes IV (Arses) (338–336)
- Rebel ruler: Khababash (c. 338–332)
- Darius III (Codommanus) (336–332)

GREEK PERIOD
332–30

332–306
MACEDONIAN DYNASTY

- * Alexander III (Alexander the Great) (332–323)
- Philip III Arrhidaeus (323–317)
- Alexander (323–309)

305–30
LAGID OR PTOLEMAIC DYNASTY

Ptolemy I Soter (305–282)

Ptolemy II Philadelphus (282–246)

Ptolemy III Euergetes (246–222)

Ptolemy IV Philopator (222–204)

Rebel ruler: **Ankhwennefer (205–186)**

Ptolemy V Epiphanes (204–180)

Ptolemy VI Philometor (180–145)

Ptolemy VIII Euergetes II (164–163)

Ptolemy Eupator co-regent **(152)**

Ptolemy VIII Euergetes II restored **(145–116)**

Rebel ruler: **Harsiese (131–130)**

Cleopatra II Philometora Soteira (130–127)

Ptolemy VII (never reigned)

Ptolemy IX Soter II and Cleopatra III (116–107/88–81)

Ptolemy X Alexander and Cleopatra III (107–88)

Cleopatra Berenice III (81–80)

Ptolemy XI Alexander II (80)

Ptolemy XII Neos Dionysos 'Auletes' (80–58/55–51)

Cleopatra VI Tryphaena and Cleopatra Berenice IV (58–55)

* **Cleopatra VII Thea Neotera Philopator and Ptolemy XIII Philopator (51–47)**

* **Cleopatra VII and Ptolemy XIV Philopator (47–44)**

* **Cleopatra VII and Ptolemy XV Caesar (44–30)**

Egypt was made a Roman province by Augustus (30 BCE)

All dates given are before Christian Era.

* Refers to the pharaos presented in the exhibition or mentioned in the publication

Adapted from the chronology published by Pierre Tallet, Frédéric Payraudeau, Chloé Ragazzoli and Claire Somaglino, *L'Égypte pharaonique. Histoire, société, culture*, Armand Colin, Paris, 2019.

Curators

FRÉDÉRIC MOUGENOT

Frédéric Mougenot is a cultural heritage curator responsible for the Antiquities and Ceramics collections at the Palais des Beaux-arts in Lille, and was formerly Domestic Life theme manager at Mucem. At Mucem, he served on committees for the exhibitions *Le Monde à l'envers: Carnavals et mascarades d'Europe et de Méditerranée* (2014) and *Migrations divines* (2015). He was co-curator of *Bonne fortune et mauvais sorts* at the Abbaye de Daoulas (Finistère) in 2016. His research is largely focused on deities and religious practices in ancient Egypt.

JOÃO CARVALHO DIAS

João Carvalho Dias is an art historian and researcher in the field of collecting at ARTIS — the Institute of Art History, University of Lisbon. As Curator of European books, drawings and prints for the Gulbenkian Collection (2014–22), he recently published *European Illuminated Manuscripts in the Calouste Gulbenkian Collection* (2020). He is currently Deputy Director of the Calouste Gulbenkian Museum.

Authors

GUILLEMETTE ANDREU-LANOË

Guillemette Andreu-Lanoë has been a scientific member of the French Institute of Oriental Archaeology in Cairo, Professor of Egyptology at the École du Louvre, and curator and then Director of the Department of Egyptian Antiquities at the Musée du Louvre. She has curated many exhibitions on Egypt: *Les Artistes de Pharaon. Deir el-Médineh et la Vallée des Rois* (Musée du Louvre, Paris; Musées Royaux d'Art et d'Histoire, Brussels; and Museo Egizio, Turin, 2002–3); *Méroé, un empire sur le Nil* (Louvre, 2010); *L'Art du contour, le dessin dans l'Égypte ancienne* (Musée du Louvre and Brussels, 2013–14); *Sésostris III, pharaon de légende* (in collaboration with Fleur Morfoisse, Palais des Beaux-arts de Lille, 2014–15) and *L'aventure Champollion. Dans le secret des hiéroglyphes* (with Vanessa Desclaux and Hélène Virenque, Paris, Bibliothèque Nationale de France, spring 2022).

MICHEL CHAUVEAU

Michel Chauveau is Director of Studies at the École Pratique des Hautes Études in Paris. A former member of the French Institute of Oriental Archaeology in Cairo, he specializes in Egyptian Demotic language and script and in the history of Greco-Roman Egypt. Notable publications include *L'Égypte au temps de Cléopâtre* ('La vie quotidienne' series, Hachette, 1997) and *Héros, sages et magiciens oubliés de l'Égypte ancienne* (in collaboration with Damien Agut-Labordère, Les Belles Lettres, 2011).

SIMON CONNOR

Simon Connor is a scientific member of the French Institute of Oriental Archaeology in Cairo. His doctoral thesis was on the subject of statuary at the end of the Middle Kingdom and in the Second Intermediate Period (Golden House Publications, 2020). He has been curator at the Museo Egizio (Turin), Andrew W. Mellon Research Fellow at the Metropolitan Museum of Art, and Research Fellow at FRS-FNRS/University of Liège. He has taken part in archaeological excavations in Heliopolis, Tanis and Dahshur.

ANNIE FORGEAU

Annie Forgeau is a historian specializing in Egyptology. She was in charge of publications at the French Institute of Oriental Archaeology in Cairo, and previously taught for around thirty years at the Institute of Art and Archaeology at Sorbonne University, Paris. The particular focus of her research has been deciphering the discourse of power as well as studying religious phenomena and cultural transitions. She is the author of *Nectanébo: La dernière dynastie égyptienne* (Khéops, 2018).

Authors

FAYZA HAIKAL

Fayza Haikal studied in Cairo and at Oxford. She has taught in Egypt, at Sorbonne University in Paris, at Sapienza University in Rome and at the Charles University in Prague. She is now Emeritus Professor at the American University in Cairo and lectures all over the world. She was the first Egyptian woman to work in Nubia during the international campaign to save the Nubian monuments in the 1960s. In the 1990s, she led the international campaign to save archaeological sites in North Sinai, during the construction of the Peace Canal. She is also the first woman to be President of the International Association of Egyptologists and has received numerous national and international awards for her many contributions to Egyptology.

JEAN-MARCEL HUMBERT

Jean-Marcel Humbert is a historian and art historian, Doctor of Letters and Doctor of Egyptology at Sorbonne University in Paris. He has been a curator and director of national museums, before becoming a member of the General Inspectorate of French Museums. His chosen field of research is Egyptomania, which he has been studying for fifty years. His work has reached a wide audience through many national and international exhibitions, several hundred articles and dozens of books. He is currently teaching at the École du Louvre, Paris.

BERNARD MATHIEU

Bernard Mathieu is Professor of Egyptology at the Paul-Valéry University in Montpellier. Specialising in classical literature, he was awarded his doctorate in Egyptology (on the love poetry of Ancient Egypt) in 1989. He was Director of the French Institute of Oriental Archaeology in Cairo from 1999 to 2004. His researches centre especially on the Pyramid Texts and the literature of ancient Egypt. He is the author of *La Littérature de l'Égypte ancienne* (two volumes published, Les Belles Lettres, 2021) and co-author, with Pierre Grandet, of *Cours d'égyptien hiéroglyphique* (Khéops, 3rd edition, 2003).

VINCENT RONDOT

Vincent Rondot is Director of the Department of Egyptian Antiquities at the Musée du Louvre and Director of Research at the French National Centre for Scientific Research (CNRS). He spent ten years in Egypt (notably at the French Institute of Oriental Archaeology in Cairo from 1988 to 1992) and five years in Sudan. He was Director of SFDAS (Section Française de la Direction des Antiquités du Soudan) in Khartoum (2004–9). An archaeologist and specialist in epigraphy, his research is concentrated mainly on the study of the god Amun's cults in Egypt and Sudan, as well as on issues relating to the Hellenization of divine iconography in Roman Egypt.

PHARAONS SUPERSTARS

MUCEM – Musée des civilisations de l'Europe et de la Méditerranée, Marseille
22 June to 17 October 2022

CURATORS
Frédéric Mougenot
and Guillemette Andreu-Lanoë

Exhibition produced by the Mucem in partnership with the Calouste Gulbenkian Foundation

SUPERSTAR PHARAOHS

Calouste Gulbenkian Museum, Lisbon
25 November 2022 to 6 March 2023

CURATORS
Frédéric Mougenot
and João Carvalho Dias

CALOUSTE GULBENKIAN MUSEUM

DIRECTOR
António Filipe Pimentel

DEPUTY DIRECTOR
João Carvalho Dias

MANAGEMENT SECRETARIAT
Fátima Vasconcelos

MANAGEMENT SUPPORT
Filipa Medeiros

ADMINISTRATIVE SUPPORT
Fernando Maia Santos
Filomena Norberto
José Leal

EXHIBITION

CURATORS
Frédéric Mougenot
João Carvalho Dias

ASSISTANT CURATOR
Patrícia Simões

DESIGN AND TECHNICAL COORDINATION
Mariano Piçarra
with the assistance of Rita Colaço
and Ana Teresa Torres

PRODUCTION
Miguel Fumega
Patrícia Simões
Rita Rebelo de Andrade
Filipa Correia de Sousa

CONSERVATION AND RESTORATION
Rui Xavier (preventive conservation)
Susana Campos
Rita Gordo
Mafalda Fernandes

COLLECTION REGISTRAR
Ana Caldeira

INSTALLATION CREW
Miguel Fumega
Inês Pereira
Paulo Santos
Bruno Cecílio
Rute Delgado
with the assistance of Gonçalo Afonso

GRAPHIC PROJECT
Panorama Design Studio

EDITION
Carla Paulino
Rosário Azevedo

TRANSLATION
Kennistranslations
(Emma Mandley)

GRAPHIC INSTALLATION
Logotexto

CONSTRUCTION
J. C. Sampaio, Lda.

LIGHTING
Manuel Mileu

AUDIOVISUAL MATERIALS
João Hora
José Gouveia
João Hipólito
Artur Machado
Miguel Morais

INSURANCE, TRANSPORTATION, AND LOGISTICS
Paulo Gregório

TRANSPORTATION
Feirexpo

CULTURAL MEDIATION
Inês Fialho Brandão
Diana Pereira
Margarida Rodrigues
Margarida Vieira Mendes
Ricardo Mendes

DIGITAL STRATEGY
Inês Fialho Brandão
Beatriz Saraiva
Francisco Amorim
Maria João Castro

ACCESSIBILITY CONSULTANTS
Brighter Films
HandsVoice
Locus Acesso

MARKETING AND DIGITAL TRANSFORMATION
Nuno Prego, *director*
Susana Prudêncio, *deputy director*
Clara Vilar
Pedro Relvas
Andreia Constantino

COMMUNICATION
Elisabete Caramelo, *director*
Luís Proença, *deputy director*
Leonor Vaz

CENTRAL SERVICES DEPARTMENT
António Repolho Correia, *director*
Maria João Botelho, *deputy director*
Mónica Teixeira

CATALOGUE

CURATORS
Frédéric Mougenot
João Carvalho Dias

ASSISTANT CURATOR
Patrícia Simões

EDITORIAL COORDINATION
Carla Paulino

EDITORIAL TEAM
Rosário Azevedo
with the assistance
of Maria Ramalho (intern)

TEXTS
Annie Forgeau **(AF)**
Bernard Mathieu
Fayza Haikal
Frédéric Mougenot **(FM)**
Guillemette Andreu-Lanoë **(GA-L)**
Jean-Marcel Humbert
João Carvalho Dias
Michel Chauveau
Simon Connor
Vincent Rondot **(VR)**

TRANSLATION
Kennistranslations (Emma Mandley,
Andrew Miller)

PROOFREADING
António Alves Martins

GRAPHIC DESIGN
Panorama Design Studio

PHOTOGRAPHY
Catarina Gomes Ferreira

PHOTOGRAPHIC ARCHIVE
Marta Areia

**IMAGE RESEARCH
AND REPRODUCTION RIGHTS**
Filipa Correia de Sousa

PRINTING
Norprint

COVER
Head of Senwosret III (cat. 22)
Calouste Gulbenkian Museum,
Lisbon, inv. 138

LEGAL DEPOT 507552/22
ISBN 978-989-9119-07-9
GULBENKIAN.PT

ACKNOWLEDGEMENTS

Calouste Gulbenkian Museum would like to thank the following institutions and private collectors who kindly lent works, to the lenders who wished to remain anonymous:

BELGIUM
Galerie Transit, Mechelen
KBR-Bibliothèque royale de Belgique, Brussels
Musées royaux d'Art et d'Histoire, Brussels

FRANCE
Baron Thénard Collection
Centre Pompidou Paris, Musée national d'art moderne – Centre de création industrielle
Collection HALMA-IPEL, Université de Lille
Collections Chambre de Commerce et d'Industrie métropolitaine Aix-Marseille-Provence
EPHE, archives du Centre Wl. Golenischeff, Paris
G. Andreu-Lanoë Collection
Hubert Cavaniol Collection, Paris
Jean-Marcel Humbert Collection, Paris
La Piscine – Musée d'art et d'industrie André Dilligent, Roubaix
Mobilier national, Paris
Mucem – Musée des civilisations de l'Europe et de la Méditerranée, Marseille
Musée d'Archéologie Méditerranéenne, Marseille
Musée d'Orsay, Paris
Musée de l'Assistance publique – Hôpitaux de Paris
Musée de la moto, Marseille
Musée des Beaux-Arts, Marseille
Musée du Louvre – Département des Antiquités égyptiennes; Département des Antiquités grecques, étrusques et romaines; Département des Objets d'Art; Département des Peintures; Département des Sculptures, Paris
Musée Georges-Labit, Toulouse
Musée Granet, Ville d'Aix-en-Provence

Petit Palais, Musée des Beaux-Arts de la Ville de Paris

ITALY
Museo Egizio, Turin

PORTUGAL
Biblioteca de Arte e Arquivos Gulbenkian, Lisbon
Biblioteca Nacional de Portugal
BLX, Hemeroteca Municipal de Lisboa
CAM – Centro de Arte Moderna Gulbenkian, Lisbon
Câmara Municipal de Sines – Museu de Sines
Cinemateca Portuguesa – Museu do Cinema, IP, Lisbon
Joana Vasconcelos Collection, Lisbon
Museu da Farmácia, Lisbon
Museu Dr. Joaquim Manso, Nazaré
Museu Nacional de Arte Antiga, Lisbon
Palácio Nacional de Mafra
Sociedade de Geografia de Lisboa
SPSS. Lda., Vila Nova de Gaia

UNITED KINGDOM
Ashmolean Museum, University of Oxford
British Museum, London
British Council Collection, London
Janet Rady Fine Art, London
Lee Miller Archives, East Sussex, England
Tate, London

REPRODUCTION RIGHTS IN THE EXHIBITION

GERMANY
Amnesty International
Universitätsarchiv Freiburg
Zentralarchiv der Staatlichen Museen zu Berlin

FRANCE
Bibliothèque historique de la Ville de Paris
Bibliothèque nationale de France, Paris
O. Cablat Collection
David G. Tretiakoff
Films sans frontières
Gaumont Pathé Archives, Saint-Ouen-sur-Seine
La Maison de la Pub, Paris
Magnum Photos, Paris
Médiathèque du patrimoine et de la Photographie
Musée du quai Branly – Jacques Chirac, Paris

PORTUGAL
RTP Arquivos
TNDM II, Lisbon

SWITZERLAND
MAH Musée d'art et d'histoire, Ville de Genève

UNITED KINGDOM
Centre for Research Collections, University of Edinburgh
Griffith Institute, University of Oxford
The Petrie Museum of Egyptian Archaeology, UCL
Ullstein bild/Getty Images

USA
Gary Fong / San Francisco Chronicle / Polaris
National Gallery of Art, Washington, DC, Gallery Archives
Oriental Institute of the University of Chicago
Paramount Pictures

CALOUSTE GULBENKIAN MUSEUM WOULD ALSO LIKE TO THANK TO
Agathe Guillou
Ana Maria Campino
Ana Teresa Santos
Anne André
Angeliki Galanaki
Carlos Azevedo
Caroline Ragot
France Bourboulon
Inês Torres
Léonore Branche
Luís Manuel Araújo
Marianne Duchesne
Mikaël Mohamed
Penelope Curtis
Rita Albergaria
Rogério Sousa
Sarah Nagaty
Sofia Mendes

In partnership with

Mucem

With the special collaboration of

LOUVRE

1822 – 2022 BICENTENAIRE

Insurance sponsor

Innovarisk UNDERWRITING

Exhibition sponsor

bankinter.

Photographic credits and reproduction rights

Amnesty International Germany / Egypt campaign 2013 / Image: El-Zeft, cat. 202, p. 42.

Akg Images / Werner Forman, fig. 4, p. 89.

AP – HP/F, Marin, cat. 98, p. 203.

Atelier Joana Vasconcelos, cat. 251, p. 11.

Biblioteca de Arte e Arquivos Gulbenkian, cat. 234, p. 103; fig. 4, p. 116; cat. 110, p. 192 (photo: Catarina Gomes Ferreira, CGF).

Biblioteca Nacional de Portugal, cat. 95, pp. 198–9; cat. 120, p. 230; cat. 121, p. 235.

Bibliothèque nationale de France, Agence Meurisse, cat. 146, p. 247.

Bibliothèque nationale de France, Agence Rol, cat. 167, p. 234; cat. 145, p. 251.

Calouste Gulbenkian Foundation. Photo: Keurhadjian, fig. 2, p. 110.

Calouste Gulbenkian Foundation. Photo: Carlos Azevedo, cat. 150, p. 128; cat. 52, p. 181.

Calouste Gulbenkian Foundation. Photo: Reinaldo Viegas, fig. 8, p. 124.

Calouste Gulbenkian Foundation/Museum Calouste Gulbenkian. Photo: Catarina Gomes Ferreira, cat. 27, p. 17; cat. 56, p. 46; fig. 1, p. 109; fig. 5, p. 119; figs. 6–7, p. 122; cat. 60, p. 165; cat. 108, p. 183; cats. 92–93–94, pp. 196–7; cat. 22, p. 217; cat. 111, p. 221; cat. 114, p. 223.

CAM – Centro de Arte Moderna, Calouste Gulbenkian Foundation. Photo: Paulo Costa, cat. 217, p. 211.

Câmara Municipal de Sines – Museu de Sines; Diogo Vilhena, cat. 9, p. 141.

CC0 Paris Musées / Petit Palais, Musée des Beaux-Arts de la Ville de Paris, cat. 84, pp. 184–187.

Centre for Research Collections, University of Edinburgh, cat. 82, p. 58.

CML/ DMC/ DRB/ Hemeroteca Municipal de Lisboa, cat. 153, p. 232; cat. 156, p. 233.

(Collection du) Mobilier National + Isabelle Bideau, cat. 116, pp. 188–9.

Courtesy of National Gallery of Art, Washington DC, Gallery Archives, fig. 3, p. 111 (reproduction); cat. 162, p. 253.

Courtesy of the British Council Collection. Photo © The British Council. © National Portrait Gallery, London, cat. 246, p. 229.

Courtesy of The Petrie Museum of Egyptian Archaeology, UCL, cat. 38A, p. 163.

Creative Commons CC BY – MRAHKMKG, cat. 48, p. 45; cat. 58, p. 57; cat. 87, p. 59; cat. 44, p. 77; cat. 74, p. 83; cat. 5, p. 141; cats. 134–5, p. 239.

Collection Le Baron Arnould Thénard, cat. 103, p. 209.

Collections CCIAMP, cat. 188, p. 30.

FMAE Photography Department, Torino, Museo Egizio, cat. 18, p. 135; cat. 16, p. 140; cat. 62, p. 167; cat. 63, p. 168; cat. 70, p. 173; cat. 97, p. 191; cat. 91, p. 195.

M. G. Lahlou & Galerie Transit, cat. 249, p. 269.

Mairie de Toulouse, Musée Georges-Labit. Cliché Rodolphe Carreras, cat. 75, p. 81.

Museu Dr. Joaquim Manso, cat. 245, p. 272 (photo: Catarina Gomes Ferreira, CGF).

Museu Nacional de Arte Antiga, cat. 96, pp. 200–1 (photo: Catarina Gomes Ferreira, CGF); cat. 100, p. 207 (© Luísa Oliveira)

Photo © Andrea Jemolo / Bridgeman Images, fig. 1, p. 50.

Photo © Centre Pompidou, MNAM-CCI, Dist. RMN-Grand Palais / Philippe Migeat, cat. 172, p. 37.

Photo © Ministère de la Culture – Médiathèque du patrimoine et de la photographie, Dist. RMN-Grand Palais / Emile Béchard, cat. 107, p. 216.

Photo © Musée d'Orsay, Dist. RMN-Grand Palais / Patrice Schmidt, cat. 127, pp. 96–7.

Photo © Musée du Louvre, Dist. RMN-Grand Palais / Christian Décamps, cat. 76, p. 79; cat. 80, p. 90; cat. 20, p. 136; cat. 33, p. 143; cat. 47, pp. 156–7; cat. 40, p. 161; cat. 61, p. 166; cat. 71, p. 169; cat. 67, p. 170; cats. 68–9, p. 171; cat. 136, p. 243; cat. 137, p. 245.

Photo © Musée du Louvre, Dist. RMN-Grand Palais / Christian Larrieu, cat. 72, p. 80; cat. 64, p. 171.

Photo © Musée du Louvre, Dist. RMN-Grand Palais / Franck Raux, cat. 37, p. 53.

Photo © Musée du Louvre, Dist. RMN-Grand Palais / Georges Poncet, cat. 50, p. 7; cat. 78, p. 85; cat. 53, p. 145; cat. 45, p. 179; cat. 11, p. 215; cat. 139, p. 231.

Photo © Musée du Louvre, Dist. RMN-Grand Palais / Hervé Lewandowski, cat. 34, p. 154; cat. 36, p. 155.

Photo © musée du quai Branly – Jacques Chirac, Dist. RMN-Grand Palais / image musée du quai Branly – Jacques Chirac, cat. 123, p. 176.

Photo © RMN-Grand Palais (MuCEM) / Jean-Gilles Berizzi, cat. 112, p. 222.

Photo © RMN-Grand Palais (musée du Louvre) / Daniel Arnaudet, cat. 99, p. 206.

Photo © RMN-Grand Palais (musée du Louvre) / Franck Raux, cat. 24, p. 139; cat. 26, p. 160; cat. 101, p. 210.

Photo © RMN-Grand Palais (musée du Louvre) / René-Gabriel Ojeda, fig. 5, p. 91.

Photo © RMN-Grand Palais (musée du Louvre) / Stéphane Maréchalle, cat. 88, pp. 68–9.

Photo © RMN-Grand Palais (PBA, Lille) / Thierry Le Mage, cat. 115, pp. 224–5.

Photo © RMN-Grand Palais (PBA, Lille) / Stéphane Maréchalle, cat. 19, p. 71; cat. 28, p. 137.

Photo © Simon Connor, figs. 1-2, p. 78.

Santos d'Almeida/ Museu da Farmácia, cat. 13, p. 138; cat. 14, p. 139.

Sociedade de Geografia de Lisboa, cat. 106, p. 218 (photo: Catarina Gomes Ferreira, FCG)

The Metropolitan Museum of Art, New York, Rogers Fund, 1934, fig. 9, p. 127.

The Metropolitan Museum of Art, Purchase Lila Acheson Wallace Gift, 1972, fig. 10, p. 130.

ullstein bild Dtl., cat. 133, p. 242.

Universitätsarchiv Freiburg, cat. 131, p. 241.

© Agence Publicis / Collection et photo Jean-Marcel Humbert, fig. 1, p. 100.

© Ashmolean Museum, University of Oxford, cat. 38, p. 162; cat. 2, p. 214; cat. 129, p. 240.

© Collection et photo Jean Marcel Humbert, cat. 219, p. 93; cat. 206, p. 95 (©Rhino Records, A Warner Music Group Company); cat. 231, p. 101; cat. 232, p. 102; cat. 233, p. 103; cat. 222, p. 104; cat. 229, p. 105; cat. 226, p. 105; cat. 205, p. 236; cat. 204, p. 237; cat. 239, pp. 266–7.

© Dorling Kindersley ltd / Alamy Stock Photo, fig. 1, p. 38.

Grey Area, 1993, Fred Wilson. Purchased with assistance from the American Patrons of Tate, courtesy of Pamela Joyner and Reginald Van Lee 2011© Fred Wilson, courtesy of Pace Gallery. Photo: Tate, cat. 244, pp. 270–1.

© Greg Kadel / Vogue Arabia, cat. 242, p. 265.

© Griffith Institute, University of Oxford, cat. 144, p. 252.

© Hervé Lewandowski / Musée Granet, Ville d'Aix-en-Provence, cat. 54, p. 51.

© Hossam Dirar, Courtesy of Janet Rady Fine Art, cat. 250, p. 273.

© Jeanchristophe Lett, cat. 230, p. 208; cat. 176, p. 259; cat. 240, p. 264.

© Jean Marquis / BHVP / Roger-Viollet, cats. 161–60, pp. 254–5.

© KBR – Coins and Medals (Collection de Hirsch) – Dagger of Pharaoh Kamose, cat. 21, p. 136.

© Lee Miller Archives, England 2022. All rights reserved. leemiller.co.uk, cat. 31, p. 149.

© Movie Poster Image Art / Getty Images, cat. 241, p. 263.

© Mucem, cat. 113, p. 223.

© Mucem / Marianne Kuhn, cat. 200, p. 29; cat. 171, p. 32; cat. 173, p. 33; cat. 198, p. 39; cats. 181–2, pp. 40–1; cat. 81, pp. 64–5; cat. 126, p. 175; cat. 117, p. 193; cat. 105, p. 213; cat. 118, p. 226; cat. 119, p. 227; cat. 155, p. 248; cat. 175, p. 257; cat. 180, p. 261; cat. 247, p. 274 (© Les Rouquines).

© Mucem / Yves Inchierman, fig. 1, p. 18.

© Musée d'art et d'histoire, Ville de Genève, cat. 104, p. 208.

© Musée d'art et d'histoire, Ville de Genève. Foto: Emile Burdet, cat. 30, pp. 152–3.

© Museum Folkwang Essen – ARTOTHEK, fig. 3, p. 88.

© Olivier Cablat 2004, cats. 193, 192, 194, 191, 190, 189, pp. 277–82.

© Paris, EPHE, archives du Centre Wl. Golenischeff, cat. 141, p. 249; cat. 142, p. 249; cat. 143, p. 250.

© René Burri/ Magnum Photos, cat. 174, p. 258.

© The Trustees of the British Museum, cat. 43, p. 76; cat. 73, p. 82; cat. 77, p. 84; cat. 79, p. 87; cat. 32, p. 142; cat. 39, p. 144; cat. 41, p. 159.

© Ville de Marseille, Dist. RMN-Grand Palais / Claude Almodovar / Michel Vialle, cat. 12, p. 138.

© Ville de Marseille, Dist. RMN-Grand Palais / David Giancatarina, cat. 1, p. 48; cat. 46, p. 176; cat. 17, p. 177; cat. 51, p. 180.

© Ville de Marseille, Dist. RMN-Grand Palais / image des musées de la ville de Marseille, cat. 102, pp. 204–5.

© Ville de Marseille, Dist. RMN-Grand Palais / Jean-Luc Maby, cat. 35, p. 150; cat. 29, p. 178.